THE DIPLOMACY OF ISOLATION

South African Foreign Policy Making

DEON GELDENHUYS

St. Martin's Press   New York

Printed in Hong Kong
First published in the United States of America in 1984

ISBN 0-312-21132-5

Library of Congress cataloging in publication data

Geldenhuys, Deon.
  The Diplomacy of Isolation.

  Includes index.
  1. South Africa – Foreign relations administration.
I. Title.
JX1865.S634G44   1984   327.68   83-40515
ISBN 0-312-21132-5

Preface

In 1984 the South African Institute of International Affairs is celebrating the 50th Anniversary of its founding. It is appropriate that this important work by Deon Geldenhuys on the formulation of South African foreign policy should be published during the celebration of the Institute's Golden Jubilee. It is tangible evidence of the development of the Institute's efforts over the past half century to promote a serious study of international issues, particularly those affecting South Africa. There has been a dearth of published material of a scholarly nature on South African foreign policy, and, in addition to this volume, the Institute is therefore hoping to sponsor the publication of further studies on aspects of the subject.

Professor Deon Geldenhuys has achieved a prominent place among the relatively few international relations scholars in South Africa, and in this volume he deals with a subject that has not previously been extensively examined, namely the setting and process of foreign policy making. In these critical times, especially, it is important to understand the process as well as the development and implications of the policy.

Foreign policy is never static; it is formed in response and reaction to all kinds of dometic and external stimuli, as this volume illustrates. Among the multiplicity of forces is the influence of powerful personalities, and Professor Geldenhuys does not avoid the necessity of dealing with the role of personalities, which in South Africa's case may have special importance.

The Institute is indebted to Deon Geldenhuys for the extensive research and study he has devoted to the preparation of this book, both during the time he spent in charge of research on the Institute's staff and since his appointment as head of the Political Science Department of the Rand Afrikaans University. It has also been a great pleasure for the Institute and its staff to have co-operated with him in the publication of the book, which will make a meaningful contribution to the further study by scholars, in South Africa and abroad, of all aspects of South Africa's foreign relations.

JOHN BARRATT
Director-General
SAIIA

Acknowledgements

Researching and writing this book have taken the best part of three years, considerably longer than I had anticipated. Analysing the making of South African foreign policy is, as I discovered only too well, a hard nut to crack (if cracked it has). Had it not been for the generous assistance of many people, this study would have taken much longer to complete – if at all.

I am greatly indebted to the large number of individuals – serving and retired politicians, diplomats and other officials, academics, representatives of interest groups, and many others – who gave generously of their knowledge and time. Some of them agreed to being quoted by name, but most cannot be identified because of their positions.

In my seemingly unending search for published material and other obscure snippets of information I could rely on the able assistance of two super-searchers: Sonja Begg of the South African Institute of International Affairs and Fanie Strauss of the Rand Afrikaans University library. Thanks are due to Bryan Bench, Mohamad Variawa and the "library ladies", all of the Institute of International Affairs, for helping so frequently and willingly with my many queries.

Parts of the draft manuscript were read by various knowledgeable people, to whom I wish to express my appreciation for their helpful comments: Prof Mike Louw, Prof Kenneth W Grundy, Prof Gerrit Olivier, Prof Jack Spence, Prof John Barratt, Dr Peter Vale, Prof Hein du Toit, Prof George Barrie, Dr Leif Egeland, Prof Napier Boyce, Mr Anthony Hamilton and Prof Robert Schrire.

The South African Institute of International Affairs commissioned this study and carried a heavy burden in its execution. Apart from those members of the Institute already mentioned, a special word of thanks is due to Joan Cameron and Janet Manson, who capably typed the manuscript through its various stages of preparation.

Marina Pearson of Macmillan publishers offered valuable editorial advice.

I owe a great debt of gratitude to my wife, Zelda, who for nearly three years had to live with "The Manuscript", but who did so with patience and understanding.

I alone carry the responsibility for the familiar sins of omission and commission committed in this book.

The following sources are gratefully acknowledged: the quotations heading Chapters 1, 2 and 6 are taken from Jonathan Green, *The Book of Political Quotes;* the one heading Chapter 3 is from MG Benham, *Benham's Book of Quotations;* those heading Chapters 4, 5 and 8 are from John Bartlett, *Familiar Quotations,* and the one heading Chapter 7 is from Jean van der Poel, *Selections from the Smuts Papers,* Vol VII.

DG

Contents

Introduction

A question that is increasingly being asked by South Africans and foreigners alike, particularly since Mr PW Botha became prime minister in 1978, is: Who makes South African foreign policy? The growing interest is in no small measure the result of Prime Minister Botha's style of government, characterised by the involvement in top-level policy formulation of numerous committees composed of political office holders and officials. Questions are repeatedly asked about the military's role in view of South Africa's security concerns and also because PW Botha had previously been Minister of Defence for over a decade. While the questions are plentiful, the answers have been few.

There are a good many studies of South Africa's articulated foreign policy, but precious little work has been done on the actual making of its foreign policy. Probably the first attempt was that of an American scholar, ES Munger, who in 1965 published his well-known *Notes on the Formation of South African Foreign Policy*. Although a commendable effort to break new ground, Munger's impressionistic "Notes" made no pretence at serious scholarship. Since then the making of South African foreign policy has featured as a chapter in GC Olivier's work, *Suid-Afrika se Buitelandse Beleid,* published in 1977. Munger's monograph focused on the Verwoerd era, and Olivier's study covered the period up to the mid-1970s. For the rest, it is a field of enquiry that has remained largely unexplored.

It can be said that there is among interested observers both an immediate practical need and an academic need for an extensive study of South Africa's foreign policy making. Broadly speaking, four related questions ought to be addressed: *Who* makes the Republic's foreign policy? *How, where* and *why* is it made? Meeting this need is no mean task. The researcher is faced with several formidable obstacles, notably a lack of published material, which is partly the result of the reluctance of those in government to reveal information on the processes, even the structures, involved in the formulation of foreign policy. It is by and large a poorly charted area to navigate. The difficulties are compounded by contemporaneity. Analysing the events of the day is a risky endeavour; the researcher "may get haply kicked in the teeth" if he follows too closely upon the heels of events, as Sir Walter Raleigh wisely admonished. Some of the information contained in this study will inevitably be dated by the time it is published, because the end of 1981 was used as the cut-off point. In many cases, subsequent developments have however been noted in footnotes.

The scarcity of relevant published material has meant that a good deal of the information presented in the book had to be obtained through a great many personal interviews with people involved with aspects of foreign policy making in South Africa. This method of gathering data admittedly has its limitations, but it was often the only one available.

Given these various constraints, this book necessarily contains many conjectural, tentative elements. The last word on the formation of South African foreign policy has certainly not been written.

The key concepts used in the book need to be clarified at the outset, for their application differs somewhat from the conventional. The terms foreign policy *making* and *formation,* used interchangeably, should be distinguished from foreign policy *formulation.* The former two are used in a generic sense, referring, in the terminology of systems theory, to inputs, conversion processes and outputs. Foreign policy formulation, by contrast, is taken to have a much more confined meaning: it refers to the formal processes within the machinery of government. Policy formulation is, in other words, a component of the wider process of policy making.

Policy formulation consists of a number of identifiable stages, as suggested in a definition by Prof Mike Louw. The first is the official foreign policy elite's (bureaucrats' and political office holders') perceptions of their environment. Second, their analyses of these perceptions, where perceptions are related to "reality" and capabilities and constraints assessed. Third, the preparation of options, which includes a cost-benefit calculation of each of the options, and the formulation of scenarios for implementation. Fourth, the making of decisions, which essentially means the final choosing among alternative courses of action. Decision making is typically the preserve of the select few; in major matters of foreign policy they would be the principal political office holders and a handful of top officials. Fifth, the implementation of decisions, a task in which the foreign ministry is a key institution among the various government agencies involved in foreign policy. Finally, the evaluation of decisions and of their implementation, a function performed jointly by those making and implementing decisions. Evaluation, which is typically based on feedbacks, involves suggesting and making adjustments to patterns of action.

Some aspects of foreign policy making in South Africa are relatively easier to research than others. The greatest difficulties occur in the investigation of policy formulation, as it involves processes conducted within formal government structures. Much of "what goes on behind closed doors" in South Africa, in both documented and verbal form, has traditionally been kept well hidden from revelation and research, at least for the statutory 30-year embargo on official documents. It is easier to examine formal structures and to identify the principal policy formulators involved and describe their perceptions than it is to assess more subtle aspects of the policy formu-

lators' analyses and the way in which options are prepared (including the more complex elements of substance). Similarly, the implementation of decisions by various government agencies is considerably easier to examine than is the evaluation of the decisions by those institutions and the political office holders. These features confirm just how much still needs to be done in the study of South Africa's foreign policy making. As for the wider aspects of foreign policy making in South Africa, information on environmental factors, such as domestic public opinion, the physical components of national power and international pressure, is fairly readily available. Assessing their impact on the policy formulators is, in view of the absence of accepted criteria, a new and challenging task.

The material in this book is organised as follows: The first two chapters are background sections. Chapter 1 presents an overview of the development of South Africa's foreign policy system from the consummation of the Union of South Africa to 1966. The object is to identify features that help to explain South Africa's foreign policy making in the years 1966-81, the period that is the main focus of the book. The second chapter briefly sketches the salient features of South Africa's domestic and external environment in the 1966-81 period; it is a description of the setting of South African foreign policy making. The next four chapters, which form the main body of the book, deal with the making of the Republic's foreign policy under Prime Ministers Vorster and Botha. Chapter 3 focuses on the role of the legislature in the process. Chapter 4 considers the role played by the political office holders in the executive. The government departments – primary among them the Department of Foreign Affairs, the former Department of Information and the Defence Force – feature in Chapter 5. Chapter 6 pays attention to the public and foreign policy making – both the "unorganised" and the "organised" public, white and black. The role of external pressure in the formation of South Africa's foreign policy, and indeed also the implications for domestic politics, are considered in Chapter 7. The concluding chapter contains some *ex post* theoretical perspectives on foreign policy making. The object of considering these perspectives at the end of the study is not merely to test their explanatory qualities with regard to the South African case, but, more important, to try to find some guidelines for a model of South African foreign policy making. If it is accepted that much empirical work has yet to be done on the formation of the Republic's foreign policy, then the more theoretical aspects need even more strengthening. The book offers some suggestions about possible components of such a model. It is an attempt to place the search for a model on the agenda, as it were.

This book admittedly leaves many empirical and theoretical questions unanswered, but this might prove beneficial in the long run in that it might encourage further systematic research in a field that is vitally important for South Africa's future relations with the outside world.

1. South Africa's Foreign Policy System, 1910-1966

History is past politics and politics is present history.　　　　　　Sir John Seeley

Compressing a discussion of South Africa's foreign policy making in the nearly six decades before 1966 into a single chapter is no mean task. For one thing, there is a good deal of revealing and fascinating material available – even without tapping the potential richness of archival sources. However, the limited requirements of a background chapter impose a certain discipline which, invariably, is not generous to the volume of data at hand.

The object of this chapter is to help explain the formulation of South African foreign policy after 1966 by reference to specific features of the preceding period. The discussion will be organised around the structures, processes and people involved in foreign policy formulation. These are the elements comprising what is being referred to here as South Africa's foreign policy system. Included in the examination of structures will be the forms of state, government and authority of South Africa, and also the country's diplomatic network abroad. In discussing the role of specific policy formulators, some consideration will be given to the influence of personal characteristics on their political behaviour. Together, the structures, processes and people reveal the locus of foreign policy decision making.

Foreign policy is, of course, not made in a vacuum, nor in monastery-like insulation from worldly influences. Policy formulators constantly respond to a range of stimuli from their environment. It is therefore necessary to take cognisance, even at this early stage, of the salient features of the domestic and external environment of South Africa's foreign policy formulators.

Since the pre-1966 period is long and packed with important developments, the discussion can be facilitated by breaking it down into two sections, drawing the dividing line at 1948. It was in that year that the National Party (or the *Herenigde Nasionale Party* as it was officially known until 1951) came to power. The National Party's ascendance opened a new chapter in South Africa's domestic politics and foreign relations: it heralded the era of apartheid. Since 1948-66 immediately preceded the period that forms the focus of this book and saw the same party in power, these years will be considered at greater length than the period before 1948.

The Years 1910 to 1948

Some implications of constitutional form and status

The Union of South Africa, consummated in 1910, was from a constitutional point of view little more than an enlarged self-governing British colony composed of four smaller self-governing colonies (the Cape Colony, Natal, Transvaal and the Orange River Colony).[1] Parliament, according to the *South Africa Act*, 1909, consisted of the King, the Senate and the House of Assembly. The Crown was represented by the governor-general who, in practice, was appointed by the King acting on the advice of a British minister. The governor-general could be given instructions by the King – again on the advice of a British minister – about signing bills or reserving signature for the Crown.

1

In addition to these functions, the governor-general served as the representative of the British government in South Africa and as high commissioner for the British territories of Bechuanaland, Basutoland and Swaziland.

The new Union's constitutional status from the outset became a major domestic political issue. Centring as they did on South Africa's ties with the United Kingdom, the country's external relations, so to speak, became a divisive issue in internal politics. South Africa's relations with the British Empire, later the Commonwealth, were to remain the principal issue in its foreign relations and at the same time a highly contentious party political one until the early 1960s. Another implication of the British connection was, of course, that the United Kingdom dominated South Africa's external milieu.

The political structures created by the South Africa Act had further important and enduring implications for South Africa's foreign relations. Following the British Westminster model, a parliamentary *form of government* – a cabinet system – was established. This arrangement in practice greatly strengthened the role of the executive branch of government over that of the legislature in policy making. In the realm of foreign policy making specifically, it is appropriate to say that the Westminster system tends to impose further restrictions on the already limited, secondary role that legislatures commonly play relative to that of executives. The *form of authority* established by the South Africa Act has over the years variously been depicted as a sectional or limited democracy, a racial oligarchy, and a pigmentocracy. The monopolisation of political power by the whites,[2] supplemented by racially discriminatory legislation in the socio-economic sphere, lies at the heart of the international unpopularity and ostracism into which South Africa began to sink after the Second World War. Foreign policy making has, of course, from the beginning been an exclusively white preserve. The unitary *form of state* selected by South Africa's founding fathers has little if any material effect on foreign policy formation. Although a unitary system typically enhances the authority of the central government *vis-à-vis* regional or provincial governments, this phenomenon is relevant mainly to domestic policy making; foreign policy formulation is in any case always the exclusive prerogative of the national government. Returning to the Union's subordinate status to Britain, a particularly important implication was that South Africa, like the other British dominions, enjoyed no international status whatsoever. Their foreign relations were handled by the British government. In practice, this meant that the British Foreign Office, *via* the Department of the Union Prime Minister and the governor-general, served as the channel for South Africa's diplomatic activity.[3] The Union merely possessed delegated powers directly to conclude administrative arrangements and agreements with other countries.[4]

The participation of the Union and the other dominions in the Versailles peace conference, their signing of the peace treaty and joining the new League of Nations, signalled the dominions' desire to express their autonomy and to attain equal status with other members of the international community. In 1923 the United Kingdom responded by agreeing that a dominion could enjoy diplomatic representation abroad and that each dominion's parliament had to ratify treaties affecting that particular country.

Since South Africa's new foreign representatives were still appointed by the British monarch in the same way as Britain's own representatives it was only to be expected that foreigners would be in some doubt as to the role and status of South African representatives abroad. This caused considerable dissatisfaction among the representatives and contributed to the eventual establishment of the Union's diplomatic service.[5]

The only permanent diplomatic representative South Africa had until 1929 was its high commissioner in London. The post was created by law in 1911. For the duration of South Africa's membership of the Commonwealth, the high commission in London remained its "principal overseas establishment";[6] even after South Africa's departure from the Commonwealth in 1961, its embassy (as it then became) in the British capital retained its pre-eminence among the country's diplomatic missions. The special position of the high commissioner's office has traditionally been reflected in the status of the incumbent: until the 1950s, the appointment had always been regarded as political. This made the high commissioner more than a diplomat; "an official minister without portfolio" is the description once given to the office-holder.[7]

In the absence of a foreign office, the Union's foreign representatives came under the auspices of other state departments, such as Finance, and Mining and Industry.[8] The high commissioner's office in London was a sub-department of the

Treasury,[9] although the high commissioner reported directly to the prime minister.

Other early South African foreign representation was the presence of an agent in Mozambique (since 1910), a trade commissioner on the European continent (appointed in 1922), a trade representative in Kenya (appointed in 1923 to serve East Africa), and a trade commissioner in the United States of America.[10] At the League of Nations South Africa was represented in the Assembly, usually by its high commissioner in London.[11] In 1933 the Union was accorded the honour of having Mr CT te Water, its high commissioner in London, elected President of the Assembly.

As the holder of the League-awarded mandate over South West Africa, South Africa also sent a representative to the annual meetings of the Permanent Mandates Commission. South Africa participated in the activities of such major international functional organisations as the World Health Organisation, the Universal Postal Union and the International Labour Organisation.[12]

The Union's foreign relations were materially affected by various moves in the late 1920s and early 1930s to clarify the dominions' constitutional status. The famous Balfour Declaration, adopted at the 1926 Imperial Conference, defined the position and mutual relations of Britain and the dominions as follows: "They are autonomous communities within the British Empire, equal in status, in no way subordinate one to another in any aspect of their domestic or external affairs."[13] It was, however, also agreed that "in the sphere of foreign affairs, as in the sphere of defence, the major share of responsibility rests now, and must for some time continue to rest, with His Majesty's Government in Great Britain."[14] South African foreign policy would, therefore, still largely be made in London, or at least bear a very strong British imprint.

Notwithstanding this constraint, the Balfour status was given legislative effect with Britain's adoption of the Statute of Westminster in 1931. South Africa incorporated the provisions of the Statute in its constitutional law with the passing of the Status Act in 1934. These two measures enabled "the transfer of the source of South African sovereignty from Westminster to Cape Town."[15] The Crown would henceforth be represented by the governor-general, appointed on the advice of the South African prime minister. The latter could also advise the King, via the governor-general, on South African affairs.[16] In 1931 Britain created the new post of British high commissioner in South Africa, an office combined with that of high commissioner for Bechuanaland, Basutoland and Swaziland.

With its independent status formally beyond any doubt, South Africa could claim the international tokens of sovereignty. The Union government was entitled, in the name of the British monarch (as South Africa's head of state), to appoint diplomatic representatives abroad and to declare war in its own right.[17]

Establishment of the Department of External Affairs

The Balfour Declaration – of which Premier JBM Hertzog was the prime mover – was a major contributory factor leading to the establishment of the Union's Department of External Affairs on 1 June 1927. The appointment of overseas representatives, Hertzog said, was an "absolute necessity": it was "the only proof which can satisfy the sentiment that we ought to behave as an independent country"; it accordingly "does not befit us as an independent country any longer to simply rely on the services of other countries"[18] – an obvious reference to Britain's diplomatic service. Practical considerations also influenced the decision to establish a foreign ministry. However limited South Africa's foreign representation had been, it still required some organisation of human and material resources. Rather than entrust the management of the Union's overseas representation to various different departments, it could be handled much more effectively by a single permanent department whose primary function it would be.[19]

Dr HDJ Bodenstein, professor of law at the University of Stellenbosch, was appointed the first permanent head, or secretary, of the new department. Apart from his other attributes[20], important considerations in the selection of Bodenstein were his expertise in international and constitutional law and his support for Hertzog's views on South Africa's constitutional status.[21] The dominant issue in South Africa's foreign relations at the time, it should be remembered, centred on the Union's ties with Britain and the Commonwealth. In July 1941 Bodenstein was succeeded by Mr DD Forsyth, a career civil servant who had previously served as secretary for South West Africa. By then, Hertzog was no longer prime minister. Following the rejection by

Parliament of Hertzog's motion calling for South Africa's qualified neutrality in the war, Smuts was in September 1939 invited by the governor-general to form a new government.

Smuts, like Hertzog, assumed personal responsibility for the Department of External Affairs. The convention that the prime minister serves as the political head of the department was to be upheld for nearly three decades.

With control of the Union's diplomatic and consular missions vested in the Department of External Affairs, the country's network of foreign representatives expanded markedly from the late 1920s onwards. One of the first states in which South Africa established a fully-fledged legation was The Netherlands in 1929.[22] This was a move with obvious symbolic significance: The Netherlands was the Afrikaners' principal country of origin and their cultural *heimat*. South Africa's London representation nonetheless retained its pre-eminent position. In fact, in 1920 it was laid down that the Union's high commissioner in London was its senior political representative.[23] Also in 1929 South Africa opened diplomatic missions in Italy and the United States. The year 1934 saw another major extension of South Africa's diplomatic network with the establishment of missions in Portugal, Belgium, France, Germany and Sweden. Four years later the Union gained full diplomatic representation in Canada and it also extended its interests to South America with the appointment of a consul-general in Argentina. In 1943 a consulate-general was opened in Brazil.[24]

Probably lesser known but particularly interesting was South Africa's establishment of a presence in "non-white" parts of what subsequently became known as the Third World. At the time, most of these territories were colonial possessions, which meant that South Africa's ties were with the colonial powers rather than with indigenous rulers. In the late 1920s the Union's agency in Mozambique was upgraded to that of a consulate-general. In 1938 a South African trade commissioner for North and West Africa was appointed in Morocco. Trade representatives were also appointed in Singapore and India, and honorary trade commissioners in Palestine and China. In the war years South Africa opened missions in the Belgian Congo and Madagascar. Another wartime development was the establishment of a South African consulate in Egypt in 1942.[25]

It is worth mentioning two particular cases of foreign representation in South Africa. The Indian government appointed an agent-general in the Union following the conclusion of the Cape Town Agreement between the two governments in February 1927. The agreement concerned the position of South Africa's Indian population, and the agent-general's duties were mainly related to matters affecting local Indians; he was therefore not a diplomatic representative in the ordinary sense of the word. In 1941, his status was however raised to that of high commissioner.[26]

In 1942 the Soviet Union established a consulate-general in South Africa. Prime Minister Smuts explained this politically controversial move on the grounds of Russia's involvement in the war against Germany. Smuts, in turn, in 1945 considered opening a South African mission in Moscow, but eventually decided against it. His growing distrust of Stalin's international intentions and the Nationalist Opposition's vehement hostility to communism probably weighed heavily with Smuts. By the same token, Smuts was unwilling to agree to Soviet wishes to upgrade their representation in South Africa to embassy status.[27]

It was not only diplomatic, consular and trade representation that South Africa built up in the late 1930s and in the 1940s. In 1938 a press officer was appointed at South Africa House in London. Although not a member of the diplomatic staff, the official was attached to the Department of the Prime Minister. The creation of this post can be regarded as the precursor of the later network of information officials abroad.[28] In 1942 South Africa appointed its first press and public relations officer in the United States.[29] Two years later information officers were appointed in Nairobi and Leopoldville.

A review of South Africa's evolving diplomatic network can hardly overlook the early and enduring practice of political appointments to diplomatic positions. This applied *par excellence* to the high commissionership in London, owing to its special status among South Africa's overseas missions. The first incumbent was Mr WP Schreiner, former prime minister of the Cape Colony (1898-1900). Another familiar name was that of the already mentioned Te Water, a Hertzog supporter who lost his parliamentary seat in the 1929 general election. Te Water served as high commissioner from 1929-1939, resigning in the wake of the fall of the Hertzog government.[30] Smuts, the incoming prime minister, appointed one of his United Party MPs, Mr SF Waterson, as

4

high commissioner. In 1942 he was succeeded by Col. Deneys Reitz, a member of Smuts's Cabinet. Next in line, in 1944, was Mr G Heaton Nicholls, Administrator of Natal and a former Senator.[31] The last of Smuts's appointees was Mr Leif Egeland, a former United Party MP – the only high commissioner who had some diplomatic experience before taking up his post in early 1948.[32]

South Africa's first trade representative in the United States was Mr Eric H Louw. Although this was not a diplomatic position, Louw was a political appointee, having been elected National Party MP in 1924. When South Africa's representation in America was upgraded to that of a diplomatic mission in 1929, Louw became Envoy Extraordinary and Minister Plenipotentiary.[33]

These were by no means the only political appointments to diplomatic positions until 1948. It should be borne in mind that without a foreign office for the first seventeen years of its existence, the Union had no experienced career diplomats available to fill diplomatic posts. Apart from that, successive prime ministers regarded certain diplomatic positions as politically important enough to merit political appointments. There have traditionally also been several other considerations behind political appointments. Such appointments have variously been used as a political reward, a means of granting *solatia* to disappointed cabinet aspirants, and a way of removing unwanted politicians or officials.[34] A celebrated case of Smuts using the diplomatic service as a "dumping ground" was his appointment of the ageing Prof. Leo Fouché, chairman of the South African Broadcasting Corporation, as South Africa's diplomatic representative in The Hague in 1947.[35]

The new post-war world

While South Africa's foreign policy formulators could derive satisfaction from the country's expanding representation abroad, the post-war environment in which the representatives operated differed profoundly from that existing before 1945.

In the pre-war years South Africa was, generally speaking, a respected member of the international community. In large measure because of the international standing of Smuts, the Union enjoyed a role and influence in international affairs quite out of proportion to its relative physical power. On the African continent South Africa was one of only three independent states and economically the most advanced. In an era when Western colonial rule was the order of the day in Africa, white rule in South Africa drew little international attention or criticism; segregation in South Africa seemed essentially consistent with colonialism in Africa.

Yet even in this favourable international environment, South Africa's racial policies struck some discordant notes. At the Imperial Conferences of 1917, 1918, 1921 and 1923 the issue of the Union's treatment of its Indian population was raised; at the 1923 meeting it actually led to acrimonious exchanges between the Indian delegate, Sir Taj Bahadur Sapru, and Smuts.[36] South Africa's racial policies also came in for indirect censure in the Permanent Mandates Commission, which from time to time criticised various aspects of the Union's administration of South West Africa, including black education, African reserves and job reservation. South Africa was in fact one of the first mandatory powers to be criticised by the commission.[37] These instances of external criticism of South Africa's actions at home and in South West Africa were trivial when compared with the torrent of international condemnation it had to face after the war. They were, nonetheless, omens of things to come.

One of the most far-reaching consequences of the Allied victory over Nazi Germany was the introduction of what can be characterised as a new international morality. The essence of the new norm is well expressed in Winston Churchill's reference to "the enthronement of the rights of man".[38] The concern for human rights is clearly reflected in the charter of the new United Nations Organisation: it contains no fewer than seven explicit references to such rights. The first reference is to be found in the preamble, which was, ironically, drafted by Smuts – leader of the very state that would first be condemned for its failure to uphold human rights. The very first article of the charter states that it is the purpose of the United Nations to "develop friendly relations among nations based on respect for the principle of equal rights and self-determination of people." The new notion of self-determination was undoubtedly a major influence in effecting a material change in the course of colonialism after the war.[39] This was of direct concern to South Africa, for it affected the Union's immediate external environment.

In the new climate of international opinion,

Smuts, his international stature notwithstanding, was unable to prevent the new United Nations General Assembly at its first session in 1946 from concerning itself with both the future of South West Africa and South Africa's treatment of its Indian population.[40] These two issues in fact soon became internationalised, and the events at the United Nations in 1946 underlined the fact that South Africa was out of step with post-war ideas on human rights; its racial policies showed up as the major cause of the Union's early setbacks at the United Nations. For Smuts, present at the General Assembly's 1946 session, it was "a bad blow"[41] and "a bitter experience"[42] to find himself in the dock of world opinion. Government supporting newspapers in the Union complained bitterly about what they depicted as malicious representations abroad of South Africa's racial policies,[43] and Heaton Nicholls, the Union's high commissioner in London, informed Pretoria in alarmist though patently exaggerated terms of "the flood of abusive and distorted anti-Union propaganda" he had to cope with in Britain.[44] What all this points to is that South Africa's racial policies were, as Hancock put it, "on the way to becoming the stuff and substance of her foreign policies."[45] It also reveals what in due course became some of South Africa's typical responses to international criticism.

The principal foreign policy formulators

Having noted some of the environmental and structural features of the South African foreign policy system in the period up to 1948, the roles of the principal individual policy formulators should now be considered. One useful guide is the practice of personal diplomacy by political leaders.

Smuts was undoubtedly the chief exponent of this. Not only did he frequently represent South Africa in international forums, but he also earned a reputation as a world statesman, enjoying an international standing not since equalled by any other South African political leader. Long before becoming prime minister in 1919, Smuts had already won acclaim in the United Kingdom for his leadership qualities and, of course, for his friendly attitude towards Britain and his commitment to the British Empire. Smuts had first shown his *bona fides* to the British in the aftermath of the Anglo-Boer War, when he emerged as a powerful force for reconciliation between the defeated Boers and the British.[46] In

1916 the British government invited Smuts to take control of the Allied war effort in German East Africa.[47] The following year Smuts became a member of the British War Cabinet,[48] and he even acted as emissary for the Imperial government in both internal and war matters.[49] General Louis Botha was still prime minister at the time, but Smuts, a minister in Botha's government since union, overshadowed Botha as the Boer idol of the British.

On the wider international scene Smuts first established a name for himself with his contribution to the establishment of the League of Nations at the Versailles Peace Conference in 1919. He published a treatise, *The League of Nations: A Practical Suggestion,*[50] and was elected to serve on the Commission of the League of Nations, where he distinguished himself as one of the architects of the new organisation.[51]

Smuts's role on the international stage was again much in evidence in his second term as prime minister (1939-1945), particularly during and immediately after the Second World War. The British government accorded him – alone among the dominion premiers – the honour of attending meetings of the War Cabinet whenever he visited London.[52] In the course of the war he paid four visits to the United Kingdom;[53] the most important matters in Anglo-South African relations were thus handled personally by Smuts and his counterpart and old comrade, Churchill.[54] As had been the case after the First World War, Smuts made a material contribution to the shaping of the new post-war world. He was appointed president of the General Assembly, one of the four large commissions of the San Francisco Conference. Among other things, it dealt with the preamble[55] to the charter of the proposed United Nations Organisation, and with trusteeship.[56]

Important though Smuts's contribution was at San Francisco, it was not nearly as significant as at Versailles. Much of the preliminary work on the new organisation had already been done by the major powers at the Dumbarton Oaks and Yalta conferences.[57] Quite apart from that, the San Francisco Conference proved to be the last international assembly that Smuts attended "with his reputation untarnished by the sins imputed to his country and to himself as its Prime Minister", in Hancock's words.[58] San Francisco, therefore, represented a watershed in South Africa's international standing; thereafter, the country steadily declined into international unpopularity and eventual ostracism.

The truth of Hancock's statement was vividly demonstrated only a year later at the first session of the United Nations General Assembly. Smuts's pride was no doubt injured by the unexpected mauling,[59] and it was probably largely for this reason that he did not attend the 1947 session of the United Nations General Assembly. Instead, he chose Mr Harry Lawrence, Minister of the Interior, to lead the Union delegation.[60]

Smuts was a faithful participator in Commonwealth Prime Ministers' Conferences (thus named after 1944), and he attended those held in 1944, 1945 and 1946.[61] In his first term as prime minister, Smuts had attended the Imperial Conferences held in London in 1921 and 1923.[62] The year 1946, it can be added, was a particularly active diplomatic one for Smuts; apart from attending the Commonwealth Conference, he later participated in the Paris Peace Conference and then went on to visit The Netherlands and Belgium, followed by his attendance of the United Nations General Assembly meeting in New York.[63]

Though one of the founding fathers of the League of Nations and a keen protagonist of the new organisation, Smuts, as prime minister, never attended any of the meetings of the League Assembly.

Hertzog, who succeeded Smuts as prime minister in 1924, attended only the 1930 session of the League Assembly.[64] As with his predecessor, the focus of Hertzog's personal diplomacy was the Commonwealth, and he attended the Imperial Conferences of 1926, 1930, 1933 and 1937.[65] For the rest, Hertzog in 1930 paid official visits to Ireland, The Netherlands and Italy, where he met Benito Mussolini.[66]

When one deals with the period of Hertzog's premiership, the remarkable pre-war diplomatic mission of Mr Oswald Pirow, his Minister of Defence, should be mentioned. Towards the end of 1938 Pirow, with the blessing of Hertzog and Smuts (the latter then Deputy Prime Minister following the formation of a coalition government in 1933 and the so-called fusion government a year later) set out for Europe in an attempt to prevent a worsening of the tensions between the Third Reich and the United Kingdom. The Hertzog government was deeply concerned about the dangers of another European war and its implications for South Africa. Pirow, offering his services as mediator, met with Neville Chamberlain, Adolf Hitler and later also Mussolini.[67] Pirow's endeavours, however, appeared to have

had little influence on the ominous course of events in Europe, because "the idea of South African mediation was unwelcome to Germany and embarrassing to the British government", according to Watt.[68]

The frequency of South African prime ministers' visits to London reflected the weight Britain carried in the making of the Union's foreign policy. Munger went so far as to argue that "the formation of major South African foreign policy was still largely in London . . . right up until 1948", notwithstanding what he called a "significant broadening out" after the Statute of Westminster and through Hertzog's emphasis on South African nationalism.[69] Although Munger's observation may in some respects be fair, it is too sweeping a generalisation to be left unchallenged.

For Prime Minister Hertzog the major foreign policy issues of the day were related to South Africa's so-called British connection and were decidedly not matters on which the Union simply took its cue from the United Kingdom. The issues were South Africa's international status as a dominion and the related questions of the Union's right to secede from the British Empire and to remain neutral in a war involving Britain.[70] To these can be added Hertzog's policy of diversifying South Africa's external economic relations, which essentially meant lessening the Union's overwhelming economic dependence on the United Kingdom. This in fact caused some uneasiness in Anglo-South African relations.[71] The way in which Hertzog handled these matters reflected what Munger called his "strong sense of South African nationalism".[72] It found expression in Hertzog's famous motto, "South Africa first"; South Africa had to seek its own identity in the world – something that militated against any notion of the Union's foreign policy simply being made for it in London.

It was nonetheless true that South Africa, under both Hertzog and Smuts, was firmly locked into the British diplomatic network, being a dominion. This enabled South Africa and the other dominions to receive British Foreign Office material. For a small dominion with sparse foreign representation, access to the facilities of a great power's world-wide and sophisticated diplomatic network was of major value. Apart from supplying information, the British Foreign Office also acted on behalf of South Africa and other dominions in dealings with countries with which they had no diplomatic ties, while Britain had. It would be fair to assume that Britain heavily influenced the dominion's policies – insofar as they had policies – towards these states.

Smuts, with his fervent commitment to the British connection, was probably content to leave the making of major South African foreign policy largely to London, in the sense that he saw a commonality of interests between Britain and the Union on major international issues. This was, above all, reflected in Smuts's support for South African involvement against Nazi Germany in the Second World War. There were, however, two issues in the realm of South Africa's foreign relations where the Smuts government did follow its own made-in-Pretoria policy, which actually caused London considerable embarrassment.

The first was South Africa's treatment of its Indian population, an issue that had direct international implications, specifically for the British Empire and Commonwealth. This issue had already caused tensions between South Africa and India at the Imperial Conference of 1917 and thereafter, and it became truly internationalised when India first raised it in the UN General Assembly in 1946. Britain was greatly concerned about the damaging effects the Indo-South African dispute could have on the Commonwealth, and probably made behind-the-scenes attempts to mediate between the two countries both before and after the war.[73]

The second was the issue of South West Africa, which after the war soon became internationalised by the UN's involvement. Although Britain in 1946 supported Smuts's unsuccessful request to the UN Trusteeship Committee for the incorporation of South West Africa into the Union, there can be no doubt that South Africa's quest for incorporation was based on the Union's perception of its own interests and not those of Britain or the Commonwealth. Least of all was it a policy prescribed by Britain. Britain's support for incorporation can largely be attributed to British regard for Smuts and a desire not to offend him.[74] Yet, it cannot but have been embarrassing for the United Kingdom to find itself the sole backer of South Africa's claims to South West Africa.

Whatever Britain's precise influence on the Union's foreign policy may have been, South African leaders in their own right still played a key role in the process. Here it should be remembered that prior to the establishment of the Department of External Affairs in 1927, the Prime Minister's Office carried the political responsibility for foreign policy; the prime minister was the *de facto*

minister of foreign affairs. After 1927 the Department of External Affairs fell under the prime minister, until a specific minister was first made responsible for foreign affairs in 1955.

Hertzog, who established the Department of External Affairs, was during his premiership undoubtedly the dominant figure in foreign policy formulation. This was mainly because the major foreign policy issues of his premiership were extensions of the principal issues in domestic politics. With Hertzog giving a clear lead on the domestic front, it was not surprising that he also dictated South Africa's foreign policy. Yet, others also carried significant weight in foreign policy making under Hertzog.

Five names can be singled out: the Secretary of External Affairs, Dr HDJ Bodenstein; the legal adviser to the Department of External Affairs, Advocate Toon van den Heever[75]; Hertzog's Minister of Finance, Mr NC Havenga; Mr Oswald Pirow, Minister of Defence (formerly of Justice), and Dr DF Malan, Minister of the Interior. Smuts's name should, of course, also be added, for he became a member of the Cabinet after 1933. Smuts could thus bring his wealth of knowledge and experience to bear on foreign policy.

Havenga had established a reputation, both in South Africa and abroad, as a highly competent minister of finance. A well-travelled man holding a major Cabinet portfolio, this former Boer commander was a very close confidant of Hertzog's.[76] Pirow, in fact the first minister to hold the defence portfolio (Prime Ministers Botha and Smuts had themselves taken responsibility for the portfolio), probably exerted considerable influence, particularly on the Hertzog government's policy in the pre-war years. A mark of Pirow's standing was his 1938 diplomatic mission to Europe. Malan, in turn, made his influence felt on matters relating to the British connection, and he was also involved in the round table discussion with India in 1927.

Although considerably less influential than the five individuals mentioned, Louw and Te Water are nonetheless also important. They occupied key diplomatic positions – already an indication of their standing in government circles – and became seasoned diplomats. Louw, it is known, frequently wrote directly to Hertzog on matters concerning South Africa's foreign relations.[77]

Smuts, indisputably the South African leader most experienced and esteemed on the international political scene, was supremely confident in foreign affairs and felt little need for advice on major issues.[78] In both his terms as prime minister, South Africa's foreign relations – which centred on the British connection – carried Smuts's firm imprint. Even under Botha's premiership, Smuts, the prime minister's political lieutenant, was the chief architect of such foreign policy as there was. In the more visible formal aspects of South Africa's external relations, Botha was, as noted earlier, virtually eclipsed by the ambitious and imaginative Smuts.

A feature of Prime Minister Smuts's handling of foreign affairs was that he frequently by-passed his own Department of External Affairs. The practice was of course facilitated by the exigencies of war and the old Smuts-Churchill comradeship. What further strengthened Smuts's position in South Africa's wartime foreign policy formulation was that he – and not the governor-general, as the constitution required – acted as Commander-in-Chief of the Union's armed forces.[79]

With Smuts effectively in sole command of South African foreign policy formulation, there were simply no other prominent figures. Mr JH Hofmeyr, Deputy Prime Minister and Smuts's right-hand-man in the Cabinet, and widely regarded as his most likely successor, is not known to have played any significant role in foreign policy formulation. If involved at all, Hofmeyr would in any case have had a supportive rather than an initiatory role.[80] Moreover, as Alan Paton, Hofmeyr's biographer, pointed out, "Hofmeyr was never to Smuts what Smuts had been to Botha, or what Havenga had been to Hertzog."[81] Other Cabinet members would have been even less involved. It should be remembered that Smuts not only dominated his Cabinet – one, incidentally, not noted for its general competence – in foreign policy matters, but in purely domestic policy making too. Smuts was, in Egeland's words, "a committee of one";[82] Bernard Friedman wrote that Smuts was "the sole arbiter in matters of policy";[83] Arthur Barlow referred to a "Smuts 'dictatorship' ", in which "Smuts was the Cabinet and the Cabinet was Smuts . . . no one else counted."[84] All three of the authors were, significantly, former United Party MPs. Smuts's was, in short, a highly personalised way of formulating foreign policy, allowing wide scope for such personal characteristics as intellectual brilliance, supreme self-confidence and a resolute political will (although the latter at times tended to be a rather erratic quality, especially in domestic policy matters). Smuts's virtual monopoly on foreign policy formulation was hardly the right kind of inducement to his Cabinet colleagues to take an active, more specialised interest in foreign affairs. Thus, when a foreign official wrote to South Africa enquiring about "those public men in your country who concern themselves with international affairs", the curt official response was: "There is only one – General Smuts."[85] Although exaggerated, the reply was not altogether flippant.

Let us turn to the role of the Department of External Affairs: Forsyth was an exceedingly reliable and dedicated civil servant. In administrative matters Smuts no doubt relied heavily on him. But Forsyth was not in any real sense an initiator or formulator of foreign policy; under Smuts that would in any case not have been possible. There is, however, one important but little-known exception: it was Forsyth who first suggested to Smuts that South Africa should hold a referendum in South West Africa to allow the people of the territory to express themselves on incorporation into South Africa.[86] (The referendum was held in 1946, producing an overwhelming majority in favour of incorporation.)[87] Among South African diplomats General Frank Theron, South African Ambassador in Rome after the war, should be mentioned. A devoted friend of Smuts, he was a man for whose abilities the Prime Minister had high regard.[88] Among the younger generation of politician-diplomats a prominent name was that of Egeland, who served as South African envoy to Sweden, Holland and Belgium before being appointed by Smuts to the Union's choice diplomatic position of high commissioner in London. But whatever their abilities and personal relationships with Smuts, these diplomats were confined to an essentially instrumental role in foreign policy, well removed from the centre of decision making. During both Smuts's and Hertzog's premierships, diplomats in the field in fact complained to their superiors about being kept in the dark by the government on major policy matters and, under Smuts particularly, being by-passed through the Prime Minister's conduct of personal diplomacy.[89]

Parliament and the public

Parliament's role in foreign affairs up to 1948 was ambivalent. On the one hand, "not the slightest interest is displayed by Parliament in the activities of our Department of External Affairs",

The Forum remarked in 1941.[90] A decade earlier much the same point was made by Hertzog in Parliament.[91] On the other hand, foreign relations loomed large in parliamentary debates, given the salience of South Africa's British connection as a party political issue. In 1939 it was in fact on a foreign policy issue – whether or not South Africa should remain neutral in the war – that Parliament forced Hertzog to resign the premiership. For Parliament to decide this ultimate issue in foreign policy – declaring war – was indeed only proper. For the rest, foreign policy decision making remained very much in the hands of the prime ministers. Smuts in fact even ignored Parliament in deciding on South Africa's membership of both the League of Nations and the UN.[92] But despite such blatant disregard of the legislature, foreign affairs continued to feature strongly in Parliament. Even during the Second World War, with South Africa actively involved on the Allied side, the Nationalist Opposition unsuccessfully moved a parliamentary motion calling for the Union's withdrawal from the hostilities.

As regards the general public's interest in foreign affairs, *The Forum* in December 1941 asserted that successive prime ministers "have sharply discouraged any inclination to discuss the Union's relationship with other lands. No sort of public opinion on world affairs has ever been created in South Africa."[93] This is a rather sweeping generalisation, which ignores the fact that South Africa's British connection for the most part overshadowed the domestic political debate. Public opinion was therefore at least sensitised to issues relating to South Africa's ties with the United Kingdom. *The Forum* may have been largely correct as far as South Africa's relations with other countries were concerned; prime ministers did not encourage public debate and there was no clear public opinion in this regard. One exception, caused by the prevailing circumstances, was South Africa's relations with Nazi Germany: in line with the deep division among the public on South Africa's participation in the war, opinion was sharply divided on the Union's attitude to Germany.

The public opinion under consideration was, of course, white opinion. As far as black, coloured and Indian opinion was concerned, reference can be made to the repeated attempts, since the early days of the Union, of local black and Indian political organisations to take their causes to the outside world, particularly the United Kingdom.

Feeling that they could find no redress for their grievances from the Union government, they tried to internationalise the issues. After the Second World War, with international opinion much more susceptible to the plight of South Africa's black, coloured and Indian population, and indeed also to that of South West Africa, the practice of appealing to outside opinion gained new momentum. This certainly contributed to the growing international hostility South Africa began encountering after 1945.

From 1948 to 1966

The international and domestic settings

As favourable and receptive as the domestic climate of white opinion in South Africa was in 1948 to the National Party's apartheid policy, so unfavourable and unreceptive was the post-war climate of international opinion. As the Nationalist government determinedly set about legislating its racial ideology in numerous spheres of life, the schism between South Africa and the international community already evident in the last years of the Smuts government was bound to widen. What greatly added to the growing estrangement was the changing composition of the international community as a score of new states emerged from the earlier Western European colonial empires.

Dr DF Malan, the new prime minister, did not accept South Africa's deteriorating international standing with equanimity. Within weeks of coming to power he appointed the retired Te Water as roving ambassador charged with combating what Malan described as the "campaign of hostility and unfairness" being directed against South Africa abroad.[94] Malan, as indeed some of his successors too, believed that international criticism of South Africa was a transient phenomenon, and within ten months of Te Water's temporary appointment, Malan confidently asserted that the roving ambassador had done "excellent work" to "put matters in the right light".[95] However, it soon became evident that the vastly changed post-war international environment was not one in which matters could that easily be "set right". South African diplomats increasingly had to contend with the unpleasant fact that the domestic political base from which they operated was a formidable if not insurmountable obstacle to improving the country's foreign relations.

10

During Malan's tenure of office (1948-1954) the legislative foundations of an apartheid society were laid with the enactment of such key measures as the *Prohibition of Mixed Marriages Act, 1949*, the *Immorality Act, 1950* (prohibiting carnal intercourse between whites and "non-whites"), the *Population Registration Act, 1950* (which provided for the classification of every South African according to race) and the *Group Areas Act, 1950* (which demarated separate residential areas for exclusive occupation by particular racial groups). Malan also paved the way for the eventual removal of the coloureds from the voters' roll in 1956, during Mr JG Strydom's premiership, after a protracted political and legal battle.[96] For blacks in the so-called reserves a three-tier system of "Bantu authorities" – a blend of traditional and Western forms of authority – was created in 1951.

Dr HF Verwoerd, who succeeded Strydom as prime minister in 1958, introduced what became known as grand apartheid, or separate development, as it was officially styled. In 1959 Verwoerd unveiled his radical "new vision" for South Africa's black peoples. This was embodied in the Promotion of Bantu Self-Government Act, which provided for the establishment of eight main homelands for each of the "separate national units" comprising the Union's black population. It was the first time that territorial separation was legislatively explicitly linked to ethnic separation. Through the extension of the "Bantu system of government", introduced in 1951, blacks in the homelands – as the reserves subsequently became known – would under white guardianship gradually develop into self-governing entities. If it was within the ability of the blacks to develop to "full independence", that would happen, Verwoerd envisaged.[97] In 1963 Transkei became the first homeland to proceed to the status of self-government.

It is particularly significant that Verwoerd openly acknowledged that international opinion influenced the government in formulating its homelands blueprint.[98] He was, furthermore, optimistic that international pressure on South Africa would abate as the success of separate development and the whites' honest intentions became evident to the world.[99] Verwoerd's admission regarding foreign opinion was remarkable, and certainly did not conform to his typically uncompromising stance on apartheid. It nonetheless raised an issue that in subsequent years became as controversial as it was important: the

effects that external pressure had on the South African government's domestic and foreign policies.

As apartheid encroached on more areas of life, the resistance of blacks, in particular, increased. In the early 1950s this found dramatic expression in the "Defiance Campaign" initiated by the African National Congress (ANC), designed to effect political change through mass non-violent disobedience. The most dramatic and tragic instance of black protest against government policies was the shooting at Sharpeville on 21 March 1960. This was followed by the government's proclaiming the ANC and the Pan-Africanist Congress (PAC) banned organisations. A dramatic new phase in black opposition to the government was introduced in June 1961, when the ANC endorsed violent resistance and created a subsidiary body, *Umkhonto we Sizwe*, to conduct a campaign of violence. The PAC also took to violence through a similar arm, called *Poqo*. For the next few years South Africa was the scene of a spate of sabotage attacks.[100]

Meanwhile the most cherished ideal of Afrikaner Nationalists – the establishment of a republic – had become reality on 31 May 1961. For some of the more ardent republicans in the National Party it was a bonus that the new Republic was outside the Commonwealth.

On the international front the omens were not good for the new Republic. South Africa's forced departure from the Commonwealth was an outstanding manifestation of the escalating international opposition to apartheid, but it was by no means the only one. The previous year, in February 1960, Mr Harold Macmillan gave his "wind of change" speech in the South African Parliament.[101] The British Prime Minister gave poignant expression to the growing alienation between Britain and South Africa, a trend reinforced by South Africa's severance of the Commonwealth tie[102] and given further impetus by the ascendance of Mr Harold Wilson's Labour Party government in 1964. The advent of the Kennedy Administration in 1961 heralded a period of unprecedented strain in relations between Pretoria and Washington. An indication of the extent to which South Africa had become estranged from its traditional Western allies was when Britain, the United States and other Western countries declared their adherence to the voluntary arms embargo against South Africa called for by the UN Security Council in 1963. South Africa's Western trading partners however refused to heed the resolutions demanding diplomatic and economic sanctions, which the General Assembly began passing with monotonous regularity from November 1962 onwards. Thus, while Western powers were becoming increasingly keen to demonstrate their distance from South Africa in political and military matters, their economic ties with the Republic remained virtually unaffected by the international controversy over the latter's racial policies. Perhaps Western powers deliberately tried to divert international attention from their advantageous economic ties with South Africa by taking public stances on political and military issues.

As Smuts had already experienced, the UN was the focal point of international hostility to South Africa. Successive National Party governments reacted forcefully to what they regarded as the UN's unacceptable and unconstitutional interference in South Africa's domestic (racial) policies. In 1951 the Union temporarily withdrew from the UN,[103] and in 1955 recalled its mission from the tenth session of the General Assembly. The following year it was decided to retain only token representation until the UN agreed to refrain from discussing South Africa's internal affairs. In 1958 South Africa resumed full participation, despite there being little lasting evidence of an "improved sentiment"[104] towards the Union. On the contrary, South Africa, a founder member of the UN and a member of 13 of the UN's 14 specialised agencies, began being excluded from several UN bodies or withdrawing under duress. Thus South Africa's membership of the Economic Commission for Africa (created by the UN's Economic and Social Council), the Food and Agriculture Organisation, the International Labour Organisation and the World Health Organisation was terminated.[105] Under such circumstances it was not surprising that Malan questioned the value of South Africa's continued membership of the UN,[106] and that the Verwoerd Cabinet gave the matter serious consideration.[107] Realising that withdrawal would not stop international condemnation of South Africa and would moreover deny the country a forum to state its case, the government decided to retain membership.

Newly independent states, particularly from black Africa, were in the vanguard of the UN campaign to ostracise South Africa. South Africa's departure from the Commonwealth was in no small measure due to the pressure of a growing number of newly independent "non-white" states in the formerly exclusively white "club". Of all the changes in South Africa's postwar external environment, those in Africa were certainly the most spectacular and far-reaching. When the Nationalists came to power, there were, together with South Africa, only four independent states on the continent. By the end of 1966 the tide of political liberation had reached South Africa's very frontiers, when Botswana and Lesotho gained independence. The year before, another neighbouring territory acquired independence of an entirely different nature, when Rhodesia issued a unilateral declaration of independence. Soon enough Britain's rebel colony found itself subjected to mandatory UN sanctions. South Africa's continued control of South West Africa placed it on a direct collision course with the UN. Following Ethiopia's and Liberia's unsuccessful attempt (1960-66) to get the International Court of Justice to rule on South Africa's administration of South West Africa, the UN General Assembly took matters into its own hands by unilaterally revoking South Africa's mandate. The Assembly also decided to rename the territory "Namibia".[108]

Elsewhere in Southern Africa the remnants of colonialism were coming under increasing pressure. Portugal's control over Angola and Mozambique not only attracted the political wrath of newly independent black African states, but Portugal also had to contend with guerrilla warfare in its African empire since the 1960s.

Despite these developments in its immediate environment, South Africa was in 1966 still left with a *cordon sanitaire* shielding it against militant black states. The cracks were, nonetheless, already evident: Rhodesia was faced with international sanctions and the Portuguese were meeting with violent resistance in Angola and Mozambique. The two other links in the chain were Botswana and Lesotho. Although they adopted a friendly stance towards South Africa and found themselves economically heavily dependent on the Republic, their independence nonetheless represented a new political era in Southern Africa.

The dilemma of formal ties with black states

When Malan identified Africa as the Union's primary diplomatic front, he was not thinking of independent black states – an idea to which he never reconciled himself – but rather of ties between South Africa and the colonial powers.

This found clear expression in Malan's Africa Charter, an anachronistic statement of policy aimed at stemming the tide of decolonisation.[109]

In many cases South Africa's only direct contact with colonial territories was through its participation in a number of inter-territorial organisations for technical co-operation. The organisations of which South Africa became a member were the Commission for Technical Co-operation in Africa South of the Sahara (CCTA) and its two main auxiliary organs, the Scientific Council for Africa South of the Sahara (CSA) and the Inter-African Bureau of Soil Conservation and Land Utilisation (BIS), all established in 1950. Under the aegis of BIS four regional committees were formed, one of which was the familiar Southern African Regional Commission for the Conservation and Utilisation of the Soil (SARCCUS), which had its headquarters in South Africa. Another well-known auxiliary organisation of CCTA to which South Africa belonged was the Foundation for Mutual Assistance in Africa South of the Sahara.[110]

The beginning of a reorientation in South Africa's attitude towards Africa followed the appointment of Mr Eric Louw as the Union's first Minister of External Affairs in January 1955. At the very beginning of his tenure Louw announced that he intended giving particular attention to the Africa section in his Department, describing it as one of the most important. Later in 1955 he reorganised the Africa section to improve contact with other African territories.[111] In 1959 a separate Africa Division was established in the Department – the first geographically based division in a ministry that had previously practised a functional division of labour.[112]

In a celebrated policy statement in March 1957 Louw urged that South Africa "must accept its future role in Africa as a vocation and must in all respects play its full part as an African power." At the same time, however, South Africa could serve as a "permanent link between the Western nations on the one hand and the population of Africa south of the Sahara on the other."[113] South Africa was, in effect, trying to bridge the gap between the ascending and declining orders in Africa by keeping one foot in each. Having nonetheless accepted, albeit grudgingly, the inevitable demise of colonialism and the birth of a new generation of independent black states, the Union was soon confronted with the question of establishing diplomatic relations with them. In 1956 Louw had cautioned that South Africa's policy in this regard

should be one of *festina lente*, adding that the matter should in any case not be discussed at that stage, but rather be left to the future.[114] A year later Strydom acknowledged that diplomatic ties between South Africa and black states would follow, but he too urged caution: the white population would slowly have to be prepared for such a development.[115] On occasion, black representatives from elsewhere in Africa did attend conferences on technical co-operation in South Africa. This prompted the Department of External Affairs to consider building "an international guest house" for foreign delegates – an establishment which, Louw acknowledged, would obviously have to be "multiracial".[116]

Verwoerd, Strydom's successor, shared the view that the domestic climate first had to be prepared for receiving black diplomats in South Africa. When the issue was raised at the fateful 1961 Commonwealth Prime Ministers' Conference, Verwoerd told his counterparts that "a little more progress" should be made with apartheid to avoid the opening of black diplomatic missions causing "confusion" and "incidents".[117] Verwoerd also added a new prerequisite for diplomatic ties with black states: an exchange of missions was "always based on existing friendships", he maintained. He cited Ghana as one of the countries thus disqualified.[118] Verwoerd apparently feared that diplomats from unfriendly black states could act as agents for political change within South Africa.[119] Should black states abandon their hostility towards South Africa, Verwoerd said, diplomatic relations could eventually be established.[120] Louw displayed greater flexibility with his statement that it was not necessary that states approved of each other's policies before entering into diplomatic ties.[121]

The only independent African state with which South Africa had formal diplomatic relations during Verwoerd's premiership was Egypt. The Union's consulate in Egypt, opened during the war, was converted to a legation shortly thereafter. In 1961, however, ties between the two states were severed.[122] Diplomatic links between South Africa and Ghana had been under mutual consideration since 1957, and Louw and President Kwame Nkrumah even reached agreement on establishing such relations in future.[123] Nothing, however, came of it, and Ghana from 1960 became increasingly hostile to South Africa's domestic political arrangements. In 1962 South Africa is said to have made an abortive attempt to establish diplomatic ties with one of the new black states, the Malagasy Republic.[124]

Probably realising the obstacles in the way of formal diplomatic relations between South Africa and black states, Verwoerd proposed that South Africa should be represented by a roving ambassador in nearby black states, and that black states, for their part, should conduct a form of *ad hoc* diplomacy with South Africa by sending members of government on missions to South Africa.[125] The idea of a roving South African envoy, like Te Water had been, was actually accepted but introduced on an *ad hoc* basis and not connected with a particular individual, although the head of the Africa Division in the Department of Foreign Affairs (as the Department of External Affairs was renamed when South Africa became a Republic on 31 May 1961) acted in this capacity.[126] (Although there is, strictly speaking, a difference between a department and a ministry, the two terms are used interchangeably in this book: the Department of Foreign Affairs is also referred to as the foreign ministry. "Diplomatic service" refers specifically to foreign ministry officials eligible for diplomatic positions abroad.)

While dealing with obstacles to diplomatic ties between South Africa and black African states, one should mention the request of the Second Conference of Independent African States, held in Addis Ababa in June 1960, that other African states should not enter into diplomatic relations with South Africa.[127] Two years later the UN General Assembly adopted a resolution calling on states to impose diplomatic sanctions against South Africa. The Organisation of African Unity, established in 1963, immediately added its voice to calls for South Africa's diplomatic isolation by requesting member states either to sever or to refrain from establishing diplomatic ties with the Republic.[128]

A particularly important element of the Africa policies of both Strydom and Verwoerd was the emphasis on the promotion of technical cooperation between South Africa and other African territories, and on South Africa's ability to provide these territories with assistance in such fields as agriculture, medicine, etc.[129] Given the various impediments to political and diplomatic relations between South Africa and the black states, Pretoria saw technical co-operation and the provision of aid as an important channel for communication and, moreover, as a possible forerunner to the eventual establishment of formal ties – thus the high premium South Africa placed on its involvement in organisations such as the CSA and CCTA.

In 1965 South Africa suffered a serious setback when the CCTA, CSA and BIS were either disbanded or absorbed into the OAU, an organisation from which South Africa was excluded. With the exception of SARCCUS, South Africa was in due course denied membership of virtually all the inter-African functional organisations in which it had so actively participated since the early 1950s.[130]

South Africa's diplomatic network

South Africa's exclusion from African technical organisations reflected its growing international ostracism, a phenomenon also manifested in the country's official representation abroad. South Africa's network of missions expanded in terms of numbers and size, and many existing missions were upgraded in status; however, a number of missions had to be closed. When the growth in the number of missions is set against the drastic increase in the number of states over the same period, South Africa's diplomatic network is seen to have actually contracted. Consider the following table:[131]

Year	UN Membership	SA Diplomatic Missions*	SA Consular Missions
1948	58	15	3
1955	76	20	6
1961	104	21	11
1966	122	23	26

*Includes SA mission at the UN

There is no need to examine these figures in any detail, but a number of salient features of South Africa's foreign representation in the 1948-66 period need to be noted briefly.

● South Africa's London representation retained its pre-eminent position. In 1950 Malan ruled that the high commissioner's office was a *de jure* institution of the Department of External Affairs, responsible for handling all political matters between Britain and South Africa and international issues involving both.[132] The mission's staff, which had steadily expanded after the war, experienced further growth after South Africa's departure from the Commonwealth. Having lost the material benefits Commonwealth members derived from Britain's world-wide diplomatic network, South Africa had to try to compensate by enlarging its representation in London and elsewhere. The severance of South Africa's links with the Crown of course meant that the British monarch no longer had to consent to the appointment of heads of missions to and by South Africa. The position of high commissioner was replaced by that of ambassador.[133]

- South Africa's representation in the United States probably showed the greatest growth of all after 1948. The embassy in Washington was considerably enlarged and new consular missions were established in various parts of America.[134] These developments reflected the growing importance of the United States in South Africa's external environment.
- South Africa was represented in fifteen states on the European mainland by the time it became a republic, compared with eight before the war.[135] All fifteen were, significantly, non-communist states. South Africa's only formal ties with a communist power were severed in 1956, when the Union government requested the Soviet Union to close its consulate-general. This move had long been expected, in view of the Nationalist government's vehement anti-communism and the growing suspicion with which the authorities viewed the Soviet mission's activities.[136]
- South Africa experienced mixed fortunes in the Middle East. Although South Africa had no formal ties with Israel, the Jewish state in 1949 opened a consulate in the Union and converted it into a legation the following year.[137] It would take a further two decades before South Africa established a consular presence in Israel. A serious setback for South Africa in the Middle East was the closure of its important mission in Egypt.
- South Africa's representation in the Belgian Congo and Kenya was terminated when the two colonies achieved independence.[138] By the end of Verwoerd's premiership South Africa had failed to establish diplomatic ties with any of the newly independent black states. Its only representation in Africa at that time was in the colonial territories of Angola, Mozambique and Mauritius,[139] and in Rhodesia.[140]
- India closed its diplomatic mission in South Africa in 1954 – at the Union government's request. This was related to the rapidly deteriorating relations between the two countries, manifested in India's imposition of a trade embargo against South Africa in 1946 and India's leading role in the UN's condemnation of the Union's racial policies.[141] The severance of ties

between India and South Africa was an early symbol of the latter's alienation from the emerging group of "non-white" nations.

Whatever the subsequent setbacks, the Department of External Affairs experienced a considerable increase in its responsibilities in the aftermath of the war, as new South African missions were opened abroad or existing ones upgraded or enlarged. To cope, the Department embarked on a major recruiting campaign immediately after the war. This produced a crop of well-educated and eager young recruits, known as "Forsyth's kindergarten". They were mostly English-speaking and probably political supporters of Smuts. Forsyth, a Smuts appointee, was retained as Secretary of External Affairs by Malan. Only in 1956 did Forsyth retire, and was succeeded by Mr GP Jooste, a professional diplomat. It was no secret that the Afrikaans-speaking Jooste was a firm National Party supporter. This is not to suggest that Jooste's political credentials were a deciding factor in his appointment; they would certainly not have counted against him, though.

Although there was sporadic criticism in National Party circles that the Department of External Affairs was too English and pro-Smuts, and that South Africa House in London lacked a South African atmosphere,[142] the incoming Malan government did not subject the Department to any overt or covert political purge. There were, however, some resignations from the Department in the wake of the Nationalist victory, presumably by officials either fearing for their careers or unable to reconcile themselves to serving Malan's government. As Minister of External Affairs, Louw scrupulously upheld the principle of political impartiality. Jooste, however, is said to have concerned himself with the political "reliability" of his officials.[143]

There can be no doubt about the political loyalties of those envoys chosen from outside diplomatic ranks. Malan replaced two of Smuts's appointees, one right away and the other within two years. The luckless Fouché was immediately removed from The Hague, and Malan selected Dr Otto du Plessis, a highly controversial political figure, for the post. This was a blunder of the first order – revealing Malan's ignorance of diplomatic propriety – for the Dutch refused Du Plessis *agrément*.[144] The other Smuts appointee replaced by Malan was Egeland, who, somewhat to his surprise and disappointment, was recalled by Malan in 1950. Egeland had hoped that his continued tenure after 1948 would create a precedent by which South Africa's principal diplomatic position would be kept outside the political reward system.[145] Like his predecessors, Malan however appointed a political ally – though in this case not a politician – Dr AL Geyer, former editor of *Die Burger*, Cape mouthpiece of the National Party.[146] In 1954 Geyer was succeeded by the already mentioned Jooste, the first ever career diplomat to serve as South African high commissioner in London.[147] An early politically motivated "diplomatic" appointment made by the Malan government was that of General Everett Poole, Deputy Chief of the General Staff, who was sent to Berlin as head of the South African Military Mission in 1948. In this case a "diplomatic" posting was unashamedly used to remove a politically undesirable English-speaking military officer who was the main contender for the post of Chief of the Defence Force.[148] Ironically, the person primarily responsible for Poole's removal, Defence Minister FC Erasmus, later found himself the victim of much the same practice.

The Verwoerd premiership saw several political appointments to diplomatic positions, which displayed the full range of typical motives behind such appointments. The appointment of Dr Hilgard Muller as high commissioner (subsequently ambassador) in London in 1961 and that of his successor, Dr CPC de Wet, in 1964, represented promotion for both these National Party MPs. Muller succeeded Louw as Minister of Foreign Affairs in January 1964, and De Wet was appointed Minister of Mines and Planning in 1967. It is significant that in the case of such political appointments, Verwoerd and his Minister of Foreign Affairs allowed the incumbents a large degree of freedom in their diplomatic posts, a reflection of the political masters' faith in their nominees' abilities (and political soundness).

There were at least three cases of unwanted politicians being "dumped" in diplomatic posts. Best known was the appointment of Erasmus, not noted for his ministerial success, as ambassador to Italy in 1961.[149] For much the same reason Dr AJR van Rhyn, Minister of Economic Affairs and Mines, found himself high commissioner in London in 1958.[150] Thus not even the distinguished London post remained immune from less than benevolent party political considerations. The third instance was the appointment of Mr FS Steyn, a seemingly up-and-coming young National Party MP – but somehow not liked

by Verwoerd – as ambassador to Belgium in 1965.[151] Another young Nationalist MP appointed to a diplomatic post under Verwoerd was Dr JJ Fouché, who in 1964 became ambassador to The Netherlands. In this case, an ambassadorship was apparently used to grant *solatia* to a politician widely regarded as aspiring to Cabinet status, but whom Verwoerd for some reason would not elevate.[152]

The information service

An overview of South Africa's foreign representation in the pre-1966 period cannot ignore the activities of the state information organisation.

The last few years of the Smuts government were a period of uncertainty and reappraisal as far as South Africa's information service was concerned.[153] The National Party's assumption of power heralded a new dispensation. In November 1948 Du Plessis (the man Holland refused to accept as South African ambassador) was appointed head of the State Information Office, which had already in 1946 replaced the wartime Bureau for Information. The new government decided that the Office should henceforth concentrate on "combating the hostile propaganda against South Africa abroad."[154] South Africa's foreign information officers, hitherto falling under the departmental jurisdiction of External Affairs, were then attached to the new State Information Office. Despite its external orientation, the Office was placed under the control of the Department of the Interior. This curious arrangement, never publicly explained, understandably caused some political controversy.

In 1949 a start was made with the reorganisation and expansion of the information service. Within a year of Du Plessis's appointment the original four information posts abroad had quadrupled. In 1953 the Union already had fourteen information offices abroad, employing some 30 full-time information officers and attachés. The majority of the new appointees were, significantly, journalists from Afrikaans newspapers. In the process of expansion the information offices in the United Kingdom and the United States remained the most important ones, both in terms of staff complement and amount of work.[155]

Shortly after Louw's appointment as Minister of External Affairs, the information service underwent yet another profound organisational change; "reorganisation" was to become a hallmark of the service. The State Information Office was transferred from the Department of the Interior to External Affairs. Louw, who then became the minister responsible for the information service, justified the move on the grounds that over 80% of the Office's work related to the dissemination of information abroad.[156] By then Mr Piet Meiring had succeeded Du Plessis as director of the Office. In 1957 the Office was renamed the South African Information Service.[157]

A word needs to be said at this juncture about the relationship between the Information Service and the Department of External Affairs. Accommodating the different approaches of the information officer and the diplomat under one roof from the outset proved a difficult exercise in co-existence. A former diplomat, Mr IFA de Villiers, wrote that the diplomat's "stock-in-trade" was confidence and trust. He contrasted that with the information officer, recruited mainly from the ranks of journalism and public relations, who "saw little merit in such dull traditionalism" and preferred "the spectacular selling methods of the advertising profession."[158] Meiring, in turn, depicted the Department of External/Foreign Affairs as "that prim, proper and pompous body" with a "tradition of aloofness", an obsession with diplomatic form and a disinclination "to get their feet wet or their feathers ruffled." The difference in approach between the two institutions "could very well have ended in disaster for us", Meiring wrote, had the Information Service not been placed under Louw. Louw prevented the Service being controlled – and "our efforts smothered" – by the Department of External Affairs, and his keenness to fight the anti-South African propagandists by "giving them hell" allowed wide scope for the Information Service.[159] These early differences between the Department of External Affairs and the Information Service were but an intimation of things to come.

South Africa's information organisation entered another new phase in November 1961, with the establishment of a fully-fledged Department of Information. The core of the new Department consisted of the former South African Information Service. The information sections of the Department of Bantu Administration and Development and of the Department of Coloured Affairs were also transferred to the new Department of Information. Mr FW Waring, one of the first two English-speakers to be brought into a National Party Cabinet after 1948, was appointed Minister of Information by Verwoerd at the end of 1961. Mr WC du Plessis, a former diplomat and at the time first director of the newly established Africa Institute, was appointed secretary of the Department of Information. Du Plessis's tenure was brief, for in 1963 he was appointed Administrator of South West Africa. His place was taken by Mr Brand Fourie, a career diplomat who had joined the foreign ministry before the Second World War.[160]

The Department of Information had a dual function: taking over the information activities abroad of the former South African Information Service, and the domestic dissemination of information previously handled by certain government departments. In the Department's foreign endeavours the United States and Britain were singled out as priority areas, with Western Europe also featuring prominently. Africa was not given high priority; the Department in any case had only one office in the "north", in Salisbury. Two further noteworthy developments were that the emphasis on influencing foreign opinion was shifted from the general public to policy makers and opinion formers, and the services of public relations firms overseas were called upon to assist the Department's efforts abroad.[161] Searching for new improved ways to convey the official "message" was to become a feature of the Department's activities.

Personal diplomacy

The conduct of personal diplomacy by heads of government in the years 1948-66 has a dual significance for the present discussion: it not only serves as a guide to the leaders' role in foreign policy formulation, but also provides a vivid illustration of the increasingly hostile international environment confronting South Africa.

After 1948 South African prime ministers became less and less involved in personal diplomacy. In the first few years of National Party rule, this was partly due to a deliberate attempt to demonstrate to the public the new government's primary concern with domestic matters. Having previously, in opposition, strongly criticised Smuts for being too preoccupied with international affairs at the expense of local issues, the National Party in power was determined not to stand guilty of the same alleged neglect. Yet, notwithstanding this self-imposed constraint, Malan was more actively involved in personal diplomacy than either of his two successors.

In his six years in office Malan attended only

two Commonwealth Prime Ministers' Conferences, in 1949 and 1953 (on the latter occasion also to attend Queen Elizabeth's coronation),[162] and sent Cabinet ministers to deputise for him at the others. Malan's other official visits abroad were to The Netherlands, West Germany, Switzerland and Italy in 1949, and Israel, Belgium, Italy and The Netherlands in 1953.[163]

Strydom and Verwoerd, by contrast, engaged in very little personal diplomacy abroad. This could to some extent probably be attributed to their preoccupation with domestic affairs, and also to initial inexperience in foreign policy matters. Another reason was the presence of a foreign minister since 1955, who could relieve the prime minister of at least some burdens in the realm of foreign affairs. There was another major factor, South Africa's low international standing and its growing ostracism. Particularly after Sharpeville, many of South Africa's traditional allies would have been reluctant to officially receive its head of government. A good illustration of the mounting isolation was South Africa's departure from the Commonwealth, something which meant the loss of the prime minister's principal forum for personal diplomacy.

During his premiership Strydom's only official visit abroad was to attend the 1956 Commonwealth Prime Ministers' Conference. Strydom, as indeed Malan, did not relish attending Commonwealth meetings and was a reluctant participant.[164] Verwoerd's only foreign visit in his capacity as prime minister was to attend South Africa's final Commonwealth Conference in 1961. (He meant to attend the 1960 conference, but was prevented by injuries sustained in an assassination attempt in April 1960.)[165] At the remaining Commonwealth leaders' meetings, ministers deputised for the two prime ministers. Symptomatic of the country's poor international standing was that the Union's information service made ambitious special efforts during Strydom's and Verwoerd's visits to London to present them to the British press and public.[166]

No National Party prime minister has ever attended a meeting of the UN General Assembly. Smuts's presence at the Assembly's very first session was, in fact, the last by a South African prime minister. The unenviable task of representing South Africa at Assembly sessions was frequently left to Louw, even before his appointment as Minister of External Affairs. In the course of his fifteen years in the Cabinet, Louw nine times led the South African delegation to the General Assembly.[167]

What might have been a major diplomatic coup for Verwoerd, had it materialised, was his private proposal to visit President Kennedy in Washington. The proposal failed to meet with a favourable response – an indication of the strains in US-South African relations and also of Verwoerd's misreading of the prevailing mood in America after Kennedy's election.[168] The highest level contact between the two states in Verwoerd's time was Louw's talks with Mr Dean Rusk, Secretary of State, in 1962.[169]

While on the subject of personal diplomacy one should mention visits by foreign dignitaries to South Africa, since the decline in these also reflected the country's steady slide into international unpopularity and ostracism.

At the highest level – which is actually above that of personal diplomacy – there was the visit of the British royal family to South Africa the year before the National Party came to power. The Nationalist Opposition effectively boycotted the visit. In 1951, however, Malan invited King George VI to recuperate in South Africa after a serious operation. Before he could take up Malan's invitation, the King died.[170] Malan's was not an invitation for a royal visit in the true sense of the word, but rather a gesture of goodwill. It was, in any case, very doubtful whether a 1947-style royal visit could have taken place after the Nationalists had come to power: it would probably have been politically inexpedient for the Nationalist republicans, and certainly politically embarrassing for the British government – more because of apartheid than republicanism, however.

The early estrangement between South Africa and Britain was borne out during a visit to the Union by Mr Patrick Gordon-Walker, Secretary of State for Commonwealth Relations, in 1951. Malan used the opportunity to complain publicly about the disparity in the frequency of South African ministerial visits to the United Kingdom and that of British ministers to the Union, and expressed the feeling that his government was being kept at arm's length by the British.[171]

A royal visitor who came to South Africa during Malan's premiership was Prince Bernhard of The Netherlands in 1954. The year before, the Dutch Prime Minister, Dr W Drees, paid an official visit to the Union.[172] Also in 1953 Australian Prime Minister Robert Menzies visited South Africa.[173]

It was not until 1960 that a Western head of government again officially visited South Africa –

the last one to do so during Verwoerd's premiership. The occasion was Macmillan's visit, which in the event was not one of which the South African government entertained pleasant memories: the "wind of change" speech was hardly an eulogy on Anglo-South African friendship.

South Africa received dignitaries from unexpected quarters in the early 1960s. In January 1961 Mr Dag Hammarskjöld, the UN Secretary-General, visited South Africa and held lengthy talks with Verwoerd. The following year saw another UN visit to South Africa, this time the ill-fated, farcical Carpio mission on South West Africa.[174] There was a touch of irony in South Africa being visited, in a time of increasing isolation, by representatives from the very organisation that was the focal point of moves to ostracise the country from the international community.

Little is publicly known about South Africa's diplomatic contacts with black African countries in the 1960s. It has, however, been revealed that two ministers from break-away Katanga secretly visited South Africa in August 1961 at the government's invitation.[175] This was probably one of the earliest cases of South Africa's secret diplomacy in black Africa. The first public diplomatic encounter between a South African prime minister and a black head of government took place in September 1966 when Chief Leabua Jonathan, Prime Minister of the soon-to-be-independent Basutoland (Lesotho), met Verwoerd in Pretoria. There was apprehension in government circles about a publicised meeting between the prime minister and a foreign black leader,[176] but the occasion proved a diplomatic success and represented a breakthrough in more ways than one. South Africa had established formal and open contact with a black leader who was, moreover, keen to co-operate with the Republic, and Verwoerd in a highly visible manner legitimised official top-level diplomatic exchanges with black African countries, a matter long shrouded in racial taboos.

Despite such diplomatic successes, the overall trend in the 1948-66 period was towards an increasing home-boundness of South African heads of government and a greater infrequency in the visits of foreign leaders to South Africa. The decline in personal diplomacy may well have enhanced the importance of conventional diplomatic channels, represented by the foreign ministry. However, these too had their limitations in a hostile world, and this realisation gave rise to the subsequent employment of what became known as unconventional diplomacy, conducted not by the Department of Foreign Affairs, but by the Department of Information.

Key foreign policy formulators

The conduct of personal diplomacy offers some guide to the principal formulators of South African foreign policy. It is by no means the only indicator, and has to be supplemented by various others. The use of such devices in trying to construct a picture of reality is essential, given the scarcity of "hard" information on South African foreign policy formulation. Among these indicators are the prime ministers' formal Cabinet responsibilities, their knowledge of and interest in foreign affairs, and the involvement of other politicians and officials in this area.

Prime Minister Malan

Malan, already 74 when he became prime minister, apparently thought that if Smuts could have carried the External Affairs portfolio together with his other prime ministerial responsiblities, then so could he.[177] National Party MPs saw Malan's decision as perfectly natural in view of established practice, and they moreover thought the portfolio was given special status by being handled by the prime minister. Geyer, who was on particularly close terms with Malan, however wrote that the main reason for the prime minister's decision to take on the portfolio was "to prevent certain problems within his parliamentary party."[178]

Malan's actual role in foreign policy formulation – despite what his considerable involvement in personal diplomacy might suggest – was not as clear-cut as that of either Hertzog or Smuts, both of whom dominated foreign policy formulation in their respective governments and were outstanding innovators in this field. A common view is that Malan lacked the interest, knowledge, experience and skills necessary in foreign affairs.[179] These qualities, with which Smuts, in particular, had been richly endowed – as will be shown in the final chapter – have an important bearing on a leader's role in policy formulation. Malan was, nonetheless, not totally uninitiated in the intricacies of international politics when he became prime minister. Probably his first real experience came as early as 1919 when he was a member of the National Party's "freedom deputation" to the United States and the

Versailles Peace Conference.[180] As a member of Hertzog's government Malan was of course exposed to foreign policy issues. He was also, as Minister of the Interior, involved in the 1927 Cape Town talks with representatives from India on the position of the Union's Indian community.

As prime minister, Malan showed no desire to play the role of international statesman, as Smuts had done. In any case, as already suggested, that was not a desirable distinction for a Nationalist prime minister in the wake of Smuts's example.[181] However, to contend that Malan "took no active part in foreign affairs, apart from attending meetings of the Commonwealth Premiers in London",[182] would not be fair. It is true that Malan regarded South Africa's relations with the Commonwealth as a matter of crucial importance, and was in fact well informed on Commonwealth affairs.[183] Given the salience of the British connection as an issue in domestic South African politics, it was only to be expected that Malan would actively concern himself with the matter. Yet this was not the only foreign policy issue in which Malan became deeply involved.

With great vigour he took up the decades-old issue of the future of the three British high commission territories of Bechuanaland, Basutoland and Swaziland. Each of Malan's predecessors had tried in vain to persuade Britain to transfer the territories to South Africa. What Malan elevated to a major foreign policy initiative turned out to be his biggest failure in this field. Malan had at the outset been warned by none other than Geyer, then high commissioner in London, that the renewed quest for transfer was doomed to failure. This Malan chose to ignore and pressed ahead with his approach to the British government, only to receive a downright rebuff.[184]

Another foreign policy matter in which Malan played a leading part was that of trying to get South Africa involved in a military pact with Western powers. Considering that the Nationalists, in opposition, had opposed South African participation in the Allied war effort, Malan's patent keenness to seek South African membership of the North Atlantic Treaty Organisation (NATO) and his pledge of support for the West in any future conflict with the communist powers may indeed appear strange. Yet it was his deep-seated opposition to communism that led Malan to renounce the National Party's wartime commitment to neutrality. On a less ambitious plane was the

Malan government's efforts to create an African defence pact with the colonial powers. Both these endeavours were unsuccessful.

Turning to other Cabinet members – the Cabinet certainly was the locus of decision making – five of them featured more or less prominently in foreign policy formulation. First, there was Havenga, then Minister of Finance (and until October 1951 leader of the small coalition partner, the Afrikaner Party) and senior member of the Cabinet. Havenga was particularly close to Malan and was in fact his choice for successor to the premiership. One indication of Havenga's importance in foreign policy matters was Malan's decision to assign his Finance Minister the thankless task of negotiating with the British government over the future of the high commission territories in 1953 – and that while Malan himself was in London attending the Commonwealth Conference.[185] Erasmus, Minister of Defence and thus involved in the search for defence pacts and in talks started with the British government on the future of Britain's naval base at Simonstown, had an obvious foreign policy role too. Erasmus, however, made no significant contribution on the wider foreign policy front, not least because Malan appeared to share widely held reservations about the Defence Minister's competence.[186] Two other ministers whose opinions Malan valued were Dr TE Dönges, Minister of the Interior, and Mr PO Sauer, Minister of Transport. Two senior men in the Cape National Party, they belonged to Malan's inner circle of confidants.[187] Both were on occasion selected by Malan to represent South Africa on international forums: Dönges led the South African delegation to the UN General Assembly in 1950 and 1951, and Sauer headed the South African team at the 1951 Nairobi conference on the defence of Africa.

Last, but certainly not least, was Louw, Minister of Economic Affairs and Mining. He was by far the most experienced member of the new government in international affairs and could therefore speak with authority. Louw would have placed a high premium on his own expertise and thus his "right" to speak on foreign policy matters, and he no doubt offered Malan liberal doses of advice. In addition, Louw was a National Party stalwart, having first been elected to Parliament in 1924. But while undoubtedly influential, Louw's contribution should not be exaggerated. He decidedly was not the principal foreign policy formulator during Malan's premiership; that

Malan was, notwithstanding his known short-comings in this field. Louw was, moreover, never particularly close to Malan – despite being a Cape MP – and relations between them were often strained.[188] It is then not surprising that Dönges instead of Louw, the more obvious choice, was twice sent to the UN.

Malan retained Forsyth as Secretary of External Affairs despite agitation in the National Party-supporting press for his replacement.[189] Forsyth served Malan with the same characteristic loyalty and dedication as he had Smuts, and they worked together closely and amicably. With his limited experience in foreign affairs, particularly regarding the more technical aspects of international relations, Malan leaned heavily on Forsyth's advice and guidance.[190] As for the substance of foreign policy, Forsyth would not have made any real contribution.

Smuts, who served as leader of the opposition until 1950, the year of his death, was not someone whose counsel on foreign affairs was sought by the new government. The Nationalists resented what they regarded as Smuts's arrogance by still acting in the fashion of official South African spokesman on the international scene. They also blamed him for allegedly undermining foreign confidence in South Africa by presenting a highly negative picture of the Nationalist government.[191] Similar charges were to be heard frequently in later years. Smuts's rapid relegation to the periphery of foreign policy making set the scene for the opposition's role (or rather lack thereof) in this field in future.

Prime Minister Strydom

Of South Africa's post-war prime ministers, Strydom left the smallest imprint on foreign policy. For this there are several possible explanations. It may have been related to his relatively short premiership (1954-58), in the last year of which he moreover suffered ill health; this would have left Strydom with even less time for foreign affairs, over which domestic issues already took precedence. Another credible reason is that Strydom's years in office were not marked by many major new developments in South Africa's foreign relations, compared with Malan's or Verwoerd's premiership. The outstanding occurrence on the foreign policy front was South Africa's conclusion of the Simonstown Agreement with Britain in 1955.[192] Preparatory talks leading to the agreement were, however, begun during Malan's term of office. Strydom is

not known to have taken a particularly active part in the shaping of the agreement, instead leaving most of it to Defence Minister Erasmus. As for the high commission territories, Strydom did not pursue the issue with anything like Malan's determination, probably realising that it would have been fruitless. South Africa's attitude towards the rest of Africa was going through a period of uncertainty and reappraisal. With colonialism in retreat and independent black states emerging, the Union was in search of a new role and identity in a rapidly changing continent.

Strydom's own lack of knowledge and experience in foreign affairs must also be mentioned. His portfolio in Malan's Cabinet – Lands – was about as far removed from the plane of high world politics as could be. These considerations probably weighed heavily with Strydom in his decision to appoint Louw as Minister of External Affairs in January 1955. Not surprisingly, Strydom explained the break with the tradition of the prime minister holding the External Affairs portfolio in different terms. He told Parliament it was impractical "that I should personally take the responsibility for the whole administration of South Africa." The demands being placed on a prime minister made it "impossible to do justice to a particular portfolio too".[193] Of course, this in itself would have been a plausible reason for relinquishing External Affairs.

By entrusting the portfolio to Louw, Strydom was not completely freeing himself of foreign affairs.[194] That, in any case, would have been impossible in a system where the Cabinet was the principal forum for the formulation of foreign policy. In a small state, particularly one in which domestic and foreign affairs were so closely interwoven – in South Africa's case it concerned both apartheid and the British connection – the head of government could simply not have afforded distancing himself from foreign policy concerns. Strydom's role in foreign policy seldom extended beyond such obligatory involvement, so to speak. He left matters largely to Louw, who was not only the Cabinet's foremost expert in international affairs, but also a close political ally of the prime minister.[195] Louw's aggressiveness in the diplomatic arena, it can be added, no doubt suited the fiery political style of Strydom, a passionate republican and apartheid hardliner. The assertive Louw, who had apparently long been aspiring to the External Affairs portfolio,[196] would have been only too pleased about the free hand Strydom gave him. With neither major new initiatives nor dramatic reverses in South Africa's foreign relations during his premiership, it was of course easier for Strydom to leave foreign affairs largely in Louw's hands. It could, however, be argued that the absence of foreign policy initiatives was partly the result of the uncharacteristic lack of active involvement on the part of the prime minister.

Prime Minister Verwoerd

Prime Minister Verwoerd, who had been one of Strydom's greatest confidants and shared many of his predecessor's political convictions, differed greatly from Strydom in the handling of foreign policy matters.

For a start, Verwoerd's ministerial portfolio – he had served as Minister of Native Affairs for eight years prior to becoming prime minister in 1958 – had been far less insulated from foreign affairs than Strydom's, given the internationalisation of South Africa's racial policies Verwoerd could also lay claim to some previous experience in foreign affairs, albeit in a completely different capacity. As editor of *Die Transvaler*, the National Party's Transvaal mouthpiece, from 1937 to 1948, he frequently commented – in typically forthright, uncompromising fashion – on such matters as the British connection and republicanism and South Africa's involvement in the Second World War.[197]

Louw, who had already been Minister of External Affairs for nearly four years when Verwoerd became prime minister, was retained in the portfolio. It is highly unlikely that Verwoerd at the time even considered the possibility of replacing Louw, for he was unrivalled in the Cabinet for expertise in foreign affairs, and he represented both experience and continuity. There was, moreover, no precedent for an incoming National Party prime minister to change drastically the composition of a Cabinet inherited from his predecessor. Louw, in addition, was a senior minister – in party political terms very much the senior of Verwoerd, who only became a Senator in 1948 – and his tough-minded approach to foreign affairs was still widely applauded in National Party circles.

In his first year or two as prime minister, Verwoerd tended to rely heavily on Louw's knowledge and guidance in foreign policy matters. One indication was Verwoerd's public speeches, which were notably lacking in major statements on foreign policy, containing little more than general declarations of friendship and goodwill. The rest was left to Louw, a man with a penchant for public statements.[198] As he gained in experience and self-confidence in this field, Verwoerd felt less need of Louw's – or anyone else's – advice, and the prime minister soon established himself as the dominant figure in foreign policy formulation.

Verwoerd's ascendance in the formulation of foreign policy was, in a sense, merely an extension into another field of the predominance he already enjoyed in many areas of domestic policy formulation. Verwoerd's supremacy in the Cabinet and the firm rein he kept on his ministers – to the extent of interfering with the discharge of their departmental responsibilities[199] – resembled Smuts's position. Verwoerd also brought some of the same personal characteristics as Smuts to bear on the premiership, such as a brilliant mind, a tremendous capacity for work and a strong political will. The latter, in Verwoerd's case, applied particularly to the pursuit of the policy of separate development, a cause to which he was tenaciously, rigidly committed. Verwoerd's supremacy in the Cabinet, it should be explained, was not based on coercion, but rather on his superb intellect and powers of persuasion. The seeming logic at his command and the sheer daunting experience of getting locked in argument with him – Verwoerd relished argumentation with ministers and senior officials – are features commonly recalled by Cabinet members and officials who served under him.[200] To all this should be added that Verwoerd, in a relatively short space of time, achieved a standing in Afrikanerdom that has never before or since been equalled by a National Party prime minister. Verwoerd, in short, had the qualities of an exceptional leader, and these made him approach foreign affairs with a strong dose of self-assurance and with single-minded dedication in championing causes he considered just.

It would be wrong to infer that Verwoerd in due course became effectively the sole foreign policy formulator and that Louw was reduced to little more than an agent or appendage. For years Louw remained highly influential and respected; Verwoerd decidedly still relied on his contributions in shaping foreign policy. Towards the end of his tenure, Louw's influence however waned considerably. With age, the Foreign Minister became notably more irritable, quarrelsome and intolerant, even among his colleagues – features not designed to enhance his standing in government circles. The years of attacks he had to endure abroad had also left Louw embittered.[201](What aggravated matters was that Louw became hard of hearing, frequently landing the irritable minister in embarrassing misunderstandings in exchanges with others.)

It is not surprising that Verwoerd on occasion either circumvented Louw for Secretary Jooste, or simply handled a foreign policy issue on his own. On the whole, Louw's role in foreign policy formulation was certainly considerably less influential under Verwoerd than under Strydom.

Louw's successor, Muller, served for nearly two years under Verwoerd before the latter's death in September 1966. Muller had probably been earmarked by Verwoerd for elevation to the Cabinet. His appointment as high commissioner in London in 1961 was already an indication that the prime minister had bigger things in mind for this popular and promising Nationalist MP, first elected to Parliament in 1958. Under Verwoerd, Foreign Minister Muller carried relatively little weight in foreign policy formulation, certainly much less than Louw. This can be explained in terms of Verwoerd's self-confidence in foreign affairs, the close working relationship between Verwoerd and Jooste, Muller's very junior status in the Cabinet, and also the differences in personality between Muller and Louw. By nature, Louw would in no uncertain terms have insisted on his "right" to make known his views on foreign policy, whereas the mild-mannered, self-effacing and cautious Muller was not one to express or impress his views in such a forthright fashion.

Although Muller's role was mostly instrumental, Verwoerd allowed him two significant innovations. The first was the new tenor introduced in Muller's speech in the UN General Assembly in 1964: conciliatory, reasoned and positive, after Louw's often offensive outbursts. Second, Muller began focusing particular attention on South Africa's relations with South American states, thus paving the way for visits he and Prime Minister Vorster later paid to the area.

A head of government's involvement in major foreign policy issues can serve as an indication of his role in policy formulation. Another reason for considering a leader's involvement is that it can reveal something about the effects of personal characteristics on policy. These are indeed useful guides in explaining Verwoerd's performance in the realm of foreign policy.

The year 1960 marked Verwoerd's debut in the world of high-level diplomacy. Macmillan's visit in January-February afforded Verwoerd his first opportunity for direct talks with a distinguished counterpart, and for measuring his political convictions and diplomatic skills against those of a foreign leader. Although they held lengthy private consultations, it was Macmillan's "wind of change" speech that provided Verwoerd with his greatest challenge, moreover one in the full glare of the public. The thrust of Macmillan's address came as an unexpected, rude shock to most white South Africans. Verwoerd, who had not been given a copy of his guest's speech beforehand – as diplomatic convention required – immediately took up the gauntlet, and his off-the-cuff reply was widely hailed in South Africa as an impressive, highly effective impromptu performance. The accolades Verwoerd received enhanced his domestic stature tremendously, and he was seen as having won his spurs in the field of international politics.[202]

The aftermath of the Sharpeville shooting in March can also be regarded as a kind of trial of strength for Verwoerd in foreign relations. The torrent of foreign criticism and unprecedented international pressure on the South African government to mend its ways domestically – supplemented in some cases by voices from within the National Party calling for reform – prompted Verwoerd's famous response that the government and leaders "will have to stand like walls of granite because the survival of a nation is at stake."[203] Far from necessitating the abolition of separate development, the unrest and violence underlined that peace, good order and friendly race relations "can best be served through this policy", Verwoerd asserted.[204] This statement illustrated Verwoerd's typical reaction in a crisis situation: far from deflecting him from apartheid, it reinforced his determination to preach and apply it more vigorously than ever, thus proceeding farther in the very direction his critics rejected.[205] Verwoerd put it thus: "The greater the pressure on us to make concessions, the more emphatic we must be in refusing to do so."[206] It is not impossible that Verwoerd invoked his "granite" stance to signal to the outside world that there was no point in exerting pressure for change in South Africa, since his government would not submit.

For Verwoerd, it should be borne in mind, the overriding, immutable and non-negotiable objective of national policies was the maintenance of a white nation in South Africa. When South Africa therefore rejected concessions in its racial policies, he explained, it was because such concessions would destroy whites' freedom, independence and survival. Friendship with other states could only be sought within the limits of South Africa's inalienable right to decide on its own domestic policies, according to Verwoerd.[207] "Without any hesitation, my choice is to have fewer friends and ensure the survival of my nation."[208] The realms of domestic and foreign affairs should in other words be separated; the exigencies of the latter should not affect the course of the former.

In expounding his homelands design, Verwoerd nonetheless, as mentioned, explicitly acknowledged the influence of external pressure – an admission that he later privately conceded to have been a mistake.[209] To have openly taken foreign considerations into account would seem to have been in conflict with a longstanding tenet of South African foreign policy, the rejection of interference by others in what was regarded as South Africa's domestic affairs. For Verwoerd such interference detracted from South Africa's sovereignty, something he was extremely sensitive, indeed obsessive, about. Even so, there is another instance where Verwoerd is said to have been influenced by external factors in a matter of domestic policy. The occasion was the visit by UN Secretary-General Hammarskjöld to South Africa in 1961. This visit also involved Verwoerd in high-level personal diplomacy; it was moreover the first ever visit by a UN chief to South Africa.

Hammarskjöld's visit was in pursuance of a UN Security Council resolution adopted in the wake of the Sharpeville shooting in 1960. It requested the Secretary-General, in consultation with the Union government, "to make such arrangements as would adequately help in upholding the purposes and principles of the Charter" (in South Africa). Having first reached agreement with Pretoria that the Secretary-General's discussion of the Council's resolution would not require prior recognition from the Union government of UN authority over its racial affairs, Hammarskjöld held no fewer than six meetings with Verwoerd in the course of his six-day visit in January.

The Secretary-General subsequently reported that his talks with Verwoerd had not yet produced any "mutually acceptable arrangement" to safeguard human rights in South Africa. In similar vein, Verwoerd told Parliament that "most divergent points of view had at times to be put on both sides". Nonetheless, Verwoerd and Hammarskjöld appeared to have found some *rapport*, and both publicly described their talks as

useful. What is more, both declared their intention to continue the consultations in future. Before this could happen, Hammarskjöld died in an air crash.

The intruiging side of the Hammarskjöld-Verwoerd meetings is the effect they were said to have had on the prime minister. Hammarskjöld underlined what he regarded as the dangerous implications of apartheid for South Africa's internal stability and its peaceful relations with other states. Several (un-named) South African diplomats are said to have remarked that no exchanges had created such doubts in Verwoerd's mind about the apartheid policy, as had his talks with Hammarskjöld. This seems to tie in with the notion that Verwoerd advanced by two years the planned date of granting Transkei self-government (which it received in 1963) because of the influence of the Secretary-General upon him.[210]

Verwoerd's next important test in foreign relations came with the Commonwealth Prime Ministers' Conference in London in March 1961. He went to the conference determined to try to secure South Africa's continued membership after becoming a republic. In the face of the vehement criticism of South Africa's racial policies expressed by many Commonwealth leaders on this occasion, Verwoerd decided to withdraw his request for continued membership, and South Africa left the Commonwealth. What may appear to have been a setback for Verwoerd in London was transformed into a triumph when some 50 000 people turned out to accord him a hero's welcome at Jan Smuts Airport.[211] Verwoerd was clearly not going to disappoint the faithful and, in a short speech, reaffirmed his approach to South Africa's foreign relations:

We have triumphed – not over another country, nor over Britain, but we have freed ourselves from the pressure of the Afro-Asian nations who were busy invading the Commonwealth. We were not prepared to allow these countries to dictate what our future should be . . . Therefore, we now go forward alone.[212]

Verwoerd ruled out a return to the Commonwealth, since that "must entail giving up the struggle of the White man to maintain himself in this country."[213] Casting a foreign policy issue in survival terms was something Verwoerd frequently resorted to; with (white) survival in

South Africa at stake, there could for him be no question of compromise.

It is significant that Verwoerd took the decision to end South Africa's Commonwealth membership without consulting his Cabinet, not to mention Parliament.[214] It was a unilateral act of far-reaching consequence, reminiscent of Smut's acceptance of South African membership of the League of Nations and the UN. And it again reflected Verwoerd's status and self-assurance in foreign policy matters – features he shared with Smuts. Louw was, nonetheless, intimately involved in the dramatic events in London, and he too basked in the glory upon Verwoerd's return.

In another major foreign policy issue Verwoerd again was the main, largely sole, actor. It concerned South Africa's response to Rhodesia's UDI.[215] Foreign Minister Muller was frequently by-passed by Verwoerd, who was in regular contact with British Prime Minister Harold Wilson through South Africa's Ambassador in London, De Wet, as intermediary. In his dealings with Wilson Verwoerd again displayed his characteristic attitude of no compromise on what he regarded as matters of principle. South Africa, Verwoerd informed Wilson, would not "sacrifice… her principles on non-intervention in the affairs of other nations and of non-aggression, including no participation in sanctions." Apart from this "moral issue", Verwoerd also told Wilson that "South Africa and its government are quite convinced that she would seal her own doom" if the Republic were to support sanctions against Rhodesia. Verwoerd explained that, in view of the poor record of countries under black rule in Africa, "realism demands that South Africa must avoid becoming co-responsible for such a possible real danger" in Rhodesia too.[216] The Prime Minister was again presenting the issue – and justifying South Africa's stance – in terms of considerations of survival.

A year before Rhodesia's UDI Verwoerd had his first confrontation with the new British Labour government over its support for the UN Security Council's arms embargo against South Africa. This immediately put a question mark over a contract between South Africa and Britain for the supply of sixteen British-manufactured Buccaneer strike aircraft to the Republic. Verwoerd saw the arms embargo as part of Western pressure on South Africa – in response to black African states' pressure on Western powers – to introduce black rule in the Republic. It was, once again, a question of survival and therefore white South Africans would not submit "because our lives are at stake."[217] In the end, Wilson agreed to honour the contract for the Buccaneers, but would allow no new arms deals with South Africa.

Another important foreign policy-related matter handled by Verwoerd was the future of the British high commission territories. In September 1963 he suggested that if South Africa were to become the "guardian" of the territories, "we could lead them far better and much more quickly to independence and economic prosperity than Great Britain can do." With the high commission territories drawn into the homelands design, Verwoerd envisaged a common market together with a "consultative political body of free Black and White states" in Southern Africa.[218] Britain rejected his guardianship proposal and decided to lead the three territories to independence its own way. Verwoerd's scheme for regional relations nonetheless formed the basis of South Africa's regional policy in subsequent years.

The issues mentioned show that Verwoerd's unflinching commitment to the ideology of separate development influenced his foreign policy behaviour. There are a number of other celebrated instances of Verwoerd's inflexibility on racial matters, specifically so-called petty apartheid, being carried over into the realm of foreign relations. The British Ambassador, Sir John Maud, in the early 1960s abolished the convention of two separate receptions to mark the Queen's birthday – one for whites only in the morning and a racially mixed one in the afternoon – and instead held a single reception open to all races. The Cabinet thereupon solemnly decided that no minister or official may attend a racially mixed diplomatic function[219] – a decision that remained in force for many years. Another instance concerned the visit of the aircraft carrier, the USS *Independence*, to Cape Town in 1965, when Verwoerd ruled that no American military aircraft with a racially mixed crew may land at South African airfields in the area. America responded by calling off the visit.[220] Another incident involving the United States also occured in 1965, when Verwoerd issued an advance warning to America, which intended siting a satellite tracking station in South Africa, that he would not allow black American personnel at such an installation.[221] Also in the same year, Verwoerd in his well-known Loskop Dam speech declared that South Africa would not receive any New Zealand rugby team with Maori players.[222] Finally, there was the largely unknown case of the visit to South Africa by the Portuguese Foreign Minister, who happened to be married to an Asiatic woman. The Cabinet seriously considered whether she should be admitted to South Africa, but Verwoerd in this case gave way and she accompanied her husband.[223]

It should in fairness also be said that Verwoerd on occasion displayed a commendable degree of flexibility in foreign policy matters, such as his decision to allow the Carpio mission to visit South Africa and South West Africa, and his meeting with Jonathan. And when at his rigid best (or worst) in foreign affairs, Verwoerd had a saving grace of sorts in that he behaved with "conspicuous courtesy and dignity", in the words of a Commonwealth prime minister.[224]

Foreign Ministers Louw and Muller

It is no exaggeration to say that combativeness and tactlessness were outstanding features of Louw's behaviour as Minister of External/Foreign Affairs. These were only compounded by his touchiness and unpredictability. On the credit side, Louw was a committed patriot and an intrepid fighter for "South Africa's cause"; he was, furthermore, a highly dedicated minister with an exceptional capacity for work. These positive attributes could, however, not mask the damage Louw's characteristic behaviour caused South Africa's foreign relations. One of the purposes of foreign policy is, after all, to try to orientate other states favourably towards the ego state.

Consider the following examples. In the absence of Verwoerd, Louw represented South Africa at the 1960 Commonwealth Conference. Following within months of the Sharpeville shooting, the proceedings of the now multiracial Commonwealth Conference were, not surprisingly, overshadowed by apartheid. Louw was involved in verbal skirmishes with several of the assembled premiers in discussions of South Africa's racial policies. Among those who took exception to Louw's conduct was Tunku Abdul Rahman, Prime Minister of Malaya, who accused Louw, in one of the meetings, of treating the prime ministers "like schoolboys". Rahman walked out of a later meeting with Louw, claiming that Louw was "uncompromising" and took apartheid "to the extreme limit of unreasonableness"; Rahman also refused to attend any further talks with him.[225] Following Louw's performance at the conference, Mr Duncan Sandys, British Commonwealth Secretary, at the 1961 Commonwealth Conference appealed to Muller, South Africa's high commissioner, that Louw be kept "under cover" for fear that his conduct could only harm South Africa's chances of remaining in the Commonwealth.[226]

A more dramatic and highly publicised show-down occurred in September 1961, when Louw addressed the UN General Assembly. He presented the Assembly with a "review (of) the African scene", in which, among other things, he questioned whether territories given independence "are ready to assume the responsibilities of statehood"; said that Western democratic political institutions could not survive in the alien African environment; claimed that many black African leaders were becoming "recruits for Moscow and Peking"; contrasted the "unrest and turmoil" in several African countries with the "quiet conditions" prevailing in South Africa; pointed to colour and other forms of discrimination in African countries; explained separate development in highly positive fashion and contrasted its achievements – for example in black education – with that of black African countries, and maintained that black African leaders attacking South Africa were doing so to gain popularity and leadership status.[227] Louw's address so incensed members of his audience that the Assembly adopted a motion of censure, after an initial attempt to have Louw's speech expunged from the record of the proceedings.[228] It should be added that although the sharpness of these utterances carried Louw's distinct imprint, they essentially reflected the official South African "view of the world". Also, Louw was not the only South African exponent – but certainly the leading one – of the practice of attacking the country's critics and comparing their domestic records with South Africa's. According to one analyst, there was an "important principle" at stake here: "those who attack South Africa should not be guilty of the same 'malpractices'."[229] Whether it was a matter of principle or mere tactics, the fact is that the practice of hitting back and drawing unfavourable comparisons were typical features of South Africa's foreign policy behaviour in Louw's time.

The feelings that Louw's conduct often aroused in foreigners were poignantly expressed by one of them: "If your Eric Louw had to read the New York telephone directory from the rostrum it would sound to his opponents as a personal insult directed at each of them."[230]

The negative reactions Louw generated abroad were not lost on Verwoerd and some other ministers, and South African diplomats were certainly painfully aware of the damage their minister's performances often caused.[231] It is interesting to reflect that whereas Louw's personal style complemented that of Strydom, it was in sharp contrast to Verwoerd's seemingly unemotive, reasoned and courteous behaviour.

An early indication of Verwoerd's unease with Louw's conduct of foreign affairs was the elaborate and enthusiastic welcome laid on for the Foreign Minister on his return from the UN in 1961 – the very session where he got a vote of censure on his speech. As Munger rightly remarked, "the flow of congratulatory statements by the Prime Minister and by the Afrikaans press almost suffocated Mr Louw in flowers."[232] That indeed seemed to have been the purpose of this carefully contrived exercise. By telling him that he had reached the pinnacle of his career, Verwoerd was trying to suggest to Louw that he should consider leaving public life cast in the mould of a hero. Louw, however, either failed to get the message or chose to ignore it. Two years later Verwoerd took the next step, a much less subtle one, when he decided not to send Louw to lead the South African delegation to the 1963 UN General Assembly. Instead, the Republic's delegation was led by Jooste, Secretary of Foreign Affairs. The move greatly upset Louw, and not long after, the 73 year old minister announced his retirement.[233]

Muller's personal style differed profoundly from Louw's and appeared far better suited to Verwoerd's own. The calm, composed and urbane Muller in some ways resembled the manner of a classical Oxford don (perhaps not an incidental characteristic of this former Rhodes scholar and Latin teacher at the University of Pretoria). South African diplomats no doubt widely welcomed their new minister's more conciliatory diplomatic style, and the actual dread with which many of them viewed a visit by Louw to the countries where they were stationed – for fear that he would upset relations with the host governments – disappeared under Muller. In one sense, however, South African diplomats had a high regard for Louw: the way in which he jealously guarded over the interests of his officials.[234] Muller they regarded as a weaker minister, not prepared to stand up for their interests to the same extent.

Other ministers

In the Cabinet, still very much the locus of foreign policy formulation under Verwoerd, two other ministers who carried significant weight in this field were Mr JJ Fouché, Minister of Defence, and Dr N Diederichs, Minister of Economic Affairs. Their respective portfolios were drawn into the realm of foreign policy particularly by the arms embargoes imposed against South Africa in the early 1960s, and the threat of economic sanctions against the country. Waring was not much of a factor in foreign policy matters, notwithstanding the relevance of his portfolio, Information. He was inexperienced in foreign affairs, a rather weak minister and, moreover, English-speaking. Although other ministers were to some extent constrained by Louw's sensitivity about colleagues trespassing on his jealously guarded domain, there was nonetheless a fair degree of Cabinet discussion on foreign affairs, with Prime Minister Verwoerd giving a decisive lead. During Strydom's premiership, a relatively uneventful period in South Africa's foreign relations, and with the assertive Louw effectively in charge of matters, there was not much incentive for other ministers to take an active interest in foreign affairs, except insofar as they related to the British connection. As prominent domestic political issues, South Africa's relations with the Crown and Commonwealth were "fair game" to National Party politicians.

The bureaucracy

Forsyth, who remained Secretary of External Affairs until his retirement in 1956, found his already meagre influence on major foreign policy issues futher eroded after Louw's appointment as Minister of External Affairs. His successor, Jooste, an imposing figure with an impressive diplomatic record, by contrast had a highly influential voice in foreign policy formulation under Verwoerd. This was in no small measure due to the particularly close relationship that developed between the two – much closer than would normally exist between the prime minister and a permanent head of department. Verwoerd set great store by Jooste's opinions, and Jooste had near boundless admiration for Verwoerd's leadership qualities.[235] Towards the end of Louw's period in office, Jooste probably carried more weight with Verwoerd than did his minister. Verwoerd's decision to send Jooste, instead of Louw, to the UN in 1963, may well have been a reflection of the special relationship between the prime minister and Jooste. In the first few years of

Muller's tenure, which coincided with the last few of Jooste's as secretary, the Verwoerd-Jooste partnership continued, thus curtailing Muller's influence in foreign policy formulation. Jooste, a stickler for form[236] and a somewhat aloof official – regarded as rather pompous by his subordinates – also kept a tight rein over his department in the ten years he was to be secretary.

It would appear that the few South African diplomats who could bring meaningful influence to bear on the foreign policy formulators were mostly political appointees – but only those who found themselves in diplomacy as a political reward. One such, not mentioned earlier, was Mr WC du Plessis (former Secretary of Information, 1961-63, and the man who, as National Party candidate, in 1948 had defeated Smuts in the Standerton constituency), who headed South Africa's diplomatic missions in Ottawa and later Washington.

Two top civil servants outside the foreign ministry should also be mentioned. Mr GJJF Steyn, Deputy Secretary of Commerce and Industries (who became Secretary of Commerce in 1967) carried particular responsibilities and played an influential role in a major foreign policy issue under Verwoerd: South Africa's relations with Rhodesia in the face of international sanctions against the rebel colony. Dr JE Holloway, one of South Africa's most distinguished officials (having served as Director of Census and Statistics, 1925-33, Economic Adviser to the Treasury, 1934-37, and Secretary of Finance, 1937-50), in the 1950s served as ambassador in Washington and subsequently as high commissioner in London. With his outstanding record, Holloway's counsel on particularly the economic dimensions of South Africa's foreign relations was probably sought by prime ministers.

The Information Service/Department of Information, although active in disseminating and obtaining information abroad, was a relatively unimportant actor in foreign policy formation in the 1948-66 period.

In the field of security, the government took a number of steps in the 1960s to co-ordinate the flow of intelligence to the political decision makers. In 1963 the State Security Committee was formed, composed of representatives of the foreign ministry, Military Intelligence and the Security Police. The committee's name was changed to the Intelligence Co-ordination Committee the following year, and it was given a permanent secretariat. This committee submitted its weekly intelligence reports to a restructured State Security Committee consisting of the Secretary of Foreign Affairs, the Chief of the Defence Force and the Commissioner of Police. The State Security Committee proved an unsatisfactory body, among other things because the various government departments failed to canalise all their intelligence through the Intelligence Co-ordination Committee, and because the State Security Committee did not meet regularly. In 1966 the structures were again changed. The State Security Committee was renamed the State Security Advisory Council and the existing secretariat was given a permanent director who also served as secretary of the new council. Mainly because of personality clashes this council – modelled on the British Joint Intelligence Committee – also failed to live up to expectations.

Parliament

With foreign policy making effectively concentrated in the executive branch of government, the legislature's influence in this area was slight. This is not to say that foreign affairs were ignored by Parliament, least of all by the House of Assembly. Topical issues in South Africa's foreign relations frequently featured in parliamentary debates in the years 1948-66, among them the pervasive British connection, South Africa's international standing and the effects of apartheid on it, relations with the UN, international pressure on South Africa, the dangers of communism, South Africa's relations with the colonial powers and independent black states, and Rhodesia's UDI. Such limited influence as the legislature could bring to bear on foreign policy making originated behind the scenes in the National Party's parliamentary caucus, rather than in the contributions of parties in open debate.

The United Party's main disputes with the government over foreign policy matters in the 1948-66 period centred on the declaration of a republic and departure from the Commonwealth (both of which the United Party oppposed), the effects of apartheid on South Africa's international position, and the Republic's relations with Rhodesia after UDI. For the rest, there was a large measure of bipartisanship, something fostered by the opposition particularly after Sir De Villiers Graaff in 1956 succeeded Mr JGN Strauss as leader. Good personal relations existed between Graaff and Prime Ministers Strydom and Verwoerd, and the well-liked, trustworthy Graaff was extensively briefed on foreign affairs, particularly by Verwoerd. Such was the understanding between Graaff and Verwoerd that the opposition on occasion agreed to the prime minister's personal appeal not to raise delicate foreign policy issues in Parliament.

It could be added that bipartisanship was perhaps also encouraged by a basic domestic political consensus between the National Party and the United Party. While the opposition was quick to blame South Africa's poor international standing on apartheid, "we reject one-man-one-equal vote absolutely", Graaff emphasised in 1963, adding the familiar lament that "we . . . cannot understand why it [one man, one vote] should be asked of us, save by those who wish to destroy our civilisation, and our standards." The United Party also came out strongly against any attempt by external forces to deny South Africa the right of finding its own solutions in its own time.[237]

Whatever the agreements or understandings between the government and the opposition, the United Party's influence in foreign policy making was marginal. Although the opposition leader was kept confidentially – and "correctly" – informed on major foreign policy issues, he was not given any meaningful voice in policy formulation; at best, he served as a sounding board. What further circumscribed the opposition's role in foreign affairs was the absence of a parliamentary standing committee on foreign affairs, a body the United Party wanted but the government rejected. Graaff was, nonetheless, on occasion an important source of information: he for example briefed Verwoerd on his talks with various Commonwealth leaders before the 1961 Prime Ministers' Conference.

The general public

Broadening the focus to the (white) general public, Munger (writing in 1965) depicted its role in foreign affairs as "minimal".[238] Yet the public cannot simply be dismissed as a factor in foreign policy making. It is possible to speak of a foreign policy "mood" on several topical issues in the 1948-66 period. One such was a fierce anti-communist mood, thanks largely to the emphasis Nationalist governments had after 1948 placed on a perceived communist menace, both domestically and externally, and on South

Africa's uncompromising anti-communist orientation. Another was resistance to what was typically portrayed as foreign interference in South Africa's internal affairs. Such moods served only to reinforce government policies both at home and abroad. Verwoerd, it should be added, deliberately and with notable success set out to promote white (Afrikaner-English) unity in the 1960s. Foreign policy issues in no small measure facilitated the enterprise. With the establishment of a republic and South Africa's departure from the Commonwealth a *fait accompli*, a major divisive issue had been removed from white politics. The mounting tide of international condemnation had an undoubted unifying effect on white South Africans, who began developing a distinct threat perception. When arguing that the government was fighting for white survival in a hostile world, Verwoerd was issuing a powerful rallying call.

Black opinion, as articulated by political organisations such as the ANC, certainly complicated matters for the South African government in its foreign relations. These movements were very active, and could indeed claim success, in promoting the internationalisation of South Africa's racial policies and the isolation of the country, particularly since Sharpeville. In this respect, the government could not have ignored black opinion. In the sense of a "positive" influence on the foreign policy formulators, however, black opinion was effectively irrelevant.

Interest groups

When one looks at the organised (white) public, the striking fact is that South Africa did not have anything like the "foreign policy community" found in countries such as Britain and the United States. In the 1948-66 period there was hardly any identifiable group of informed and influential people outside government who provided significant inputs in foreign policy making. Munger found that "intellectual circles" in South Africa "are well removed from the formation of (foreign) policy." Universities accordingly made little if any real contribution to providing the policy formulators with intellectual inputs. There was in any case little serious local scholarship on foreign policy issues. The Africa Institute in Pretoria, initiated by the *Akademie vir Wetenskap en Kuns* and a number of universities, and established by parliamentary statute in 1960 to promote scientific studies of African affairs, rendered services to government – who supported it financially – but these were "primarily fact-producing and not policy-making". The independent South African Institute of International Affairs, established in 1934, was even further removed from foreign policy making circles; Munger playfully compared its influence with that of the John Birch Society on the Johnson Administration.[239]

The Afrikaans press, not to mention the English anti-government press, likewise had "very slight impact" on policy making, according to Munger.[240] Louw nonetheless maintained close relations with the press, regarding it as having instrumental – or publicity – value rather than innovative. As noted earlier, he had a predilection for publicity. The Afrikaans pro-government press, specifically, played an instrumental role in the sense of serving as a sounding board or preparing public opinion for new, perhaps unpopular, government moves. In the late 1950s this applied particularly to the thorny issue of black diplomats being stationed in South Africa.[241]

A celebrated case of an Afrikaans newspaper expressing itself on South Africa's foreign relations was *Die Burger*'s editorial, "The Overseas Catastrophe", on 7 April 1960. In the wake of the Sharpeville shooting, South Africa's foreign relations were in "acute danger", the paper warned, emphasising that the country's international status and relations had become wholly dependent on the handling of race relations domestically. Unless South Africa accelerated the "positive aspects" of its racial policies "in accordance with the haste of history", the Union would be faced with "permanent status as the world's polecat". This forthright assessment was apparently not welcomed in government circles.[242] Verwoerd's already noted reaction to the events of early 1960 would indicate that he was unmoved by *Die Burger*'s dire warning. *Die Burger*, it can be added, was during Verwoerd's premiership the most imaginative and venturesome of all Afrikaans papers in its handling of foreign affairs. For the rest, the typically docile and submissive Afrikaans press played a largely acclamatory role.

The local English press, although without any real influence on foreign policy, was a frequent source of annoyance to the government, who vigorously berated anti-Nationalist newspapers for contributing to South Africa's low standing abroad by its attacks on the government. Even worse were the foreign newspapers, whose reporting and comment on South Africa so concerned (and incensed) the government that a special press commission was appointed to investigate their coverage on South Africa. After a protracted inquiry the commission in 1964 presented its voluminous report, confirming the government's charges of unfair treatment being meted out to South Africa by the overseas press.[243]

Turning to other interest groups, Munger found that even the family of Dutch Reformed Churches, often very influential on domestic policy issues, was not a factor in foreign affairs. Much the same situation applied to labour and farmers' organisations. The South African business community was virtually the only non-official group of significant strength which from time to time may have helped to shape foreign policy. The role of business was however very limited because, as Munger noted, "the broad business influence simply supports steps which make South Africa popular and opposes those which make it unpopular."[244] The Department of External/Foreign Affairs nonetheless valued the role businessmen could play in providing useful contacts abroad and the potential of trade in paving the way for the flag.

The South Africa Foundation, established at the end of 1959, funded by the business community and active in the area of foreign relations, is unlikely to have carried much weight with the policy formulators – least of all with Verwoerd, who seemed to entertain suspicions about the motives and political leanings of some leading sponsors of the Foundation.[245]

The lack of influential interest groups in the realm of foreign policy should be seen against the background of the general scarcity of interest groups having the ear of the South African government (when compared with the United States or Britain, for example). Another factor is that Verwoerd, in particular, was not a prime minister to have encouraged or welcomed "outside" participation in foreign policy formulation (nor, for that matter, in domestic policy making). Instead, he would have relied on his own ability and judgement and the contributions, if required, of those surrounding him in the Cabinet and top echelons of the civil service. There were, however, exceptional cases when Verwoerd did solicit expert outside opinion. One such was the South West Africa issue, where he sought the views of such eminent jurists as Advocate DP de Villiers, Judge JT van Wyk and Professor JP Verloren van Themaat.[246]

There was one major exception to the general rule of meagre interest group influence in the making of South African foreign policy: the *Afrikaner-Broederbond*. Although this secret, exclusively Afrikaner organisation had already been founded in 1918, it was only after the National Party's election victory thirty years later that the Broederbond was in a position to exert direct and substantial influence over government policies. Hertzog had found himself seriously at odds with the Broederbond in the 1930s, and Smuts had in December 1944 invoked his wartime emergency powers to issue an ultimatum to public servants who were Broederbond members to resign from either the public service or the Bond. After 1948 things looked quite different. Not only was Malan's the first ever all-Afrikaner Cabinet in the Union's history, it was also one of which all but two members were Broederbonders. The two exceptions were, perhaps surprisingly, Havenga and Louw,[247] but their exclusion was unlikely to have diminished their influence in government.

By the time the Nationalists came to power the Broederbond was well prepared to make its influence felt in certain areas of foreign policy. Since 1940 the organisation had been occupying itself with the promotion of the republican ideal. After 1948 this was pursued with renewed vigour. Following talks in December 1959 between Verwoerd (himself a Broederbonder, needless to say) and Dr PJ Meyer, head of the Broederbond, it was agreed that the organisation would begin preparing the *volk* for the declaration of a republic.[248] The Broederbond should "accept co-responsibility for the establishment of a republic", Verwoerd maintained.[249] On the important question of Commonwealth membership the Broederbond's view was that "practical considerations at the time" would determine whether a republic would be established outside the Commonwealth. Yet it was made absolutely clear that "departure from the Commonwealth as soon as possible remains a cardinal aspect of our republican aim."[250]

Although preparing the way for a republic was the major foreign policy-related matter with which the Broederbond concerned itself until 1961, other aspects of foreign affairs received some attention. In 1960 the organisation began commissioning studies by experts – all Broederbonders, of course – on such topical issues as South Africa's relations with Britain, the high commission territories and, later, the Central African Federation. Then, in the mid-1950s, the Broederbond defined a three-fold future task for itself: promoting the republican ideal; exerting a "christianising and civilising influence" in Africa, and "conveying a message of hope to confused Western countries, where liberalism and communism conduct the struggle against the Afrikaner and the white of our country."[251] This was followed in the early 1960s with the formation of various task groups to conduct studies on salient issues of the day. Among these "watch-dog committees", as they have been labelled, were an Africa Committee and an Africa and World Committee. The composition of the two committees was significant. The former was chaired by Professor PFD Weiss, Director of the Africa Institute, and counted among its members the former diplomat WC du Plessis; De Wet, later ambassador in London and Cabinet minister and Mr PJ Cillié, editor of *Die Burger*. The Africa and World Committee was chaired by Broederbond head Meyer, and its members included two later Cabinet members – Mr SP Botha and Dr PGJ Koornhof – and Colonel (later General) HJ van den Bergh, South Africa's security chief. There was also a task group to combat communism and liberalism and other perceived evils; the struggle against the communist menace was indeed given high priority by the Broederbond.[252] The topics that were studied were notably ambitious and included one on how South Africa should maintain itself as a white state in the prevailing international political climate.[253]

All this was no mere academic or educational exercise. The Broederbond made a memorandum on the general political situation in Southern Africa available to the Department of Foreign Affairs, and decided that a study document on the high commission territories would be publicly distributed – with the aid of the Department of Information, no less.[254] But the Broederbond also went further than policy-oriented studies and became involved in foreign relations on the ground, so to speak. The organisation gave assistance to the moderate Basutoland National Party of Chief Leabua Jonathan both before and after the territory's general election of 1965. This assistance included training party officials in election techniques and strategy. Jonathan presumably remained unaware of the true source of all this calculated generosity – which by 1968 amounted to some R15 000[255] – but the South

African government was certainly aware of the Broederbond's venture, and most likely encouraged it too.

The Broederbond's involvement in foreign affairs should be set in the context of the organisation's special relationship with successive Nationalist governments. Professor AN Pelzer, who in 1968 wrote the Broederbond's official history (which was published only in 1979), noted: "Since 1948 every prime minister has been a member of the movement and although all their doors perhaps have not stood equally wide open, talks between the UR (Executive Council – the Broederbond's highest authority) and the prime minister or members of his cabinet took place regularly."[256] Shortly after his election as prime minister in 1958 Verwoerd told a national meeting of the Broederbond that it was not only his privilege but also "my duty to draw closer by my presence the ties that always existed unobtrusively between our Afrikaner organisation and our Afrikaner government."[257]

It would indeed be tempting to view the National Party government as the Broederbond in power. The problem about equating the two in such a manner is that it implies that government policies were designed by the Broederbond, or that the government was for all its actions ultimately accountable to the Broederbond.

Although there can be no denying that the Broederbond was tremendously influential in government policy making, this does not mean that it necessarily dictated government policies. In the foreign policy field, it is very difficult to be categorical about the Broederbond's precise influence or to cite specific instances of policies initiated by the organisation. The Broederbond was nonetheless active in this area and the policy formulators in government certainly paid due attention to views expressed by the organisation. The government would, at least, not have launched a major foreign policy initiative without sounding out the Broederbond – which, of course, is quite different from getting clearance from the organisation.

This touches upon the Broederbond's instrumental role of mobilising support for government policies, whether domestic or foreign. For this the Broederbond was uniquely equipped: in 1966 it had 7 452 members (compared with 5 997 in 1961), carefully selected to represent Afrikaners from numerous walks of life, in many instances the leading men in their respective fields.[258]

A final word to add is that the Broederbond's role and influence was, understandably, much more pronounced in domestic politics than in foreign affairs.

2. The Setting of Foreign Policy in the Era of Vorster and Botha

There is one thing solid and fundamental in politics – the law of change. What's up today is down tomorrow.
Richard Nixon

The main focus of this book is on the making of foreign policy in the BJ Vorster and PW Botha premierships. It covers the period 1966-81, three years after PW Botha's assumption of power. Although the PW Botha premiership still continues and his first three years in office is a relatively brief period (compared with his predecessor's twelve years), it is nonetheless long enough to identify important new institutions and styles in foreign policy formulation on the one hand, and elements of continuity on the other.

The object of this brief, intermediary chapter is to sketch in broad outline the salient features of South Africa's internal scene – the "domestic base" of foreign policy – and its external milieu in the years 1966-81. Together they provide the necessary context in which to examine the formation of South African foreign policy under Vorster and Botha. These fifteen years have in fact witnessed many major developments on both the domestic and international fronts which have had profound implications for South Africa's foreign policy.

The Domestic Setting

Following Verwoerd's assassination in September 1966, Adv. BJ Vorster, Minister of Justice, was elected prime minister by the National Party's parliamentary caucus.

Vorster, a lawyer by profession, was first elected a National Party Member of Parliament in 1953. After five years in Parliament, Verwoerd in 1958 appointed him Deputy Minister of Educa-

tion, Arts and Science and of Social Welfare and Pensions. (Another National Party MP appointed as a deputy minister at the same time was Mr PW Botha, who was given the portfolio of the Interior.) In 1961 Vorster became Minister of Justice in Verwoerd's Cabinet. Already at the time Vorster was branded by the *Rand Daily Mail* as one of the National Party's "young extremists".[1] In his five years as Minister of Justice, Vorster established an awesome reputation as a resolute and ruthless law-and-order man. The drastic legislative and other measures he took had the desired result in terms of suppressing internal violence and restoring tranquillity after the traumatic events in the wake of Sharpeville. Vorster's right-hand-man in these years was his close friend and fellow-internee in the Second World War, Brig. HJ van den Bergh, head of the Security Police. When elected prime minister on 13 September 1966, Vorster was only thirteenth in order of precedence in the Cabinet.[2]

Prime Minister Vorster, to many people's amazement, soon displayed a remarkable degree of political flexibility compared with Verwoerd's typical "granite" stance. While undoubtedly subscribing to the basic tenets of separate development, Vorster did not display the same unmerciful consistency as Verwoerd in rigorously applying apartheid to virtually all facets of human interaction in South Africa. Vorster was prepared to make concessions in some, admittedly peripheral, areas of race relations. Vorster's deviation from aspects of thoroughgoing Verwoerdian apartheid seemed to show that he lacked Verwoerd's unwavering sense of purpose.

The late 1960s was a period of great white confidence in South Africa's ability to ride out the storms and provide a secure future for its white inhabitants. Vorster typified the mood of self-assurance when he said in 1968 at the seventh anniversary of the Republic:

> It seems as if it was only yesterday that supporters, as well as opponents, of the Republic wondered what the future of the Republic would be. Now after seven years, South Africans have the answers to most – if not all – of their questions. Doubts have gone and fears have vanished.[3]

Perhaps the mood of confidence to some extent inspired Vorster to show a measure of flexibility in domestic politics; with a secure domestic base and high white morale he could afford to be seen to be magnanimous and conciliatory.

The first demonstration of Vorster's new flexibility – or pragmatism, as it was usually referred to – was his announcement of a change in sports policy in April 1967. The government would no longer prescribe to other countries who may or may not be included in sports teams visiting South Africa. This was a clear departure from Verwoerd's uncompromising insistence on all-white foreign teams only. But having taken a step forward, Vorster the very next year took a decisive one backwards. He refused permission to a British MCC cricket team that included Basil D'Oliveira, a coloured formerly from Cape Town, to tour South Africa.[4] Vorster's action heralded the severance of South Africa's traditional cricket ties with Britain. This was by no means South Africa's first international sports link to be broken: already in 1964 South Africa was denied participation in the Olympic Games. Since then, South Africa has experienced growing sports isolation. It was a highly ironical development because South Africa, which started to politicise sport by subjecting it to apartheid, increasingly found other governments interfering with their sportsmen's contacts with South Africa.

Small though it was, Vorster's change in the sports policy in 1967 was sufficient to cause unease in National Party circles, also among MPs. What added to their concern about Vorster's political direction was the "outward movement" on which he embarked in 1967. The focal point of the outward movement was Africa, where Vorster hoped to establish a *modus vivendi* with black states. The new initiative produced early benefits:

in January 1967 Vorster met Prime Minister Jonathan of Lesotho and in September 1967 diplomatic ties were established with Malawi. Not all Nationalists were pleased about the diplomatic breakthrough with Malawi, for they feared the prospect of black diplomats residing in white South Africa. What had in the late 1950s been largely an academic discussion about exchanging diplomats with black African states, became a reality a decade later and revived the debate. By the end of the 1960s the divisions within the National Party, its parliamentary caucus in particular, could no longer be concealed. Vorster stood at the centre of the conflict. There was a sense of betrayal among a group of Nationalists; they felt that Vorster, who had all the necessary credentials to serve as a faithful disciple of Verwoerd, had deviated from the straight and narrow ideological path.

Matters came to a head at the Transvaal National Party congress in September 1969 when delegates had to declare themselves openly on the government's sports policy and on diplomatic ties with black states, in addition to the government's policies of encouraging (white) immigration and promoting Afrikaans-English co-operation. On three of the four issues the congress gave a unanimous verdict, but 18 delegates either voted against or abstained on the issue of the government's sports policy. Among those against were four Nationalist MPs, including Dr Albert Hertzog whom Vorster had in 1968 dismissed from the Cabinet because of his suspected implication in right-wing dissidence directed against Vorster. The four MPs were expelled from the National Party and in October 1969 established the *Herstigte Nasionale Party* (HNP) under Hertzog's leadership.[5]

Vorster called an early election for April 1970 with the obvious intention of crushing the HNP. In this he succeeded admirably, for the HNP failed to win a single parliamentary seat. Yet the election was a mixed blessing for the prime minister, because the National Party suffered its first serious electoral setback since 1948. The National Party lost eight seats to the opposition United Party which, for the first time in 27 years, managed to improve on its previous parliamentary standing.[6]

Despite the HNP's poor performance at the polls and its relatively low profile over the next four years, the mere fact of its continued existence remained a constant reminder of the political divisions within Afrikanerdom. These divisions in fact extended to within the National Party, which had failed to purge itself of all right-wing dissidents. The cleavages therefore did not neatly correspond with the party divisions; there was a broader based rift between the so-called *verligtes* and *verkramptes*; the enlightened, even progressive elements versus the bigoted, arch-conservative group.

If Vorster seemed to have "gone soft" on sports policy – which saw a further change in April 1971 with the allowance of "multinational sport" in South Africa[7] – he certainly lived up to his tough reputation in the very area he had first established it, namely security matters. The already formidable armour of security legislation was further strengthened with measures such as the *Suppression of Communism Amendment Act*, 1967 and the *General Law Amendment Act*, 1969. A particularly important piece of legislation was the *Public Service Amendment Act*, 1969, which provided for the establishment of the Bureau for State Security. Popularly known as BOSS, the Bureau was made directly responsible to the prime minister and was, significantly, headed by General HJ van den Bergh.[8]

Vorster also continued, through various legislative measures, to reinforce what Heard has termed the "general apartheid edifice". Political apartheid, for example, was further extended by the *Prohibition of Political Interference Act*, 1968, which made it an offence to belong to and assist a racially mixed political party. This was part of a new package of legislation that also included the *Separate Representation of Voters Amendment Act*, 1968, which finally ended all coloured representation in the House of Assembly, and the *Coloured Person's Representative Council Act*, 1968, in terms of which a partly elected, partly nominated coloured council (CRC) with limited subordinate powers of legislation was created. *The South African Indian Council Act*, 1968, gave statutory authority to the Indian Council already established in 1964, but which remained wholly nominated with advisory powers only.[9] In 1974 half the Council's members became elected, the other half nominated.[10]

By trying to channel coloured political participation through the CRC, the government unwittingly opened a Pandora's box. Already in the first election for the CRC, the strongly anti-apartheid (coloured) Labour Party scored a decisive victory and used its position to in effect wreck the "apartheid institution". In an effort to resolve the acute dilemma over the political status of the coloureds, as well as to examine their socio-economic position, the government appointed the Theron Commission of Inquiry in 1973. In its report submitted in 1976 the Commission recommended, among other things, that satisfactory forms of direct coloured representation should be created at the various levels of government and that South Africa's Westminster system of governmnent should be changed to suit the requirements of a plural population.[11] The government, while accepting the vast majority of the Commission's 178 recommendations, rejected direct coloured participation in existing national, provincial and local authorities for whites. A Cabinet committee, chaired by PW Botha, was nonetheless appointed to investigate changing South Africa's system of government in pursuance of the Theron Commission's recommendation in this regard.[12]

While separate development, particularly as it related to coloureds, was in a process of reappraisal as its shortcomings became only too obvious, Vorster closely followed the course Verwoerd had marked out for the blacks. *The Black States Constitution Act*, 1971, was designed to accelerate the constitutional development of the homelands by stipulating that special legislation of the South African Parliament was no longer required to replace homelands' territorial authorities with legislative assemblies and thus to confer self-governing status. Before the end of 1972 seven other homelands had joined Transkei as self-governing entities, namely Ciskei, KwaZulu, Lebowa, Venda, Gazankulu, Bophuthatswana and QwaQwa.[13]

No sooner had the government embarked on what was to be a long process of constitutional reform involving whites, coloureds and Indians, when South Africa and the world were made acutely aware of the position of another crucial segment of South African society, the so-called urban blacks. On 16 June 1976 violence erupted in Soweto, heralding months of large-scale and widespread racial turmoil. It left a trail of death and destruction and dramatically underlined the depth of racial cleavages in South African society. The protracted violence severely undermined white confidence. The deteriorating economic climate and fresh memories of South Africa's involvement in the Angolan war served to strengthen a public mood of gloom. In these inauspicious circumstances the independent Republic of Transkei was born in October 1976 – the first homeland to pursue separate development to its much vaunted logical conclusion.

The year 1977 was yet another dramatic one. In August the special Cabinet committee to consider constitutional alternatives reported. The committee proposed separate Parliaments and Cabinets for the whites, coloureds and Asians; a Council of Cabinets consisting of members of the three Cabinets, and an advisory President's Council to act as a "brains trust" to the Council of Cabinets and the State President.[14] Blacks were excluded from the proposed new deal. The next month saw the death in detention of Mr Steve Biko, leader of the black consciousness movement. In October, in a massive security clampdown under the Internal Security Act, the government declared 18 organisations unlawful and served banning orders on over 40 people. Three newspapers were likewise banned. In the wake of these events the UN Security Council imposed its first mandatory arms embargo on South Africa. Meanwhile, a second homeland, Bophuthatswana, had received its independence in October.

Against the background of drastic security action at home and sharply escalating international censure, in which the Carter Administration featured prominently, a general election was held in November 1977. Vorster cited three reasons for the election: the voters should be given an opportunity to express themselves on the dissolution of the United Party in July, on the government's new constitutional proposals and on external interference in South African affairs. In the event, the National Party made external pressure, from the United States in particular, the central issue. For the first time since the Nationalists came to power a foreign relations issue dominated a general election. It highlighted the interrelationship between domestic and foreign affairs and, indeed, the extent to which external influence had penetrated the South African political system. The National Party scored an impressive electoral triumph, emerging with 134 of the 165 parliamentary seats – the highest proportion ever gained by any one political party in South Africa. The newly-formed Progressive Federal Party (PFP) became the official opposition, holding 17 seats. The New Republic Party, successor of the United Party, won 10 seats. (In the 1974 general election the then Progressive Party had increased its number of seats from one to seven at the expense of the United Party.) The HNP again fared badly and failed to come near winnng a single seat.[15]

South Africa's foreign relations again featured on the domestic political scene the following year, when the so-called Information scandal for months dominated the headlines. The Erasmus Commission of Inquiry into the affairs of the Department reported misappropriation of state funds and considerable financial losses sustained by the state through the Department's attempts to purchase American newspapers and its setting up of a local newspaper with official funds. Both Vorster and Dr CP Mulder, Minister of Information, were found by the Commission to bear responsibility for the irregularities in the Department. Vorster was by then State President, having resigned as prime minister in September 1978 – citing health reasons – before the Erasmus Commission produced its damaging findings. These led Vorster to resign as State President after only eight months in office. Mulder too resigned from the Cabinet.

Following Vorster's resignation as prime minister, the National Party caucus elected PW Botha, Minister of Defence since 1966 and Cape leader of the Party, as its national leader and prime minister. Unlike Vorster who was unanimously elected as prime minister, PW Botha was opposed by Mulder and Mr RF (Pik) Botha, Minister of Foreign Affairs. (To avoid confusion, the two Bothas will always be referred to as PW Botha and Pik Botha.) In what was a bitterly contested election, PW Botha won only on the second ballot. Mulder's chances were widely believed to have been jeopardised by strong rumours implicating him in the Information scandal.[16] An interesting feature of the election was the preference expressed by the white public. An opinion poll showed that whites generally heavily favoured Pik Botha.[17] He no doubt owed his public popularity to high visibility and a dramatic, forceful political style. Far from confining himself to foreign affairs, the Foreign Minister was deeply involved in domestic politics.

When PW Botha came to power, white South Africans still found themselves caught in the mood of gloom that had set in with the Soweto riots. What aggravated the sense of foreboding was the sharply escalating international pressure South Africa had to endure, particularly over Namibia. Economic sanctions seemed to loom large. Despite such heavy odds, the new prime minister soon inspired a new mood of expectation among a great many whites and even other races with his strongly reformist rhetoric. He challenged his white audiences to "adapt or die", and tried to show blacks his *bona fides* by undertaking an unprecedented grand tour of the black homelands and Soweto. A new relationship between government and the private sector was also fostered by PW Botha, culminating in the Carlton Conference (Johannesburg) of November 1979 and repeated two years later with the Good Hope Conference (Cape Town).[18] The new partnership between government and business flowed from the prime minister's emphasis on economic co-operation and development in Southern Africa. This, in turn, was a key element of his proposed constellation of Southern African states.

On the constitutional front the 1980 parliamentary session saw legislation to give effect to the recommendations of the Schlebusch Commission which investigated a new constitution for South Africa. The Senate was abolished and an advisory President's Council composed of nominated whites, coloureds and Indians was established to pursue work on a new constitution. For the first time racial groups other than whites were formally drawn into the search for new constitutional arrangements. A black advisory council composed of representatives of the homelands and urban black communities was envisaged by the government, but proved stillborn because of fierce black resistance to a separate council.[19] "Grand apartheid" was meanwhile running its destined course, with Venda in September 1979 becoming the third homeland to opt for independence, followed by Ciskei in December 1981. This left six self-governing (non-independent) black homelands.

In the socio-economic sphere PW Botha's initial reformist pronouncements raised widespread hopes that the government would abolish or at least ease apartheid legislation. The area where most progress was made in this regard was labour, following the recommendations of the Wiehahn and Riekert commissions of inquiry.[20] Sport has ever since Vorster's first changes in 1967 become increasingly non-racial – "normalised", in official nomenclature. However, highly contentious discriminatory legislation such as the Group Areas Act, Population Registration Act, and the Mixed Marriages and Immorality Acts remained on the statute book.

Prime Minister PW Botha's first three years in office produced different reactions from different people. While many were disappointed that he was making too slow progress down the road of political reform, others maintained that he was

already going too fast. The extent of right-wing opposition to the prime minister's political course was vividly demonstrated in the general election of April 1981. The National Party fared badly compared with the previous election, losing eight seats, six of them to the PFP and two to the NRP. The HNP, though again failing to win a single seat, made a spectacular advance by capturing 13,84% of the vote, compared with only 3,21% in 1977. The other right-wing party, former Minister CP Mulder's National Conservative Party, polled a mere 1,38% of the vote and failed to win a seat.[21] As with Vorster, right-wing opposition from within Afrikanerdom to PW Botha was not merely evident outside the National Party, but also clearly within. Limited and cautious though his moves on political reform have been, they were nonetheless sufficient to cause considerable tension in Nationalist ranks.[22]*

A significant feature of the 1981 election was the prominence of foreign policy issues relating to Southern Africa. The HNP made great play of South Africa's relations with particularly Zimbabwe, Mozambique and Zambia, and challenged the government to take a stronger line against hostile black states supporting, whether in word or in deed, "terrorism" against South Africa. The government was also charged with "feeding the terrorists" by exporting South African maize to neighbouring black states. Terrorism was, understandably, an issue with great emotional content among white South Africans, and this the HNP exploited to the full. Diplomatic ties with black states were no longer an issue, perhaps because of the realisation that there was no real chance of South Africa entering into such relations with black states other than independent former homelands.

A final and very important feature of the PW Botha administration is its heavy emphasis on South Africa's security. This has typically found expression in the need for a "total national strategy" to resist a "total onslaught" on the country. The onslaught is presented as having both

---

* In March 1982 17 MPs left the National Party following an open right-wing revolt against PW Botha. The principal reason for the most serious split in Nationalist ranks since 1948 was the government's plans for constitutional reform involving whites, coloureds and Indians. The rebel MPs subsequently formed the Conservative Party and Dr AP Treurnicht, previously a member of PW Botha's Cabinet, became its first leader.

internal and external dimensions, ultimately under the direction of communist powers. The total national strategy involves the mobilisation of South Africa's total physical and human resources in a national endeavour to thwart the onslaught. As of old, it is again survival that is seen to be at stake, but with a significant difference: the government now argues that the security and survival of whites and blacks alike are being threatened by a common enemy, thus compelling them to join forces in countering it.[23] The internal threat was dramatically underlined in the course of 1980, when the ANC launched armed attacks on police stations, a bank and the SASOL oil installations. Also encompassed under the total national strategy has been the initiation of a thoroughgoing "rationalisation" of the civil service to ensure efficient government. This has affected not only the execution of policy but in a very material fashion also the formulation of policy in key areas, including foreign policy.

This overview of South Africa's internal scene in the period 1966-81 has revealed several examples of the interrelationship between domestic and foreign affairs. First, Vorster's outward movement was launched at a time of strong white confidence in South Africa's economic power, military strength and future in general. Second, the outward movement had domestic repercussions in the form of white objections to black diplomats being stationed in South Africa. The divisions that this issue caused in Afrikaner ranks were an intimation of things to come. Third, foreign affairs were the dominant issue in the 1977 general election, thereby reflecting the extent to which South Africa's political system has become penetrated by extraneous influences. Fourth, the Information scandal drew aspects of South Africa's conduct of foreign relations into the domestic political debate. Fifth, a perceived external threat against South Africa became part and parcel of domestic politics in terms of PW Botha's notion of a "total national strategy". Sixth, foreign affairs again featured prominently in the 1981 general election, in a manner clearly reflecting the growing white preoccupation with matters of security.

The External Milieu

The period 1966-81 saw dramatic changes in South Africa's international milieu, particularly in its immediate regional environment. The changes were overall in a direction unfavourable to (white) South Africa's perceived interests. Thus the *cordon sanitaire* of white-ruled and moderate black countries still surrounding South Africa in the late sixties has been replaced by a string of independent black states nearly all highly antagonistic towards South Africa and openly supportive of the aims and in many cases also the actions of South African exile movements fighting for the overthrow of the South African government. The optimism about a *rapprochement* with black African states, which was inherent in the outward movement, in due course gave way to a preoccupation with that most basic of state objectives, security in a hostile environment.

In the late 1960s, however, South Africa's domestic base was so secure that it felt ready to face the world with renewed confidence and approach Africa from a position of strength. The emergence of moderate and friendly governments in neighbouring Botswana, Lesotho and Swaziland (the first two became independent in 1966, followed by Swaziland in 1968) and also in distant Malawi seemed to augur well for a South African attempt at establishing a *rapprochement* with nearby black states.[24] For the first time South Africa was able to give effect to its long-standing offer of aid and assistance to black states. It was on such non-political ties, together with trade links, that the Republic relied to draw the countries of Southern Africa closer together.[25]

The outward movement was not merely confined to Southern Africa, however. South Africa soon appeared to be attracted to bigger "diplomatic stakes" than surrounding black states, namely a *rapprochement* with black states farther north and outside South Africa's immediate sphere of interest and influence. Success on the wider African stage, South Africa hoped, would have a spill-over effect improving its foreign relations over a broad front. It had by then, after all, become conventional wisdom to argue that the key to an improvement in South Africa's standing in the world was an improvement in its relations with black African states.

The outward movement, it is important to note, was closely related to South Africa's concern about its regional security. By orienting other countries favourably towards the Republic, it was hoped, they could be prevented from becoming a security risk. There was indeed cause for concern about South Africa's security, even in the halcyon days of the outward movement. The destruction of a guerrilla training camp of the South West

African People's Organisation (SWAPO) in northern Namibia in August 1966 by South African security forces[26] heralded the beginning of what developed into a protracted low-intensity war between South African and SWAPO forces. Following UDI and mandatory UN sanctions, embattled Rhodesia depended for its very survival on the economic lifeline provided by South Africa.[27] South Africa also supported Rhodesia in another way, by despatching police units there in 1967, ostensibly to intercept ANC insurgents *en route* to South Africa,[28] but in reality to assist Rhodesian security forces counter sporadic guerrilla incursions launched by black nationalist organisations. Evidence also points to limited South African military involvement in counter-insurgency operations in Angola and Mozambique since the late 1960s.[29] Despite the absence of formal defence agreements, these circumstances produced a powerful cohesive force between the white-ruled parts of Southern Africa.

The importance of security considerations was also borne out in Vorster's statement that the Republic would not tolerate what he described as terrorism or communist domination in Southern Africa and was determined to fight it even beyond the country's borders.[30] Another way in which South Africa sought to combat a perceived communist threat was to offer non-aggression pacts to black states in 1970.[31] Such agreements – for which there were no takers, except for independent former homelands several years later – would have meant that the black countries involved would deny insurgents facilities for operating against South Africa.

Despite some initial successes in the early 1970s,[32] the dialogue initiative, as the outward movement subsequently became known, soon ran aground, primarily because of the OAU's intervention to block any moves towards a *rapprochement* between South Africa and black African states. This, together with the unresolved Rhodesian and Namibian issues, led South Africa to lower its sights and concentrate on consolidating its position in Southern Africa and finding regional solutions to the area's conflicts. In February 1974 Vorster spoke of a "power bloc" of sovereign independent states developing in Southern Africa.[33] Later he introduced the concept of a "constellation of politically completely independent states" maintaining close economic ties.[34] The other way of safeguarding South Africa's position in Southern Africa was through seeking settlements to the issues of Namibia and Rhodesia. This led to the *détente* initiative, a joint endeavour between South Africa and Zambia to try to resolve the Rhodesian issue. In Namibia, South Africa in September 1975 initiated the Turnhalle constitutional conference, in which all ethnic groups were for the first time drawn into the process of plotting Namibia's political future. These moves were no doubt inspired by a sense of urgency in view of Portugal's liquidation of its African empire. South Africa was deeply concerned that the independence of Angola and Mozambique might create a power vacuum in the region or, worse still, produce hostile communist-backed regimes in the two countries. As it turned out, the Lisbon *coup d'état* in April 1974, which set in motion Portugal's retreat from the continent, was a watershed in the history of Southern Africa and indeed in South Africa's foreign relations.

Despite the new emphasis on South Africa's immediate external environment, Vorster had not given up his interest in establishing contact with black states farther afield. Two of his most spectacular diplomatic coups in Africa during this time involved distant states, namely the Ivory Coast, where Vorster visited President Felix Houphouet-Boigny in September 1974, and Liberia, whose President William Tolbert received Vorster in February 1975.[35] The high-water mark of Vorster's *détente* initiative was reached closer to home, however, with the Victoria Falls conference in August 1975 between the Rhodesian government and black nationalists. Also present were the two architects of the historic meeting, Vorster and Zambian President Kenneth Kaunda.[36] To help create a favourable climate for the conference, South Africa had in August 1975 withdrawn its police units from Rhodesia.[37]

The era of *détente* was short-lived, its demise caused primarily by the collapse of the joint South African-Zambian settlement initiative for Rhodesia, and South Africa's intervention in the Angolan war, 1975-6. Southern Africa now entered a period of rapidly escalating conflict, with outside powers actively involved: the Soviet Union and Cuba in the military field and the Western powers on the diplomatic front. South Africa participated in a new Western peace initiative in the region, despite its severe disappointment, even bitterness, about being left in the lurch by the United States in the Angolan war.[38] Three rounds of talks were held between Vorster and Dr Henry Kissinger, American

Secretary of State, in West Germany, Switzerland and South Africa in June and September 1976, with Rhodesia the focal point. The upshot was the acceptance of black majority rule within two years by Mr Ian Smith, Prime Minister of Rhodesia. Britain thereupon convened a conference in Geneva between the Rhodesian government and black nationalist parties to pave the way to a final resolution of the Rhodesian issue. The conference, however, proved abortive and the war continued.[39]

Of secondary and less immediate concern to the United States in its new diplomatic role in Southern Africa, but nonetheless matters of great importance, were Namibia and the situation in South Africa itself. In Namibia the Turnhalle conference failed to attract any international recognition as a genuine constitutional conference. SWAPO, which did not participate, continued its armed struggle. With Angola in MPLA hands, the United States feared that an escalation of the war in Namibia could provide new opportunities for the Soviet Union and its Cuban allies. In South Africa itself the widespread unrest and violence in black townships began to erupt on the eve of the first round of talks between Vorster and Kissinger, thus thrusting the Republic's serious domestic political problems to the fore.

The year 1977 was a bleak one for South Africa internationally. The advent of the Carter Administration in January, with its emphasis on human rights, soon brought sharp new tensions in American-South African relations. In May 1977 Vorster held talks in Vienna with Vice-President Walter Mondale, an occasion that revealed fundamental differences between the South African and American governments over South Africa's domestic policies.[40] It also appeared that the Carter Administration was not prepared to follow Kissinger's piecemeal approach to resolving Southern African issues by subordinating Namibia and South Africa's domestic situation to a Rhodesian settlement. Instead, America now wanted to see simultaneous advance on all three. The mounting tide of international pressure on the Republic culminated in the UN Security Council's imposition of a mandatory arms embargo against the country in November 1977.

As if the arms ban was not enough, the threat of economic sanctions kept hanging ominously over South Africa's head because of the lack of progress in resolving the Namibian conflict. In April 1978 prospects for a settlement improved, however, when South Africa accepted a set of Western proposals. As it soon turned out, this was but a brief interlude of optimism in a protracted, tortuous cycle of negotiation characterised by delays, vacillation, setbacks and progress. Numerous rounds of talks were held between representatives of South Africa, the five Western powers forming the "contact group", and the UN. Two rounds of talks, chaired by UN representatives, were held in Geneva in November 1979 and January 1981 to try to iron out differences between the parties over the UN-endorsed settlement package. The meetings, attended by South Africa, internal Namibian political parties, SWAPO, the frontline states and the five Western powers, proved abortive.[41] A crucial factor consistently bedevilling a settlement has been a lack of trust all round. South Africa, for its part, is distrustful of the UN's ability to act as an impartial arbiter, and at times Pretoria has also voiced deep misgivings about the Western powers' role as honest brokers. In addition, South Africa fears an outcome that might produce a SWAPO regime in Windhoek. What certainly did not help the international settlement drive but instead created new tensions between South Africa and the Western powers was South Africa's decision to override Western objections and stage an internal election for a constituent assembly in Namibia in December 1978. SWAPO refused to participate, preferring to continue its armed struggle.

In Rhodesia there had been even less progress towards an international settlement by the time PW Botha became prime minister. The Rhodesian government launched its own domestic settlement initiative leading to the so-called internal agreement of March 1978 between the Smith government and three internal black leaders. In April 1979, following a general election, Bishop Abel Muzorewa became the first black prime minister of Zimbabwe-Rhodesia. The Patriotic Front, composed of Mr Robert Mugabe's Zimbabwe African National Union (ZANU) and Mr Joshua Nkomo's Zimbabwe African People's Union (ZAPU) were excluded from both the 1978 settlement and the election the following year. The war consequently continued.[42]

The situation in Southern Africa thus offered South Africa's incoming prime minister little cheer. There was no end to the wars in Rhodesia and Namibia in sight; instead, the conflicts escalated. South Africa also had to contend with the threat of sanctions over Namibia as the Western settlement initiative repeatedly ran into difficulties. What aggravated matters for the Republic was that its *cordon sanitaire* had been broken by the independence of Angola and Mozambique under regimes highly antagonistic towards South Africa. These features led PW Botha to place renewed emphasis on safeguarding South Africa's embattled position in Southern Africa. His regional designs in essence represent a defensive strategy; circumstances forced South Africa to retreat behind the perimeters of Southern Africa. Thus PW Botha's concept of a constellation of Southern African states – as his scheme for regional relations became known – is part and parcel of the "total national strategy".[43] Although the prime minister inherited the concept of a constellation of states from his predecessor, he has given it a substance previously lacking and he has, through it, elevated the promotion of closer regional ties in Southern Africa to a major foreign policy initiative. In one of the earliest authoritative statements on a constellation, Foreign Minister Pik Botha in March 1979 envisaged between seven and ten states representing 40 million people south of the Kunene and Zambezi Rivers joining forces in a formal constellation and devising "a common approach in the security field, the economic field and even the political field."[44] The grouping would have included Botswana, Lesotho, Swaziland, Rhodesia, Namibia and South Africa and its three independent former homelands (Transkei, Bophuthatswana and Venda). It was hoped that Zambia too would join and the possibility of including even Mozambique was left open.[45]

South Africa's envisaged grand regional constellation failed to materialise, mainly because the political and ideological divisions between the Republic and internationally recognised black states are such that the latter are unwilling to formalise relations with Pretoria much further, least of all in the military and political areas. In addition, there was no chance of these black states, members of the OAU, joining a formal association with non-recognised former "Bantustans", Rhodesia and South African-controlled Namibia as their full and equal partners. Thus Botswana, Lesotho and Swaziland – the first two's often strident criticism of South Africa a far cry from their friendly relations with the Republic in the late 1960s – served notice that they would not consider joining a formal grouping with South Africa as long as the latter adhered to its prevailing racial policies.[46] These considerations apply even more strongly in the case of Zambia and Mozambique.

An even more important setback to the constellation plan was that it was overtaken by events in Rhodesia. At the British-chaired Lancaster House Conference in late 1979 the Muzorewa government and the Patriotic Front reached agreement on an independence constitution and a ceasefire. The UN Security Council lifted all economic sanctions on 21 December, the day the ceasefire was signed. In February 1980 elections for 20 white members of the new House of Assembly were held, while the black voters went to the polls a week later. Mugabe's ZANU-PF scored a landslide victory, winning 57 of the 80 seats, followed by 20 for Nkomo's Patriotic Front and a mere 2 for Muzorewa's party. On 18 April the independent Republic of Zimbabwe was born with Mugabe as prime minister. An early indication of the new government's attitude towards South Africa was the latter's exclusion from the independence ceremony and the presence instead of SWAPO, the ANC and PAC.[47]

In line with his implacable opposition to apartheid and his support – albeit moral and political – for the "liberation struggle" in Namibia and South Africa, Mugabe has made it plain that Zimbabwe has no intention of joining any South African-designed constellation of states. Instead, Zimbabwe, along with Botswana, Lesotho, Swaziland, Mozambique, Angola, Zambia, Malawi and Tanzania, joined forces in the Southern African Development Co-ordination Conference (SADCC). SADCC was designed to reduce the nine black states' dependence on the South African economy and transport network by jointly strengthening their own. The grouping has been dubbed the counter-constellation – a designation that in itself reflects the black states' opposition to South Africa's proposed constellation.

These developments left South Africa with no other option but to amend some of its ideas on a constellation and reduce an initially grandiose design to what became essentially a device to restructure relations, politically and economically, between present and former parts of the South African state. In its scaled down form, the constellation has been formalised between South Africa, Transkei, Bophuthatswana, Venda and

Ciskei. Like SADCC, the constellation was given substance in 1980. As other homelands become independent, they too are bound to join the constellation.[48]

From the preceding discussion it is obvious that Southern African affairs represented South Africa's major foreign policy preoccupations for the best part of the 1966-81 period. There are, however, other important features of South Africa's external environment that should be mentioned briefly. The state of South Africa's relations with Western countries fluctuated greatly since the late 1960s. At that point South Africa, realising that it was being kept politically and militarily at a distance by Western powers, began questioning whether it should maintain its traditional alignment with the West.[49] South Africa began to focus increasingly on relations with powers in the southern hemisphere, thus the expansion of diplomatic and economic ties between the Republic and Latin American countries in the 1960s and Vorster's visit to Uruguay and Paraguay in 1975. Other links that South Africa also began strengthening, partly in response to what it saw as Western indifference to South Africa's value as an ally, were those with Israel and Taiwan. In April 1976 Vorster paid an official visit to Israel, and PW Botha visited Taiwan in October 1980.[50]

Despite South Africa's dissociative moves, Western countries still dominated South Africa's external environment in terms of diplomatic importance and trade links. There was thus no chance of South Africa turning its back on its traditional allies; what did develop was a kind of love-hate relationship. Very often the political climate depended on progress in Namibia: the better the prospects for a settlement, the friendlier the relations between South Africa and the West. Government changes in Western states have also influenced the state of bilateral relations. For example, South Africa's relations with the United Kingdom improved to some degree when a Conservative government came to power in 1979. This has been even more true of South Africa's relations with the United States following the installation of the Reagan Administration in January 1981.

3. The Head of State and the Legislature

Can it be maintained that a person of any education can learn anything worth knowing from a penny paper? It may be said that people may learn what is said in Parliament. Well, will that contribute to their eduction?

Marquis of Salisbury, 1861

In terms of the *Republic of South Africa Constitution Act,* 1961, the national legislature, known as Parliament, consisted of the State President, the Senate and the House of Assembly. The top echelon of the executive included, according to the Constitution, the State President, Executive Council (or Cabinet) and deputy ministers. The *Republic of South Africa Constitution Fifth Amendment Act,* 1980, abolished the Senate and provided for a new body, the President's Council. This new multiracial advisory body is, however, not a substitute for the Senate, since their respective functions are completely different. The object of this chapter is to assess the role of the head of state and the two chambers of Parliament in the making of foreign policy. Attention will be paid not only to the formal, public features of the houses of Parliament's involvement with foreign policy, but also to the more important informal, behind-the-scenes proceedings.

The State President

According to the Constitution the State President is vested with both legislative and executive powers. He is one of the two component units of Parliament (or three, before the Senate was abolished). Although executive government of South Africa "in regard to any aspect of its domestic or foreign affairs" is vested in the State President, he acts on the advice of the Cabinet. Being a nominal head of state means that his role in foreign affairs is largely ceremonial. In terms of

the State President's constitutional powers, he appoints and accredits, receives and recognises ambassadors, plenipotentiaries, diplomatic representatives and other diplomatic officers, consuls and consular officers; enters into and ratifies international conventions, treaties and agreements; declares war and makes peace. He is also commander-in-chief of the South African Defence Force and appoints ministers and deputy ministers. Elected by an electoral college consisting of members of the House of Assembly (and Senate, when that was still in existence), the State President holds office for seven years. Only a white is eligible for election as head of state. Since the State President acts in foreign, as in domestic, affairs on the advice of the Cabinet, his role in foreign affairs is essentially instrumental, giving effect to government decisions. He has no role in the making of those decisions, except where legislation is involved, in which case the State President's assent is required before it can be enacted. Apart from the common duty of appointing and receiving diplomats, the State President may also get involved in the conduct of foreign policy by paying state visits abroad.*

To date the Republic has had six State Presidents. The first, Mr CR Swart (1961-1967), paid no state visits while in office. Dr TE Dönges, elected in January 1967 to succeed Swart, died

---

*In terms of the new Constitution approved by Parliament in 1983, the State President will be an executive president combining the offices of head of state and head of government. His role in foreign policy will therefore correspond with that of the prime minister at present.

before he could be inaugurated. The next incumbent, Mr JJ Fouché (1968-1975), visited Iran in October 1971 to attend the 2 500th anniversary of the Persian Empire. The same month he was received by President Franz Jonas in Austria. Fouché also paid an official visit to Malawi in March 1972. Dr N Diederichs, who served as State President from 1975 until his death in August 1978, did not pay any state visits abroad. He was, however, present at the independence ceremonies of Transkei in October 1976 and Bophuthatswana in December 1977. It should be mentioned that Diederichs, who served as Minister of Finance for eight years before becoming State President, had established a high reputation in international banking and financial circles. During this time he among other things received the Order of the Knight of Great Cross from the Italian government, became a freeman of Paris and was named Business Statesman of the World by the Harvard School of Business in 1973.[1] Vorster, in his eight months as State President (1978-9), made no official trips abroad, not even to independent former homelands. Mr Marais Viljoen, who became State President in June 1979, represented South Africa at Venda's independence celebrations in September 1979 and Ciskei's in December 1981, and paid a state visit to Bophuthatswana in March 1981. In twenty years, therefore, South Africa's State Presidents have paid only eight official visits to other countries, including former homelands. This remarkable homeboundedness of the head of state is a reflection of the degree of South Africa's ostracism from the international community. It also indicates the very limited significance of the largely ceremonial office of State President in the conduct of South Africa's foreign policy.

The Senate

At the time of its abolition on 31 December 1980 the Senate had 51 members, of whom 43 were indirectly elected and the others appointed by the State President. In its 70-year existence the composition of the Senate was frequently changed and its powers amended. These features reflected the controversies that for long raged over the *raison d'être* of the Senate, particularly after the National Party took power in 1948. The Nationalists went to great lengths to convert the Senate into a submissive chamber that would in no way obstruct them in pursuing their chosen

policies. Rather than functioning as a house of review where party political divisions would not be as prevalent as in the lower house, the Senate in many respects became as partisan a body as the House of Assembly. (The National Party at the time of the Senate's abolition held no fewer than 40 seats, including all eight nominated seats.) The political cleavages in the Assembly were reflected in the upper house, and debates in the two chambers were consequently to a large extent duplicatory. What is more, the powers of the Senate were restricted by those of the House of Assembly, making the lower house very much the dominant of the two chambers. The Senate's overall role in the legislative process was, therefore, not particularly significant over the last three decades – a feature that contributed to its eventual demise. It is against this background that the Senate's role in foreign affairs has to be considered.

The Senate could invite the Minister of Foreign Affairs, or any other minister, for that matter, to participate in a debate on his particular parliamentary "vote" or ministerial portfolio. Ministers' votes were not automatically placed on the order paper of the upper house, as was the case in the lower house. In practice ministers were seldom invited to present their votes in the Senate. Muller, in the more than ten years between Vorster's assumption of the premiership and Muller's own retirement in March 1977, had his vote debated only twice in the Senate, in 1967[2] and 1976.[3] Muller nonetheless appeared in the Senate on other occasions, for example to make a statement on a particular foreign policy matter [4] or to participate in a debate on legislation dealing with foreign affairs.[5] Pik Botha, who took over as Minister of Foreign Affairs on 1 April 1977, never had his vote debated in the Senate. However, he participated for the government in the censure debate in the Senate in 1979[6] and on occasion spoke on legislation relating to his portfolio.[7]

Foreign affairs was not a subject that attracted a great deal of attention in the Senate in the 1966-81 period. Apart from the few occasions when the Foreign Affairs vote and legislation emanating from the Department of Foreign Affairs were debated, there was precious little in-depth discussion of issues relating to South Africa's foreign relations. Such matters did, however, feature to a limited extent in the customary censure debate and when votes such as Defence and Information[8] were on occasion considered. Questions directed at the Minister of Foreign

Affairs were an exceptionally rare item on the Senate order paper.

A feature of Senate debates on foreign affairs was the high degree of bipartisanship between the governing party and the opposition. Until its dissolution in July 1977, the United Party had been the official opposition. Thereafter its successor, the New Republic Party, became the opposition in the upper house. At the time of its dissolution the United Party held ten of the then 55 seats in the Senate, against the National Party's 43 and the Progressive Reform Party's two. The New Republic Party held nine of the 51 seats of which the Senate was composed at the time of its abolition. The Progressive Federal Party had a single seat, and there was also a lone Independent member.

Opposition foreign affairs spokesmen in the Senate openly acknowledged the large degree of consensus between the two sides on foreign policy issues. In 1976 when the Foreign Affairs vote was debated, Senator HFB Oelrich, leader of the opposition in the Senate, reminded the Minister of Foreign Affairs that "when it comes to matters of the safety of the State, or defence or foreign affairs, we often find ourselves *ad idem* with what the government does". Oelrich pointed out that the United Party did not simply blame South Africa's problems with the international community on the government's policies: "We do not say: 'We told you so' . . . We have today to deal with the accomplished fact that South Africa finds herself in a difficult, separate and disturbing position."[9] In 1979 Senator JL Horak, Chief Opposition (NRP) Whip, gave Pik Botha the assurance that regardless of party politics, "our approach to foreign affairs . . . specifically to the assault upon our country by the enemies that surround us, is very similar to that of the government."[10]

Not only were these bipartisan sentiments reflected in Senate debates on foreign affairs, but the debates themselves were noted for being generally calm, reasoned and dignified. Whereas petty politicking often featured in Assembly discussions of foreign affairs, that rarely applied in the Senate. This was probably partly attributable to the fact that the United Party and later the NRP, and not the PFP, was the official opposition. The Progressive Federal Party (PFP) was born out of the merger in September 1977 between the Progressive Reform Party (PRP – itself the product of a merger between the Progressive Party and the Reform Party in 1975) and six former United Party MPs led by Mr JD du P (Japie) Basson. After the PFP had become the official opposition in the Assembly, the sharpness and even acrimony of government-PFP differences on domestic policies tended to be reflected in foreign affairs debates. Had the PFP also been the official opposition in the Senate, there might have been less consensus on foreign affairs and the debates might have been less free of partisan rhetoric and point scoring. In practice, however, the PFP's sole member in the upper house, Senator LED Winchester, told Foreign Minister Botha that "while we differ politically in South Africa, we are entirely on the same side when it comes to putting our case in the outside world."[11]

Foreign Affairs provided a rare exception to the rule of partisanship that generally prevailed in the Senate. Nonetheless, Senate debates on foreign affairs, although different in style, were in substance largely duplicative of those held in the House of Assembly because of corresponding party political cleavages – even though the party lines were notably less strongly drawn in the Senate than in the Assembly when it came to foreign affairs. With the Senate also composed on party lines, it would have been unrealistic to have expected the upper house to place a profoundly different or unique stamp on foreign affairs. This is not to say that senators' contributions to the discussion of foreign affairs were necessarily unimaginative or meaningless. On the contrary, significant contributions were in the last number of years of the Senate's existence made by senators such as AM van Schoor, Dr DJ Worrall, LF Poorter and PHS van Zyl on the government side, and senators Horak and Oelrich from the opposition benches. But despite the quality of some of the speeches, their actual impact on foreign policy was marginal, and in any case even smaller than those made in the Assembly.

Those National Party senators actively interested in foreign affairs had greater opportunity to play a role in this field outside the formal debates in the chamber. The vehicle was the National Party's Senate study group on foreign affairs. No fewer than 26 Nationalist senators belonged to the study group in its final year, including a committee of four under the chairmanship of Senator AM van Schoor. Because the group was so large in relation to the number of National Party senators, it is only to be expected that not all members of the study group actively participated in its proceedings or, for that matter, displayed keen interest in foreign affairs. All senators, it should be explained, had to belong to five study groups; there was a group corresponding with each ministerial portfolio. Van Schoor's election to the Senate in 1974 blew new life into the National Party's involvement with foreign affairs in the upper house. A former editor of the Johannesburg Afrikaans daily, *Die Vaderland,* and a regular radio commentator on international affairs, Van Schoor managed to revive his colleagues' interest in an area they at times tended to neglect.

The Nationalist senators' foreign affairs study group met on an *ad hoc* basis during Senate sessions. The Minister of Foreign Affairs seldom attended these meetings. Occasionally there were joint meetings with the foreign affairs study group for National Party members of the lower house; members of the Senate's study group could attend the meetings of their party colleagues' group in the Assembly, but not *vice versa.* Since the Minister of Foreign Affairs was usually present at meetings of the Assembly foreign affairs study group and at joint meetings of the study groups of the two chambers, these occasions provided Nationalist senators with their most important potential opportunity for influencing foreign policy. In practice, the influence was however meagre.

Two of the NRP's nine senators (the number at the time of the Senate's dissolution) formed a joint Foreign Affairs study group with three of their colleagues in the House of Assembly. Mr George Bartlett, MP, was convenor of the group. In the days of the United Party its members in the Senate had also formed a joint Foreign Affairs study group with their colleagues in the lower house.

The House of Assembly

Before examining the House of Assembly's role in South Africa's foreign policy making, it would be useful to refer briefly to some general views on the role of representative legislative bodies in the conduct of states' foreign policies, and then to focus on the British experience. The role of the British Parliament, specifically the House of Commons, provides a useful frame of reference for examining the role of the South African lower house. The House of Assembly is structurally and procedurally to a large extent modelled on its British counterpart.

The involvement of the legislature in foreign policy has long been a contentious matter. Its ability to concern itself with foreign policy matters was already criticised by John Locke, who argued that a state's foreign relations were of such an exceptional nature that the legislature should even be by-passed.[12] Joseph Frankel took the view that "as large clumsy bodies parliaments cannot effectively exercise initiative and their participation upsets diplomacy." He referred to the problems of ignorance, the need for secrecy and the fact that the legislature was not always in a position to give immediate attention to urgent matters.[13] Nonetheless, the democratisation of Western polities coupled with the general recognition of the close interplay between domestic and foreign policies have meant that the legislature – as a representative organ – can no longer be overlooked in the conduct of a democratic state's foreign policy. In a totalitarian or authoritarian state, by contrast, the legislature's role amounts to little more than expressing unqualified approval and acclaim for the foreign policy already made by the executive.

The British Parliament's consideration of foreign policy concerns is substantially different from the way it deals with domestic matters and its influence over foreign affairs is much smaller than over internal matters. There are several reasons for this situation. First, as Richards pointed out, "the essence of foreign policy is negotiation rather than legislation", thus limiting the opportunity for parliamentary scrutiny. Second, foreign affairs are usually of less concern to Members of Parliament and the public generally than immediate social and economic issues. Politicians and public alike are accordingly less informed on foreign than domestic issues. "Save at times of great crisis", Richards added, "foreign policy tends to be overlaid by other issues." Having examined the various sources of information available to MPs – official publications, trips abroad, institutional assistance (particularly from the headquarters organisations of the major political parties), and the Commons' library – Richards concluded with the following indictment: "In spite of – or perhaps because of – the facilities available to Members of Parliament, it is difficult to resist the conclusion that many are ill-informed about international problems." Unless they are well informed MPs can hardly be expected to exert "effective influence and scrutiny over public affairs".[14] Third, a bipartisan approach to foreign policy that exists on many major issues can often restrain parliamentary debate. Fourth, the need for secrecy, to which the executive regularly alludes, not only inhibits debate but also shields ministers from parliamentary criticism. A final constraint on Parliament's role in foreign affairs is the general consideration noted earlier, the common notion that the legislature is not really suited to handle the day to day dynamics of foreign policy, and the need for speedy responses to rapidly changing situations.[15]

In view of these factors the two main areas of formal parliamentary authority – the approval of legislation and of public expenditure – are not normally relevant to foreign policy issues. The bulk of parliamentary time devoted to British foreign policy is taken up by general debates, questions and ministerial statements. These are all important, for they allow Parliament to be kept informed on international affairs; the executive's actions in the field of foreign affairs can be subjected to some degree of scrutiny, and ministers are in turn provided with an opportunity to explain policy and respond to criticism; and the government is enabled to gauge opposition thinking and to muster parliamentary support for its policies. Because of party loyalty, such support from within the ruling party is virtually automatic. Parliament can of course only perform these functions when in session; in recess, its influence over foreign affairs is effectively nil. Overall, Richards found, the British Parliament's record on foreign policy matters is certainly "unimpressive".[16]

South Africa's lower house was until recently composed solely of members directly elected by the voters according to the single member constituency system coupled with the relative majority (or first-past-the-post) method of voting. The *Republic of South Africa Constitution Fifth Amendment Act,* 1980, ended the tradition of a fully directly elected second chamber. In addition to 165 directly elected members – the previous composition of the Assembly – provision was made for four members nominated by the State President, of whom one shall be nominated from each province, and a further eight members elected by the 165 directly elected MPs according to the principle of proportional representation. After the general election of April 1981, the National Party held 131 of the 165 elected seats, while all four of the members nominated by the State President and seven of the eight indirectly elected members belonged to the National Party. Of the total number of 177 seats in the Assembly, the National Party therefore held 142 against 27

for the PFP (including one indirectly elected) and eight for the NRP. During Vorster's premiership, when three general elections were held, the National Party each time gained an overwhelming majority of Assembly seats.

Opportunities for debating foreign affairs in the Assembly

The National Party's overwhelming numerical superiority in the House of Assembly constitutes a material constraint on the chamber's role in foreign affairs and further enhances the dominance of the executive. With the National Party known for its strict internal discipline, the Cabinet can normally count on the support of the party's parliamentary caucus in both foreign and domestic policy matters. This is not to say that there are no intra-party differences on foreign affairs; these, however, would usually be resolved in caucus and hardly ever find expression in debates in the chamber. What all this points to is that the National Party's parliamentary caucus in practice plays a more important – or perhaps more accurately a less unimportant – role in influencing foreign policy than do the public proceedings of the House of Assembly.

When examining the House of Assembly's consideration of foreign affairs, it is well to be reminded of Carl Friedrich's well-known dictum: "Speech is the essence of parliamentary activity, it is the very lifeblood of parliament's body politic." The Assembly provides a number of major opportunities for speech-making on foreign affairs, most notably during the annual Foreign Affairs vote. Foreign affairs understandably also features prominently in the discussion of the Defence vote and, when the Department of Information still existed as a separate ministry with its own minister, also the Information vote. The customary censure debate at the beginning of each new parliamentary session and also the Prime Minister's vote invariably deal with foreign policy matters among the wide range of subjects broached in the course of the debates which stretch over several days; domestic issues are, however, dominant.

The accompanying table shows the approximate time (in hours) spent on the votes of Foreign Affairs and Information (at first two separate votes, but later combined with the creation of a single enlarged Department of Foreign Affairs and Information) and Defence in a selected number of parliamentary sessions. Normally the

Assembly meets for about five months annually.

YEAR	VOTE			
	Foreign Affairs	Foreign Affairs and Information	Information/ Information Service	Defence
1980	–	8½	–	6¾
1979	7	–	2½	6½
1977	8¾	–	3½	7
1976	5¾	–	4½	6½
1974	8¼	–	4½	6¾
1970	5½	–	4¼	5¾
1968	4	–	1¾	4

Inter-party conflict and consensus on foreign policy

The National Party and the United Party

When one examines the nature and content of Assembly foreign affairs debates, the question of consensus between government and opposition parties naturally arises. A significant change, or deterioration, in the relationship between the two sides has occured after the PFP replaced the United Party as official opposition. Although the domestic political divisions between the United Party and the Nationalists had not been as deep as between the latter and the PFP, the United Party nonetheless tried to keep its distance from the government on aspects of foreign policy.

Japie Basson, the opposition's chief spokesman on foreign affairs, in September 1970 went so far as to state that his party was generally speaking not in favour of bipartisanship on foreign policy:

> The reason is quite obvious. We make no secret of it. We are not in favour of a bipartisan attitude for the simple reason that the government is associated with the policy of apartheid, which has created an extremely unfavourable image of South Africa. In the interests of South Africa we on this side, as the alternative government, do not want that albatross around our necks.[17]

Basson's statement touched on the basic and lasting point of disagreement between the government and the United Party on foreign affairs: the influence of South Africa's domestic political order on its foreign relations. The United Party was in no doubt about the cause of South Africa's international difficulties. The situation in which the Republic found itself, Basson suggested in 1974,

> is attributable solely to the realities of the government's statutes and policy which force apart and humiliate people in our country on the basis of race and colour.[18]

Committed to domestic policies rejected by the rest of the world, the government was incapable of improving South Africa's foreign relations, the United Party argued.[19] Foreign policy initiatives, such as Vorster's idea of a "power bloc" of states in Southern Africa, were consequently bound to fail, for they would be "brought up short by the policy of colour apartheid of the government".[20]

In the United Party's view the only way out of South Africa's international dilemma lay in a new domestic political order, based upon the idea of a racial federation; it would bring "a new light for South Africa in the darkness abroad", Basson confidently predicted.[21] Needless to say, the government disputed opposition claims that its idea of a racial federation would be any more acceptable than apartheid abroad, or that it would improve South Africa's international relations. If anything, the United Party's policy was "even far less acceptable to the outside world" than the government's since it was widely regarded as one of "baasskap", Muller countered. While admitting that the government's domestic policies were not acceptable internationally, Muller still insisted that "the root of our problems in the international sphere is not the Government's [race relations] policy." That, he said, was merely "a pretext". The real explanation, the Foreign Minister maintained, was to be found in the evil machinations of the "non-White extremists" and particularly the "communists" who aimed their attacks at South Africa's whites and who coveted the Republic "as a sphere of influence".[22]

The link between South Africa's domestic and foreign policies could, however, not so easily be dismissed. The opposition's harping on this theme clearly touched a raw Nationalist nerve. It found expression in government spokesmen, Vorster included, referring ad nauseam to Smuts's setbacks at the UN in 1946 in an attempt to prove that South Africa's international difficulties predate the advent of the Nationalist government with its apartheid policy.[23] The further argument was that attacks on South Africa would have grown in vehemence even if the Nationalists had not come to power in 1948, because no South African political party committed to "upholding the position and influence of the Whites in South Africa" could have escaped international censure.[24] Basson's unconvincing rejoinder was that Smuts, had he remained in power, would have made the necessary "adjustments" to meet the demands of the post-war world.[25] Another typical Nationalist response was Muller's suggestion that people attributing South Africa's problems in the world to its racial policies "are definitely not in good company" since their actions are prejudicial to South Africa's interests.[26] The government's sensitivity was furthermore reflected in assertions that it was improper to drag apartheid into foreign affairs debates since it did not belong there, coupled with the notion that it was "quite fruitless" to discuss the unacceptability of South Africa's domestic policies to the outside world.[27]

The assumption underlying the latter view was the familiar one that no white South African political party could ever hope to satisfy international demands about the Republic's political system. Yet, paradoxically, Muller on occasion said that if the feud between black African states and South Africa could end, the Republic would be able to give its "undivided attention" to the implementation of separate development "and it will enable us to get away from those things which our critics do not like and which we do not like either."[28] Although this statement implicitly acknowledges the connection between South Africa's domestic and foreign policies, it is a linkage that has more often than not been denied. Muller came in for opposition criticism on this score, when Basson told him he too infrequently spoke about the domestic-foreign policy connection and the necessity of domestic political changes if South Africa wanted to survive the storms threatening it. Basson urged the Foreign Minister to exert more political influence "to bring about those essential changes and formations among his own people and in South Africa."[29] In view of Muller's low internal political profile and his aloofness from the party political mêlée – quite apart from other possible considerations – he was hardly the man to champion openly the cause of political reform. That was to be left to his successor.

This basic disagreement between the National Party and the United Party introduced another contentious matter, the extent of South Africa's international isolation. The government took strong exception to the opposition's repeated charges that the Republic's isolation was constantly growing. Thus Muller told the House of Assembly in 1970 that

we should guard against buttering up South Africa's enemies with hackneyed references to South Africa's isolation, which in actual fact is confined to certain countries and a few spheres which are not vital to South Africa.[30]

Four years later Muller was still berating the opposition for "playing into the hands of our enemies, encouraging our enemies and doing South Africa a disservice" by continuously drawing attention to the Republic's isolation. Although assuring opposition members that he was not questioning their "patriotism",[31] Muller was nonetheless sailing close to the wind. In subsequent years, after the PFP had become the official opposition, the government would display much less restraint in casting doubts on opposition members' loyalty to South Africa. This kind of reaction, together with the charge that opposition criticism of the government is harmful to South Africa's interests, flows from a tendency to equate the National Party with the state and from a stubborn belief that the National Party is the sole articulator and guardian of the national interest.

The dispute over South Africa's international isolation in turn raised the question as to whether the government presented Parliament with an accurate picture of South Africa's foreign relations. The opposition, curiously enough, alternately criticised Muller for displaying "too much optimism" and always talking about South Africa's diplomatic "breakthroughs",[32] and for being too "gloomy" and pessimistic.[33] True, Muller frequently recounted in detail the number of foreign dignitaries, particularly from black African states, who had officially visited South Africa in the preceding months, and the number of visits South African ministers and senior officials had paid abroad. The object was always to counter opposition charges about South Africa's mounting international isolation.[34] On other occasions Muller presented a rather sombre picture of South Africa's position in the world, explaining that "it is my duty to do so." Even then the rider was that successive National Party governments had "under very difficult circumstances" not only "maintained" South Africa's position internationally but actually succeeded in "improving" it.[35]

When proudly revealing the statistical records of South Africa's diplomatic interaction with other states, Muller was usually careful to keep a veil of secrecy over the identity of the foreign individuals and countries involved. In 1974 he told the House of Assembly that it was unfortunately impossible to take members into his confidence and disclose more information on South Africa's foreign relations:

> By preserving confidentiality in respect of contracts entered into on a confidential basis, one creates confidence in the minds of those involved in the matter. One would not like to shake their confidence and frustrate and thwart the progress that has been made.

As if to console the opposition, Muller added that he dared not even take the National Party caucus into his confidence all the time.[36] Particularly when matters such as South Africa's relations with black African states and the Republic's procurement of arms were raised by the opposition, Muller cut the discussion short by saying that these were "delicate matters" that ought not to be publicly discussed and were best left to "the good judgment of the Government".[37] Realising the major constraint thus imposed on parliamentary consideration of foreign affairs, the United Party repeatedly called for the establishment of a standing committee on foreign affairs, where sensitive matters could be confidentially discussed.[38] Muller rejected the proposal on the very grounds on which it was based, the need to maintain confidentiality.

The constraints imposed by South Africa's internal policies on its foreign relations featured in another important area of disagreement between the government and opposition: South Africa's possible establishment of diplomatic ties with other states, particularly black African. This involved several aspects, the first of which was the government's stand that diplomats could be exchanged with distant black African states, but not with South Africa's immediate neighbours. "That is so because it is impossible to communicate directly with those distant countries as we do in the case of our . . . neighbouring states", Muller explained in 1968, "and incidentally, this direct method is much cheaper."[39] Malawi, with which South Africa established diplomatic relations in 1967, was then presumably regarded as a "distant" state. The United Party, favouring reciprocal diplomatic representation also with neighbouring black states, argued that diplomatic ties go further than mere inter-governmental contact. "It is something which penetrates to the ordinary levels of the population", Basson said, and is essential to create friendly relations between the various countries' peoples.[40] Some years later the government changed its position and agreement was reached with Lesotho to exchange consular representatives. Nothing, however, came of it, essentially because of Lesotho's unwillingness to go ahead.

The second matter concerned the government's establishment of a so-called diplomatic suburb in Pretoria. The United Party opposed the idea, arguing that it would be viewed with suspicion abroad; it would, in short, be seen as a suburb for black diplomats, segregated from white residential areas.[41] Muller maintained that diplomatic suburbs were to be found in various other countries and gave the assurance that "nowhere in the world are there first and second class diplomats, not here in South Africa either." All diplomats, regardless of colour, would therefore enjoy the same privileges and immunities.[42]

Finally, there was the government's practice of boycotting racially mixed social functions arranged by foreign diplomatic missions in South Africa. The United Party in 1968 appealed to the government to drop its objections and attend.[43] Muller, however, reaffirmed the government's stance:

> When both white and non-white South Africans – please note, South Africans – are invited to receptions held by foreign organisations, we do not attend those receptions, and we do not approve of them.

But, he added, the government had no objection to functions attended or given by "non-white diplomats".[44] This practice demonstrated the government's rigid adherence to the precepts of Verwoerdian separatism, extending it also to the realm of diplomacy. In subsequent years the practice was dropped.[45]

The areas of disagreement on foreign affairs between the United Party and the National Party were of secondary importance when compared with the issues on which a broad consensus prevailed. Despite Basson's rejection of bipartisanship, the United Party in practice displayed a large measure of agreement with the government on such key foreign policy issues as South West Africa/Namibia and Rhodesia.[46] The opposition nonetheless on a number of occasions from 1970 onwards exhorted the government to "display greater initiative" in resolving the South West Africa/Namibia dispute in consultation with the UN.[47] As for Rhodesia, the United Party began moderating its original pro-UDI sentiments towards the late 1960s. By 1975 the opposition was earnestly appealing to the government to use all its influence to find a peaceful settlement and avoid a devastating race war in Rhodesia. Fears were also expressed by the United Party that South Africa, because of the presence of its police in Rhodesia, might get drawn into a large-scale guerrilla war.[48] As it turned out, the government shared these concerns. Government and opposition also closed ranks in the House of Assembly on what Muller typically termed the "onslaughts from abroad".[49] The United Party was no less insistent than the National Party on South Africans' right to decide their own future without being dictated to from outside.

The National Party and the Progressive Federal Party

Before considering bipartisanship on foreign affairs between the government and the PFP as official opposition, it is worth noting a number of areas of disagreement between them in preceding years.

The first, dating back to September 1974 (when the then Progressive Party held seven seats in the House of Assembly), concerned Nationalist attacks on Mr Colin Eglin, leader of the party, over his talks with five black African heads of state. In the vanguard of the critics was PW Botha, Minister of Defence, who assailed Eglin for sitting around the table with "terrorists" and falling over his feet in front of President Kaunda of Zambia. For good measure, PW Botha called Eglin's patriotism into question.[50] Eglin saw his visits as creating goodwill for South Africa.[51] Muller, in sharp contrast to his Cabinet colleague, was not opposed to members of opposition parties visiting other states provided "they have the right object in view," and not "cheap party-political gain". Muller moreover recognised that members of the other parties had access to countries closed to the government, and he thought it necesary "to put our heads together, to stand together and to think of South Africa's interests".[52] PW Botha's sharp attack on Eglin was nonetheless an intimation of things to come.

A vivid illustration of the divisions over foreign affairs between the government and the Progressive Reform Party, as the Progressive Party subsequently became known, was the January 1976 Assembly debate on South Africa's involvement in the Angolan war. Vorster revealed that

amid all the official secrecy surrounding South Africa's role in the war, he did from time to time inform the leader of the opposition, Graaff, of what was happening. Vorster "gave very serious consideration" to informing the PRP leader, Eglin, too, but decided against it "because I was afraid to run the risk". It was not that he did not trust Eglin, Vorster explained, but because Eglin and members of his party "go along with people I do not trust." Who they were, Vorster did not say.[53] It should be added that whereas Graaff expressed reservations about South Africa's involvement in the Angolan war, particularly regarding the government's objectives (or lack of them), he was far more guarded than Eglin, who declared openly that the government's decision to get embroiled in the Angolan war was "an error of political judgement . . . which could seriously prejudice and jeopardise the future security of South Africa."[54]

A recurring area of disagreement between the Nationalists and the Progressives was South Africa's relations with the West, and the United States in particular. Since the late 1960s sporadic suggestions have been made by some members of the Cabinet that South Africa ought to consider becoming a non-committed country rather than maintaining the tradition of openly siding with the West.[55] This was clearly in response to what was seen as Western indifference to South Africa's value as an ally. Following the Angolan war and South Africa's resentment of the West's, specifically America's, failure to support the Republic's engagement in the conflict, government members returned to the notion of reconsidering South Africa's traditional Western alignment in favour of a more "neutral" posture or even some understanding with the People's Republic of China.[56] Eglin instead argued in favour of "an active and vigorous association with the West" and urged an end to a "hollow posture" of disinterest in or hostility towards the West. He also disputed frequently heard claims from government members that the West had lost its will to oppose Soviet actions in Southern Africa and was prepared to sacrifice Rhodesia, Namibia and South Africa. Eglin perceived no such lack of will on the part of the Western powers, saying that they were in fact making a "constructive effort" to counter Soviet influence. He went further to maintain that the West's desire to see the abolition of racial discrimination in South Africa flowed from the belief that this feature, in the eyes of black African states, provides a justification for Soviet involvement in Southern Africa.[57]

These differences between the government and the PRP were thrown into sharper focus on the issue of South Africa's relations with the United States under the Carter Administration. In June 1977 Eglin in the House of Assembly mentioned the talks that Vorster, accompanied by Pik Botha, held with American Vice-President Walter Mondale in Vienna the previous month. Eglin saw the essence of Mondale's message to Vorster embodied in the phrase "full political participation and the removal of discrimination". "If those are the prerequisites for good relations with the West", Eglin said, "those are also the prerequisites for real peace in South Africa and in Southern Africa." Yet Eglin maintained that Mondale had made no demand that South Africa should introduce political change and had not tried to prescribe any particular political system.[58] Pik Botha, after quoting at length from Mondale's statements at a press conference following the talks with Vorster, concluded that the Americans "want us to remove the whole basis of the structure of our society." They wanted to remove South Africans' right to govern themselves, and for the Foreign Minister this meant that "one's nation's survival is at stake." In such circumstances the removal of discriminatory measures would not satisfy the Carter Administration; not even the PRP, Pik Botha intimated, would be able to satisfy an American "demand for 'one man, one vote' ".[59]

Some months earlier a Nationalist MP, Mr GF Botha, in a totally unsubtle fashion resorted to the established practice of casting suspicions on the patriotism of people in opposition ranks. At issue was an address delivered by Dr ZJ de Beer, executive director of the Anglo American Corporation and member of the PRP's federal executive committee (and later PFP MP) at an investment conference in Johannesburg in December 1976. If he were a foreign investor looking clinically at South Africa, De Beer had said, he would refrain from investing in the Republic until the country looked safe for private enterprise. That, in turn, would only occur once essential political reforms had been implemented.[60] Such a statement, Botha asserted brazenly, "is absolute treason against South Africa in the times in which we are living."[61]

Following the general election of November 1977, the newly-formed Progressive Federal Party (PFP) became the official opposition. It was, as mentioned earlier, an election dominated by foreign policy issues, specifically South Africa's relations with the United States under the Carter Administration. Given the strains in US-South African relations and the anti-American sentiments evident among the white electorate, opposition parties had to tread warily on the issue of relations with the United States. An "American connection" was a particularly undesirable attribute in the then prevailing political climate. In April 1979 Eglin fell victim to a shrewd design by the Foreign Minister to tar the opposition leader with the American brush. The celebrated incident was a telephone conversation Eglin held with Mr Donald McHenry, American UN ambassador and chairman of the Western "contact group" on Namibia. Pik Botha in the House of Assembly charged that after he had given Eglin "extremely confidential information" in a briefing on the international negotiations over Namibia, Eglin telephoned McHenry in New York "to check up on me and on my word". In so doing, Eglin had allegedly conveyed to McHenry the confidential information supplied by the Foreign Minister. Eglin was said to have subsequently made a speech in the Assembly based on what McHenry had told him, thereby rejecting the Foreign Minister's views. This showed, Pik Botha claimed, that Eglin was "hand in glove" with someone who was an "enemy" of South Africa, and his actions had made the Minister's negotiating position on Namibia "more difficult".[62]

Eglin, bitterly resenting the suspicions cast on his integrity and commitment to South Africa, denied that he had conveyed any secret information to McHenry. There was nothing clandestine about the telephone call, he said, and explained that it was merely to get clarity on UN proposals for a Namibian settlement. The official opposition had a duty to keep itself informed on "sensitive foreign policy issues, above all Namibia", and his talk with McHenry was a "genuine and a positive attempt" to do just that.[63] What detracted from Eglin's explanation, however, was that he failed to tell Pik Botha of his conversation with McHenry when he saw the Foreign Minister the following day. Even more important was that none other than McHenry mentioned Eglin's telephone call to South Africa's envoy at the UN and apparently expressed annoyance about Eglin's action. The envoy in turn reported the matter to the Foreign Minister.[64]

As a foreign policy issue *per se* the "McHenry affair" was not of great consequence, yet it was assiduously exploited for party political purposes.

It is not without significance that the incident was raised in the Assembly almost six weeks *after* it had occurred. The *persona dramatis* was the Foreign Minister, who ventured to suggest that there was "no previous example in our constitutional history of such an abominable, blatant, arrogant breach of confidence against a member of the government" as that of Eglin's against Pik Botha himself.[65] As a party political ploy the McHenry affair proved devastatingly successful, for it was a major cause of the subsequent downfall of the hapless Eglin as leader of the opposition. The whole episode underlined the potency of South Africa's relations with the United States (under the Carter Administration) as a factor in domestic politics. As so often in the past, government spokesmen also turned this incident into a test of an opposition party's loyalty to South Africa.

The McHenry affair, together with the continuing debate on the Information debacle, took relations between government and official opposition to probably their lowest post-war ebb. One political commentator remarked on the "inter-party slanging, bitterness, personal insults within the bounds of parliamentary language, and genuine anger".[66]

Another PFP MP, Mr Dave Dalling, has also been the target for similar suspicions on matters pertaining to South Africa's foreign relations. In January 1981 the *New York Times* published a letter written by Dalling, in which he expressed severe criticism of the homelands policy. The Foreign Minister took Dalling to task in the Assembly for writing to a foreign newspaper known for its "vilification" of South Africa, "and he slings mud at his own country, at the Black leaders in this country and at this Government."[67] The inference was clear: a member of the official opposition had acted in a fashion that was both disloyal and damaging to the interests of the country as a whole. The government recognises a very thin line – if at all – between criticism of its policies and a blanket condemnation of the country *per se*. Some months later Dalling, the PFP spokesman on sport, again attracted the wrath of Nationalists when he questioned the wisdom of allowing the South African rugby tour of New Zealand to proceed in the face of opposition in the host country. Dr Gerrit Viljoen, Minister of National Education, sharply rebuked Dalling and again invoked the question of loyalty to South Africa.[68]

There are probably a fair number of similar incidents that illustrate how PFP disagreement with the government on both domestic and foreign policy matters has frequently been cast in the mould of disloyalty towards South Africa. Only one further example of this practice deserves mention. In the middle of 1981 Dr F van Zyl Slabbert, leader of the PFP, addressed a meeting of the Ebert Foundation in Bonn on the role of the parliamentary opposition in South Africa. In the House of Assembly the prime minister subsequently, through innuendo, suggested that Slabbert had secretly said things abroad that he was not prepared to say publicly in South Africa. This was a transparent attempt to discredit the opposition by casting doubts on its leader's patriotism. In a bitter exchange with the prime minister Slabbert threatened that PFP MPs would no longer receive guests of the Department of Foreign Affairs and Information "if our patriotism, if our loyalty, if our integrity as South Africans are questioned." The prime minister's curt response was: "I think it would be better if you did not see them."[69] A few days later Slabbert dropped his threat.[70]

Looking at the areas of consensus next, the most important one was Namibia. Like the government the PFP on occasion also voiced its criticism of the actions of the Western contact group in the search for an international settlement.[71] Government and opposition had established some understanding on the Namibian issue, and the PFP expressed appreciation of the efforts of the Minister and Department of Foreign Affairs to provide the opposition with detailed documentation. Basson (then a PFP MP) took this as evidence of Parliament "being taken into consideration far better as a Parliament" on Namibia, since PW Botha had become prime minister.[72] On a wider regional front, the PFP supported PW Botha's idea of a constellation of Southern African states and argued that stability in Southern Africa and closer ties between South Africa and surrounding black states were essential as "a springboard of constructive action for our foreign policy".[73] Some common ground was also found on the notion of South Africa being threatened from outside. "Our right to exist as a country and our right as South Africans to work out our own destiny are actually in dispute", Mr Harry Schwarz said in June 1979, and pointed to sanctions as the greatest threat.[74] But having acknowledged the existence of an external threat, the PFP was quick to add that domestic political reform was a principal way of resisting it. PFP members among themselves however appeared to differ on the question of external dangers.[75]

South Africa's attitude to the United States was not always a source of disagreement between the government and the PFP. An outstanding example of consensus concerned the American spy plane incident raised by the prime minister in the House of Assembly in April 1979. The official aircraft of the American diplomatic mission in South Africa had secretly been photographing sensitive strategic installations in South Africa, the prime minister revealed. Eglin joined in the condemnation of the American action, calling it "shocking and reprehensible, even more especially because it came from a country with whom we had friendly diplomatic relationships." The PFP, he said, was *ad idem* with the government in not tolerating any such violation of South African sovereignty.[76]

The National Party and the New Republic Party
When one looks at the NRP's parliamentary stand on foreign policy it will suffice to record that its major disagreement with the government centred on the effects of apartheid on South Africa's external relations. Like its predecessor, the United Party, the NRP time and again blamed the government's racial policies as the primary cause of South Africa's poor international standing. In expressing this opinion, NRP MPs were notably forthright: "the root cause of most of our problems in our foreign relations", Mr George Bartlett, the party's spokesman on foreign affairs, said in May 1980, "is racism".[77] Injecting an avowedly party political note, NRP members have portrayed the government as being immobilised by its right wing when it came to introducing political reforms; the government was therefore incapable of doing the necessary to improve South Africa's foreign relations.[78] Of lesser importance was the NRP's taking issue with the government over the latter's frequent attacks on Western powers.[79] It was nonetheless apparent that NRP MPs were far less inclined than some of their colleagues in the PFP to try to explain or rationalise, or even defend, the actions of Western powers – notably the United States – in their dealings with South Africa.

The principal areas of general agreement between the government and the NRP were Namibia, the promotion of closer co-operation in Southern Africa, and the seriousness of external threats or onslaughts against South Africa.[80] Regarding Southern African relations it is instructive that a central tenet of NRP policy has always been its "federal/confederal system": a federation of South Africa that would link up with other independent states in Southern Africa (including independent former black homelands) in a confederation.[81] What the government envisaged with a constellation of Southern African states was therefore essentially the same as the confederation proposed by the NRP. In due course, the two parties began calling the same design by the same name when the government started equating its constellation with a confederation.[82]

Relations between the prime minister and opposition leader
When one considers the consensus between the government and opposition parties on foreign policy, it should be borne in mind that the South African Parliament does not have any formal inter-party machinery for the discussion of foreign policy matters, particularly those of a sensitive or confidential nature. There was, nonetheless, a tacit convention that vital issues touching on South Africa's security – notably Namibia and to a somewhat lesser extent Rhodesia – would not be made subjects of division.[83] For the rest, it proved impossible to keep politics out of foreign affairs debates. Even the government in time came to acknowledge that South Africa's peculiar international difficulties could not be explained or debated in isolation from domestic political realities. In this sense, foreign affairs debates were discussions of "the foreign policy of apartheid". Differences between the government and opposition parties on domestic matters were therefore extended to the realm of foreign policy.

The absence of an inter-party parliamentary body concerned with foreign affairs does not mean that opposition parties are simply denied access to confidential information on South Africa's foreign relations. It has already been mentioned that Eglin was confidentially briefed by the Foreign Minister on the Namibian issue. It was not uncommon for the Foreign Minister – whether Pik Botha or Muller – to inform the opposition parties' leaders and also some of their spokesmen on foreign affairs in this manner. There was also a tradition for the prime minister to take the leader of the official opposition into his confidence on sensitive foreign policy matters. Vorster faithfully upheld this convention with regard to Graaff. Thus Graaff was confidentially briefed by Vorster on such highly delicate matters as the prime minister's talks with leaders of black African states and South Africa's involvement in the Angolan war. It was noted earlier that Vorster did not likewise brief Eglin on Angola because he considered it too risky. Despite being political adversaries Vorster and Graaff enjoyed a cordial relationship based on mutual trust and respect. There is little evidence of a similar affinity between Vorster and Eglin. Graaff, it should be explained, commanded wide respect in National Party circles for his charm, dignity and unstinting loyalty to South Africa. Stemming from a prominent political family, Graaff was a veteran politician, having first been elected to Parliament in 1943 and becoming United Party leader in 1956. The amicable relationship between Graaff and Vorster as opposed to the rather strained, distant relationship between Vorster and Eglin should probably also be seen in the context of domestic political differences. These were much deeper between the National Party and the PFP than between the former and the United Party or subsequently the NRP.* Parliamentary exchanges on domestic political issues between the government and PFP were often characterised by their acrimony, whereas National Party-United Party debates over the years tended to lose a good deal of their earlier bitterness.[84]

---

* The United Party, like its successor, the NRP, favoured a race federation. For the white group the United Party proposed at least four legislative assemblies empowered "to take important decisions that cannot be overridden by the federal assembly or any of the legislative assemblies for other race groups." In a strongly decentralised federal system the federal assembly would only deal with those matters "it is agreed between all the groups are of common concern to all groups". The whites' "presently majority contribution" to South Africa's development would be safeguarded at federal level through a system of representation "based on a voice for everyone but a louder voice for those who contribute most in economic welfare." (United Party, "Does the United Party Have a Policy for Whites?", Roneoed, Division of Information and Research, Johannesburg, May 1975, 9pp.) The PFP proposes a geographic federation, but one that would make provision for the "plural nature" of South Africa's population structure. This can be done by constituting the federal assembly on the basis of proportional representation of political groupings and the introduction of a minority veto in the assembly (PFP, "The PFP Policy: Consensus Government", official publication, updated, 8pp.)

Relations between Prime Minister PW Botha and Eglin were even worse than between Vorster and Eglin. In February 1979 PW Botha bluntly told Eglin over the floor of the House: "Don't you show your face in my office again." Three weeks later PW Botha repeated the prohibition.[85] The prime minister was reacting to an insinuation by the opposition leader that the Cabinet – notwithstanding government denials – had known about the irregularities in the former Department of Information. PW Botha insisted that he would only accord Eglin the treatment to which the leader of the opposition could customarily lay claim once Eglin had apologised to the Cabinet. At the time it was suggested that the prime minister's stand was inspired by more than Eglin's utterances over the Information issue. PW Botha also felt annoyed about Eglin's visits to black African states closed to members of the government and ordinary citizens, it was said.[86] The situation improved after Slabbert had succeeded Eglin as leader of the PFP in 1979, but serious tensions in due course developed between Slabbert and the prime minister, particularly after the April 1981 general election. As already discussed, these strains were evident in the field of foreign affairs.

Nationalist perceptions of opposition parties attitudes

In personal interviews with ordinary National Party MPs[87] it was evident that their strong antipathy towards the PFP because of its domestic policies also extends to the realm of foreign policy. They widely believe that the opposition's stance on domestic political issues is related to foreign opinion. Cabinet members[88] differ in their views on the extent to which external considerations supposedly influence the PFP. Opinions range from the view that the PFP adopts an "absolutely servile attitude" to foreign pressure and is "absolutely manipulable" by external opinion, through criticism that the opposition fails to take a strong stand against foreign interference in South African affairs, to disapproving references to the frequent foreign visits of PFP MPs. Ministers are in general agreement on the principal source of external influence on the PFP: the United States under the Carter Administration, or the "American connection". The McHenry affair is seen by Nationalist politicians as the ultimate confirmation that the PFP – or most members of the opposition, at any rate – are in cahoots with the Americans.

Another subject, often closely related to foreign affairs, that ministers (also in personal interviews) cited as a further example of a lack of bipartisanship between the government and opposition, concerns South Africa's national security. A view frequently expressed is that some PFP MPs display a degree of insensitivity, even recklessness, with regard to the Republic's security. The charge is, in other words, that opposition members act in a way detrimental to the interests of the country and not merely of the ruling party. It must be remarked that a great many Nationalists, both ministers and ordinary MPs, very often tend to perceive opposition criticism of the policies and actions of the government in the realms of foreign affairs and security as questionable, unworthy and in some ways disloyal. Such reactions are the product of a tendency to see national interests as National Party interests. Nationalist politicians nonetheless concede that some PFP MPs' attitudes towards South Africa's interests are above suspicion. The two names most frequently mentioned are Basson and Schwarz. Basson in 1980 resigned from the PFP, probably to pre-empt expulsion because of his decision to accept nomination to the President's Council in the face of the PFP's refusal to serve on it. There is good reason to believe that the PRP/PFP, as its numbers in Parliament grew, experienced marked internal differences on some foreign policy issues, such as the role of foreign pressure in promoting domestic change in South Africa and the nature and seriousness of external threats against the country. Basson and Schwarz belonged to what can conveniently be designated the more conservative faction in the party.

A noteworthy opinion, also expressed in interviews with ministers, is that the NRP has made a far more positive contribution than the official opposition in Assembly discussions on foreign affairs and security matters. The special 30-minute Assembly debate on the ANC sabotage attack on SASOL installations in June 1980 is cited as an example of the NRP's more constructive and less ideologically oriented approach when compared to that of the PFP, to issues of national security.

It can be said that before the PFP became the official opposition, its influence on South Africa's foreign policy was probably effectively nil. Thereafter, the position did not change materially. Given the fundamental differences beween the PFP and the government on domestic policies, the National Party's reservations about the PFP's position on foreign policy issues and the animosity characterising their parliamentary relationship, the opposition is poorly placed to exert any real influence on foreign policy. These negative features tend to outweigh the positive elements of bipartisanship in the realm of foreign policy. Should a standing inter-party foreign affairs committee be established in Parliament, it might offset some of the disadvantages suffered by the PFP – or virtually any opposition party, for that matter. But the mere creation of structures cannot ensure any significant PFP influence on South African foreign policy. That seems to require a larger measure of convergence of National Party and PFP domestic policies, a substantial degree of trust on the part of the National Party in the PFP's loyalty to South Africa, and an accompanying improvement in their general relationship. But even under such favourable conditions the extent of an opposition party's influence on foreign policy may in the final instance depend on the wishes and whims of the prime minister.

The NRP, despite not being the official opposition, probably has more influence than the PFP on foreign policy – or, more accurately, is not as uninfluential. The reasons are precisely the converse of those explaining the PFP's virtual irrelevance. First, there is much more – and in the 1980s growing – agreement between the National Party and the NRP on domestic policies, specifically racial matters, than between the NP and the PFP. Second, the NRP has never had a major dispute with the government on foreign affairs comparable to the Eglin-McHenry controversy. Third, Nationalists undoubtedly have much greater faith in what they would see as the patriotism of NRP MPs than in their PFP counterparts. Finally, parliamentary relations between the government and the NRP are generally vastly better than between the Nationalists and the PFP. The result is that the government is more likely to turn a sympathetic ear to NRP views on foreign policy than to those of the official opposition. Even so, the NRP's influence on foreign policy making is at best marginal.

The effects of secrecy

A major factor that effectively circumscribes the House of Assembly's role in the foreign policy making process is the government's perceived need to maintain secrecy on aspects of South

Africa's foreign relations. Two outstanding recent examples have been South Africa's involvement in the Angolan war (1975-6) and the activities abroad of the former Department of Information.

The Government initially deliberately tried to shroud the participation of South African forces in the Angolan war in a veil of secrecy. While the government succeeded in shielding many of its activities in Angola from the South African public, foreign audiences, ironically, were kept well informed on the South African involvement thanks to the international news media. It soon became apparent that the official restrictions on news fuelled rumour, confusion and concern among the (white) public and could not be maintained for any length of time. It was therefore not surprising that South Africa's involvement in the Angolan war overshadowed the no-confidence debate in the House of Assembly in January 1976. As the first ground for his customary motion of no-confidence, Graaff in fact cited the government's failure "to take the public into its confidence, and to motivate it adequately, in regard to the government's actions and objectives in Angola."[89] Graaff himself suffered no similar lack of information on the Angolan venture, for he had in the preceding months been confidentially briefed by Vorster.

In censuring the government for its actions in Angola the two opposition parties found much common ground. A key argument was the government's concealment of information from the public, which had destroyed a traditional bond of trust between government and people. In essence it revolved around the public's right to know what government was doing; in this particular case, what the government's strategic objectives in Angola were and what had been achieved politically and militarily.[90] This consideration also found expression in the argument that government had a duty to consult Parliament "whenever the government acts beyond the bounds of defence against aggression and involves the country in a war which may lead to an attack on us."[91] It was furthermore asserted that the government did not have the "right" to involve South Africa militarily beyond its own borders without having consulted Parliament.[92] The crux of the government's response was that more information could not be divulged "because the matter was delicate and because we were not alone in our involvement in this", in Vorster's words. Vorster said that the restrictions on information "worried me as it worried everybody

else",[93] while the Minister of Defence explained that the public's "right to know" was circumscribed by diplomatic and military considerations.[94]

If the Angolan war showed the government's disregard for Parliament in a matter of grave public importance – it involved the use of the Defence Force in a war on foreign soil – the very experience apparently made the government anxious not to repeat the treatment meted out to Parliament. This may well have been the result of the criticism that the government had incurred in Parliament. In mid-1979, when the Rhodesian bush war was raging and with persistent rumours that South Africa might get militarily involved, PW Botha declared that if foreign military intervention in Rhodesia assumed such proportions that South Africa's perceived interests became threatened, Parliament would be convened to consider appropriate action by the Republic.[95] In the event no such situation materialised, thus leaving the Angolan war as the only example in the immediate past of the executive involving South Africa in foreign military operations on a sizeable scale without the legislature's blessing. The government's decision to send South African police to Rhodesia in 1967 – on the pretext of intercepting guerrillas *en route* to South Africa – had also been taken without first consulting Parliament.[96] Compared with the subsequent military involvement in Angola, the police action in Rhodesia was on a minor scale and its significance more symbolic than strategic.

A less symbolic intervention in Rhodesian affairs was revealed by the (Durban) *Sunday Tribune* on 16 August 1981. South Africa had secretly supplied 400 motor vehicles, worth some R2 million, to assist Bishop Abel Muzorewa's United African National Council (UANC) in the April 1980 election. This was in a vain bid to prevent Mr Robert Mugabe winning. Prior to this support the former Department of Information had also secretly channelled R800 000 to the UANC. The Minister of Foreign Affairs refused to explain this interference in the affairs of another country either to the press or Parliament.

The vexed question of the executive's accountability to the legislature in the conduct of covert actions abroad is also highlighted by the so-called Information scandal. The role of the former Department of Information in the conduct of South Africa's foreign policy is considered in the following chapter; here the concern is with Parliament's involvement in a particular aspect of executive actions on the international plane.

In 1973 the Department of Information drew up a five-year plan for a secret propaganda offensive. The Department of Defence would serve as a conduit for the R50 million allocated for the venture. The details of the offensive were secretly worked out by the executive – or at least by some members of it – and Parliament was merely informed in 1973 that a restructured Department of Information had launched an unorthodox psychological war against South Africa's enemies abroad.[97] Secrecy was to be a hallmark of the foreign activities of the Department of Information. While insisting on the need for secrecy the Minister of Information, Dr CP Mulder, nonetheless gave Parliament repeated assurances that his Department was making great strides in improving South Africa's foreign relations, particularly in Africa.[98]

It was only in December 1978 that Parliament could assert its authority over the activities of this particular branch of the executive. The occasion was an extraordinary session of Parliament, convened to discuss the report of the Commission of Inquiry into Alleged Irregularities in the former Department of Information (Erasmus Commission). The report laid bare what a former senior Information official depicted as his Department's "masterplan for bribery, deceit and infiltration in the media, political circles, churches, labour unions, publishing houses, cinemas and every other possible avenue of publicity and influence peddling."[99] The focal point of the Assembly debate was not the Department of Information's activities abroad, but its clandestine activities on the home front, above all its setting up of *The Citizen* newspaper with government funds.

The debate was nonetheless of relevance to South Africa's conduct of foreign policy. A major charge of the PFP and NRP against the government was that the Information affair had humiliated the public and the institution of Parliament. They accordingly insisted that the government agree to "restore a fundamental principle in our system of government, namely the accountability of the executive to this Parliament."[100] As had been the case when the Assembly debated the Angolan war in January 1976, the opposition parties strongly defended Parliament's and the public's "right to know" what government was doing. In response PW Botha acknowledged that "the Government considers Parliament to be the highest authority in the country and that, humanly speaking, it is accountable to Parliament for its deeds from beginning to end."[101] The government's insistence that it should have secret funds at its disposal was supported by the other parties, on condition that adequate control be exercised over such funds and that they be used only to serve the country's interests, particularly its national security interests.[102] The government, when under attack from opposition ranks, made great play of external onslaughts on South Africa and also invoked the familiar strategem of casting doubts on the patriotism of some of its parliamentary critics.[103]

Having noted the main thrusts of an Assembly debate heavy with laudable declarations on all sides about the proper role of the legislature in the affairs of government, one has to ask whether the Information debacle materially strengthened Parliament's role in the conduct of foreign policy. The short answer is, probably not. True, Parliament's watchdog role over the financial implications of government activities – both domestic and foreign – has been reasserted. This, however, does not mean that Parliament will in future exert any more influence than previously over the substance of foreign policy; as an innovator its role is still at best peripheral. This has left Parliament, as before, as a forum for the government to inform, expound and mobilise support for its foreign policy; opposition parties can enquire about, criticise and propose alternative courses of action.

When one explains the South African legislature's lack of real influence in foreign policy making, it should be borne in mind that the government has consistently refused to submit regular white papers or other forms of continual reporting on foreign affairs to Parliament. The Department of Information submitted annual reports to Parliament, but these failed to reveal much because the Department's major foreign activities were conducted clandestinely. The government, as mentioned, rejected repeated calls by the United Party for the establishment of a parliamentary standing committee on foreign affairs, citing the need for secrecy and confidentiality on the diplomatic front. Louw had first rejected such a committee as early as 1955, largely on the grounds of secrecy.[104]

To summarise, Parliament's role in the conduct of South Africa's foreign policy was very restricted in the 1966-81 period. This is partly attributable to the Republic's parliamentary form of government based on the British Westminster model, which tends to strengthen the executive at the expense of the legislature. Apart from the lack of an American-type system of checks and balances, Parliament's influence is further undermined by the government's preoccupation with confidentiality and by strict party discipline, particularly in the National Party. Not only does the discipline inhibit inter-party discussion in the Assembly, it also creates the impression that Nationalist MPs are fully united on foreign policy issues. There were certainly intra-National Party differences on foreign affairs, but these surfaced – and were resolved or suppressed – in the National Party caucus, specifically in the caucus's Foreign Affairs study group.

To conclude this discussion Foreign Minister Pik Botha's exposition of the matter should be mentioned.[105] He welcomed it that parliamentary debates on foreign affairs were "subdued", something he attributed to the sensitive nature of the issues involved. Debating the question of which party's policies would be acceptable to the outside world was futile, Pik Botha reiterated, since none could satisfy international opinion. Where such debates nonetheless took place, they in no way contributed to improving South Africa's foreign relations and moreover often had the result of hardening the opinion of the majority of whites against constructive foreign criticism; this, in turn, "has a negative effect on the Government's efforts to make adaptations to domestic policy." (It is rather difficult to follow this line of argument, because it is not clear why whites should become less receptive to positive foreign criticism when hearing that alternative domestic policies would be more acceptable internationally than the government's own policies.) The Foreign Minister went on to argue that in view of the special situation in which South Africa found itself internationally the less said in Parliament about internal differences, "the better it is for South Africa." (This statement seems to deny the possibility that liberal parliamentry criticism of the government's domestic policies might serve as some encouragement to segments of Western opinion.) The task of his Department, Pik Botha maintained, was being "exceptionally complicated" by the fact that parliamentary debates were mostly conducted for purely party political purposes, resulting in statements being made (by implication by the opposition parties)

"abounding in generalisations, one-sidedness, exaggerations and emotional pronouncements". The "revolting caricature images" thus created of government policies have "extremely negative consequences" abroad for South Africa. (This contention on the one hand seems to exaggerate the influence of the white parliamentary opposition on foreign opinion, and on the other underestimates – or perhaps even ignores – the negative effects of the government's domestic policies on South Africa's foreign relations.)

The parliamentary National Party and foreign policy making

The caucus

The formal, public features of the House of Assembly's involvement with foreign affairs present only part of the picture of the legislature's role in this area. Those parliamentary activities conducted behind the scenes are actually of more importance in the conduct of South Africa's foreign relations than the public proceedings of the Assembly. The body to consider is the National Party's parliamentary caucus, particularly its Foreign Affairs study group.[106]

Because of the veil of secrecy surrounding National Party caucus discussions it is virtually impossible to make a thorough assessment of its role in foreign policy making. What is certain is that the caucus is not a policy making body in foreign affairs. It is little more than a forum for the prime minister and Minister of Foreign Affairs to explain government policies and actions and to mobilise support, if necessary. Vorster and PW Botha have made great efforts to keep the caucus informed on foreign affairs. The latter introduced a new practice of convening a caucus meeting outside parliamentary sessions to keep Nationalist MPs and provincial councillors briefed on government policies during the parliamentary recess. There are, however, limits to the extent to which the party's MPs are kept informed on foreign affairs. Because of their sensitive – or, perhaps, politically embarrassing – nature, some matters are bound to be withheld from the caucus. The government is probably also wary of the possibility of leaks from the caucus.

There is, generally speaking, little real caucus discussion, not to mention debate, on foreign policy issues. Instead it is usually a matter of policy statements by the prime minister and Minister of Foreign Affairs, and their answering questions put by MPs. Very often the information is provided *ex post facto;* the caucus is simply confronted with a *fait accompli.* The chances of MPs openly challenging the government's position on foreign relations are exceedingly small. This may be because the caucus is generally in agreement on fundamental foreign policy issues – which is not to deny some differences of opinion among MPs on aspects of the government's conduct of South Africa's foreign relations. Another reason may be that the caucus in any case seldom witnesses intense debates and sharp divisions of opinion on major government policies. The authority that ministers, and the prime minister in particular, command in the caucus at least partly explains this phenomenon. The political risks an MP may run in openly challenging the government is a further inhibitory factor.*

All this means that there is essentially a one-way flow of communication on foreign affairs in the caucus: from the prime minister and Minister of Foreign Affairs to ordinary MPs. In this process the prime minister is the dominant figure, with the Minister of Foreign Affairs playing a complementary or supportive role. That foreign affairs does not generally produce intense discussion in the caucus is not to say that it is regarded as unimportant. Foreign policy has indeed at times commanded a good deal of attention in the caucus. In recent years Namibia, Rhodesia, the "terrorist" threat and the danger of sanctions against South Africa featured prominently. Although the salience of foreign policy concerns largely depends on circumstances, foreign affairs can in the general run of caucus proceedings probably be rated among the four most important issues dealt with, the others being the perennial racial issue, economic matters and security.

The role of the National Party caucus in foreign affairs can be summarised as being at best marginal. It does not innovate policy or, least of all, formulate it. Instead the caucus's role is reactive and instrumental; it reacts to the extent that members ask questions; it is instrumental in the sense that MPs are expected to expound and defend government policies and actions on the floor of the House of Assembly and among their constituents.

---

* The most dramatic breakdown of caucus unity occurred with the revolt of a group of right-wing Nationalist MPs in February 1982.

The Foreign Affairs study group and Pik Botha's peculiar position

The focus now has to be narrowed from the National Party's parliamentary caucus as a whole to the study group on Foreign Affairs. The following analysis of the group's activities is based on its composition in 1980.

The Foreign Affairs study group was one of 24 such groups in 1980. They were all extensions of the National Party's caucus, and each group corresponded with a ministerial portfolio. The general object of the study groups was to provide MPs with an opportunity to consider policy matters in greater depth than was normally possible in full caucus meetings and to provide a forum for discussion between ministers and ordinary MPs. As the designation "study group" implies, members were supposed to familiarise themselves with the various aspects of the ministerial portfolio with which a particular group corresponded. Ideally a study group would have consisted of MPs "specialising" in the particular area of ministerial responsibility. National Party MPs had to join a minimum of five and a maximu... of seven study groups, but were free to participate (without voting rights) in the activities of groups of which they were not members. Membership of a particular study group was voluntary and lasted for the duration of a parliamentary session. There has, however, been a remarkable continuity in membership of the various groups, with major changes in composition normally only occuring after general elections when new MPs joined the caucus. Although there was no official limit on the number of MPs per group, the low fifties was tacitly regarded as the maximum in order to prevent a group becoming too large and drawing MPs away from other less popular study groups. Members of each study group elected a committee which also served for a parliamentary session.

In 1980 the Foreign Affairs study group, composed of 51 members including a committee of three, was the third largest study group. The two largest groups, each with 52 members, were those for Defence and National Security, and for Co-operation and Development. These were significant features, reflecting the importance MPs attached to security and racial matters. It is interesting to note that half the members of the Foreign Affairs group in 1980 also belonged to that for Defence and National Security. The smallest study groups in 1980 were Indian Affairs (eight members), Posts and Telecommunications (ten) and Health (eleven).

To facilitate its work the Foreign Affairs study group was subdivided into four geographically-based sub-groups, each with its own chairman: Africa, the Americas, the Near, Middle and Far East, and Europe. Membership of a sub-group was again voluntary and ranged from 9 to 25; participation in sub-group meetings was open to all National Party MPs.

In common with other study groups, the Foreign Affairs group normally met once a month during a parliamentary session, which meant meeting roughly five times a year. The committee at times held separate meetings with the Minister of Foreign Affairs. The four sub-groups also held their separate meetings at irregular intervals. Meetings of the full Foreign Affairs study group were usually very well attended with anything up to 90 MPs and Senators present, making it one of the National Party's most popular study groups.

The actual reasons for National Party MPs' deciding to become members of the Foreign Affairs study group are significant, for they already reveal something of the group's role in the conduct of foreign policy. It seems safe to say that the majority of the members were genuinely interested in foreign affairs – which is not to say that they were particularly well informed or had a special understanding of the subject. In many cases this interest was related to the high salience of South Africa's foreign relations, and particularly the concern of MPs about events in Southern Africa. The person of Foreign Minister Botha to some extent also accounted for MPs' interest in the Foreign Affairs study group. On the one hand, his charismatic political style and high public profile attracted MPs to the group; for them it was the study group "where things really happen". On the other hand, a small number of MPs joined the study group to try to keep some check on a minister with whose political views they disagreed. This essentially applied to right-wing or *verkrampte* MPs, who perceived Pik Botha as a super-*verligte*, or as something of a dangerous liberal in National Party terms.* These *verkrampte* members of the study

group maintained that some of the other members joined merely because they were "ideological allies" of the Foreign Minister, and not because of any particular interest in or knowledge of foreign affairs. In addition to these various categories of members there were those, to be found in most study groups, who simply joined the Foreign Affairs group because they *had* to belong to at least five study groups.

Members of the Foreign Affairs study group entertained widely differing views about their role in the making of foreign policy. There was a minority that had rather exaggerated ideas about the study group's input, and they typically argued that the group played an initiatory role in the sense of generating ideas that the government and the Department of Foreign Affairs took seriously and acted upon. For them, the study group served as a kind of foreign policy think tank. A related view was that the study group at the time (1980) did not play much of an initiatory role but was, presumably with the blessing of the minister, moving in that direction. The majority view in the group was, however, that it served as little more than a forum for the Minister of Foreign Affairs to expound government policy and mobilise support for it. At best, they argued, the study group provided a sounding board for the minister. An interesting observation was that *verligte* MPs were strongly represented among study group members who rated the group's role in foreign policy making very low: only a few *verligtes* thought the group made a material contribution.

The latter (majority) views indicate that the study group's influence on foreign policy making was about as limited as that of the caucus as a whole. Communication was similarly largely a one-way flow from minister to MPs. The study group also laboured under such constraints as government secrecy on aspects of foreign policy, the fact that foreign affairs produced very little legislation and thus limited opportunity for study group scrutiny, and the dynamic and complex nature of international politics. Since the study group normally met only once a month during a parliamentary session, it was hardly in a position to remain *au fait* with the fast changing world of foreign relations. It should also be added that only a minority of study group members were really active and took the trouble to become reasonably well informed, within the constraints noted, on foreign affairs. For the rest, members were little more than passive spectators, whatever their motives may have been in joining the group.

*The terms *verligte* and *verkrampte* were coined in 1966 by Dr Willem de Klerk, then of the University of Potchefstroom. He distinguished between two kinds of Afrikaners: the *verkramptes* (narrow-minded Afrikaners) opposed change in general and in race relations in particular, whereas the *verligtes* (enlightened ones) were too hasty in their advocacy of change.

It should, in fairness, be said that there was substantially more discussion on foreign policy matters in the study group than in the general caucus. MPs were afforded much greater opportunity to put questions to the minister and they probably felt less inhibited than in the caucus, with the prime minister and the rest of the Cabinet present, in airing their views. Foreign Minister Pik Botha has had to contend with critical opinions on issues such as Namibia and Rhodesia and on his publicly stated opposition to racial discrimination.[107] There was more to the occasional critical question directed at Pik Botha than meets the eye. It was an indication of the strong misgivings some members of the study group had about the Foreign Minister's political sentiments. On the positive side, study group members have on occasion made constructive suggestions that may have found their way into practice. These would, however, have been the exceptions.

The role that a study group plays in the formulation of government policies largely depends on the attitude of the minister concerned towards the group. It has already been noted that members of the Foreign Affairs study group held divergent views on their role in foreign policy making. When relating these views to the person of Foreign Minister Botha, one again discovers a range of opinions among study group members on the minister's supposed attitude towards their group. There were those who maintained that Pik Botha rated the group's contribution highly and valued their opinions. Others adopted a neutral opinion, arguing that the Foreign Minister, like any other minister, for party political reasons had to take note of his study group. A negative extension of this view was that Pik Botha regarded the Foreign Affairs study group as no more than an irritant to be tolerated. The importance of such perceptions – irrespective of whether they were accurate – is that they condition action: members of the study group would hardly have been encouraged to take an active interest in its proceedings if they believed the minister did not take the group seriously.

How then did Foreign Minister Botha see the study group's role? There can be little doubt that the group offered Pik Botha a valuable platform to explain policies and actions and to seek support. Because of what some Nationalist MPs depicted as the Foreign Minister's low "lobby profile" (referring to the lobby inside the Parliament building) and his being rather inaccessible to backbenchers, the study group

became an important channel of communication between the minister and ordinary MPs. In study group meetings Pik Botha in fact tried hard to obtain members' understanding or support for his policies and actions. This, however, was no mean task because the minister was faced with a good deal of opposition and suspicion among study group members, as in the party caucus generally. Such resistance was a compound of domestic and foreign policy considerations which sprang from the fact that Pik Botha had a high profile on the domestic political scene and was deeply involved with highly contentious foreign policy issues.

The domestic component of the dissatisfaction in National Party ranks with Pik Botha, which was the more important of the two, was related to the *verlig-verkramp* dichotomy in the party. The *verkrampte* element saw the Foreign Minister as a leading *verligte* and they objected particularly to his statements in favour of abolishing petty discriminatory measures; for them it was a short step to questioning Pik Botha's commitment to the whole separate development design. The other intra-party factor that counted against the Foreign Minister was his "wanton arrogance", as it was seen, in having stood as a candidate for the premiership in 1978 and – worse still – having thereby thwarted the chances of Dr CP Mulder, favourite of the *verkrampte* wing. One consideration that, it has been widely speculated, encouraged Pik Botha – then only 46 and a Cabinet member for under two years – to contest the premiership against two such senior party leaders as PW Botha and Mulder was the wide public support for his candidature: he was very much the "people's choice" for prime minister.[108] Pik Botha cut a charismatic figure in the public eye. He was anything but an aloof Foreign Minister preoccupied with international politics and divorced from domestic politics. Instead, he was as much a "hustings" politician as any other minister. Key issues in South Africa's foreign relations at the time, notably the search for international settlements in Namibia and Rhodesia and the threat of sanctions against South Africa, helped ensure that the Foreign Minister enjoyed a particularly high public profile.

For his political opponents within the National Party – and in the Foreign Affairs study group too – Pik Botha's continued high public visibility after his defeat in the election of the prime minister was seen as a deliberate campaign on his part aimed at personal political gain, or "PPG", as it was called. A frequently cited instance of the Foreign Minister's PPG activities was what was disparagingly labelled the "Pik and Cliff show" – a reference to the not infrequent television interviews the minister had with Mr Cliff Saunders, a reporter of the South African Broadcasting Corporation.

As regards the external dimension of the intra-party opposition to the Foreign Minister, his critics typically claimed that he was obsessed with and afraid of foreign opinion and pressure. He was, moreover, charged with "intimidating" the study group, the caucus and the voters generally with the big stick of international punitive measures against South Africa in order to force domestic political change. This is highly ironical, for here the Foreign Minister was being blamed by his own MPs for supposedly doing what he frequently denounced the opposition for: being an accomplice of sorts of external critics demanding political reform in South Africa.

These features are recounted in some detail because they had a bearing on Foreign Minister Botha's conduct of South Africa's foreign policy. Under Muller such considerations hardly applied, if at all. First, it has to be said that the exigencies of party politics and grass-roots popularity might have complicated Pik Botha's conduct of international negotiations; the sensitivities of the "home audience" might at times have been difficult to reconcile with the need for high-level bargaining and compromise. Second, because there were Nationalist MPs who suspected Pik Botha of image building, they were bound to have judged his statements on foreign affairs in this context. Third, they tended to see his warnings on external pressure as amounting to blackmail designed to coerce the caucus into agreeing to domestic policy changes that not only external opinion but Pik Botha himself supposedly wanted to see. What all this adds up to is that the Foreign Minister's credibility was placed in jeopardy. When he therefore pointed to external dangers a good many Nationalist MPs were likely to have discounted them by a certain margin to allow for the Foreign Minister's alleged PPG manoeuvres and scare-cum-intimidation tactics. What added to doubts about the credibility of such warnings by Pik Botha was that they were made so frequently, but that the grim dangers seldom seemed to materialise. Such false alarms made it particularly difficult for caucus supporters of the Foreign Minister to convince others that he was merely doing his duty, uninfluenced by ulterior motives, by telling MPs and the public at large the unpleasant truth about South

Africa's precarious international position. For their part, *verligte* followers of Pik Botha were quick to blame the "Connie Mulder mafia" in the caucus for attributing these nefarious motives to the Foreign Minister.*

Not only the Minister of Foreign Affairs but also his Department had to take note of the Foreign Affairs study group. Reconciling party political interests with those of the professional foreign service officers in the Department may well have been a difficult exercise. It is hard to escape the impression that among senior officials in the Department of Foreign Affairs the study group on Foreign Affairs was generally neither kindly nor highly regarded, but rather seen as something of an amateur, politically motivated intruder into a domain best left to the experts. Mr Brand Fourie, Director-General of the Department, was known to remain aloof of the group. Senior officials of the Department have, nonetheless, been invited to address the study group. Another form of interaction between the group and the Department of Foreign Affairs was that the former has produced a good many political appointees to the diplomatic service. No fewer than three members of the 1979 Foreign Affairs study group were appointed ambassadors in that year: Dr P Bodenstein to The Netherlands, Dr DJ de Villiers to the United Kingdom and Mr PD Palm to Venda.

Apart from the officials of the Department of Foreign Affairs, other outsiders have on occasion been invited to address the study group, including Ambassador William B Edmondson of the United States, Chief Minister Lennox Sebe of Ciskei, Mr Rowan Cronjé, an Afrikaner member of the Zimbabwean Parliament and former deputy minister in the Smith government, Dr JH Moolman, then Director of the Africa Institute, and Mr Cas de Villiers, then head of the now defunct Foreign Affairs Association, a front organisation of the former Department of Information. These speakers addressed the group over several years, which would indicate that outsiders were only rarely invited. The infrequent use of outside specialists to brief the study group was partly due to lack of time, since the full group met only about five times in the course of a parliamentary session. Another reason may well

---

* Following the split in the National Party in early 1982, it is safe to assume that most of Pik Botha's right-wing critics in the Nationalist caucus found a new home in the Conservative Party.

have been that there was some resistance from within the study group to being exposed to experts' views which might be in conflict with those of certain members. This kind of aversion was particularly evident among the more *verkrampte* study group members, whereas *verligtes* tended to favour a larger degree of interaction with outside specialists. Outside speakers, it should be added, were invited by the committee, but it is known that Pik Botha has on occasion suggested a particular person to be invited, probably because he thought a specific "message" ought to be delivered to the study group. The limited use of outside experts was even more pronounced in the four sub-groups of the Foreign Affairs study group.

The verlig-verkramp divide

Now that the intra-party criticism of Pik Botha has been noted, it would be useful to consider the respective strengths of *verligte* and *verkrampte* MPs in the National Party's caucus and the Foreign Affairs study group. One attempt at measuring these cleavages was made by Christopher Hill of the University of York, and published in *The Times*, London. Using Hill's rating of individual Nationalist MPs[109] one can classify members of the 1980 Foreign Affairs study group into Hill's four categories, ranging from most *verlig* (category 1) to most *verkramp* (category 4). The following table shows the *verlig-verkramp* rating for the NP caucus as a whole and for the Foreign Affairs study group.

Category	Caucus	Study Group
1	14 (10,5%)	8 (15,7%)
2	42 (31,6%)	13 (25,5%)
3	42 (31,6%)	17 (33,3%)
4	35 (26,3%)	13 (25,5%)
	133	51

The *verlig-verkramp* division in the study group thus roughly corresponded with that in the caucus as a whole. It is significant that whereas Pik Botha was rated in category 1, both the chairman and vice-chairman of the Foreign Affairs study group in 1980 (Mr F Herman* and Dr WD Kotzé respectively) were placed in category 4.

In personal interviews conducted with both

---

* Herman joined the Conservative Party following the split in the National Party in 1982. He was by then no longer an MP, having previously been appointed to the President's Council.

members and non-members of the National Party's Foreign Affairs study group (in 1980/1) a clear correlation was found between their views on domestic and foreign policy issues. Described very loosely, a *verkrampte* domestic stance has a "hawkish" foreign policy extension, whereas a "doveish" posture is the foreign policy corollary of a *verligte* domestic position. A simple yet typical illustration of these linkages is the following: a Nationalist MP who harbours misgivings about the government's moves away from racial discrimination and about the possible involvement of other races in central political decision making is bound to oppose the selling of maize to certain neighbouring states on the grounds that it amounts to "feeding the terrorists"; an MP favouring an acceleration in domestic political liberalisation can be expected to support economic and other ties between South Africa and surrounding black states in the interests of peace, prosperity and stability. It should be added that not all *verkrampte* Nationalist MPs are hawkish, nor are all the *verligtes* doveish. There are exceptions and permutations, but the tendency of a domestic-foreign policy linkage is unmistakable.

The *verlig-verkramp* controversy also featured in the selection of National Party speakers for foreign affairs debates in the House of Assembly. It was a function of the Foreign Affairs study group to nominate speakers; normally only members of the group spoke on foreign policy matters. Those who wished to participate informed the study group committee, which selected a number of speakers and then submitted its list to the party whips. Alternatively the committee itself could ask specific members of the study group to speak in debates. *Verligte* members maintained that the *verkrampte*-oriented committee gave preference to speakers sharing *verkrampte* sentiments. In the 1980 parliamentary session 18 members spoke, nine each in Hill's two *verligte* and two *verkrampte* categories. *Verligte* members' suspicions about the committee manipulating participation in debates to the advantage of *verkramptes* were therefore unfounded as far as the 1980 parliamentary session was concerned. The same finding applies to the 1979 Foreign Affairs vote in the Assembly. If anything, *verligtes* were actually advantaged in the 1980 session because, according to Hill's scale, the *verlig* (categories 1 and 2) : *verkramp* (categories 3 and 4) ratio in the caucus as a whole was 56:77 in that year.

Nationalist MPs' knowledge of foreign affairs

When assessing MPs' role in foreign policy making one must consider their knowledge of and involvement in foreign affairs. As Richards remarked, parliamentarians cannot reasonably be expected to exert meaningful influence over public affairs unless they are well informed.[110] In 1980 a written questionnaire was sent to National Party MPs (excluding ministers and deputy ministers) to gain factual information in this regard. Over 70% responded to the questionnaire.

The press proved to be one of the principal sources of information for Nationalist MPs. Nearly 70% of the 1980 Foreign Affairs study group members claim to read four or more papers daily (roughly an equal number of Afrikaans and English papers). For non-members the corresponding figure is 40%, while another 50% indicated that they read two or three papers daily, giving definite preference to Afrikaans papers. (Of the 134 members of the National Party caucus in 1980 only two did not have Afrikaans as their first language.) It should be explained that with the exception of the Johannesburg daily, *The Citizen,* all the major English-language newspapers in South Africa oppose the National Party, whereas all the major Afrikaans newspapers support the ruling party. Asked to rate the quality of South African newspapers' coverage of international affairs, over 80% of the study group members depicted both the Afrikaans and English press's reporting in this regard as either "good" or "fair". In the "bad" category Afrikaans and English papers are virtually level with 10% each. As for the top end of the scale – "very good" – 10,5% of the study group respondents place the English press in this category, against only 2,6% for the Afrikaans press. Among study group members the English papers apparently have the edge over the Afrikaans ones in the quality of reporting on international affairs. Non-members of the study group gave much the same ratings, except that 15,4% placed Afrikaans papers' coverage in the "very good" category. This is perhaps because non-members have a less discerning eye than study group members for the quality of the coverage.

Over half the members of the study group and no less than 85% of non-members do not regularly (at least once a week), if at all, read one or more foreign newspapers. This can obviously not be attributed to language difficulties: British and American newspapers pose no problems in this regard. What makes the finding all the more remarkable is that 56,6% of the study group members claimed to be able to read one or more foreign languages (other than Afrikaans, English and indigenous African languages), as against 42,5% for non-members. Insofar as foreign newspapers are read by Nationalist MPs, German papers (which may well have included the English-language *German Tribune*) are the most popular, followed by the British press. As far as news magazines are concerned, *To the Point* was by far the most popular among members and non-members of the study group, followed by *Time* and *Newsweek* a good distance behind. *Der Spiegel* has an insignificant number of readers. *To the Point,* first published in South Africa in 1972 and secretly funded by the government, ceased publication in December 1980, ostensibly because of financial difficulties.

When it comes to reading non-fiction books on international affairs, including South Africa's foreign relations, MPs present a highly flattering picture of themselves, with virtually all respondents saying they read such books. Some 40% of the study group members admit doing so seldom, whereas 57% say they read either often or regularly. This is hard to accept and allowance should be made for exaggeration, particularly among non-members. There seems to have been an attempt to create a good, if not entirely accurate, picture of reading habits.

MPs were next asked to indicate which, if any, local and foreign academic journals on politics (the domestic politics of South Africa and other states, foreign policies and international politics generally) they read or were at least familiar with. 31,6% of study group members and 75% of the non-members failed to respond to this open-ended question. Among the study group members who replied the best known journals are those published by institutes of the University of Potchefstroom (*Die Wêreld in Oënskou* and *Nuus oor Afrika*), followed by the Africa Institute *Bulletin* and some of its other publications, and *South Africa International,* published by the South Africa Foundation. Less well known, but still worth mentioning, are publications put out by the Southern Africa Forum (previously the South African Freedom Foundation, a front organisation of the former Department of Information) and the South African Institute of International Affairs. Foreign academic journals hardly feature at all. Essentially the same institutions feature in a related open-ended question that asks MPs to list those South African research institutions dealing with international affairs with whose activities they are familiar. The only one that needs to be added to those mentioned above is the Institute for Strategic Studies at the University of Pretoria. When one considers that the library of Parliament is reasonably well stocked with academic journals dealing with various aspects of politics, the MPs are remarkably ignorant.

Foreign embassies in South Africa are another source of published information available to MPs. Judging by the MPs' responses, the United States embassy is by far the most active in providing information, followed by those of Germany and France way behind, with the United Kingdom running a very poor fourth. Virtually all members of the Foreign Affairs study group say they regularly read such material and regard it as useful. Among non-members opinion on the usefulness of the material is mixed but the majority view corresponds with that of study group members.

As for contact with foreign visitors to South Africa, there is a striking difference in the extent to which members and non-members of the Foreign Affairs study group are exposed to foreigners. Whereas over 40% of study group members meet (socially and/or officially) an average of more than five foreign visitors a month, virtually no non-members have this measure of contact. The rest of the study group members see fewer than five foreign visitors a month. Roughly half the visitors whom study group members meet are referred to them by the Department of Foreign Affairs, but very few of the foreigners seen by non-members are handled by the Department. It therefore appears that the Department, when selecting Nationalist MPs to meet foreign guests, gives preference to members of the Foreign Affairs study group.

Foreign visits by MPs represent another important source of information and understanding of international affairs. With few exceptions, all members of the National Party's Foreign Affairs study group had been abroad (Namibia and independent former homelands excluded) by 1980, most of them more than once, whether before or since becoming MPs. Among non-members 65% had been abroad. The foreign visits that study group members had undertaken since entering Parliament were mostly related to their being MPs and members of the Foreign Affairs study group. (It was suggested in

Nationalist caucus circles that some MPs might have been influenced to join the Foreign Affairs study group by the possibility of travelling abroad.) In 1980 the South African Parliamentary Association arranged eight foreign tours, involving 28 MPs of all parties. The tours were to North and South America, the United Kingdom and Western Europe, the Scandinavian states, Taiwan and Hong Kong. There was no tour to African states, but the possibility was mentioned of the National Party's Foreign Affairs study group arranging one to the independent ex-homelands.[111] A conscious effort, with the blessing of the Minister and the Department of Foreign Affairs, was in fact made to take MPs of all parties abroad to acquaint them with South Africa's international environment and the difficulties the Republic experienced.

The states most frequently visited by study group members (based on 1980 findings) are Britain, Germany, France, other Western European countries, and the United States, in that order. Israel ranks well behind these states, with Taiwan much further down the list. To illustrate : 94% of the study group members who had been abroad visited the United Kingdom, against only 9,1% for Taiwan. Much the same situation applies in the case of non-members of the study group. There is, however, a significant difference between members and non-members regarding visits to African countries (Namibia and independent former homelands excluded): 42,4% of study group members who had been abroad visited African states, as against only 25% for non-members. The United Nations in New York is not a particularly popular foreign attraction for Nationalist MPs: by 1980, only 54,1% of study group members and 20,5% of non-members who had been abroad had visited the UN.

When one considers these findings and reads Nationalist MPs' contributions in Assembly debates on foreign affairs, a rather mixed picture of their knowledge and understanding of the complexity of international politics and South Africa's international position emerges.

There have undeniably been impressive, well-reasoned contributions in recent years from MPs such as Dr DJ Worrall* (the former Senator who

*Worrall left Parliament in October 1980 to become chairman of the constitutional committee of the President's Council. In February 1983 he took up his present appointment as South African ambassador in Australia.

had been a professor of political science), Dr Jan S Marais, Mr KD Durr and Mr WC Malan[112] (from the Randburg constituency). But there were also contributions at the other end of the spectrum, and some of the poorest speeches in recent years – emotive, unimaginative, simplistic and slogan-laden – were made by the members of the committee of the Foreign Affairs study group.[113] In fairness it must be conceded that it would have been entirely unreasonable to expect all Nationalist spokesmen on foreign affairs to be experts in the field. As Nationalist MPs not unreasonably pointed out, their compulsory membership of five different (and often quite unrelated) study groups made it extremely difficult to specialise in any one particular area. During parliamentary sessions heavy demands are made on MPs' time by Assembly debates, caucus and study group meetings and a variety of other parliamentary duties. In addition they have constituencies to care for. Further constraints on their creativity in the field of foreign affairs are imposed by strict party discipline and, not least, by their commitment to a domestic political order so obviously at odds with international opinion. National Party MPs do not have the benefit of a party research organisation to assist them in studying foreign affairs either. In short, the incentives for taking trouble to obtain a special knowledge and understanding of foreign affairs are few, and the constraints plentiful. Many lacklustre, stale contributions from government benches in foreign affairs debates are therefore only to be expected.

To conclude this discussion of the parliamentary National Party's role in foreign policy making it can be said that neither the party caucus as a whole nor the Foreign Affairs study group produces any major positive input. Their role is instrumental: they provide useful forums for the government to announce and explain, to sound out its followers in regard to policies and actions, and to mobilise support. Far from being initiatory, the caucus and the study group would be more likely to indicate in broad terms the limits of what is acceptable. Given the divisions among National Party MPs and Pik Botha's own peculiar position within the party, the caucus and study group may even have served as a brake on the Foreign Minister and the prime minister.

This detailed analysis of the study group, it should be reiterated, is based on its composition in 1980. Following the April 1981 general election its composition changed considerably, and

membership increased to 55. Kotzé, formerly vice-chairman, became chairman in the place of Herman who was appointed to the President's Council. Whether these periodic changes* would materially enhance the study group's role in foreign policy making is open to question. Successive study groups would labour under much the same constraints as the 1980 group. For one thing, it is highly questionable whether the mere fact of new faces brings with it greater knowledge and understanding of foreign affairs.

The parliamentary opposition and foreign policy making

Opposition parties, it has already been argued, can through the formal workings of Parliament bring precious little influence to bear on foreign policy. This is in no way offset by the existence of "private" intra-party structures to consider foreign affairs, similar to those of the parliamentary National Party.

The United Party, the official opposition until its dissolution in 1977, also had a Foreign Affairs study group as part of its parliamentary caucus. In its final year the group was chaired by Basson, with Mr IFA de Villiers as secretary. Meetings were open to all UP members in both the House of Assembly and the Senate. The party's leading spokesmen on foreign affairs in the Assembly understandably came from the ranks of the study group, among them Messrs Basson, IFA de Villiers, JI de Villiers and NJJ Olivier.

More important for the purposes of this book is to look at the foreign affairs machinery created by the present official opposition, the PFP. In 1980 its MPs had a Foreign Affairs study group of nine members under the chairmanship of Basson (who had in 1977 joined the PFP). Following Basson's resignation from the PFP in 1980, IFA de Villiers (who had also joined the party in 1977) became chairman of the study group. The study group's membership was enlarged to 14 after the PFP's gains in the 1981 parliamentary election. This made the Foreign Affairs group the largest of the party's 19 study groups. Upon his retirement from

---

*The split in the National Party in 1982 resulted in nine members leaving the study group to join the Conservative Party. The committee however remained intact: Kotzé (chairman), Terblanche (vice-chairman) and Mr Louis Nel (secretary). Kotzé was subsequently appointed ambassador to Bophuthatswana. In 1983 Nel, a known *verligte*, served as chairman.

politics in 1981, De Villiers was succeeded as chairman by Eglin. The object of the group, which met on an *ad hoc* basis and allowed non-members to attend, was to provide a forum for PFP MPs specialising in foreign affairs to exchange ideas and information and to plan strategy and tactics for Assembly debates on foreign affairs.

Apart from Basson, the PFP's leading spokesmen on foreign affairs were IFA de Villiers, Eglin and Schwarz. Basson, a veteran politician of many loyalties (he was first elected to Parliament in 1950 as a National Party representative), had already made his mark as a foreign affairs spokesman when in the United Party. De Villiers was a former South African diplomat and a man who spoke with authority and conviction on foreign policy. Eglin had been PFP leader from 1971 to 1979. Schwarz, another long-serving MP who had previously been in the United Party, was a skilful parliamentary debater, and also a leading opposition spokesman on finance and economic affairs.

PFP MPs' lack of influence on foreign policy having been acknowledged, it is nonetheless interesting to compare their knowledge of and involvement in foreign affairs with that of their Nationalist counterparts. PFP MPs were in 1980 sent the same written questionnaire as National Party MPs. Of the 19 opposition MPs, 14 returned their questionnaires, a 74% response. The 14 respondents included all the members of the Foreign Affairs study group. Because of the small number of MPs involved, no distinction will be drawn between the responses of members and non-members of the PFP's Foreign Affairs study group.

Like Nationalist MPs, opposition members are avid readers of the local English and Afrikaans press. Their respective ratings of the press's coverage of international affairs however differ significantly. No PFP respondent gives either the Afrikaans or English language press a "very good" rating. A full 62% rate the Afrikaans press's reporting as "bad", compared with 7% for the English press. Well over half the PFP MPs think the English press's coverage of international affairs is "fair", with only a third of them regarding it as "good". Roughly 30% of the respondents rate the Afrikaans press's reporting as "fair" and a mere 7% describe it as "good". As for reading patterns, 64,3% of the MPs indicated that they regularly read foreign newspapers, a considerably higher figure than for Nationalist MPs. The most popular foreign newspapers

among PFP MPs are from the United Kingdom and the United States. Among news magazines *To the Point* comes a very poor third after *Time*, by far the most popular, and *Newsweek*. Like the Nationalists, all PFP respondents claim to read non-fiction books on international affairs, half of them doing so either often or regularly.

PFP MPs, like the Nationalists, fared poorly when asked to list local and foreign academic journals on politics, with over 40% failing to reply. Significantly, research institutions and journals from the University of Potchefstroom do not enjoy the prominence among PFP MPs they do among Nationalists. Instead, the South African Institute of International Affairs and its publications head the list, followed by the Africa Institute and the South Africa Foundation.

PFP MPs have considerably more contact with foreign visitors to South Africa than their Nationalist colleagues, and the minority of these visitors are referred to them by the Department of Foreign Affairs. Opposition members also travel abroad more frequently than those in the National Party, with the United Kingdom, Western European countries and America the states most often visited. A noteworthy feature is that nearly 70% of the respondents had visited African countries (Namibia and independent former homelands excluded), a considerably higher figure than for Nationalist MPs. Over 70% of the PFP MPs had visited the UN in New York, again a much higher percentage than for National Party MPs.

The United States, Germany and France head the list of foreign embassies sending PFP MPs regular informational material. Like their Nationalist colleagues in the Foreign Affairs study group, PFP MPs also regard this information as useful and claim to read it regularly.

Apart from these various sources of information on foreign affairs, one should also mention the PFP's Research Department under the directorship of Mr NJJ Olivier, MP, a former University of Stellenbosch professor. Although the bulk of the institution's work is on domestic political matters, it assists MPs on foreign affairs too. This benefit available to PFP MPs is however neutralised, if not outclassed, by Nationalist MPs' access, via the Minister of Foreign Affairs, to information from the foreign ministry.

The NRP, which in 1980 had ten representatives in the House of Assembly and nine in the Senate, also has a Foreign Affairs study group, composed of two Senators and three MPs.

The study group, similar in purpose to those of the PFP and National Party, does not contain the same expertise in foreign affairs as the PFP's group. Lacking the research back-up of the official opposition, NRP MPs have to rely on their own resources. The few NRP representatives' time and energy are severely taxed, and this inevitably limits the degree to which they can specialise in any particular field. Yet despite being so thinly stretched, the NRP MPs are no less informed, interested or involved in foreign affairs than either members of the National Party's Foreign Affairs study group or PFP MPs.

There is no need to devote much attention to the South African Party (SAP), a conservative offshoot of the United Party, which in its brief existence (1978-80) had three MPs. Upon the SAP's dissolution its MPs joined the National Party. One of the three, Mr JWE Wiley, MP for Simonstown, has long been a prominent figure in foreign affairs debates in the House. English-speaking Wiley consistently took a hard line on such issues as Namibia and Zimbabwe and South Africa's relations with the United States.[114] In many respects his views on foreign affairs were as "hawkish", if not more so, than those of the *verkrampte* members of the National Party's Foreign Affairs study group. Wiley in due course became a member of the study group.*

---

* In 1982 Wiley was appointed Deputy Minister of Environmental Affairs and Fisheries.

4. The Executive: The Political Actors

"What war?" said the Prime Minister sharply. "No one has said anything to me about a war. I really think I should have been told. I'll be damned," he said defiantly, "if they shall have a war without consulting me. What's a cabinet for, if there's not more mutual confidence than that? What do they want a war for, anyway?"
                                                                Evelyn Waugh, *Vile Bodies*

The prime minister and his Cabinet ministers are the political actors discussed in this chapter. They are all, in terms of the South African Constitution, members of the legislature; the Cabinet is accountable to Parliament. As is typical in a Westminster system such as South Africa's, the legislature's role in foreign policy making is strictly limited, certainly far more so than in America's presidential system. The formulation of foreign policy is first and foremost the function and indeed the prerogative of the executive. Certain members of the Executive Council, as the Cabinet is styled in the South African Constitution, understandably play a more influential role than others in the formulation of foreign policy.

An assessment of the role of the prime minister and his ministers in South African policy formulation generally is no mean task, because precious little is publicly known about the processes involved. The difficulty is worse when the present or the immediate past is being examined. Given the acute lack of published material, the ensuing analysis is based on numerous personal interviews with serving and former Cabinet members and senior government officials closely involved with foreign policy making. This method of information gathering has its obvious limitations, but under the circumstances it was the best and indeed only option available.

The Prime Minister

As the head of government the South African

prime minister is the key figure in the formulation and implementation of government policies both at home and abroad. Even if the prime minister does not always play an initiatory role in policy formulation nor always finds himself directly involved with policy implementation, he is nonetheless ultimately responsible for the actions of the government.

Vorster and PW Botha: Some comparisons

A useful point of departure is to consider the knowledge and experience of foreign affairs that Vorster and PW Botha have brought to bear on policy making. Before being elected prime minister in 1966, Vorster had served for five years in Verwoerd's Cabinet as Minister of Justice, and prior to that for three years as Deputy Minister of Education, Arts and Science and of Welfare and Pensions.[1] As a member of the Cabinet, Vorster had of course been exposed to foreign policy matters. The way he handled the Justice portfolio certainly had implications for South Africa's foreign relations. For example, measures to combat what was regarded as communist activities in South Africa – something Vorster did with determination and evident success – often adversely affected the Republic's image abroad. When he succeeded Verwoerd, Vorster could not, however, claim any substantial direct knowledge or experience of foreign affairs, even though he had a keen interest in it. Fortunately for the new premier, he had an experienced Foreign Minister in the person of Muller. What perhaps also eased matters for Vorster on the foreign policy front was that South Africa had weathered remarkably well the international storms in which it found itself in the early 1960s, and domestically the situation had stabilised after the upheavals in the wake of Sharpeville and the banning of the ANC and PAC.

Whereas Vorster had not featured in foreign relations prior to becoming prime minister, PW Botha by contrast had regularly ventured into this field in his 12 years as Minister of Defence. This is not surprising, since defence matters have a direct bearing on foreign policy and *vice versa*. It was particularly during the House of Assembly's annual discussion of the Defence vote that PW Botha dealt at some length with foreign policy concerns. Two notable features of such discourses, which were normally focused on the strategic aspects of international relations and the threats facing South Africa, were PW Botha's frequent references to published works by well-known foreign authors (more often than not of rather conservative political inclination) and his at times strident condemnation of Western powers for their policies towards both South Africa and the communist bloc.[2] PW Botha was also directly involved in foreign affairs on his visits abroad in his capacity as Minister of Defence – an experience not shared by Vorster in his term as Minister of Justice. On the face of it, when PW Botha became prime minister he was far better equipped for foreign policy matters than his predecessor. He therefore probably felt less need than Vorster for the guidance and advice of the Foreign Minister, in this case Pik Botha (who had been appointed by Vorster in 1977). But while previous knowledge and experience may be an advantage, they are not vital prerequisites for a prime minister to become active and indeed successful in the foreign policy realm.

Because of the peculiar link between South Africa's domestic and foreign policies, any prime minister is bound to become actively involved in foreign policy matters.[3] This connection, it should be remembered, not only refers to the effects of South Africa's domestic policies on its foreign relations, but equally to the influence of extraneous factors on internal developments. But while the prime minister is thus compelled to engage himself in foreign policy concerns, his main preoccupation remains internal affairs, above all the racial issue. Also high on his domestic agenda are party political matters, for the prime minister remains national leader of his party. For both Vorster and PW Botha the spectre

of right-wing resistance to or even revolt against their policies – both domestic and foreign – from within the National Party has often loomed large.[4] With these divergent responsibilities and interests to attend to there are strict limitations on the time the prime minister has for foreign affairs. This may particularly apply to his intake of information on which decisions are eventually based.

What tends to obfuscate the picture of South African foreign policy formulation is that the policy is commonly identified with the prime minister of the day and, to a lesser extent, with his Foreign Minister. Although the prime minister as head of government is ultimately responsible for foreign policy, it is wrong to attribute all initiatives to him personally or to him and the Foreign Minister jointly. In many instances foreign policy initiatives originate elsewhere in the machinery of government.

The identification of foreign policy with the person of the prime minister is encouraged by the fact that he regularly deals with it in Parliament and in public. Foreign affairs usually feature prominently in prime ministerial speeches when the no confidence motion and the prime minister's vote are debated annually in the House of Assembly. Also in public addresses, notably at National Party congresses, the prime minister as a rule devotes considerable attention to foreign policy matters. These observations apply as much to Vorster as PW Botha. Regular American presidential-style press conferences are an uncommon phenomenon in South Africa. Only rarely does the prime minister call a press conference on foreign – or even domestic – policy issues; it requires some major occurrence.[5]

It is probably the prime minister's involvement with summit diplomacy, more than anything else, that in the public mind identifies him with foreign policy. This applies particularly to Vorster, who was next to Smuts the South African prime minister most active and mobile on the international diplomatic scene. Very early in his premiership Vorster gave notice that he was going to accord high priority to improving South Africa's international position. Two immediate manifestations were his moves to relax Verwoerd's rigid segregationist sports policy and his launching of the "outward movement". From the outset the new prime minister got involved in personal diplomacy in Southern Africa. For example, he met Lesotho's Prime Minister Jonathan in January 1967[6]; received a ministerial delegation from Malawi in March and held talks with Mr Ian Smith, Prime Minister of Rhodesia, in October 1967 – all in South Africa.[7] In 1970 he visited Malawi and Rhodesia. Much more dramatic were his secret diplomatic forays into black Africa in the 1970s to meet with Presidents Felix Houphouet-Boigny of the Ivory Coast, Leopold Senghor of Senegal and William Tolbert of Liberia. No less momentous was his meeting with Zambia's President Kenneth Kaunda at the joint South African-Zambian-sponsored Victoria Falls Conference between the Rhodesian government and its black nationalist opponents in August 1975. The meeting with Kaunda represented the high-water mark of the *détente* initiative aimed at resolving Southern African conflict situations. *Détente,* like the preceding dialogue initiative – as the outward movement became known in due course – was virtually exclusively identified with Vorster. The search for peace in Southern Africa also involved Vorster in personal diplomacy with foreign representatives such as Britain's Foreign Secretary Mr James Callaghan, and its UN Ambassador Mr Ivor Richard. In 1976 Vorster held three rounds of talks with Dr Henry Kissinger, American Secretary of State, in West Germany, Switzerland and South Africa. A Rhodesian settlement was the focal point of the deliberations. In 1977 Vorster met Vice-President Walter Mondale of the United States in Vienna. On this occasion Namibia and South Africa's domestic situation, apart from Rhodesia, featured prominently.

Earlier, in 1970, Vorster had made what were officially billed as "private" visits to Portugal, Spain, France and Switzerland. He nonetheless held talks with leaders of the states, but except for the Portuguese, the meetings were handled in a very low-key fashion by the host governments. In 1975 Vorster became the first South African premier to visit South America, with an official visit to Paraguay (reciprocating Paraguayan President Alfredo Stroessner's visit to South Africa the previous year), followed by a brief "strictly private" visit to Uruguay. The next year Vorster officially visited Israel.

The list is probably not complete. It is particularly with regard to secret high-level diplomacy that a good deal more may well have taken place than has subsequently become known. Nonetheless, enough has been said to show a profound contrast between Verwoerd's home-boundness and his relative lack of personal diplomatic activity (even on home ground) and Vorster's active involvement in summit diplomacy.

During his first three years in office Prime Minister PW Botha has not been engaged in much high-level diplomacy, at least as far as is publicly known. Within a fortnight of his election, PW Botha received the Foreign Ministers of the five powers constituting the Western contact group on Namibia. In 1980, following a visit to South Africa by the Taiwanese prime minister, PW Botha paid a return visit to the island. In June 1981 Mr William Clark, American Deputy Secretary of State, saw the prime minister in Pretoria on the Namibian issue.

The frequent meetings between the South African prime minister and the heads of government of independent former homelands should also be mentioned. This kind of diplomatic interaction is however at a level quite different from that discussed above.

The prime minister's involvement in summit diplomacy, to reiterate an earlier point, does not necessarily mean that he is the prime architect in South Africa of such exchanges. Yet it must at once be acknowledged that some of the major foreign policy initiatives since 1966 can rightly be attributed to Vorster and PW Botha. The notion of an outward movement originated with Vorster, although its substance as far as South Africa's relations with countries in the region were concerned closely resembled ideas already propounded by Verwoerd.[8] For the development of South Africa's close relations with Malawi, Vorster deserves the credit.[9] He played a key role in setting up the 1975 Victoria Falls conference. Changes to South Africa's sports policy, begun in the late 1960s and with obvious implications for foreign relations, were initiated by Vorster.

The problem, however, comes with Vorster's diplomatic exploits in the 1970s, notably his visits to Francophone Africa, Liberia and Israel. In the first and last cases the initiative went out from the Department of Information, with Vorster in effect only coming in towards the end to set the seal on Information's painstaking preparatory work. In the case of Liberia the Department of Foreign Affairs played the key role to arrange Vorster's visit. The prime minister's visits to Paraguay and Uruguay were, in turn, primarily the result of Muller's personal endeavours over a decade to promote closer ties between South Africa and South American states.[10] (The roles of these two departments and other state organisations in the conduct of South Africa's foreign policy are examined in the following chapter.)

The Minister of Foreign Affairs was a key figure in the Vorster Cabinet's deliberations on foreign policy. Muller, with his considerable experience of international affairs, was Vorster's key advisor in the Cabinet on foreign policy matters. They in fact worked very closely, Muller usually seeing Vorster every second day or so. The unassuming, mild-mannered Muller played nothing of the "Dulles-like role"[11] of Louw, his predecessor; Muller was in a way the confidant in his master's shadow. This often left Vorster acting as a kind of "super-Foreign Minister", a phenomenon not uncommon in a Cabinet system of government.[12]

In April 1977 Pik Botha succeeded Muller as Foreign Minister. Prior to his elevation to the Cabinet, Pik Botha served as South African ambassador to both the United States and the UN. During this time he enjoyed what was for a diplomat an extraordinarily close relationship with the prime minister. It is known in South African government and diplomatic circles that Pik Botha regularly telephoned Vorster from the United States – something on which the ambassador prided himself. The result was that when Pik Botha became Foreign Minister he was much closer to the prime minister than such a very junior Cabinet member would usually have been. Combined with his forceful, assertive style and his fresh diplomatic experience, the new Minister of Foreign Affairs was well placed to exert considerable influence on foreign policy formulation at Cabinet level.

Vorster's leadership style

Unlike Verwoerd's undisputed domination of the Cabinet and his inclination to dictate to ministers, Vorster's position was that of *primus inter pares*. He proved a particularly skilful chairman of the Cabinet, inviting wide discussion on a topic and then in the end giving a firm lead. Whereas Verwoerd acted like a presidential figure "above and apart from his Cabinet colleagues", Vorster's style conformed more to the team concept of Cabinet government in which, "while the Prime Minister is leader, he is heavily dependent on his colleagues."[13]

Some qualifications should, however, immediately be added. The team concept of government was certainly not always upheld by Vorster. It did not operate in at least two major foreign policy issues, South Africa's involvement in the Angolan war and the Department of Information's venture into the world of clandestine propaganda. In both cases the principal political decisions were taken by Vorster and one or two ministers while the Cabinet as a whole was largely kept in the dark. Another feature of Vorster's leadership style was his heavy reliance on the advice of his old friend and head of the Bureau for State Security, General HJ van den Bergh. The result of all this was that decision making under Vorster was not infrequently a rather haphazard process involving only a tiny number of participants – a far cry from a structured team concept of government allowing for inputs from a variety of interested parties. This state of affairs can perhaps partly be explained in terms of Vorster's failing health in the 1970s and the consequent impairment of his ability to exert effective control over government decision making.[14] More fundamentally it revealed a serious lack of decisive leadership on Vorster's part.

It is significant to note which ministers were primarily involved in the Angolan issue and the so-called Information scandal – two matters that profoundly and adversely affected South Africa's foreign relations. They were the Minister of Defence, PW Botha, and the Minister of Information, Dr CP Mulder, respectively. They were two strong-willed characters, senior members of the Cabinet and leaders of the National Party in the Cape and Transvaal respectively. Their portfolios had a direct bearing on foreign relations and neither hesitated to make his influence felt in this area.

An interesting anecdote is that Vorster, well before his eventual retirement from the premiership in September 1978, on several occasions in his inner circle raised the possibility of stepping down. According to Mr MC Botha, Minister of Bantu Administration and Development in the Vorster Cabinet and a member of the inner group, Vorster early in 1975 and quite frequently thereafter, mentioned the possibility of retirement. Cabinet members prevailed upon him not to resign and – what is particularly significant – Vorster commonly cited foreign policy considerations to explain postponements of his intended retirement. Among these were Rhodesia, Namibia and the Angolan war in 1975/6 and, in early 1977, the retirement of Foreign Minister Muller. In view of South Africa's troubled international position and the need for continuity in its foreign policy, Vorster thought it inopportune to step down in the wake of Muller's departure.[15] When Vorster eventually retired, ironically, it was in the midst of intense international negotiations and intermittent crises over a Namibian settlement.

There is also a less charitable explanation of Vorster's first postponement of his retirement plans in the mid-1970s, with foreign considerations again at the centre. Vorster's dramatic diplomatic sorties into black Africa, starting with his visit to Houphouet-Boigny and Senghor, captured the imagination of the South African public and were a tremendous boost to his domestic political standing. These achievements were not lost on international opinion either.[16] Vorster had virtually overnight become an international statesman of sorts. This new status, so the explanation goes, so enthralled Vorster that he shelved plans for any immediate retirement. Exponents of this view note with glee that not only did the initiative for the Francophone rendezvous not emanate with Vorster, but that he was both highly sceptical and reluctant to follow up with a personal visit the groundwork done by the Department of Information.

South Africa's involvement in the Angolan war and the Department of Information's secret propaganda offensive are two outstanding examples of a seriously deficient decision making process under Vorster. Falling firmly within the ambit of foreign policy, the two cases bear closer scrutiny.

Vorster and the Angolan war
No definitive study on South Africa's military involvement in the Angolan war has yet appeared. The official secrecy in which the matter is still shrouded greatly complicates such an investigation, particularly for South African scholars. For the purposes of the present study this largely unexplored and uncharted area is entered with the very limited objective of trying to explain how the political decisions regarding South Africa's involvement had been taken. First, it is necessary to sketch in broad outline, from such information as could be obtained, the sequence of events on the ground, so to speak. Against this backdrop an attempt will be made to reconstruct the decision making process that culminated in some 2 000 South African troops penetrating hundreds of kilometres into Angola.

• Long before the Portuguese decolonised Angola towards the end of 1975, South Africa already had a limited military presence in the north of Namibia to counter SWAPO insurgency.

SWAPO guerrillas infiltrated into Namibia by two routes: the main one was directly from Zambia, the other was from Zambia via Angola. As early as 1967 the Defence Force began taking over security functions from the South African Police in the northern part of the territory. South Africa's other direct interest in the border area was the construction of hydro-electric projects at Calueque and Ruacana, undertaken in partnership with Portugal. South Africa's co-operation with the Portuguese colonial authorities had also taken another completely different form. Since at least the early 1970s, South Africa had been covertly supplying arms and helicopters and also a limited number of pilots to the Portuguese forces fighting the Angolan guerrilla movements. While the Portuguese were keen on receiving logistical support from South Africa, they remained wary of operational assistance, preferring to do the actual fighting themselves. Being a Western colonial power obstructing the course of African liberation was enough of a political handicap for Portugal; fighting openly under the same banner as the "apartheid regime" would merely have aggravated matters. South Africa received no direct *quid pro quo* for its military support, but saw it as a worthwhile investment to help safeguard a vital link in the *cordon sanitaire* shielding it from hostile black African states.

• Portugal's decision to withdraw from Angola was viewed with grave apprehension in Pretoria, particularly in military circles. The main fear was that a political and military vacuum might be created and then exploited by SWAPO and, worse still, by communist powers. Added to South Africa's concern was the fact that the three guerrilla movements that had previously fought the Portuguese, subsequently became locked in a power struggle, greatly increasing the opportunities for communist interference.

• Robin Hallet, in a highly readable but speculative account of South Africa's involvement in the Angolan war, presented the following picture of the Angolan situation and its wider ramifications at the beginnig of August 1975:

> Massive military support flowing from the Soviet Union, Cuba and Eastern Europe to the MPLA; increasing alarm in Zambia and Zaïre; a bitter debate over Angola in the American State Department culminating in a decision to counter the Russian threat by

supporting the FNLA and UNITA; and finally increasing tension on the Angola-South West Africa border.[17]

The mounting tension on the border was caused by the presence of MPLA forces, which had begun moving to the south of Angola in sizeable numbers in order to gain control of the area and keep rivals out.

• Workers at the hydro-electric schemes in August 1975 reported being harassed and threatened by the forces of the MPLA. With its control of Angola on the verge of total collapse, the Portuguese colonial administration was in no position to safeguard the workers and the sites. South African forces stepped in to provide the necessary protection, thus establishing a military presence on Angolan soil. The South African presence in Angola took another form: setting up and safeguarding refugee camps at Chitado and Calai for the thousands of Portuguese and Angolans fleeing south to escape the mounting tension and instability into which Angola was sliding.[18]

• Sporadic cross-border skirmishes occurred between South African and MPLA forces. The latter were regarded by the South Africans as insufferably aggressive and provocative, and South African troops on a number of occasions pursued fleeing MPLA guerrillas onto Angolan soil. Even so, MPLA activities were more of an irritant than a serious military threat. At that stage (August 1975) much the same applied to SWAPO's ventures, despite the opportunities created by the chaotic conditions prevailing in southern Angola. It is interesting that South Africa had previously been very cautious about hot pursuit operations against SWAPO for fear of incurring the displeasure of Portugal. The Portuguese colonial authority, sensitive about its control over Angola, would never concede that its territory was being violated by SWAPO, nor would it allow South African forces free access to track down SWAPO guerrillas. In the event, the occasional South African military foray into Angola was conducted clandestinely, without Portuguese authorisation.

• According to a Defence Force statement, South African forces in the course of a hot pursuit operation – it was not revealed whether the MPLA or SWAPO was being pursued – came across Cuban weapon and ammunition dumps, "which placed the security situation of southern Angola and the water schemes in a completely different light."[19] Although the statement did not mention where and when the find was made, it may be that it was in the course of a reported military operation towards the end of August – evidently in response to fire directed against South African positions from across the border – during which the South African forces temporarily (for a day or two) occupied the district capital of Pereira d'Eca.[20] Considering that the town was situated some 150 kilometres east of the Kunene River dam, such an operation would indicate that South Africa had considerably extended its operational area in Angola; it may even have been part of an attempt to establish a buffer zone of sorts, freed of SWAPO, MPLA and Cuban forces, north of the Angola-Namibia border.

• Meanwhile, UNITA and the FNLA appealed to South Africa for military support against the rival MPLA and its communist backers. The MPLA – against which UNITA on 21 August formally declared war – was at the time active in south-central Angola, UNITA's traditional sphere of influence. South Africa agreed "to give help and support on only a limited scale". UNITA at that stage had only a ramshackle fighting force: sizeable in numbers but hopelessly unorganised and untrained, and armed with primitive, ineffective weapons. On 24 September the South African Army sent an officer to advise UNITA on training and reorganisation, and he was soon followed by a team of 18 instructors and a small consignment of arms.[21] South Africa's decision to step in to check the MPLA was welcomed in a number of important quarters abroad: Zaïre (which actively supported the FNLA), Zambia, the Ivory Coast, the United States and France.[22] With such influential (covert) backers, South Africa felt greatly strengthened in its decision to increase its involvement on the side of the pro-Western UNITA movement.

• From the South African troops' first encounters with MPLA forces, "it became obvious", according to a Defence Force statement, "that the struggle, with strong Cuban support [for the MPLA], began to take on a conventional colour." Consequently, a squadron of armoured cars with crews was sent into Angola in mid-October, the statement recorded.[23] By that time South Africa had also established and staffed two training camps inside Angola to train UNITA fighters.

• In the course of October and early November the South African forces, together with their

UNITA allies and FNLA elements (combined in two battle groups code-named "Foxbat" and "Zulu"), scored impressive military gains against their MPLA and Cuban enemies. Southern Angola came under the control of South Africa and its allies, as did the important centres of Benguela and Lobito. Operations were subsequently extended into central Angola. In northern Angola the picture looked entirely different: the FNLA forces fared disastrously on the battle field, one reason being – according to the South African Defence Force – the FNLA leadership's disregard for the military advice offered by South Africa.[24] FNLA forces were at one stage only about 20 kilometres north of Luanda. In their advance they relied greatly on three heavy guns with crews provided by South Africa. This handful of military personnel were the only South Africans to have come literally within striking distance of Luanda.

• This, then, was the situation when war-torn Angola became independent on 11 November. The military successes of the South African and UNITA forces were achieved with very limited South African manpower. According to the Defence Force, South African forces comprised only "about 300 advisers/instructors and personnel" and a selection of arms.[25] Hallett, however, quoted a press report that claimed that 1 200 to 1 500 troops were already active in Angola towards the end of October.[26] If the official figure might be suspected of being too low, the latter figures were probably greatly exaggerated. More important than this dispute, however, were strong indications that South Africa at that stage considered withdrawing its forces from Angola.[27] In the end it was decided to stay. In this decision South Africa may well have been influenced by an appeal from Dr Jonas Savimbi, the UNITA leader, that the anti-MPLA forces should hold their ground until the OAU had taken a vote on Angola at its summit in mid-January 1976.[28] Certain moderate black African leaders supported Savimbi's views, while some senior American officials urged the South Africans to keep their forces in Angola.

• A drastic escalation in South Africa's involvement in the Angolan war occurred in the wake of the black state's independence. The number of South African military personnel rose to nearly 2 000, additional battle groups were formed and heavy arms brought in.[29] The South Africans with their UNITA allies launched a determined offensive against the MPLA and

Cuban forces, resulting in a number of major battles which, on the whole, went strongly in favour of the South African side.[30] "The days immediately after independence", Hallett recorded, "were to be the MPLA's darkest hour."[31] There is a theory that the South Africans' northward thrust may have been their part of a giant pincer operation designed to wrest Luanda from the MPLA and its Cuban allies. South Africa and UNITA would move in from the south, it was said, and a force composed of FNLA forces and others (presumably Zaïreans), with American logistical backing, would march on the capital from the north. This theory implies some understanding between South Africa and the United States that the latter would participate – certainly by providing arms, if not more – in an assault on Luanda. However, there is no firm evidence of any such understanding having been reached between the two countries. There was, in other words, no co-ordinated South African-American plan to capture Luanda.

• In the wake of its impressive military successes South Africa suffered a decisive setback. On 19 December the United States Senate voted by a convincing majority to ban further American military aid to the anti-MPLA movements in Angola.[32] South Africa had hoped that the United States would not only provide the FNLA and UNITA with arms, but also sell the Republic certain sophisticated weapons required for its Angolan offensive. The Senate decision more or less pulled the carpet from under South Africa's feet; it was a watershed for Pretoria. Having pinned its hopes on American support, South Africa was deeply disappointed and greatly angered by the Senate's decision. It should, however, be noted that South Africa had earlier (before the Senate decision) begun showing public signs of displeasure with the paucity of American aid.[33] With all hope of increased United States involvement destroyed by the American Senate, South Africa probably calculated that an assault on Luanda would require much more military muscle than it had in Angola, particularly in view of the drastic increase in the number of Cuban troops and quantity of Soviet arms.[34] The presence of sophisticated Soviet MiG fighter aircraft was of particular concern to the South African military. But apart from not stepping in to provide South Africa with the necessary military hardware, the United States also appealed to South Africa not to attack Luanda.[35] Although South Africa may, with some difficulty, have been able to muster the forces and firepower required to capture Luanda, Pretoria probably wanted at least the open diplomatic backing of the United States for such a dramatic action. Another consideration militating against South Africa going it alone was that the FNLA offensive in the north had virtually collapsed, largely because of the movement's sheer military incompetence. In the event, South Africa had little option but to discard any idea of marching on Luanda. The distance to the Angolan capital was in any case considerable and an advance would have been fraught with logistical problems, not the least of which was the crossing of rivers where bridges had been blown up by retreating enemy forces trying to halt the South African advance. The farthest point north that South Africa and its UNITA allies reached was about 50 kilometres north of the inland town of Cela; at the coast Nova Redondo was the farthest point reached, some 300 kilometres from the capital.

• The next major development occurred on the diplomatic front with the OAU summit conference held from 10 to 13 January 1976. South Africa had hoped that the meeting would help to resolve the Angolan conflict in a manner compatible with the Republic's interests – which meant at least involving UNITA in a government of national unity. In the event, the conference ended in deadlock: 22 member states voted for recognising the MPLA as Angola's government, and 22 against. Although Pretoria took comfort from the failure of the radical African states to get the summit to recognise the MPLA as government and to demand South Africa's withdrawal from Angola, the fact of the matter is that the OAU did not contribute to a settlement of the conflict either. With the OAU's inability to inspire a political solution "an accomplished fact", a Defence Force statement noted, "the RSA forces, except for a limited number of protective forces in south Angola, had to withdraw by 22 January 1976."[36] By that time, it should be added, the effects of the massive Soviet/Cuban military build-up had become painfully evident: the FNLA forces in northern Angola were in full retreat, and UNITA forces in southern and central Angola came under heavy pressure from the MPLA and Cuban forces.[37] For South Africa the military cost of continued involvement would obviously have become much higher, perhaps prohibitively so. What no doubt further dampened South African enthusiasm for continuing the war was the growing rift between UNITA and FNLA, which

already in December started becoming violent.

• In March 1976 South African forces were finally withdrawn from Angola into Namibia, following assurances – conveyed through intermediaries – from the MPLA regime that there would be no interference with the construction of the Ruacana and Calueque projects.[38]

Because of the South African government's continued reticence on the nature and extent of the Republic's involvement in Angola, the preceding reconstruction of events inevitably contains conjectural elements. This also applies to the following reconstruction of the South African decision making process, about which even less is publicly known. To piece together a picture of what *possibly* happened, the researcher has to rely on the relatively few and moreover vague official statements, on the pitifully few published accounts of events and on information obtained (confidentially) from persons who were *au fait* with the decision making.

The Lisbon *coup d'état* on 25 April 1974 and the subsequent decision to decolonise Portugal's African empire held profound implications for South Africa. The Defence Force, with Military Intelligence in the vanguard, felt strongly that the Republic should involve itself in some way to influence the course of events in Angola in a direction favourable to the Republic's interests. Well before the colony's independence, Military Intelligence had put out feelers to three liberation movements – MPLA, FNLA and UNITA – to try to establish their respective attitudes towards South Africa. The MPLA was found to be implacably hostile, whereas the other two organisations, UNITA in particular, proved quite amenable. Should the MPLA come to power, Military Intelligence concluded, South Africa's security interests in Namibia might be seriously jeopardised. Towards the end of June 1975 the Defence Force produced a document setting out the implications of alternative courses of action that South Africa could follow towards Angola. The document was submitted to Defence Minister Botha who, in turn, passed it on to Vorster for final consideration. It took the political decision makers some months to come up with a major decision on how to handle the Angolan situation.

South Africa meanwhile had to contend with the effects of the unsettled conditions prevailing in southern Angola. In the process of establishing a restricted military presence immediately north of the border, South African troops came under fire from Angolan guerrillas. Defence headquarters in Pretoria and subsequently the Minister of Defence were informed of the attack. Following consultations with Vorster, PW Botha is said to have instructed the Defence Force that the attackers should be decisively driven off. If true, this event had a dual significance: a political decision opening the door to offensive military operations in Angola had been taken, and the two principal (if not the only) political decision makers who were to control South Africa's military involvement in the Angolan war – code-named "Operation Savannah" – were identified.

The Department of Foreign Affairs from the outset found itself largely excluded from decision making on South Africa's Angolan venture. The foreign ministry's religious adherence to the principle of non-interference in other countries' internal affairs was the very antithesis of the Defence Force's belief that South Africa should take a hand in shaping Angola's destiny. Foreign Affairs wanted South Africa to adopt the same "hands off" attitude it had (ostensibly) displayed when the Portuguese left Mozambique. The military saw major differences between the situations in Mozambique and Angola: in Angola three rival liberation movements were fighting for political power and creating opportunities for communist involvement and for a SWAPO presence on Namibia's northern border. In Mozambique FRELIMO had been the sole heir to political power.

The foreign ministry's relegation to the sidelines was evidenced by their hearing of the Defence Force's first major offensive north of the Angola-Namibia border – presumably the operation in and around Pereira d'Eca – only when the Portuguese government handed South Africa's ambassador in Lisbon a note of protest over the action.

The next phase in South Africa's involvement in Angola represented a significant escalation: instructors/advisers and arms were despatched to UNITA and the FNLA. Although the military aid was very limited, it meant that South Africa had actually entered the Angolan civil war, supporting two of the three belligerents. This major decision may have been taken in response to the document prepared by the Defence Force in June. Vorster and PW Botha were certainly involved with the decision, but it is doubtful whether the full Cabinet was party to it.

The crucial question is, what were the political objectives behind the decision to commit South African forces to a foreign war? What did South Africa hope to achieve by supporting UNITA and the FNLA? The military and also Vorster and PW Botha took the view that South Africa had to try to steer events in Angola in a direction beneficial to its own interests. A major obstacle was the MPLA, violently opposed to South Africa and manifestly Marxist in its ideological leanings. Even when one accepts these considerations, a host of questions remain. If South Africa wanted to prevent the ascendance of a Marxist regime in Luanda and the formation of what Vorster subsequently called "a string of Marxist states across Africa from Angola to Tanzania",[39] how was this to be done? Was it South Africa's intention to drive the Cubans out of Angola, thus freeing the country from a communist presence? And thereby clear the way for a UNITA-FNLA regime in Luanda? Or did South Africa want to help the anti-communist forces to hold their own against the MPLA and thus promote the chances of a government of national unity (as envisaged in the Alvor and Nakuru Agreements)?[40] Or was it Pretoria's intention to help set up a separate UNITA-controlled state in southern Angola – one freed of SWAPO? In the event, not one of these possible objectives was achieved. What is clear, paradoxically, is that South Africa lacked a clear political objective when it decided to become an active participant in the Angolan civil war. This had serious implications, because without a definite objective it was difficult, if not impossible, to execute military actions and commit resources in a planned fashion, or to make reliable cost-risk calculations.

A different avenue to follow in trying to make sense of South Africa's military involvement in Angola is to identify some of the key forces that influenced the decision makers. On the external side, these were the United States, a handful of moderate black African states, UNITA and the FNLA. Perhaps South Africa hoped to impress its *détente* partners in Africa and the Western powers with its resolve to stand up to communist aggression. South Africa could only have been encouraged by the statement of the American Secretary of State, Kissinger, that Soviet and Cuban support for the MPLA was a "serious matter" and that Washington would not tolerate Moscow's "hegemonial aspirations" in Angola.[41] Domestically the driving force behind the Republic's involvement was undoubtedly the military. White public opinion hardly featured in any demonstrable way on the question of South African participation in the Angolan war. The public was in any case kept largely in the dark on the true state of affairs, thus making it exceedingly difficult for public opinion to make itself known. It is true that an opinion poll conducted after South Africa had withdrawn from Angola showed that a majority of whites supported the government's Angolan policy.[42] Gratifying though such *ex post facto* support may have been for the government, white public opinion could hardly have been a source of strength and encouragement for the government at the time of South Africa's actual involvement; the public was deliberately denied information by the decisions makers and was exposed to a flood of rumours about events in Angola.

It should be said that there were powerful domestic voices raised against South Africa's involvement in the Angolan war, notably from the head of the Bureau for State Security, General HJ van den Bergh, and from the Department of Foreign Affairs. Their reasons for dissenting were different. In military circles a cynical view was taken of Van den Bergh's opposition. He was bound to oppose most things suggested or undertaken by the Defence Force, it was said – an indication of the tensions between the two institutions. Initially Van den Bergh had however advised Vorster that South Africa should provide arms to the anti-MPLA movements in Angola. Van den Bergh had also been in personal contact with leaders of these movements, and actually tried to make his Bureau rather than Military Intelligence the main vehicle for South African involvement in Angolan affairs. In due course Van den Bergh came out against further South African participation in the Angolan war. It was apparently at the stage when strong indications emerged that the United States might end its involvement in the conflict. The Central Intelligence Agency (CIA) may well have given Van den Bergh warning about such an eventuality. Without American logistical backing, he concluded, South Africa could not hope to prosecute the war against the MPLA and Cuban forces successfully.

The Department of Foreign Affairs, the real "doves" in the affair, feared international political repercussions: the Soviet Union might be drawn deeper into the conflict in response to South Africa's involvement, thus raising the awesome prospect of a South African-Soviet military showdown; South Africa could endanger *détente* by fighting in a black African state and ran the risk of being branded an aggressor by the OAU and the UN; South Africa's intervention would undermine its oft-declared commitment to the principle of non-interference. In the event, the foreign ministry's concerns were overridden by the military's strong agitation for South African military involvement in Angola.

Once a top-level political decision had been taken to commit South African military personnel and arms to the conflict in Angola, the Defence Force devised a four-phase plan for a military offensive. It was an operational plan, identifying specific military targets and calculating the resources required to achieve them. The phases were progressively more ambitious: phase 4 provided for the capture of Luanda, the ultimate military objective. The decision to escalate from one phase to another was left to the political decision makers, Vorster and PW Botha. For the day-to-day operational control of the South African involvement in Angola a special committe composed of military chiefs was set up in Pretoria. Representatives from the Department of Foreign Affairs and the Bureau for State Security were on occasion invited to participate in meetings of the committee. Their presence may have been little more than symbolic, since the Defence Force saw the Angolan war as very much *its* responsibility.

Amid all the operational planning, the political objectives of South Africa's military involvement still remained unclear. This meant that the political decision makers were uncertain whether to permit South African forces to proceed from one phase of the four-phase plan to another; more seriously, they may even have been uncertain whether South Africa should continue its military involvement in Angola. Crucial political decisions urgently needed by the commanders in the field were often slow to materialise, thereby hampering military operations. Apart from the lack of clear political direction, the Defence Force was inhibited by the political leaders' insistence that South African loss of life had to be avoided. With the South African government pretending that its forces were not involved in the Angolan war, it would have been hard put to explain a sudden spate of casualties to the public. Given these serious deficiencies in political leadership on the one hand and operational exigencies on the other, it is not surprising that military commanders at the front on occasion overstepped the line. Caught in the momentum of the war, they escalated their actions beyond the point agreed to by the political decision makers.

Against this background the following admission that Vorster made to Parliament on 30 January 1976 acquires its real significance:

> I want to be very candid about this, it is rather difficult . . . when you chase a man away to decide when to stop. That, candidly, is a difficulty. Naturally it must be left to the people who are responsible for doing the job to decide how far you are going to chase away the man, knowing that if you chase him away a short distance he may come back. I make no bones about the fact that we chased him a very long way, and I take full responsibility for that.[43]

The "man" being chased could certainly not have been SWAPO, judging by the extent of the "chase"; MPLA and Cuban forces were being pursued. Vorster's statement confirmed that tactical military considerations had become supreme – a feature understandable enough in the absence of clear political objectives. Whatever the extent of "unauthorised" escalation, South African forces were given permission by Vorster and PW Botha to proceed to the third phase of the plan of action. This included capturing the towns of Cela and Nova Redondo – targets that were in fact reached by the South Africans.

It was when the South African forces were executing the third phase of their offensive that the United States Senate blocked any further American military involvement in Angola. American logistical support – and supplies of heavy arms – that South Africa had fervently hoped to obtain to bolster its military capability had effectively been embargoed. This left Pretoria with a crucial political decision: should South African forces be allowed to proceed with phase 4 of the offensive? Or should they instead begin pulling back? A decision was not only urgently needed by the South African forces at the front, but also because Parliament was going into session in the new year, and the country was rife with rumour about the involvement in Angola (fuelled, of course, by the virtual blackout on information).

In the event, a decision in principle was taken in either late December or early January to withdraw the South African forces from Angola. Vorster and PW Botha were again the two key figures involved. It is quite possible that Hilgard Muller, General Magnus Malan, Chief of the Defence Force, and others were also present on this occasion. The troops would, however, remain in Angola until the OAU summit, it was decided, in the hope that African leaders would help to settle the Angolan conflict in a way agreeable to South Africa and its Angolan allies. By maintaining a temporary presence, South Africa hoped to strengthen the position of UNITA and the FNLA in a possible settlement. Any idea of trying to displace the MPLA and the Cubans from Luanda – that is, implementing phase 4 – had by then been abandoned. By the end of December there were indeed strong public indications that South Africa was prepared to pull out. PW Botha issued a statement to the effect that South Africa "would almost certainly reconsider its involvement in Angola" if its interests in southern Angola (a reference to the hydro-electric schemes) were safeguarded and SWAPO attacks into Namibia were halted.[44] Apart from the obvious military or security implications of such assurances, they could also have served as face-saving devices.

Such, then, was the situation that Vorster early in January 1976 presented to a startled Cabinet at its first meeting after the long Christmas holiday. Whatever misgivings ministers might have expressed when learning the true state of affairs concerning South Africa's involvement in Angola, the Cabinet presented a solid front when the government's handling of the Angolan issue was challenged by the opposition parties in the parliamentary no-confidence debate at the end of January. The National Party caucus had meanwhile also been put into the picture by Vorster and PW Botha. By the time Parliament debated the Angolan war, the earlier decision on withdrawal had come into effect, following the OAU meeting in mid-January – despite signs of second thoughts about the withdrawal among decision makers, not least the military.[45]

Both Vorster and PW Botha and also Foreign Minister Muller gave Parliament numerous reasons for and objectives of South Africa's intervention in the Angolan war.[46] Most of these may be regarded as *ex post facto* rationalisations. A particularly significant statement of Vorster's was that the Angolan war had confirmed a lesson South Africa had previously learned, "when it comes to the worst, South Africa stands alone."[47] Vorster obviously had Western powers, specifically the United States, in mind, thus confirming the high hopes South Africa had vainly placed in American support.

If the preceding reconstruction of the decision

making process is in essence correct, it reveals profound deficiencies in top-level decision making on a matter as vital as involvement in a war on foreign soil, as witness the serious miscalculation of American moves and indeed of the American mood. This raises questions about the origins and quality of the information on which the decision makers acted. The role of South Africa's ambassador in the US, Pik Botha, is inevitably called into question. It can also be asked whether Soviet and Cuban intentions were accurately assessed. Did the decision makers, for example, anticipate the massive Soviet and Cuban support for the MPLA? On a different level, one should mention the government's failure to consult Parliament. A little known fact is that Vorster and PW Botha had toyed with the idea of convening a special session of Parliament towards the end of 1975 to inform MPs *in camera* of events in Angola. They eventually decided against taking Parliament into their confidence for fear of leaks from opposition (specifically PRP) ranks. It was, however, not only Parliament that was ignored; neither the National Party caucus nor the full Cabinet was consulted or enjoyed the two principal decision makers' confidence. The leader of the opposition, De Villiers Graaff, was nonetheless one of the very few politicians to have been given confidential briefings by the prime minister.

The gravest weakness of South Africa's Angolan venture was the lack of clear political objectives. This greatly complicated political decision making and adversely affected the prosecution of the war. Another serious deficiency was the absence of a well structured process of decision making. The various interested parties within the executive branch of government had unequal opportunities for making their views known. The military, including the Defence Minister, had a disproportionate and decisive influence, thus virtually monopolising decision making on involvement in the war. The Department of Foreign Affairs, it has already been suggested, had serious reservations about the venture. In the haphazard way in which decisions were made there was no system of inter-departmental checks and balances. The "hawkish" voices long had the field almost to themselves, with the "doves" able to make their influence felt only very late in the day.

The way in which the Angolan issue was handled at the highest political level inevitably calls the prime minister's leadership into question.

His was, after all, the ultimate responsibility. There can be little doubt that the team concept of Cabinet government hardly applied in this case. For the most part decisions were taken by the prime minister and one other minister. PW Botha, it would appear, was the driving force behind their joint decisions, a man whose strong views more often than not prevailed. This has led to the frequently heard but unfair charge that South Africa's intervention in Angola had been PW Botha's "personal venture", that he had taken exceptional liberties and virtually unilaterally got South Africa embroiled in a foreign war. The truth is that Vorster had from the outset been deeply involved in the political decision making regarding South Africa's role in Angola. Vorster later told Parliament he had "full confidence" in PW Botha, adding "I was with him all the way."[48] It would have been quite inconceivable for the head of government not to have been a party to such far-reaching decisions as involving South Africa in a war beyond its borders. Be that as it may, the point is Vorster displayed a preference – or weakness – for unstructured decision making involving only one other person or a very small group. In the case of the Angolan war his principal adviser and fellow decision maker was PW Botha. In other instances Van den Bergh had been the prime minister's main if not sole adviser. Insofar as Vorster had been involved in decision making on the Department of Information's clandestine activities, he was again surrounded by only a handful of advisers and other political decision makers. (It is a moot point whether decisions taken in this manner implicate the Cabinet as a whole, that is, whether joint Cabinet responsibility applies to decisions taken by the prime minister and at least one other minister.)

The preceding account challenges the version[49] which has it that on the Angolan war Vorster had been assisted by a group of his "closest advisers", including the Minister of Defence, the Secretary of Foreign Affairs and the head of the Bureau for State Security, and "assisted by the intermittent participation of military and military intelligence staff." It was only towards the end of South Africa's involvement in the Angolan war that the foreign ministry, for example, managed to exert any significant influence over events. Both the Secretary of Foreign Affairs and the head of the Bureau for State Security had been largely outmanoeuvred by the military, who for long virtually monopolised the bureaucratic advisory function. **Military and military intelligence staff** were of course deeply involved, indeed more than intermittently. The contention that South Africa's entire Angolan operation "was monitored by a small group surrounding the Prime Minister", might refer to the special committee of military chiefs mentioned earlier. This was, however, a "technical" group concerned with the operational side of the war and not with formulating political objectives. The State Security Council, which could have played a "political" monitoring role, was never a prominent forum for decision making under Vorster.

The climax of South Africa's military involvement in Angola coincided with the Christmas vacation, during which Cabinet members too were away from office. This may have added to the way in which the Angolan crisis was handled (or mishandled) at the highest level; if so, it is a further serious indictment of governmental decision making under Vorster.

South Africa's involvement in the Angolan civil war was not the only instance of the military prevailing over its critics in government on the question of military action in Angola. In May 1978 the South African security forces launched a massive strike against SWAPO bases in southern Angola. The operation, code-named "Reindeer", inflicted heavy casualties on SWAPO. Operation Reindeer was the first large-scale South African military strike into Angola since Operation Savannah in 1975-6. The decision to launch large-scale pre-emptive and follow-up operations into Angola had reportedly been taken in December 1977 at a meeting at Vorster's seaside cottage near Port Elizabeth. Among those present were senior military officers; Defence Minister PW Botha was presumably also there. Vorster is said to have been "not too enthusiastic" about cross-border military operations, not least because of the recent memories of South Africa's involvement in the Angolan civil war. But he acknowledged the necessity of such actions in view of the build-up of SWAPO forces inside Angola and the movement's stepped-up incursions into Namibia.[50]

The driving force behind the political decision to launch Operation Reindeer must have been the Defence Force, supported by PW Botha. Pik Botha and Foreign Affairs are said to have expressed grave misgivings, fearing international repercussions, particularly UN sanctions. In the end, the military had their way. Not only was the raid a great military success, but the dire diplomatic consequences failed to materialise. In Foreign Affairs circles, Operation Reindeer was seen as a great political triumph for PW Botha's party political standing (a fillip he probably needed after the Angolan war) and it again greatly strengthened the military's influence in foreign policy formulation. By proving the diplomatic "wets" (to borrow a British expression) wrong, the military could claim that Foreign Affairs possessed no monopoly on understanding international affairs and was moreover unduly concerned about possible diplomatic reprisals. Operation Reindeer paved the way for further raids: by the end of 1982 some eight known large-scale incursions into Angola had taken place, the most important being "Operation Sceptic" in 1980. It is highly likely that many clandestine raids into Angola have also been launched.[51]

In sharp contrast to South Africa's military involvement in Angola in 1975-6, any such overt intervention was refrained from when the Portuguese handed the government of Mozambique over to the Marxist liberation movement FRELIMO, led by Samora Machel. It has however been claimed that South Africa became involved in clandestine military activities in independent Mozambique. According to one source South African Military Intelligence spearheaded a campaign of subversion against the FRELIMO regime. This allegedly involved the setting up of a fake anti-FRELIMO liberation movement, the *Resistência Nacional Mocambicana* or Mozambique National Resistance (MNR) in 1976. Sabotage attacks carried out in the name of the MNR were said to have been undertaken by South African soldiers. In due course, the story went, Military Intelligence began recruiting black Mozambicans who had fallen foul of the FRELIMO regime to serve in the MNR. Only then did the movement begin to take on a life of its own, but still with South African material support.[52] The account does not mention whether the alleged actions had the blessing of the prime minister and Cabinet. The Minister of Defence would almost certainly have known of and agreed to these clandestine actions – assuming that the claims are largely true. Whatever the involvement or non-involvement of Vorster and the Cabinet, such use of a military instrument of foreign policy would have underlined the increasing prominence of the military in the conduct of South Africa's foreign policy.

The South African military, no doubt supported by their minister, had their way in involving South Africa in an earlier foreign military conflict in the Biafran war (1967-70). Allegations of South African involvement are not new,[53] but the details are extremely sketchy. A hitherto unrevealed version of events contains many new elements. Military Intelligence, it is said, in the late 1960s took the view that South Africa should try to establish a diplomatic foothold in an English-speaking state in the heart of black Africa. When the Ibo people unilaterally tried to secede from the Nigerian federation and establish the state of Biafra, Military Intelligence saw an opportunity to win friends for South Africa by supplying the secessionists with arms and offering moral support. Should the break-away attempt succeed, the new state would be heavily indebted to South Africa. Vorster agreed to provide Biafra with clandestine military support.[54] Whether Foreign Affairs and the Cabinet were consulted is not certain. South Africa's military assistance took the form of arms and a small number of military advisers. It was only towards the end of the civil war, when it became obvious that the Biafran rebellion was collapsing, that the Republic stopped its military support. If there had been any South African collusion with a foreign intelligence service in Biafra, the chances are that the French were involved, rather than the American Central Intelligence Agency.

Vorster and Information's secret ventures
In contrast to South Africa's involvement in the Angolan war, a great deal has been said and written about the Information affair. It has to date been the subject of two books.[55] There have been several official inquiries into the matter, notably by the Erasmus Commission. Parliament was summoned for a special two-day session in December 1978 to consider the Erasmus Commission's first report. But despite all these exposures, a complete picture of the former Department of Information's activities has not been made public. This applies not only to the secret projects – a number of which have been retained after the Department's dissolution in mid-1978 – but also to the top-level decision making that paved the way for the Department's secret propaganda war. Finding reliable, detailed information on these subjects is still a major problem for researchers. Very few people – whether politicians or officials – with first-hand knowledge of Information's inner workings are willing to reveal details for publication. Consequently, the following account relies very heavily on only a limited number of sources

(identified in the endnotes). This is far from satisfactory, since much of the information thus obtained could not always be verified. Nonetheless, the overall picture that emerges is probably fair and credible.

In this section the concern is with decision making about Information's activities abroad. It is, in other words, an attempt to identify the *locus* of decision making on a particular aspect of South Africa's foreign relations. In the next chapter something will be said about the substance of a number of the former Department's foreign programmes.

Perhaps the following analysis should be prefaced by remarking that if South Africa could have become involved in a war in a foreign country without the whole Cabinet being informed, it is not really surprising that something similar could have happened with regard to an extensive clandestine propaganda offensive abroad and indeed at home. One difference is that more Cabinet members knew of Information's secret activities than of South Africa's involvement in the Angolan war. In the former case the prime minister, for one, featured prominently in the inner circle of the initiated.

To try to reconstruct the decision making process regarding the Department of Information's clandestine activities, one must sketch in broad outline the context in which decisions were reached.

Although secret information projects are popularly associated with Dr Eschel Rhoodie, who became Secretary of Information in August 1972, at least two major secret programmes had been started under his predecessor, Mr Gerald Barrie: the establishment of the news magazine *To the Point* in 1971 and the appointment of Heinz Behrens, a public relations expert in West Germany, to feed positive reports on South Africa to the German news media.[56] The Minister of Information had since August 1968 been Dr CP Mulder.

An important development that convinced Mulder of the necessity for drastically stepping up his Department's secret operations abroad was an extensive foreign tour he and Barrie undertook in 1971. One of its purposes was to investigate the nature of what Mulder depicted as the "propaganda onslaught" on South Africa, and to devise ways and means of countering it. The essence of their findings was that the international propaganda offensive against South Africa was well organised, highly sophisticated and generously funded. On the face of it, South Africa's own information effort abroad was wholly inadequate in content and finance. In a report submitted to the prime minister it was recommended that South Africa, having no alternative, should immediately and actively get involved in the propaganda war and employ the same methods as its opponents.[57] (The terms "propaganda" and "information" are used interchangeably when referring here to the activities of the Department of Information.)

Mulder also used his foreign tour, during which he visited South Africa's information posts in Western Europe and the United States, to scout for talent to fill a number of senior positions at Information's head office. Among these was the secretaryship of the Department, for Mulder had grown impatient with Barrie's approach to his task. A forestry graduate, Barrie was known as a dedicated and accomplished official, but also a typically cautious, meticulous book-of-rules one. In Mulder's eyes Barrie lacked both the experience and innovativeness the minister sought in his Department's top official. In looking for new blood to rejuvenate the Department of Information, Mulder was particularly impressed with three Information officers : Eschel Rhoodie, based in The Hague; his brother, Dr Deneys Rhoodie in London, and Mr LES de Villiers in New York. These men, Mulder established, shared his views on the necessity of overhauling the Department of Information to equip it for a new propaganda offensive.[58] In due course Eschel Rhoodie was brought in as special adviser to Mulder, while Barrie was still secretary. When Barrie was in July 1972 promoted to Auditor-General, the top civil service position, Eschel Rhoodie succeeded him as Secretary of Information. (Unless otherwise indicated, all further references to "Rhoodie" mean Dr Eschel Rhoodie.) Rhoodie's appointment was no easy matter. He was Mulder's firm choice, the minister insisting that a "professional" and not a mere "administrator" was required to head the Department in its offensive. The Public Service Commission, by contrast, held out for a career civil servant ready for promotion. In the end the Cabinet resolved in Mulder's favour.[59] Rhoodie maintained that he accepted the post offered by Mulder on condition that he be allowed to conduct a covert propaganda offensive.[60] Once installed in office, Rhoodie appointed his brother Deneys and De Villiers as his two deputies.[61]

Meanwhile, Vorster had agreed to Mulder's recommendations for a new clandestine informa-tion campaign abroad. The case for resorting to a massive secret venture was strengthened by the findings of the world-wide market analysis that the Department had secretly commissioned in 1973, undertaken by Richard Manville Inc. of New York at a cost of R280 000. The wide-ranging survey of the international images of 14 states, including South Africa, revealed that the Republic fared little better than Uganda. Manville himself was brought to South Africa to present his findings to a very select audience including Vorster, Mulder, Finance Minister Dr N Diederichs, Foreign Minister Muller and heads of government departments.[62]

In the knowledge that conventional diplomacy and information activities had left South Africa with an international image not much superior to Uganda's, Vorster in 1973 agreed that the Department of Information could, for an initial five-year period, embark on a covert propaganda offensive financed from secret funds. R15 million a year was to be allocated for this purpose. Diederichs was intimately involved because of the obvious financial implications. Rhoodie was instructed to prepare a memorandum outlining the aims and some of the methods to be employed in the secret propaganda exercise.[63]

For the small circle of people involved with planning Information's new covert operations there was no doubt that the actions in fact had to be performed clandestinely; they simply could not be carried out effectively in the open.[64] Secrecy in this sense meant that the "targets" of the secret operations and the public at large – in South Africa and abroad – should not know that the South African government was behind these actions. But there was also another even more controversial question about the secrecy: should the Cabinet, beyond approving funds, be given details of all Information's secret projects? And what about the Department of Foreign Affairs, which had an obvious interest in the activities abroad of a sister department? In the end Vorster decided to confine the secrets to a very small number of people, and not to reveal details to the full Cabinet. Rhoodie[65] has suggested a range of considerations that led Vorster to this decision. First, the prime minister wanted to protect the fact that Information had already in the early 1970s improperly been receiving funds secretly channelled from the Bureau for State Security.[66] Second, the Department of Foreign Affairs, specifically the extremely cautious Secretary, Brand Fourie, would have had grave reservations about many of Information's secret activities. Third, Foreign Affairs should be left largely in the dark so that South African diplomats abroad should not be compromised by the clandestine activities of their Information colleagues and should therefore be able to deny any knowledge of these operations. Fourth, there was a strong feeling of dissatisfaction and impatience, shared by Vorster and Diederichs, about the results achieved by Foreign Affairs' conventional diplomacy, and a feeling that this Department should consequently be bypassed in certain instances. Finally, Vorster was extremely concerned that Information's secrets should remain secret: two ways of ensuring this would be to limit knowledge to as few people as possible and to circumvent normal public service financial regulations to avoid detection.

Having opted for this secrecy, Vorster in December 1973 in his own name sent out a circular to the Ministers and Secretaries of Foreign Affairs, Bantu Administration, Economic Affairs, Police, Mining, Immigration and Sport, setting out the task of the Department of Information. The letter was in fact drawn up by the Rhoodie brothers and De Villiers, with Vorster doing little more than adding his signature. Since this was a key document, it is worth quoting from it at some length. "In view of the increasing political and propaganda onslaughts against the Republic, both in intensity and extent, as well as the unorthodox and sophisticated nature of these attacks", the letter began, "it became necessary to adapt the functions of the Department of Information accordingly in an effort to promote the national interest and to ensure national security." The Department was responsible for conveying previously announced government policies and all relevant information concerning South Africa and South West Africa "in all possible ways" to the people of other countries, in particular to opinion formers and decision makers. It was left to the Minister of Information to "determine which methods, means and actions, either public or secret, are necessary to attain these goals." He would, however, consult with the prime minister "on the important information aspects and projects" and would consult with members of the Cabinet "on those matters in which they may be involved", it was promised, and the Minister of Foreign Affairs was specifically mentioned.[67] This letter was obviously very ingeniously drafted, for it officially gave the Minister of Information as near to a blank cheque as could be. The stamp of

prime ministerial approval had in effect been put on unconventional or unorthodox methods of winning friends and influencing people.

A sample of what unconventional methods entailed in the eyes of Information's masters was given to Vorster, Diederichs and Mulder by Rhoodie in February 1974 when he was called upon to expound on the memorandum he had submitted on proposed secret activities. Rhoodie's scheme of things was approved, thus officially launching South Africa's secret propaganda war.[68]

There have been repeated assertions that there was a small inner group that was privy to much of Information's secrets. It was said to have been an "informal" Cabinet committee composed of Vorster, Mulder and Diederichs[69] – popularly referred to as the "Committee of Three" by the private secretaries of the members involved.[70] The object of the committee was supposed to be the continuing monitoring and approval of Information's secret projects. Claims about the existence of such a committee have been vehemently denied by several Cabinet members, including Vorster. From the investigations of the Erasmus Commission it is evident that there was no Cabinet committee, in the strict sense of the word, that concerned itself with Information.[71] In its report the Commission nonetheless seemed to leave open the possibility that an informal, *ad hoc* group might have met from time to time to consider Information's secret ventures. It is instructive to note Vorster's own testimony, in which he revealed that at a Cabinet meeting on 12 March 1974 it was decided that he, Diederichs and Mulder would form a "committee" to finalise the amount of money to be allocated to Information.[72]

Mulder maintains that informal meetings between him, the prime minister and Minister of Finance took place from time to time, usually in Pretoria late in the year, around September/October, after the parliamentary session and the annual round of National Party congresses.[73] Rhoodie, who is said to have attended these meetings, normally gave a report on his Department's activities. In October 1977 – when the first reports of alleged irregularities in Information's operations had already been made by the Auditor-General – Rhoodie arranged an elaborate audio-visual display of what the Department was engaged in. Vorster, Mulder and Senator Owen Horwood (who had succeeded Diederichs as Minister of Finance in 1975), as well as Rhoodie, his deputy De Villiers and General HJ van den Bergh, head of the Bureau for State Security, were present.[74] These meetings, it would seem, were essentially opportunities for Rhoodie to report back to the Committee of Three, rather than an in-depth review of a past year's projects with a view to deciding what to continue, discontinue, amend or add. These decisions appear to have been left largely to Rhoodie.

Van den Bergh's involvement in Information's clandestine operations is not surprising. He was probably Vorster's closest confidant and key adviser, and he made his considerable influence felt in both domestic and foreign affairs. As head of the Bureau for State Security – thus formally responsible to the prime minister – he no doubt had a keen appreciation of the need for secrecy in government actions. Van den Bergh can in fact be regarded as a key figure in Information's covert ventures. It was with the Mulder-Rhoodie-Van den Bergh triumvirate, with De Villiers close at hand, that the real planning and execution of the Department's secret programmes rested, rather than with the so-called Committee of Three. A notable absentee in all this was, of course, the Foreign Minister. His exclusion was explained by the considerations, mentioned above, behind the decision to confine Information's secrets to such a small circle. This is not to say that the Minister and Secretary of Foreign Affairs were kept totally in the dark about Information's secret activities. At bureaucratic level some of these operations were revealed to Foreign Affairs.[75] The information thus conveyed was very limited and carefully vetted. Excluded from the Committee of Three, the Department of Foreign Affairs – whether through its Minister or Secretary – was simply not in a position to exert material influence over the conduct of the secret propaganda offensive. This, of course, was the very situation that Mulder and Rhoodie desired, for it left them with the free hand they wanted.

A further vital aspect of the secret propaganda campaign was the way it was financed. Since the enterprise was conducted clandestinely, there was no public knowledge of how it was financed – that was only revealed once the so-called Information scandal had broken into the open. Secret state funding of secret projects, using other state institutions as conduits, is not a feature unique to the Rhoodie-style propaganda offensive launched in 1974. This had already occurred in the early 1970s, it will be recalled, before Rhoodie became

Secretary of Information. Vorster later claimed full responsibility for these early arrangements.[76] The funds thus channelled were however paltry when compared with the investment made in the five-year propaganda exercise initiated in 1974: R15 million per annum had been promised by Vorster and Diederichs, as opposed to the R293 000 secretly transferred from the Bureau for State Security to Information in the 1973-4 financial year.[77] To have asked Parliament to allocate this money openly for the Department of Information to use secretly was not politically expedient from the point of view of the government, or at any rate of those members involved with Information's financial arrangements. There was simply no chance that the opposition parties would have agreed to vote such amounts for Information's secret activities. In the opposition parties and press it was frequently alleged that the Department of Information was merely a government propaganda organ. A massive secret programme would only have added to their suspicions. The government, for its part, was also keen to avoid a parliamentary debate in which it might have to reveal aspects of the secret operations; above all it wanted to protect the fact that Information would also be active, clandestinely, on the domestic front. Another consideration was that any public announcement of secret Information activities would have encouraged the anti-government (English-language) press to expose front organisations and thus defeat the object of such bodies. Information's programmes were, after all, not protected under the Official Secrets Act.[78]

Once the possibility of funding Information's secret operations through normal parliamentary means had been ruled out, it was decided to use the Defence Special Account as a vehicle for transferring the funds to the Bureau for State Security, which would in effect act as Information's banker. This account had its obvious attractions: it was not subject to public scrutiny or parliamentary debate.[79] As for the decision makers involved with these arrangements, the Erasmus Commission found on the evidence before it that Vorster had known all along about the methods of funding secret activities.[80] Vorster's statement that he only in May 1978 became aware of the financial arrangements, seems difficult to reconcile with his already mentioned testimony about the Cabinet meeting of 12 March 1974 and the subsequent formation of a three-man committee to decide on the funding of the Department of Information. PW Botha told both the Erasmus Commission and Parliament that he had from the outset objected to the Defence Special Account being used as a conduit[81] – a contention that Vorster, in turn, disputed.[82] Be that as it may, the use of the Defence Special Account was eventually terminated owing to PW Botha's objections, and legislation was passed in 1978 to provide for a Secret Services Account. Not only Information but various other departments too are entitled to funds for secret projects from this new source.[83]

The question of responsibility for the financial arrangements for the secret propaganda war is an important guide to the knowledge certain figures had of Information's clandestine operations. The Erasmus Commission found that Vorster "must have known everything in connection with the Department's funds and its most important projects."[84] Mulder, as political head of the Department, was likewise implicated.[85] Horwood, allegedly the other (living) member of the Committee of Three (Diederichs died in 1978, when State President), was absolved from responsibility for the projects or their financial arrangements.[86] It is however known that Horwood at least once – in October 1977 – together with Vorster, Mulder and Van den Bergh, attended a meeting where Rhoodie reported on the secret operations.[87] What is also worth noting is that the Erasmus Commission found that it was "highly unlikely" that the secret Information projects would not have been mentioned to Vorster to support requests for funds.[88] Would this not have applied to Horwood too? Diederichs, it would appear, was from the outset intimately involved with both the financing and the substance of the clandestine actions.[89] Knowledge of Information's programmes need not necessarily imply that a person had been involved in the decision making preceding the operations; he may simply have been informed after the fact. Such decisions rested with the Mulder-Rhoodie-Van den Bergh triumvirate, to which the name of De Villiers can justifiably be added, although he was an official of lower rank than Rhoodie and Van den Bergh.

Although Vorster's full Cabinet was not *au fait* with the details of Information's covert actions, Mulder on occasion, in line with the December 1973 document, briefed Cabinet colleagues whose portfolios gave them a direct interest in a particular Information project. Some ministers participated, probably unwittingly, in meetings abroad arranged by Information's front organisations.[90] There were also occasional liaison and even co-operation at secretary level, one example being a covert propaganda campaign against SWAPO in Namibia, involving the Department of Information, the Defence Force and the South African Broadcasting Corporation.[91]

The question of collective Cabinet responsibility for what the Erasmus Commission called "irrefutable indications of large-scale irregularities and exploitation" of Information's R64 million secret fund,[92] nonetheless featured prominently in the special Assembly session in December 1978. It was in the first instance not Information's secret operations abroad on which the opposition parties tackled the government, but rather on the funding of the Johannesburg daily, *The Citizen*, from the secret funds to the tune of R32 million. "In the light of collective responsibility", Mr Vause Raw, the NRP leader, argued, "every single Minister shares joint responsibility for everything that was done by Dr Connie Mulder and for everything that was done under his control as a member of the Government." Whereas ignorance of what happened could be a mitigating factor, Raw maintained, "it does not absolve the Government from its responsibility."[93] Ignorance was indeed Prime Minister Botha's and other ministers' first line of defence: "Dr Mulder never informed the Cabinet in regard to these [irregular] activities of the Department of Information; not me, nor any of my colleagues", PW Botha insisted.[94] For this reason, Mr AL Schlebusch, Minister of the Interior, declared, the argument with regard to collective responsibility was "totally null and void".[95] In its final report in May 1979 the Erasmus Commission confirmed the government's contentions with its finding that Vorster, like Mulder, had for more than a year withheld knowledge of irregularities in government administration from Cabinet colleagues – at a time when allegations of maladministration in the Department of Information were already being made in public – and that Vorster had also failed to call Mulder to order.[96] Mulder, for his part, tried to dissociate himself before the Commission from the irregularities in his Department on the grounds that he was the political head and had regarded administrative matters and projects as "detail"[97] – and by implication left them to his officials. It is worth noting that Vorster considered that inter-departmental co-ordination involving Information's activities had taken place primarily at secretary level and not in the Cabinet.[98] While this might not have been an unusual arrangement, it seems rather unlikely that departmental heads could liaise on matters on which their political masters were not informed at Cabinet level.

Vorster and Mulder in the end bore the political brunt of the whole Information debacle. Vorster in June 1979, in the wake of the final Erasmus Report, resigned as State President after a mere eight months in office. Mulder, perhaps mainly because of the Information affair, lost the race for the premiership and was subsequently forced to resign from the Cabinet by PW Botha.[99] Earlier, in June 1978, Rhoodie had been prematurely retired – in effect dismissed – as Secretary of Information.[100]

In summary, it can be remarked that the decision making process relating to Information's secret ventures revealed some important analogies with that of the Angolan war: the obsession with secrecy; the confinement of political decision making to very few people; the lack of a range of inputs from various interested parties within government – notably Foreign Affairs – and the corresponding absence of a system of inter-departmental checks and balances; and the prime minister's lack of firm direction and control.

PW Botha: "organisation man" in action

When considering Prime Minister Botha's role in the conduct of South Africa's foreign relations, a constraint is that one does not have the benefit of hindsight as in Vorster's case; at the time of writing PW Botha had been in office for three years.

Initiatives, images and preoccupations

By the time he became prime minister in September 1978, PW Botha had enjoyed considerable exposure to foreign affairs in his long tenure of the Defence portfolio. Yet ministerial exposure and experience are no guarantee for prime ministerial success in foreign policy. By the same token it can be argued that an unfortunate earlier venture into foreign affairs – such as getting embroiled in a foreign war – need not necessarily serve as a guide to a new prime minister's conduct of foreign policy.

Just as Vorster's name became popularly identified with certain foreign policy initiatives – whether rightly or wrongly – some recent moves on this front have been attributed to Prime Minister Botha. This applies above all to the notion of a constellation of Southern African states. PW Botha, however, is not the father of the idea: Vorster had already expressed it in 1975. It would nonetheless be true to say that PW Botha elevated the concept of a constellation to a new prominence and gave it a substance previously lacking.[101] What can more rightly be linked to his name is the "total national strategy" – which has both domestic and foreign policy dimensions – designed to counter what is portrayed as a "total onslaught" on South Africa.[102] The terminology is not all that strange, considering that PW Botha had long served as Minister of Defence and had already in that time begun using such concepts.[103]

Although identified with Prime Minister Botha, neither the constellation design nor the total national strategy has managed to capture the public imagination in the same way as Vorster's *détente* initiative. The explanation is obvious: an element of the spectacular or dramatic is still lacking. PW Botha holding a constellation summit meeting in Pretoria with only the leaders of independent former homelands in attendance has nowhere near the same impact as, for example, Vorster's meeting with Kaunda at the Victoria Falls in 1975. PW Botha visited Taiwan – an event accompanied with massive publicity in the South African media – but this has not yet earned him the statesman's image Vorster had enjoyed in South Africa prior to his political demise. It is relatively early days yet for PW Botha in the premiership and he might in due course – like Vorster – become the embodiment of South African foreign policy.* This might, however, be somewhat complicated by the fact that his Minister of Foreign Affairs maintains a particularly high public profile and has, moreover, become the (white) people's favourite politician.[104] In Hilgard Muller, Vorster faced no similar challenge.

South African prime ministers' reputation among the voters is in the final analysis determined by their performance in the domestic arena. This is nowhere better illustrated than in Smuts's electoral defeat in 1948, when his international reputation if anything proved a political liability. The concern Malan had about repeating Smuts's "mistake" of allegedly

---

* On 30 April 1983 PW Botha met with Kaunda in Botswana to exchange views on the situation in Southern Africa.

engaging in international diplomacy at the expense of domestic duties today hardly applies in view of the extent of South Africa's international ostracism. Instead it is conceivable that South African prime ministers would welcome an opportunity to demonstrate to the electorate and the international community that the Republic is not all that isolated and that its leaders are still received in international councils. Yet Vorster was in many cases a very reluctant participant in African diplomacy,[105] an unwillingness born probably not of fear of seemingly neglecting his domestic responsibilities, but rather of ignorance of the need for and value of top-level personal diplomacy in Africa – and perhaps even of his aversion to flying! But once persuaded to become involved, Vorster greatly boosted his political reputation at home. The point is that diplomatic exploits may indeed be desirable and politically rewarding at home, but are by no means indispensable. This means that PW Botha's relative lack of highly visible, imaginative diplomatic ventures need not be a domestic political handicap.

To date PW Botha has been preoccupied with and has had his political reputation shaped by domestic concerns. Two matters in which he has featured particularly prominently are domestic political reform and the so-called rationalisation of the public service. Both are of direct relevance to this study.

In his first year in office the prime minister struck a strong reformist note in racial policies and raised expectations both internally and abroad that far-reaching political change was in store. Action however lagged behind rhetoric and even the rhetoric itself in due course became rather subdued.[106] Should the reformist spirit however be revived and expressed in substantial liberalisation in racial policies,* there may be some foreign policy benefits, if only a temporary and limited respite in international pressures on South Africa. This may provide PW Botha with an opening to embark on a spell of personal diplomacy – perhaps partly as a reward from outside for his domestic achievements. Of course, PW Botha may also earn himself a diplomatic *quid pro quo* through an internationally agreeable

settlement of the Namibian independence issue.

The second area of interest is the prime minister's drive to rationalise the public service. This has, among many other things, had a material effect on the structures of foreign policy decision making. The key to understanding the reorganisation is PW Botha himself.

In his many years as Minister of Defence, PW Botha became well acquainted and impressed with the management system operating in the South African Defence Force. It appeared far more dynamic and effective than the system employed in the public service generally. As Defence Minister PW Botha had established a reputation as an able administrator and he probably not merely learned from but also contributed to Defence Force management practices. Prior to his election to Parliament in 1948 PW Botha had been a National Party organiser in the Cape Province, and an accomplished one at that.[107] An "organisation man", PW Botha in his acceptance speech upon his election as prime minister not surprisingly committed himself to clean and efficient administration.[108] This statement also had a broader significance, being made in the midst of the Information debacle.

The prime minister's preoccupation with state administration should be seen against the background of the notion of a total national strategy. The policy framework of such a strategy is expressed in the "12-point plan", first enunciated by PW Botha in August 1979. The eleventh point concerns "the maintenance of effective decision making by the State, which rests on a strong Defence Force and Police Force to guarantee orderly government as well as efficient, clean administration."[109] The rationalisation of the civil service and indeed also of top decision making structures is part and parcel of the total national strategy.[110]

The first phase of a comprehensive three-phase rationalisation programme was launched in 1980 and affected the pinnacle of the power structure. The Office of the Prime Minister was considerably strengthened. A Cabinet secretariat was for the first time created. Five permanent Cabinet committees were formed in the place of the twenty *ad hoc* ones that had operated in the Vorster administration. The second phase of rationalisation commenced in April 1980, when the existing 39 government departments were consolidated into 22. The final phase, to be implemented gradually, involves a rearrangement

* In 1982 the National Party approved a new constitutional blueprint based on the recommendations of the President's Council. The proposed three-chamber parliament for whites, coloureds and Asians will probably be established in 1984.

of functions and finance between the new departments.[111]

Many of the *ad hoc* Cabinet committees in Vorster's time had simply never been formally dissolved upon completion of their particular assignments, and their very number was bound to have created problems of co-ordination. Under the new dispensation the Cabinet committees no longer merely handle specific *ad hoc* issues, but each is responsible for a demarcated segment of the total field of government responsibilities. They now also meet at regular intervals. The Cabinet committees became integral components of the actual governmental decision making process, having in 1979 been given the power to make decisions and not merely recommendations for consideration by the full Cabinet. Another significant departure from previous practice is that a minister may refer a particular matter directly to a Cabinet committee, instead of first going to the Cabinet, from where it had to be assigned to a Cabinet committee for further consideration.[112]

The five permanent Cabinet committees are the following: National Security (known as the State Security Council, SSC), Economic Affairs, Social Affairs, Internal Affairs and Finance.* The SSC differs from the others in that it was created by law in 1972. The statutory members of the SSC are known, but not all those who participate in SSC meetings. The prime minister can invite or co-opt whoever he pleases. The four other Cabinet committees were created solely by executive action and their precise composition has never been officially revealed. It is nonetheless known that the four are chaired by ministers – the SSC is chaired by the prime minister – whose ministerial portfolios correspond with the areas of responsibility of the respective Cabinet committees. Thus it is safe to assume that the Cabinet Committee for Finance is chaired by the Minister of Finance, and that for Internal Affairs by the Minister of Internal and Constitutional Affairs. The standing members of these four Cabinet committees are appointed by the prime minister, presumably on the grounds of their respective ministerial portfolios' relevance to the various committees' fields of activity.

An outstanding feature of the Cabinet committee system is the presence of senior officials as permanent members of the committees. These officials at the same time constitute permanent working groups – or a working committee, in the case of the SSC – that on a regular inter-departmental basis and with the co-option of other officials give further expert attention to matters serving before or referred by the Cabinet committees. Each Cabinet committee, in other words, has a working group/ committee composed of officials.[113]

The officials who chair the working groups/ committees of the Cabinet committees for National Security, Economic Affairs, Social Affairs and Internal Affairs – and who are thus full-time members of the respective Cabinet committees – are also the heads of four of the planning branches in the Office of the Prime Minister. With the establishment of these bodies the Prime Minister's Office was obviously strengthened. The planning branches are connected with the Cabinet committees as follows:

Planning Branch linked with *Cabinet Committee*

Security	State Security Council
Economic	Economic Affairs
Social	Social Affairs
Constitutional	Internal Affairs

There are two further branches, Physical and Scientific, whose heads serve in the Planning and Scientific Advisory Councils respectively.[114]*

The State Security Council (SSC)
The principal Cabinet committee, and for this book the most important one, is the SSC. To understand its significance requires an explanation of some of its structural and functional features.

---

* The number of Cabinet committees has subsequently been reduced to four. The former Cabinet Committee for Finance was merged with that for Economic Affairs, and the Cabinet Committee for Internal Affairs became the Cabinet Committee for Constitutional Affairs. It is not certain who chairs the new Cabinet Committee for Economic Affairs, neither is it known who chairs that for Social Affairs. The Cabinet Committee for Constitutional Affairs is in all likelihood chaired by the Minister of Constitutional Development and Planning. The new Department of Constitutional Development and Planning came into being in August 1982.

---

* With the establishment of the Department of Constitutional Development and Planning, all the planning branches except that for Security were transferred to the new department. The Security Planning Branch was transferred to the Secretariat of the SSC.

The SSC stands apart from and above the other Cabinet committees for a number of reasons. First, it is the only Cabinet committee created by law – the *Security Intelligence and State Security Council Act,* 1972 – although it is not referred to as such in the legislation. Second, it is the only committee chaired by the prime minister. Third, the Council concerns itself with a far wider range of issues than any of the other Cabinet committees. Its statutory responsibility is to advise the government on the formulation and implementation "of national policy and strategy in relation to the security of the Republic" – an assignment broad enough to embrace virtually every area of government action both at home and abroad. Whereas the SSC under Vorster tended to confine itself to strictly security matters, its scope has since drastically expanded. Foreign policy is one of the many areas falling firmly within the ambit of the SSC. Both the Minister and Secretary of Foreign Affairs are among the Council's permanent members. Another indication of the SSC's enhanced status is that it meets fortnightly throughout the year, as opposed to its irregular *ad hoc* meetings under Vorster. Fourth, the SSC has its own secretariat, whereas the four other Cabinet committees have a joint one situated in the Office of the Prime Minister.* Fifth, meetings of all Cabinet committees except the SSC are open also to ministers who are not members, and they may freely participate in the deliberations. Finally, the SSC is exempt from the rule that the decisions of all Cabinet committees have to be circulated as appendices to Cabinet minutes and are subject to confirmation by the full Cabinet.[115]

Besides the prime minister as chairman, the following are by law permanent or standing members of the SSC: the Ministers of Defence, Foreign Affairs, Justice, and Police (since renamed Law and Order), and the senior Cabinet minister if he has not already been included under the above portfolios. The law also provides for the co-option of other ministers. In practice two or three ministers have become "co-opted" on a more or less standing basis, one being the Minister of Industries, Commerce and Tourism.

In practice, the SSC plays a role in policy formu-

lation that is far more substantive than the limited function entrusted to it by law. When the Council presents a recommendation to the Cabinet for final approval, that recommendation carries the prime minister's stamp of authority. At least five other ministers would also have been involved in the Council's formulation of the recommendation. It is moreover supposed to be a recommendation based upon expert bureaucratic inputs, and one reached after presumably thorough discussion to which various interested agencies contributed. An SSC recommendation is therefore a blend of political insights and technical expertise. Under these circumstances it seems highly unlikely that the full Cabinet – which in any case will not have the same volume of background information available as the SSC – will turn down or materially amend an SSC proposal. The fact that the prime minister as a rule orally conveys all SSC recommendations or advice to Cabinet, and that the Cabinet formally has the final say, may be of little more than symbolic significance.

Apart from its *de jure* advisory function, the SSC may actually take decisions (as may the other Cabinet committees). The Cabinet would normally indicate the parameters within which the Council may take decisions. Given the salience and urgency of security concerns, the SSC may well enjoy a fairly wide decision making brief. If these decisions are then submitted to the Cabinet by the prime minister – at his discretion – the Cabinet only enters the picture *ex post facto*. Notwithstanding the similarities between Cabinet committees, it is apparent that the SSC enjoys a special position among them; it is at least *primus inter pares*.

The quality of the Council's recommendations and decisions of course depends to no small degree on the quality of the information on which the decision makers act. The bureaucrats play a crucial role here. Five top officials are by law permanent members of the SSC: the heads of the National Intelligence Service, the Police and the Defence Force, and the Directors-General of Foreign Affairs and Justice. Other heads of departments may be co-opted. Bureaucratic input into the SSC is furthermore provided for through the Council's working committee, composed of about 11 heads of departments and the chairman of the working groups of the other Cabinet committees.

The bureaucracy plays another key role in the operation of the SSC. The head of the Security Planning Branch, General AJ van Deventer – a

---

* Each Cabinet committee was subsequently given its own secretariat. The Secretariat of the SSC is certainly considerably larger than any of the others, consisting of about 45 people in 1983.

career military officer on secondment to the Branch – acted as secretary to the Council, and his Branch provided the secretarial infrastructure. In due course the Branch was absorbed into a new, separate secretariat of the SSC. Van Deventer became head of the secretariat and thus remains the secretary of the SSC. To have a subject placed on the Council's agenda, the head of a department has to work through Van Deventer. A minister who sits on the Council may, however, take a matter directly to the Council and need not submit it to the secretary first. The significance of Van Deventer's position is that he can in effect act as a "gate-keeper" and thus to a certain extent regulate the input reaching the SSC. That this key post has been assigned to a professional soldier can hardly have been coincidental: not only some of the military's management methods but also its manpower has been drafted into top-level decision making.

Under Prime Minister Botha the SSC has undoubtedly become a highly important body in the formulation of South African foreign policy. It owes its role in foreign policy at least partly, and rather ironically, to the Angolan war. According to General Magnus Malan, Minister of Defence, Angola "focused the attention on the urgent necessity for the State Security to play a much fuller role in the national security of the Republic than hitherto." An inter-departmental committee was appointed urgently to consider "the formulation of strategy on the national level" and the organisational structures required for the purpose.[116] It is difficult to place any other construction on this statement but that the Angolan debacle underlined the need in top government circles – still during Vorster's premiership – for regularised and formalised decision making procedures allowing for the consideration of all relevant interests. Put differently, it means preventing decision making on matters of vital national interest being usurped by a particular individual or agency in government.

The result of these investigations was the creation of what became known in official nomenclature as a "national security management system". Although its origins are to be found in the Vorster era, it is only under Prime Minister Botha that this new system has effectively been put into operation. Its component units are the SSC, the working committee of the Council, the Security Planning Branch in the Prime Minister's Office, a number of inter-departmental committees, a number of "joint management

centres charged with implementing and monitoring the various strategies emanating from the system", and the National Intelligence Service to provide "the essential strategic background".[117] The inter-departmental committees, numbering no fewer than 15, operate under the aegis of the SSC. Although there is not one specifically charged with foreign affairs, the 15 cover a remarkably wide spectrum. Consider the following examples of committees: Political Action Committee, Co-ordinating Economic Committee, Manpower Committee and Cultural Action Committee. There are nine joint management centres spread over different regions (for example, Western Province, Southern Cape, Western Transvaal and Witwatersrand). A further four are responsible for certain Southern African countries, including Namibia. All joint management centres are composed of senior officials, the four external centres probably composed of representatives from government departments closely involved with South Africa's relations with surrounding countries; Defence and Foreign Affairs are likely to feature in the latter groups.

The very terminology selected for this cluster of decision making and planning bodies invariably conveys the impression that it is heavily military-oriented both in composition and activity. Although the military imprint is clearly discernible in the new structures, it would be an exaggeration to ascribe the changes solely to a new military influence in South African policy formulation. PW Botha had long been an "organisation man" in his own right; his years in the Defence portfolio certainly influenced his views in this regard, but they did not originate there. Also, a thorough reorganisation of the civil service had long been on the cards in the Public Service Commission (subsequently renamed the Commission for Administration), the central government personnel agency. The assumption of power of an administratively-minded prime minister, together with the Information affair and the earlier Angolan war, provided the necessary impetus for a thoroughgoing restructuring of the executive.[118]

A related popular notion is that the new structures are the vehicle for the military's involvement in policy formulation in both domestic and foreign affairs. Yet, while a military input into policy making has now been formalised, so has that of other government institutions. To see the SSC as being dominated and dictated to by

93

the military would be grossly unfair. As Malan's earlier quoted statement tends to suggest, the Council at least partly owes its present character to an acknowledgement of the deficiencies and dangers involved in the military's dominance of decision making on South Africa's involvement in the Angolan war.

It is worth pointing out that South Africa's SSC is by no means a novel instrument for policy co-ordination and policy formulation. In the United States the National Security Council, set up by law, is designed to advise the President on the integration of domestic, foreign and military policies relating to national security. Consisting of the President and the Secretaries of State and Defence, among others, it in effect formalises the role of the American military in foreign affairs. In the United Kingdom a parallel yet more powerful body is the Defence and Overseas Policy Committee. Its membership is made up of the Prime Minister, Foreign Secretary, Minister of Defence, Chancellor of the Exchequer and a few other ministers, with military leaders attending in an advisory capacity. Unlike the American National Security Council, the Defence and Overseas Policy Committee can actually take decisions on matters of vital security. The two institutions represent examples of an attempt to co-ordinate "two separate and distinct decision-making groups", the military and civilian, in policy formulation.[119]

What, then, are the implications of the new decision making structures for the formulation of South African foreign policy?

First, the formalisation and regularisation of decision making might help counter the tendency to *ad hoc* foreign policy formulation. Through the SSC and its various subsidiary bodies the possibility of co-ordinated longer-term planning on an inter-departmental basis has been created.

Second, although the Cabinet is formally the *locus* of decision making, its role in some major foreign policy decisions cannot be divorced from the SSC. The Council often provides the cue to the Cabinet, which does little more than ratify SSC recommendations. Where the SSC does take the final decision, it is the *locus* of decision making. Under Vorster the *locus* often shifted from one institution to another – Defence Information and Foreign Affairs – instead of drawing the various threads together at the centre. An early manifestation of the SSC's central role in foreign policy matters under PW Botha (although this particular case was not exclusively concerned with foreign

relations), was that it took the decision in late 1978 to appoint an inter-departmental (Pretorius) committee to investigate the then disbanded Department of Information's secret projects. The committee reported to the Council, which finally resolved whether or not a particular project should be continued.[120]

Third, checks and balances have been built into the new system through the permanent presence of various ministries. This theoretically reduces the chances of any one party or group – whether Defence or Foreign Affairs or some other department or individual – monopolising decision making and acting with virtual impunity. Of course, there is no absolute guarantee that Angolan or Information-type debacles will not recur. In the final analysis it rests with the prime minister to ensure that the various relevant interests are adequately represented and considered on the Council, and sectional domination avoided.

Finally, and related to the previous point, foreign policy formulation has unquestionably lost any semblance of exclusiveness, of being the preserve of the select few – the prime minister, Minister of Foreign Affairs and a few top professional diplomats. A previously jealously guarded – even if on occasion blatantly intruded into – domain has been formally opened up to a range of other political and bureaucratic elites. Foreign policy formulation has become firmly locked into the new national security management system. Thus, on the one hand, the traditional foreign policy elite, specifically the Minister and Director-General of Foreign Affairs and some senior officials, have seen a decline in their influence in foreign policy formulation, or at least a contraction of their area of jurisdiction, so to speak. On the other hand, Foreign Affairs has in a sense been compensated for this loss by being given a formal say in such other vital fields of government as defence. What Foreign Affairs in other words lost in exclusiveness in one area, it gained in access to others.

While the new decision making structures have in some ways diminished the influence of both the Cabinet as a whole and of the traditional foreign policy elite in the formulation of foreign policy, the status and influence of the prime minister has not been similarly affected. If anything, his position has been enhanced. He is indisputably in charge of the SSC and has thus ensured that key foreign policy decisions have been bought firmly under his ultimate control.

An outstanding feature of the whole SSC apparatus is that it has introduced a new team concept of government. The team has a permanent form, composed of a select group of political office-holders and top officials. Crucially important is the corps of professional civil servants specifically assigned to the task of providing expert inputs from various fields to the team of decision makers. One of PW Botha's main innovations has been the formal involvement of expert officials in the policy formulation process, in both domestic and foreign affairs. A new technocratic element has in fact emerged within the South African bureaucracy.

A significant result of the SSC network has been that PW Botha does not have a personal confidant or adviser playing the kind of role Van den Bergh did under Vorster. The prime minister's principal adviser on the broad front of foreign policy is Foreign Minister Pik Botha, with Secretary Fourie close at hand. The military have made their influence felt in more defined areas, above all on Southern African matters. A key figure is Defence Minister Malan, a professional soldier who served as Chief of the Defence Force when PW Botha was Minister of Defence. His appointment to the Cabinet, straight from the Defence Force, can be seen as yet another manifestation of PW Botha's technocratically oriented style of government. Some observers have gone further, portraying Malan as something of a new *éminence grise* – PW Botha's own "HJ van den Bergh". Those who incline to this view probably see it as more than a coincidence that both Malan and Van den Bergh were from the security establishment. At this stage it seems unlikely that Malan is playing a role in policy formulation that stands above and apart from his contribution as a member of the SSC.

Given the novelty of the sweeping changes to the highest structures of government, it is difficult to make a fair assessment of their impact in terms of the quality of the decisions reached. Should such an assessment be made, it would be well to do so against the background of the official rationale for the Cabinet committee system: to reduce the workload of the already overburdened (full) Cabinet; to promote collective Cabinet responsibility by familiarising and involving ministers with decision making in other areas of government than their own, and improving the quality of decision making.[121]

Set against these considerations is the likelihood that at least some ministers would not take kindly to ostensibly relinquishing part of their authority over their ministries to their colleagues.[122] There are also those sceptics who see PW Botha's plethora of committees, working groups and planning branches as a substitute for decisive leadership. The prime minister, so the argument goes, is afraid of stepping out and giving a firm lead; he is obsessed with having his "back covered" by others, both politicians and professional experts. The extent to which bureaucrats have been drafted into policy formulation is an aspect to which these critics object particularly strongly. For them – and this reveals something of their identity – the formulation of policy is the preserve of politicians, whereas the officials are there to implement the policies.

An entirely different but still hardly benevolent explanation of PW Botha's style of government relates to his legendary quick temper.[123] This has earned him the nickname "Pangaman" (Axeman) among senior Information officials. Alternatively he has been called "The Bald Eagle",[124] an allusion that apparently has to do with both his psychological and physical features. PW Botha is no doubt painfully aware of this (psychological) disability – as are his parliamentary opponents – and his very system of government by committee and the heavy reliance on expert inputs may go some way towards preventing rash decisions being taken in moments of ill-temper. This, at any rate, is the explanation sometimes heard. More seriously, PW Botha's excitable nature is of relevance to a study of foreign policy because it *might* have a material influence on the way he conducts himself in the loaded atmosphere of international diplomacy.

In view of the SSC's important role in major foreign policy formulation, one can justifiably ask whether foreign policy issues still feature prominently at meetings of the full Cabinet. The first point to underline is that the Cabinet has strictly limited time available to deal with any particular matter. It normally meets once a week for about three hours, and being composed of 19 ministers as well as the prime minister, it clearly has a vast range of issues and interests to consider. One among very many areas of ministerial responsibility, foreign affairs receives its share of attention and, depending on the importance of the issue(s) involved, has on occasion featured prominently or even predominantly. A case in point is Namibia, on which there may well have been considerable Cabinet discussion, but this would inevitably have been inhibited if the SSC had already considered the matter and produced a recommendation. It is therefore rather difficult to avoid the impression that the full Cabinet might to some extent have been reduced to a rubber-stamp in major matters of foreign policy. It should also be borne in mind that Cabinet procedure has been formalised under Prime Minister PW Botha, which means that a matter can be discussed in full Cabinet only if a minister has it placed on the agenda; if not, a minister is allowed only a very brief statement, without ensuing discussion.

Defining the role of the Cabinet in foreign policy formulation during Vorster's premiership is rather difficult. Since the SSC did then not play the pivotal role it subsequently assumed, the Cabinet as a whole was potentially well placed to play a much greater role in foreign policy than under PW Botha. The problem, however, is that so much in the foreign policy field happened outside the Cabinet. As South Africa's involvement in the Angolan war and the Information debacle showed, the full Cabinet was at least in two major instances largely excluded from the decision making process. Vorster's secret diplomatic ventures to black African states were mostly revealed to the full Cabinet only after the event. Another constraint on the full Cabinet's involvement in foreign policy formulation was Vorster's heavy reliance on Van den Bergh. In spite of all these limitations, Vorster regularly allowed for substantive Cabinet discussions on foreign affairs, and on the whole perhaps provided more opportunity than his successor. Discussion is of course not synonymous with decision, but Vorster's Cabinet was the forum for important foreign policy decisions, such as on the Namibian issue. Even so, the Cabinet was merely one, albeit officially the highest, of several centres of foreign policy decision making. Far from being a defined process neatly focused on a single decision making body, foreign policy formulation was dispersed, with several elites simultaneously but separately and even competitively involved.

Foreign Minister Pik Botha

In the preceding discussion some reference was made to the role of Foreign Ministers Muller and Botha in the conduct of South African foreign policy. Muller also featured in a previous chapter, having first served as Foreign Minister under Verwoerd. It now remains to take a closer look at Pik Botha's role as Minister of Foreign Affairs.

Pik Botha had been a professional diplomat before turning to politics. As a Foreign Affairs official he first came into public prominence when he served on the South African legal team in the International Court of Justice's hearing of the South West Africa case in the 1960s. He too, like his predecessors Louw and Muller, holds a law degree (although Muller was in the first instance a classicist). It is interesting that as an official Pik Botha had served under Brand Fourie who in 1966 became Secretary of Foreign Affairs; 11 years later Pik Botha became Fourie's political master.

In 1970 Pik Botha entered politics and successfully contested the Wonderboom (Pretoria) seat for the National Party in a parliamentary by-election. A feature of his campaign was its strongly *verligte* thrust, despite the constituency being conservatively inclined. Pik Botha gave further substance to his *verligte* image when in his maiden speech in the House of Assembly he argued that South Africa should to a greater degree heed the Universal Declaration of Human Rights of 1948.[125]

After four and a half years on the parliamentary benches, Pik Botha was in September 1974 appointed South Africa's Permanent Representative at the United Nations. A year later he was given the post of ambassador to the United States, and he served in this dual capacity until his elevation to the Cabinet. In an address to the UN Security Council on 24 October 1974, shortly after taking up his appointment, South Africa's new representative introduced a theme that made headlines:

> I want to state here today very clearly and categorically: My Government does not condone discrimination purely on the grounds of race or colour. Discrimination based solely on the colour of a man's skin cannot be defended. And we shall do everything in our power to move away from discrimination based on race or colour.[126]

This statement, which conformed with Pik Botha's own *verligte* utterances when in politics, should in the first place be seen in the context of South Africa's *détente* initiative with black African states. Only the day before the ambassador's address, Vorster had made his famous "Southern Africa at the cross-roads" speech in the South African Senate.[127] These were carefully planned moves to set the scene for *détente*.

In the 30 months he was based in the United States, Pik Botha became an ardent exponent of an assertive, indeed aggressive, highly visible diplomatic style. Performances such as televised verbal duels with American public figures contrasted sharply with the low profile, hyper-cautious style that was the order of the day in South African diplomacy. The new note injected by Pik Botha nicely complemented the method of forceful overt political salesmanship that the Department of Information applied alongside its covert propaganda ventures. It is difficult to escape the impression that in his high-profile diplomatic endeavours in the United States, Pik Botha also had a South African audience in mind. His labours were certainly not lost on the "folks back home". In this time Pik Botha also developed a particularly close relationship with Prime Minister Vorster.

In April 1977 Vorster elevated Pik Botha to the Cabinet, making him Minister of Foreign Affairs. From the very outset the new Minister found himself in the thick of domestic party politics. *Rapport*, the Afrikaans (pro-government) Sunday newspaper, boldly proclaimed that his return to politics meant that "*verligtes* get a leader".[128] He indeed became the *verligtes'* flag-bearer in the Cabinet and immediately served notice that he was not going to emulate his predecessor's aloofness from internal party politics. In his very first handling of the Foreign Affairs vote in the House of Assembly in June 1977 he declared his willingness "to effect quite a number of changes within our group relations and to suspend quite a number of measures which are marring relations." He was frank enough to add that his views were meeting with resistance from some of his colleagues, and that he still had to convince them. The other important admission he made concerned external dangers. He claimed that "I can frequently see the foreign threats more clearly than some of my colleagues", but he in effect conceded that others did not share his perceptions on the nature of the threats and the need for internal political adjustments in response.[129]

Another important feature of Pik Botha's first parliamentary statement as Foreign Minister was that he openly admitted the link between South Africa's foreign relations and its domestic policies. South Africa's international difficulties, he told the House of Assembly, "began in 1948 and . . . the cause of it was that the NP

Government which came into power then was equated with a crowd of race-haters."[130] But having acknowledged this connection and declared the government's determination to remove measures "humiliating" to other races, the Minister went on to assert that neither the policies of the government nor the opposition parties had any chance of satisfying the demands of South Africa's "enemies".[131] Nonetheless, Pik Botha, unlike his two predecessors, came out openly and vigorously on the side of the political reformers. The fact that the theme of domestic political change featured so prominently in his speeches under the Foreign Affairs vote[132] was a further clear acknowledgment of the link between domestic and foreign policies and a significant departure from his predecessors' anxiety to keep domestic politics out of foreign affairs debates.

Pik Botha's maiden ministerial statement contained what have become enduring features of his political behaviour: his active involvement in party politics under a *verligte* banner and his concern with external threats to South Africa. On both counts he came up against strong opposition from within the National Party. His bid for the premiership in no way improved his standing with these critics. They thought that on top of being ideologically deviationist and dangerously obsessed with external opinion, he was politically over-ambitious, even opportunistic. The general (white) public however held decidedly different views about the Foreign Minister. He had established himself as the "people's politician", opinion polls showing him as the public's firm favourite among the members of government.[133]

For the present study the Foreign Minister* was asked about the implications of playing the dual role of party politician and diplomat.[134] In his response he underlined the harmful effects of domestic affairs on South Africa's foreign relations. He was often "painfully aware" of the damage a decision on domestic matters would have on the country's foreign relations, and saw it as his task "to speak out on those harmful consequences and to ensure that the damage

---

* Following the amalgamation of the Department of Foreign Affairs and the former Department of Information in April 1980, Pik Botha's official designation became Minister of Foreign Affairs and Information. Although it is strictly speaking incorrect to refer simply to the Foreign Minister, this form is both convenient and conventional and will be used in this book.

internationally is weighed up against the necessity of taking the particular decision." He conceded that some institutions or individuals took decisions without these considerations in mind, or were simply ignorant of the potential damage to South Africa's foreign relations. The Republic's three-tier system of authority (central, provincial and municipal) made it difficult to ensure that decision makers in provincial and municipal institutions were continuously informed of the international implications of their actions; this was a matter necessitating attention, the Foreign Minister said. In the final analysis, however, "the conflict between the promotion of foreign relations and internal events damaging those relations" was unavoidable. The exigencies of foreign policy were, in other words, not easily reconcilable with domestic political demands.

Pik Botha's domestic political behaviour is of relevance to the conduct of South African foreign policy. There is always the risk that diplomatic dealings may become complicated if a particular representative's mind is weighed down by concern over the impact of his actions on his standing in his political party and with the public. The Foreign Minister's constant harping on the theme of external dangers confronting South Africa has already earned him the image of an alarmist in party ranks and undermined the credibility of his frequent warnings about foreign threats. It might be that the public too has begun treating his warnings about the perils facing South Africa with some reserve. This, however, does not seem to have affected his popularity. A possible explanation is that the public tends to be more impressed with the *way* in which Pik Botha says things than with *what* he actually says; style counts more than substance.

The Foreign Minister's preoccupation with foreign threats also has implications for South Africa's relations with the very states supposed to be threatening the Republic. A classic example occurred in November 1980.[135] On his return from discussions with West European governments on the Namibian issue, the Foreign Minister made dramatic statements about the "inevitability" of imminent sanctions being imposed by the Western powers against South Africa. The supposed sanctionists denied this, and nothing has yet happened to prove Pik Botha's warning. Needless to say, such events served only to confirm the Foreign Minister's propensity for alarmist rhetoric. It is said in government circles that the prime minister in the course of 1981 instructed Pik

Botha to contain such pronouncements, realising that they may well be counter-productive.

It is interesting that despite their obvious differences in style, Muller strongly favoured Pik Botha as his successor. Muller knew full well that Pik Botha was going to adopt a forceful, extrovert style, the very antithesis of Muller's own. Having been in office for 13 years, Muller thought the time had come to again have an Eric Louw of sorts as Foreign Minister. Muller explained that his own cautious, low-key style had managed to stabilise and even improve South Africa's international position – economic sanctions and further isolation had been warded off – but he thought the Republic would benefit from a new face and a new style after all his years as Foreign Minister. Most of his foreign contemporaries had moreover left or lost office by then.[136] When asked about his own style, Pik Botha specifically mentioned that Muller wanted to see him as his successor, and that they had in fact worked together "very closely" during Muller's tenure,[137] when Pik Botha served as an official and later as ambassador to the United States and the United Nations.

The role and influence of a foreign minister in the conduct of foreign policy are largely dependent on the latitude he is given by the head of government. What complicates an assessment of Pik Botha's particular position is his high public profile. In the public mind, he rather than Prime Minister Botha is the embodiment of South African foreign policy. However, visibility and volubility are not necessarily in proportion to influence. Pik Botha is PW Botha's main adviser on the broad foreign policy front. The Foreign Minister is also a key foreign policy formulator in his own right, but on Southern African affairs in particular his influence is considerably circumscribed by the powerful military input. The involvement of the inter-departmental SSC places further constraints on the traditional role of the Foreign Minister by introducing a new team concept of foreign policy formulation.

A little known, rather amusing feature of Pik Botha's handling of his portfolio is his keenness to keep his Cabinet colleagues informed on international affairs and on his and his Department's activities. Full Cabinet meetings are not, in the prime minister's view, the appropriate forum and moreover lack the time for elaborate personal briefings by individual ministers. The Foreign Minister thereupon introduced a novel way of conveying the desired information: a regular briefing paper circulated to all members of the Cabinet. Compiled by members of the Department of Foreign Affairs, the circular is jokingly referred to by foreign ministry officials as the "Dear Colleague letter" (after its heading). Cabinet colleagues have dubbed it "Pik's newspaper", and frequently make fun of the latest edition of the "newspaper" before going into Cabinet meetings. On a more serious note, some ministers view the "Dear Colleague letter" with reservation, arguing that they too could have started issuing circulars to colleagues about developments in their own ministries. Pik Botha's venture is, in short, seen as an exercise in image building, trying to impress on his colleagues just how active he and his Department are, and that he is "the right man in the right place". The Foreign Minister's curt explanation of his circular was that he continuously kept the Cabinet informed on all important foreign developments affecting South Africa; for the rest, he had "no comment on internal procedures regarding my ministry".[138] Another interesting household feature is the slogan Pik Botha has had printed on official correspondence within his Department. It reads, in both English and Afrikaans: "The Minister is proud of his Department." The effect on departmental morale is not known. (The waiting-room outside his office, by the way, is covered from floor to ceiling with photographs and cartoons of himself.)

It is not inconceivable that the "Dear Colleague letter" is at least partly a response to Pik Botha's awareness of the misgivings some of his Cabinet colleagues entertain about his handling of foreign affairs. The main one is the Foreign Minister's supposed obsession with external pressures and his tendency to exaggerate their danger to South Africa. This has led to the familiar view (already encountered among ordinary National Party MPs) that Pik Botha is using the "big stick" of foreign pressure to try to promote domestic political change. A related contention is that the Foreign Minister "overplays" the sanctions threat over Namibia. Another reservation concerns Pik Botha's dramatic style. As one minister remarked, Cabinet members involved daily with important issues are not as impressed as ordinary MPs and the public with the style of the Foreign Minister. Finally, there are doubts whether his performances on public platforms – where it is all "thunder and lightning" in the words of one minister – can be reconciled

with the demands of high-level diplomacy. It should immediately be added that there are also those Cabinet members who enthusiastically endorse the way Pik Botha handles foreign affairs and who indeed see him as "the right man in the right place at the right time".

Other Members of the Cabinet

Since the military input carries such weight in foreign policy formulation, it is appropriate to begin with the role of the present Minister of Defence. What adds importance to the present incumbent is that this particular portfolio was previously held by the prime minister. For a time after becoming prime minister, PW Botha still retained responsibility for Defence. When he eventually decided to relinquish the portfolio, it was to be expected that he would be particularly selective in choosing a successor. In Magnus Malan PW Botha got someone with whom he had worked closely in the Defence Force, and whose views on politics and strategy were consistent with the prime minister's. Like the prime minister, Malan is known as an "organisation man", having been responsible for a major overhaul of Defence Force management in his time as Defence Chief (1976-80).

In his public utterances, the new Defence Minister has placed particular emphasis on two themes. First, the dangers of the total onslaught on South Africa and the need for countering it with the total national strategy. He is a great exponent – even if in rather dull text-book fashion – of the notion of a national security management system. Second, South Africa in its fight for survival can rely for only 20% on military means, the remaining 80% being political. The view that the answer to South Africa's problems is predominantly political and not military was already being propounded by Malan in his days as head of the Defence Force, and indeed also by others before him. In practice the military do not merely confine themselves to their 20% share, but, as will be seen in Chapter 5, also involve themselves in the remaining 80% through so-called civic action programmes.

In foreign policy Malan and the military probably take a considerably tougher stance than the Department of Foreign Affairs. The military would typically be less concerned than the diplomats about potential international diplomatic repercussions flowing from the use of the military instrument of foreign policy. Their major concern would be the basic one of security. The military have probably injected a good deal of scepticism into discussions on the utility of diplomatic persuasion in South Africa's relations with seemingly hostile or intransigent neighbouring states. South Africa's military raid on ANC targets in the Maputo area in January 1981 provides an outstanding example of the decision makers having concluded that diplomatic means had indeed failed to persuade the Mozambican authorities not to allow the ANC to establish bases in the country.[139] Once the threshold of military action against a South African exile movement on foreign soil had been crossed, this kind of raid could easily be repeated.* In the use of this instrument of foreign policy the military could claim a major say.

A related issue on which the military probably hold a much more hawkish view than Foreign Affairs is the vexed one of using economic levers for political purposes in relations with hostile black states. Whereas Foreign Affairs might tend to take a broader (regional and international) and longer-term view of the potential consequences of manipulating economic ties for political purposes, the military would incline to "quick fix" actions on this front, largely undeterred by adverse international reactions. Should economic levers, like diplomatic means, fail to produce the desired results, it of course again focuses on the "final arbiter" and its immediate master.

The use of economic instruments in the conduct of foreign policy has to involve the minister responsible for South Africa's external trade. That falls under the ministerial portfolio of Industries, Commerce and Tourism. Trade is a particularly important component of South Africa's foreign relations[140] and in many instances the Republic's only channel of communication with countries with which it has no diplomatic ties. Trade is, in short, a vital link with the outside world in a situation of relative political isolation. South Africa's strong economic ties with Western powers, in particular, serve as a powerful constraint on their supporting economic sanctions

against the Republic. Nonetheless, the threat of economic sanctions and indeed the reality of selective trade bans against South Africa have long been major concerns of its foreign policy formulators. Here it is worth bearing in mind that South Africa's is a relatively open economy: of the gross domestic product of R36 832 million in 1978, exports of goods and services accounted for R13 244 million, and imports for R11 888 million.[141] In the Southern African context the economic dependence on the Republic of a score of surrounding black states offers the former a considerable measure of potential leverage.[142] The importance of this particular ministry in overall decision making is reflected in the more or less standing co-option of the minister concerned on the SSC.

Closely related to the direct interest of the Minister of Industries, Commerce and Tourism in foreign policy formulation is that of the Minister of Mineral and Energy Affairs. The Republic's mineral and energy resources are not only a vital component of its own economy, but also an important factor in the economies of several foreign powers. In 1980, for example, South Africa produced more than 50 different mineral commodities worth R14 993 million (US $ 18 140 million). Directly and indirectly, mining accounted for some 26% of South Africa's gross domestic product. A feature of the Republic's mineral industry is that it is predominantly export-oriented with an average of 85% of revenue being earned abroad. Minerals in 1979 accounted for some 73% of South Africa's total exports, underlining their dominant position in the national economy.[143]

In terms of value of annual mineral output, South Africa ranks as the third largest mineral producing country in the West (assuming here that South Africa belongs to the Western community) after the United States and Canada. South Africa is the largest supplier, in terms of quantity, of various categories of non-fuel minerals, namely precious metals and minerals (platinum, gold and gem diamonds), steel and alloying mineral commodities (vanadium, manganese and chrome ore), and a number of processed mineral products. In addition South Africa is one of the Western world's major suppliers of industrial minerals and products, such as vermiculite, industrial diamonds and fluorspar.[144] In the field of energy, South Africa rates as the world's largest exporter of power station coal, with a figure of 26 million tons in

---

*In December 1982 a South African military task force attacked several ANC targets in Maseru, Lesotho. Only five months later, in May 1983, the South African Air Force attacked what it reported as ANC hideouts in Maputo. Mozambique however claimed that civilian targets were hit.

1980. This position will be greatly enhanced when coal exports are increased to 44 million tons per annum by the mid-1980s. South Africa is also the second largest exporter of uranium, accounting for 20% of Western countries' supply.[145]

While these figures are undoubtedly impressive, it has to be acknowledged that the importance of South African minerals to Western economies – or, to put it differently, their dependence on South African minerals – is a matter of considerable dispute in the importing countries.[146] The controversy is essentially politically induced, relating primarily to the question of economic sanctions against South Africa and secondarily to the possible interruption of supplies from South Africa in the event of domestic instability. For the Republic, mineral exports hold potential as an instrument of foreign policy. Although there have in the past been sporadic suggestions in government circles that South Africa might use its minerals as a political lever in the face of external pressures and threats, official policy has remained firmly against manipulating supplies in this fashion. Instead, buyers have frequently been reassured that South Africa intends upholding its reputation as a reliable supplier.[147] The policy of keeping the mineral supply lines open has obvious political utility.[148] There has, nonetheless, been some disquiet among foreign buyers of South African minerals about the possibility that the Republic might begin to interfere politically with supplies.[149]

The Minister and Department of Mineral and Energy Affairs are involved with South Africa's foreign relations in another crucial area, the procurement of oil. Its importance is obvious enough, given South Africa's restricted access to the world oil market because of supplier embargoes.[150] A corollary of securing oil imports has long been official endeavours to reduce South Africa's dependence on imported energy resources. This has led to the establishment of the Republic's own oil-from-coal industry, SASOL. In developing this commercially viable technology, South Africa has created a new potential foreign policy instrument in the form of selling its know-how to foreign countries. Another foreign dimension in the energy field is South Africa's purchase of electric power from Mozambique's Cabora Bassa hydro-electric scheme.

In any country the finance minister features in the conduct of foreign policy in the sense that he has a key role in providing the financial means required. In South Africa this function became the object of intense political controversy due to the Information affair. At issue were the provision of funds for controversial secret domestic and foreign propaganda operations, and the irregular and clandestine means of channelling funds to the Department of Information. This, in turn, raised the highly contentious question of the extent to which the former and present Ministers of Finance had actually been informed of – and even helped to determine – the purposes for which the secret funds were used. Diederichs, there is little doubt, had been an early and ardent advocate of Information's secret propaganda offensive. On a completely different level, a finance minister becomes involved in his country's foreign relations through such matters as the raising of foreign loans, membership of the International Monetary Fund and, particularly in South Africa's case, gold sales. Diederichs, for example, had earned the cognomen "Mr Gold" for his unstinting promotion of the role of gold in the international monetary system.

The Minister of Manpower Utilisation (previously Labour) has in recent years come to play an increasingly prominent role in South Africa's foreign relations. First, there is mounting international pressure aimed at changing the Republic's labour practices; second, the government is patently keen to publicise its labour reforms abroad; and third, South Africa's large-scale importation of labour from neighbouring states has become a political issue in the region. The Minister of Manpower Utilisation, Mr SP Botha, has been closely identified with official moves to remove ideologically motivated constraints on the utilisation of labour in the wake of the reforms recommended by the Wiehahn Commission of Inquiry into labour matters. Publicising the new labour dispensation abroad as a means of countering foreign pressure has become a matter of high priority for SP Botha. (South Africa has long since ceased to be a member of the International Labour Organisation – a tie severed over apartheid.) What has added to his influence in this area of foreign relations is his status as the senior Cabinet minister – something that also ensures him a permanent seat on the SSC.

In the particular context of South Africa's relations with Southern African states the Ministers of Agriculture and Fisheries and of Transport Affairs have important contributions to make. Agriculture features because of South Africa's export of food, particularly maize, to surrounding black states. This has become the subject of domestic political controversy, the charge (from right-wing parties) being that South Africa is "feeding the terrorists" by supplying food to states sympathetic to and even providing sanctuary to "terrorists" fighting the Republic. The government publicly rejects such allegations and defends food exports to black states. There can nonetheless be little doubt that the government is keenly aware of the potential political leverage offered by supplying food to economically vulnerable and politically antagonistic black countries in Southern Africa.[151] Transport Affairs has become relevant as a result of South Africa's so-called transport diplomacy in Southern Africa. In short, it means that the Republic maintains close transport links with politically hostile black states in the region, even to the extent of providing technical expertise to these countries. (Transport diplomacy, which became firmly identified with the general manager of South African Railways, Dr JGH Loubser, will be considered in more detail in the next chapter.) As with food, the reliance of many black African states on South Africa's transport network provides the Republic's foreign policy formulators with a potential political lever.

The Ministers of Industries, Commerce and Tourism, of Mineral and Energy Affairs, of Finance, of Agriculture and Fisheries and of Transport Affairs are not permanent members of the SSC. They may, however, be co-opted when matters directly concerning their portfolios are under consideration. It must be added that the issues being discussed need not necessarily have implications for South Africa's foreign relations, but may be of purely domestic concern.

In view of the intimate connection between South Africa's international fortunes and developments on the home front, the remaining ministers' handling of their respective portfolios may indeed have an impact on the Republic's foreign relations. Most relevant are those ministerial portfolios directly concerned with blacks, coloureds and Indians, namely Co-operation and Development (involved only with blacks, both in the homelands and urban areas); Education and Training (responsible for only black education and training); and Internal Affairs (among other things responsible for the coloured and Indian population groups). The Internal Affairs ministry is also important because its other duties include

immigration and the issuing of travel documents to South Africans wishing to go abroad and to foreigners wanting to visit South Africa. The way in which the latter responsibility is being discharged has frequently caused serious political controversy both within South Africa and overseas.

The Ministers of Police (subsequently renamed Law and Order) and of Justice should also be mentioned. Their portfolios (the two had long been combined and entrusted to a single minister) have frequently been in the forefront of international criticism of events in South Africa. Highly contentious matters such as indefinite detention without trial, banning orders and the activities of the Security Police fall within their jurisdiction. These two ministers are, in terms of law, standing members of the SSC. Foreign policy considerations do not account for their membership of the Council, but their sitting around the same table with the Minister and Director-General of Foreign Affairs might at least offer an opportunity of continually exposing them to the potential and actual implications of their domestic actions for South Africa's foreign relations.

Cabinet members also involve themselves with foreign policy in a different, well-publicised fashion. South Africa's foreign relations in the mid-1970s – during Vorster's tenure – appeared to have become "free game" for ministers and other Nationalist politicians, who liberally indulged in often conflicting public pronouncements on the subject. The main spokesmen were, not unexpectedly, the prime minister and the Ministers of Foreign Affairs, Defence and Information, and they were enthusiastically joined by some other Cabinet colleagues. A feature of the profusion of utterances was a strong antipathy towards Western powers. This is explained by the state of South Africa's relations with these powers: it was the period after the Angolan war, followed by the Soweto riots, Biko's death, the October 1977 security clampdown and the UN Security Council's mandatory arms embargo against the Republic.[152] The familiar theme of questioning the Republic's traditional Western alignment gained new currency. Some politicians suggested that South Africa should consider adopting a non-aligned posture between East and West; others alluded to the Republic's siding with other "outcast" or "pariah" states in a new bloc, while there was even a suggestion that South Africa establish relations with the People's Republic of China. Even if one allows for the exigencies of electioneering at the end of 1977, it still remains a remarkable phenomenon that as vital a matter as South Africa's foreign relations could have become the subject of such loose rhetoric. Perhaps it reflected both the lack of firm direction in South Africa's foreign policy and Vorster's inability to exert his authority over ministers in foreign policy matters.

The Minister of Information often found himself in an invidious position *vis-à-vis* his Cabinet colleagues, including the Foreign Minister: being responsible for Information, he was in a sense a spokesman for the government. It was simply inconceivable that the Minister of Information, particularly when abroad in his official capacity, could have refused to express himself on a particular aspect of government policies, whether domestic or foreign, on the grounds that it fell outside his ministerial jurisdiction. The unwritten rule in the Vorster government was that the Minister of Information (Mulder) may only expound already announced government policies and may not prescribe or anticipate policies.[153] That such a demarcation could easily have led to friction with ministers jealously guarding their domains against infringement by their colleagues is only too obvious. There is one celebrated example of Mulder encroaching in this fashion, the wronged party being none other than Defence Minister PW Botha. Following his address to the Washington National Press Club in mid-1975, Mulder was asked about the possibility of defence links between South Africa and the United States. He replied that America did not need to develop base facilities at great expense at Diego Garcia because South Africa's Simonstown naval base was available to Western allies. On reading reports of Mulder's statement, PW Botha is said to have become so incensed that he immediately demanded of Vorster that he put an end to Mulder's interference with defence matters.[154] Ironically, Mulder had essentially repeated what PW Botha had said earlier in Parliament, and the dust settled when Mulder subsequently pointed this out to his colleague.[155]

The Informal Political Elite

The informal political elite are political office-bearers in supposedly representative political institutions outside Parliament, but established by the white legislature. The bodies are black homeland governments and the national councils for the coloured and Indian population groups, created to represent the three population groups not represented in Parliament. These institutions are of course subordinate to Parliament, the sovereign body. The members of the four white provincial councils are excluded from the list of the informal political elite because the foreign policy formulators do not seem to regard them as significant actors in the policy making process and, moreover, because their respective electorates are also represented in Parliament.

In terms of government thinking the rationale for drawing representatives of other racial groups into the foreign policy making process – even if only to convey the official "view of the world" rather than a real exchange of opinion – is the common threat facing all South Africa's peoples. The total onslaught, so the argument goes, is ultimately directed at all racial groups: they have to join forces in a total national strategy to counter a "communist-inspired onslaught" aimed at destroying all "democratic power structures" and imposing a "subject communist-oriented Black government".[156] Often coupled with official warnings of the threats facing South Africa are lamentations about the public's supposed ignorance of or indifference to the seriousness of these dangers;[157] the concern is not merely about whites' attitude, but also those of the "moderate" sections of the coloured, Indian and black communities.[158]

On the basis of their involvement in the constellation of states, both the independent former homelands of South Africa and the self-governing (non-independent) homelands have claims to be heard in the formulation of South African foreign policy. Two key features of the Republic's constellation design are the notion that "moderate" countries in Southern Africa should join forces against a common "marxist threat", and that they should co-operate not only in economic matters but indeed also in the military and political fields.[159] The component units of the constellation – or confederation, as it was subsequently styled – are South Africa and independent former homelands as full members, while the non-independent homelands would in South Africa's scheme of things be given associate membership. The point, therefore, is that the (independent) partners of the constellation/confederation are supposed to develop a common foreign policy, and that the associate members seem entitled to a voice in Pretoria's foreign policy.

The reference to a common foreign policy between South Africa and the independent ex-homelands needs to be qualified in view of their peculiar international status. With their independence receiving *de jure* recognition from South Africa only, these territories are effectively excluded from normal international political interaction. To speak of their having foreign policies – except towards South Africa and one another – therefore tends to imply much more than actually exists. Given these constraints, together with the fact that South Africa serves as the non-recognised states' link with the outside world, the former homelands' influence in shaping a common foreign policy for the constellation/confederation – and by implication influencing South Africa's foreign policy – appears to be strictly limited. The heavy economic dependence of the ex-homelands on South Africa can only strengthen Pretoria's predominance.

An early example of the constellation partners adopting a common stand in an external issue concerned Namibia. Following a meeting between the Foreign Ministers of South Africa, Transkei, Bophuthatswana and Venda in January 1981, a joint declaration pledged their "firm and unambiguous support for the democratic parties of South West Africa/Namibia" – that is the internal anti-SWAPO parties – and "fully endorsed" the parties' position in the international settlement negotiations.[160]

Jealous of their independence and "equal" status with South Africa as fellow members of the constellation/confederation, the independent former homelands are bound to insist on being consulted by South Africa on major foreign policy matters, particularly those affecting the whole of Southern Africa, such as Namibia. In turn, South Africa would probably, to display its good faith towards its constellation/confederation partners, to some extent oblige, even if the significance is more symbolic than substantive. The implication again is that the independent former homelands are of minor significance in the formulation of South African foreign policy; they are more likely to enter the picture *ex post facto*. In matters of foreign relations South Africa is after all immeasurably more important to the ex-homelands than *vice versa*. For its part, South Africa may only further complicate the already perplexing nature of its foreign relations if it openly starts to conduct foreign policy also in the name of its constellation/confederation partners.

Leaders of the self-governing homelands seem to have even less access than those of the independent former homelands to South African foreign policy formulators. In what was hailed an "historic occasion", the Foreign Minister in April 1979 at a briefing session attended by eight homelands leaders informed them on international affairs, particularly the Namibian and Rhodesian issues. The two-hour meeting was, however, not solely for the purpose of imparting information on foreign affairs; also present were the Minister and several officials of the (then) Department of Plural Relations and Development. It was nonetheless the very first occasion at which the Minister of Foreign Affairs formally informed homeland leaders on foreign policy matters. Pik Botha added to the general air of satisfaction generated by his unprecedented venture by declaring that black leaders would henceforth regularly be briefed on South Africa's foreign relations.[161] Nothing, however, seems to have come of this undertaking.

The Minister of Foreign Affairs admitted[162] that formal discussion between his Department and homeland leaders "seldom" took place. Regretting that the kind of meeting mentioned above was not held more often, he offered the telling explanation that "there are unfortunately only 24 hours in the day." He added that his Cabinet colleagues responsible for the affairs of the other racial groups "are of course completely familiar with the most important foreign currents and they, where appropriate, convey the necessary background information to the leaders involved." This statement is open to serious question. It is doubtful whether the ministers involved are in fact as *au fait* with foreign affairs as suggested, particularly since they are not permanent members of the SSC. They would in any case not be nearly as directly involved with foreign policy formulation as the Foreign Minister, and are therefore poor substitutes for him in briefing representatives of the other racial groups. The very fact that it is left to the ministers responsible for black, coloured and Indian affairs to convey the "necessary background information" may be taken as an indication of the value the government attaches to these informal political elites in the foreign policy process.

The comments on the lack of black homeland leaders' involvement in the conduct of foreign policy apply equally – if not more so – to coloured and Indian leaders, not to mention representatives of urban black communities. It is paradoxical that this situation should apply to coloured and Indian representatives in view of the fact that coloureds and Indians are permitted to join the Department of Foreign Affairs and Information on an equal basis with whites. Coloureds and Indians may in future become involved in the process of foreign policy formulation if they are drawn into top-level political decision making under a new constitution.

In an interesting exercise in multiracial diplomacy the South African delegation to the UN in 1974 included Chief KD Matanzima, Chief Minister of the then self-governing Transkei, Dr MB Naidoo, a member of the South African Indian Council, and Mr DR Ulster, a coloured educationist. Officially they were presented as "advisers" to the South African representatives. The significance of their brief presence at the UN was, however, little more than symbolic. It was designed to demonstrate to the local black, coloured and Indian communities what South Africa had to endure at the UN and that not only white South Africans were in the firing line. The move was probably also related to Pik Botha's statement in the Security Council that year that the South African government was committed to move away from racial discrimination; a multiracial UN delegation might then symbolise this undertaking. No similar delegation has since been sent to the UN.

The involvement of blacks, coloureds and Indians in the conduct of foreign policy confronts the government with a political dilemma. It constantly expounds the theme of inter-racial co-operation and harmony as essential components of its total national strategy. However, the other races are still excluded from participation in political decision making at central government level. How, then, can politically unrepresented groups be drawn into foreign policy making? Even if they were to become involved, a complicating factor may be that consensus on foreign policy issues between the various racial groups would be difficult to achieve in view of their profound differences on domestic matters.

A vivid illustration of the conflicting perceptions of the white and black political elites on a key foreign policy issue relates to how South Africa should react if a neighbouring state provided sanctuary to ANC insurgents operating against the Republic. The government's answer was provided in the military strike against ANC targets near Maputo in January 1981. Chief Gatsha Buthelezi, Chief Minister of KwaZulu and leader of Inkatha, vehemently denounced the attack – in which a number of ANC members and two South African soldiers died – as a tragedy that "creates intense hatred, hardens feelings and makes reconciliation between Black and White more and more impossible to realise." Not even those blacks committed to peaceful change in South Africa "can be jubilant about the death of our kith and kin," he said. Buthelezi saw the deaths as a result of the conflict existing in South Africa "because of white intransigence." Blacks did not share the prime minister's view that communism threatened peace in South Africa, he maintained, but they believed instead that it was white racism.[163] Buthelezi's views were not kindly received in National Party circles, although at least one Afrikaans newspaper, *Beeld*, took the point that white and black reactions to the Maputo raid differed widely.[164] The PFP and NRP both declared their support for the attack.[165]

In his response to the military action Dr Cedric Phatudi, Chief Minister of Lebowa, raised the question of black involvement in decision making on such matters. He suggested that blacks should be represented on the SSC.[166] This kind of proposal is not new. At the time of the Angolan war Basson, then the United Party's chief spokesman on foreign affairs, said in Parliament that it had become a matter of the "greatest urgency" that the government should create "permanent machinery so that White and non-White may consult one another in matters of peace and war so that joint action may be taken against the dangers threatening our country."[167] The call went unheeded. This is not at all surprising, considering that the government has never been amenable to the idea of creating such machinery in Parliament itself.

There can be little doubt that Buthelezi's reaction to the Maputo raid reflected the general attitude of the black population, if not of coloureds and Indians as well. The government's decision to launch the attack was, by contrast, warmly applauded by the vast majority of whites. This raises the complex problem of the role of public opinion in foreign policy making – a particularly perplexing matter in South Africa in view of the racial cleavages in society. A subsequent chapter considers the nature of South African public opinion on foreign policy issues and its impact on the policy formulators.

5. The Executive: Government Departments and Subsidiary Bodies

A government of statesmen or of clerks? Of Humbug or Humdrum? Benjamin Disraeli

To discuss the role of civil service institutions in the foreign policy making process separate from that of their respective political heads or ministers is to some extent an artificial division. For one thing, the contribution of a minister may be materially influenced by the quality of information provided by his officials. Then, top civil servants, through the State Security Council, have become involved in policy formulation to a degree previously unknown. Nonetheless, a principal distinction between the respective roles of politicians and officials remains that politicians are accountable to Parliament and the electorate, officials not. Related is the (theoretical) possibility that the government may be replaced by another, whereas the civil service is a relatively permanent institution and its officials are normally not subject to political dislodgement.

In Chapter 4, passing reference was made to the contributions of public service institutions and their permanent heads in the formulation of South Africa's foreign policy. The present chapter focuses in some detail on their roles, the key department obviously being that of Foreign Affairs and Information (as it has been known since April 1980). Since there were previously two separate departments, each active in the conduct of foreign policy, the former Department of Information's role also requires examination. Prominent among the remaining institutions are the security services, namely the Defence Force and the National Intelligence Service (previously the Bureau for State Security). Ordinary civil service departments such as those responsible for foreign trade and for transport have important

contributions to make. Many of these and other official institutions also enter the foreign policy field through their representatives abroad.

The Department of Information

Some months before Vorster became prime minister in September 1966 the Department of Information received both a new minister and secretary: in April Senator J de Klerk succeeded Waring as minister, and in July Mr FG Barrie became secretary in the place of Fourie, who was appointed secretary of Foreign Affairs. De Klerk, in turn, was succeeded by Dr CP Mulder in August 1968. Mulder's appointment marked a significant upgrading in the status of the Department of Information, for it was no longer merely a ministry added to the minister's other portfolios, but ranked first among Mulder's; thus he was named Minister of Information, of Social Welfare and Pensions, and of Immigration. The decision to enhance Information's status was probably related to Vorster's subsequent announcement that a comprehensive information campaign was to be directed at foreign governments and international organisations to counter "ignorance" and inform them about the South African government's racial policies.[1]

The new style of the 1970s

The Department of Information soon embarked on what officials depicted as a "provocative new propaganda campaign" to improve South Africa's image abroad, mainly through large-scale press advertising. The Department's budget was doubled from R3,2 million in 1966 to R6,7 million in 1971, its staff was expanded and in 1969-70 four new offices were added to the existing 19 abroad.[2] It was also at this time that the Department became engaged in secret projects. In Germany, a public relations expert, Heinz Behrens, was appointed on a secret retainer to feed the media with positive articles on South Africa. In 1971 Information was involved with setting up the news magazine, *To the Point,* with official funds. The Department had its "front man" on the editorial staff to keep an eye on its investment. He was none other than the deputy editor, Eschel Rhoodie. Two years later the magazine established an international edition, *To the Point International.*[3]

It was only after Rhoodie's appointment as Secretary of Information in September 1972 that the Department embarked on a large-scale secret propaganda offensive. The new secretary immediately set about overhauling his department for its new task. Within a year, Information had eight instead of the original four divisions.[4] Particularly significant was the addition of the new Division for Planning and Special Projects. Headed by LES de Villiers, it was to be the nerve-centre of the Department's covert propaganda war.[5]

Rhoodie's appointment was in many ways remarkable. He was brought in from the "outside" (having ostensibly left Information to join *To the Point*) and appointed over the heads of many senior officials in line for the secretaryship – much to the chagrin of the Public Service Commission. Aged 39, he was one of the youngest departmental heads ever.[6] Rhoodie was neither a member of the National Party – though no doubt a supporter – nor of the Broederbond.[7] But he had very decisive attributes, such as being bright and dynamic and having considerable foreign experience as an Information officer. Also, he had written a number of books dealing with aspects of South Africa's foreign relations.[8] Like Mulder, Rhoodie was frustrated by the way in which both the Departments of Information and Foreign Affairs operated abroad. The two men saw eye to eye on the need for a new aggressive and unorthodox propaganda strategy. Mulder assured Parliament that his new secretary was "above all an expert who knows his subject and has the necessary drive and dynamite to take his department to great heights."[9] Drive Rhoodie certainly had:

among his colleagues he was known as boundlessly, indeed obsessively, ambitious. The United Party, too, welcomed Rhoodie's appointment.[10]

The Department of Information's new professional management gave an early public indication of an unprecedented new phase in the conduct of South Africa's foreign relations. In the Department's 1973 annual report Rhoodie boldly declared that in a world in which weapons such as bribery, vilification, insinuation, indoctrination and propaganda were being used against South Africa, the Department of Information would rule "no means, no channel and no tactic" out of order in fulfilling its designated task of influencing foreign opinion formers and decision makers.[11] This message was amplified by Mulder when he told Parliament in 1974 that his department "has now gone on the offensive." This followed an earlier statement that Information would not always act defensively.[12] By then, Vorster's written guidelines for the Department had been circulated.[13]

Before some of Information's foreign projects can be considered, it should first be explained *why* it was decided to resort to so-called unconventional methods. The key is the way the Department of Foreign Affairs handled (or mishandled) South Africa's international relations, as perceived by the architects of the Department of Information's propaganda offensive.[14]

Their first point of criticism was that South Africa's foreign policy was conducted in such a low-key fashion "as to be almost underground".[15] Instead of standing up and fighting South Africa's critics, Foreign Affairs' watch-word was caution. South African diplomats abroad should do nothing to "rock the boat" or attract unnecessary attention – even if it meant not displaying the South African flag outside a mission.[16] By adopting such a low profile, South African diplomats in effect became hostages of the host governments. Hyper-cautious ambassadors severely constrained the activities of Information officers, again for fear of attracting hostile attention. The obsession with keeping an extremely low diplomatic profile was primarily the product of South Africa's peculiar international position. But it also suited the styles of Hilgard Muller and especially Brand Fourie – both known for their particular caution in foreign policy and their aversion to controversy.

Second, and flowing from the previous point, Foreign Affairs representatives were faulted for their limited contacts with opinion leaders and policy makers in their host countries. To maintain their low profile they often tended to restrict their contacts to the particular countries' foreign offices.

The third complaint concerned the lukewarmness, if not actual hostility, of many South African diplomats towards government policies. How, it was asked, can someone actively promote something for which he has no enthusiasm? A clear manifestation of the anti-government sentiments of diplomats was said to be the fact that a good many of them, having left the foreign service, became active in opposition politics.[17] It is worth bearing in mind that many of the diplomats against whom such criticism was levelled had joined the Department in the immediate post-war years, when Smuts was still in power; at least some of them had been ardent admirers of Smuts (and until well into the 1950s entertained great hopes of the National Party government being defeated at the next election). This perceived state of affairs led Rhoodie to remark wryly that if a black government in 1960 came to power in South Africa, it would not need to make too many changes in the diplomatic corps.[18] Far from seeing the Department of Foreign Affairs' political neutrality in appointing diplomats as a commendable feature, the Information fraternity saw it as potentially and actually harmful to promoting South Africa's cause abroad.[19]

Fourth, the commitment of some diplomats to South Africa was questioned, largely on the grounds that many retired diplomats settled permanently abroad. Under much the same banner was criticism of those foreign wives of South African diplomats who failed (or refused) to identify with South Africa and who could not speak Afrikaans.

The fifth objection was more substantive, that Foreign Affairs was paying too much attention to the UN and in the process neglected other areas of vital concern to South Africa abroad. The main external threat facing the Republic, Information reasoned, was that its opponents tried to force it into greater isolation. To counter this required fighting on many more fronts than at the UN – and using new means.

The sixth point is related to the fifth: Information thought South Africa's general foreign policy orientation needed reconsideration. South Africa was so Western-oriented, it was said, that Western powers took the Republic "for granted" and the latter meekly allowed itself to be misused and abused by indifferent Western powers. Instead, it was suggested, South Africa should less readily commit itself to the West and seek to build bridges with other middle and small powers who were either non-aligned in the East-West divide, or were, like South Africa, outcast states. Another Information idea was that the Republic, in pursuit of a more independent stance in international politics, should make overtures to the People's Republic of China. A hallowed South African foreign policy principle with which issue was also taken was that of non-interference. With other countries freely interfering in the Republic's domestic affairs, it was argued, it made little sense for South Africa to refrain rigorously from doing the same in return. If others interfered, so Information contended, South Africa had every right to respond in kind.

Finally, and this was the crux of Information's complaints against the Department of Foreign Affairs and traditional diplomacy, South Africa's position in the world had become progressively worse over the past decades. The endeavours of Foreign Affairs had not managed to stem the tide of international condemnation and growing ostracism. For Information's new masters there was a clear-cut case to supplement conventional diplomacy with unconventional or unorthodox means.

In a new propaganda strategy, Information suggested, South Africa should both overtly and covertly play its "strong cards" in a bid to counter international hostility, notably in the West. These included South Africa's strategic minerals, its role as a supplier of food to black African states, and its SASOL oil-from-coal process. For Rhoodie a major reason for playing South Africa's strong cards was that it had been proven over decades that the policy of separate development could not be "sold" abroad.[20] Therefore South Africa should concentrate instead on those features it could promote internationally.

The constraints imposed by South Africa's racial policies were not ignored. When planning the secret propaganda war, Rhoodie told Vorster that the domestic corollary would have to be a major effort to eliminate racially discriminatory measures and practices. Racism, he maintained, had become the principal social and political evil in the world.[21] It was particularly with regard to the political status of the coloureds that Rhoodie thought major changes were essential, and he favoured giving them and the Indian community representation in Parliament. He even formed a private discussion group composed of academics, officials and others to try to promote changes to government policies on this score. Rhoodie's "liberal" endeavours were apparently an early source of strain between him and Vorster.[22]

Mulder, a politician known for his conservative leanings, was by contrast an ardent exponent of separate development. He acknowledged that the policy was a stumbling block to South Africa's foreign relations, but saw this as being caused by the caricature made of the policy abroad. The way out of the dilemma was by correcting the distorted image through improved salesmanship, and not by tampering with the fundamentals of separate development. This was not the only matter on which Mulder and Rhoodie were in basic disagreement. Mulder did not share his secretary's views on the political status of coloureds and Indians either. Mulder insisted that once concessions on the principle of "separate freedoms" were to be made for the coloureds and Indians, the whole policy might as well be abandoned.[23] With his political head holding such views, one pillar of Rhoodie's dual approach to his task – a secret propaganda offensive and promoting domestic political change backstage – was obviously severely weakened. What aggravated matters for Rhoodie was that the government, despite lofty declarations, appeared unable or unwilling to meliorate the harsh realities of racial discrimination. In his department's annual report for 1976 Rhoodie expressed veiled criticism of the government's attitude and voiced a sense of frustration. Writing in the aftermath of the Soweto riots, Rhoodie said that foreign opinion on South Africa would not easily be influenced "except by imaginative large scale moves . . . in the implementation of government policy to move away from racial discrimination."[24] For the rest, the Department's annual reports quite understandably faithfully expounded (and rationalised) the policy of separate development.[25]

Faced with formidable political constraints on the domestic front – as Foreign Affairs had long been – Information had good reason to play South Africa's strong cards. These limitations probably strengthened Information's conviction that it had to resort to unconventional methods to promote South Africa's cause in a hostile world unreceptive to the official, overt political message of the white-ruled Republic.

It was not only with the Department of Foreign Affairs that Mulder and Rhoodie found fault, but indeed also with the way in which the Department of Information had previously conducted its operations. Indulging in such ventures as making films on South Africa's fauna and flora was regarded as a waste of time and irrelevant to the challenges facing the country from abroad. It was also wholly inadequate for the Department of Information to serve as little more than a press information service in foreign countries. Diederichs went so far as to label the Department "a glorified post office".[26] Like Foreign Affairs, Information had not previously succeeded in countering South Africa's increasing international isolation. The Department of Information's new masters saw their ministry encumbered by a mass of public service financial arrangements. Lest they undermine the new covert propaganda operation, these regulations had to be changed – or flaunted.

These, then, were some of the major considerations out of which developed Information's new strategy for the 1970s. Its overt and covert activities spread over an impressively wide field of countries and projects. The ultimate object was to influence key decision makers and opinion formers abroad to act in a fashion conducive to South Africa's perceived interests or, alternatively, to refrain from prejudicial actions. With the Department proceeding from the assumption that "it is better to have others speak up for South Africa than to have its own government do the talking,"[27] the need to employ covert means was obvious. It meant creating ostensibly independent instruments of communication to convey an official message. The way in which the Department managed to enlist people abroad to assist its cause was "by appealing to their own greed, selfishness or desire for importance and self-aggrandisement," in the words of De Villiers, head of Information's Planning and Special Projects. Put differently, it meant that South Africa, through Information's secret propaganda offensive, was to "buy, bribe or bluff its way into the hearts and minds of the world".[28]

Sight should not be lost of the fact that the Department of Information, next to its massive clandestine operations, actively engaged in greatly expanded and highly visible overt propaganda activities. The Department conducted a form of aggressive high-profile diplomacy also aimed at policy makers and opinion leaders abroad. Parliament, kept in the dark about Information's covert operations and secret funding, voted steadily increasing allocations for the

Department's public activities: from under R4 million when Mulder became Minister, Information's budget soared to R10,7 million in 1974 – R3,2 million less than the R13,9 million granted to Foreign Affairs.[29]

An interesting feature of the expansion that took place in Information's personnel was the employment of Indian and coloured officials. Like whites, they too underwent a departmental training course and were eligible for overseas postings. In South Africa, however, they were employed in Information offices or sections involved with their respective population groups. Following a government decision in 1971 that information departments could be established in the black homelands, the Department of Information in subsequent years trained home-land blacks to man the information services of homelands due to become independent.[30]

Relations with the Department of Foreign Affairs

The simultaneous involvement of the Departments of Foreign Affairs and of Information in the conduct of South Africa's foreign relations on the political and diplomatic planes was no easy exercise in co-responsibility. Vorster's guidelines of December 1973 were anything but precise in demarcating the Department of Information's functions. The vagueness of the wording, as the drafters of the document must have hoped, worked strongly in Information's favour; it contained little protection for Foreign Affairs. There was, nonetheless, an established understanding between the two departments that Information would not engage in official dealings with foreign governments and ministries of foreign affairs, leaving that to the Department of Foreign Affairs. The Department of Information would concern itself, for example, with opinion makers outside government. In practice this rule was often broken by Information, notably in its contacts with government leaders of the Ivory Coast, Senegal and Israel. Vorster endorsed these ventures into high-level diplomacy.

The Department of Foreign Affairs did not view with equanimity the Department of Information's assertive intrusion into what was traditionally the diplomats' domain. Members of South Africa's diplomatic corps entertained serious misgivings about Information's activities abroad. Information's public relations approach to diplomacy was for them the antithesis of their established low-key and ultra-cautious approach. The diplomats saw in it a lack of professionalism and experience, and easily attributed this to the considerable number of former journalists in the Department of Information. It is difficult to avoid the conclusion that a strong element of professional jealousy influenced Foreign Affairs' views on Information's endeavours, for it is a fact that the latter engineered some remarkable diplomatic breakthroughs, such as Vorster's visits to the Ivory Coast and Israel. It is also true to say that Information's high-profile activities in some foreign countries created a much greater awareness of and probably interest in South Africa; Information put South Africa on the map, as it were. Attracting attention is, however, often an undesirable achievement in the eyes of the diplomats.

A serious point of friction between the two departments was the remarkable feature that ambassadors were not fully informed of the activities of their missions' Information officers. The reason was to prevent ambassadors from being compromised by Information's secret propaganda ventures. The diplomats should, if the need arose, be able to disclaim any responsibility for the unorthodox fashion in which some of their subordinates acted in a host country.

The inter-departmental – and consequently intra-embassy – tensions occasionally found public expression. In 1970 a United Party MP claimed that relations between Foreign Affairs and Information were strained, only to be told by Mulder that there was the closest co-operation between the two.[31] The tension became much greater after the Department of Information embarked on its massive clandestine propaganda offensive. In 1975 it found expression in a heated, rather amusing controversy sparked off by an editorial in *To the Point,* in which some pointed questions were asked about the Department of Foreign Affairs. "Can the Republic of South Africa afford a diplomatic service where opposition to the government of the day is common-place?", it was asked. "Or one whose stance is so neutral that if a man like Buthelezi were to take over he would not need to make sweeping changes [in the foreign ministry]?"[32] Hilgard Muller denounced the editorial as a stab in the back of South Africa's diplomats.[33]

The Afrikaans newspaper, *Rapport,* strongly hinted that the attack may have been Rhoodie's work since, the paper claimed, special links existed between the Department of Information and *To the Point.* Although Rhoodie had been associated with *To the Point* prior to becoming Secretary of Information, it was not publicly known at the time that the magazine received government funds. Rhoodie, who publicly distanced himself from the editorial, took *Rapport* and *Beeld,* which repeated the *Rapport* story, to the Press Council for falsely alleging that there was a close connection between Information and *To the Point* and for insinuating that the editorial concerned had been inspired by Rhoodie. This resulted in their being fined.[34] Once the so-called Information scandal broke and state funding of *To the Point* was acknowledged, the government decided to exonerate the newspapers.

From time to time the opposition repeated allegations in Parliament about tensions between Foreign Affairs and Information.[35] In response Mulder rejected such claims "with the utmost contempt", adding that co-operation between the two departments was "as sound as it could possibly be". Each had its own task and own instructions, which were not in conflict but "complementary to one another". Mulder also said that regular discussions – "weekly, and even more frequently" – took place between the two ministers and the two departmental heads involved.[36] Whether the inter-departmental co-operation *was* in fact as close is open to serious doubt. Foreign Affairs officials, notably ambassadors, complained of not being kept informed on Information's foreign activities.[37] Information officials, in turn, accused Foreign Affairs of deliberately withholding vital information on South Africa's foreign relations, such as ambassadors' reports. (Information officials abroad consequently began submitting their own situation reports to their head office.) Official acknowledgment of the strained relations between the two departments eventually came in May 1980 after they had been amalgamated. Foreign Minister Pik Botha conceded that "the greatest distrust and ill-feeling" existed between officials of the two formerly separate departments. He singled out Rhoodie as the main culprit of the tensions, saying it "would require hours" to furnish all the facts "on the trouble he caused between Foreign Affairs and Information".[38]

In official circles a celebrated case of Foreign Affairs-Information discord concerned Mr JSF (Frikkie) Botha, South African ambassador in Washington, 1971-5. Botha was a highly experienced professional diplomat who had had two previous tours of duty in the United States in the 1950s and 1960s. In the eyes of Information's masters Botha was the archetype of the old school diplomat – as his customary bow tie was supposed to symbolise. The Department of Information associated low visibility with limited contacts, and portrayed Botha as something of a diplomatic recluse. What might have added to Information's reservations about the envoy was that he was said to be a United Party supporter, although he was Afrikaans-speaking. Enter Mr HJ Bekker as information officer in Washington in 1973. An energetic exponent of his department's brand of aggressive high-profile diplomacy (combined, of course, with clandestine unconventional diplomacy), Bekker was soon on a collision course with the ambassador. Bekker's chiefs in Pretoria were pleased with what they regarded as his success in reaching out to a wider audience than Botha and in gaining access to politicians and opinion leaders ignored or otherwise omitted by the ambassador, whom they saw as a virtual captive of the State Department. In South African diplomatic circles, by contrast, the approach adopted by Bekker was regarded as often crude, unprofessional and counter-productive. It was in any case doubtful whether Bekker could have matched Botha's understanding of the American political process and the network of contacts he had built up over many years of duty in the United States. Although an experienced information official (having joined in 1963), Bekker was a newcomer to the American scene. What greatly added to the tensions in the Washington embassy was that Botha was often deliberately left in the dark about the activities of Information representatives. Yet it would appear that Ambassador Botha, true to Foreign Affairs form, tended to be over-cautious and he too on occasion misread the American mood. A case in point was Mulder's meeting with Mr Ronald Reagan, Governor of California (1967-1974), in Sacramento in January 1974. Botha reportedly took the view that Information should not place a Cabinet minister in an embarrassing position by having him associate with a right winger who was politically a spent force.[39] The South African press was not slow in uncovering the discord Mulder's diplomatic venture to the United States – which included a meeting with Vice-President Ford – created between Information and Foreign Affairs.[40] Relations between the ambassador and Bekker eventually became so strained that Botha is said to have asked his head office to arrange Bekker's removal. The upshot was that Mulder apparently agreed to transfer Bekker from Washington on condition that Foreign Affairs remove Botha. The two representatives were transferred more or less simultaneously in mid-1975.

Wedded as it was to conducting South Africa's foreign relations through conventional diplomatic channels, the Department of Foreign Affairs did not take kindly to Information's so-called backdoor diplomacy. Yet, it has to be conceded that in identifying the targets for this kind of diplomacy, Information – whether by coincidence or design – succeeded in selecting a number of future political leaders: in the United States not only Ford and Reagan, but indeed also Mr Jimmy Carter,[41] while in Australia De Villiers held discussions with Messrs Killen and Peacock, soon to become Defence and Foreign Ministers respectively, and in New Zealand he had met with Mr Robert Muldoon, who subsequently became prime minister.[42]

In at least the cases of Carter and Muldoon the foreign policy benefits for South Africa proved negligible. Relations between South Africa and the United States under the Carter Administration in fact became so bad that Vorster in August 1977 publicly appealed to the American people, over the head of the American government, to exert their influence to change official policy towards South Africa.[43] This call was decidedly not the approach to South Africa's foreign relations that would have appealed to the mandarins in Foreign Affairs. However, it fitted in with the brand of diplomacy Pik Botha had practised in the United States, and with the Department of Information's aggressive high-profile diplomacy.

Pik Botha's predecessor as ambassador had been none other than Frikkie Botha. Informing Mulder and Rhoodie of Pik Botha's appointment as ambassador, Vorster is said to have remarked, "You wanted an activist, now I'm giving you one."[44] This is not to say that Information was instrumental in getting Pik Botha selected for the position. Vorster had probably been aware of the feud between Frikkie Botha and the Department of Information, and he must have shared the latter's view that it would be appropriate to appoint a politician to the ambassadorship in Washington, one who would adopt an approach different from that of Frikkie Botha. Information was happy with the choice of Pik Botha, for they expected his manner would in many ways conform to their own kind of high-visibility diplomacy in the United States. Before taking up his new assignment, Pik Botha was briefed by Mulder and Rhoodie on the Department of Information's activities in America.[45] The new ambassador did not disappoint those favouring a new outgoing, assertive South African diplomatic presence in the United States. Pik Botha proved the very antithesis of his predecessor, for his peculiar blend of visibility and volubility soon drew the attention of a wide spectrum of American opinion. Ambassador Pik Botha was in effect more than a diplomatic representative – he was also South Africa's principal public relations officer in the United States.[46]

Open and secret projects

After this fairly lengthy discussion of the context of the Department of Information's activities, the nature of its programmes can now be considered. For the purposes of this book it will suffice to present a catalogue of the more important ventures on which information could be obtained.

The Department's overtly conducted activities do not require much attention for they were generally known and annually reported to Parliament. In 1977, the year before the Department of Information was dissolved, it maintained offices in 18 countries, the United States being the focal point with offices in five different centres. The methods and aids employed by information officers both abroad and domestically included personal discussion, personal appearances on radio and television, the compilation of radio programmes and the publication of journals. Overseas, numerous publications – among them the well-known *South African Panorama* and *South African Digest* – were distributed to 100 000 readers every month. Acting as official host to "top-flight leaders of opinion" from foreign countries was a major element in the Department's overt activities, and in 1977 it received 138 such visitors from 17 states.[47]

It is often forgotten that the Department of Information also had a fully-fledged Interior Division, which in 1977 maintained offices in 16 different centres in South Africa, and another four in Namibia. In the Department's annual report for 1977 the Interior Division's functions were described under the self-explanatory headings of "Liaison with Black Communities", "Liaison with Whites", "Liaison with Coloureds" and "Liaison with Indians". Liaison with black communities included involvement with Bophuthatswana's independence celebrations and attempts to defuse the tensions in urban black areas. Liaison with coloureds and Indians focused on publicising the government's new constitutional proposals. The Department's publications division was responsible for 21 regular publications in South Africa and Namibia, with a total circulation of nearly 850 000.

What made the Department of Information famous – or infamous – was its indulgence in secret propaganda activities. These eventually proved to be the Department's undoing. The exact number of secret projects is uncertain, but it was clearly in excess of 150.[48] While the majority of the projects were directed at foreign targets, there were a good many that were solely domestically oriented. Many of Information's clandestine actions are still shrouded in complete secrecy,[49] one reason being that some of the projects are still in operation today.

For the sake of convenience the major secret projects will be listed by country. Some operations merit elaboration in that they involved "high politics" in the sense of directly implicating heads of government.

United Kingdom

One of the first Information front organisations to be established was the Club of Ten in London in mid-1973. Using a retired British judge, Mr Gerald Sparrow, as its letter-head name, the organisation was designed to front for newspaper advertisements – placed in the British, American and European press – conceived by the Department of Information.[50]

The Department became involved in British party politics through "Operation Bowler Hat", the code-name for a project aimed at secretly financing, through a Conservative Party supporter, visits to South Africa by British MPs. Of a different nature was Information's paying two Labour MPs to lobby for South Africa in the House of Commons and to spy on anti-apartheid organisations, thus enabling the Department to mount "disinformation and disruptive" operations against such groups.[51]

The Department of Information tried to gain influence by heavily subsidising and expanding the activities of the Foreign Affairs Research Institute in London and distributing its publications world-wide. At least one publication of the Institute for the Study of Conflict – dealing with the Cape sea route – was sponsored by Information. Plans were made to set up a Human Rights Foundation in both the United Kingdom and South Africa, and for an Atlantic Council to be based in London and involving such public figures as Lord Carrington.[52] Nothing seems to have come of these plans.

The British media was another of Information's targets. The Department was prepared to commit millions of rands to purchase the publishing giant Morgan Grampian. This was then to serve as a basis for taking over newspapers like The Observer, and eventually a television station. In the event, Information indirectly acquired only a 30% interest in Morgan Grampian, which it again sold shortly thereafter.[53] Following its failure to purchase the Investors Chronicle in London, the Department bought the Investors Review. The idea was to get an influential financial journal to propagate British investment in South Africa and to counter the activities of the anti-investment lobby. Also in London, Information funded a new magazine called African Development.[54]

France

The Department of Information's secret activities in France focused on the setting up of interest groups and buying into publications. The Amis des communautés Francaises-Sud Africaines was established in France, and a similar French-South African organisation in the Republic. Information also took the initiative in forming the French-South African Chamber of Commerce. Ambitious plans to buy the well-known publications L'Express and Paris Match failed, but the Department managed to obtain (and finance) a number of others, including Courier Austral, France Eurafrique and Le Monde Moderne.[55]

West Germany

Information began secret operations in West Germany even before the Department embarked on its massive secret propaganda offensive under Rhoodie. His predecessor had appointed Heinz Behrens, a public relations expert, on a secret retainer. Later the services of a public relations concern in Hamburg and another in Frankfurt were employed to conduct for Information an expensive PR-campaign directed at West German politicians. Through its front organisations, both political and academic, the Department arranged a series of conferences on South Africa in West Germany. Over R100 000 was provided annually to 30 pro-South African organisations in West Germany, and about R700 000 per year was secretly spent on lobbying and public relations.

In the publications field, Information held discussions with the Springer publishing empire on buying shares;[56] whether anything materialised in uncertain.

Norway and Sweden

With the help of sympathetic Norwegian politicians, an existing political organisation was expanded and a weekly publication launched. Known as "Project Agnetha", it eventually led to the establishment of a political party that managed to win four seats in the Norwegian Parliament.[57]

United States of America

To assist in its massive clandestine operations in the United States Information employed two lobbyists, Messrs Donald de Kieffer and Tom Shannon, from a large legal firm. They concentrated their efforts on American politicians, getting them to meet with South African leaders. A public relations consultant, Sydney S Baron, was also engaged to promote South Africa's interests in America.[58] In four years the Department of Information paid over R2,1 million for these various services.[59] Baron's corporation claimed to have played an important role in the electoral defeats of Senators Dick Clark and John Tunney, known for their outspoken opposition to the South African government.[60] Other American politicians were provided with financial support channelled from the Department of Information. One of them, ironically, was Jimmy Carter; the amount involved was however insignificant.[61]

A subsequently well-publicised and highly contentious secret project in America was Information's bid to buy into the newspaper market. In September 1974 the Department made available the equivalent of $10 million for the purchase, in collaboration with American publisher, Mr John McGoff, of the *Washington Star*. The attempt failed and Information thereupon, through McGoff, acquired the *Sacramento Union*. The Department also provided $1,35 million to McGoff for the purchase of a controlling interest in United Press International and Television Network, a company that supplied television material worldwide.[62]

Among various other secret projects in the United States were financing the publication of books,[63] sponsoring investment seminars on South Africa, financing special supplements on

South Africa in the ranking American financial journal, *Business Week*, and organising an interest group known as "Americans Concerned with South Africa".[64]

Reference has already been made to Information arranging, through its "backdoor diplomacy", a meeting between Mulder and Gerald Ford. The way Information went about setting up the meeting reportedly displeased the Vice-President's office. Other instances of Information's resort to "backdoor diplomacy" in the United States apparently also tended to antagonise precisely those people it wanted to befriend.[65]

People's Republic of China

The Department of Information's dealings with China fall into an entirely different category from those activities listed above. South Africa has no official relations with China, a communist state. Information's overtures to China represented a fundamental departure from South Africa's traditional rigid adherence to the rule of no formal inter-government relations with communist states. The approaches to the People's Republic of China were based on the assumption that South Africa needed to change it traditional Western orientation and adjust to the new realities in great power relations.

The Department of Information saw opportunities for South Africa in China's changing attitude towards the United States. Arguing that the Soviet Union, not China, is the expansionist power and a threat to Africa, Information thought in terms of some grand anti-Soviet coalition in which both South Africa and China would feature. There was also an awareness of the potential economic benefits South Africa might derive from ties with China. South Africa's close relations with Taiwan, it was confidently assumed, need not be jeopardised by links with mainland China. Another consideration for turning towards Peking was South Africa's alienation from the West. Resentful of what was typically viewed as Western indifference or unjustified hostility to South Africa, Information strongly favoured loosening the Republic's Western alignment.

To put these ambitious ideas into practice, Rhoodie arranged contacts with the Chinese ambassadors in The Netherlands and Canada. Vorster was particularly apprehensive about a relationship with the Chinese, fearing an adverse reaction from his white electorate. Nonetheless he allowed Mulder to fly his famous kite about "my enemy's enemy is my friend", and Rhoodie arranged for Professor Chris Barnard, the heart surgeon, to meet with China's ambassador in The Hague. Should the Chinese open the door to South Africa, Barnard would be the first unofficial envoy. Rhoodie received word that the Chinese were prepared to establish some contact with South Africa, and that Peking would in due course send a specific public signal as confirmation. The signal came, and Vorster was asked to give the green light for Barnard's visit to China. The prime minister, concerned about possible negative public reaction, first hesitated and then refused. This version of events is Rhoodie's.[66] Mulder blamed the collapse of the Chinese initiative on the South African press, which made a great issue of his statement about "my enemy's enemy". The publicity given to his pronouncement and indeed also the ridicule heaped on it were said to have made further progress impossible.[67]

Israel

Undoubtedly one of the Department of Information's greatest diplomatic coups was the tangible strengthening of South Africa's relations with Israel, culminating in Vorster's official visit to the Jewish state in April 1976.

"Operation David", as the Israeli initiative was code-named, was explained by its architects in terms of their perception of South Africa's and Israel's international position. The Department's thinking was on a grand geo-strategic scale. Israel and South Africa were seen as the two pillars supporting the Free World's strategic interests in the Middle East and Africa respectively. They were both surrounded by numerically vastly superior hostile nations. Should one or the other succumb to external pressure, the chances were that the Arab and African states would join forces against the other. The Free World would not survive a global Marxist onslaught if it lost its two strategic pillars in the Middle East and Africa, it was postulated.[68] Another notion, not entirely reconcilable with the foregoing, was that South Africa, Israel and other medium-sized powers should form a grouping of their own; it would, essentially, have been an association of outcast states. On a much less ambitious plane was the idea that, in view of the special relationship between Israel and the United States, South Africa's relations with America might benefit from establishing close links with Israel.[69]

The Department of Foreign Affairs was deeply apprehensive about closer ties with Israel. It maintained that the Israelis were strongly opposed to South Africa, as their actions in the United Nations and support for black African states had shown. That Israel was not amenable to upgrade the two countries' missions to the status of embassies was seen as further evidence of Israel's uninterest in strengthening relations with South Africa. Foreign Affairs also raised a completely different consideration, that South Africa might antagonise Arab states and endanger its oil supplies if it strengthened its ties with the Jewish state.[70] Vorster too was highly sceptical about the chances of improved relations with Israel, not only on the grounds of Israel's publicly expressed hostility to South Africa's domestic policies, but also because of Vorster's belief that he would be personally unacceptable to the Israelis. Because of his war-time internment, Vorster feared, his image in Israel was that of a Nazi sympathiser.[71]

Following the 1973 Yom Kippur war between Israel and Arab states and the severance of diplomatic ties between black African countries and the Jewish state, the prospects for a new relationship between South Africa and Israel improved markedly. Rhoodie, who had in the meantime maintained links he had previously established with some prominent Israelis, embarked on a vigorous new diplomatic venture to strengthen relations between the two countries.[72] Officially authorised by Vorster to involve himself in this field, Rhoodie in two years paid some 14 visits to Israel. Vorster in due course began sensing the real possibilities of improved relations with Israel and privately expressed his interest in visiting the country.[73] An indication of the emerging *rapprochement* between South Africa and Israel was Mulder's meeting with Israeli Prime Minister Yitzhak Rabin in June 1975. The Department of Information's painstaking bridge-building culminated in Rabin inviting Vorster to officially visit Israel. Vorster procrastinated, probably because of Foreign Affairs' reservations about his visiting Israel. Eventually, under strong pressure from Rhoodie, Vorster accepted his Israeli counterpart's invitation.[74]

When he visited Israel in 1976, Vorster took Hilgard Muller and Brand Fourie along, leaving Mulder and Rhoodie behind. "Unorthodox diplomacy had made the visit possible and ortho-dox diplomacy had taken over when the trumpets sounded and the guards of honour stepped to the front", LES de Villiers remarked wryly.[75] By including Foreign Affairs and excluding Information from his delegation, Vorster perhaps wanted to console the former for having been left out in the cold while Information worked on a remarkable diplomatic breakthrough. Vorster's visit proved a resounding success and he could again bask in the glory of statesmanship. Several agreements were concluded between the two countries, including the establishment of joint Cabinet committees to discuss co-operation in various fields.[76] (It is often wrongly stated that South Africa's representation in Israel was upgraded from that of a consulate-general, opened in March 1972, to an embassy following Vorster's visit. In fact, the upgrading had taken effect in December 1975.)

Arab states

The Department of Information's contact with Arab states had a two-fold purpose: to promote dialogue between them and South Africa, with one eye no doubt on oil supplies, and to obtain overflying rights for South African Airways. If South African aircraft were permitted to overfly Africa instead of taking the long route round the bulge of the continent to Europe, it would have meant a saving, at the time, of some R9 million annually.[77]

Rhoodie visited Jordan, Morocco and Egypt. His partner in the endeavour to open up an African air corridor for South African Airways was General van den Bergh. Between them he and Rhoodie were said to have cleared the way for South Africa right up to Egypt and the Sudan. These two countries were to have been approached in tandem: Van den Bergh was to meet the Sudanese head of state, General Gaafar Mohamed Nimeiri, at the end of 1976, and Rhoodie arranged to follow up his earlier meetings with Egyptian officials in Montreal, Canada, with a visit, together with Mulder, to Cairo. The South African party's visit to Egypt had an abrupt ending, for they were asked to leave within 24 hours, thus preventing their scheduled meetings with Egyptian representatives. The reason for the unexpected reception, according to Rhoodie, was a special Arab League meeting that had suddenly been called in Cairo. In due course the story of Mulder's and Rhoodie's abortive visit to Egypt leaked out in the South African press, causing a further setback to contacts with the Egyptians. In January 1978 it was arranged for Mulder to fly to Egypt to try to mend the fences. He was also due

to proceed to Morocco, Jordan and Israel. Vorster, according to Rhoodie, inexplicably cancelled Mulder's visit.[78]

African countries

Some of the Department of Information's most spectacular diplomatic successes were in Francophone Africa, where its endeavours culminated in Vorster's meeting with the Presidents of the **Ivory Coast** and **Senegal.** The Department's contacts with French-speaking African states were again related to the attempt to obtain overflying rights for South African Airways, as well as aimed at winning friends among moderate black states. These states, it was hoped, would speak up in the OAU in favour of dialogue and co-operation with the Republic. A diplomatic breakthrough in black Africa would in turn benefit South Africa's foreign relations over a wide front, for it is conventional foreign policy wisdom that the Republic's road to international acceptability runs through black Africa. The states to which it would direct attention, Information decided, had to be those that carried diplomatic weight in Africa and beyond. The Ivory Coast and Senegal were particularly attractive, for their presidents were moderate and respected elder statesmen of Africa. Information was of course not the only department engaged in diplomatic overtures towards black African states. The Department of Foreign Affairs was conducting its own quiet diplomacy while Van den Bergh was particularly active in Southern, East and Central Africa.[79]

Believing that South Africa could gain diplomatic access to some French-speaking African states, Rhoodie in 1973 embarked on "Operation Wooden Shoe". A sceptical Vorster gave Rhoodie a virtually free hand to approach these states. The Department of Foreign Affairs, true to form, would not believe direct top-level contacts with the Francophone countries possible. Using Mr Bernard Lejeune, a French journalist working in South Africa and one of Information's first secret collaborators, as a go-between, Rhoodie conveyed messages via the Paris ambassadors of Senegal and the Ivory Coast to their respective presidents. Early in 1974 Rhoodie met President Leopold Senghor of Senegal in Paris. The upshot was that Senghor expressed his willingness to meet Vorster within 14 days in Paris or Dakar. Before Rhoodie set out for Paris, a doubtful Vorster had said that if Senghor should agree to talks with him (Vorster) it would be a great breakthrough and he would accept; however, when informed of Senghor's reaction, Vorster hesitated, declaring that he first had to consult the Cabinet. From Paris Rhoodie went on to the Ivory Coast and saw President Felix Houphouet-Boigny, who likewise agreed to meet Vorster. Houphouet-Boigny was also prepared to grant South African Airways landing and overflying rights, provided it was kept quiet.[80]

After some persuasion from Van den Bergh, Vorster decided to meet Senghor and Houphouet-Boigny.[81] Rhoodie returned to convey Vorster's acceptance to the two leaders, and in May 1974 Senghor and Houphouet-Boigny held their historic secret summit with Vorster in the Ivory Coast.[82] Included in the South African party were Van den Bergh, Foreign Affairs Secretary Fourie and Rhoodie. Although Rhoodie, Fourie and also Mulder subsequently visited the Ivory Coast, the whole initiative began to lose force after Vorster's visit. Rhoodie blamed it squarely on Vorster, for not following up his May 1974 talks with further personal diplomacy with the two presidents.[83] It seems doubtful whether this is the only explanation. More fundamentally, Vorster and his hosts had widely diverging objectives: the South African Prime Minister sought to promote *détente* with the black African states and improve South Africa's position in Africa and elsewhere, whereas Senghor and Houphouet-Boigny probably saw dialogue as a means of peacefully persuading South Africa to mend its ways domestically and to promote settlements of the Rhodesian and Namibian issues. Nonetheless, when Vorster's journey to the Ivory Coast subsequently became public, it immensely enhanced his political standing in South Africa and also earned him some international credit.

The dubious means that Information was prepared to employ in its unorthodox diplomacy were vividly illustrated in "Operation Playboy". The principal target – and a very willing one at that – was President James Mancham of the **Seychelles**. The project took its code-name from the flamboyant politician's lifestyle. The primary instrument that Information used was, apparently, bribery. In 1975, the year before the Seychelles, a British island colony in the Indian Ocean, was to become independent, Rhoodie first met Mancham in Paris. Pro-Western Mancham badly needed assistance in the forthcoming presidential election against his leftist rival, Mr Albert René, who was believed to be receiving funds from foreign sources. Rhoodie

offered to provide Mancham's political party with a printing press, in addition to an annual R25 000 to be paid to Mancham personally. In return South Africa would expect an independent Seychelles to continue providing landing rights to South African Airways, to maintain trade links with South Africa and to keep the Soviet Union at bay. As leader of a state belonging to the OAU, Mancham would also be required to provide South Africa with information on the OAU's activities. In the event, Mancham won the election in June 1976 and became the first president of the independent Seychelles, having duly received both his printing press and cash payment. After independence Mancham received at least one more payment in return for his services. In June 1977 Operation Playboy came to grief when Mancham was unceremoniously deposed by none other than René. Ironically, it is likely that some of the South African money had found its way to René – who served as prime minister under Mancham – in a vain bid by Mancham to buy the ambitious René's favour and thus safeguard his own position.[84]

Another secret Information project that fell victim to the vicissitudes of African politics is "Operation Chicken" in **Rhodesia**. It involved providing, with Vorster's blessing, R800 000 to the United African National Council (UANC). The operation was based on the premise – propounded among others by Allegheny Ludlum Industries, a major American importer of Rhodesian chrome – that although Bishop Abel Muzorewa was the leader of the UANC, Mr James Chikerema, a senior office-holder, was the power behind the throne and that he would in due course replace Muzorewa. Chikerema was therefore the main target of the South African support, and the secret project took its code-name from the main beneficiary. The money was to be used to help the UANC win the election following Rhodesia's internal settlement of March 1978. In return for the financial support Chikerema was expected to ensure – assuming the UANC ruled an independent Zimbabwe – that trade and diplomatic links would be maintained with South Africa and that there would be no interruption in the flow of traffic and tourism between the two countries after independence.[85] The UANC won the internal election in April 1979, but Chikerema subsequently left the party to form his own, the Zimbabwe Democratic Party. A much more serious setback for South Africa was the fact that the UANC's rule was very temporary. In the election of February 1980, following the Lancaster House Agreement, Mr Robert Mugabe's Zimbabwe African National Union (ZANU) won a landslide victory, emasculating the UANC.

In the **Malagasy Republic** the Department of Information secretly financed two election campaigns of a Cabinet minister who, Information believed, was a politically moderate man willing to co-operate with South Africa.[86]

The Department of Information's secret activities in **Namibia** should also be mentioned. Together with the Defence Force and the South African Broadcasting Corporation, Information embarked on a radio propaganda campaign to discredit SWAPO. The Department was also responsible for clandestinely distributing propaganda material in northern Namibia, SWAPO's stronghold.[87]

Some of Information's secret projects in **South Africa** itself are of relevance to this book, since they touch on aspects of the Republic's foreign relations. These essentially involved the establishment of front organisations. In the broad political field, two "independent" organisations, the Foreign Affairs Association and the Southern African Freedom Foundation, were formed; also, the Institute for the Study of Plural Societies was established at the University of Pretoria. The three bodies were engaged in producing "academic" analyses of domestic political issues for local and foreign distribution, arranging international conferences and building contacts with prominent foreigners. Information also secretly provided funds for the Institute for Strategic Studies at the University of Pretoria and the Centre for International Politics at the University of Potchefstroom. A publishing concern, Valiant Publications, was established to produce and distribute "academic" studies on Southern Africa, both internationally and domestically. To promote South Africa's return to international sport the Committee for Fairness in Sport was established as a front organisation.[88]

Finally, Information's involvement in ecumenical matters. Through a front organisation, the Christian League of Southern Africa, a new international church body was created as a counter to the World Council of Churches, and it set up offices in London and Washington. "Project Bernard" cost Information several hundred thousand rand. The Dutch Reformed Church was also drawn into the campaign against the World Council of Churches, with Information providing over R150 000 to its Ecumenical Bureau.[89]

An assessment of Information's secret projects

Although incomplete, the preceding overview of the Department of Information's ventures into the realm of South Africa's foreign relations highlights a number of important features. First, Information officials were left with a remarkable degree of freedom of action by their political superiors or, perhaps in some cases, simply took exceptional liberties. Second, there is no denying the innovative role played by Rhoodie; in many instances he can justly be described as the architect of foreign policy initiatives. Third, the statesman-like image that Vorster gained from his visits to the Ivory Coast and Israel is in sharp contrast to his initial scepticism and reluctance about making the visits. Although Vorster set the seal on these Information breakthroughs, he did not initiate them. Neither did Vorster appear to have made much effort to follow up his dramatic diplomatic achievements with further bold steps to keep up the momentum. Fourth, the Department of Foreign Affairs remained very much in the background in Information's major diplomatic initiatives. Bypassed and indeed surpassed by Information in its unorthodox and daring way of winning friends, Foreign Affairs was in some instances reduced to a helpless spectator, but at times one that acted as a brake on Information's activities. Fifth, although the merits of some of the targets and methods of Information's secret projects can readily be questioned, the spectacular successes achieved have to be acknowledged. The failures and blunders should however not go unremarked. Sixth, Information's often grandiose conception of international politics consisted of a strange compound of wishful thinking, naïveté and hard-headed *realpolitik*. In the end, it was probably the much more basic considerations of *realpolitik* rather than ambitious visions that shaped Information's actions on the international political scene. Finally, Information's involvement with South Africa's foreign relations revealed serious shortcomings in overall foreign policy formulation. *Ad hoc,* short term diplomatic successes, however impressive, can hardly be substitutes for clear foreign policy ends and defined means. It also has to be said that Information was in many instances patently ill-equipped for clandestine activities. These would have been much better left to government agencies with the means thereto, namely the intelligence services.

If others had doubts about Information's way of conducting diplomacy, the Department and its minister radiated confidence – for a few years, at any rate. In its annual repørt for 1974 the Department stated that by the end of the year there had been "a distinct shift of opinion" regarding South Africa in official circles and among opinion leaders in most Western states and even in several African and Latin American countries.[90] For Mulder the vehemence of attacks on South Africa was but a measure of Information's success: "The more we put the facts across, the more fanatic our real enemies become."[91] The year 1975, the Department declared, was probably the best in the last decade in terms of positive news coverage.[92] In May 1976 a confident Mulder assured the House of Assembly that "1976 will also be a good year." South Africa was "gradually beginning to reap the benefits which flow from the implementation of its policy of separate development", he explained. When the policy has been carried through to its much vaunted "full consequences", such as the forthcoming independence of Transkei (in October 1976), separate development "will be acceptable to the world". Mulder went on to praise the effectiveness of the Department of Information's endeavours, and he took it as a compliment for the Department that the UN's Special Committee against Apartheid requested an increase in its budget. "It is therefore as clear as crystal that we are succeeding", Mulder boasted.[93] These statements are particularly significant, for they show that if Mulder was amenable to unorthodox propaganda methods, the message to be propagated remained orthodox separate development. In the event, Mulder's promising prognosis for 1976 was proven disastrously wrong. At the end of 1977 the Department reported that when the UN General Assembly had decided on 14 December to proclaim 1978 as International Anti-Apartheid Year, "it brought to a climax the worst period of anti-South African publicity and hostility in the country's history."[94] What of course happened in the meantime, were the Soweto riots, Biko's death in detention and the October 1977 banning of several organisations, newspapers and individuals. The 1977 annual report was, incidentally, the Department of Information's last, for six months later it was disbanded.

Not everyone in government shared Information's assessment of its achievements. In March 1980 Foreign Minister Botha launched a broadside against Mulder's and Rhoodie's secret diplomatic ventures, asserting that no foreign government's attitude towards South Africa had been changed as a result, nor had any parliament or international organisation been persuaded to adopt a more sympathetic posture towards the Republic. No noteworthy success or break-through had been achieved by Information; instead, South Africa's friends had been deterred by the Department's unorthodox methods. He was in effect saying that R60 million in taxpayers' money had been wasted. South Africa, moreover, had to pay a heavy price in "integrity, self-respect and dignity" because of Information's actions.[95] This bland condemnation lacks credibility in the face of the government's decision to maintain a large number of the former Department's secret projects, following an inter-departmental investigation into them. "Numerous projects launched by the department over the years have been and still are sound projects", the prime minister said in December 1978, adding that "it would be the utmost form of irresponsibility to terminate those projects or to make them public."[96]

Obtaining the opinion of retired foreign policy formulators on Information's contribution to South Africa's foreign relations proved an impossible task. Vorster, when asked whether Rhoodie had opened any doors for him in the diplomatic world, pointed out that he had held talks with Prime Minister Jonathan of Lesotho and had visited Malawi "years before" Rhoodie became Secretary of Information. He nonetheless acknowledged that Information, together with "other departments", had been involved in the case of the Ivory Coast.[97]

What complicates or, perhaps more aptly, distorts public discussion on the merits or demerits of Information's clandestine actions is that the whole issue has become intensely politicised. The Information affair became locked into party political rivalry between the National Party and Mulder's National Conservative Party, and of course also between the National Party and the parliamentary opposition. Add to this the feature of sharp personality clashes, particularly between the former masters of Information and their present critics in government, and it is not surprising that the verbal duels have generated more heat than light.[98]

The Department of Foreign Affairs and Information

The foreign ministry of a state, Lerche and Said noted, "constitutes the primary grouping of expertise on international matters within the government."[99] Composed of permanent civil servants, the foreign office also provides continuity amid changes in political leadership. Its primary function is of a dual nature: it is responsible for the execution of foreign policy, but is also involved in the process of policy making. Although these are clearly two closely related processes, a distinction can nonetheless be drawn between foreign policy and diplomacy. The former, according the Padelford and Lincoln, refers to "the overall course of action a country proposes to follow in its foreign affairs backed by supporting programs," whereas diplomacy is "the primary instrument for carrying out a state's foreign policy with other states with which it is at peace."[100]

The role of the foreign ministry in the decision making process normally lies in formulating policy recommendations for the political decision makers. In so doing, officials may of course influence eventual decisions in a very real sense. In South Africa's case, through the operation of the State Security Council, bureaucrats are no longer merely confined to an advisory role but have become formally involved in decision making as such. The diplomatic function of the foreign office involves a two-way communication process, with its own staff abroad and with foreign diplomats stationed in its own country. In discharging these responsibilities, foreign ministry officials are constantly engaged in making "a vast number of policy decisions, at all but the highest level of importance".[101] A further connection between policy making and diplomacy is that policy recommendations may well originate in a state's missions abroad.

Not only do diplomats become engaged in foreign policy making, but policy formulators also conduct diplomacy. Summit diplomacy between heads of government and meetings between foreign ministers are common phenomena. One implication of the political actors' involvement in diplomacy is that it tends to curtail the diplomats' traditional role in the conduct of interstate relations.

Apart from its conventional dual-natured policy making and diplomatic function South Africa's Department of Foreign Affairs and Informa- tion, as the very name suggests, also has an information function. This might seem a perfectly natural addition or it might even be implied in the conduct of diplomacy; if so, the term Information in the Department's official designation is superfluous. What makes the Information side of the Department's activities unique is not in the first instance that it was previously handled by a separate department, but rather that the information function has a specific domestic dimension alongside its foreign operations.

Structural features

In the days of the two separate Departments, of Foreign Affairs and of Information, there were occasional suggestions and rumours about their possible amalgamation. In 1970, for example, a United Party spokesman, having alleged that poor relations existed between the two Departments, suggested that Information be amalgamated with Foreign Affairs since the former lacked justification for a separate existence.[102] In the early 1970s, as Information increasingly began to venture into high-level diplomacy, there was talk of amalgamating it with Foreign Affairs, presumably to avoid duplication or to protect Foreign Affairs' traditional domain. One factor that might have worked against such a development was the insistence of Mulder and Rhoodie that a public undertaking be given that Information officials should, in the event of amalgamation, be afforded equal opportunities to become ambassadors; in other words, they should be assured that they would not play second fiddle to the career diplomats.[103] In 1976 there was a rumour that Foreign Affairs would instead be absorbed by Information: Rhoodie, it was said, was destined to become Secretary of Foreign Affairs.[104]

When the two eventually merged to become the new Department of Foreign Affairs and Information on 1 April 1980, it came about because of circumstances unforeseen in any previous talk of amalgamation. The Department of Information had become the victim of its own unorthodox actions and the Department was delivered to Foreign Affairs on a platter. Recreating the Department of Information as the Bureau for National and International Communication and subsequently calling it the Information Service of South Africa[105] were merely intermediary steps to its ultimate destiny, a merger with Foreign Affairs. For Brand Fourie the wheel had turned full circle: after 14 years he was again head of South Africa's official information apparatus, but now it was merely part of a much greater empire.

Prior to the formation of the enlarged Department of Foreign Affairs and Information, South Africa's foreign ministry had been structured in a conventional fashion. The breakdown into divisions was both geographically and functionally based. The structure was geographical as far as bilateral relations were concerned, with one of two divisions dealing with Africa and the other with the rest of the world. (Until a major restructuring in 1969 the Africa Division had been the only geographically organised one.) A separate multilateral division was responsible for international organisations. Legal matters, protocol and administrative (including staff) matters were each handled separately. For the rest, the Department was structured along functional lines, consisting of sections responsible for political, economic and consular matters.[106]

The amalgamation of the Departments of Foreign Affairs and of Information was occasion for another thoroughgoing reorganisation of what had been Foreign Affairs. Not only was the former Department of Information added, but the typically foreign ministry machinery was overhauled too. (The reorganisation of Foreign Affairs would have taken place irrespective of the merger with Information. The wide-ranging rationalisation of the civil service would also have affected Foreign Affairs.) Yet, as the chart on pp. 124-5 shows, some geographical and functional structures of the old Department of Foreign Affairs were retained. Under the Director-General, formerly styled Secretary, were now two Deputy Directors-General in charge of the Directorates Africa and Overseas Countries.

The Directorate Africa is broken down into three functional branches, namely economic and development co-operation, political services Africa and Africa information. The economic and development co-operation branch, a new one, reflects the government's preoccupation with the promotion of economic co-operation in Southern Africa. The Africa information branch is an inheritance of the former Department of Information. The political services Africa branch, by contrast, is a "true" Foreign Affairs unit. Its two divisions are responsible for Southern Africa and the rest of Africa respectively. The former is broken down into two sub-divisions that clearly reflect the changing political landscape of the region: one deals with the so-called TBVC countries, that is, the former black South African

homelands of Transkei, Bophuthatswana, Venda and Ciskei; the other handles Namibia, Botswana, Lesotho and Swaziland, borders and land consolidation matters. It is strange that the two latter concerns are not part of the TBVC subdivision, for they are issues typically related to the creation of independent homelands. It is interesting that "Southern Africa", as defined above, excludes Zimbabwe, Mozambique, Angola, Zambia and Malawi.

The Directorate Overseas Countries consists of three branches – political services overseas countries, media production and liaison services, and overseas information – and their various divisions. The latter two branches were formerly part of the Department of Information. The political services overseas countries branch is, like the corresponding branch in the Directorate Africa, an original foreign ministry institution. A feature of the geographical breakdown of the political services overseas branch is the wide areas of responsibility entrusted to the component units. One division embraces not only North and South America, but also the Middle East, South-East Asia, the Far East and Australasia. The two Americas are dealt with by a sub-division, with all the other areas mentioned jointly handled by the other sub-division. The second division of the political services overseas branch is responsible for the whole of Europe (Eastern, Central – including Scandinavia – and Western) and international organisations, and consists of only two sub-divisions (Europe and international organisations).

South Africa's diplomatic missions abroad occupy a special position on the organisational chart, as is indeed customary. In practice a particular mission would liaise closely with the particular division or section dealing with the host country involved. Separate provision is made for handling legal matters, administration (including training) and protocol and consular matters (combined).

The planning division is new, having been established in April 1978. It is headed by a deputy director who reports directly to the Director-General.

Functional features

Merely sketching the structural outline of the Department of Foreign Affairs and Information is of strictly limited value. The functional, dynamic dimension has to be added. In attempting to examine some operational features of the foreign ministry – as the new expanded Department will be referred to for the sake of convenience – some formidable constraints have to be recognised. The inner workings of the ministry have traditionally been well shielded from public view; it has, in effect, been a rather secluded arm of government. What adds to the problem is that the annual foreign affairs debate in the House of Assembly focuses more on foreign policy issues than on the actual functioning of the Department. Furthermore, Foreign Affairs in its previous form had never been the object of Information-type exposures.

The discussion that follows is not confined to the foreign ministry in its enlarged (post-April 1980) form, but also covers aspects of the period from 1966 onwards.

The departmental head

The Department has for the whole period under consideration been headed by Brand Fourie. A long-serving official – he joined the diplomatic service in 1938 – Fourie is the doyen of departmental heads. His services in 1977 earned him an honorary doctorate from the Rand Afrikaans University (and he officially uses the title). As South Africa's senior civil servant and for so long head of a key state department, Fourie is probably privy to a greater amount of confidential information than any other civil servant. In this regard, his position is enhanced by his being, *ex officio*, a standing member of the SSC, chairman of the External Trade Relations Committee and a member of the Atomic Energy Board. The Foreign Trade Relations Committee is an inter-departmental body composed of directors-general and their advisers, and concerns itself with both the economic and political dimensions of South Africa's foreign trade. The Atomic Energy Board is the statutory governing body of the state-controlled nuclear energy organisation.

Fourie has the reputation of an extremely hardworking, dedicated and loyal public servant. He possesses an enormous knowledge of international affairs, having been a professional diplomat for many decades. Fourie and Mr Donald Sole, South Africa's ambassador in Washington, were the last two representatives of the pre-war generation of South African diplomats still in office in 1981. Fourie was particularly close to Vorster who, in turn, had a particularly high regard for Fourie. In the foreign ministry it is widely said that their relationship was

so close that Foreign Minister Muller had often been by-passed in communications between the prime minister and the secretary.

Having been its head for so long, Fourie has understandably placed a firm personal stamp on his department. He holds the reins very tightly and is loath to delegate authority, thus giving rise to the familiar saying in the foreign ministry that Fourie is running a "one-man show". Another symptomatic expression is that Fourie plays his cards so close to his chest that they might be stuck to it. Among his subordinates he has the image of a distant, rather autocratic head. With the foreign ministry so closely identified with Fourie, its management style is bound to change under a successor.*

Although a key figure in the formulation of foreign policy, Fourie is not someone noted for his innovative ability. This is at least partly related to his legendary caution, a characteristic so strong that it tended to stifle innovation and imagination over a wide front in the Department. If his predecessor, Jooste, was obsessed with dignity and formality, Fourie's obsession is with caution. (Jooste, for a time after his retirement in 1966, served as the government's adviser extraordinary on foreign affairs. The unprecedented appointment is probably explained by Verwoerd's very close relationship with Jooste. Retaining the imposing Jooste's services in this capacity could hardly have been welcomed by the new incumbent.)

If Fourie does not impress as an innovator in foreign policy, he certainly enjoys a high standing as a diplomat. Foreign diplomats who have been involved in negotiations with Fourie, particularly on Namibia, speak highly of him as an accomplished negotiator and one with an impressive command of the facts.

The Directorate Overseas Countries

Two of the three branches of the Directorate Overseas Countries, media production and liaison services, and overseas information, were formerly part of the Department of Information. Some

---

*On 1 May 1982 Fourie was succeeded as Director-General by Mr J van Dalsen, who had previously been one of the two Deputy Directors-General. Van Dalsen, who had joined the diplomatic service in November 1945, reaches the compulsory retirement age of 65 in March 1985. Upon his retirement Fourie was given the extraordinary appointment of ambassador in Washington for a fixed period of two years.

STRUCTURE OF THE DEPARTMENT OF FOREIGN AFFAIRS AND INFORMATION

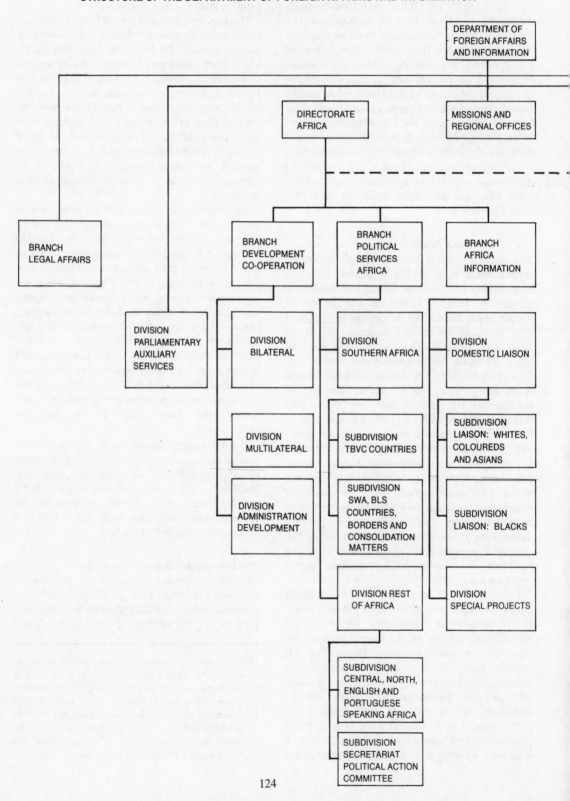

DEPARTMENT OF FOREIGN AFFAIRS AND INFORMATION

DIRECTORATE AFRICA

MISSIONS AND REGIONAL OFFICES

BRANCH LEGAL AFFAIRS

BRANCH DEVELOPMENT CO-OPERATION

BRANCH POLITICAL SERVICES AFRICA

BRANCH AFRICA INFORMATION

DIVISION PARLIAMENTARY AUXILIARY SERVICES

DIVISION BILATERAL

DIVISION SOUTHERN AFRICA

DIVISION DOMESTIC LIAISON

DIVISION MULTILATERAL

SUBDIVISION TBVC COUNTRIES

SUBDIVISION LIAISON: WHITES, COLOUREDS AND ASIANS

DIVISION ADMINISTRATION DEVELOPMENT

SUBDIVISION SWA, BLS COUNTRIES, BORDERS AND CONSOLIDATION MATTERS

SUBDIVISION LIAISON: BLACKS

DIVISION REST OF AFRICA

DIVISION SPECIAL PROJECTS

SUBDIVISION CENTRAL, NORTH, ENGLISH AND PORTUGUESE SPEAKING AFRICA

SUBDIVISION SECRETARIAT POLITICAL ACTION COMMITTEE

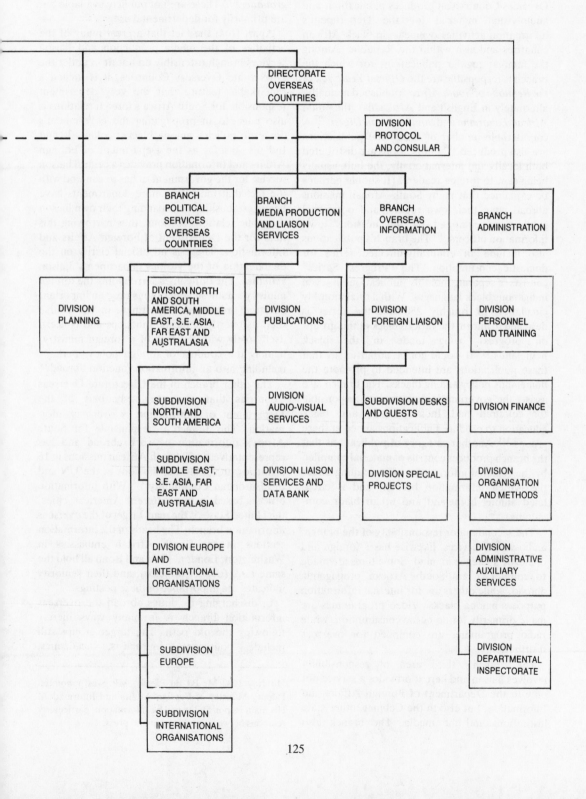

DIRECTORATE
OVERSEAS
COUNTRIES

DIVISION
PROTOCOL
AND CONSULAR

BRANCH
POLITICAL
SERVICES
OVERSEAS
COUNTRIES

BRANCH
MEDIA PRODUCTION
AND LIAISON
SERVICES

BRANCH
OVERSEAS
INFORMATION

BRANCH
ADMINISTRATION

DIVISION
PLANNING

DIVISION NORTH
AND SOUTH
AMERICA, MIDDLE
EAST, S.E. ASIA,
FAR EAST AND
AUSTRALASIA

DIVISION
PUBLICATIONS

DIVISION
FOREIGN LIAISON

DIVISION
PERSONNEL
AND TRAINING

SUBDIVISION
NORTH AND
SOUTH AMERICA

DIVISION
AUDIO-VISUAL
SERVICES

SUBDIVISION DESKS
AND GUESTS

DIVISION FINANCE

SUBDIVISION
MIDDLE EAST,
S.E. ASIA, FAR
EAST AND
AUSTRALASIA

DIVISION LIAISON
SERVICES AND
DATA BANK

DIVISION SPECIAL
PROJECTS

DIVISION
ORGANISATION
AND METHODS

DIVISION EUROPE
AND
INTERNATIONAL
ORGANISATIONS

DIVISION
ADMINISTRATIVE
AUXILIARY
SERVICES

SUBDIVISION
EUROPE

DIVISION
DEPARTMENTAL
INSPECTORATE

SUBDIVISION
INTERNATIONAL
ORGANISATIONS

observations have already been made about the third branch, political services overseas countries.

Although the media production and liaison services branch falls under the Directorate Overseas Countries, it produces publications and audio-visual material for the Department's information activities overseas, in black African countries and also within the Republic. Among the familiar regular publications for which the branch is responsible are the *Official Yearbook of the Republic of South Africa* (published annually, alternately in English and Afrikaans), the *South African Panorama* and *South African Digest*.[107] A considerable number of occasional publications are also produced.[108] Publications are distributed both locally and internationally, the bulk usually being sent to foreign readers. (It should perhaps be explained that many South African missions abroad issue their own regular and occasional publications compiled by the missions' own information officers.[109] The branch's publications also include an ethnically-directed series for domestic consumption. The "Progress Series" consists of separate monthly publications in seven indigenous black languages. With a total monthly circulation of roughly 250 000, the series is designed to inform the various black ethnic groups on progress being made in the black homelands.[110] It would not be unfair to say that these publications are intended to promote the homelands policy among blacks. The branch also assists the government departments responsible for coloured and Indian affairs and black education to produce publications aimed at these groups.[111] Another category of publications that the branch produces consists of material compiled by the regional information offices falling under the Africa information branch, and is circulated among homeland and urban black communities.[112]

The second major responsibility of the branch, audio-visual services, likewise has a foreign and domestic audience in mind. Some films are made to counteract anti-South African propaganda abroad, while others are for internal information purposes among blacks. Video programmes are made primarily for domestic consumption, while radio programmes are compiled for overseas distribution.

The branch's third area of responsibility involves liaison and here it provides a service not only to the Department of Foreign Affairs and Information, but also to the Cabinet, other state institutions and the media. The branch also operates a databank that channels information through a daily news bulletin telexed to South African missions abroad, and through three publications, *Spectrum, Focus* and *Backgrounder*.[113] These are not publicly available but are primarily for departmental use.

Apart from the fact that a great many of the activities of the media production and liaison services branch ostensibly do not fit in under the Directorate Overseas Countries, it is indeed a remarkable feature that the very department responsible for South Africa's foreign relations is also engaged in propagating the government's domestic policies among blacks, coloureds and Indians. Insofar as the Department of Foreign Affairs and Information provides a central liaison service for the government, it has to contend with the fact that more and more departments have begun establishing or expanding their own liaison or public relations sections, thus narrowing this field for the Department of Foreign Affairs and Information. There is no official clarity on the demarcation of the various departments' liaison activities. The difficulties surrounding the foreign ministry's domestic operations raise an important question: might the Department in due course shed its overtly domestic functions and concern itself solely with the task of a foreign ministry, namely the conduct of foreign policy, perhaps including also an information function abroad?*

The other branch in the Directorate Overseas Countries that was previously part of the Department of Information is overseas information. This branch is responsible for South Africa's information network abroad and has representatives in 23 South African missions in 16 countries, including the missions at the UN and the European Community.[114] With information officers based in five different American cities, the United States is the main target of the overseas information branch. The heads of the information sections in the South African embassies in Washington, London, Paris and Bonn all hold the same rank (deputy director), and their seniority indicates the importance of these postings.

In discharging its duties abroad the overseas information branch is in many ways merely following the old path. The target groups still include politicians, journalists, academics,

---

*In July 1982 Mr BJ du Plessis, MP, was appointed Deputy Minister of Foreign Affairs and Information. His main responsibility will be Information, particularly relations between government and press.

businessmen, trade unionists and clergymen. The "selling points" feature such familiar themes as South Africa's strategic location, its mineral resources and its value as a trading partner, its importance as an exporter of food, and a more recent one, the government's plans for domestic political reform. The overseas information branch is still largely staffed by career officials formerly attached to the Department of Information. At the time of writing they are all white, although the branch is open to coloureds and Indians. To assist it in its overseas operations, the new Department decided to retain the services of a professional lobbyist and a public relations consultant in the United States[115] and a similar consultant in West Germany. Secret information projects continue to be carried out abroad, but their exact number is not known. Having stated its conviction that the end does not justify the means, the government undertook to exert strict control over the secret operations to prevent a recurrence of the previous financial irregularities and unacceptable unorthodox practices.[116]

An important change that the amalgamation of Foreign Affairs and Information brought about is that information officers may no longer act abroad without keeping their ambassadors fully briefed.

The Directorate Africa

Two of the three branches of the Directorate Africa require some consideration, since they constitute important new components of the foreign ministry. The third, the political services Africa branch, is the counterpart of the political services overseas countries branch, and is an established section of the foreign ministry.

The Africa information branch consists mostly of officials of the former Department of Information who had been involved with domestic activities. The branch concerns itself primarily with information programmes in South Africa and its former homelands. In the rest of the continent the branch's main function seems little more than that of a post office, sending out information material about South Africa. It does not have representatives in any African state, not even in the independent former homelands. The Africa information branch is specifically structured for internal operations, with a domestic liaison division consisting of a sub-division for liaison with whites, coloureds and Indians, and one for liaison with blacks. The main domestic task is regarded as the cultivation of sound race relations, which in fact means promoting government policies. Included in the policies package are the South African government's plans for a constellation of Southern African states, which have been propagated among the independent ex-homelands. In its domestic undertakings the Africa information branch frequently collaborates closely with other government departments. Thus it has been involved with the police, security police, the Department of Justice and the Department of Education and Training in programmes aimed at defusing tension in urban black areas. Such "psychological actions", as they are styled, are handled by the special projects division, as are other secret projects. The bulk of these are domestically oriented, with very few directed at black African states other than former homelands.

Not only does the designation of the Africa information branch imply much more than it actually involves, but the branch's activities reveal more clearly than those of its counterpart, the overseas information branch, and the related media production and liaison services branch, a remarkable duality in the functions of the Department of Foreign Affairs and Information. It is a department that on the one hand conducts negotiations with representatives from the great powers, and on the other launches clandestine propaganda activities in urban black areas. In the sense that domestic racial issues are of direct relevance to South Africa's foreign relations, these two widely divergent pursuits are distantly related. It would, however, be stretching a point too far to use that as the rationale for the Department of Foreign Affairs and Information's dual character. Instead, it would seem that the merger of the two departments combined features that hardly belong together.

The economic and development co-operation branch, headed by a chief development adviser, was established in 1979 and consists of three divisions: bilateral, multilateral and development administration. Most of the personnel in the branch are professional economists, of whom a good many had previously been employed by either the Bureau of Economic Research, Co-operation and Development (BENSO – an influential, semi-official research organisation-cum-think tank), or the Corporation for Economic Development (a public corporation engaged in development projects in black homelands). Although the branch's functions of promoting economic co-operation and directing development assistance are defined in regional

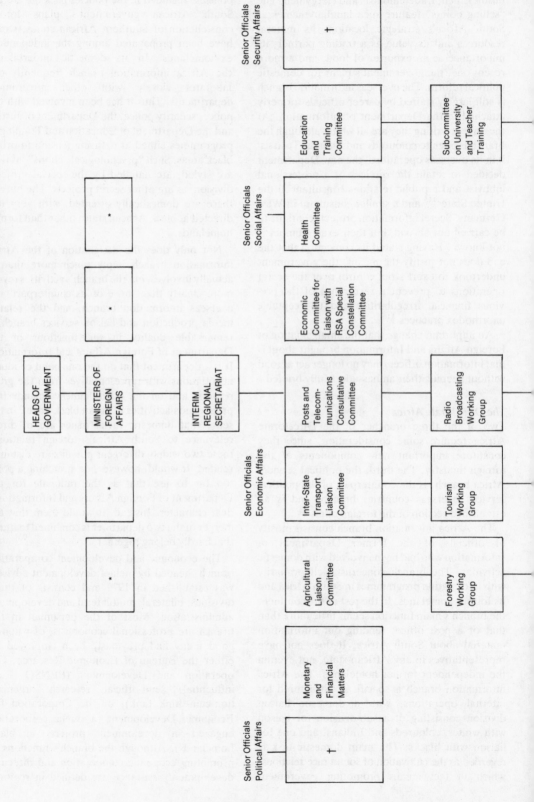

CONSTELLATION OF SOUTHERN AFRICAN STATES CONSULTATIVE STRUCTURES

128

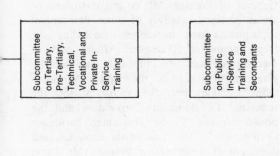

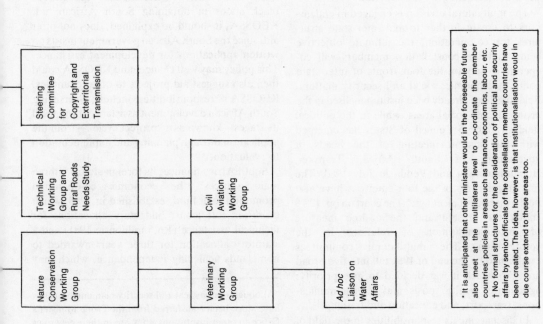

(Southern African) terms, it concerns itself in practice mostly with the independent former homelands. Other countries such as Malawi and Lesotho – which are not members of the constellation of states – nonetheless benefit from the branch's programmes.

The multilateral division in the economic and development co-operation branch serves as the interim regional secretariat of the constellation. The idea is that a permanent regional secretariat, staffed by officials from the constellation's member states, will in due course be established to provide the necessary secretarial support, administrative continuity and co-ordination of constellation activities. The need for a secretariat is evident, considering that the four constellation partners – South Africa, Transkei, Bophuthatswana and Venda – had by mid-1981 already established 19 multilateral functional committees and working groups at senior official level. Upon achieving independence in December 1981 Ciskei became the fifth member of the constellation.

The multilateral division is engaged in endeavours to create further formal inter-state structures for co-operation, the ultimate objective being that the constellation members will co-operate closely on the four fronts of inter-state political, economic, social and security matters. Relations have already been institutionalised in the economic and social areas, while in the political field an embryo Council of States has emerged with the summit meeting of the heads of government of South Africa, Transkei, Bophuthatswana and Venda in July 1980. The foreign ministers of the four countries have also held a number of meetings.* The chart on pp. 128-9 shows the present and the desired measure of institutionalisation of relations in the constellation. The multilateral committees established by the end of 1981 fall into five broad areas to which it was decided to give priority: agriculture, health, posts and telecommunications, transport, and education and training.[117]

In discharging its responsibilities in the field of development assistance, the economic and development co-operation branch works in tandem with the inter-departmental committee for economic and development co-operation

(known by its Afrikaans acronym, KEOSSA).[118] Requests for official South African aid are channelled to the branch, which then submits them to KEOSSA. Established in 1979, KEOSSA is an advisory body chaired by the Director-General of Foreign Affairs and composed of about 30 representatives of other government departments and institutions (including the Departments of Transport Affairs and of Agriculture, and the physical and security planning branches in the Prime Minister's Office*), and also institutions such as BENSO, the Industrial Development Corporation and the privately-owned Credit Guarantee Insurance Corporation.** The head of the economic and development co-operation branch (Mr Deon Richter) features prominently on KEOSSA and was one of its principal architects.

KEOSSA concerns itself virtually exclusively with development assistance for South Africa's ex-homelands, but there is said to be growing interest from some other (internationally recognised) black states in obtaining South African aid. KEOSSA, it should be explained, does not offer aid, since the South African government insists on written applications for development assistance. This policy may well change, and KEOSSA could then also suggest aid projects to other countries. KEOSSA's responsibilities include overseeing South African development assistance through all its stages – known as a "project cycle" – from the application through planning and implementation to evaluation.

South Africa finances its foreign aid from three main sources: the economic co-operation promotion loan fund, established in 1968, which disburses soft loans; budgetary allocations for technical assistance (R6,5 million in 1981) and a statutory allocation for three years awarded to homelands achieving independence, which may

---

*Although the physical and security planning branches have since been transferred from the Prime Minister's Office to other institutions, they are in their new roles still represented on KEOSSA.

**The Industrial Development Corporation (IDC) was established in 1940 mainly to help finance new industries and expand and improve existing ones. It is funded largely from government sources. Credit Guarantee Insurance Corporation of Africa Limited is a South African company owned by a consortium of leading insurance companies, banks and financial institutions. Its major business is the insurance of export and domestic credit risks. Export credit risks are underwritten in co-operation with the government.

---

*In November 1982 another summit was held between the leaders of the "SATBVC" countries (South Africa and the former homelands). In May 1983 a multilateral Development Council of Ministers was inaugurated, and it will serve as an umbrella policy making body.

thereafter be converted to budgetary assistance.

Development assistance is of course widely used as an instrument of foreign policy by industrialised countries. In South Africa's case it has so far had a strictly limited application, since the Republic's official aid flows primarily to its independent former homelands. States such as Malawi and Lesotho have, however, also received development assistance from South Africa. Apart from the Minister of Foreign Affairs some other ministers also have a role to play, depending on the nature of the aid. Thus agricultural aid would involve the Minister of Agriculture and Fisheries, transport aid concerns the Minister of Transport Affairs, and so forth. It is conceivable that major aid projects are considered by the SSC. As for bureaucratic input into decision making on foreign aid, the two key bodies would be the economic and development co-operation branch in the foreign ministry and the inter-departmental KEOSSA.

The planning division

The idea behind the planning division was to create an in-house think tank that would perform a continual and thorough analysis of international issues, particularly as they affect South Africa. Its work is intended to be policy-oriented, which means that it would, for example, formulate alternative policy options and in some cases recommend specific courses of action. The division would, ideally, through anticipation, innovation and recommendation, equip the foreign policy formulators to move away from a reactive *ad hoc* conduct of foreign policy, and instead to formulate longer term policy ends and select the appropriate means. The intention is to staff the division with officers freed from day-to-day office duties to allow them to devote their full attention to the planning division. In a sense, members of the division should stand apart from the operational units of the ministry. An important requirement for the division's success is that it has to enjoy special access to the head of the department and via him to the minister.

In practice the planning division found itself absorbed in day-to-day foreign policy issues at the expense of longer term, thoroughgoing policy studies. It is particularly with the Namibian issue, South Africa's major foreign policy preoccupation, that members of the division have been directly concerned. This is probably largely because many of them have long been involved with the issue and their knowledge is still required. Another reason may be that the Foreign Minister included in his team on the Namibian issue officials who are closest to him – and the planning division houses some of them. On Namibia specifically the planning division is, with the exception of Secretary/Director-General Fourie, the foreign ministry's main source of expertise and no doubt an influential voice in policy formulation.

The first head of the division was Mr NP van Heerden, who was subsequently appointed ambassador in West Germany. He was succeeded by Mr JA Eksteen, who for a time combined the post with that of South Africa's UN ambassador.* The planning division consists of only six officials. Van Heerden and Eksteen, both in their forties, were two of the most prominent members of the new generation of South African diplomats. Their heading the planning division and becoming ambassadors at a relatively early age reflect their standing in the foreign ministry. They have both been deeply involved with the international negotiations over Namibia.

In existence for a relatively short period and preoccupied with Namibia, the planning division's impact on the wider foreign policy front has been very limited. It is quite possible that the division has also had difficulty getting its *bona fides* accepted within the foreign ministry. There is bound to be apprehension about a seemingly elitist unit that concerns itself with matters falling within the sphere of responsibility of other divisions.

To be really effective in policy formulation the planning division has to ensure that its contributions reach the SSC. This can be done in two ways. Both the Foreign Minister and the departmental head are standing members of the Council, and the head of the planning division often attends meetings of the working committee of the SSC, whether jointly with the Director-General or as his representative. As such, the planning head is more than an influential departmental adviser. He belongs to the bureaucratic outer circle of foreign policy formulators (the SSC being the inner circle), since the Council's working committee has the power to make certain decisions, also on foreign affairs. If a decision is

---

*In a surprise move, Eksteen was in early 1983 appointed Director-General-designate of the South African Broadcasting Corporation. He was succeeded as head of the planning division by Mr DW Steward, previously South Africa's UN ambassador.

considered important enough, it is referred to the SSC for approval.

Training

Departmental training of foreign service officers used to be handled by a division within the administration branch. It was only in 1969 that a formal training unit was established in the foreign ministry. Prior to that, foreign service cadets were given *ad hoc* lectures, leaving a great deal to in-service training.[119]

Following the merger between Foreign Affairs and Information, the training programme for the diplomatic service had to be somewhat adjusted to meet the needs of the expanded department's branches concerned with information activities. In the days of two separate departments, each had its own training unit. In 1981, for the first time, a single comprehensive training programme catering for the political and information branches was introduced. The cadets are all treated equally; no-one is trained specifically for either political or information duties. Having completed their training, cadets are eligible for service in the political, consular, information or protocol section.The training period lasts between 12 and 18 months. Some seven or eight months of the time are spent on full-time training at the training centre in Pretoria, the rest is in-service training. Three officials with the rank of counsellor are responsible for training.

Thirteen cadets enrolled for the new training course begun in 1981. This is a significant drop from the average annual intake of 20 that Foreign Affairs had in the past. Among the 13 was the first coloured cadet in the foreign service; the Department of Information, however, had coloured and Indian officers abroad. In 1981, as on previous occasions, training was also offered to blacks from a homeland destined to become independent – in this case from Ciskei.*

An established requirement for selection as a foreign service cadet is possession of an academic degree. The cadet course has its own strong academic content, with courses in diplomacy, economics, politics, constitutional and international law, and a foreign language. It is particularly in the course in politics (which includes such subjects as South Africa's constitutional and policy-making structures; the politics of black African states and of the great

---

*In 1982 the Department enrolled 17 trainees (one of whom was a coloured) and 23 in 1983.

powers; international organisations and topical international issues) that considerable use is made of academics and other outside experts to lecture the cadets. For the rest, courses are conducted by the training division personnel and other foreign ministry officials, with some involvement of representatives from other departments and state institutions. Apart from the more academic side, the cadet training programme also has a practice-oriented dimension, officially styled "functional training". This includes a course in communication, a product of Foreign Affairs' merger with Information.

Foreign representation

A highly visible and indeed prestigious element of a foreign ministry is its network of missions abroad. South Africa is represented abroad by diplomatic and consular missions. Although these are two different forms of representation, the Department of Foreign Affairs and Information draws no distinction between diplomatic and consular personnel. They all belong to one and the same foreign service and they may serve in both diplomatic and consular capacities.[120]

A feature of South Africa's representation abroad is that it is thinly spread. In the period since 1966 South Africa's diplomatic network has expanded in absolute terms, but has contracted when related to the growth in the number of internationally recognised states. Consider the following table[121]:

Year	UN membership	Number of countries in which SA has diplomatic missions
1966	122	22
1975	144	29
1980	154	28
1982	157	29

In addition to the 28 countries in which South Africa in 1980 had diplomatic representation, it was represented in 15 or more at consular level only (including the non-state entities of Hong Kong and Reunion) and by only trade representatives in two more (Mauritius and Ireland). Among the 28 states mentioned were South Africa's three independent former homelands, but not Zimbabwe, which severed diplomatic links with South Africa following independence in April 1980. The Republic in 1980 also maintained permanent diplomatic missions at the UN in both New York and Geneva, and at the European Community in Brussels. In countries where South Africa enjoyed only consular representation, consular missions performed some diplomatic functions, too. The fact that South Africa has only consular representation in countries such as Norway, Denmark, New Zealand and Japan, reflects adversely on the state of relations with them. In many of the states where South Africa maintains embassies it also has consular representation.

As regards foreign representation in South Africa, 24 foreign countries in 1976 had diplomatic missions, and 26 in 1981. The latter figure includes Transkei, Bophuthatswana and Venda. (In 1982 28 countries, including four ex-homelands, maintained diplomatic missions in South Africa.)[122]

The geographical distribution of South Africa's foreign representation underlines the country's isolation from major segments of the international community. In 1980 South Africa had embassies in seven of the then nine EC member states, and had either consular or trade representation in the remaining two. In nine other European states, all non-communist, South Africa was also represented. It maintained no official links with any communist state. In the Americas, South Africa had embassies in the United States and Canada and some form of representation in 13 Central and South American states. In Australasia, South Africa was represented in Australia and New Zealand; in the Far East, in Japan, Taiwan and Hong Kong. Nowhere is South Africa's diplomatic isolation more vividly reflected than in Africa, where the Republic in 1980 enjoyed diplomatic relations with only one internationally recognised black state, Malawi. South Africa lost its representation (consulates-general) in Angola and Mozambique when they became independent in 1975. The diplomatic links South Africa had with Zimbabwe-Rhodesia before independence were subsequently replaced by mutual trade representation. In the Middle East, South Africa was represented only in Israel after 1974, the year in which the Republic's consulate-general in Lebanon was closed.

The distribution of South African missions abroad clearly reveals the Republic's heavy Western fixation, its traditional foreign policy posture. The significance of the Western powers in the Republic's external environment is further borne out by the size and number of South African offices in particular Western states. In terms of staff complement, the five largest missions in 1980 were London (229), Paris (70), Bonn (54), Washington (51), and The Hague (35).[123] South

Africa also maintained more than one consular mission in four of these countries: two in the United Kingdom; nine in the United States; seven in West Germany and three in France.[124]

Not only the Department of Foreign Affairs and Information has representatives abroad. Attached to many South African diplomatic or consular missions are also a host of representatives from other state institutions, notably military attachés, trade representatives, immigration officers, agricultural counsellors, scientific counsellors, cultural attachés, labour representatives and agents from the National Intelligence Service. The attached personnel normally report directly to their head office in Pretoria, but they are nonetheless responsible to the head of the mission where they are stationed. There have been frequent calls from these and also from other (unrepresented) official institutions to have their own representatives abroad. At one stage there was even talk of appointing sports attachés at some South African missions.

The Department of Foreign Affairs and Information in 1981 employed 697 people at its head office in Pretoria and 1 555 abroad. Of the total number of employees of the Department 596 were classified as foreign service and information officers; the remainder were administrative and auxiliary personnel, a large number of them locally recruited people working in South Africa's missions abroad. With the merger of the Departments of Foreign Affairs and of Information in 1980, 536 officials formerly attached to Information joined the new enlarged ministry.[125]

The convention of appointing politicians to ambassadorial posts has in recent years been maintained. Like before, the ambassadorships that went to political appointees were particularly those in the United States, United Kingdom and Western Europe. National Party politicians who have in the last decade been appointed as ambassadors include Pik Botha (Washington and the UN); Dr CPC de Wet, Dr DJ de Villiers and Mr SJM Steyn (all London); Mr B Coetzee (Rome); Mr LA Pienaar (Paris); Mr JH Visse (Berne); Mr PH Meyer (Vienna) and Dr P Bodenstein (The Hague). A new diplomatic field, particularly for politicians, opened with the granting of independence to black homelands. South Africa's first ambassadors to Bophuthatswana and Venda, Dr WL Vosloo and Mr PD Palm respectively, were formerly National

Party MPs. As always the government probably had a variety of motives in appointing these politicians to diplomatic posts. In some cases it was obvious promotion for an MP, an intermediary step before being elevated to the Cabinet; Pik Botha and De Villiers fall into this category. Alternatively ambassadorships may be used as a convenient means of easing out of office Cabinet ministers whose services are, for whatever reason, no longer required or desired; Coetzee[126] and Steyn, and to some extent De Wet (for his second term in London) probably earned their diplomatic "honours" in this way. In other cases a diplomatic appointment may be a consolation for an MP failing to enter the Cabinet, or a way of removing a caucus member who has fallen foul of the party leadership.

Whatever the reasons for such appointments, there is a convention that not more than four or five ambassadorships (excluding those in the former black homelands) be filled at any one time by political appointees. The official view is that there is no strict "quota" for political appointments, but an "understanding" that the number of political appointees should not be so great that professional diplomats feel they are being pushed out.[127] While the career officials display great understanding for the practice of political appointments, they understandably strongly resent the diplomatic corps being used (or abused) as a "dumping ground" for unwanted politicians. To aggravate matters, such politicans often fail miserably in diplomacy too. Yet, as professional diplomats readily acknowledge, many political appointees prove highly successful ambassadors. From the career diplomats' point of view political appointments may actually have some advantages: the politicians may bring in new ideas; politicians gain first-hand experience of what diplomatic duties involve; and they may help to promote understanding between the foreign ministry and Parliament.[128]

South Africa in 1980-81 was nearing the end of an era in its diplomatic service, as the ranks of officials who entered it in the early post-war years or even earlier – when Smuts was still in power – were rapidly thinning out. Many of those who joined in this period were strong supporters of Smuts and were to some extent perhaps even attracted to the foreign service by Smuts's standing as an international statesman. Among recently retired members of the old generation of South African diplomats – a predominantly English-speaking generation and one that produced a fair number of ambassadors – a strong lack of identification with National Party policies is evident. There is also a feeling of sorrow at having seen, at first hand, South Africa slide into ever greater isolation over the years. For this phenomenon the Nationalist government is held primarily responsible. The government is said to have failed to give its friends overseas – and South African diplomats abroad – encouragement through (changing) its domestic policies and actions.

Two of the very few members of the old generation diplomats still serving in 1981 were Fourie and Sole. The most senior of South African diplomats in the field – having joined the foreign service in 1938 – the able, hard-working Sole enjoys a high regard in both South African and foreign diplomatic services for his abilities. Sole distinguished himself on the international diplomatic scene through his role as the South African representative on the board of governors of the International Atomic Energy Agency and, in 1959-60, as chairman of the board. With this generation of diplomats disappearing, South Africa's diplomatic service will soon be staffed exclusively by officials who joined after the National Party had come to power. They will have had no experience of the (relatively) "good old days" in South Africa's foreign relations, instead knowing the country only as something of an international outcast.

Since the old (Smuts) generation of diplomats consisted of so many English-speakers, a word needs to be said about the position of English-speaking officials in the foreign ministry after 1948. The fact that so many of them became ambassadors[129] would seem sufficient evidence that they were not discriminated against. It was, nonetheless, argued by some of them that Afrikaners received preference when it came to key ambassadorships – they were on the inside track, so to speak – and that London, for one, would not be entrusted to an English-speaking official. A more commonly held view is that the position of departmental head is strictly reserved for an Afrikaner. Such notions are based on the fact that the secretaryship of the Department has been in Afrikaner hands since 1956 and the head of South Africa's mission in London has since 1950 been an Afrikaner.

In Washington, by contrast, two recent ambassadors were English-speaking: Sole and one of his predecessors, Mr HLT Taswell. The two appointments are explained, by those claiming Afrikaners were advantaged, as being exceptional: Sole was an outstanding diplomat, and Taswell was known for his pro-government political leanings. While it might be true that political considerations influenced (professional) diplomatic appointments to the London and Washington posts, this certainly does not apply as a general rule. Both Afrikaans and English-speaking diplomats known to support opposition parties have reached the top rungs of the diplomatic ladder. But despite such indications of political and language equality, the other features mentioned suggest that Afrikaners and Nationalists – but particularly Afrikaner-Nationalists – are in some important respects "more equal" than other officials. Related to claims about discrimination against English-speakers, especially anti-government English-speaking diplomats, is the contention that some of these officials were painfully aware of the suspicion with which they were viewed by ordinary Nationalist MPs and even Cabinet members. This was apparently not a widely shared experience, or at any rate not one that caused much concern among English-speaking diplomats. That there were Nationalist politicians unhappy with the political leanings of some diplomats is, however, entirely conceivable.

While on the subject of ambassadorial appointments, reservations have often been expressed about the foreign ministry's professional judgement. Attributes such as language skills, and knowledge of and interest in particular countries and regions are said to be insufficiently weighed. There is a saying among diplomats that South African missions have become like magistrates' offices, with a constant coming and going of heads, some well equipped for their duties and others singularly ill prepared. Of course, it has to be recognised that it is simply impossible to please everybody all the time. Yet it would seem that the particular qualities of diplomats have on occasion not been acknowledged or effectively utilised, and that they were sometimes placed in inappropriate posts abroad.

As regards the relations between the "men at the front" and the "men at home" Munger wrote that "Pretoria keeps very tight reins on those stationed abroad."[130] This is a sweeping generalisation and does not correspond with the experience of many retired ambassadors. Munger cited as an exception the then head of the mission in Sweden, Mr AAM Hamilton. Hamilton had in fact been given a relatively free hand to improve the very poor relations between South Africa and Sweden following the disappointing performance of his predecessor in the post. South Africa's ambassadors in South America were also given considerable scope to expand the Republic's relations with states in the region. The diplomats in the field who probably enjoyed the greatest measure of freedom were the political appointees for whom ambassadorships were political rewards or promotions. The head office of the foreign ministry could hardly keep a tight rein over an ambassador who is an up-and-coming protégé of the Prime Minister. Other ambassadors' freedom of action might have been deliberately curtailed by Pretoria where it was considered prudent for them to adopt a low profile in their host countries so as to avoid attracting unnecessary and unfriendly attention.

A particularly important contention of Munger's that requires consideration is that South African ambassadors as a general rule "do not carry as much weight in the formation of South African foreign policy as they do for some nations."[131] The concern here is not with the extremely vaguely formulated comparison in Munger's statement – which would in any case be difficult to verify – but rather with the actual contribution of ambassadors to policy formulation. Foreign policy recommendations may well originate in a state's missions abroad. Former South African ambassadors hold widely divergent views on the weight attached to their situation reports by head office and the policy formulators. On the one hand, there are those who confidently state that their reports received due recognition at head office and were also read by those in high authority. On the other hand, it is known that diplomats abroad have a habit of wondering aloud "what the cadets in Pretoria are going to think of my report". An often heard complaint is that ambassadors seldom get any feedback on their reports, thus leaving them in the dark about the reception they had received at head office. One explanation that has been offered for the lack of feedback is that the foreign ministry is too highly centralised, leaving too few people with the authority to respond.

The importance that the policy formulators attach to ambassadors' submissions is probably influenced by a number of considerations: the professional standing of the particular ambassador; the topicality and quality of the ambassador's contribution; the political sentiments of the author of a report (these might either add weight to his submission or detract from it); and the availability of other sources of information and expertise on the issue at hand. Ambassadors' contributions, however important, are by no means the only ingredient in the making of policy decisions. Domestic political considerations, for example, also feature and may very often not be kind to the exigencies of foreign policy, to which the ambassadors would draw attention. Given this complicated picture, it is difficult to formulate a reliable general rule about the weight ambassadors carry in South African foreign policy formulation.

As regards the flow of communication from Pretoria to its diplomats in the field, a frequent complaint of ambassadors has been that they are not kept sufficiently informed on government policies and intentions. Even if the volume of information material sent to ambassadors is impressive – particularly since Pik Botha became Minister – and contains elaborate *ex post facto* reviews of government policies, it is notably weak on explaining the reasons behind decisions and outlining the government's intentions. While it might be politically expedient for the government to be reticent on these two matters, it only serves to complicate the already arduous task of South African ambassadors operating in hostile foreign environments. A glimpse of better things to come on the domestic front could bring welcome relief to South African diplomats labouring under heavy political pressure abroad. The lack of "deep" background information leads to the feeling that the government is unwilling to take ambassadors into its confidence.

The major means used to brief ambassadors are a regular departmental circular, *Policy Review,* and conferences of ambassadors. Conferences take two forms: a general conference, usually held annually in a foreign country, attended by the Foreign Minister and the head of the department, and on occasion by the Prime Minister; and regional conferences attended by ambassadors stationed in a particular region. Vorster, for example, was present at an ambassadors' conference in South America when he visited countries in the area in 1975, and at another in Bonn in 1976 on the occasion of his visit to West Germany to meet Kissinger. PW Botha has not attended any meeting of South African ambassadors abroad. The value of the regular conferences with the Foreign Minister is a matter of dispute. There is a feeling among ambassadors that the flow of communication is largely one-way, with little opportunity for a real exchange of views. For this situation Fourie is blamed: as chairman of the meetings, he is said to have exercised rigid control over the agenda and proceedings. Some ambassadors have nonetheless used the occasion of general conferences to express their dissatisfaction to Foreign Minister Muller about their being insufficiently briefed on government policies and intentions. Ambassadors who have no reason for complaint on this score are the political appointees, who enjoy close personal relations with key policy formulators. This enables the representatives to be better informed on government thinking than ambassadors generally. Two recent examples are De Wet (London), a former Cabinet minister and close friend of Vorster, and Pik Botha (Washington), who had also been on close terms with Vorster.

A factor that might have contributed to ambassadors feeling inadequately informed on developments on the home front is that long, uninterrupted periods of service abroad make them lose touch with the nuances of the situation in South Africa. The Department has no hard and fast rules on the length of foreign tours of duty. Nonetheless a diplomat normally qualifies for home leave after three years (or two years, or in some cases even annually for someone serving in a tropical country), and then usually returns to his post for a further 18 to 24 months. Thereafter a person is normally kept at head office for anything from two to four years. There are exceptions to this general practice, and diplomats are on occasion transferred directly from one mission to another, without an interim tour of duty in Pretoria.

An "occupational hazard" to which South African diplomats (and also information officers) are probably more consistently exposed than any of their foreign counterparts is a "tremendous emotional hammering"[132] caused by the international disapprobation of their government's domestic policies. The intensity of the hammering varies from place to place, being particularly acute at the UN and in European states such as Sweden and The Netherlands.

The government's racial policies, as South African ambassadors widely acknowledge, are not a saleable commodity abroad, least of all their many blatantly discriminatory features. In some countries there may however be some understanding for the rationale of the separate development grand design – the creation of black homelands – but this is undermined by the political status given to the Indian, coloured and urban black communities, and by petty apartheid measures and practices. What aggravates the situation for South Africa's foreign representatives – and this is indeed a general complaint – is a seeming lack of direction on the government's part: for example, in 1974 at the UN it publicly committed itself to remove racial discrimination, but has done precious little to give effect to the undertaking. A further complicating and highly frustrating factor with which diplomats have to contend is ill-considered pronouncements by South African politicians. Designed for the home audience, remarks that are racist in intent or effect often cause South Africa severe embarrassment abroad.

So serious a political handicap are the government's racial policies that diplomats widely believe no amount of sophisticated or unorthodox marketing would in the end have made the product internationally acceptable. The Department of Information's efforts, it is argued, were doomed to failure. While it can be remarked that it is easy for diplomats to be wise after the Information debacle, there is no denying the misgivings that ambassadors all along had about Information's activities, particularly its so-called unconventional diplomacy. In many instances the heads of missions were not informed about the pursuits of their Information personnel, and this was strongly resented by ambassadors and caused tension between them and the Information officers. In only one or two exceptional cases did an ambassador manage to bring the Information section firmly under his control.

To conclude the discussion of South Africa's diplomatic service it is worth noting how former ambassadors view their foreign ministers. There is high regard for Hilgard Muller's personal qualities; his quiet, gentlemanly diplomatic style is widely seen as particularly suited to South Africa's peculiar international position. After the aggressive, brusque Louw who gave so much offence to foreign diplomats and politicians, Muller gave South African diplomacy a new respectable image abroad. It is, however, also said that Muller tended to be too accommodating, showing a lack of tenacity and drive in international negotiations. As the political head of the foreign ministry Muller fared rather poorly in the eyes of his former subordinates. He is typically regarded as a weak protector of his department's interests (a feature that earned him an unpublishable nickname in the Department); the Department of Information's intrusion into the diplomatic domain is cited as the example *par excellence* of Muller's weakness.

As regards Pik Botha, there is appreciation for his vigour and dedication, but reservations about his theatrical style. While his style may initially impress foreigners, it is said that Pik Botha takes things too far and in due course this enlists negative reaction abroad. As one seasoned former diplomat explained, Pik Botha talks too much and too easily; he has a propensity for making categorical statements that often force him to back down later, thereby undermining his credibility.

Esprit de corps

What intrigues many present and former officials is the relationship between Pik Botha and Secretary Fourie, bearing in mind that the Minister had long been a subordinate of Fourie's. The general belief is that relations are rather strained, with the ever cautious Fourie cramping his forceful Minister's style, as it were. Their differences permeate the rest of the Department to the extent that officials are labelled as being either a "Pik man" or a "Brand man". Such a division must inevitably have a negative impact on the Department's *esprit de corps*.

Among the Minister's men is a small circle of relatively young officials whom Pik Botha grouped around himself, known as the "Washington Mafia" or "Pik's kindergarten". It consists of officials who served under Pik Botha in Washington and at the UN. Two of them have since become ambassadors: Van Heerden in Bonn and Eksteen at the UN. Appointed as UN ambassador in 1979 (having served at the UN under Pik Botha, 1974-6), Eksteen was at 37 South Africa's youngest ambassador.[133] A third member is Mr DW Auret who served at the UN under Pik Botha and has subsequently been posted to the planning division. Auret has long been involved with the Namibian issue. It might be that the professional fortunes of Pik's kindergarten will be closely tied to the political fortunes of the Minister – something that might in future prove a mixed blessing to the officials concerned. Among foreign ministry officials not part of the inner circle there is considerable resentment about what is seen as the Washington Mafia's favoured treatment. This feature can only undermine departmental morale. The Foreign Minister, it should be pointed out, denies the existence of such an inner group.[134]

Among the South African public Eksteen is probably one of the country's best known professional diplomats because of the extensive publicity given in the local media to his role at the UN. This kind of public exposure, which contrasts sharply with Foreign Affairs' traditional aversion to publicity, is a product of Foreign Minister Botha's period. Under him the Department has become much more accessible to the media than ever before. The ministry does not have an official spokesman, as for example the US State Department, but there is a branch responsible for liaison services. In practice, however, the media liaise directly with the official(s) involved with the issue in question, such as Eksteen on Namibia.

Greater departmental exposure to the media fits in well with Pik Botha's own high visibility in domestic politics. The Minister's high public profile and his controversial championing of *verligte* causes have had implications for his department. The ministry, too, has easily been labelled a bastion of *verligtheid*-cum-liberalism, particularly by the Minister's right-wing critics. The former Department of Foreign Affairs had certainly been politically the most enlightened of all government departments on the overriding political issue of racial policies. Since the merger with the Department of Information the picture may have changed somewhat, since it is known that many Information officials incline to the conservative political views of their erstwhile Minister.

While discussing *esprit de corps*, one can justifiably ask how smoothly the amalgamation of the former Departments of Foreign Affairs and Information is working. In the diplomatic service there is evident satisfaction at Information being "brought under control". The former Foreign Affairs has decisively reasserted itself in the foreign policy making process, with the remains of Information effectively reduced to an instrumental role. In this respect the merger between the two departments has not produced a new partnership, but served to re-establish Foreign Affairs' authority. Perhaps it is then more appropriate to talk of Information having been absorbed by Foreign Affairs.

Among long-serving information officers the new dispensation is viewed with apprehension. There is a discernible feeling of being discriminated against and regarded as second-rate officials by their old Foreign Affairs colleagues. A typical complaint is that at a South African mission abroad a member of the political (diplomatic) branch may enjoy a higher status with greater material benefits (e.g. an official vehicle) than an information officer who is his senior in rank. A development galling to information personnel is that some ambassadors seized upon the merger between the two departments as an opportunity to exert excessively strong control over their missions' information officers, as if to get their own back for the years Information had disregarded ambassadors' authority. The relations between the two formerly separate departments are "as in a forced marriage", an experienced information official said. Suggestions about strains between the two have also surfaced publicly from time to time.[135]

Shortly after the formation of the Department of Foreign Affairs and Information Pik Botha announced that former Information officials would also qualify for ambassadorships – a statement that apparently displeased some diplomats.[136] By the end of 1981 no such official had yet become an ambassador. As far as could be established, two ex-Information officials holding key positions in the Department of Foreign Affairs and Information have been offered ambassadorships: the one in Portugal and the other in Venda. Neither accepted: in the one case, personal considerations (of which his superiors could hardly have been unaware) made it impossible for the official to accept a position abroad; in the other case, the official concerned was an authority on black languages – but not that spoken in Venda. The offers made to the two officials are therefore seen as a rather cynical exercise, apart from the fact that a post in Venda is probably the very lowest rung on the diplomatic ladder. In the meantime their continued absence from the rank of ambassadors tends to feed the suspicions of Information personnel. Not surprisingly, quite a few former Information officials resigned in the wake of the amalgamation with Foreign Affairs, fearing that their career prospects had been considerably diminished.

The foreign ministry and the State Security Council

The elevation of the SSC to a key organ in foreign policy formulation has meant that the foreign ministry, like others, now finds itself in a new decision-making milieu in which new rules apply. The adjustment has not always been easy for Foreign Affairs. On the one hand, there is the uneasy feeling, even resentment, among foreign ministry officials that they are frequently "browbeaten" by the well-organised and determined – some would say ruthless – military elite. On foreign policy matters, specifically Southern African issues, Foreign Affairs and the military are indeed the two main actors on the SSC and its working committee. Some foreign ministry sensitivities may well have been offended by the military, but that decidedly does not mean that the military dominates foreign policy decision making on the Council. One of the advantages Foreign Affairs sees in the SSC system is that it offers a potential safeguard against any one state institution acting in a unilateral fashion on matters of vital national interest. The Council provides a central forum where a range of interested parties can in a regularised and formalised fashion contribute to decision making. The foreign ministry is thus represented not only on the Council itself and its working committee, but also on various inter-departmental sub-committees of the SSC where it can claim a legitimate interest. On others it can ask to be co-opted when relevant matters come under consideration. The most positive self-assessment of Foreign Affairs' role in the SSC system is that the Department is recognised by the other participants as being at least first among equals on foreign policy issues. Although other ministries have been given a voice in foreign policy formulation, it is said that this feature in the end makes for more balanced decisions. This observation also applies to decision making on other matters where the foreign ministry can express its views; these often involve pointing out the possible international repercussions of domestic policies and actions. As for the argument that the Prime Minister strengthened the military's position on the Council because of his having been Defence Minister, it is said in foreign ministry circles that PW Botha has been very successful in freeing himself from the military embrace and that he acts as a more or less impartial chairman of the SSC – while still giving the Council a firm lead.

An interesting side-effect of the SSC's role in foreign policy formulation is that it serves to undermine what Lerche and Said depict as the "aura of preferment", which foreign ministry officials in many states enjoy because of the nature of their responsibilities. It would nonetheless be true to say that South Africa's foreign ministry personnel still form part of "the inner bureaucratic elite within the government".[137] A powerful recent entrant into the inner circle has been the military.

Finances

The accompanying table shows the budgetary allocations for the Departments of Foreign Affairs and Information respectively in select years, and the budget for the single Department of Foreign Affairs and Information.[138]

Year	Foreign Affairs	Information	Foreign Affairs and Information
	R million	R million	R million
1970/71	8,25	5,73	—
1974/75	13,85	10,65	—
1977/78	33,90	15,37	—
1980/81	—	—	234,81
1981/82	—	—	340,95
1982/83	—	—	525,70

It is not only the Department of Information that engaged in secret activities and had financial sources other than the above allocations at its disposal. Already in 1965 an item marked "secret services" appeared on the Department of Foreign Affairs' budget. In 1965 and 1966 R500 000 was earmarked for what Foreign Minister Muller explained as the promotion of the Republic's foreign relations "in unorthodox fashion".[139] The *Foreign Affairs Special Account Act*, 1967, provided for funds to be spent on secret activities at the discretion of the Minister of Foreign Affairs. Unlike Information, the Department of Foreign Affairs has managed to keep its secret operations strictly secret, even down to the money involved. A further source was made available to the new Department of Foreign Affairs and Information through the already mentioned *Secret Services Account Act*, 1978, The funds thus available were mainly spent on secret "information" projects – to use departmental jargon – while the funds provided for by the 1967 legislation were used for "political" activities.

Since 1970/71 the departmental budget has provided for a different kind of expenditure under the heading "assistance to and co-operation with foreign countries". The following amounts were provided for in a number of select years:

1978: R13,6 million
1980: R136,6 million
1981: R218,4 million
1982: R434,0 million

The bulk of the funds were spent on economic, agricultural and indirect financial assistance and on seconding officials to independent ex-homelands. Since 1968 the foreign ministry has also had access to a loan fund, established by law, set up to promote economic development. Although former homelands have been the major recipients of loans and grants from the fund, Lesotho, Malawi, Mauritius and the Central African Republic have also benefited.[140]

The Defence Force

When considering the involvement of bureaucratic groups in the formulation of foreign policy, "special attention needs to be paid to the role of the military", Jensen wrote. "As international conflict becomes more ubiquitous and national security is seen as a more critical issue, one might expect to see the military assuming a more prominent role in such policy."[141] This expectation has become reality in South Africa.

Total onslaught and total national strategy

The Defence Force's growing involvement in policy making has been the product of the security situation in Southern Africa. The Defence Force has since the 1960s been involved in a guerrilla war on Namibia's northern border. SWAPO's military offensive is seen in Pretoria as a manifestation of a communist threat ultimately directed at South Africa. The long perceived communist menace assumed a greater reality and urgency in the course of the 1970s. A watershed event was the collapse of Portugal's African empire. South Africa became embroiled in the resultant civil war in Angola, as did several thousand Cuban soldiers. More recently the Defence Force has become involved in protecting South Africa's own frontiers against ANC insurgents. In January 1981 the Defence Force launched its first known military attack on ANC targets on foreign soil, when it raided ANC establishments near Maputo.

It is against the background of growing threats to South Africa's security that the military began talking of a "total onslaught" on the Republic, and of the need for a counter-strategy. The latter opened the door to the military to involve itself with major decision making on both foreign and domestic matters.

The 1973 White Paper on Defence first introduced the concept of a "total strategy", as it was then styled. It emphasised "the interaction and inter-dependence" of "three basic elements", namely internal policy, foreign policy and defence policy. "The last is determined by the preceding two, but these, in turn, cannot be developed properly unless they are sustained by a sound and adequate defence policy."[142] South Africa's national defence, the 1975 Defence White Paper explained, could not be based entirely or even primarily on military capability, but the latter was vital to ensure a "firm base from which the State can employ its other means". In a foreign policy context, it means that the preparedness of the Defence Force "is a guarantee that a policy of weakness and appeasement need not be followed"; domestically, it provides a guarantee that South Africa "will solve its problems in an orderly manner and without interference" (from outside).[143] These statements acknowledge the limitations on the role of the military instrument in safeguarding South Africa's internal and external security, and imply that the ultimate answer is political. The task of grappling with the political problems is however not to be entrusted to politicians alone. Far from being confined to the role of a neutral guardian of the peace or holder of the fort, the military would, thanks to a "total national strategy", become an active participant in political decision making.

The 1977 Defence White Paper, which was largely devoted to an exposition of the concept of a total national strategy, offered the following definition:

> The comprehensive plan to utilize all the means available to a state according to an integrated pattern in order to achieve the national aims within the framework of specific policies.[144]

A crucial feature of a total national strategy is that it embraces the totality of state structures and functions.

As Minister of Defence, PW Botha has been an ardent exponent of a total national strategy, but it was only after he had become prime minister that the concept really became operationalised. The utilisation of the state's "means" is to be done through a national security management system, with the SSC at its centre. Magnus Malan defined the means of the state in terms of "four power bases", the political/diplomatic, the economic, the social/psychological, and the security base.[145]

The "national aims" are not new: they are set out in the preamble to the South African constitution and include safeguarding the inviolability and freedom of the Republic. The "specific policies" are not new either, having first been expressed in a concise, if not precise, "12-point plan" by Prime Minister PW Botha in August 1979. The plan articulates 12 policy objectives for a broad spectrum of government activities at home and abroad. Of particular relevance are point 9, which declares South Africa's "firm determination to defend itself against interference from outside in every possible way"; point 10, which favours "a policy of neutrality", as far as possible, in superpower conflict; and point 11, which commits the government to "the maintenance of effective decision making by the State, which rests on a strong Defence Force to guarantee orderly government as well as efficient, clean administration".[146]

Structure of the "defence family"

The Defence Force is composed of the Permanent Force, the Citizen Force and the Commandos. The latter two consist of all non-career members of the Defence Force, such as volunteers and national servicemen. The Permanent Force comprises the Army, Navy, Air Force and Medical Services and their respective supporting services. In October 1981 the Permanent Force consisted of 33 000 members, and the number of national servicemen (called up for two years) was 58 000.[147] The chiefs of the four services – Army, Navy, Air Force and Medical Services – report to the Chief of the Defence Force, who in turn is responsible to the Minister of Defence. Apart from his command function, the Chief of the Defence Force is also head of the Department of Defence, thus carrying the same responsibilities as the directors-general of other state departments. General Constand Viljoen in September 1980 succeeded Malan as Chief of the Defence Force, when the latter was appointed Minister of Defence.

Within the wider Defence Force establishment, it is necessary to single out the institutions producing the men and ideas influencing policy making. The only institution providing academic training is the Military Academy at Saldanha Bay. The Academy, which houses the Faculty of Military Science of the University of Stellenbosch, offers first and subsequent degrees in Military Science. In 1981 150 students attended the Academy. The percentage of graduate officers in the Permanent Force stood at 16,3% in 1981, excluding the Medical Services and the Chaplain-General's staff. With these included the figure rose to 36,5%. Any inquiry into the existence of an intellectual elite among South Africa's professional soldiers would have to focus on the 16,3% graduates, since neither medical officers nor chaplains would normally make a politically relevant contribution to the Defence Force's role in national policy making.

The aim of the South African Defence College, situated in Pretoria, is to train selected officers for senior command and staff appointments. Their training includes the study of military strategy, joint operations and related aspects of national security. The College also offers combined courses in warfare for the various services of the Defence Force.

The third institution to be mentioned is the planning sub-division of the operations division. Situated at Defence Headquarters in Pretoria, the sub-division is charged with, among other things, defining the Defence Force's role in the total national strategy, formulating co-ordinated strategies for government departments and undertaking strategic research.[148]

Finally there is Military Intelligence, established in 1960. Precious little is publicly known about the composition and functions of this body. Its official designation has since 1971 been the Military Intelligence Section (MIS) and its head has since 1974 been known as the Chief of Staff: Intelligence. MIS is engaged in assessing the threat against South Africa by analysing the military intentions and capabilities of potential enemies. It is commonly overlooked that the *Security Intelligence and State Security Council Act,* 1972 (which also provided for the establishment of the SSC), empowered Military Intelligence to engage in covert counter-intelligence activities within the Republic as well as to collect intelligence outside the country in a covert manner.

Military Intelligence's role in South Africa's intelligence community has been a matter of dispute, particularly in the Vorster administration. There was considerable rivalry between the various intelligence agencies, with the Bureau for State Security trying to extend its domain at the expense of others. PW Botha's elevation to the premiership saw MIS strengthening its position, whereas its main rival, the Bureau for State

Security, had its wings clipped.

Besides being a (white) "people's army" and, moreover, one involved in actual combat, the Defence Force's importance in society is further enhanced by its receiving a large slice of the national budget. After the rapid escalation in military expenditure in the early 1960s, the annual Defence allocation remained relatively constant from 1964 to 1973.[149]

The 1973/4 Defence budget stood at R470 million (13,5% of state expenditure and 2,5% of GNP), and escalated sharply to R1 712 million for 1977/8 (19% of state expenditure and 5,1% of GNP). The allocated amount for 1977/8 was, however, not spent because of the effects of the 1977 UN arms embargo on South Africa's overseas arms purchases. This downward trend was only reversed in the 1980/81 financial year, with a defence budget of R1 890 million. For the 1981/82 financial year the Defence Force's allocation stood at R2 465 million.[150]

An outstanding feature of South Africa's defence effort in the past two decades has been the country's growing self-sufficiency in armaments. In the early 1970s an estimated 70% of the defence budget was spent on arms imports; a decade later it was only about 15%.[151] This has been directly related to an international arms embargo against the Republic. By law it is the task of the Armaments Corporation of South Africa (ARMS-COR)* "to meet as effectively and economically as may be feasible the armaments requirements of the Republic." A state corporation, ARMSCOR is the official and sole procurement agent of armaments for the Defence Force. Apart from a number of wholly-owned subsidiaries – established mainly for strategic and economic reasons – ARMSCOR co-operates closely with the private sector. ARMSCOR's declared procurement policy has as its very first priority "the maximum utilization of the private sector in the RSA and the utilization of ARMSCOR subsidiaries as main contractors who in turn subcontract the local private sector to a maximum degree." In 1978 ARMSCOR and its subsidiaries used 800 main and subcontractors in the private sector; four years later a figure of 3 000 was reported. In 1978 ARMSCOR and its

subsidiaries employed nearly 19 000 people (of whom nearly 11 000 were white); four years later it reportedly employed 28 000. In addition ARMSCOR indirectly provided some 100 000 employment opportunities in the private sector. In the early 1980s ARMSCOR was said to rank among South Africa's top 20 companies on performance, with assets of R1 200 million. The corporation's link with private enterprise is further embodied in its ten-man board of directors. Appointed by the State President and responsible to the Minister of Defence, the board includes only two public service representatives: the Chief of the Defence Force and the Director-General of Finance. The chairman is from the private sector, as are several other directors. Their names have not been officially revealed for fear that it might harm their foreign business interests.

ARMSCOR is, as one observer put it, a "paradox: a state corporation run almost exclusively by private enterprise."[152]

Given the growth of South Africa's arms industry, a sizeable segment of private enterprise has acquired a material stake in armaments production. To speak of a "military-industrial complex" in the American sense of the word seems an exaggeration. But there is no doubt a military-industrial partnership, which gives each side a vested interest in what the other is doing. The partners may, moreover, actually exert some influence over each other. The military's armaments requirements may have influenced business decisions in the private sector. Much more difficult is whether the private sector influences military decisions other than on a purely logistical level (where, for example, the availability or otherwise of certain arms and equipment may have a very real effect on the military's operational capabilities). Any suggestion that private sector firms benefiting from arms manufacturing are successfully influencing the government not to relinquish control of Namibia and thus to ensure the continuation of the war would be extremely difficult to sustain. Even so, the military-business link is not one that can be entirely ignored when considering certain top-level strategic decisions. Should ARMSCOR in future succeed in developing a sizeable export capability, the military and the private sector would jointly add a new dimension to South Africa's foreign relations.

A final member of what is officially styled the

---

*In April 1977 the present Armaments Corporation of South Africa (Pty) Ltd was formed out of a merger of the Armaments Production Board (established in 1964) and the Armaments Development and Production Corporation (established in 1968).

"defence family" is the Defence Advisory Council. Its declared aim is to advise the Minister of Defence on defence matters "as these affect the national interest" – a meaningless formulation that probably entails advice on labour utilisation and the application of business practices in the Defence Force, among other things. The Council's composition again reflects the close relationship between the military and the private sector. It is chaired by the Minister of Defence and counts top businessmen among its members. In contrast to the anonymity of business leaders serving on ARMSCOR's board, the names of the members of the Defence Advisory Council have been made known publicly.[153]*

Action on the domestic front

Institutionally the military are well placed to make substantive inputs into decision making over a wide field. The most important institution is the SSC together with its network of supporting bodies, including the 15 inter-departmental committees and the various joint management centres. The secretariat of the SSC has a representative on KEOSSA, as do a number of government departments.** The Defence Force, along with other departments, is represented on the Central Consolidation Committee which was appointed in 1979 to formulate proposals for

---

*Although the Council had been established some years earlier, PW Botha, then Minister of Defence, revealed its composition to Parliament on 1 May 1980: Dr FJ du Plessis (Sanlam); Dr WJ de Villiers (General Mining); Dr JA Hurter (Volkskas); Mr GWH Relly (Anglo American); Mr AM Rosholt (Barlow Rand); Mr C Saunders (Tongaat Group); Mr R Lurie (Johannesburg Stock Exchange); Mr BE Hersov (Anglo-Transvaal); Mr I McKenzie (Standard Bank); Mr RJ Goss (SA Breweries); Mr JG van der Horst (Old Mutual); Dr FJ Cronje (Nedbank) and Mr J Wilkins (SA Agricultural Union). The Defence Advisory Council was not reappointed upon the expiry of the above members' term on 31 March 1982. Defence Minister Malan explained that the Council had become superfluous as a liaison body between the Defence Force and industry, following the restructuring of the Defence Manpower Liaison Committee. Chaired by the Chief of Staff: Personnel, the Committee includes representatives from national employers' organisations. (Nat 80's, National Party, August 1982. Die Afrikaner, 23/3/1983, speculated that the Defence Advisory Council – a body of "money magnates" – had not been dissolved.)
**In 1982 the Defence Force joined the ranks of departments represented on KEOSSA.

submission to the government on the consolidation of the black homelands.

On some domestic political issues the military adopt a reformist public posture expressed in the familiar dictum that South Africa's struggle for survival depends for only 20% on military means and for 80% on political means. The expression is commonly associated with Namibia, where the South African Defence Force has been engaged in a concerted "hearts and minds" campaign among blacks in an effort to counter SWAPO influence. Winning hearts and minds is of course an old doctrine in guerrilla warfare, but one of relatively recent origin in the specifically South African context. Perhaps the first to talk in this idiom was General RC Hiemstra, albeit only after he had retired as chief of the Defence Force in 1972. The Defence Force was not and could not be strong enough to protect South Africa if political action did not help to secure the home base, he said. This allusion to race relations was at the time not received kindly in government circles.[154] Since then top military officers have repeated the theme many times, making it part of South African political vocabulary.[155] In military parlance the hearts and minds campaign is referred to as "civic action". Under this rubric the Defence Force makes its contribution to the 80% struggle.

In 1974 an organisation was created in the Army to conduct "civic action" programmes in Namibia. A sub-section for civic action was established in January 1978 under the Chief of Staff: Operations of the Defence Force. According to the 1979 Defence White Paper, civic action involves those activities of the Defence Force, together with other departments, "directed towards medical and socio-economic facets in areas subjected to a variety of onslaughts". Such actions are based on the simple premise that "a population whose basic needs are provided for is less vulnerable to enemy propaganda." Under its civic action programmes the Defence Force provides physicians, teachers, agricultural experts, administrative personnel and other specialists to "developing areas" in both Namibia and South Africa. Dispensing such aid is an executive function performed mainly by the Army; the sub-section civic action is charged with the planning and co-ordination of programmes.[156]

In March 1980 the directorate of civic action, as it was then known, found itself at the centre of a political storm over its meddling in white party politics. A "psychological action plan", among other things designed to "nullify" opposition attacks on PW Botha, then Minister of Defence, in the coming Defence budget vote in Parliament, was leaked to the *Sunday Times*. The document was signed by the Director-General of civic action, Major-General Phil Pretorius, on behalf of the chief of the Defence Force. In a particularly bitter parliamentary debate over the action plan, the PFP suggested that the Defence Force had made the party into an "enemy" and that the Defence Force ran the risk of acquiring the image of the National Party in uniform. The government dissociated it from the document and denied any involvement in or prior knowledge thereof. A Defence Force board of inquiry, set up to investigate the matter, found no wilfulness or negligence by anyone concerned with the document. Conceding that parts of the document could "reasonably be interpreted as encroachment on the party political terrain", the board found that "serious errors of judgment" had been made by some people.

The upshot of the controversy was that the directorate of civic action was abolished, but the civic action programme is continued by other bodies within the Defence Force.[157]

With regard to the relatively enlightened stance that the military seems to take on racial matters, it would probably be fair to say that logistical considerations also help to shape the military's views. Faced with constant manpower problems on the one hand and a growing external threat on the other, cold calculation told the military that whites alone cannot carry the defence burden. Consequently the Defence Force in the 1970s began enlisting blacks, coloureds and Indians on a voluntary basis (white males are subject to compulsory military training). Coloured and black units have since seen active duty on the Namibian battle front.[158] It seems a natural corollary that, having been "liberalised" in this regard, even if under force of circumstance, the military would wish to demonstrate its *bona fides* to the black population groups by striking a reformist political note. White right-wingers have not taken kindly to these developments, and the HNP has tried to make political capital out of the Defence Force's allegedly dangerous "integration" policy.

The *Defence Act*, 1957, as amended, is an illuminating piece of legislation, for it not only caters for the Defence Force's manpower requirements, but also outlines the force's domestic duties and thereby reveals the nature of perceived threats to the Republic's internal security. Thus article 92 contains the following self-explanatory heading: "Mobilization of Citizen Force, Reserve and Commandos for the combating of terrorism, internal disorder or other emergency". These duties conjure up the image of a uniformed soldier manning a roadblock – something that has become a reality of life in South Africa.

It is not only the white citizenry that can be drawn into the defence effort by law, but also private enterprise. In terms of the *National Key Points Act*, 1980, the Minister of Defence may declare any place or area a "national key point" if it is considered "so important that its loss, damage, disruption or immobilization may prejudice the Republic". The owner of such premises is obligated to undertake security precautions and to furnish the Minister with "any information" he may require on the premises. The further disclosure of information on a national key point is strictly regulated by the Act. The *National Supplies Procurement Act*, 1974, and the *Petroleum Products Amendment Act*, 1979, also impose obligations and restrictions on private firms with regard to such matters as production and trade. These laws are not without international ramifications, for they implicate also foreign corporations in safeguarding the "security of the state".

The military and foreign relations

The Defence Force's main preoccupation in the field of South Africa's foreign relations has been with threats to the security of the Republic and Namibia posed by guerrillas or insurgents operating from bases in neighbouring states. Since the introduction of Cuban troops into Angola in 1975 an additional concern has been that outside forces – specifically communist – would become actively involved on the side of SWAPO and even the ANC. Repeated military attacks on SWAPO in Angola – and on Angolan targets – and raids on ANC targets in Mozambique amply demonstrate the Defence Force's uncompromising stance on what it regards as vital security matters.

In its approach to regional strategy the military seems to have adopted what can conveniently be designated a "hawkish" posture. Although there are certainly ill-defined "areas of grey", the essence of the ideal-typical form of hawkishness has become apparent. The hawks start from the premise that South Africa possesses only two credible and effective instruments to ensure its security in the Southern African context, namely military and economic muscle. Should black states endanger the Republic's security, tough military and economic punitive measures ought to be taken. The hawks are concerned that South Africa should not lose the ability to use these levers against black states; hence the familiar notion that it is in South Africa's interests that surrounding black states should remain economically dependent on South Africa. They should likewise remain militarily weak and vulnerable. If the black states succeeded in loosening their economic ties with South Africa to a meaningful degree and in developing a reasonable military capability, the fear is that they would become more assertive, even provocative, in their relations with South Africa – such as by providing sanctuary to the ANC – because they would no longer be as vulnerable to South African economic and military pressure. To prevent the black states strengthening themselves economically and militarily, the hawks would argue, South Africa can manipulate economic ties and support disaffected groups at least to the extent that a hostile regime would be compelled to concentrate its energies and resources on fighting the rebels. The hawks believe that the black countries, while in a state of domestic weakness and instability, will be less able to threaten South Africa's security.

The hawks tend not to be impressed with political or diplomatic considerations in their formulation of a regional strategy. They take a rather cynical view of world opinion with its ritualistic condemnations and threats of punitive measures against South Africa. For the hawks immediate security interests are of paramount importance. In a sense their approach to regional strategy is that of an eye for an eye: if black states are committed to destabilising* South Africa through their support for the ANC and their advocacy of sanctions and South Africa's further international isolation, the Republic ought to reciprocate in kind. It is therefore a case of meeting destabilisation with destabilisation – or "let us destabilise them lest they really succeed in destabilising us." The hawks also tend to adopt a rather intolerant attitude on black states'

incessant declamations of political antagonism towards South Africa. These states, the hawks maintain, have to be made aware of the limits of political expediency or exigency.

The radical hawkish views have certainly not always found expression in political decisions. For one thing, the presence of the foreign ministry on the SSC and its working committee has served as something of a brake on the Defence Force's hawkish inclinations. Compared with the military, Foreign Affairs can be depicted as "doveish" in its approach to regional strategy. The doves share most of the hawks' concerns about threats to South Africa's security and they may well support the limited use of economic and military instruments to safeguard the Republic's perceived interests. The doves are nonetheless particularly sensitive to adverse international reaction to South Africa's use of punitive measures against black states, particularly if such measures amount to the drastic action of destabilisation. Destabilisation is an option to be exercised only in dire circumstances. The threat of destabilisation, the doves hope, serves as an effective deterrent. They see the Republic's military capability as reinforcing the diplomatic instrument of foreign policy: South Africa can talk to black states from the proverbial position of strength. In formulating a regional strategy, the doves furthermore place heavy reliance on economic links as a determinant of political behaviour. They see the black states' close economic ties with South Africa as an incentive to them to adopt a reasonable or moderate attitude towards the Republic, which essentially means not endangering its security. South Africa, the doves believe, can trade regional economic prosperity against security.

While some decisions on South Africa's relations with black Southern African states may have been a compromise between hawkish and doveish views, the fact remains that the military instrument of South Africa's foreign policy has become an operational one, and this has given the institution handling it a legitimate voice in deciding on its application.

The picture that emerges of the Defence Force's "political role" is that of an institution that is *verlig* and flexible in its views on the domestic situation, but tough and uncompromising in its external orientation. Although it might seem a contradictory dualism, the combination of moderation and militancy makes sense in South Africa's peculiar domestic and regional settings. To allow for (relatively) peaceful domestic

---

* For the purposes of this book it is suggested that the (political) objective of destabilisation is to effect profound political changes in the "target state". These may or may not involve structural change – which means dislodging the regime in power – but certainly involve major changes in the target state's behaviour, specifically towards the "destabiliser".

political change in a direction and at a pace determined by the government, the process has to be protected against external threats which could upset it. The two are also related in another way. Through domestic reform, it is hoped in official circles, the threats to South Africa's security will to some extent be reduced in that some of the causes for people taking up arms against the government might be eliminated.

The military's involvement in South Africa's regional relations also has a more amicable, co-operative side to it. The vehicle is the constellation of states. Prime Minister Botha has envisaged that the constellation partners would co-operate in the area of security, among others.[159] A bilateral non-aggression pact already exists between South Africa and each of the independent former homelands.[160] The idea, in official South African circles, is that the parties should institutionalise co-operation in security matters through regular meetings of the ministers responsible and the establishment of multilateral committees of senior officials.[161] At that stage the existing bilateral non-aggression treaties might be complemented or perhaps replaced by a multilateral defence pact between all the members of the constellation. Whether or not such developments take place, and notwithstanding the fact that the non-aggression treaties do not commit South Africa to the defence of the former homelands, it is safe to assume that it will not stand by idly if the security of one of these territories is seriously threatened, whether from within or externally.

Farther afield the South African military would be particularly interested in the Republic's relations with those states willing to co-operate, overtly or covertly, in the military field. This applies especially to the procurement and development of arms. Israel and Taiwan are frequently mentioned in this regard. Although its precise nature is uncertain, there can be little doubt about military co-operation between South Africa and these two states. South Africa's relations with Israel and Taiwan have been greatly strengthened in recent years, not least because they too, to a greater or lesser degree, find themselves with South Africa in the league of outcast states. The three countries also share a pronounced sense of external threat, each finding itself confronted by one or more numerically superior hostile neighbours. In cementing ties with Israel, the South African Defence Force has either been completely uninvolved or deliberately remained well in the background. The military's

role in cultivating the Taiwanese connection is uncertain, but it is conceivable that military considerations have from the outset weighed heavily in the decision to strengthen South Africa's ties with the island.

The Defence Force is also engaged in international relations of sorts through its military attachés abroad. South Africa in the early 1980s maintained military representation in 18 states. The stationing of South African military representatives has become a contentious political issue in a number of countries, and the Republic has had to withdraw its military attachés from some of them in recent years. A host country's termination of South Africa's military representation is essentially an expression of opposition to the Republic's domestic policies. A different kind of politicisation of South Africa's military relations occured in the case of the United States in April 1979. Following the South African security authorities' discovery that the official aircraft of the American ambassador in South Africa had been taking unauthorised photographs of sensitive installations, three United States military representatives were expelled from the Republic. The Carter Administration retaliated swiftly by ordering two South African military attachés to leave the United States.[162] Military representation was, however, not permanently broken by either side.

Two years after the "spy plane" incident US-South African relations ran into another controversy in which the military again featured. After the United States had long refused South African military officers visas to enter the country in their official capacities (except to take up appointments as military attachés), four senior officers in March 1981 managed to slip through the net. They were Lieutenant-General PW van der Westhuizen, head of Military Intelligence, and three of his colleagues. They reportedly carried a secret report on Soviet military involvement in Southern Africa,[163] and apparently hoped that the information might encourage closer American ties with South Africa, not least in the military field. The group managed to meet Mrs Jeane Kirkpatrick, America's ambassador to the UN. This meeting and the officers' mere presence in the US caused a political furore. They were alleged to have entered America "under false colours", in Kirkpatrick's words,[164] although they had been formally invited by the American Security Council to attend a meeting.[165]

The Civilian Intelligence Network

"Since intelligence on some security matters is vital", to restate a truism, "states feel impelled to develop appropriate services even at great cost." Operating secretly, intelligence services tend to assume important political roles in many countries. Not only do they develop into key centres of power in domestic politics, but they even conduct foreign relations independently of their countries' foreign ministries. Another not uncommon phenomenon is that the military and civilian authorities develop separate, at times competing, intelligence organisations.[166]

These general observations provide an apt summary of the record of South Africa's intelligence services over the past two decades. The three institutions involved are the already mentioned Bureau for State Security (since twice renamed), Military Intelligence, and the Security Police. Suspicion, competition and duplication often characterise the relationship between South Africa's intelligence agencies.[167] All three engage in covert intelligence gathering both within South Africa and abroad. Areas of responsibility are often poorly defined and even ignored. Personality clashes between intelligence heads further complicate matters.

The Bureau for State Security (unofficially dubbed "BOSS") was established in 1969. Its predecessor, launched in the early 1960s in the midst of a concerted sabotage campaign by underground resistance movements, was known as Republican Intelligence. This was not a legally constituted body, but merely a clandestine extension of the Security Police, the latter then headed by Colonel HJ van den Bergh.[168] (The Security Police, originally known as the Special Branch after its British model, was established in 1947.) The Minister of Justice, under whose portfolio the Security Police fell, was Vorster. When the Bureau for State Security was formed, Vorster, then prime minister, appointed Van den Bergh as its first head. The two men had a longstanding friendship dating back to their internment by the Smuts government in the Second World War. In the early 1960s they made a name for themselves in suppressing the wave of sabotage that swept the country in the wake of the banning of the ANC and PAC. Vorster saw to the necessary legislation to allow for drastic action against those seen to be undermining state security; Van den Bergh with awesome efficiency rounded them up.

The Bureau of State Security's functions, as spelled out in the *Security Intelligence and State Security Council Act*, 1972, entail a very wide brief. Among other things, the Bureau is to "collect, evaluate, correlate and interpret national security intelligence" with the purpose of identifying any threat or potential threat to state security; to involve itself with departmental intelligence at the request of any state department; to submit a "national intelligence estimate" concerning any threat to South Africa's security to the State Security Council; to formulate, also for the Council, "a policy relating to national security intelligence" and to co-ordinate the flow of security intelligence between government departments involved with aspects of state security. Given these functions, the Bureau for State Security is indisputably the primary intelligence service. In practice, the Bureau encroaches on what both the Security Police and Military Intelligence consider their respective areas of responsibility. It is even said that Vorster wanted Van den Bergh's Bureau to absorb the gathering of military intelligence.[169] Be that as it may, the fact is that a particularly close personal relationship had long existed between Vorster and Van den Bergh, and this was probably a key factor in explaining the Bureau's rise to an important centre of power on the domestic scene.

The Bureau's intrusion into the military's domain is one reason for the strained relations that are widely known to have existed between PW Botha, then Minister of Defence, and Van den Bergh. Other reasons may have been Van den Bergh's position as Vorster's closest confidant and adviser – the Bureau for State Security reported directly to the prime minister, thus further enhancing Van den Bergh's standing with Vorster – and the security chief's willingness to take issue openly with Cabinet members, notably PW Botha. Van den Bergh rather than Vorster or any other Cabinet member, it was said, was prepared to stand up to the headstrong, often impetuous Minister of Defence.

A highly revealing picture of the influence Van den Bergh (known by such nicknames as the "Tall Man" or "Tall Hendrik" – references to his imposing height – and "Long Ear") exerted over Vorster was presented by the Erasmus Commission. He was depicted as the "power behind the throne", a man who not only exercised great influence over Vorster, but who at times made his decisions for him. He used his office and his personal relationship with Vorster to try to influence the course of events in South Africa. So strong was his position in the power hierarchy that even Cabinet members on occasion channelled matters through him to the prime minister. But Van den Bergh was not always Vorster's trusted adviser and informer. He sometimes withheld certain facts from the prime minister, sometimes only selected facts were provided and at times he ignored Vorster's instructions. Even more chilling is that Van den Bergh was unscrupulous enough to put pressure on an investigating official to produce a false report on irregularities in the former Department of Information, perhaps with a view to exonerate Mulder and thus enhance his chances in the election of Vorster's successor in September 1978. Van den Bergh presented a sinister picture of the Bureau for State Security to the Erasmus Commission, declaring: "I have enough men to commit murder if I tell them to kill . . . I do not care who the prey is."[170] Mrs Helen Suzman, PFP MP, responded by branding Van den Bergh as "South Africa's very own Heinrich Himmler".[171] The government accepted the findings of the Erasmus Commission.[172]

The Erasmus Commission's remarks about Van den Bergh were, of course, made in the context of the investigation into the affairs of the former Department of Information. The Commission presented ample evidence of Van den Bergh's involvement with Information's secret domestic ventures, but very little was said about the security chief's role in Information's secret projects abroad.

Van den Bergh and Rhoodie enjoyed a close relationship characterised by mutual respect and trust and a belief in conducting South Africa's foreign relations by unorthodox means. Van den Bergh can perhaps even claim some credit for Rhoodie's appointment as Secretary of Information, for he strongly supported it in the face of opposition from the Public Service Commission.[173] Van den Bergh was closely involved with Information's secret propaganda offensive, being informed about many of the key projects and conceivably helping to plot some of them. He was "an enthusiastic participant in Dr Mulder's and Dr Rhoodie's schemes", to cite the Erasmus Commission's unflattering tone.[174] The Bureau for State Security provided a conduit for secret funds destined for Information. Van den Bergh also added his weight to Information's activities when he helped persuade a reluctant Vorster to follow up Information's contacts with Francophone African leaders with a personal visit to the Ivory Coast.[175]

The West African initiative was part of a wider joint Department of Information-Bureau for State Security diplomatic exercise. The object was to cultivate links with black African states with a view to establishing an air corridor for South African Airways (thus obviating the need to take the expensive route round the bulge of Africa), and reaching a *rapprochement* with moderate member states of the OAU. There was said to be an understanding that Rhoodie would focus on the Francophone states and Van den Bergh on Southern, East and Central Africa.[176]

Van den Bergh was particularly active in Southern Africa as an emissary of Vorster's in the *détente* era of the 1970s. Van den Bergh played a major role in arranging the historic Victoria Falls summit between Vorster and Kaunda in August 1975.[177] There are indications that Van den Bergh was also engaged in various other top level secret contacts with black African states – among them Gabon and Zaïre – but no details are available.[178] As an emissary of the prime minister Van den Bergh was second to none, because of his close personal ties with Vorster. But Van den Bergh was much more than an agent. He was very much part of the decision making elite, but was not a member of a team: he had direct access to the prime minister and found himself unencumbered by the "normal channels" of government. Van den Bergh has, quite appropriately, been depicted as Vorster's *alter ego* and the *éminence grise* of the Vorster premiership.[179]

There has in recent years been a spate of "revelations" about the more ominous side of the Bureau's undercover activities abroad. It has, among other things, been alleged that the Bureau was involved in organised political break-ins in the United Kingdom and also in the sex scandal that led to the downfall of Mr Jeremy Thorpe, leader of Britain's Liberal Party.[180] Whether such claims are true, partly true or false, the Bureau was engaged in clandestine operations abroad – a normal pursuit of intelligence organisations the world over.

Notwithstanding the uncomplimentary picture the Erasmus Commission gave of Van den Bergh, as well as the Bureau for State Security's apparent involvement with dubious covert operations abroad, Van den Bergh's influence on South Africa's foreign policy was generally constructive. He displayed keen appreciation of the dynamics of African politics and was exceptionally well informed, particularly on regional affairs. His was to some extent a moderating voice against that of the military. It is not a case of Van den Bergh and his Bureau being "doveish" in their stance on foreign policy issues, specifically those relating to security. What distinguished their position from the military's was that they were more susceptible to the nuances of a situation and more subtle in their choice of means to be used – even if these included some rather unpleasant methods of conveying the desired message to a foreign state or individual.

Like Vorster, Mulder and Rhoodie, Van den Bergh too fell from grace because of the Information affair. His final exit was not without a touch of the bizarre. Immediately upon his retirement as head of the Bureau for State Security in June 1978, Vorster appointed him to evaluate the secret projects of the then just disbanded Department of Information.[181] Here, then, was a man who had been deeply involved in Information's clandestine operations, now commissioned to assess those very activities. By the end of September Van den Bergh had completed his assignment. Thereafter his fall into ignominy was both dramatic and rapid. Of all the indictments in the first Erasmus Report, which was made public in December 1978, those relating to Van den Bergh were the most sensational and damning.

When PW Botha became prime minister, South Africa's premier intelligence agency knew that a major change in its role and status was in store. Not only the history of conflict between the new prime minister and Van den Bergh came into the picture. There were also the Erasmus Commission's findings on the former security chief and PW Botha's comprehensive reorganisation of the civil service to support the need for restructuring the intelligence service. The framework into which it had to fit was the total national strategy and its national security management system.

Van den Bergh was succeeded by Mr Alec van Wyk, a professional intelligence officer. In September 1978 the Bureau's name was changed to the Department of National Security (which produced the popular acronym DONS, hardly more flattering than BOSS). These were, however, merely interim moves before the intelligence service finally reached its destiny in the PW Botha administration. This stage followed in June 1980, when Dr LD Barnard took over as Director-General of what then became known as the National Intelligence Service. The 30-year old

Barnard was a complete newcomer to intelligence work – he served as Van Wyk's understudy for six months before taking over – having been Professor of Political Science at the University of the Orange Free State. The peculiar compound of Machiavellianism and Calvinism that characterises Barnard's writings on international relations[182] – his field of speciality – was probably less of a consideration in his appointment than his being a bright young Afrikaner academic, qualified in a discipline with obvious relevance to intelligence work, and someone displaying the "right" political predisposition. The fact that he was a complete outsider coming from academia was certainly also a consideration, for it underlined the new role that PW Botha had earmarked for South Africa's central intelligence organisation.

Whereas the Bureau for State Security under Van den Bergh had become heavily "operationally" oriented with clandestine intelligence gathering, allegedly engaging in "dirty tricks," both within South Africa and abroad, and even conducting high-level diplomacy, Barnard's National Intelligence Service appears to have reverted to the agency's original purpose: to serve as the central intelligence think tank, concentrating on co-ordinating and evaluating intelligence gathered by its own personnel and that of other relevant state institutions. The National Intelligence Service operates in terms of the same law that was supposed to determine the functions of the Bureau for State Security. Barnard can probably be expected to stick to the "book of rules", and he is unlikely to emulate Van den Bergh either in the sense of an advisor on foreign policy (among other things), or as a diplomatic emissary of the prime minister. What also acts as a constraint on the National Intelligence Service is that it – through the SSC – has to contend with various other highly influential institutions in the formulation of policy. One such is the military, whose own intelligence service has gained influence under PW Botha's premiership.

Institutions Involved with External Economic Relations

The government department most closely involved with South Africa's international trade is the Department of Industries, Commerce and Tourism. It consists of two directorates, one for industries and the other for commerce and tourism. The latter, the directorate of interest here, comprises a foreign trade relations division and an export trade promotion division. The foreign trade relations division involves itself on a multilateral level with the administration of South Africa's participation in the General Agreement on Tariffs and Trade (GATT) and several international commodity arrangements, and is also concerned with such UN activities as the United Nations Conference on Trade and Development (UNCTAD). The division also administers South Africa's bilateral trade agreements. The division maintains three offices abroad staffed by economic attachés: Geneva (dealing with GATT), Brussels (for the EEC) and Washington (for the United States only). The export trade promotion division has trade representatives stationed in 33 offices in 27 countries. They liaise with state institutions and private sector organisations in the host countries with a view to promoting South African exports.

The Minister of Industries, Commerce and Tourism is not a standing member of the SSC, but has become a more or less permanently co-opted member. The Department has another channel to the SSC through its representation on the Council's working committee. The Minister and Director-General of the Department are standing members of the Cabinet committee for Economic Affairs, which is chaired by the Minister of Manpower Utilisation.* The foreign ministry has no standing representation on this Cabinet committee but can be co-opted, and its representatives have on occasion been co-opted onto the inter-departmental working group of the committee.

A highly influential body in the economic arena, including South Africa's foreign trade relations, is the Prime Minister's Economic Advisory Council. It was established in the early 1960s to co-ordinate co-operation between the public and private sectors and to advise the government on current economic issues. It is composed of representatives of national employers and employees' organisations in the private sector, senior civil servants, outside economic and financial experts and representatives from the Indian and coloured communities. Among the departmental heads serving on the Council are the Director-General

of Foreign Affairs and Information and the chief of the Defence Force. Their involvement is an indication of the Council's very wide sweep.

Within the government service a principal advisory body in the field of economic politics is the economic planning branch in the Office of the Prime Minister. Among the broad spectrum of matters dealt with by the branch is the drawing up of South Africa's Economic Development Programme. An important feature of the revised edition of the 1981-7 programme is its emphasis on regional economic co-operation across political boundaries. The concept of functional economic units based on economic factors is part and parcel of the constellation of states plan. The economic planning branch is formally linked with various other official institutions involved with economic planning. The head of the branch is also chairman of the Prime Minister's Economic Advisory Council;* he is a member of the Cabinet committees for Economic Affairs and Finance and their respective working groups, and of the working committee of the SSC. The chairman of the SSC's working committee is, in turn, a member of the Economic Affairs working group. Two other particularly important institutions on which the economic planning branch is represented are the Special Constellation Committee and the Foreign Trade Relations Committee.

The establishment of the Special Constellation Committee was announced by PW Botha in July 1980 at a meeting of the heads of government of the then four constellation partners. Dr GPC de Kock, governor of the South African Reserve Bank, was appointed as co-ordinator of constellation affairs and head of the committee. Professor JA Lombard, an economist from the University of Pretoria, was named deputy co-ordinator. The high-powered Committee, which has direct access to the prime minister, co-ordinates South Africa's constellation activities and also serves as a top-level think tank on matters of regional co-operation. Approaching co-operation between the constellation members from a typically functionalist perspective, the Committee operates through the following five working groups: monetary matters; fiscal matters;

---

*The Cabinet committee for Economic Affairs has subsequently been merged with that for Finance. The new committee retained the designation Economic Affairs.

*The economic planning branch was transferred to the new Department of Constitutional Development and Planning in August 1982. The same year Dr SS Brand became chairman of the Economic Advisory Council. In 1983 Brand was appointed chief executive of the newly established Southern African Development Bank.

the Southern African Development Bank; development co-operation; and labour utilisation. The various government departments and other institutions involved with these matters are represented on the working groups. The chairman and secretary of each group form the Special Constellation Committee. Prominent among the institutions involved in the work of the Committee is the foreign ministry's KEOSSA: its head sits on four of the five working groups and also on the Committee itself. The composition of the Special Constellation Committee is another illustration of the technocratic features of PW Botha's style of government. But using expert officials in this particular instance might also have been due to another consideration: the government perhaps hoped that it would be easier for officials than politicians to gain the co-operation of black countries – ideally also those not formerly part of the Republic – for South Africa's plans for regional economic interaction.

An inter-departmental body that predates the various institutions created under the PW Botha administration is the Foreign Trade Relations Committee. Chaired by the Director-General of Foreign Affairs and Information, it is composed of departmental heads and their advisors; some of the Directors-General are permanent and others co-opted members. As the name suggests, the Committee is designed to provide co-ordination between the various departments with an interest in South Africa's foreign trade relations. In practice the Committee in the past apparently tended to cast its attention much wider than strictly trade matters, and dealt with more overtly political concerns too. In this way the Committee allowed for a degree of co-ordination between at least some of the departments involved with aspects of South Africa's foreign relations.[183] With the emergence of the wide range of inter-departmental bodies referred to, the Foreign Trade Relations Committee may well have found that its field had narrowed considerably, or that a number of the other institutions mentioned also involved themselves with some of the matters dealt with by the Committee. It can be said with reasonable certainty that the issues of economic sanctions against South Africa, the Republic's use of economic levers in its foreign relations and the question of its preferential trade agreement with Zimbabwe all featured in the Committee's deliberations. These matters are likely to have been considered also by the Cabinet committee

for Economic Affairs and the SSC, together with their respective supporting bodies, and perhaps even by the economic planning branch in the Prime Minister's Office. Whereas the Foreign Trade Relations Committee only advises ministers, Cabinet committees may take decisions.

Three other institutions involved in South Africa's foreign trade require brief mention. The Private Sector Export Advisory Committee, appointed by the Minister of Industries, Commerce and Tourism, is composed of representatives from the private sector and provides for liaison with the public sector. The Standing Committee for Export Incentives, chaired by the director of export trade promotion in the Department of Industries, Commerce and Tourism, is composed of an equal number of representatives from the public and private sectors. The Export Credit Guarantee Insurance Underwriters Committee, also chaired by the director of export trade promotion, has members from the private and public sectors, including the foreign ministry, and is concerned with insurance for private South African companies engaged in foreign trade.

The importance of foreign trade as a factor in South Africa's overall foreign relations has already been illustrated in facts and figures in a previous chapter. South Africa's heavy reliance on external trade – it represents about 63% of the GDP, one of the highest proportions in the Western world[184] – is a source of both strength and weakness. It is a strength insofar as other states' reliance on trade with South Africa constrains them in considering punitive action against the Republic. To trade interests must of course be added the investments of foreign companies in South Africa. Even so, such an open economy remains vulnerable to external economic pressure exerted for political purposes. In Southern Africa the economic dependence of black states on South Africa[185] provides the latter with a useful foreign policy instrument.

Institutions Involved with Mineral and Energy Matters

Although the Department of Mineral and Energy Affairs has not joined the ranks of the foreign ministry, the Defence Force and the major intelligence service in the inner circle of state institutions involved with foreign policy formulation, its field of responsibility makes it an important factor in foreign relations.

For each of the Department's two major areas of responsibility there is an advisory policy committee. The Energy Policy Committee was formed in 1974, following the world oil crisis. Composed of the heads of various government departments and other state and semi-state institutions involved with energy matters, it was designed to advise the government on the formulation of an energy policy.[186] The intention was that the Committee's composition would be changed to provide also for private sector participation. The private sector is represented on the Minerals Policy Committee, created in 1980. Chaired by the Minister of Mineral and Energy Affairs, the eight-man committee – which includes four representatives from the public sector – advises the government on all aspects of the minerals industry and on the formulation of a minerals policy. Among the matters that the committee is likely to have considered – though most probably not endorsed – is South Africa's use of minerals as a political lever in its foreign relations.

Although the Minister of Mineral and Energy Affairs is not a permanent member of the SSC, he can of course be co-opted if necessary. Liaison between his department and others normally takes place through the Energy Policy Committee and a number of other inter-departmental committees which deal with particular aspects of minerals and energy, such as the stockpiling of oil. The Department of Mineral and Energy Affairs furthermore participates in the activities of some of the Cabinet committees and their subsidiary bodies.

As the Department's name suggests, it is broken down into two divisions, Mineral Affairs and Energy Affairs. In the former division a particularly important body is the Minerals Bureau. Formed in 1975, its object is to advise the government on the formulation of policies to ensure optimum utilisation of South Africa's mineral resources, in the sense of their contribution to the national economy. This involves the Bureau in collecting world-wide mineral intelligence. With more than 40 professional posts and eight mining counsellors serving in South African missions abroad,[187] the Minerals Bureau provides the essential hard data on which South Africa's minerals policy is based.

The Energy Affairs Division, which is responsible for the planning and provision of energy, handles four different sources and forms of energy: coal, liquid fuels, electricity and uranium/nuclear energy. Each of these has relevance for South Africa's foreign relations. The Republic is one of the world's leading coal exporters. As far as liquid fuels are concerned, the country's procurement of oil is of course complicated by the existence of oil embargoes. To reduce its dependence on foreign oil supplies, South Africa has long since developed its own oil-from-coal industry, and its advanced technology in this field may well be a commodity for which there is a demand from abroad. Electricity has an international dimension through South Africa's providing power to eight neighbouring territories, and in turn purchasing electricity from Mozambique's Cabora Bassa hydro-electric power project.[188] South Africa's generation of nuclear power has become a matter of some international controversy in view of the country's refusal to sign the Nuclear Non-Proliferation Treaty. For the outside world the issue is whether or not South Africa intends using its nuclear technology for military purposes too.

A number of semi-state institutions are also involved with meeting South Africa's energy needs. The Electricity Supply Commission (ESCOM), a public enterprise founded in 1922, supplies some 90% of South Africa's total energy needs, and is also responsible for selling South African electricity to neighbouring territories. Electric power is generated almost exclusively from coal, but ESCOM is busy erecting South Africa's first nuclear power station in the Western Cape.[189] Two public corporations are involved specifically with nuclear energy research and application. The Atomic Energy Board, already established in 1948, took its research reactor into service in 1965. The Uranium Enrichment Corporation was formed in 1971 following the Atomic Energy Board's development of a unique process for the enrichment of uranium. The Corporation operates its own uranium enrichment plant. In 1981 it was decided that the two institutions would in future be administered under a single corporate structure.[190]

In the field of liquid fuels the Department of Mineral and Energy Affairs is responsible for the strategic fuel fund, which is used for stockpiling oil. South Africa's well-known oil-from-coal industry, SASOL, was set up with government finance in 1950. In 1981 this public corporation had two plants in operation, with a third coming into production in 1982. Then there is the Southern Oil Exploration Corporation (SOEKOR), a state-financed company established in the 1960s to undertake a search for natural oil in South Africa.[191]

Although these various public institutions active in the minerals and energy fields may not hitherto have featured prominently in foreign policy making as such, they are important institutions in South Africa's overall foreign relations. Moreover, the Department of Mineral and Energy Affairs and bodies such as the Atomic Energy Board, the Uranium Enrichment Corporation, SASOL and ESCOM have at their disposal potential instruments of foreign policy that can be actively employed in pursuit of political objectives. In such an event the institutions handling the instruments are bound to gain in influence in policy formulating circles. It should, however, not be forgotten that some of the bodies mentioned also deal with vital aspects of South Africa's physical vulnerability, oil being the primary example. This, too, has obvious political implications.

Transport Organisations

Like so many other aspects of South Africa's foreign relations, its transport links with the outside world have also become politicised by the international controversy over apartheid. Already in 1963 African states imposed a ban on landing and overflying rights for South African aircraft. The year before, the UN General Assembly had adopted its first sanctions resolution against South Africa, which called, among other things, on member states to close their ports to all South African vessels and to refuse landing and passage facilities to South African aircraft. Such resolutions have since been passed regularly and, indeed, have been implemented by a great many states. It will be recalled that one of the main objectives of the former Department of Information's diplomatic ventures in Africa was to secure overflying and landing rights for South African aircraft. In the case of the Ivory Coast, it succeeded.

Notwithstanding isolation attempts, South Africa's transport links with the black states of Southern Africa feature prominently in its regional relations. Surrounding black states find themselves to a greater or lesser degree dependent on South Africa's transport network. They are, however, through the Southern African Development Co-ordination Conference (SADCC), actively engaged in attempts to reduce this dependence and make themselves economically much less dependent – ideally, independent – of South Africa. South Africa, for its part, tries to promote co-operation with these very states in the transport field – a foreign policy initiative that has become known as "transport diplomacy".

The chief agent in the conduct of transport diplomacy is the South African Transport Services. (In September 1981 the South African Railways and Harbours Administration changed its name to the South African Transport Services.) This is one of two separate state organisations for which the Minister of Transport Affairs carries ministerial responsibility; the other is the Department of Transport Affairs, whose functions include such civil transport matters as aviation and road transport.

The use of transport links for bridge-building in the subcontinent can be traced back to the late 19th and early 20th centuries.[192] More important is that South Africa recognised the potentially cohesive effects of its transport links with the emerging black states of the 1960s.[193] Modern South African transport diplomacy has been popularly identified with the co-operation in transport matters between South Africa and Mozambique in the wake of the latter's independence in 1975. Transport diplomacy is also commonly associated with Dr JGH Loubser, General Manager of South African Railways/ Transport Services since 1970.* With all the attention focused on Mozambique, little mention is ever made of a major exercise in transport diplomacy in August 1975. It was the occasion of the Victoria Falls conference, where Vorster tried to persuade Smith and Kaunda to reopen the border between Rhodesia and Zambia – closed by Rhodesia in 1973 – to allow for a free flow of rail traffic from South Africa to Zambia and *vice versa* via Rhodesia. Vorster was prepared to act as guarantor of an agreement between the other two. Smith was prepared to reopen his border, but Kaunda refused.[194] Three years later, in October 1978, Kaunda agreed to open the Zambian side. It then took very little time for a transport agreement to be signed between the South African and Zambian railways and for rail traffic to start moving again.[195]

The South African-Zambian agreement was concluded between the two countries' railways authorities and not the governments themselves. That indeed is a principal feature of the transport diplomacy identified with Loubser: it is conducted

---

*Loubser retired in January 1983 and was succeeded by Dr EL Grové.

by officials on a technical-cum-business level. In the case of Mozambique, its transport organisation in February 1979 concluded a business agreement with South African Railways. The agreement was, however, only the official, formal seal on the close co-operation in which the two railways had been involved since Mozambique's independence.[196] So successful has transport diplomacy been with Mozambique that there are South African officials stationed in Maputo to see to the Republic's railway, trade and customs interests. There is no foreign ministry representative among them.[197] Transport diplomacy also extends to Zaïre, Botswana, Lesotho, Swaziland and Zimbabwe, although in the latter case it might be somewhat undermined by the political tensions between Pretoria and Harare. Co-operation extends beyond railways, with South African Airways maintaining pool partnerships with the national airlines of Botswana, Lesotho, Swaziland, Zimbabwe, Malawi and Mozambique.[198]

Since Loubser is the main exponent of transport diplomacy, it is important to note his definition of it. The definition is based on the premise that a state's transport infrastructure is one of the major factors from which it derives bargaining power. Loubser sees transport diplomacy as "the art of applying the transport potential of the country to perform a maximal role in its relations with other countries for its own benefit as well as that of others." Conscious of black African states' suspicions about its motives, South Africa offers assistance only when requested, and then provides it in the form of a business transaction for which the recipient pays "a fair price". Furthermore, assistance is offered in a way that would stimulate development and not offend the recipient's pride in its independence. Although Loubser on the one hand declared that he was opposed to transport being used to achieve "non-economic objectives", he on the other hand saw South Africa's transport system as "a highly strategic deterrent to political isolation and a key to relations with Africa in transport as well as other fields." He then went on to say that the Railways' involvement in black African states provided "unique opportunities" not available to any South African government department or private institution; consequently, "I cannot but use these opportunities to the full to the benefit of South Africa in various areas and particularly in the political ["staatkundige"] field." This is probably related to Loubser's contention that transport diplomacy can pave the way "for the development ["ontplooiing"] of the outward policy and perhaps also the constellation of states."[199]

That transport diplomacy indeed has more than mere economic objectives in mind is not at all surprising. After all, there can be no transport diplomacy without the government's blessing and active backing. As Loubser himself suggested, the government is aware of the potential political benefits to be derived from what he termed an "open line" policy.[200] In accordance with the functionalist approach to co-operation, transport diplomacy would hopefully spill over into other areas of inter-state co-operation and contribute to better political understanding, if not ultimately active co-operation in this field too.

The importance of transport links in South Africa's regional relations is reflected in Loubser's regular participation, as a co-opted official, in the proceedings of the SSC. This tends to conjure up a picture of transport links being manipulated for non-economic purposes, particularly to punish or coerce a black state. It is certainly not inconceivable that transport has thus been used as a political lever. It is only to be expected that those actually operating the instrument would be drawn into the political decision making on its use.

To infer that Loubser was invited to sit on the SSC essentially to receive orders, as it were, on the political manipulation of transport links, would be grossly unfair. For one thing, these links need not be purposely manipulated to be politically useful. And then Loubser's high personal standing in government and public service circles makes it extremely unlikely that he could have been reduced to such a subservient, merely executive, role. His stewardship of South Africa's largest public enterprise has earned him a formidable reputation, further enhanced by the obvious achievements of his transport diplomacy. These attributes assured Loubser of an influential voice in formulating South Africa's policies towards the states of Southern Africa. He can be reckoned among the foreign policy "doves", championing the view that economic considerations to a large degree shape political behaviour. The deliberate manipulation of transport links for political purposes is something Loubser probably would have resisted, fearing that it might undermine transport diplomacy. (Loubser reportedly had misgivings about the government's decision in September 1981 not to renew the lease of 25 diesel locomotives to Zimbabwe[201] – something Zimbabwe saw as a punitive action.)

154

The preceding discussion has centred on South Africa's relations with internationally recognised black states. The involvement of South Africa's official transport organisations in the constellation of states should also be mentioned. In May 1980 an inter-state transport liaison committee, composed of senior officials from the four constellation countries, was formed. This umbrella committee has since appointed tourism, technical and civil aviation working groups.[202]

The Department of Manpower Utilisation

The Department of Manpower Utilisation (previously Labour) is important to this book for a familiar reason: *its* field of responsibility, too, has become internationally politicised. Labour and industrial relations is an area that has traditionally been materially affected by the discriminatory features of the government's racial policies. What contributed to this becoming an issue of international proportions is that many major foreign companies operate in South Africa and are thus subjected to officially regulated labour arrangements. This is of concern not merely to the local subsidiaries but also to the mother companies that face mounting criticism over their South African operations. International concern about the situation has, among other things, led to so-called disinvestment campaigns and to a number of codes of labour conduct – the EEC Code, the Sullivan Principles (United States) and a Canadian code – applicable to foreign corporations operating in South Africa.

Another international or, to be more precise, regional dimension to the South African labour scene is the employment of several thousand migrant labourers from neighbouring states. In 1978 the figure stood at 327 051, of whom 258 017 were employed in the mining sector. The countries involved were, in order of number of migrants, Lesotho, Mozambique, Malawi, Botswana, Rhodesia/Zimbabwe, Zambia and Angola, plus a number of unidentified others.[203] Migrants from South Africa's independent former homelands are not included in the above figures: the numbers of migrant labourers from Transkei and Bophuthatswana in 1978 were estimated at 265 200 and 180 900 respectively.[204]

The large-scale employment of their nationals is of course a highly visible feature of black states' economic dependence on South Africa, although the degree of this particular form of dependence varies from state to state. To reduce and ultimately end the export of labour to South Africa has long been an ideal of many of the black Southern African states. With the emergence of SADCC, new impetus has been given to the desire. There have also been unilateral actions in this regard, such as Kaunda as early as 1965 prohibiting Zambians from taking up employment in South Africa; Banda in 1974 terminating a mine labour agreement between Malawi and South Africa (with only very short-term effects)[205], and Zimbabwe in February 1981 announcing that employment organisations may no longer recruit Zimbabweans to work in South Africa. South Africa was not long in responding to the Zimbabwean decision by declaring that employment contracts for (black) Zimbabweans presently working in the Republic would not be renewed.[206] Zimbabwe made no secret that its decision was largely, if not exclusively, politically inspired. South Africa, in turn, could hardly have acted solely or even mainly for economic reasons. Labour, too, has therefore become an instrument of foreign policy.*

As is the case with transport, South Africa need not deliberately manipulate its labour links with black states to derive political benefits. The mere fact that these states rely on the South African labour market – in many cases formalised through bilateral labour agreements[207] – and that their labourers' remittances are important sources of national revenue, has obvious political implications for the black states in their relations with South Africa.

The involvement of the Department of Manpower Utilisation in the constellation of states should also be mentioned. Following the decision of the heads of government of the four constellation member countries in July 1980 to set up a special committee to consider tertiary education and the training of manpower, an education and training committee was formed. It is a multilateral body composed of senior officials,

---

*In 1982 South Africa began imposing strict new controls on the employment of Mozambicans in the Republic. Later the same year South Africa threatened to curtail the employment of Lesotho citizens if Lesotho failed to act against ANC "terrorists" on its soil. The threat was made after South African forces on 9 December 1982 launched a commando raid against ANC targets in Lesotho's capital.

and has since split its activities into three sub-committees.[208]

South Africa's labour arrangements have a further international dimension. The government is patently keen to publicise as widely as possible the labour reforms initiated by the Commission of Inquiry into Labour Legislation (the Wiehahn Commission), which began its investigations in 1977. The Minister of Manpower Utilisation has, for example, held discussions with representatives from the International Labour Organisation (of which South Africa has since 1966 not been a member) in this regard.

Recently the Department of Manpower Utilisation began appointing labour attachés at South African diplomatic missions. The new process of de-ideologising labour arrangements in South Africa, it may be said, has probably been influenced by more than domestic economic considerations; the government could hardly have lost sight of the international pressures directed at South Africa's racially discriminatory labour and industrial relations regulations.

The Department of Agriculture

An obvious way in which a state's agriculture ministry features in its foreign relations is through the export of agricultural produce. In South Africa's case agricultural products contribute approximately one fifth of the total value of exports, excluding gold.[209] What gives South Africa's agricultural exports added significance is that a sizeable proportion finds its way to black African states that maintain official trade embargoes against the Republic or, at least, openly discourage trade. Since South Africa does not publish country-by-country statistics on its trade with black Africa, reliable information on the volume and destination of agricultural exports is virtually impossible to obtain. It is nonetheless certain that South Africa exports food to a large number of black African states, the bulk of it probably going to those in Southern Africa.[210]

Because of the political hostility of black states to South Africa, the export of food to them has developed into something of a political issue in the Republic. This is typically expressed in the emotive slogan that the government is "feeding the terrorists" by providing food to states believed to be giving active support to insurgents operating against the Republic. This view – with its accompanying demand that food supplies to these states be stopped – is primarily, but not exclusively, propagated by (white) extreme right-wing political groups. The government publicly refused to change its policy of selling food – as a business transaction – to black states. Yet the South African government is no doubt keenly aware of the foreign policy implications of the Republic's position as an important supplier of food to black states. It provides South Africa with another potential political lever, but – as with labour and transport – it need not be deliberately manipulated to be politically useful. The foreign policy benefits of selling food to politically hostile black states must, in the government's view, outweigh the domestic criticism that it attracts.

South Africa's state agricultural organisations are involved in official co-operative ventures with some neighbouring black countries. These include South African agricultural control boards marketing certain agricultural products of Botswana, Lesotho and Swaziland overseas, and also providing them with technical aid.[211] An important vehicle for inter-state co-operation on agricultural matters is the Pretoria-based Southern African Regional Commission for the Conservation and Utilisation of the Soil (SARCCUS). A number of black states, including Botswana, Lesotho, Swaziland and Malawi, are members, together with South Africa.

The constellation of states also embraces co-operation in the field of agriculture between the member countries. A multilateral agricultural liaison committee, composed of senior officials, was constituted in June 1980, and has subordinate working groups for forestry, nature conservation and veterinary matters.[212]

The ministry of agriculture maintains its own representation abroad, with agricultural counsellors stationed in Paris, London, Washington, Canberra, Brussels, Bonn and at the UN in Geneva.[213]

Other Government Departments

There are a host of other government departments whose activities intentionally lead them into the field of South Africa's foreign relations. While some of them may make a significant contribution to foreign policy making, it would be *ad hoc* and confined to specific issues.

The ministry of finance, by holding the purse strings, has an obvious indirect influence on the conduct of foreign policy. The ministry in its own right maintains wide-ranging international contacts, for example through South Africa's membership of the International Monetary Fund (where the South African Reserve Bank acts as agent for the government) and in seeking loans on the international money market. Nearer home the ministry is involved with the constellation's multilateral committee for monetary and fiscal matters, composed of senior officials.

Various other departments are also engaged in the constellation's network of multilateral technical bodies. For example, the Department of Water Affairs, Forestry and Environmental Conservation is represented on the forestry working group (a subsidiary body of the agricultural liaison committee); the Department of Posts and Telecommunications participates in the posts and telecommunications consultative committee and its supporting bodies; the Department of Health in the health committee and the Departments of Education and Training and of National Education in the education and training committee and its sub-committees. Some of these departments also engage in foreign relations of sorts beyond their involvement in the constellation. The Department of Posts and Telecommunications has an obvious additional international dimension to its functions; the Department of Water Affairs, Forestry and Environmental Conservation has been involved in protracted talks with Lesotho on a joint water project, and the Department of National Education is responsible for the appointment of cultural attachés abroad.

There are other government departments that occasionally inadvertently stray onto the international scene because their domestic actions have international political repercussions for South Africa. The actions are usually in the fields of race relations and state security. The most important of these departments have been identified in the previous chapter. It is certainly a remarkable feature that the domestic actions of a state's official institutions have become so thoroughly internationalised.

6. The Role of the Public

Ten persons who speak make more noise than ten thousand who are silent.   Napoleon Bonaparte

The role of the people in the formation of foreign policy is in academic literature, as in political debate, a contentious subject. There are, on the one hand, scholars who see the public making little or no positive contribution, if not actually being a hindrance, to foreign policy making. On the other hand, there is the notion that in a democracy also a government's foreign policy should be subject to popular control.[1] The dialectic essentially deals with the political role of the people as "an unorganised whole", that is, with public opinion as it is commonly understood. This is only one possible level of analysis. The other is to consider the public's role as articulated by organised groups, which in effect serve as intermediaries between government and people.[2]

The distinction between the organised and unorganised public is very basic. Holsti has refined the concept "public" as it relates to foreign policy making. In a pyramidal construction, Holsti distinguished three layers of people. There is a "small top layer of the . . . public that is reasonably well-informed, articulate, and interested, although not necessarily more prone [than the public at large] to change basic attitudes when subjected to new information, propaganda, or dramatic events abroad." Ranging in size between one and fifteen per cent of the population, the "attentive" public's interest and involvement in foreign policy is not spread evenly over the whole foreign policy spectrum. There may in fact be several different attentive publics, one for international commerce, another for agriculture, a third for a specific region of the world, and so forth. The attentive public, Holsti went on to argue, represents probably the only segment of society that actually introduces ideas for consideration by the foreign policy formulators.[3]

Holsti's attentive public – which is not an original concept[4] – corresponds with what has also been termed the "informed public",[5] and with that section of society that creates "positive" public opinion. The positive element flows from the informed views of the attentive public and finds expression in the organised activities of interest groups, political parties and mass media.[6] Interest group activity, it should be said, is generally less pronounced in foreign than domestic affairs.

Within the confines of the attentive public, it is possible to identify the unofficial foreign policy elite, which would include leaders of interest groups active in foreign affairs (such as trade organisations), prominent representatives from the media, recognised experts from non-official research institutions, and other academics. In the United Kingdom common social and intellectual backgrounds – the "old school tie" – are important characteristics of this foreign policy elite and indeed of the British political elite generally.[7] To be counted among the unofficial foreign policy elite does not necessarily mean that someone has the ear of the policy formulators. Thus a further distinction can be drawn between "insiders" and "outsiders", individuals and groups who are recognised by government as a source of information and advice, and others who do not enjoy this close relationship. Their respective relationships with the policy formulators tend to influence their methods, the insiders being "protective" in advancing their cause, and the outsiders "promotional" by dramatising their cause and "taking it to the hustings". The decision makers see instrumental value in the insiders, by using them to develop and help implement government policies – something that directly affects group behaviour.[8]

Holsti divided the rest of the public into two layers. The intermediate layer, comprising between 30% and 50% of the total population, holds established attitudes towards foreign countries, has some knowledge of a limited range of issues and some ability to express opinions if asked. The bottom layer, in some cases representing 70% or more of the public, is apathetic, uninformed and non-expressive on most issues.[9] Research into public opinion in various countries has convincingly shown that "specific knowledge of international affairs is quite limited within the mass public", in the understated words of Abravenal and Hughes.[10]

Holsti's bottom layer – to which other analysts might put an even higher figure than 70% – represents what has been labelled "negative" public opinion, "associated with the pollster's view of public opinion in which the emphasis is upon numbers rather than the status or activity of the opinion holders".[11] Negative public opinion has also been depicted as a "mood", one that prescribes the limits within which foreign policy can be formulated. "Such mood", Frankel warns, "can exclude all practicable choices and leave the decision-makers with prohibitions alone."[12] Others, however, take a more charitable view. Almond, for example, sees the function of the public in a democratic policy making process as setting certain policy criteria in the form of generally shared values and expectations.[13]

Whatever the general public's role in foreign policy making is or should be, a vital point is that public opinion "is important if the political leaders believe it to be so."[14]

A peculiar South African problem, which first has to be clarified before examining the local public's role in foreign policy making, is whether the public is synonymous with the Republic's total population or merely part of it. The simple answer is that is depends on how the policy formulators define the public. Although the government is accountable to an exclusively white electorate, it does not mean that the views of the blacks, coloureds and Indians are necessarily ignored. Instead, the government is faced with the dilemma of how to respond to an emerging body of articulate black opinion expressing itself increasingly on foreign policy issues. To complicate matters for the government, this feature coincides with a noticeable hardening of white political attitudes – also on some key foreign policy issues – as manifested in the impressive growth of support for right-wing political groups in the early 1980s. Under these circumstances it would be appropriate to speak of several "unorganised publics" in South Africa, just as there are also a number of different "organised publics".

The Organised Public

The business community

When Prime Minister PW Botha in October 1980 told a congress of the Association of Chambers of Commerce (ASSOCOM) that "my government places more emphasis on free enterprise and on the utilisation of the free market mechanism than any previous South African government",[15] he was not overstating the case – at least as far as the post-1948 period is concerned. There has indeed been a thaw in relations between government and private sector since PW Botha came to power. Under Vorster the relations were rather cool and distant, the former prime minister being a great believer in the old adage that "the business of business is business", and that politics should be left to the government, which has a popular mandate to pursue its chosen policies.

PW Botha's new relationship with the business community can be explained in terms of the all-pervasive total national strategy. Part of it is what the prime minister calls a "national economic strategy" aimed at achieving a series of "national economic objectives". Among these are the protection of the economy against external economic, political and security threats ("a large part of the total onslaught on the RSA is directed at the economic field") and the promotion of economic development in and co-operation between the countries of Southern Africa.[16]

The former objective can again be related to the notion of a national security management system, designed to manage South Africa's four power bases as an integrated whole. One of these is the economic power base, and its function is defined by Malan as the provision of manpower, material means and finance for the state to fulfil its welfare and security functions. Total national strategy, Malan has emphasised, can never be a matter exclusively for the public sector; the security management system therefore makes provision for the involvement of the private sector.[17] One way in which this is presumably done is through the appointment of leading figures from the private sector to the Defence Advisory Council and ARMSCOR's board.[18] Such appointments should also be seen in the context of the special relationship that has since the 1960s been developing between the business sector and the military thanks to the burgeoning arms industry.

The promotion of regional economic development and co-operation is the other main area in which the prime minister hopes to foster a mutually beneficial partnership between government and business. Development co-operation between governments, PW Botha explained, "benefits private enterprise in the long term by contributing to order and stability in the region". Governments can only "create a framework", while "the greatest real contribution" to the extension of inter-state co-operation can be made by the private sector.[19] A key component of the framework is an oft-repeated government commitment to the free enterprise system.[20] This has led to the issuing of a declaration to promote private investment by the heads of government of South Africa, Transkei, Bophuthatswana and Venda in July 1980, in which the signatories undertook to adhere faithfully to some basic tenets of free enterprise.[21] The parties to the declaration already reveal the effective geographical parameters of the South African government's plans for regional economic interaction involving the private sector. The prime minister appealed to the local business community to concentrate its investments and the transfer of expertise on South Africa's "traditional area of responsibility", namely independent former homelands, in addition to the self-governing homelands.[22] To promote economic development on this sub-regional scale – and to encourage private sector involvement – the government introduced the new concept of regional development co-operation transcending political borders, which means the creation of functionally defined economic regions.[23]

In its original conception the constellation was a highly ambitious, even grandiose design, with visions of between seven and ten states south of the Kunene and Zambezi rivers joining forces in a community of nations.[24] Despite the heavy political odds, the ideal of attract-ing internationally recognised black states in Southern Africa to the constellation remains. Thus two key joint public-private sector enterprises created as part of the constellation – the Development Bank of Southern Africa and the Small Business Development Corporation – are not restricted in their activities to South Africa and its former homelands.[25] Whether the constellation of states is defined in sub-regional or wider terms, the fact remains that the South African government has realised that it needs to harness the resources of private enterprise in pursuit of its plans for regional co-operation. Aware of the political and ideological obstacles to a broad-based regional constellation involving South Africa and internationally recognised black states, the government probably sees the private sector as a potential "neutral agent". Businessmen can hopefully build bridges across the political and ideological divides and prepare the groundwork for eventual inter-state co-operation at government level. The business community, for its part, has expressed strong support for the government's constellation ideas.[26]

The ceremonial inauguration, amid great fanfare, of the government's closer relationship with the private sector, and indeed of its attempts to involve the business community in the constellation design, was the so-called Carlton conference (called after the venue, Johannesburg's Carlton Hotel) in November 1979. The conference was convened by the prime minister (and arranged by the Department of Foreign Affairs) to consult business leaders "on how we can all co-operate in mobilising the extensive resources of our community towards the best advantage for our country, our region, and all its inhabitants". In attendance were the whole Cabinet and heads of government departments. The list of names from the private sector read like a Who's Who of South African business. Particularly significant was the inclusion of black businessmen. Following the prime minister's keynote address,[27] a select number of businessmen were given the opportunity to make statements. Mr HF Oppenheimer, chairman of the Anglo American Corporation, gave expression to the general air of optimism created by the conference: "It marks the beginning of a new relationship between State and private business in South Africa", he said. The concept of a constellation of Southern African states "attracts us all, and businessmen will want to help."[28] But apart from their voicing these sentiments, the assembled business leaders also highlighted a number of major immediate problems exercising their minds, notably those of unemployment, the severe shortage of skilled manpower, taxation measures and economic decentralisation. Not forgotten, least of all by the black businessmen, were the socio-political aspects of the government's discriminatory racial policies.[29] Foreign policy issues, insofar as they featured in the discussion of the constellation concept, were relegated to the periphery.

In due course the high hopes of the Carlton conference gave way to a sense of disillusionment in business circles. There was a detectable feeling of having been let down, even used, by the government; the prime minister had "nobbled" them, as a representative of organised commerce expressed it.[30] Some businessmen, for so long left out in the cold by the government, were perhaps mesmerised by the prospect of rubbing shoulders with the political leaders, of becoming insiders, to use textbook terminology. The disappointment that set in was in the first instance certainly not because the much vaunted constellation which eventually materialised was on a much more modest scale than the government had originally envisaged and business leaders had hoped. Instead, it was felt that the government had not delivered domestically, particularly on political reform. The unease of the private sector found expression at the so-called Good Hope conference (named after the venue, Cape Town's Good Hope centre) in November 1981. Called by the prime minister as a follow-up to the Carlton conference, and with PW Botha and his Cabinet in attendance, business leaders vented their impatience with the slow pace of political reform. A number of other important domestic socio-political issues also featured at the conference, for example housing, labour mobility and training and the removal of racial discrimination. Whereas a key theme at the Carlton conference had been the creation of a highly ambitious regional constellation of states, the Good Hope conference concerned itself with the more modest and immediate objective of economic decentralisation. The prime minister unveiled details of the government's new decentralisation scheme. 1 April 1982 was set as the target date for the implementation of the new deal, which would divide South Africa into eight development regions. On the whole, the sense of euphoria and the high expectations that the Carlton conference had generated among businessmen had two years later given way to a more sober, realistic

assessment by the business sector of where it stood with the government.[31] Even so, the relationship between business and government under PW Botha remains closer than at any time since 1948.

Apart from the high profile, summit-like liaison between the policy formulators and businessmen, an established and highly important channel is the Prime Minister's Economic Advisory Council. Two other forums for consultation, the Private Sector Export Advisory Committee and the Standing Committee for Export Incentives, have also been mentioned. Private sector influence in foreign policy matters, specifically regarding Southern Africa, might be brought to bear in the Southern African Development Bank and the Small Business Development Corporation. There is of course also ongoing *ad hoc* contact, on a formal and informal level, between the government and the business community. On the official side the main participants, as far as South Africa's foreign trade is concerned, are the ministers and departments of Finance and of Industries, Commerce and Tourism. The foreign ministry has in the past tended to remain rather aloof from the business community, while the latter in turn regarded the Department's understanding of the private sector's needs as, at best, suspect. PW Botha's new relationship with the business community has apparently produced a greater appreciation in foreign ministry circles of businessmen's role in South Africa's external relations. This is particularly evident in the planning division of the Department of Foreign Affairs and Information, which is keenly aware of the valuable feedback to be gained from well-travelled businessmen.

On the wider international front there are many areas of common interest between the South African government and the local business community. First and foremost, there is the need to avoid sanctions. In cases where trade bans have been imposed against South Africa, the public and private sectors would liaise, if not effectively cooperate, on ways to overcome such restrictions. With its international network of business contacts the private sector serves as a useful sensor to pick up early signs of political interference with trade links with the Republic. South African businessmen moreover have access to many states closed to official representatives from the Republic. South Africa's peculiar international position precludes the realisation of the old mercantilist philosophy that trade follows the flag. The traders themselves often have to pave the way, the flag being unwelcome either to lead or follow the trade. With many countries trade links represent South Africa's only channel of communication, and this gives businessmen a unique role in the conduct of the Republic's foreign relations. Oppenheimer's well-publicised meeting with Prime Minister Mugabe shortly after Zimbabwe's independence was a dramatic illustration of doors that opened to a South African businessman while remaining firmly shut to government leaders. What made this meeting rather special was that the Anglo American Corporation's sizeable economic stake in Zimbabwe made the Oppenheimer empire a factor to be reckoned with by Mugabe's socialist government.

In the South African private sector there is acknowledgement of the special role businessmen can – some would say should – play, given the country's international political ostracism. This has produced the notion of "business diplomacy", with the businessmen acting as "ambassadors of prosperity". They play that role not only where the flag is totally absent, but wherever South Africa finds itself under pressure. The essence of the message they convey, according to an exposition of business diplomacy, is that "prosperity accelerates the rate of positive change" within South Africa.[32]

The business community is certainly not oblivious to the close interplay between South Africa's domestic policies and its foreign relations. After all, many of the difficulties that South African businessmen experience abroad are related to the internal situation. It can also be argued that some of the very features of the domestic order that have a negative influence on the private sector's foreign ventures are also obstacles to their internal operations. At issue are ideologically motivated restrictions on the utilisation of black labour, particularly. This presents the business community with a dilemma: whether, and how, to make representations to government. An interesting new development appears to be taking place in this regard: because of the closer relationship PW Botha has forged with the private sector, business leaders might have become "protective" rather than "promotional" in putting their case to the government. Acting in a promotional fashion, they might fear, could damage their new relationship with the government. Alternatively they might feel satified that they now enjoy good access to the policy formulators and that there is no need to "go public".

It might be useful to identify some of the prominent members of the business community who can bring material influence to bear in foreign policy making. Included are individual businessmen, enterprises and organised business. Such input as they make would probably not be via the foreign ministry in the first instance, but rather through the Minister and Department of Industries, Commerce and Tourism.

There are a number of prominent organised groups whose activities also embrace external trade. The Johannesburg-based Association of Chambers of Commerce (ASSOCOM), formed as early as 1892, is engaged in the promotion and development of South Africa's trade, commerce and industries. Among its various categories of members are some 100 chamber members representing over 16 000 individual business firms.[33] The Federated Chamber of Industries (FCI), seated in Pretoria, was established in 1917 to promote the interests of the manufacturing industry. Eight affiliated regional chambers of industry, 20 national employers' organisations and a number of statutory bodies (including ARMSCOR) form the bulk of its membership.[34] The *Afrikaanse Handelsinstituut* (AHI), founded in 1942, is an exclusive association of Afrikaans business interests in all sectors of the economy, excluding agriculture. Based in Pretoria, the institute counts some 190 local chambers of commerce among its affiliated members, in addition to about 600 business members ranging from small enterprises to such giant conglomerates as Gencor and the Rembrandt Group.[35]

All three organisations are represented on the Prime Minister's Economic Advisory Council and the Private Sector Export Advisory Committee. The FCI and AHI have committees for external trade, among various others, while ASSOCOM has a foreign trade section and also serves as secretariat for the South African Council of the International Chamber of Commerce (ICC). Apart from ASSOCOM, the FCI and AHI count among the South African members of the ICC. Some of the large local chambers of commerce – such as those in Johannesburg, Cape Town and Durban – in themselves represent influential sections of the business community. Johannesburg's, for example, has 3 500 institutional members, representing a wide range of business concerns. Liaison with foreign trading partners is one of the services the Johannesburg Chamber of Commerce offers its members.[36]

An organisation engaged solely in the promotion of external trade is the South African

Foreign Trade Organisation (SAFTO). Although nominally a private sector organisation, SAFTO receives 18% of its revenue from state funds.* Established in 1963 and based in Johannesburg, SAFTO's objective is to assist companies in developing their own international marketing capabilities by offering various services relating to foreign trade. SAFTO in 1981 had 950 individual company subscribers. The organisation structures its export promotion activities on a geographic basis. The eight areas, ranked in order of resources and energy devoted to each, are Latin America, Africa, North America, Far East and Australia (equal), Middle East, Europe and Indian Ocean islands.[37]

A representative body of a different nature is the Chamber of Mines. Some 200 mines and six major mining finance houses – Anglo American Corporation, Anglovaal, Gencor, Goldfields, Johannesburg Consolidated Investments and Rand Mines – are members of the Chamber. Long the bane of Afrikaner-Nationalists, who portrayed it as a bastion of Anglo-Jewish economic power and pernicious liberal political influence, the Chamber of Mines has in recent years become "respectable". This was well illustrated in the government's invitation to the Chamber President, Mr DA Etheredge, to make a prepared statement at the Carlton conference. For its part, the Chamber has expressed an interest in the constellation idea and appointed an in-house committee on future economic development co-operation in Southern Africa.[38] As the representative organisation of the mining industry, the Chamber engages in activities of direct relevance to South Africa's foreign relations. The industry's exports are of course a principal earner of foreign exchange. The Chamber is responsible for selling gold to the South African Reserve Bank, which in turn markets it. The Chamber also sells gold on the open market in the form of a specified quantity of Kruger Rands. Labour is another area in which the Chamber features, its members employing several thousand migrants from surrounding black states. The Chamber of Mines also ventures into South Africa's foreign relations through its foreign information service in New York, run by a public relations consultancy in the city. The object is to promote the South African mining industry abroad and, when necessary, to attract foreign investment.

Foreign business interests in South Africa are represented by various bodies organised on an inter-country basis. Among the largest are the South Africa-Britain Trade Association (SABRITA),[39] the American Chamber of Commerce in South Africa (AMCHAM),[40] and the South Africa-German Chamber of Industries.[41] Operating under the aegis of ASSOCOM are the South Africa-Republic of China Chamber of Economic Relations, the South Africa-Israel Chamber of Economic Relations and the South Africa-South America Chamber of Economic Relations. There are also representative chambers for France, Belgium and Austria, among others. These various trade organisations are there to promote the interests of their member companies, foreign corporations doing business in South Africa. A major function that this has in recent years entailed is to protect their members against political pressures from their home countries. In South Africa the trade organisations have traditionally taken a very low political profile, acting in their dealings with government in a "protective" fashion. Yet they cannot be regarded as "insiders" in any way; their methods are, rather, born of caution not to offend the host government. The chambers serve as a useful channel of communication between the public sector and the foreign business community in South Africa, they provide a valuable source of information on aspects of South Africa's external business-political environment, and they help to protect the Republic's foreign trade interests. A significant recent development has been that some of these organisations have become publicly involved in social programmes designed to benefit blacks[42] – something probably not unrelated to foreign political pressures on their member companies.

When one turns to individual business enterprises and businessmen, it should be borne in mind that many of those who might bring influence to bear on government policies on domestic economic and even political matters, might not carry much weight when it comes to foreign affairs. Since PW Botha's assumption of office, new opportunities have nonetheless been created for the private sector to make its views known to the foreign policy formulators.

It is certainly more than a coincidence that two business leaders invited to deliver keynote addresses at the Carlton and Good Hope conferences were Oppenheimer and Dr AE Rupert. Not only is Oppenheimer widely

---

*This figure was reduced to 12% in 1983.

regarded as the principal spokesman of the English-speaking business sector, he also chairs South Africa's largest transnational corporation. Rupert, the leading Afrikaner businessman, heads another transnational corporation, the Rembrandt Group. Rupert certainly has far greater entrée to the policy formulators than Oppenheimer ever had. A former opposition MP and open supporter of the PFP, Oppenheimer has long been an outspoken critic of the government, although in recent years noticeably less so. Oppenheimer's is nonetheless a voice to be heeded in foreign policy circles, if only because of the economic power he wields internationally. Rupert, by contrast, is an insider among the business elite, a man whose views are much sought after by the policy formulators. In the realm of foreign policy, Rupert is particularly influential in the regional context: his corporation has for some years been providing various forms of assistance to surrounding black states, notably Lesotho, and more recently he has been the architect of the Small Business Development Corporation. Rupert has, however, not always been an insider. It is known that Verwoerd had serious differences with him, not least because of Rupert's mildly "liberal" reputation.

A manifestation of the new government-business partnership under PW Botha is the involvement of the private sector with the defence effort. The Defence Advisory Council and in all likelihood also ARMSCOR's board include some of the country's top businessmen. If the government has enough confidence in these men to enlist their expertise in such a crucial and sensitive area as defence, it can be argued that the government would also take note if they express themselves on foreign policy matters.

Another rather obvious rule of thumb that might help identifying insiders among businessmen is that the policy formulators are probably more susceptible to the views of those business leaders who are fairly openly supportive of the government. One such may well be Mr Basil Landau, Chief Executive of Union Corporation and a member of the President's Council (1981-3). In the banking sector, top executives of the Afrikaans banking group Volkskas are probably better placed to influence government than, for example, those of a multinational bank.[43]

While the prime minister developed a new relationship between government and big business, the foreign ministry nurtured its own contacts with the private sector. The Depart-ment's planning division has taken the lead in trying to place departmental contact with the business community on a more formal, regular footing. Even so, it appears that most of the interaction between individual businessmen and particular Foreign Affairs officials is *ad hoc*.

Whatever successive prime ministers' attitudes towards the private sector may have been, Parliament has traditionally counted a good many businessmen among its members. Stultz, in a comprehensive analysis of the backgrounds of all those elected or nominated to the two Houses of Parliament between 1910 and 1970, found that 18% of the members of the House of Assembly were businessmen by profession, the third largest category after farmers (24,4%) and lawyers (20,4%).[44] It was mentioned earlier that 11 members of the National Party's 1980 Foreign Affairs study group were businessmen by profession. With the exception of Dr Jan S Marais, former head of Trust Bank, the others were involved in relatively small business enterprises or in subordinate positions in larger concerns. The scarcity of top-flight businessmen would seem to be a feature of business representation within the parliamentary National Party as a whole. True, the party has had a number of wealthy businessmen in its parliamentary ranks and in the Cabinet, but these have been proportionately fewer in number than the prominent businessmen associated with major companies who have sat on the opposition benches. Three former opposition MPs were connected with the Anglo American Corporation: Oppenheimer, Dr ZJ de Beer and Mr G Waddell. This link with the opposition – first the United Party and since its formation the Progressive Party (subsequently PRP and PFP) – has long made the Anglo American Corporation highly suspect in government circles. Only under PW Botha has South Africa's principal transnational corporation come in from the cold.

Labour

Although organised labour may not bring significant influence to bear on South Africa's foreign policy making, it cannot be ignored as a factor in the country's overall foreign relations. The reason is twofold: the Republic's system of labour relations has become greatly internationalised, forming part of the wider political controversy over apartheid; and the fledgling black trade union movement in South

Africa has become a force to be reckoned with – and not only in labour matters.

South Africa's exclusion from the International Labour Organisation and the introduction of codes of conduct for foreign companies operating in South Africa are only two of the better known manifestations of the international controversy over labour arrangements in the Republic. To counter the wave of foreign criticism the government vigorously publicised the labour reforms introduced as a result of the recommendations of the Wiehahn Commission. One of the many changes flowing from the Commission's proposals has been statutory recognition of blacks' trade union rights. Although various legal constraints are still imposed on trade union activity generally, the reforms provided an impetus for the formation of numerous black trade unions. Along with unionisation went a spate of strikes and industrial unrest affecting a wide spectrum of the economy. Some of the firms most severely affected have been transnational corporations.[45]

Black trade unions articulate not merely their members' labour or economic interests. In view of black's political status in society, the politicisation of the black trade union movement – notwithstanding a legal prohibition in this regard – could hardly have been avoided. For exile movements like the ANC, the new unionisation of blacks no doubt presents a potentially useful channel of influence. Since the black unions cannot hope to become "insiders" to the government, they are bound to advance their causes by "promotional" means. Their credibility among their members in any case demands highly visible, dramatic actions by the unions. This may well involve taking their causes to international opinion. The irony of such a situation is inescapable: the South African government may find itself being "prosecuted" internationally by its own creation.

As regards the white trade union movement, it has in recent times begun to reflect the political divisions within Afrikanerdom. On the one hand there are Afrikaner-dominated trade unions that have adopted notably *verligte* stances on the highly emotive issues of black labour advancement, job reservation and racially mixed unions. On the other hand, the growth in right-wing radicalism has been reflected in the trade union movement, particularly among mineworkers. The white miners' intransigence has already produced a farcical "international" incident in 1980/1

when the right-wing Mineworkers' Union resisted President Mangope's call for the abolition of all job reservation on mines in Bophuthatswana. Particularly the prospect of black miners acquiring blasting certificates – something the union has traditionally opposed in South Africa – upset the white mineworkers.[46] Just as the black trade unions may get caught up in wider political issues, right-wing white unions may use their industrial muscle for political purposes. In this situation, too, there is an irony: the Afrikaner trade union movement, particularly the miners, played a crucial role in the National Party's electoral success in 1948; in the 1980s some white unions, with the miners in the vanguard, have become implacable opponents of the "liberal" National Party.

Should industrial unrest escalate still further, it may well affect South Africa's international economic interests. It could undermine an established economic "selling point" abroad, namely the Republic's record of industrial peace owing to a well-disciplined labour force. Although this might at present seem an unlikely scenario, the point is that organised labour is bound to become an increasingly important factor in South Africa's foreign relations, one that cannot be ignored by the policy formulators.

Agriculture

White farmers have traditionally played a highly significant role in South African politics. It is from their ranks that most MPs, by occupation, come: no less than 24,4% of the MPs elected from 1910 to 1970 were farmers (followed by lawyers and businessmen).[47] The farming community is also disproportionately represented in the House of Assembly because of the familiar practice of weighted rural constituencies. And then, of course, Afrikaner farmers have long been a strong source of National Party support.

The agricultural sector's contribution to the national economy is not particularly impressive if measured in terms of its share of the GDP: in 1979 it accounted for only 6,3%. The picture looks different when agriculture's contribution to South African exports is considered: it stood at 18% of total exports in 1979.[48] Between a quarter and a third of the country's agricultural production normally finds its way to the export market. Another important contribution of the agricultural sector to the national economy is the provision of employment opportunities: the

166

country's estimated 70 000 farmers employ approximately 1,25 million people, making it the largest employment sector.[49]

The South African Agricultural Union (SAAU) is the representative body of South African farmers. It is a voluntary organisation composed of affiliated and associated members. The former category includes the provincial agricultural unions, which are in turn divided into district unions and finally farmers' associations. The associated members are agricultural co-operatives.[50] The SAAU is represented on such official bodies as the Prime Minister's Economic Advisory Council and the Private Sector Export Advisory Committee.

Although organised agriculture is understandably preoccupied with immediate domestic matters affecting farmers, it has not been inactive on the foreign relations front. At the request of the government, the SAAU in October 1980 arranged through the Orange Free State Agricultural Union that 20 000 hectares of land in Lesotho be tilled and sown with grain by four Free State farmers' co-operatives.[51] It was not the first operation of its kind: in 1968, in the wake of Vorster announcing his "outward movement", farmers in the Orange Free State spontaneously undertook a ploughing expedition for the benefit of Lesotho's farmers.[52] The South African farmers are, to extend the fashionable term, conducting agricultural diplomacy. The SAAU also provides assistance on a substantial scale to Bophuthatswana, and has offered its services to the other independent ex-homelands and to the self-governing homelands. Given this involvement in regional relations and considering the fact that agricultural development is one of the most pressing needs of neighbouring black states, the SAAU felt offended when it was not invited to attend the Carlton conference. Two years later the SAAU was however represented at the Good Hope conference.

The matter of food exports to politically hostile black states, which right-wing political groups have tried to politicise, seems very much a non-issue in the ranks of organised agriculture. The SAAU is expressly opposed to any political interruption of food sales to black states, arguing that the Southern African export market is the most rewarding one for South African food producers. While a good many farmers no doubt share the political views of the *Herstigte Nasionale Party*, considerations of material self-interest prevent their supporting the party's opposition to

what it disparagingly refers to as "mealie diplomacy".[53]

An aspect of South Africa's relations with surrounding black states that is of real concern to farmers is the use of neighbouring territories as springboards for terrorist attacks on South African targets. Particularly farmers in the outlying border areas of the Eastern Transvaal and Northern Natal are vulnerable. Should insurgents start attacking border farms, the government would for security and also domestic political reasons be compelled to react forcefully and visibly against the neighbouring state involved. This might, ironically, result in the food lever being used to protect the very sector that produces the food and has a very material interest in its being sold.

Churches

South African churches reflect both the country's international political ostracism and the divisions within society at large.

Particularly the Afrikaans churches, above all the white *Nederduitse Gereformeerde Kerk* (NGK), the largest of the family of Reformed churches, have in the past two decades become notably isolated from the ecumenical movement. The Afrikaans churches in fact have become caught up in the international controversy over apartheid, and are seen abroad and also by other local churches as endorsing apartheid. For their part the Afrikaans Reformed churches view the ecumenical movement, in particular the World Council of Churches, as having become unacceptably politicised and violently anti-South African.

In earlier times the NGK extended its activities over a wide geographical area, with its missionaries working in such far-flung countries as the Sudan and Nigeria. However, with the onset of independence in Africa, the church's international network contracted. At the beginning of the 1980s it found itself confined to Southern African countries, the outposts being Malawi, Zambia and Zimbabwe. The church's links with Malawi were, interestingly enough, cited by Vorster as one of the reasons for his selecting Malawi as the main target of his early political overtures to black states.[54]

Domestically the NGK enjoys an unchallegeable numerical superiority in membership. According to 1970 census figures, nearly 1,5 million whites belonged to the NGK (roughly 40% of whites belonging to religious denominations); second largest was the Anglican Church with about 400 000 members. The other two Reformed churches, the *Gereformeerde Kerk* and the *Nederduitsch Hervormde Kerk*, followed way behind with 114 000 and 192 000 members respectively.[55] Occupying such a pivotal position in the Afrikaner community, the NGK is bound to exert considerable influence in society at large. Historically the NGK has closely identified with Afrikaner nationalism and the National Party. The church is, it has been said, the National Party at prayer. Such influence as the NGK has exerted over government policies has been limited to domestic matters. It has had precious little to contribute on foreign affairs, not only because these are of less immediate concern than domestic issues, but also because of the church's own international isolation. Foreign issues that have however in recent years concerned the NGK were Rhodesia/Zimbabwe and Namibia, where uncertainty over the political future of whites inevitably calls the position of the NGK in the two territories into question. The government is certainly aware of the NGK's concern in this regard.

A completely different and for it embarrassing way in which the NGK recently became involved with foreign policy matters was when its Ecumenical Bureau was drawn into the Department of Information's secret campaign against the World Council of Churches.

Among the churches that have long been seriously at odds with the government over its racial policies are most of the so-called English churches and the "daughter churches" in the *Nederduitse Gereformeerde* family of churches. The English churches have mostly become non-racial in their membership, whereas there are separate NG churches for each of the four main racial groups. (Among coloureds the *NG Sending-kerk* has by far the largest single following – 28,5% – while the Methodist Church occupies this position among blacks – 11,9%.)[56] The heavily strained relations of some of these churches with the government set severe limitations on the measure of "positive" influence they are able to exert in policy making, whether on domestic or foreign matters. Nonetheless, these churches are important factors in South Africa's foreign relations for a number of reasons.

First, a number of them maintain close links with the World Council of Churches. This is a source of tension between them and the government (and also the NGK), mainly because of the World Council of Churches' support for South African exile movements under its programme to combat racism. The churches' membership of the South African Council of Churches (SACC) further sours relations with the government, given the long record of antagonism between the SACC and the government. Second, some of the leaders of the English and black churches have publicly expressed sympathy with – if not active support of – international attempts to curb investments in South Africa and to institute boycotts against it. Such views are, of course, diametrically opposed to those of the government. Third, a number of these churches have come out in support of whites objecting to military service on conscientious grounds. In addition there are churches that have declared their intention of ministering to both sides in the war in Namibia. Again the cause for conflict with the government is obvious enough. Finally, as spokesmen for South Africa's black population groups, the English and black churches certainly play a role in sensitising and indeed shaping foreign opinion on South Africa.

Universities and research institutes

In his well-known monograph on the making of South African foreign policy in the Verwoerd era, Munger remarked that the policy formulators lacked help from the universities in understanding more about the United States and about the rest of the African continent. There was no major academic study by a South African scholar on political developments in Africa, Munger noted. An important reason for this state of affairs, he suggested, was the inferior status of political science in South Africa. As for research institutions, he mentioned only the South African Institute of International Affairs and the Africa Institute, neither of which carried significant weight in foreign policy making.[57]

Within a decade the situation has improved to the extent that one can with justification talk of an intellectual elite in the field of foreign policy. Although relatively small in numbers, its members – based at universities and research institutes – include a good many well-informed, widely travelled, alert and critical scholars who produce a steady output of studies on international affairs.

Again, the general standing of political science in South Africa has had much to do with it. As an academic discipline, political science has in the past two decades come into its own in South Africa, with hardly a university not offering it as a fully-fledged degree course. At a number of universities international politics/relations is taught as a separate course to political science, whereas at others it forms part of the political science syllabus. The University of the Witwatersrand was the first to introduce such a separate course in international relations with the establishment of the Jan Smuts Chair in International Relations in 1962. The general practice, however, is that the two courses are presented by a single teaching department. The establishment of the Political Science Association of South Africa in 1973 symbolised the discipline's coming of age in the Republic.

Munger singled out Africa and the United States as two areas in which South African academics were notably lacking in thorough knowledge. With regard to Africa generally, Munger's observation is still valid more than a decade later. There has been no comprehensive publication on modern African politics comparable to, for example, Vernon McKay's *Africa in World Politics* (1963). South African historians have, however, been active in writing the continent's history.[58] Any such work published in Afrikaans is of course of value to an extremely confined readership. (A particularly prolific writer on African politics is a former South African, Mr Colin Legum, assistant editor of the London weekly, *The Observer*.) A number of local studies of varying quality on South Africa's relations with the United States have been published over the last decade or so. Although some of these were the products of the intense strains in US-South African relations in the Carter era, the upsurge in interest in ties with the United States reflects the latter's growing importance in the Republic's external environment.[59]

Local political scientists have made considerable strides in the study of Southern African affairs. A good deal has lately been published on aspects of South Africa's relations with black states in Southern Africa, and a number of books on Namibia have appeared.[60] There are other scholars who involve themselves with more general foreign policy studies, one of whom produced the first truly comprehensive work (in Afrikaans) on South African foreign policy, with a section on the making of policy.[61] There is also the monograph on South Africa's foreign policy – *Republic under Pressure* – produced in the mid-1960s by JE Spence, a South

African-born academic resident in Britain.[62] Topical issues in South Africa's foreign relations have also received attention, with sanctions being one recent example.[63] A feature of many of these studies is that they are not merely fact-producing but indeed policy-oriented.

There has over the past decade or so been a proliferation in institutions engaged in research and publication in the field of international affairs. A number owe their existence to the former Department of Information, which created them as front organisations, while some existing bodies were financially supported by the Department. The Foreign Affairs Association and the South African Freedom Foundation were fronts for the Department of Information. Apart from their research and publications functions, they were also involved with promotional work, such as bringing prominent visitors to South Africa. The Foreign Affairs Association was disbanded after three and a half years in the wake of the Information debacle, but the South African Freedom Foundation survived and changed its name to the Southern Africa Forum. In its new guise the organisation continues its research and promotional activities and moreover remains on the Treasury's payroll, now openly so. The Forum is today only partly financed by the government, with funds also coming from the private sector. Other institutions that previously received secret funds from Information and were subsequently openly getting public money are the University of Pretoria's Institute for Strategic Studies and the Centre for International Politics at Potchefstroom University. The latter, which also receives financial support from the *Rapportryers*, an Afrikaans cultural organisation, often tends to adopt a rather popular, for-the-man-in-the-street approach to international affairs. The Institute for Strategic Studies can be depicted as a policy-oriented academic research institution, leaning heavily towards the Defence Force.

There is a host of other university-based research institutions that concern themselves with international affairs. The Rand Afrikaans University maintains the Institute for American Studies – the only one of its kind in South Africa – and a Centre for the Study of Islam. The latter, of which there is a similar one at the University of Durban-Westville, concerns itself also with the international political implications of the rise of Islam. At the University of South Africa (UNISA) a good deal of commendable work of direct relevance to South Africa's foreign relations has been produced by the Verloren van Themaat Centre for Comparative and International Law. The University of the Witwatersrand has the African Studies Institute, while a similar unit at the University of Potchefstroom is known as the Institute of African and Bantu Studies *(Instituut vir Afrikanistiek).** The Institute for Contemporary History at the University of the Orange Free State is not noted for either the quantity or quality of its publications on international affairs, but rather for the first-rate computerised press information retrieval system it operates and for its impressive political archive – both of inestimable value for research into South Africa's foreign policy. Finally, there is Stellenbosch University's Institute for the Study of Marxism, the youngest of all the research bodies mentioned.

Although they are not prominent in the study of international affairs, it can be expected that at least some of the institutions involved in futures research will in due course increasingly enter into this area. Best known is the Unit for Futures Research at the University of Stellenbosch, which has hitherto been heavily preoccupied with economic issues. Potchefstroom University in 1981 established an Institute for Future Studies, which focuses mainly on socio-economic matters. The Human Sciences Research Council, a corporate body outside the public service, contributes to futures research through its regular journal, *RSA 2 000 – Dialogue with the Future*. A private body, SYNCOM, has undertaken some policy-oriented futures research in both politics and economics.

The already mentioned BENSO, together with the South African Bureau of Racial Affairs (SABRA) and the South African Institute of Race Relations (SAIRR), concern themselves with aspects of South Africa's foreign relations particularly in the Southern African context. The first two are strongly *status quo*-oriented, with BENSO actively expounding the homelands policy and the constellation theme, and the ultra-conservative Afrikaans SABRA inclining towards rigid Verwoerdian separate development. The English-oriented SAIRR, by contrast, has an established liberal reputation and is an outspoken opponent of the government's racial policies.

*In 1983 the Institute of African and Bantu Studies merged with the Centre for International Politics and the Institute for South African Politics to form the Institute for Political and African Study.

A word should also be said about the present standing of the South African Institute of International Affairs (SAIIA) and the Africa Institute, the only two research bodies featuring in Munger's study. Munger compared the SAIIA's influence on the foreign policy formulators with that of the John Birch society on President Johnson's Cabinet. This is an apt summary of the SAIIA's position during the Verwoerd era; not surprising considering that it tended to reflect "educated, English-speaking United Party views".[64] Although the SAIIA more than a decade later still has something of an upper-class, English-oriented and liberal image, it has come a long way since its "John Birch days". At least in foreign ministry circles, the SAIIA enjoys some recognition as a reputable independent research body (it receives no public funds). Its enhanced status is probably as much due to its increasing output, its higher public profile and the capable directorship of former diplomat Professor John Barratt, as to a new receptivity to outside views on the part of the foreign ministry. The SAIIA finds itself in a unique position among local institutions active in the same field, in that it maintains branches in eight main centres in South Africa (to cater for its members by arranging meetings, etc.), and enjoys good international contacts, which it partly owes to its origins as one of a chain of similar institutes established in member countries of the Commonwealth.

Munger depicted the leadership of the Africa Institute and its work as "strictly *persona grata* with the National Party hierarchy".[65] Although it cannot today as readily be identified with the government as in the early 1960s, the state-funded but autonomous Africa Institute nonetheless stands much closer to the government that the SAIIA, for example. The Institute has on occasion been entrusted with policy-oriented research by the government or a particular ministry. Officially styled a research organisation and information centre, the Africa Institute is a multi-disciplinary body covering a wide spectrum of the natural and human sciences in its work. The focus of its research has in recent years been on Southern Africa, but it intends widening its scope.

However impressive the list of institutions and whatever merit their work may have, such features are no guarantee that their voices are being heard by the foreign policy formulators. The influence that the academic community can exert ultimately depends on the policy formulators. The greater degree of recognition that the foreign ministry has over the last few years been according the intellectual elite may be related to PW Botha's style of government, which has led to a much greater acknowledgement than ever before of the value of outside expert advice in policy making. In a number of instances the experts – also from academic ranks – have formally joined the public service; for example, those who left academia for appointments in the constitutional planning branch in the Office of the Prime Minister. The advice of "armchair politicians", as Vorster once referred to academics, was not particularly sought after by the former prime minister when it came to sensitive political issues; the notion that policy formulation is the business of elected politicians acting in terms of a popular mandate was the general rule of the day.

The foreign ministry's greater receptiveness to the views of the intellectual elite was given expression by the planning division. Apart from *ad hoc* contacts with academics, the division attempted to establish semi-formal, regularised communication through annual round table discussions with selected representatives from the ranks of universities and research institutions. The idea was that those in the Cape Town area would meet during the parliamentary session held in the city, followed by a similar meeting with others in the Johannesburg-Pretoria area later in the year. The procedure was followed for only a year or two, and then fell into disuse. These arrangements fell far short of a standing advisory group, something the foreign ministry has never had.

Among the intellectual elite, as among businessmen, there are insiders and outsiders, to use a categorisation outlined earlier. Although it is difficult to be precise about who the insiders are, a few names stand out, such as Professor GC Olivier of the Department of Political Science and International Relations at the University of Pretoria; Dr GME Leistner, Director of the Africa Institute, and Professor John Barratt of the SAIIA. Their views certainly carry considerable weight and are sought after in the foreign ministry. The outsiders include those academics who do not enjoy the same entrée to the foreign ministry – one possible reason being the latter's dislike of their views – and who express their ideas in a "promotional" rather than a "protective" fashion. Then there are those academics who tend to adopt a low profile and do not fit either of these categories, but whose views are nonetheless noted

by the foreign policy formulators. One such is Professor DT Kunert of the Department of International Relations at the University of the Witwatersrand, a man whose writings have impressed none other than the prime minister.[66]

Given the importance of the military in foreign policy making, academic voices with influence in military circles should also be noted. It is not possible to be categorical, but is seems safe to say that the Institute for Strategic Studies at the University of Pretoria plays a role here. Its first director, Professor MHH Louw (since retired), is a highly respected political scientist and his views are certainly taken seriously in military circles. He was succeeded by Professor M Hough. Another is Mr DFS Fourie, attached to the Department of Political Science and International Relations at UNISA and a specialist in strategic studies. The Rand Afrikaans University has a chair in National Strategy. The holder, General H de V du Toit, was formerly head of Military Intelligence. Like the foreign ministry, the Defence Force has in recent years displayed a greater openness towards the academic community, and has been keen to enlist the services of academics in, for example, officer training courses.

In conclusion, it must be said that the involvement of academic experts in an advisory capacity offers no guarantee of better or more balanced decisions. The fact that they are being invited to make their views known to the policy formulators nonetheless indicates that the latter feel a need for input from the academic community. If nothing else, South Africa's precarious international position may have persuaded the policy formulators to mobilise the country's best brain power in the realm of foreign policy. In the economic field this has long been done.

The Afrikaner Broederbond

The Afrikaner Broederbond occupies a unique position among interest groups; the elitist organisation counts virtually the entire Cabinet and very many ranking civil servants among its members. "Since the Afrikaner Broederbond got into its stride it has given the country its governments", Mr HB Klopper, one of the founders of the secret organisation, boasted at its 50th anniversary in 1968. "It has given the country every Nationalist Prime Minister since 1948."[67] The understanding between Broederbond and government "has always been of the best", according to Prof AN Pelzer, a senior member of the organisation and its official biographer. He attributes this "fortunate state of affairs" to the fact that "the political leaders were normally members of the Afrikaner Broederbond and the problems were discussed in a spirit of brotherhood."[68] The relationship between successive National Party governments – also those of Vorster and PW Botha – and the Broederbond has always been intimate, by virtue of overlapping membership. Against this background it might be tempting to see the government as the Broederbond in power, or the Broederbond as the power behind the throne. To do so would, however, be a grave over-simplification of the relationship between the two. Under Vorster a significant change in the Broederbond's status set in: it was, as Serfontein convincingly illustrated, relegated from a "co-partner of the National Party" to a "support organisation".[69] The Broederbond was being used by the government as an agent of sorts – a far cry from the organisation dictating government policies. This development had important implications for the Broederbond's role in both domestic and foreign policy matters.

Early in Vorster's premiership it already became apparent that the extremely close ties that had existed between the Broederbond and the Verwoerd government had fallen on hard times. The tensions within the National Party were, not surprisingly, reflected in the Broederbond, where expression was also given to reservations about the new premier's "deviationist" tendencies, such as the liberalisation of the sports policy and the outward movement with its implication of black diplomats being stationed in South Africa. Both Vorster and his right-wing critics took their respective causes to the Broederbond, thus drawing the supposedly cultural organisation firmly into Afrikanerdom's political infighting. As in the National Party, Vorster eventually also prevailed in the Broederbond: at the end of 1972 the organisation was finally purged of HNP supporters within its ranks, following the example set by the National Party. This is not to say that the organisation had completely freed itself of all right-wing elements; like the National Party, the "purified" Broederbond also continued to harbour *verkramptes* who entertained misgivings about some of Vorster's domestic and foreign policies. The important point, nonetheless, is that Vorster in the years 1969-72 managed to place his political leadership beyond question in both the

National Party and the Broederbond. Far from his political leadership being challenged from within the Broederbond, Vorster could henceforth by and large rely on the organisation to sanction his policies.[70]

It is possible to be categorical about these events in the obsessively secretive Broederbond thanks to two impressively detailed exposés of the organisation.[71] They filled a long felt void in the search for reliable information on the role of a particularly important institution in the South African political process. Previously, assessments of the Broederbond's political input were more often than not mere guesswork, lacking in accuracy and authority. In his study on South African foreign policy making Munger in passing references dismissed the Broederbond as "much overestimated" and "not particularly significant on the foreign policy level".[72] His comments applied to the Verwoerd period. Although the Broederbond's influence was significantly less in foreign than domestic policy matters, Munger had nonetheless greatly underestimated the organisation's role in the realm of foreign policy.[73] And in domestic politics the Broederbond's role during Verwoerd's premiership could hardly be over-estimated.

This sketches the context in which the Broederbond's political role in the Vorster era should be viewed, but it must be stressed that the organisation, despite its reduced status, remained "the reinforced scaffolding of the fortress of Afrikaner nationalism". [74] There was close and continuous interaction between the government and the Broederbond, on the clear understanding that on the political level the government was the senior party in this partnership. For the Broederbonders in government – which in practice meant nearly all Cabinet ministers – their fellow Broederbonders provided a valuable sounding board – a "secret opinion poll"[75] – and could also serve as reliable "agents" to prepare the political groundwork within Afrikanerdom for new or amended government policies, and to promote them afterwards. With the 11 910 members it had in 1977 the Broederbond was well placed to fulfil these functions, for its members held numerous top positions in professions that exerted great influence in shaping public opinion, such as journalism, education and the church. Overall, the Broederbond included an impressive number of prominent Afrikaners.[76]

The partnership between the government and the Broederbond was mutually beneficial and indeed regarded as essential by both sides. The Broederbond "is convinced that the [National] Party is the best means of promoting our political ideals", Dr PJ Meyer, then head of the organisation, declared in 1970.[77] Some years later the new Broederbond chief, Professor G van N Viljoen, said the organisation's principal function was to "activate, motivate and guide our members, many of whom carry high-level responsibility for making and directing policy and thus are busy every day 'about the Afrikaner Broederbond's business'."[78] That business essentially remained the same over the years, namely "securing stable political control for the Afrikaner."[79] Such statements were of course made in confidence, designed for Broederbond consumption only.

A political issue with obvious foreign policy implications that greatly preoccupied the Broederbond in the late 1960s and early 1970s was changes to the government's sports policy. Vorster moved away from Verwoerd's rigid adherence to racially segregated sport by, among other things, allowing racially mixed sports teams from abroad to visit South Africa. In what was probably a carefully designed move to cover his back against a possible right-wing backlash, Vorster actually involved – and thus implicated – the Broederbond in devising liberalising changes to the sports policy. In the end, Vorster could count on the Broederbond to spread the message that so-called multi-national sport was the new name of the game.[80]

Among the other matters that featured in what Viljoen called "regular discussions at high level" – meaning the government and the Broederbond's Executive Council – were the *détente* policy, South Africa's relations with Rhodesia and Mozambique, the Turnhalle conference in Namibia, and matters of security.[81] In February 1976 Broederbond members were told that the Executive Council had decided to establish a "special committee on foreign relations, particularly on relations with Africa". It would provide members with "the necessary expert information" and, evidently as a think tank, would formulate suggestions on strategy and convey tactical information to the prime minister to assist him in his pursuit of *détente* with black African states.[82] The formation of such a group was nothing new. Already in 1963, as mentioned in Chapter 1, a range of task groups or watchdog committees had been established by the Broederbond, dealing among other things with

foreign affairs. It was through such committees of experts – which often included political leaders – rather than acting organisationally as the Broederbond, that the organisation achieved its greatest successes, Viljoen suggested.[83]

In the 1970s the Broederbond also concerned itself with other topical issues in South Africa's foreign relations. By the time the ramifications of the international oil crisis of 1973 were being felt over a wide front, the Broederbond had already examined South Africa's future capital requirements. A few years later, when international sanctions against South Africa loomed large because of Namibia, the Biko incident and the October 1977 security clampdown, the Broederbond had already done its homework with an investigation into the role of foreign investment in South Africa and the country's self-defence in a hostile world.[84]

Another way in which the organisation expresses itself on foreign affairs is through its national congresses, held every two years. They take the form of political party congresses in that resolutions are passed on aspects of government policies. With Cabinet ministers usually in attendance, such expressions of Broederbond opinion are noted in the highest councils of state.[85] Delegates are also briefed on the foreign policy issues of the day; for example, at the October 1978 congress a paper was presented on "the total onslaught against South Africa in the international field".[86]

The peculiar link between the government and the Broederbond explains why the Executive Council was made privy to confidential information on South Africa's involvement in the Angolan war in 1975/6, when Parliament and the public were deliberately kept in the dark by the government. But while the Executive Council was being kept "well up to date" by some Cabinet members on events in Angola, it was told that in "a situation like the one in which our country currently finds itself, it is absolutely unthinkable that detailed information of a confidential nature [on Angola] can be extended to our general membership."[87]

As the government used the Broederbond to develop support for changes to its sports policy, the organisation was instrumental in explaining aspects of foreign policy. Rhodesia is a classic example, where Vorster deployed the Broederbond to counter possible negative reaction to changes in Pretoria's policy towards the Smith regime. The man selected to prepare Broederbond members for things to come was Van den Bergh, head of the Bureau for State Security. The choice was shrewd, for this old comrade of Vorster's was the last man who could be suspected of selling out whites. In a secret circular of February 1975 he bluntly stated that South Africa had to abandon its traditional attitude towards Rhodesia and accept the inevitability of black rule in an independent Zimbabwe in the immediate future. Van den Bergh warned that South Africa would attract the "everlasting hate" of black Africa if it did not accept a black majority government in the neighbouring territory. The real enemy of Southern Africa was communism, Van den Bergh added, and South Africa needed to co-operate with black African states in countering this threat. A Rhodesian settlement was therefore essential.[88] The following year Broederbond chief Viljoen took the exercise a step further when, in a circular, he accused the Rhodesian government of duplicity, double talk and a lack of integrity in the settlement negotiations. South Africa would involve itself in the Rhodesian issue only if it were in its interests, Viljoen said, and pointedly added that South Africa would not back the rebel colony in all circumstances.[89]

These various Broederbond ventures into the realm of foreign affairs during the Vorster premiership were on a much more limited scale than the organisation's involvement with domestic political issues. Foremost among these were, not surprisingly, race relations.[90]

The two exposés of the Broederbond on which the preceding discussion is based were published very soon after PW Botha became prime minister. They consequently contain hardly any information on his relationship with the organisation. There is no other published material to rely on either. This makes an accurate assessment of the Broederbond's present role in policy making virtually impossible. There are, nonetheless, some pointers that may serve as a rough guide to the state of affairs in the PW Botha era.

What has not changed is the familiar feature of a National Party Cabinet composed almost entirely of Broederbonders. Only two members of PW Botha's first Cabinet were not members of the secret organisation.[91] Following subsequent changes to the Cabinet, it is possible that the only non-Broederboder is Mr OPF Horwood, Minister of Finance and the sole English-speaker. In December 1978 the new prime minister told the House of Assembly that he was a member of the Broederbond, and "proud of the fact".[92] It was no revelation, but merely the confirmation of a known fact. But pride notwithstanding, PW Botha certainly wants to keep the organisation at least as well in check as his predecessor had managed to do – if not actually maintain a more distant relationship with the Broederbond.[93] Perhaps an intimation of things to come was an unprecedented public statement PW Botha had already made in 1968, when he declared that the National Party would not allow itself to be dictated to by any other power when it came to policy; the Broederbond, he made it plain, was an "outside organisation".[94] In April 1981 the prime minister, with reference to the Broederbond, insisted that his government "does not take instructions from anyone other than the party we belong to". Any representations from other organisations would nonetheless be considered "on merit". He could give the assurance, he said, "that I am a free man and that I am acting as a free man as Prime Minister of this country."[95] While it might be said that such statements were made for political consumption and ought not to be taken at face value, they do gain some credibility when considering PW Botha's style of government. He is open to outside advice, but then primarily from professional experts. Nonetheless, PW Botha is certainly keenly aware of the instrumental value of the Broederbond: a sounding board and a superbly placed agency to mobilise support for government decisions.

What might have added to the more distant relationship between PW Botha and the Broederbond was the election of Prof CWH Boshoff in September 1980 to succeed Viljoen as head of the organisation. Boshoff, a Pretoria University theologian, is a man of pronounced conservative views – even in National Party terms – on the key issue of race relations. He is moreover chairman of SABRA, a body that stands well to the right of the PW Botha government. Boshoff, his Broederbond position notwithstanding, can certainly not have been a valued confidant or counsellor of PW Botha. The differences between the Broederbond chief and the prime minister should be seen in the context of the divisions that have plagued the National Party since PW Botha's assumption of office. It is extremely unlikely that the dissension would not have been reflected in the Broederbond. Any struggle for the "soul" of the Broederbond – a far more intense battle than that waged by Vorster some years earlier, because the revolt against PW

Botha is much greater – would probably have inhibited the organisation in its political exertions.

It was earlier suggested that a further constraint on the Broederbond's political innovation is PW Botha's style of government. In this respect the SSC is an important factor. Although the majority of the SSC's members are probably Broederbonders, it cannot be assumed that they simply follow a "Broederbond line" on the Council; as an organisation the Broederbond in all likelihood does not have a defined position on all or even most major foreign policy issues. Even so, the government must be well aware of its "duty" to keep fellow-Broederbonders informed on government thinking. Because of the differences between PW Botha and Boshoff, the communication could – in contrast with the Vorster era – be taking place at a lower level.* Between PW Botha and Viljoen, however, no such tensions exist; the latter was in fact earmarked by the prime minister for high political office. In August 1979 Viljoen, previously Rector of the Rand Afrikaans University, was appointed Administrator-General of Namibia. A year later PW Botha elevated Viljoen to the Cabinet as Minister of National Education.

Of all the organisations considered in this chapter, the "Super-Afrikaners", as the Broederbonders have been called,[96] are no doubt the supreme insiders when it comes to government policy making. More than any other organisation, the Broederbond is protective in promoting its cause; it is, after all, a secret society.

Other non-partisan interest groups

South Africa Foundation

The South Africa Foundation was formally established in December 1959, sponsored by a group of leading South African businessmen. They were drawn together by the perceived need to present a "true picture of South Africa" to a world becoming increasingly critical of and indeed hostile to the country. Thus was born "the diplomacy of private enterprise".[97] The continuing business connection has over the years

*Boshoff's tenure as head of the Broederbond came to an abrupt end in July 1983 when, in what seems a palace revolution, he was replaced by Professor JP de Lange, Rector of the Rand Afrikaans University. Whereas Boshoff is a *verkrampte* flag-bearer finding himself at odds with the government's constitutional reforms, De Lange is a noted *verligte*.

been reflected in the Foundation's presidency and in the composition of its council, the governing body, and the board of trustees, which reads like a Who's Who of South African business. A good many prominent personalities from such fields as academia, law, sport and medicine are listed among the Foundation's over 300 trustees. It is a singularly impressive line-up comprising English and Afrikaans speakers, Nationalists and non-Nationalists (also a fair sprinkling of Broederbonders), whites and blacks.

Financed entirely – and very generously – by private enterprise, the Johannesburg-based Foundation maintains its own overseas representation with permanent offices in Washington, London, Paris and Bonn. It also conducts its foreign activities through a network of MM (Man-to-Man) committees, each responsible for contacts with a particular country.[98]

Being what Foundation President WH de la Harpe Beck has termed "an information and communication organisation", the South Africa Foundation has the dual function of presenting the facts about South Africa to the world on the one hand, and on the other analysing and explaining the nature and aims of foreign pressures on South Africa "to engender a responsible and sophisticated reaction to such pressures amongst South Africans themselves". Part of the Foundation's external function of promoting good relations between South Africa and other countries is to keep the Republic's international lines of communication open. Thus the Foundation has tried countering attempts to increase South Africa's political isolation, encourage disinvestment and impose economic sanctions. The means employed are research, the distribution of "unbiased information" and direct contact "at top level throughout the world".[99] These commitments have not prevented the Foundation developing an academic character in recent years, as its research projects and publications testify.[100] The Foundation is therefore no mere promotional organisation for South African business interests – "an arm of the business community", as Munger depicted it[101] – but it can also lay some claim to being a reputable independent research institution, its activities in many ways resembling those of the SAIIA, for example.

Although the Foundation is primarily concerned with South Africa's foreign relations, it recognises that external attacks on the country are based on the domestic political situation and that the Republic's international image is largely "made in South Africa itself". But even so, there has since the Foundation's early days been a clear division between those who maintain that the organisation should state South Africa's case on the basis of the political *status quo,* and others who see the Foundation as a means of promoting change in government policies, above all its racial policies.[102] Lately the Foundation has openly identified with the voices calling for more rapid – albeit incremental and cautious – political liberalisation in South Africa. But any political flavour brings its inevitable controversies: foreign critics have depicted the Foundation as a slick apologist for the *status quo* in South Africa, whereas South Africans variously criticise it for not defending the Republic vigorously enough against external pressures,[103] for being too "liberal", or for being a "capitalist"-inspired defender of the *status quo.*

As far as the Foundation's influence on government is concerned, it is well known that Verwoerd had serious reservations about the organisation and kept it at a distance, also from the foreign ministry. In Verwoerd's time the Foundation's voice was "quite a minor one", considering the great stature of its board and its financial outlay, Munger observed.[104] The Foundation has since certainly received greater recognition from the foreign policy formulators as a factor in South Africa's foreign relations. The foreign ministry, for instance, is keenly aware of the value of the Foundation's network of contacts abroad. The foreign ministry and the former Department of Information no doubt saw the Foundation as a valuable ally in promoting South Africa's interests in a hostile world, particularly because of the Foundation's independence from government. There had, for example, been regular consultations between Information and the Foundation.[105] Useful though it may have been, the relationship between the foreign ministry and the Foundation has not always been smooth in recent years. Probably the most serious differences between the Foundation and the government – specifically the foreign minister – occurred in 1981 and concerned the Von Wechmar incident. At the South Africa Foundation's annual convention in Cape Town that year Dr RF Gruber, Director of the Foundation's Bonn office, criticised Pik Botha's angry reaction to the treatment Baron von Wechmar had earlier meted out to South Africa in the UN General Assembly. The foreign minister's attack on Von

Wechmar was "most regrettable and undeserved", Gruber said, and had harmed South Africa's relations with West Germany. Pik Botha had moreover offered the West German government "some gratuitous advice" regarding Von Wechmar's position as Bonn's representative at the UN.[106] It is known that the foreign minister did not take kindly to Gruber's utterances – just as he had taken strong exception to newspaper criticism of his attack on Von Wechmar[107] – and the episode must have placed considerable strain on the relations between the foreign ministry and the Foundation.

As far as positive inputs into foreign policy making from the South Africa Foundation's ranks are concerned, these come not so much from the Foundation as an organisation, but rather from prominent individuals associated with it. The influence they bring to bear (and this applies to domestic as well as foreign policy making) is derived not from their Foundation connections in the first place, but from their standing in other spheres quite unrelated to the Foundation. (To say that these people carry weight not *because of* but rather *despite* their involvement with the Foundation would be a rather unkind cut.) With PW Botha's overtures to the business community, new opportunities for access to the policy formulators have been created for the Foundation's principal domestic constituency.

United States-South Africa Leader Exchange Programme (USSALEP)

USSALEP, Munger suggested, generated important feedback regarding foreign policy. This was done through the South Africans who had visited the United States under the exchange programme.[108] Between USSALEP's founding (in 1958) and 1980 over 250 "leaders and potential leaders" from South Africa had spent some time in the United States under the association's various exchange programmes. The object of these efforts was to "promote authentic communication and the broadening of options within and between South Africa and the US."[109] Although the many South African visitors to the United States may have gained valuable insights into US-South African relations, and may on their return have played an educational role of sorts in this regard, their views may not have reached the policy formulators at all. For someone to carry weight with the policy formulators requires attributes completely unrelated to a USSALEP connection. As for the organisation itself, USSALEP's management committee consists of a number of people prominent in the foreign affairs field, such as Advocate DP de Villiers, managing director of Nasionale Pers, Barratt of the SAIIA, and Olivier, the Pretoria University political scientist. Such influence as they may have in foreign policy making exists quite independently of their associations with USSALEP; nor does their presence give USSALEP as such any significant weight in foreign policy making.

Sports organisations

Sport is the area in which attempts to isolate South Africa have probably been most successful and the impact most widely felt within the country. In response, local sports organisations have launched a two-pronged offensive to regain admission to international sport or to stave off further isolation. On the one hand, attempts are made at international level, through inter-national sports bodies, to put the case for South African participation in world sport. On the other, some South African sports organisations campaign for accelerated "normalisation" of sport within the country, not least in an attempt to strengthen their claims to international competition. Prominent among the local bodies attempting to break their international isolation and break racial barriers at home are the South African Rugby Board, the South African Olympic and National Games Association (representative of 25 Olympic and 13 non-Olympic sports bodies), the South African Cricket Union, the South African Tennis Union and the Football Council of South Africa. By trying to keep South Africa in international sport, these bodies are doing precisely the opposite of the South African Council on Sport (SACOS), a body about which more will be said in the next chapter. To date, it would appear that SACOS and international groups agitating for South Africa's increased sports isolation have had the upper hand. On the domestic front, the other bodies perhaps deserve credit for the desegregation of sport – although their endeavours cannot be divorced from the realities of isolation.

White political parties

Much has been said in Chapter 4 about the role of the parliamentary parties in the making of foreign policy. Of interest here are the contributions of the non-parliamentary, grass-roots section of the National Party and of the *Herstigte Nasionale*

Party (HNP), which is not represented in Parliament. The PFP and NRP, already so marginal in their parliamentary influence on foreign policy, carry even less weight in their non-parliamentary capacities and are therefore not discussed here. The National Conservative Party can also be overlooked because of its insignificant impact on the electorate, and because it moreover turned out to be shortlived.*

The National Party

The most visible way in which National Party supporters can express themselves on the specifics of party policies in the presence of the policy formulators is the party's annual round of provincial congresses. Each branch or divisional council, depending on the particular province, sends a certain number of delegates to the congresses, and the delegates are invited to table motions for discussion.

In the late 1960s foreign policy issues featured prominently, notably at the Transvaal congresses. The 1967 congress became known as the "black diplomats congress" because of the salience of the issue of diplomatic ties with black African states. The controversy was closely tied up with the smouldering right-wing revolt in the Transvaal National Party. Matters came to a head at the Transvaal congress of 1969, and foreign policy issues loomed large. Delegates were asked to affirm their support for the government's policies on Afrikaans-English co-operation, diplomatic ties with black states, immigration and allowing visiting national sports teams that might include blacks. The handful who refused left the National Party to form the HNP. The right-wing revolt and the consequent split in the ruling party did not act as a brake on the government: diplomatic ties with Malawi, established in 1967, remained and Vorster in 1970, as part of the outward movement, paid an official visit to that country. The government also continued its cautious incremental moves towards the "normalisation" of sport in South Africa.

After the strains they caused in the late 1960s, foreign policy issues for a time receded into the background. Although they still regularly appeared on the list of motions tabled at National Party congresses, they did not attract much attention and were least of all divisive. Instead

---

*The Conservative Party, into which the NCP dissolved, was only formed in March 1982 and thus falls outside the time scope of this book.

they were – as typically happens at the congresses – supportive and acclamatory. Foreign policy issues again came strongly to the fore at National Party congresses in the years 1976-8, a period when South Africa's international standing reached the lowest point since the early 1960s. Although the mounting tide of international censure, culminating in the UN arms embargo, exercised delegates' minds, they could find no fault in the Vorster government's handling of the situation. As the November 1977 general election clearly demonstrated, Vorster had correctly read the electorate's mood on the question of external pressure on South Africa. Following a familiar cyclical pattern, the high level of interest in foreign policy levelled off soon after PW Botha had come to power. Not only did the grave external threats of the 1976-8 period appear to have subsided, but the new prime minister's domestic political initiatives overshadowed the National Party congresses in the next few years. Insofar as foreign policy issues made their customary appearance on the agenda, motions and speeches were supportive rather than apprehensive or critical. The most important issue in this regard was the "terrorist threat", but the prime minister's tough stance – typically expressed in terms of the total national strategy – gave the rank and file little to complain about. Namibia also featured prominently among the annual foreign policy issues, but again the government's oft-repeated resolve not to hand the territory to a "Marxist terrorist organisation" (SWAPO) at the point of a gun was well attuned to the delegates' sentiments.

An important feature of National Party congresses' involvement with foreign policy matters which emerges from the preceding overview is that delegates' contributions are neither particularly original nor innovative, and they typically express the prevailing foreign policy mood. This mood manifests itself in a hard line on issues relating to South Africa's external security.

The Herstigte Nasionale Party

That foreign policy considerations featured strongly in the founding of the HNP in October 1969 was an omen of things to come. It was, however, not until the 1981 general election that the HNP was in a position to propagate its policies with notable success. In the interim the party failed to make any meaningful impact on the electorate, as witness its dismal performances in the 1970, 1974 and 1977 general elections. The

HNP's dramatic progress in the 1981 election was, however, not in the first instance attributable to its stand on foreign policy issues or, for that matter, voter disaffection with the government on this score. Instead, the major plank in the HNP's platform – and indeed its main drawing card – is a policy of unadulterated, old-style apartheid. The PW Botha government is portrayed as watering down apartheid and forsaking the true principles of Afrikaner nationalism as articulated by Malan and Verwoerd. The foreign policy corollary of this brand of domestic ultra-conservatism is extreme "hawkishness". The HNP leader, Mr JA Marais, for example, demands that neighbouring black states harbouring anti-South African insurgents be set an ultimatum to get rid of these elements, failing which South Africa would attack militarily.[110] The HNP also makes great play of Namibia – or South West Africa, as it insists on referring to the territory – and charges the South African government with being weak and manipulable in the face of external pressure. Die Afrikaner, mouthpiece of the HNP, took the government severely to task for the way it was conducting the war against SWAPO. The war had to be ended swiftly, the paper demanded, and that could be done only through a decisive military victory. South Africa had the capability to do so. Die Afrikaner derided the government for wanting to end the war through a settlement reached around the conference table. Referring to the government's notion that the struggle in Namibia could be only 20% military and 80% political, the paper wrote that "the HNP says the struggle against the terrorists must be a 100% military struggle."[111] The government's alleged submissiveness to foreign pressure, the HNP tried to convince the electorate, was a symptom of its dangerous "liberalism" on domestic racial matters. The HNP plays these foreign policy issues in a high key, adding force to its stand on domestic issues. By freely mixing domestic and foreign policy issues, the HNP has managed to create a politically highly potent compound: the party appeals to the electorate's racial prejudices, its real concern for security and indeed its instinct for survival. So skilfully did the HNP exploit foreign policy issues that to a large extent it dictated the terms of the election debate on them.

But the foreign policy ingredients did not primarily account for the success of the HNP's election package. The external dimension has little effect without the domestic component; the former merely reinforces the appeal of the latter.

The government is in any case far less vulnerable to the HNP on foreign than domestic policies – but with one exception: Namibia. In linking the fate of whites in Namibia with that of whites in the Republic, the HNP is sowing in fertile ground, for there is widespread apprehension among white South Africans about the future of Namibia and the impact of events there on their own situation. A Namibian independence settlement resulting in a SWAPO regime could be a political bonanza of the first order for the HNP – a vindication of its charge that the government is selling out the whites in the territory. All this may have served as a further brake on the South African government in its involvement in the Western-led settlement initiative.

Black, coloured and Indian political organisations

Banned and exiled movements

Of all the organisations discussed in this chapter, the starkest contrast is between the Broederbond and the various predominantly or exclusively black organisations based abroad and composed largely of South African exiles. Whereas the Broederbond is dedicated to safeguard Afrikaner political control, these other movements are committed to the overthrow of the white government. Broederbonders enjoy a special, intimate relationship with the government, while members of the black organisations are *personae non gratae,* banned and in exile.

Foremost among the anti-government forces are the ANC and PAC. They were banned by the South African government in 1960, and subsequently went both underground in South Africa and into exile. Going into exile proved everything but a flight into the political wilderness. Following the lead of the OAU, the UN General Assembly in December 1968 conferred recognition on "the South African liberation movement" in its "legitimate struggle" against apartheid.[112] From this point it was only a short step for the General Assembly to condemn the South African government to illegitimacy and declare it unfit to represent the people of South Africa. Again taking its cue from the OAU, the General Assembly elevated the "liberation movements" to the "authentic representatives of the overwhelming majority of the South African people". The ANC and PAC, both specifically recognised, were said to struggle "for the seizure of power by the people", and the Assembly

declared legitimate their use of "all available means".[113] The next move was to accord the so-called liberation movements observer status at the UN. Material support for the ANC and PAC in their struggly against the South African government has been forthcoming from various quarters. Some Western states are providing what is termed humanitarian aid, whereas black African and communist states contribute materially to the actual armed struggle. The two movements have also been allowed to establish representation in Western, communist and black African countries.

Given their international status, the so-called liberation movements have become important factors in South Africa's foreign relations. They are instrumental in shaping the Republic's external environment, for example in trying to influence foreign opinion – both government and public – on South Africa. In concrete terms, this has typically involved agitation for South Africa's further isolation in all areas of inter-state contact and for the imposition of mandatory economic sanctions. The two exiled movements are however not in the first instance a foreign policy concern for Pretoria, but rather a domestic political and security one: the ANC in particular enjoys sizeable support among blacks and is moreover engaged in violent resistance in South Africa. Some Western business enterprises with interests in South Africa have for their part recognised the ANC as an important political force. In what was for the ANC something of a coup, its President, Mr Oliver Tambo, in 1981 met top representatives of the largest American transnational corporations operating in South Africa.[114]

Black African states' support for the "liberation struggle" against South Africa has profound implications for the Republic's relations with particularly its neighbouring states. Pretoria's primary concern has been that surrounding countries would serve as springboards for insurgency against South Africa. Mozambique, for example, has provided the ANC's military wing, *Umkhonto we Sizwe,* with bases from where attacks against the Republic can be launched or at any rate planned. This led to the South African Defence Force's commando raid on ANC targets near Maputo in January 1981. While other neighbouring states, including Zimbabwe, have refused the ANC facilities for insurgency, they have all declared their solidarity with the ANC; the movement has been allowed to open offices and ANC supporters and others have been given sanctuary as political refugees. (In the wake of the 1976 riots an estimated 10 000 blacks illegally left South Africa.)[115]

Of the exiled movements, the ANC is by far the most important. It is the oldest, best organised and most active domestically and internationally. As a political and "military" force, the ANC far outclasses its old rival, the PAC. They are by no means the only two exiled organisations with an impact on South Africa's foreign relations. The South African Communist Party, banned in 1950, has since been active in exile. Over the years a close relationship has developed between the Communist Party and the ANC, manifested among other things in overlapping membership. The extent of the Communist Party's influence over the ANC has long been a matter of some controversy. In Pretoria's book there is no doubt on this score: the ANC is "controlled" by the South African Communist Party and "subsidised and supported by Communist Russia and her satellites", according to PW Botha.[116] A recent arrival on the exile scene is the Black Consciousness Movement of Azania, which in 1979 set up offices in London and elsewhere. Two years earlier, in a mass security clampdown, a whole range of black consciousness organisations were banned in South Africa. Because of internal divisions, poor organisation and differences with the ANC, the exiled Blanc Consciousness Movement has proven a very marginal organisation in influencing South Africa's external milieu.

Exiled organisations with a narrower focus than the above-mentioned four are the South African Non-Racial Olympic Committee (SANROC) and the South African Congress of Trade Unions (SACTU), both based in London. SANROC actively and not without some success campaigns for South Africa's further isolation from international sport, while SACTU professes to be the voice of the black trade union movement of South Africa.

A constant thorn in the South African government's flesh is the network of anti-apartheid movements abroad. South African exiles were engaged in the formation of the oldest and largest of these, the British Anti-Apartheid Movement, and exiles feature among the office holders in some of the various anti-apartheid movements.

The influence that the banned and/or exiled movements have on South African foreign policy is neither direct nor what might be termed positive. Illegal in South Africa, or at any rate operating from abroad, these organisations are inevitably highly "promotional" in advancing their causes, trying to enlist international sympathy. They thus exert pressure on Pretoria via the international community – apart from such direct pressure as flows from acts of terrorism in South Africa. The influence they exercise is not "positive" in the sense that their views are not solicited by the South African policy formulators, for the two sides' objectives are in fundamental conflict. Yet, and this is the point to emphasise, exiled movements are important actors in South Africa's external environment and in fact help to shape that environment.

Legal organisations

A wide range of black, coloured and Indian political organisations operate legally in South Africa. They are mostly group-based, that is, exclusively or predominantly black, coloured or Indian. Among blacks there is a further breakdown into homeland or ethnic-based organisations, urban-based organisations and national non-ethnic organisations. In their political leanings the black, coloured and Indian political movements range from those boycotting any co-operation with whites and involvement in government-created political institutions, to others seeking inter-racial accommodation and participating in official racial or ethnic-based institutions. Of course, not nearly all of these organisations are relevant to a study of South Africa's foreign policy.

By far the largest in terms of numbers is Inkatha, led by Chief Gatsha Buthelezi, Chief Minister of KwaZulu. Its membership has in recent years variously been estimated at 200 000 and 300 000.[117] Although officially styled a "national cultural liberation movement", Inkatha operates as a de facto Zulu political movement. In its endeavours to present itself as a credible mass political organisation representing black South Africans, Inkatha has "gone international". Buthelezi, a frequent visitor abroad, has managed to gain some recognition for himself and Inkatha as legitimate spokesmen for a section of the black population. Buthelezi has thus achieved an international standing of sorts not reached by any other homeland leader. In 1980 Inkatha decided to establish a mission abroad to promote the movement internationally. Inkatha's moves on the international stage may have been at least partly inspired by a desire to build up the organisation to one meriting the same kind of recognition abroad as the ANC. While there is undoubtedly a large measure of competition and conflict between Inkatha and the ANC, the two have also sought to reach an understanding. Meetings between Inkatha and ANC leaders were held on foreign soil in 1978 and 1979, following which Buthelezi spoke hopefully of a united front of black opposition to apartheid. While Inkatha and the ANC have a common objective of "liberation", the two would pursue different strategies, Inkatha's being the non-violent promotion of change. Nothing tangible came of these ideas and relations between Inkatha and the ANC deteriorated markedly during the following years.[118]

Two important themes that the Inkatha leader has expounded to foreign audiences are that peaceful change is still possible in South Africa, and that economic sanctions and disinvestment would not further the cause of black South Africans. This is of course a message dear to the heart of the South African government, which, particularly through the former Department of Information, enthusiastically marketed it abroad.

Inkatha is one of the four constituent members of the South African Black Alliance, the others being the Coloured Labour Party, the Indian Reform Party and the Inyandza National Movement of KaNgwane. Established in 1978 with Buthelezi as chairman, one of the Alliance's main objectives is a national convention at which all races and parties would jointly shape a new South African political system. Apart from Inkatha, the Labour Party is the only Alliance partner that represents a major political force, being the dominant party among coloureds. Outspoken in its opposition to apartheid, the Labour Party favours non-violent forms of external pressure to promote political change in South Africa. Thus the party at its 1979 conference expressed itself in favour of economic sanctions and the continuation of the sports boycott against South Africa.[119]* Now it must be said that the views of coloured and also Indian

political parties – whatever their following in South Africa – probably carry much less weight abroad than those of organisations representing blacks, particularly militant black organisations. Coloureds and Indians are regarded as minority groups, relatively unimportant when compared with the black majority.

All the legal parties mentioned are involved in government-created political institutions based on race or ethnicity. Among those refusing any such involvement, the most prominent is the Azanian People's Organisation (AZAPO), heir to the Black Consciousness Movement banned in 1977. Established in 1979 AZAPO is an exclusively black organisation and one of the aims it has set itself is "to work towards the unity of the oppressed for the just distribution of wealth and power to all people of Azania".[120] Azania is the name the organisation uses for South Africa, even in its "pre-liberation" state. AZAPO has extended its boycott politics also to foreigners involved with South Africa as part of a strategy to isolate the country in as many areas as possible. For example, it is AZAPO policy not to talk to officials of the five Western powers engaged in the Namibian settlement initiative, and the organisation boycotts foreign artists performing in the Republic.[121] South African policy formulators experience these "international" actions of AZAPO as little more than annoyances. Compared with the ANC, AZAPO plays at best a marginal role in influencing South Africa's external milieu in a direction unfavourable to Pretoria. What detracts from AZAPO's influence both at home and abroad are running internal feuds and tensions with established black political organisations.[122]

Finally, SWAPO should also be mentioned here, although it is a Namibian "liberation movement". SWAPO is not a banned organisation in Namibia, but its legal political activities in the territory are far less prominent than its guerrilla war. Internationally SWAPO enjoys a standing easily surpassing that of the ANC. The OAU and the UN recognise SWAPO as the sole authentic representative of the Namibian people, and the organisation participates in the Western settlement drive in Namibia as a primary party along with South Africa. Given the international salience of the Namibian issue, SWAPO is an even more important factor in South Africa's external environment that the ANC.

---

*In January 1983 the same Labour Party decided to participate in the proposed tri-cameral Parliament for whites, coloureds and Indians. Shortly thereafter the Party withdrew from the South African Black Alliance.

The Mass Media

Under this heading attention will be focused on the effects of the South African press, radio and television on the foreign policy making process.

The press

Any attempt to assess the political influence of the local press must at the very outset take cognisance of the fact that the South African press cannot be treated as an undifferentiated whole. Instead, it reflects the various cleavages evident in South African society – race, language and political affiliation. There is, invariably, a "white" press and a "black" press. The white press, in turn, can be broken down into the "Afrikaans" press and the "English" press, a division that largely corresponds with the distinction between the "Nationalist" or government-supporting press, and the "opposition" press. These basic divisions caution against generalisations on the political role of the press as a whole. Some sections of the press are in fact more influential – or perhaps less uninfluential – than others in affecting public policy.

Structure and political support
Ownership of South African newspapers is concentrated in the hands of four large private press groups. The Argus Printing and Publishing Company owns a number of English and also black newspapers, among others *The Star* (Johannesburg), *Daily News* (Durban), *The Argus* (Cape Town), *Pretoria News* (Pretoria), *Sunday Tribune* (Durban), *Sowetan* (Johannesburg; for blacks), *Ilanga* (Durban; for blacks) and *The Cape Herald* (Cape Town; for coloureds). South African Associated Newspapers (SAAN) owns the remaining major English newspapers. These are the *Rand Daily Mail* (Johannesburg), *The Cape Times* (Cape Town) and *Sunday Times*, *Sunday Express* and *Financial Mail* (all three Johannesburg). SAAN and the Argus group are, however, interlinked. In 1971 the two agreed on an exchange of shares, which gave the Argus group a 31,25% share in SAAN, while the latter obtained a seven per cent interest in the Argus group.

All the leading Afrikaans newspapers are likewise owned by two publishing houses, Nasionale Pers, who owns *Die Burger* (Cape Town), *Beeld* (Johannesburg), *Die Volksblad* (Bloemfontein) and *Oosterlig* (Port Elizabeth), and Perskor, with *Die Transvaler* and *Die Vaderland* (Johannesburg), and *Hoofstad* and *Oggendblad* (Pretoria). The two groups jointly own the only Afrikaans Sunday newspaper, *Rapport*, while Perskor also has an English daily, *The Citizen*, and two lesser black publications.[123]

The present complexion of the South African press can be explained in terms of the greatly different origins of the English and Afrikaans newspapers. Many of the existing English newspapers were established in the latter part of the nineteenth and early years of the twentieth century. The local English newspapers then championed the cause of British imperialism, modelled themselves on Fleet Street and served as "the direct instruments of financial and commercial power".[124]

The Afrikaans press only came into being in the second decade of this century, in the wake of the formation of the National Party in July 1914. The Afrikaans newspapers were born "in times of strife and tribulation" for the Afrikaner people,[125] and "out of political necessity and distress".[126] The *raison d'être* of the Afrikaans press was to champion the cause of Afrikaner nationalism in partnership with the National Party, the Afrikaans churches and Afrikaans cultural organisations. The Afrikaans press, as Elaine Potter aptly put it, "was filled with evangelical zeal and kindled the flame of a cause".[127] The relationship between press and political vehicle was particularly close: *Die Burger,* which was launched by Nasionale Pers in July 1915, was accepted by the Cape National Party as its mouthpiece.[128] In 1917 Nasionale Pers acquired *Die Volksblad,* which became the National Party's mouthpiece in the Orange Free State. In 1937 the newly established Voortrekkerpers launched *Die Transvaler* as the mouthpiece of the "Purified" National Party in the Transvaal. (Voortrekkerpers in 1971 merged with Afrikaanse Pers, established in 1915 and publisher of *Die Vaderland,* to form Perskor.)[129] The intimate link between press and party can also be seen in the fact that two newspaper editors subsequently became leaders of the National Party and prime ministers: Malan, first editor of *Die Burger,* and Verwoerd, first editor of *Die Transvaler.*

As regards publications for blacks, the recent (Steyn) Commission of Inquiry into the Mass Media noted that "there is no truly black press in South Africa." Following nearly 50 years of an independent, black-owned black press, the early 1930s saw the beginning of a white take-over, albeit private white entrepreneurs rather than giant newspaper conglomerates. Only later did the Argus group and Perskor enter the black newspaper market.[130]

Until the National Party came to power in 1948, the English press had been solidly pro-government and the Afrikaans press largely anti-government (some Afrikaans newspapers – not belonging to any of the three Afrikaans press groups already mentioned – supported the United Party government of Smuts). Since 1948 the reverse situation has obtained, with the English papers *en bloc* anti-government (except for the government's own creation of three decades later, *The Citizen)* and the Afrikaans press predominantly pro-government.

For many years after 1948 the major Afrikaans newspapers faithfully and very literally continued to live up to their purpose of National Party mouthpieces. Only in the 1960s did a somewhat independent stance *vis-à-vis* the National Party begin to emerge in the ranks of the pro-government Afrikaans press. This development followed after the realisation of one of Afrikanerdom's and the National Party's most cherished ideals: the establishment of a republic, freed from the "British connection", in 1961. It was, however, an independence within narrow confines, for the Afrikaans press remained faithful to the basic tenets of government policies. Such differences as emerged were mostly on matters of style or interpretation of official policies, rather than substance – with one important exception: *Die Burger* was prepared to challenge Verwoerd on the political future of the coloureds. Nasionale Pers papers were also prepared to discuss openly the emerging rifts within the National Party. Something that may well have constrained at least some Afrikaans papers in their dealings with the government was the fact that Cabinet ministers sat on the boards of both Perskor and Nasionale Pers, a phenomenon that exposed the newspapers to "sporadic taunts of being a 'kept' press". It was left to Prime Minister PW Botha, who had been a director of Nasionale Pers, to put an end to the practice of ministers holding newspaper directorships.[131]

A different manifestation of independence in the ranks of the Afrikaans press followed the establishment of the HNP in 1969. The breakaway party soon established its own weekly newspaper, *Die Afrikaner.* In championing the reactionary cause, the paper is no less zealous than National Party mouthpieces had been in the early days of the party. By the time *Die Afrikaner* emerged on the scene, Afrikaans papers that did not support the National Party had long since disappeared.*

The National Party in subsequent years gained two new voices – but not mouthpieces, a status reserved for the three established Afrikaans dailies already mentioned – with the launching in 1979 of the Afrikaans Sunday paper, *Rapport* (the result of an amalgamation of two competing weeklies) and the Johannesburg daily *Beeld,* in 1974.

As regards the English newspapers, their relegation to opposition politics proved a rather traumatic experience and their new role after 1948 has been highly contentious. In 1961 Morris Broughton, former editor of *The Cape Argus,* remarked on a "type of negativeness" displayed by the English press. Like the Afrikaans papers, the English also had "a common outlook and a single orientation".

> They are unanimously in opposition, anti-Nationalist, greatly preoccupied with politics and frankly and forcefully partisan, however this last might be qualified. Yet they have lost the political struggle. They cry incessantly in varying and eloquent voices. They cry down the wind. Where they seek to be effective, they are dismayingly ineffective. Their political aims have become imprecise, ill-defined. They are no longer able to influence the course of events and, though still largely unaware of it, have become the last thing they intended to be and that which they avowedly most oppose – a source and perpetuator of division on every plane, social, economic, political and spiritual.[132]

Fourteen years later Potter, in a study of the "political role" of South African newspapers, wrote that the English press had determinedly "kept the vocabulary of democracy, and the concept and fact of dissent alive." It was nonetheless "unable to stop the advance of repression in the society", Potter observed, and was "virtually impotent in respect of influencing government policy and the functioning of the State apparatus."[133] This inability of the English

---

*In May 1982 a new anti-government Afrikaans newspaper appeared on the market when the newly formed Conservative Party launched its mouthpiece, *Die Patriot,* a fortnightly paper.

press is but a reflection of the political impotence of English-speaking South Africans over the last three decades.[134] The Steyn Commission judged the role of the English press from a rather different angle and expressed a view that would be widely echoed in National Party circles: the English press is guilty of "an over-critical and highly partisan presentation of everything the government says and does".[135] The Commission did, however, point out that the English press is never aligned with opposition parties in the same manner as the Afrikaans papers are tied to the National Party. Although supporting opposition policies, the English press "obviously feels no obligation to give support to all opposition methods or tactical compromises."

The English press, it can therefore be said, is not a vehicle of opinion whose views are sought and seriously considered by the policy formulators. The English press finds itself in this position despite the fact that it is widely read by Afrikaners and is well ahead of the Afrikaans newspapers in circulation figures.[136] Clearly, therefore, readership – even when it includes the Afrikaner elite – is no indicator of press influence on government policies. This is not to say that the English newspapers can simply be ignored by government. Their investigative journalism is one aspect of which the government has to take note – the exposure of the so-called Information scandal was in large part the work of English newspapers. Such influence upon government can be termed negative in the sense that it is unsolicited and indeed unwelcome, yet too important to dismiss.

The generalisations on the English press of course do not apply to *The Citizen*. Founded and funded by the Department of Information, the paper is unashamedly pro-government and intended as an English antidote to the liberal *Rand Daily Mail,* which had the English morning market to itself. After being taken over by Perskor, *The Citizen* continued to plough its lonely furrow as the sole English newspaper supporting the government; as a Perskor paper it could hardly have been expected to do otherwise.

Not only newspapers' attitude to the government determines their role in policy making, buy also, and more important, the policy formulator's attitude towards the press, specifically their stance on the question of press freedom. The government has on numerous occasions declared its commitment to press freedom, with the explicit proviso that the press fulfil its "obligations" to the country and people;

the press should not abuse its freedom and harm South Africa's "interests". The government has just as often charged the press – specifically the English and black newspapers – with deliberately ignoring its duties in this regard.[137] Apparently the government thinks that not even the 25 Acts concerning national security matters and which, in the words of the Steyn Commission, "have a direct or indirect inhibiting effect on the media",[138] sufficiently constrain the press. Neither, apparently, is the voluntary control that the press exercises over itself through the South African Press Council and its Press Code considered adequate.[139]

The government's displeasure with the behaviour of the press, specifically the English and black press, caused a number of celebrated confrontations over the last decade.[140] The most serious occurred in October 1977, when the government banned Johannesburg's main black papers, *The World* and *Weekend World,* in addition to detaining *The World*'s editor and banning the editor of the *Daily Dispatch*. These actions were part of a massive security clampdown in which 17 black consciousness organisations were banned. *The World,* South Africa's largest daily newspaper with a circulation of some 178 000, was succeeded by *Post*. In January 1981 *Post* ceased publication following a government refusal to renew its "registration" after the paper had failed to appear because of a labour dispute; many saw the government's decision as a technical banning.

Another manifestation of strained relations between government and press can be seen in the appointment of a number of official commissions of inquiry into the press or mass media generally. The latest, the Steyn Commission, was appointed in 1980 to "inquire into and report on the question whether the conduct of and handling of matters by the mass media meet the needs of the community, and, if not, how they could be improved." Government concern about press behaviour is, however, not a recent phenomenon. In 1950 the Malan government appointed a commission of inquiry into the press, which took over a decade to produce its report – a product better known for its quantity (it was too voluminous to publish) than its quality.

Coverage of foreign affairs
NP and PFP Members of Parliament, it will be recalled, have different views on the quality of the Afrikaans and English newspapers' reporting on

international affairs. Opposition MPs have a low opinion of the Afrikaans press's coverage compared with the Nationalists' views; PFP members rate even the English press's reporting lower than do National Party MPs. The Steyn Commission noted that a standing criticism of the South African press "in the past" had been a relative neglect of foreign news. The last decade has seen great changes, the Commission reported, to the extent that "serious newspapers now probably give their readers much more foreign, and especially African news, than they really want, need or are capable of digesting." How the Commission reached this remarkable conclusion is not explained. Nonetheless, the Argus Company was singled out for its "network of foreign news and feature services of excellent quality". The Afrikaans newspapers, with very few of their own correspondents abroad, rely mainly on stringers. The placing of Afrikaans press correspondents abroad is noteworthy: they are nearly all in the United States and Britain. Another source of foreign news, shared by all important newspapers in South Africa, is the services of the South African Press Association (SAPA), the co-operative national news agency. Through SAPA they receive the international services of Reuters and Associated Press, sometimes supplemented by *Agence France-Presse* and *Deutsche Presse-Agentur*.[141]

To try to get some picture of the substance of foreign news reported in the local press, a content analysis of foreign reports carried in two Pretoria dailies in May 1976 can be used.[142] They are the *Pretoria News* (English) and *Hoofstad* (Afrikaans). (Foreign reports are defined as reports dealing purely with an event in another country or between other countries, and reports on the outside world in which South Africa featured.) Foreign reports represented 35,4% of all the news reports carried by the *Pretoria News* in May 1976; for *Hoofstad* the figure was 25,3%. The geographical distribution of foreign news was highly significant: no less than 57% of the *Pretoria News'* foreign reports came from Britain and the United States, with the former accounting for a full 37%. If reports from other English-speaking countries were added, the figure rose to 75,3%. In the case of *Hoofstad,* the major foreign source was also Britain with 21,6% of all foreign reports; together with the United States the figure stood at 41,7%, and increased to 66,7% when reports from all English-speaking countries were added. The analysis shows that the two dailies carried the bulk of their foreign news on only five countries: Britain, the United States, Rhodesia, France and West Germany. Taken by region, most foreign reports were from Europe, followed by America, Africa, Asia/Oceania and the Middle East. The distribution of the foreign news reports undoubtedly gave the readers of the two papers a totally distorted picture of the world, in the sense that only events in the English-speaking world would have seemed to be of importance.

While on the subject of foreign news coverage, it is worth mentioning that South African newspapers have on occasion championed certain external causes. Recent examples are particularly the Afrikaans press's enthusiastic support for Rhodesia's so-called internal settlement of March 1978 (involving the Smith government and a number of internal black political parties) and for the Democratic Turnhalle Alliance (DTA; a multiracial political alliance born of the Turnhalle constitutional conference of the mid-1970s) in Namibia. Whereas English newspapers were generally more guarded, albeit sympathetic, on these two issues, some of them have as keenly as the Afrikaans newspapers championed the cause of UNITA in Angola. In each case the newspapers can be said to have adopted a stance conforming to the government's own views. A quite different cause, indeed more of a crusade, was undertaken by *The Citizen* in 1977. Under the title "Secret US War on South Africa" the paper ran a series of "startling disclosures on the secret war which the Carter administration is waging against South Africa". *The Citizen* presented it as a sinister plot, in which the Trilateral Commission was a prime mover.[143]

As regards the reverse situation, foreign press reporting on South Africa is a subject that has long exercised the minds of the policy formulators. As early as February 1947 Heaton Nicholls, South Africa's high commissioner in London, wrote to the secretary of External Affairs in Pretoria that he had to cope with a "flood of abusive and distorted anti-Union propaganda" in Britain.[144] Government-supporting (pro-Smuts) newspapers at the time complained bitterly about what *The Star* depicted as foreign criticism "based on the general assumption that some kind of moral twilight envelops the European mind".[145] After 1948 foreign press reporting became increasingly "negative" and has been a constant thorn in the flesh of the ruling National Party. The Press Commission appointed in 1950 devoted a great deal of time and energy to content analyses of overseas newspapers' reporting on South Africa – merely to confirm what the government had long been saying.[146] In later years the Department of Information monitored foreign press coverage of South Africa and annually presented its assessment. In its 1974 annual report, for example, the Department stated that during that year "the increase in positive news coverage continued as it did during 1973." Although the Republic still encountered a mass of adverse reporting, the report boldly proclaimed that South Africa in 1974 "had its best year on radio, television and in the press for the past three decades."[147] The year 1975 was rather confusingly rated as "probably the best year for South Africa the past decade in terms of positive news media coverage."[148] The satisfaction was shortlived, for the Department in 1976 reported despondently that foreign media coverage in that year had been "very negative".[149]

As far as the quantity and content of foreign news reporting on South Africa were concerned, the Press Commission, which examined the years 1950-55, reported that only four countries in that period received substantial quantities of "general" and "political" news from South Africa: the United Kingdom (74,09%), the United States (18,46%), India (4,30%) and Australia (2,12%). Of the reporting done in the British press on "politics and race" in South Africa, the Commission rated a mere 9,42% as "good", the rest being variously "very bad", "bad" and "faulty".[150] Nearly three decades later the British press is probably still top of the league in respect of the amount of coverage of South African affairs. In West Germany an analysis of the three leading national dailies' foreign news coverage in 1978/9 revealed that while South Africa had certainly been the "leading newsmaker in Africa," it represented an average of only 2,37% of the three papers' foreign news. This figure was considerably lower than that for Spain and Austria, for example.[151] That South Africa is not the focus of attention of the West German press, or probably of the world press generally, is not to deny that political developments in South Africa have a high news value abroad and may under particular circumstances dominate foreign reporting.

A prerequisite for adequate local press coverage of South Africa's foreign affairs is, of course, sufficient access to reliable information. One practically universal problem for the press is that governments commonly regard aspects of foreign relations as "mysteries of state" in which neither press nor Parliament should meddle. In many instances secrecy is imposed by law – and South Africa certainly has a sizeable quota. A difficulty of a different nature is that some South African newspapers enjoy greater access than others to official sources of information. The Steyn Commission plausibly suggested that the English press, because it had since 1948 opposed the government, has "very little in the way of government 'sources'". The Afrikaans press, while having greater access, "did not often use its knowledge of government activities without the express permission of the government."[152] Given the government's secrecy and its reluctance to share private confidences with the English press, the latter adapted itself to this situation by relying heavily on the Afrikaans newspapers as a source of information, and on public statements for its understanding of government.[153]

In the recent past the *cause célèbre* of government secrecy on a foreign policy matter was South Africa's involvement in the Angolan civil war. Invoking the provisions of the Defence Act, the government carefully regulated the dissemination of information to the public on South Africa's role in Angola. It produced the absurd situation that the South African public was kept largely in the dark on developments in Angola, while the world media was giving extensive on-the-spot coverage of the Republic's participation in the war. A significant feature of the local reporting was that *Die Burger* and its sister newspapers in Nasionale Pers were notably better informed – or less uninformed – about the activities of South African forces than were other Afrikaans papers, not to mention the English press. A credible explanation is that *Die Burger* had far better, if not exclusive, access to official military sources: the paper is the National Party's Cape mouthpiece; PW Botha was Cape leader of the Party and director of Nasionale Pers – and he was Minister of Defence.

Apart from deliberately withholding information from the press and public, official institutions' inability or unwillingness to provide information is often due to a "lack of governmental expertise", in the words of the Steyn Commission. There is a widespread "inability to grasp the importance of the information and public relations function", the Commission reported, and this finds expression in the absence of an "integrated, central information and communication policy". To illustrate its point the Commission referred to a large-scale South African military operation in Angola in August/September 1981. The Defence

Force's handling of the press side of "Operation Protea", the Commission said, displayed a lack of expertise and understanding of both the domestic and international effects of "non-coordination and tardiness in the release of information".[154]

Not only on the military aspects of the Republic's foreign relations does the South African press find itself particularly hamstrung. Two other related areas in which the press's freedom of reporting is severely circumscribed by law are South Africa's activities in the nuclear field and its procurement of petroleum products.

The outstanding example of government failure to keep a cloak of secrecy over foreign activities – or of press success in exposing secret government activities in the foreign policy realm – was the Information affair. Of course the Department of Information was not only involved in secret projects abroad; the biggest "scandal" concerned its financing of a local newspaper. Nonetheless, English newspapers in the finest tradition of investigative journalism also managed to uncover a massive irregular clandestine propaganda campaign which the Department had been conducting abroad.

The question of newspapers' access to information on foreign policy matters has another more spectacular or sensational side to it, namely deliberate leaks of official information to the press. A case in point has been the publication, particularly in Afrikaans newspapers, of information on the Namibian settlement talks. Western negotiators have on a number of occasions taken exception to highly sensitive information finding its way into local newspapers. They tend to see a connection between the occurrence of leaks and the state of negotiations: press revelations coincide with an unfavourable turn of events for South Africa.

The Afrikaans newspapers' special relationship with the government has not only made them privy to particular kinds of information, but they have on occasion also played an instrumental role, helping the government prepare or educate the public concerning the domestic implications of a change in foreign policy. The outstanding example was the Afrikaans press's endeavours to pave the way for the outward policy of Prime Minister Vorster. The white public had to be prepared particularly for the prospect of black diplomats being stationed in South Africa and, moreover, breaking the social barriers of apartheid.[155] Another case that deserves mention was the Afrikaans press's attempts to sell to the (Afrikaner) electorate Vorster's changes to the sports policy.

A more difficult question to consider is the influence the Afrikaans press has exerted on the government in the realm of foreign policy. It is not possible to be precise on this score or to cite specific examples of successful influence. Such influence as is exercised is probably not so much through the printed word as behind the scenes. In this regard newspaper editors would be the key figures, and the extent of their "private" influence would depend on their personal relationship with the decision makers. A case in point is that of Mr PJ Cillié, editor of *Die Burger*, who is likely to have had the ear of PW Botha when the latter was Minister of Defence. (Cillié retired in 1977.) Apart from a long personal-cum-political association with PW Botha, Cillié also enjoyed a special relationship with the Cape National Party: he was given observer status on the Party's head council.[156] Another highly influential figure from the same ranks is Advocate DP de Villiers, Managing Director of Nasionale Pers. An eminent jurist – he was a member of the South African legal team at the World Court case on South West Africa in the 1960s – and leading *verligte*, De Villiers is close to the National Party establishment in the Cape Province. There may well be a number of other Afrikaans editors and journalists who enjoy close relationships with particular policy makers, and not necessarily the prime minister. Dr WJ de Klerk, editor of *Die Transvaler* (1973-82), and a leading *verligte* Afrikaner intellectual, probably stands close to the PW Botha government.

As regards the English press, it has since 1948 frequently been accused by the government of carrying a large part of the responsibility for South Africa's poor international standing. The typical argument is that the English press serves as a major source of information on South Africa for the foreign press; being anti-government, the English press's "negative" reporting has been creating a distorted image of South Africa abroad. The "positive" Afrikaans press, by contrast, has been unable to play a role in shaping external opinion because of the language difficulty. These familiar views have recently been expressed by the Steyn Commission, which referred to the local English press as "the main mirror in which South Africa is reflected in the outside world". The Commission stated it as an "unfortunate and incontrovertible fact" that foreign attacks on South Africa are largely inspired by "reports and comment" emanating from within the country. South Africa thus suffers from what the Commission depicted as "malicious 'stereo-typing'", a phenomenon for which it clearly held the English press mainly responsible.[157] Afrikaans newspapers too have openly blamed their English counterparts for contributing to what one called a "steady barrage of unfavourable information and opinion, which gradually builds up into an impenetrable wall of hostility" against South Africa.[158] Afrikaans newspapers, like the government, have since 1948 displayed a particular sensitivity to foreign criticism, particularly if it emanates from South Africa's traditional Western allies.[159] The English press, in turn, has unceasingly emphasised what it sees as the harmful effects of government policies on South Africa's international reputation.[160] The local English-language press adopts much the same attitude as that taken by *The Times* of London when it as far back as 1958 rather arrogantly commented on the Nationalist government's frequent complaints about British press reporting on South Africa: "faces have no valid complaint against mirrors."[161]

Editorial comment on foreign policy issues: some case studies

The object of examining press reaction to a number of foreign policy issues is not merely to get some picture of South African press comment on external issues, but also to compare the responses of the Afrikaans or pro-government and English or anti-government newspapers.

The first event selected is the Portuguese *coup d'état* of 25 April 1974. South African newspapers were quick to see the potentially far-reaching consequences it had in store for the Republic. The prospect of fewer Portuguese soldiers protecting vulnerable borders against guerrillas *en route* to South Africa and Rhodesia "could mean a severe escalation of the war in the south", the *Rand Daily Mail* predicted.[162] Should independence come to Angola and Mozambique, two buffer territories could be transformed into countries with "hostile terrorist governments" in power, *Die Transvaler* warned. The paper saw a great political challenge to South Africa in these external developments. Pointing out that the National Party had just been given a further mandate for its policy of "separate freedoms" – a general election had been held on 24 April – *Die Transvaler* hopefully suggested that eventual autonomy for the peoples of Angola and Mozambique fitted in with the South African

homelands formula.[163] *The Star* interpreted the "real lesson" of the Portuguese coup rather differently. Not only did "true security begin at home", but military means alone could not defeat political disaffection. "Make reform meaningful enough to your own populace, give them a real stake in the future", *The Star* submitted, "and there is no need to fear insurgency."[164]

The way in which English newspapers relate foreign policy issues to domestic politics was again illustrated in their comments on the historic meeting between Vorster and Kaunda at the Victoria Falls on 25 August 1975. While acknowledging that the meeting was something of a diplomatic coup for Vorster, the *Rand Daily Mail* emphasised that South Africa could only ensure acceptance in Africa and elsewhere if "change" is introduced at home – "and certainly faster and more significant change than is happening at present."[165] In similar vein *The Star* wrote that it did not "begrudge" Vorster the accolades he deserved for his diplomatic achievements, but added that "our only real hope for the future lies in our ability to change, to create a just society." Admitting that change had already been taking place, the paper advocated that change should go both faster and deeper "if domestic detente is to keep pace with African detente".[166] *Die Transvaler,* by contrast, highlighted the diplomatic significance of the Vorster-Kaunda meeting, saying that it symbolised a bridge across the great divide between the white South and the black North, and could be a turning point in Southern African affairs. "It can show the world what can be achieved if co-operation is substituted for conflict."[167]

The next issue is one of the most dramatic, even traumatic, foreign ventures in which South Africa had been engaged since the Second World War: involvement in the Angolan war in 1975/6. South African forces eventually withdrew from Angola towards the end of March 1976. On 3 March the *Rand Daily Mail* called on the government to "quit the war we can't win. The chances of withdrawing from Angola with clean hands are long gone. But the dangerous risk of getting them bloodier yet . . . grows every hour we continue to dally on foreign soil", the *Mail* warned. Following Vorster's announcement that South African troops would be out of Angola by 27 March, the same paper editorialised under the heading, "Angolan blunder: the reckoning". The reckoning was "given", for the venture had been characterised by "misjudgements, mistakes, miscalculations and precipitation of possible disastrous consequences still to come". For all this, the *Mail* asserted, "three men must bear primary responsibility": Vorster, PW Botha and Pik Botha.[168] Both the tone and content of *Die Transvaler*'s and *Die Burger*'s comments differed profoundly from the *Rand Daily Mail*'s. There were those in South Africa who reproached the government for its handling of the Angolan affair, *Die Transvaler* conceded, but went on to dismiss most of the criticism as being politically inspired. The majority of "the South African population" (blacks too?) supported the government's action, the paper insisted. The sacrifices in terms of money and loss of life, *Die Transvaler* proclaimed, were worth it. The most important lesson to be learnt from South Africa's "enforced involvement" in Angola was that the country was thrown on its own resources to defend its borders.[169] *Die Burger* advanced the argument that South Africa's departure from Angola could produce "substantial diplomatic dividends". By pulling out, South Africa would deny the Soviet Union a handy propaganda weapon and would thus make a new contribution towards focusing international attention on Soviet imperialism in Africa.[170]

In 1976 the South African prime minister embarked on a new round of personal diplomacy. In the highest level contact between the South African and American governments for decades Vorster had three different meetings with Dr Henry Kissinger, American Secretary of State, between June and September 1976. Unfortunately for Vorster the first meeting, held in West Germany, coincided with the Soweto unrest in June. With this background well in mind, the *Rand Daily Mail* referred to the "racialism of apartheid" as the main stumbling block between South Africa and the United States. With a touch of irony the *Mail* remarked that Vorster seemed willing to promote black majority rule in Rhodesia and Namibia "in an effort to buy more time for separate development at home". America's dilemma, the paper said, was that it could not give South Africa "full support" without visible evidence of domestic political change.[171] Under the caption "Successful deliberation", *Die Burger* presented the first Vorster-Kissinger meeting as something of a watershed. For South Africa it represented "a spectacular break-out from the hostile walls of isolation" and showed clearly that the period in which South Africa had been perceived as expendable was passing. The

West was displaying a new concern about the Soviet threat in Southern Africa and was also acknowledging that no effective counter-strategy could be attempted without South Africa's co-operation. South Africa's involvement also flowed from its loyalty to the "cause of the West" and its implacable opposition to communism. It was because of factors such as these, *Die Burger* maintained, that not even "an extremely unfortunate event such as the black riots" could have jeopardised the Vorster-Kissinger talks. This did not mean that South Africa need not be concerned about the unrest; it had to pay attention to its "domestic task", because the Republic's "increasing responsibility in Southern Africa demands it".[172] *Die Transvaler*, while similarly headlining its editorial "Vorster success", was more guarded in its assessment and did not fail to point to the domestic implications of the situation in Africa, notably the Soviet threat. Whites should with greater broad-mindedness help blacks fulfil their aspirations, whereas black leaders should heed the consequences of situations that enabled the Russians to intervene – an allusion to Angola and Mozambique.[173]

The following year saw another high-level meeting between South Africa and the United States. Vorster in May 1977 met with Vice-President Walter Mondale in Vienna. This time there was no talk of any diplomatic breakthrough for Vorster. By all accounts, the meeting hit heavy weather, highlighting severe strains in South Africa's relations with the United States under the Carter Administration. For *Die Transvaler,* known for its often flamboyant language, the Vienna summit flashed the red light: seat belts had to be fastened because "storms lay ahead" in South Africa's foreign relations. In more sober terms *Die Burger* suggested that America's involvement in Southern Africa, as well as in South Africa's domestic policies, was entering "a new intense phase". Mondale's uncompromising stance on apartheid, the *Rand Daily Mail* argued, "pitches this country into an entirely new era in its international relations". But there the agreement between the two Afrikaans papers and the *Mail* ended. The *Mail* in notably sympathetic fashion sketched the American position in Vienna, and took issue with Vorster over his "implacable stand", arguing that he ought to have adopted "the far more flexible attitude" he displayed on the Namibian issue.[174] The two Afrikaans newspapers were sharply critical of the American attitude towards South Africa and Africa generally. If Africa were to be saved from Moscow's designs, *Die Burger* maintained, "greater and more intelligent" American and Western involvement than in the immediate past was imperative. The paper ventured to suggest that American policy formulators had more to learn about Africa from South Africa than vice versa.[175] *Die Transvaler* likewise argued that South Africa should use the opportunity of dialogue to convince the United States more than ever before "that its simplistic view of matters will lead to disaster for the country and all its people." The paper nonetheless recognised the need for domestic political adjustments to accelerate the process of "normalisation" – but then "within the broad framework of national policy".[176]

The UN Security Council's imposition of a mandatory arms embargo against South Africa in November 1977 provides another clear illustration of the widely differing reactions of the Afrikaans and English press to foreign policy issues. The grounds on which the embargo was imposed – South Africa's "acts of aggression" against neighbouring states – were branded "the great lie" by *Die Burger*. It was a falsehood conjured up by "hostile black states" who wanted to draw the UN into their campaign aimed at destroying white rule in South Africa. The Western powers subscribed to the great lie, because they shortsightedly judged it to be in their interests to do so.[177] *Die Transvaler* focused on the embargo's "clarion call", which was that South Africa should become increasingly self-reliant in armaments. The arms ban would also "make us more determined than ever before to defend with all our might what we have created."[178] The *Rand Daily Mail,* by contrast, posed the question why "the entire world condemns us with this unprecedented unanimity" when so many wrongs were committed elsewhere? The simple answer, the *Mail* suggested, was "race". The paper lauded the "momentous unanimity" on this particular moral issue as "another step forward" for mankind. The time had come for the abolition of racial discrimination as a factor in official policy, the editorial concluded, for institutionalised discrimination was in any case doomed.[179] *The Star,* while noting that international criticism of South Africa had reached a crescendo with the arms embargo, was far more restrained than the *Mail* in its assessment of the implications. What "responsible statesmen" in the West were demanding of South Africa was not overnight

transition to black rule but "a reasonable, sincere and serious commitment to change". The absence of such a commitment and government denials that there was anything wrong in the present system were, however, driving South Africa's friends in the West "to despair".[180]

Examining press comments on the drawn-out Namibian dispute would be a major exercise. Here only one particular event is selected, the so-called internal elections in Namibia in December 1978. *The Star* warned that "go-it-alone" elections would in the long run benefit only SWAPO and its backers. Worse still, "unilateral action could plunge South Africa into a sad, protracted, no-win-no-lose war."[181] The *Rand Daily Mail* inclined to SWAPO's contention that the December elections were designed to place the DTA in the position of a *de facto* internal government able "to threaten a UDI" should the UN become too persistent about involving SWAPO. It was a "ploy" that could never work. The only lasting solution in Namibia was one that included SWAPO as the "biggest and best-organised of all black political movements"; SWAPO had to be involved "either as a majority or a minority power".[182] *Die Burger,* noting with great satisfaction that over 80% of the electorate had voted in Namibia, saw it as "a powerful demonstration by the South-Westers against SWAPO and what it stands for". The election showed SWAPO and the world that the organisation's support had been exaggerated and that it was a myth that SWAPO was the only representative of the people of the territory. *Die Burger* went on to hint that the envisaged constitutional assembly, strengthened by these factors, might consider alternatives to the UN settlement plan.[183]

The final case study concerns the outcome of the Rhodesian pre-independence election in 1980. The mood of the Afrikaans press was captured in a cartoon in *Die Burger* which depicted a red bear drawing tighter a giant belt across Southern Africa, and another in *Die Transvaler* which showed a huge hammer and sickle spanning the sub-continent from coast to coast. *Die Burger* made no secret of its deep mistrust of the moderate posture adopted by prime minister-elect Mugabe. The paper warned that Mugabe's reasonableness should not mislead South Africans, for a "Marxist" was now in power. "Some time or other his Red masters will want to use him as a pawn in the strategic game they are playing in Southern Africa."[184]

Both the Afrikaans and English newspapers devoted considerable attention to the domestic implications for South Africa of Mugabe's victory. It meant a clear ascendance for the "extremists" in black ranks, *Die Transvaler* wrote. The distinctive mark of the victors in the election was violence and it was the gun that touched political hearts. South Africa should act to deny its enemies the opportunity for violence by engaging in domestic reform.[185] *Beeld* took up the same theme, arguing that Mugabe's victory flowed "from the barrel of the gun". Yet, even allowing for intimidation and war fatigue, Mugabe's victory could not have been as overwhelming "if he did not embody the black population's aspirations and therefore become embraced as their leader and liberator." If South Africa wanted to avoid becoming "the next", it should not like Rhodesia try to swim against the tide of African history, but should talk to black leaders willing to do so while there was still time.[186]

The *Rand Daily Mail* and *The Star* went much further than *Beeld*. Rhodesia's lesson for white South Africans, the *Mail* suggested, was that "they cannot escape reality by silencing opponents and preventing newspapers from revealing the true position facing them."[187] *The Star* maintained that the message for South Africa from black Africa "has never been spelt out more clearly" than in the Rhodesian election: "It is that whites in this country have the straight choice of either talking to the blacks here, of discussing real power-sharing *now*, or of eventually having to fight them." The paper exhorted the government to negotiate directly and immediately with the "real black leaders", some of whom were imprisoned, detained or banned.[188] In sharp contrast to the Afrikaans newspapers, which generally took a gloomy view of Zimbabwe's prospects under Mugabe's leadership, the *Rand Daily Mail* as early as 10 March 1980 ventured the opinion that if a peaceful Zimbabwe "goes forging ahead" – as seemed increasingly likely – it would be a cause for envy for South Africans. Apart from "international and political factors", the new Zimbabwe was well placed to enter markets in Africa closed to South Africa. Zimbabwe would also join the proposed Southern African economic community (SADCC), from which South Africa would be excluded. "We should view this as yet another of the penalties we must suffer as a result of Nationalist racial policies", the *Mail* concluded.

It is instructive to note the reaction of the Johannesburg black daily, *Post*, and its Sunday edition, to events in Rhodesia. (*Post* succeeded the banned – and in South Africa unquotable – *World*.) Like the Afrikaans and English papers, *Sunday Post* commented on the surprise Mugabe's victory caused in South Africa. With evident glee *Sunday Post* observed that the election results "hit Pretoria like a tornado".[189] Under the caption "What a defeat!", *Post* derisively commented on the fate of "poor Bishop Abel Muzorewa". His "worst possible blunder", *Post* asserted, was his close links with the South African government.[190] The lesson to be learned from the Rhodesian experience, *Sunday Post* commented, was that "no society and no community would forever sustain and support leaders imposed upon them", as had been the case with Bishop Muzorewa.[191] *Post* called on the government to hold a national convention, which would include Nelson Mandela, the imprisoned leader of the ANC. For too long the government had been insisting that it was talking to elected black leaders, meaning homeland leaders. It was wrong for the government to accept them as speaking for all blacks, the paper maintained.[192]

Although editorial comments from only five white newspapers have been cited, the papers were selected so as to try to represent the broad spectrum of the white press. The two English or anti-government newspapers, *Rand Daily Mail* and *The Star,* belong to SAAN and the Argus group respectively. With one exception, all the comments from Afrikaans pro-government newspapers are from *Die Burger* and *Die Transvaler*, owned by Nasionale Pers and Perskor respectively. When comparing the Afrikaans and English papers' comments on the various foreign policy issues just considered, a number of significant differences emerge.

First, whereas the Afrikaans papers tend to interpret outside events as confirming the basic correctness of South Africa's domestic racial policies – although agreeing that implementation could be speeded up – the English press typically sees the same events as underlining the urgent need for profound political change, usually in a direction away from the government's. Second, the English newspapers are quick to diagnose apartheid as the major, if not the sole, cause of South Africa's international ills; remove this, and the Republic would be restored to international respectability. The Afrikaans papers, while sometimes acknowledging the link between domestic and foreign policy, hope for an improvement in South Africa's foreign relations despite apartheid; thus their emphasis on South Africa's loyalty to the West, its anti-communist orientation and its indispensable role in the search for peace in Southern Africa. Third, the Afrikaans dailies are inclined to attribute a mixed bag of unsavoury motives to foreign criticism of South Africa, whereas their English counterparts often read remarkably benign motives into particularly Western pressure on the Republic. The English papers also favour South Africa's taking more note of, even accommodating, some foreign demands, as opposed to an at times defiant stance by Afrikaans newspapers. Finally, the English press characteristically presents dramatic foreign policy events as cause for self-examination among white South Africans, whereas the Afrikaans papers read into the same developments a need for greater South African self-reliance and an encouragement to (white) South Africans to defend their position with determination against whatever hostile forces threaten them.

News magazines

To conclude the discussion on the press, it is worth mentioning two local English-language news magazines, which certainly did not share the English press's general political attitudes. *News/Check*, which appeared from 1962 to 1971, was edited by Mr Otto Krause, a prominent and somewhat controversial Afrikaans journalist. It was published by Checkpress, an independent company formed by English and Afrikaans businessmen. *News/Check* was in many respects a forerunner of *verligte* thought, and its political views were certainly well ahead of those of any other publication with pro-government sympathies. The magazine paid considerable attention to foreign affairs, with Africa its primary focus. *News/Check* was an early advocate of what subsequently became Vorster's outward movement. Given its *avant garde* political outlook, *News/Check* understandably enjoyed a very uneasy relationship with both Verwoerd and Vorster, who made no secret of their dislike of the magazine's "liberal" inclinations. The other news magazine was *To the Point*. It was set up with government funds. Nonetheless, being the only local magazine of its kind during its brief existence, *To the Point* was a useful source of information on foreign affairs, particularly developments in Africa, which received extensive coverage.[193]

Radio and television

The South African Broadcasting Corporation (SABC), established as a public corporation in 1936 under an Act of Parliament, controls radio and television broadcasts in South Africa. The SABC runs 16 radio programme services, including the English and Afrikaans services, Radio Bantu with its seven commercial services in different black languages, and the external service. Beaming its programmes to the outside world, the external service is on the air for over 150 hours a week and broadcasts in English, Dutch, German, French, Portuguese, Spanish and a number of African languages. In 1980 over 9,7 million adults tuned in each weekday to the SABC's various radio services. Over five million are listeners to the services for blacks. An interesting statistic is that the SABC's 16 radio services broadcast news in 17 languages in some 270 bulletins, making a total of 18 hours of news broadcasting per weekday.

Apart from its editorial offices in South Africa, the SABC maintains offices in only London and Washington. (Like the press, the SABC in this regard has a strong Anglo-Saxon orientation.) For the rest, foreign news is supplied by international press agencies and some forty professional correspondents (and a varying number of amateur correspondents) in African countries and elsewhere.

The television service only came into full operation in January 1976. The single-channel service, devoting equal time to Afrikaans and English programmes, caters for white viewers. A separate channel broadcasting in black languages was inaugurated in 1982. In 1980 TV attracted a daily viewing audience of 3,4 million, of whom 2,2 million were whites.[194]

Important for the purposes of the present study is the relationship between the SABC and the government. The 1936 Act gave the SABC autonomy, but legislation enacted since 1969 has removed the legally enshrined limitation on direct government interference in the affairs of the SABC. In a clear indictment of government moves, the Steyn Commission referred to "uneasiness with regard to the ability of the SABC to maintain its autonomy and consequently also its credibility in respect of its internal broadcasting activities." A furore over the SABC and its chairman in mid-1981 was seen by the Commission as indicative of the government's desire "to achieve a position of more direct control over the SABC". Ministerial responsibility for the SABC has since 1936 changed hands several times. In 1980 it was entrusted to the Minister of Foreign Affairs and Information. The Commission reported that "the motivation for the last change was unclear and had given rise to considerable speculation." It can be added, parenthetically, that the "Pik and Cliff show" mentioned in an earlier chapter acquired a new significance and symbolism in many people's eyes when Pik Botha assumed ministerial responsibility for the SABC.* The Steyn Commission objected to the SABC falling under the direct control of a state department. To ensure "autonomy and impartiality", the Commission recommended "crown office" status (as in the United Kingdom) for the SABC.[195]

Given the formal, legalised relationship between the SABC and the government, it is not surprising that the corporation has been widely criticised for its servile attitude towards the government. Even the Steyn Commission remarked that the SABC "is sometimes uncritically for the government".[196] Apart from other possible reasons for wanting the SABC to serve as "his master's voice", the government clearly thinks that the need for a total national strategy demands a national broadcasting corporation that can be relied upon to help counter the perceived total onslaught.

The SABC is certainly uniquely placed in South African society to entertain, inform and educate. Insofar as it exerts political influence, it is supportive of the government. Although much of this support might in a sense be genuine and spontaneous – reflecting the political loyalties of top officials – a good deal of it may also be directly inspired by the government itself; the government may, in other words, use the SABC as an agent of sorts to convey a particular "message" to the public. In the realm of foreign affairs specifically, the SABC's role is largely acclamatory and supportive. Incisive, open-minded analyses of international affairs and of issues in South Africa's foreign policy have been few and far between. The television service offers precious

little even approximating, for example, the BBC's "Panorama" programme or CBS's "Sixty Minutes". On radio a notable exception is the English service's "Radio Today", an early morning topical affairs programme – its heavy British fixation notwithstanding.

The Unorganised Public

White public opinion

An obvious prerequisite for an assessment of the impact of public opinion on foreign policy is some knowledge of the content of public opinion in the realm of foreign affairs. Measuring public opinion in this particular field has hitherto received only scant attention from scholars of South African foreign policy. For the purposes of this book an opinion survey was specially commissioned.[197]

The survey was confined to whites. Financial considerations admittedly played a major role in the decision to measure only white public opinion. It is, however, possible to make a case for this restriction on academic grounds. Since South Africa's foreign policy formulation is the exclusive preserve of the white elite, it can be argued that insofar as the foreign policy formulators take cognisance of domestic public opinion, they would first and foremost consider white opinion. However, the opinion of blacks, while certainly carrying much less weight than white opinion, cannot be completely ignored by the foreign policy formulators. Apart from the already mentioned phenomenon of an increasingly articulate body of black opinion on foreign policy matters, the link between external opinion on South Africa's domestic policies and local black opinion is only too obvious. Ideally, therefore, the opinion survey should have included black respondents. There are, however, surveys of black opinion that have been conducted elsewhere, which provide some clues to black views on foreign policy matters. These will be considered after the analysis of white public opinion.

To discover the content of white public opinion on foreign policy matters, the survey first set out to determine how informed the adult white population was with regard to foreign affairs. Second, opinions on a number of salient foreign policy issues were measured, particularly those matters that revealed respondents' threat perceptions and also their hawkish/doveish

---

*The controversy surrounding government control, more specifically Pik Botha's, over the SABC again flared up with the appointment of Mr JA Eksteen as Director-General designate of the SABC in February 1983. Pik Botha revealed that he had suggested the name of Eksteen – a senior official in the foreign ministry – to the SABC Board as a possible successor to the retiring Director-General.

inclinations. Finally, the survey investigated correlations between opinion on these aspects and on certain contentious domestic political issues.

In an assessment of the white public's knowledge of foreign affairs, respondents were asked to provide the names of eight incumbents holding prominent public positions in South Africa and abroad. The results, arranged from best known to least known (with the percentages of correct responses) were as follows:

Position	Incumbent	Percentage
Prime Minister of Britain	(Mrs Margaret Thatcher)	94,4
Prime Minister of Zimbabwe	(Mr Robert Mugabe)	88,2
President of Mozambique	(Mr Samora Machel)	74,6
SA Minister of Defence	(Gen. Magnus Malan)	72,9
Prime Minister of New Zealand	(Mr Robert Muldoon)	69,5
President of France	(Mr Francois Mitterand)	56,3
Director-General: SA Department of Foreign Affairs and Information	(Dr Brand Fourie)	41,8
President of Botswana	(Dr Quett Masire)	5,5

The fact that foreign leaders such as Thatcher, Mugabe, Machel and Muldoon are so well known is accounted for by their featuring very prominently in South Africa's foreign relations, thus becoming household names. Fourie's poor rating was something of a surprise, considering that he – although a public servant – receives a good deal of media exposure over the Namibian issue. Masire is virtually unknown probably because he does not feature nearly as prominently (nor, presumably, as menacingly in white eyes) as either Mugabe or Machel. It is interesting that for every respondent who correctly named Masire, roughly two others mistakenly provided the name of Chief Lucas Mangope, President of Bophuthatswana, the independent former homeland.

In response to the question, "What does UN resolution 435 deal with?", just over 60% of the respondents correctly related it to Namibia. A higher proportion of correct answers followed the next question, which asked what the abbreviations ANC and SWAPO stood for. 77,5% knew the former meant the African National Congress, while a further 12,9% used "Council" instead of "Congress". The South West African People's Organisation also proved well known, with 87,1% of the respondents providing

the correct answer. (Although the ANC is strictly speaking a domestic political organisation, it was included here because it is banned in South Africa but continues to operate openly in exile.) The respondents were finally asked whether the United States allowed South Africa to purchase military arms. 66,6% correctly indicated that the US did not, whereas 28% thought it did.

The survey revealed that men were generally better informed than women. No similarly distinct trend emerged with regard to two other commonly introduced variables, namely language (Afrikaans and English) and party political preferences (National Party – NP; Progressive Federal Party – PFP; New Republic Party – NRP; Herstigte Nasionale Party – HNP, and National Conservative Party – NCP).

Too much should not be read into the relatively high level of correct responses to the four questions. They were all admittedly simple and dealt with topical matters of immediate relevance to South Africa. Perhaps the results do no more than confirm the general rule that the public at large is well informed only on those foreign policy issues that are of direct concern or heavily publicised and relatively simple to comprehend.

More important and certainly more interesting than probing the public's level of knowledge, is a study of perceptions. The questionnaire focused on the white community's perceptions of threat and on possible ways of combating the perceived threat. Selecting these features seemed well justified in view of the government's preoccupation with a "total onslaught" and the need to respond with a "total national strategy".

Because an opinion poll presents a snapshot picture taken at a specific time under a particular set of circumstances, the value of opinion surveys is greatly enhanced when they are repeated at regular intervals and their findings compared. The present survey, having been conducted for the first time, bears no such comparison. There are, nonetheless, a number of independent earlier surveys which can usefully be compared with the results of the present one.

The extent to which white South Africans have become threat conscious is clearly borne out in the present survey, which found that in each case over 70% of the 1 999 respondents disagreed with the statement, "The communist threat against South Africa is exaggerated by the government"; agreed that "The government of Zimbabwe constitutes a threat to South Africa's safety"; and agreed that "A terrorist war as in South West Africa will in time also develop in South Africa".

An opinion survey of South Africa's (white) power-elite (the sample consisted of 349 members of the elite in the political, administrative and economic sectors of society) conducted in 1966/7, found that the respondents underestimated the importance of the ascendance of black nationalism as a potential threat to South Africa's future political development (a mere 9% saw it as a threat), and exaggerated the threat of world communism (73% regarded it as a threat).[198] This finding is difficult to reconcile with the results of an opinion poll conducted in 1964, which showed that the "colour issue" was rated as "the greatest problem facing South Africa today" by 73% of the respondents. Only 3% put "communism" at the top of the list.[199] Another poll conducted two years later found that the race problem still rated as the main one (65,2%), while communism slipped to a mere 1%.[200] Whatever the explanation for the apparent contradictions, there can be no doubt that whites perceived the "communist threat" as very real in the 1970s.

A nation-wide study of Afrikaans opinion in 1975 asked respondents to rate the importance of the "threat of communism and terrorism" on a 10-point scale. Over 80% rated it 10 out of 10, and 90% felt that the threat had grown more important over the previous five to ten years.[201] Important though it was, the communist menace did not blind the public to other external threats. It is only necessary to recall white South Africans' dim view of Western powers' policies towards the Republic a few years ago. In an opinion survey conducted among white voters in October 1977 – a time when South Africa's relations with Western powers, above all the United States, were at a particularly low ebb – 47% of the respondents saw the prevailing Western attitude towards the Republic as a moderate threat to white security and 32% considered it a serious threat; an insignificant number thought it a positive influence.[202] The already mentioned opinion survey of 1966/7 had produced a comparable finding: no less than 84% of the respondents perceived a lack of understanding for South Africa in the Western world as the greatest threat to the Republic's future.[203]

The October 1977 poll showed that white voters generally considered black unrest in the urban areas (e.g. Soweto 1976), black-ruled Angola and Mozambique, border conflicts and developments in Rhodesia as posing more serious threats to white security than international pressures;

the contrasts were, however, not profound. Schlemmer concluded from the survey's findings that "perceptions of external pressure combined with the other perceived dangers to white security . . . create a feeling of pessimism about the future of South Africa."[204] This impression corresponds with the present survey's findings that 75% of the respondents think a Namibia-style "terrorist war" will in due course also develop in South Africa. Similarly, an opinion survey that Market and Opinion Surveys undertook for a local newspaper group in April 1980 revealed that over 70% of the roughly 2 000 respondents agreed that "there were difficult times of war and internal unrest ahead in South Africa."[205] Further evidence of white South Africans' own prophesies of gloom is to be found in a comprehensive study of South African attitudes conducted by three West German scholars attached to the Bergstraesser Institute.[206] They compiled the following index of whites' "fear about the future", comparing responses over several years:

	June 1974	June 1976	October 1976	July 1977
	%	%	%	%
No fear	25	22	18	17
Slight fear	30	28	22	26
Pronounced fear	27	26	29	30
Very strong fear	18	23	31	27

The authors concluded that "the majority of white South Africans are quite fearful for their future: afraid that they might lose power, and afraid of what might happen then." One ingredient of this fear is the perception, shared by 65% of the respondents, that the chances are that "eventually there will be a black uprising in South Africa" – a notion that corresponds with the present survey's findings on the certainty of a terrorist war in South Africa.[207]

The decidedly hawkish inclinations of the white public are manifested in the support for tough South African responses to perceived external threats. White South Africans are thereby adopting notably hard-line stances on some of the major foreign policy issues of the day. Consider the present survey's findings that over 80% of the respondents agree that South Africa should militarily attack "terrorist bases" in neighbouring states (as it had done with the ANC base near Maputo in January 1981); over 70% support an embargo on food exports to black states that "support or harbour terrorists"; more than 70% believe South Africa can win the war against SWAPO in Namibia, and some 60% are against

South Africa negotiating directly with SWAPO to reach a settlement of the conflict in Namibia.

Although a clear majority of respondents on each of these issues take a hawkish position, thus pointing to the consensus-building qualities of external threats, this feature should not be allowed to mask the revealing finding that language and party political affiliation are significant divisive factors. The survey showed consistently greater support from Afrikaans-speakers than from English-speakers, and from NP followers than from PFP followers, for striking terrorist bases in neighbouring states and for stopping food exports to states supporting terrorists. The differences between these sub-groups are particularly pronounced on the question of South Africa's ability to win the war against SWAPO: over 80% of the Afrikaans-speaking respondents and 80% of NP supporters think South Africa can prevail, compared with only about 47% of the PFP supporters and roughly 60% of the English-speakers. Similarly, English-speakers and PFP supporters are less threat conscious than Afrikaners and NP supporters; this applies to both the communist threat against South Africa and the threat Zimbabwe poses to the Republic's security.

As regards sub-groups based on age, the survey found no great variation in the opinions of four different age groups – 16-24, 25-34, 35-49 and 50 years and older – resembling the differences between the language and political sub-groups. The widest margin of difference was between 68,0% and 83,6%, the percentages of those in the 50-plus age group and the 25-34 group respectively, who agreed that a Namibian-style terrorist war would eventually develop in South Africa. For the rest, the margin was seldom more than about 5%. The similarities in opinion notwithstanding, the 16-24 year olds emerged as the most doveish age group. For example, 40% of the respondents in this age group agreed that South Africa should negotiate directly with SWAPO (against roughly 38% for all respondents); 31,6% agreed that South Africa could not win the war against SWAPO (against 25,4%); 18,8% disagreed with the statement that South Africa should attack terrorist bases on foreign soil (against 16,6%), and 28% disagreed with the option of banning food exports to black states harbouring terrorists (against 23,5%). Although a clear majority of 16-24 year olds in each case opted for a hawkish line, the minorities were certainly not insignificant – particularly considering that South Africa's national servicemen were largely drawn from this age group. No single age group could similarly be classified as markedly and consistently more hawkish than others; the top position in the hawkish league (in terms of percentage of hawkish responses) alternated between the remaining three groups.

Again, these results bear comparison with those of other surveys previously conducted. Particularly relevant are the findings of the West German scholars. In 1977 they asked white respondents' views on the prospect that "South Africa might face war from outside and unrest from inside in the future". Nearly 75% were in favour of fighting; some 20% wanted to avoid conflict by making political concessions, and a mere 2% selected the third response option, "we should rather leave the country" if matters get out of hand. The differences of opinion between the language and party political sub-groups were marked: only 10% of Afrikaners were in favour of adapting politically against 33% among English-speakers; 85% of NP supporters were ready to fight, whereas some 75% of PFP supporters preferred making concessions.[208] As far as Namibia is concerned, the opinion survey of 1964 found that 61% of the respondents were prepared to "personally take up arms to keep South West Africa on the existing basis" (that is, administered by South Africa). Nearly the same proportion rejected any United Nations presence in the territory.[209] Such early opinions were an intimation of the present hard line adopted by white South Africans on the Namibian issue, now that arms have in fact been taken up. The white public's propensity to support hawkish foreign policy options was also illustrated in an opinion poll in May 1976 on South Africa's involvement in the Angolan war. A full 64% of those questioned said the government had been right in sending South African forces into Angola; only 18% thought the action was wrong, and another 18% offered no opinion. Support for the government's Angolan policy was stronger among Afrikaners (70%) than English-speakers (55%). It is worth adding that 46% of all respondents felt that the government had failed to keep the public properly informed on events in Angola.[210] A final indication of white South Africans' uncompromising attitude towards external forces is contained in the already cited opinion poll of October 1977. In response to the statement, "South Africa should ignore world opinion and follow its own course",

84% of government supporters expressed agreement against 67% among NRP and 47% among PFP followers.[211]

Some of the figures quoted above tend to suggest some connection between respondents' perceptions of foreign policy issues and their party political loyalties. The present survey revealed that supporters of the NP, HNP and NCP, as well as Afrikaners as a group, were more pronounced in their support for hawkish foreign policy actions and registered stronger threat perceptions than PFP and NRP followers and English-speakers generally. Now given the divisions that plagued the NP at the time the present opinion survey was conducted (February 1982), it cannot simply be assumed that NP supporters were largely in agreement on contentious domestic political issues. It was therefore necessary to test respondents' views on a number of specific domestic issues, which would reveal their *verligte* or *verkrampte* inclinations. (For the purposes of this chapter, the terms *verlig(te)* and *verkramp(te)* are not confined to Afrikaners only, but include all whites holding certain political views.) These inclinations were then compared with their foreign policy perceptions to see whether there was a correlation between the two.

The first statement, measuring domestic political opinion, read: "The time has arrived for coloureds and Indians to sit with whites in the same Parliament." Just over 60% of the respondents agreed, and 37% disagreed. A remarkable 75,1% disagreed with the second statement, "White children should not participate in sports meetings with children of other population groups"; 23,5% agreed. The final statement, "Cinemas should be open to all population groups", drew the following response: 54,7% disagreed and 43,8% agreed. Using convenient political shorthand, one can say that the percentage of *verkrampte* responses to the three statements were, respectively, 37%, 23,5% and 54,7%. Not unexpectedly, English-speakers and supporters of particularly the PFP and to a slightly lesser degree the NRP featured strongest among respondents adopting *verligte* views. Among the four age groups, the 16-24 year olds consistently registered the largest *verligte* response, although the margin of difference between the four was on the whole small. More important, though, for the purposes of this discussion, is to cross-tabulate the *verkrampte* and *verligte* respondents' respective reactions to the three statements with their answers to some of the foreign policy questions, specifi-

cally those that reflect the respondents' hawkishness or doveishness.

The accompanying table illustrates the responses of the *verkramptes* – those who disagreed that coloureds and Indians should join whites in Parliament (740 in all), agreed that school sport should be segregated (470), and disagreed that cinemas should be desegregated (1 094) – to five selected foreign policy issues.

	Disagree Mixed Parliament (N=740) %	Agree Segregated Sport (N=470) %	Disagree Open Cinemas (N=1 094) %	All Respondents (N=1 999) %
Disagree that communist threat is exaggerated	89,7	90,2	88,9	79,9
Agree on Zimbabwe threat	78,4	80,6	77,9	70,5
Agree on attacking terror bases	90,3	89,4	85,6	81,1
Agree on ban of food exports	81,9	83,0	79,7	72,4
Disagree that SA can't win SWA war	87,8	84,3	83,0	72,3

The table shows, for example, that of the 740 respondents (out of a total of 1 999) who opposed the idea that coloureds and Indians should sit in Parliament, nearly 90% disagreed that the government exaggerated the communist threat. Similarly, 83% of those who agreed that white children should not participate in racially mixed sport, also agreed that South Africa should stop food exports to black states harbouring "terrorists".

It will be noted that the respondents in question were not wholly consistent in either their *verkrampte* views (on some of the three issues there was a stronger *verkrampte* reaction than on others) or their hawkish inclinations (the level of hawkishness varied on the five foreign policy issues). These features are not surprising and the variations were, moreover, very limited on the foreign policy issues. More important, however, is the fact that *verkrampte* respondents consistently displayed a greater degree of hawkishness than the respondents generally (that is, than the 1 999). It can be concluded that although respondents generally took decidedly hawkish views on foreign policy issues, *verkrampte* respondents were even more inclined to do so. There was, in other words, some correlation between internal *verkramptheid* and external hawkishness.

The 61% of the respondents – 1 220 – who agreed that coloureds and Indians should enjoy parliamentary representation, can be taken as a good example of a *verligte* response to a domestic political issue. A cross-tabulation of responses to domestic and foreign policy issues shows that of these 1 220 respondents 67,5% agreed that Zimbabwe threatened South Africa's security; 50,4% agreed that South Africa should negotiate with SWAPO; 34,1% agreed that South Africa cannot win the war against SWAPO; 77,7% agreed that terrorist bases on foreign soil should be attacked, and 68,5% agreed that South Africa should not export food to states hosting "terrorists". *Verligtes*, therefore, tended to be only marginally less hawkish on foreign policy issues than the white population as a whole.

Having probed the nature of white public opinion, one now has to consider some of its implications for foreign policy making. A point to keep in mind is that public opinion is important to the policy formulators only if they believe it to be so. By the same token it can be argued that the policy formulators might have their own perception or reading of public opinion, which need not correspond with an objective measurement as expressed in an opinion survey. A government's foreign policy might therefore not be in tune with public opinion because of its misreading of popular opinion. Of course, a government may also choose deliberately to ignore public opinion on some issues, whereas on others there may be an effective absence of public opinion. On the basis of the opinion surveys quoted above, it however appears that the white public's threat perceptions fit in well with the government's notion of a total onslaught on South Africa. It would even seem that the government's frequent exhortations that the public should wake up to the seriousness of the threat facing the country are superfluous. In both the government's and the public's perception of the threat, communism looms large. The opinion surveys also show that white South Africans take a particularly gloomy view of the country's future, perhaps much more negative than the government would prefer. (Consider the opinions on the inevitability of a terrorist war, of internal unrest and of a black uprising.)

The white public is notably militant in its views on how to respond to perceived external threats. This feature certainly does not support Walter Lippmann's familiar criticism that public opinion is typically inclined to favour the "soft options" in foreign policy[212] – except if "soft" can be taken to mean apparently simple, uncomplicated if violent options. It can be concluded that forceful and visible South African actions against "hostile" black states – such as attacking terrorist bases on their soil and stopping the export of food – are likely to enjoy wide (white) public support. The general call is, indeed, for *kragdadigheid* in the conduct of foreign policy – the very characteristic that has long been a hallmark of the Nationalist government's actions in the domestic political arena.

As for Namibia, the public's belief that South Africa can win the war against SWAPO, together with opposition to direct talks with SWAPO, could have far-reaching domestic as well as foreign policy implications. It should be conceded that opposition to South Africa's negotiating directly with SWAPO does not necessarily mean that the public disagree with indirect talks through third parties. Such negotiations have in fact long been taking place through the Namibia settlement initiative of the five Western powers. There is, however, reason to doubt whether the public is fully convinced of the need for resolving the Namibian issue through negotiations. Faith in a military solution is running strong. Given this confidence, an early negotiated settlement that produces a SWAPO regime may well create considerable domestic political difficulties for the South African government. A strong hawkish-cum-conservative backlash, spilling across party lines, is certainly not inconceivable. The charge would be that the government, had it militarily held out longer, could have defeated SWAPO on the battle field and destroyed it as a political force. To date the government has done precious little to prepare the public for a negotiated end to the Namibian conflict, and least of all for an unfavourable outcome.

Where a display of *kragdadigheid* also has strong public appeal is in the reaction to foreign pressure. An uncompromising, defiant attitude by the government fits in well with public opinion on this score. Consider the October 1977 opinion poll already referred to, which found that 84% of government supporters agree with the contention that South Africa should ignore world opinion and pursue its own political course.[213] Prime Minister Vorster accurately read the prevailing mood, and fought the general election of November 1977 mainly against the "hostile" outside world, specifically the Carter Administration.

In an earlier chapter it was noted that National

198

Party MPs' domestic political views strongly correlate with their foreign policy stances; the *verkramptes* tend to be more hawkish and the *verligtes* more doveish than the public generally. Similar correlations among the public at large are revealed by the present opinion survey, although the strongest "hawks" are to the right of the NP and the strongest "doves" to its left; NP followers on the whole are nonetheless markedly militant in their foreign policy views.

For all the forcefulness displayed by the white public generally, it should not be overlooked that language and party political loyalties represent major divisive forces. Thus English-speakers and followers of the PFP in particular are generally inclined to hold considerably less militant and defiant views than Afrikaners and NP followers, not to mention supporters of parties to the right of the NP. While it is probably true to say that a larger degree of consensus exists among white South Africans on foreign policy issues than on domestic political issues (save for such "extreme" questions as black majority rule, on which whites are virtually united in their opposition), there are nonetheless significant cleavages in opinion on foreign policy matters – and these run along language and party political lines.

The "other" public opinion: blacks, coloureds and Indians

Black public opinion, although of secondary importance, cannot be ignored by the formulators of South African foreign policy. Assessing the role of the three groups' opinions in foreign policy making is, however, a difficult task. First, there is a lack of "hard" information on the nature of their opinions in the realm of foreign affairs. Second, the role of black public opinion – whatever its nature – in the policy making process generally is largely unknown and unexplored; in the foreign policy field the problem is even more acute. One is then left to extract from the available data on black, coloured and Indian opinion those aspects that are relevant to foreign policy, and to try to assess their implications for policy making.

Beginning with black (African) opinion, one can first refer to views on the present political order, to form some idea of the public support that the policy formulators can command when formulating policy in the name of South Africa. Apart from such dramatic, highly visible demonstrations of political disaffection as the Soweto riots, blacks' opposition to the *status quo* has been well tabulated in several opinion surveys. The basic sentiments have been expressed in a number of ways. For example, the survey that the Bergstraesser Institute conducted among urban blacks in 1977 found that 57% of them agreed that the demonstrations in Soweto and elsewhere the previous year "were a good thing for the future of South African people". Support was strongest among black pupils and students, of whom 71% over the country as a whole thought the demonstrations a good thing.[214] An opinion survey undertaken by the Quail Commission, which in 1980 reported on the future of the then self-governing Ciskei, discovered "a very substantial pool of discontent with high violence" among Xhosas; the prevailing political situation was identified as one of the major contributing causes.[215] In similar vein, the Buthelezi Commission, which investigated the future of KwaZulu/Natal, reported on the basis of opinion surveys that "it is quite clear that a stage has been reached where a very large majority of South African Blacks indicate that they are either 'unhappy' or 'angry and impatient' with the present situation in the Republic of South Africa."[216]

As for perceived alternatives to the existing political order, the Bergstraesser study established that 83% of urban blacks thought "South Africa should be one place for all people . . . Blacks and Whites . . . should be allowed to vote."[217] The Quail Commission's opinion survey showed conclusively that a unitary state for the whole of South Africa on a one-man one-vote basis represented the first preference of 90% of Ciskeians, both urban and rural. To be fair, the Quail Commission also found that several options in which homelands featured as political entities – but not with their then existing status – commanded substantial support among Xhosas generally.[218]

Another indication of blacks' lack of identification with the political system can be found in their support for particular political organisations and leaders. The Buthelezi Commission noted that the reputations and profiles of black leader figures have been in a state of flux since the massive urban unrest in 1976. What has nonetheless remained remarkably stable has been the particularly high degree of support for leaders of the banned ANC. Consider the following table, which compares the rank-order of leader support on the Witwatersrand, as found in four separate studies:[219]

	1977[1]	1979[2]	1980[3]	1981[4]
Chief Gatsha Buthelezi (KwaZulu/Inkatha)	1	2	4	2
ANC leaders	2	2 or higher	1	1
Dr Ntatho Motlana (Committee of Ten, Soweto)	0	1	3	3
Bishop Desmond Tutu (Religious leader, Soweto)	0	3	2	3
Black consciousness leaders	4	not asked	4	4
Homeland leaders collectively	3	3	not asked	5

1. Bergstraesser study
2. Quail Commission
3. Study by Lawrence Schlemmer, using a comparable sample
4. Buthelezi Commission

Investigating the choices of organisations or parties that black South Africans considered will be important in their lives, the Buthelezi Commission found that on the Witwatersrand the ANC headed the list with 37%, followed by 35% for black consciousness organisations such as AZAPO, the Soweto Committee of Ten with 17% and Inkatha or the Black Alliance with 16%. In the KwaZulu or Natal area, however, Inkatha or the Black Alliance dominated with 54%, followed by the ANC way behind with 16%.[220] There are, in other words, considerable regional differences in the support patterns of the various organisations. That Inkatha has its power base in KwaZulu or Natal is not surprising, for it is a Zulu "cultural liberation movement" led by Buthelezi.

The above findings on the ANC's popular support might be questioned because the surveys were confined to particular geographic areas; they were not countrywide. That the findings nonetheless point to a wider trend is confirmed in an opinion survey published in September 1981.[221] It was conducted by English-language newspapers among blacks in Johannesburg, Durban and Cape Town. Some 40% of the respondents said they would vote for the ANC in a parliamentary election. Second was Inkatha, which drew 20% support, followed by 11% for AZAPO and 10% for the banned Pan-Africanist Congress (PAC); the ANC thus attracted roughly as much support as the other three organisations combined. Although not strictly comparable, a 1977 survey conducted among blacks in Johannesburg, Durban and Pretoria showed 22% support for the ANC and double that for Inkatha. What is clear is that the ANC's position improved substantially between 1977 and 1981, whereas Inkatha's weakened correspondingly. The ANC's standing in 1981 was also reflected in the survey's finding that Mr Nelson Mandela, the ANC's imprisoned leader, enjoyed "towering popularity", being liked by 76% of the respondents. He was followed by Dr Ntatho Motlana, chairman of the Committee of Ten, with 58%, and Buthelezi with 39%.

Whatever the reservations about these findings,[222] there can be no doubt that "the nature of black South African politics has changed over the past five years and that this has very real implications for the future of our society", in the words of the Buthelezi Commission. As for the ANC's growing support, the Commission said it was not possible to say to what extent this phenomenon was a fashionable, rather superficial trend, or to what extent it manifested a firm political commitment among blacks generally. Earlier surveys suggested it was a mixture of the two, "and the degree of commitment and the significance of the support must not be underestimated."[223]

Having noted black South Africans' rejection of the present political order and their strong support for the radical ANC – one should however not forget that Inkatha is no supporter of white minority rule either – the next aspect to consider is the ways in which blacks perceive that desired political changes could or should be brought about.

To begin with, one can refer to the finding of the Bergstraesser study that although a majority of urban blacks in 1977 felt "helpless as individuals", a minority regarded the blacks as a group without hope, "and only a small minority still believe that a liberation movement has no prospects of success." The survey also established that a clear majority of urban blacks – 65% – are still for peaceful negotiated change, but a full 25% had "already written off the possibility of peaceful change".[224] Four years later the Buthelezi Commission's opinion survey posed the following question: "Now thinking about South Africa, if there is no change in the lives of black South Africans in another ten years, what do you think will happen?" Fully 87% of the KwaZulu/Natal respondents expected either war, revolution, intervention from outside, military incursions by guerrilla forces, or strikes, riots and boycotts; on the Witwatersrand virtually *all* respondents gave similar answers. Asked in an open probe what other things would happen, 99% of the respondents in KwaZulu/Natal and also on the Witwatersrand spontaneously mentioned revolution. "Revolution", the Commission said, stating the obvious, "is certainly no longer the topic only of frustrated intellectuals and armchair radicals."[225] Further support for this contention can be found in a Markinor opinion survey conducted towards the end of 1981. Nearly 25% of the (urban) black respondents supported the contention that "the entire way our society is organised must be radically changed by revolutionary action." A slightly higher proportion, 31%, favoured gradual reforms. A related finding is that nearly half the urban blacks believed there may be "certain circumstances where terrorism is justified". Only 20% of the respondents rejected terrorism outright, whatever its motives.[226] These findings correspond with those of a Marplan survey of black opinion on the terrorist siege of a bank in Pretoria in January 1980, in which a number of the attackers were killed. Nearly 75% of the people in Soweto felt either strong or qualified sympathy for the terrorists; of them, 37,9% regarded the raiders as heroes. Fully 75% thought the action would in some way benefit blacks in the future. Nonetheless, 58% of the Soweto respondents did not approve of the raid itself, thus indicating reservations about this form of action.[227]

Black South Africans' political perceptions have been significantly influenced by foreign events, especially in South Africa's immediate regional environment. "The displacement of white authority first in Mozambique and Angola and more recently in Zimbabwe must have had a powerful demonstration effect on the thinking of rank and file black South Africans", the Buthelezi Commission reported. Presented with a number of concrete suggestions that rationalise Mugabe's ascendancy, the one attracting by far the strongest support from blacks in KwaZulu/Natal and the Witwatersrand alike, contended that he and his men won against the whites "because of their own strength and courage".[228] A 1980 Markinor opinion survey among urban blacks revealed that they overwhelmingly supported Mugabe as leader in Zimbabwe. His reputation was based on the perception that he was a freedom fighter promoting blacks' interests, that he was courageous and intelligent and a dynamic personality.[229] The impression that black attitudes on Mugabe's rise to power created, according to the Buthelezi Commission, "is one which would seem to suggest to black South Africans that there is a possibility of a violent overthrow of the government, provided that neighbouring African countries were to lend support to insurgency." The older notion that white power is "immutable and too formidable to confront", is therefore being significantly changed.[230]

As regards the political opinions of coloureds and Indians, the overall impression created by a number of opinion surveys is that the two groups' political disaffection is pronounced, but that they are less radical than the blacks in their choice of an alternative political order and the means of achieving it.

A Markinor survey among South Africa's four racial groups towards the end of 1981 pointed to strong criticism by coloureds and Indians, and indeed by blacks, of state institutions such as Parliament, the army and the police. The coloureds' low degree of identification with present-day South Africa was also revealed in the finding that only about 50% of them were proud to be South African; most Indians declared themselves proud, but their degree of enthusiasm was somewhat lower than that of whites. A more dramatic illustration of political disaffection was the Markinor finding that only approximately 25% of the coloureds said they were prepared to fight for their country, as against roughly half the Indians; 80% of the whites, by contrast, would fight for South Africa. Among blacks the figure was 26%.[231] On the question of defending South Africa against outside aggression, a 1974 opinion survey among Johannesburg's coloured community had shown that a majority (54%) would fight for South Africa, whereas some 43% would remain neutral.[232] Although these figures differ substantially from Markinor's, they nonetheless reveal that even before the great upheavals of 1976, a large proportion of coloureds did not identify themselves with the Republic.

Despite strong expressions of political disaffection, opinion surveys have found that large segments of the Indian and coloured communities appear either politically uncommitted or apathetic. A survey among Indians in Durban found that the long existing Natal Indian Congress (linked to the ANC in the Congress Alliance in the 1950s, but today still a legal body) is the only political movement with a sizeable following – and then with only 24% support. Indian parties participating in government-created ethnic institutions can count on a pitiful 5% or 6% support. Almost half those interviewed were politically uncommitted. Among coloureds in Cape Town a 1981 opinion survey established that the anti-apartheid (coloured) Labour Party enjoyed 30% support, with the ANC coming a poor second with 8%. Nearly half the respondents either had no party political preference or said they would not vote (in a hypothetical election).[233] A newspaper opinion survey conducted in 1981 made the interesting finding that most of the coloureds and Indians supporting the ANC had reservations about straightforward majority rule as propagated by the organisation. This feature is probably related to the finding that as many as 75% of these two groups do not regard themselves as "black".[234] Given these moderate inclinations, it comes as a surprise that Markinor found that only about 33% of the coloureds are prepared to reject terrorism outright; 41% indicated that there may be circumstances where terrorism is justified. Among Indians, by contrast, 41% believed that terrorism, whatever the motive, must be condemned; 25%, however, indicated that terrorism may be justified under certain circumstances.[235] What these seemingly contradictory findings point to is that coloureds and Indians lack a coherent political identity. One possible implication is that the two groups might be swayed politically to identify closer with either the black or the white "side".*

This lengthy review of black, coloured and Indian opinion is necessary to try to obtain a reliable picture of the three groups' political perceptions – a task all the more important because of and indeed complicated by their exclusion from the parliamentary franchise as a means of political expression. What, then, are the implications for foreign policy making of the three communities' lack of identification with the political *status quo?*

• The South African government's international legitimacy must necessarily be undermined by its apparent lack of legitimacy in the eyes of the majority of the South African population. The UN General Assembly has already condemned the South African government to "illegitimacy" and elevated the "national liberation movement" to the "authentic representative" of the South African people.

• Flowing from the first point is the fact that there is a definite link between international opinion on South Africa and domestic black opinion. The international community, typically portrayed as hostile, unreasonable and prejudiced by Pretoria, is in a sense articulating or at any rate echoing

domestic black opinion. This is not to say that the foreign champions of black rights necessarily have the black groups' interests in mind in the first instance. The South African government, by contrast, is widely seen abroad as representing merely the interests of the white minority.

• Both the notions of a total onslaught on South Africa and a total national strategy as an essential antidote are undermined by the deep political divisions between whites and the black groups. The idea of a total onslaught, led by communist forces, will lack credibility for as long as blacks, coloureds and Indians see their principal "opponent" as a white minority government. It is then not surprising that a majority of blacks and coloureds, according to opinion surveys, are unwilling to defend South Africa militarily, and large proportions of them take a sympathetic stand on what whites overwhelmingly and unconditionally reject as "terrorism". The South African government would therefore find it virtually impossible to mobilise all the country's human and material resources to present a solid front against perceived external threats.

• South African blacks, in particular, are everything but insulated from external events, least of all from events elsewhere in the region." They widely applauded and took courage from the displacement of white regimes in Mozambique, Angola and Rhodesia. Whereas white South Africans view the ascendancy of black rulers in these countries with apprehension, if not outright dismay, black South Africans greeted them as liberators, and see in these developments some intrinsic value for their own struggle against white rule.

• Government concern about the impact on local black opinion of an internationally agreed independence deal for Namibia, specifically one that produces a SWAPO government, has certainly been a major constraint on Pretoria in its dealings with the five Western powers. The demonstration effect is bound to be fairly dramatic, particularly when the South African government itself is perceived as having abdicated under duress, or having succumbed to a "liberation movement".

• Whereas white South Africans would overwhelmingly support forceful actions against black states perceived as hostile to the Republic, and against foreign "terrorist" bases, blacks, in particular, but also coloureds and Indians, are likely to view such moves with considerable disfavour, if not outright hostility.

---

*The coloured Labour Party's decision in January 1983 to accept the government's new constitutional guidelines can be interpreted as an identification with the whites rather than with the excluded blacks.

To conclude, South Africa's foreign policy formulators find themselves in the invidious position of facing an unsympathetic world community without the backing of the majority of the South African people. Far from being passive, various black political organisations actively work for the radical transformation of the South African polity and in the process dispute the right of the (white) government to formulate policy for South Africa as a whole. It is not a case of the policy formulators being caught between two opposing forces, one domestic and the other foreign. Instead, internal black opinion and international opinion to some extent make common cause against South Africa's white rulers. Just how important a factor external pressure is in South Africa's foreign policy making is considered in the next chapter.

7. The External Milieu: Foreign Pressure

The world does not know or understand us, and we feel this deeply, even when we are conscious that we are much to blame in it all.

Jan Smuts, 1947

In contrast to the relatively recent recognition of the "domestic sources" of foreign policy by scholars and policy formulators, the influence of external factors on foreign policy formation has long been acknowledged. It was a widely held notion, until not many decades ago, that foreign policy is in essence a state's reaction to events and forces beyond its borders. Today it is a truism that the foreign policy of a state is shaped by factors in both the domestic and international environment.

The two settings cannot be regarded as neatly separable sources of influence, for there is close interplay between them. National political systems have become penetrated by extraneous influences to the extent of affecting domestic policies. The internal affairs of some states have, in turn, become internationalised. The traditional doctrine of national sovereignty and domestic jurisdiction has not prevented a blurring of the boundaries between domestic and international affairs.[1] The interaction between the internal and external environment can usefully be explained by the concept of linkage. In terms of Rosenau's formulation, a linkage is "any recurrent sequence of behaviour that originates in one system [the national or the international] and is reacted to in another" – thus his notion of "boundary-crossing responses".[2]

South Africa provides a dramatic illustration of the internationalisation of a domestic situation. From facing mild censure of its racial policies in the early post-war years, South Africa three decades later has to contend with a UN convention declaring apartheid a punishable crime against humanity.[3] The convention represents one of numerous forms of international pressure on South Africa. Others include repeated verbal denunciations and exhortations, punitive measures such as a mandatory international arms embargo, and international support for organisations bent on effecting a political transformation in the Republic through violent means. Foreign pressure means deliberate actions undertaken by external political actors with the purpose of persuading or coercing the South African government either to abandon certain policies and actions or, alternatively, to behave in a particular fashion. This can apply to its actions both at home and abroad. In the terminology of linkage politics such outside pressures are known as direct environmental outputs: intentional behaviour designed by the external environment to evoke a response from the target polity.[4] In another sense, these outputs or pressures are indirect, not aimed directly at the South African government. Pressure may be directed at a variety of foreign and local institutions, including foreign governments and transnational corporations, believed to be helping Pretoria sustain its policies.

Just as the channels vary, so the sources of external pressure on South Africa span a wide spectrum; foreign governments are only one among several sources. As Rosenau points out, polities do not have "undifferentiated external environments".[5]

Whatever the sources and routes, external pressure on South Africa has implications for the country's domestic and foreign policies. Its foreign policy is conducted in a highly unfavourable external milieu, while its domestic policies likewise run into heavy and tangible international opposition.

A Brief Anatomy of Foreign Pressure on South Africa

From the inception of the UN, South Africa found itself subjected to international pressure on two fronts: its domestic racial policies and the status of South West Africa. In time, the form of UN pressure changed significantly. The General Assembly began with cautiously formulated "requests", "urgings" and "invitations" to South Africa to heed international opinion. Perceiving persuasion to be ineffective, the General Assembly in April 1961 resorted to coercion, requesting states to consider taking "separate and collective action" against South Africa.[6] In November 1962 the Assembly passed its first resolution calling for specific diplomatic and economic sanctions against the Republic.[7] The following year the Security Council joined the move for punitive measures against South Africa by calling for an arms embargo.[8]

By adopting these resolutions – which related to apartheid and not South West Africa – the UN not merely claimed a right to involve itself in South Africa's domestic affairs, but moreover expressly declared that the situation, if continued, could endanger international peace and security. The punitive measures called for were designed to isolate South Africa diplomatically, economically and militarily.

Although the General Assembly from 1962 onwards passed sanctions resolutions against South Africa with monotonous regularity, it was not until 1976-8 that the international clamour for sanctions again reached, if not exceeded, the intensity it had in the first half of the 1960s. By this time the basis for sanctions demands had widened considerably, and the Security Council in November 1977 took the drastic step of imposing a mandatory arms embargo. The resolution concerned referred to the South African government's "resort to massive violence and killings of the African people", and declared that its policies and actions were "fraught with danger" to international peace and security; South Africa's procurement of arms was said to actually constitute a threat to world peace; there was mention of South Africa's "military build-up" and "persistent threats of aggression" against neighbouring states, and it was alleged that the Republic was "at the threshold of producing nuclear weapons".[9] The grounds on which the Council based its decision were, however, not the only ones that the advocates of sanctions cited in their endeavours in 1976-8. Other major reasons for sanctions were South Africa's "illegal occupation" of Namibia; its support for the "illegal" Rhodesian regime and its "repeated acts of aggression" against neighbouring states, particularly Angola and Zambia.[10] While the Rhodesian issue has since disappeared from the international agenda, the other two charges are still commonly made in support of sanctions against South Africa.

To sum up, the UN clearly perceives a situation requiring collective and mandatory punitive measures against South Africa in terms of chapter 7 of the UN charter. At issue are aspects of both South Africa's domestic and foreign policies. The only international organisation that can resort to enforcement action on a world-wide scale, the UN is obviously the principal centre of foreign pressure on South Africa. In its campaign against the Republic, the UN has established a network of institutions, absorbing a not insignificant amount of time, energy and money. Established bodies in the UN family have joined the offensive by instituting "social sanctions" against the Republic, that is, excluding it from their membership. This form of isolation is "the international equivalent of exile", in Bissell's words. Since the 1960s, South Africa has been forced to withdraw from the International Labour Organisation, the Food and Agriculture Organisation and the World Health Organisation; it withdrew voluntarily from UNESCO; it was suspended from the Economic Commission for Africa and excluded from the conferences of various specialised agencies. South Africa was furthermore banished from the UN General Assembly in 1974.[11]

While pressure on South Africa can be said to coalesce in the UN, there are a host of other actors also exerting pressure. An indication of the wide field over which the actors are spread can be gleaned from the list of participants at the UN-OAU-Nigerian-sponsored World Conference for Action against Apartheid, held in Lagos in August 1977. Present were 112 governments, 12 inter-governmental organisations, 51 non-governmental organisations and five liberation movements.[12] In the same year the South African Department of Information reported that in the United States alone 79 organisations were actively operating to "discredit" the Republic, to put pressure on the United States Congress for punitive measures against South Africa and to force American companies to disinvest in the Republic.[13]

The various state and non-state actors apply or propagate a vast array of measures against South Africa. These range from states openly giving material support to the armed "liberation" struggle, through voluntarily maintaining trade embargoes against the Republic, to more or less subtle forms of diplomatic pressure. Non-governmental organisations,[14] prominent among them the anti-apartheid movements and the World Council of Churches, involve themselves in such actions as providing humanitarian and material aid to the so-called liberation movements, in addition to appealing to foreign governments to impose punitive measures against South Africa and pressurising foreign companies to withdraw from the Republic. At the UN, two of the major measures used against South Africa are punishment and isolation. Their main champions are the black African states. Punishment, according to Bissell, involves a movement to impose economic sanctions against the Republic, whereas isolation is essentially a "social sanction". Among the various other forms of pressure on South Africa which the African states try to apply through the UN, are moves to "educate" world opinion on apartheid, obtain legitimacy and aid for the so-called liberation movements, and enforce "legal sanctions" in the form of the Convention to Abolish All Forms of Racial Discrimination and the Convention on the Suppression and Punishment of the Crime of Apartheid.[15] There is no need to compile a full inventory of the measures, for it is already evident that South Africa has to contend with an actively hostile external environment in which numerous pressures are at work to persuade or, more commonly, coerce the Republic to mend its ways both at home and abroad.[16]

More important than the means of external pressure are its objectives. It should immediately be said that there are two sides to this matter: the objectives as formulated by those exerting the pressure, and the same objectives as perceived by the target state, South Africa.

There is general international agreement that South Africa's racial policies are unacceptable (or "repugnant" or "abhorrent", as they are commonly labelled in official jargon) and should be abandoned. But while there is consensus at what might be termed the moral level, there is no similar consensus on the precise nature of an acceptable alternative political arrangement, except for a very basic agreement that it should not be based on race or ethnicity.

The resort to coercion against the Republic springs from the conviction that the South African political system is relatively static and impervious to liberalisation through internal dynamics.[17] A related view is that, in the short run, neither revolution from within, nor fundamental government-initiated reform, nor "liberation" through the efforts of black African states is likely.[18] External forces, so the argument goes, therefore have to be employed to transform the South African political system. Failure to do so would not simply perpetuate an unacceptable *status quo*, it is said, but existing racial tensions may well unleash a racial war in Southern Africa which might engulf the whole continent and involve the superpowers. This apocalyptic prognosis demands preventive international action. It all amounts to an externally sponsored exercise in nation-rebuilding.[19]

Of course, not all states endorse this rationalisation of coercion. On the one hand, there may be those who do not see coercion as a means of avoiding large-scale conflict, but who are promoting it to serve their own interests. On the other hand, some Western states profess that the South African political system can undergo meaningful political reform without external coercion, through internal dynamics combined with external encouragement and persuasion. Common to both points of view is nonetheless the notion that the prevailing political order is unacceptable and needs to be replaced.

An analysis of the various political objectives that other states and foreign organisations hope to achieve through exerting pressure on South Africa, would be a study in itself. Since the UN is the primary focus of international pressure on South Africa, the objectives articulated by the organisation will be considered. A feature of the UN's formulation of objectives has been its radicalisation. The UN's only major attempt to date to define the objectives of its campaign against apartheid has been the appointment of a group of experts in December 1963 "to examine methods of resolving the present situation in South Africa". Chaired by Mrs Alva Myrdal, the group cautiously advocated a national convention which would hopefully lead to a federal system with safeguards for individual rights.[20] These relatively moderate proposals soon made way for radical demands.

The present era of UN objectives was heralded by a General Assembly resolution of November 1969 which recognised the "legitimacy" of the struggle of the "oppressed people" of South Africa "for the exercise of their inalienable right of self-determination, and thus to attain majority rule based on universal suffrage." Particularly significant was the declaration that the agent to bring about this transformation was not the South African government, but the "national liberation movements".[21] The Assembly condemned the government to illegitimacy and elevated the ANC and PAC to the "authentic representatives" of the vast majority of South African people.[22] A further pointer to the political order sought by the General Assembly is found in its persistent rejection of "Bantustans" as being, among other things, prejudicial to the territorial integrity of the state and the unity of its people, and designed to perpetuate white minority rule. By insisting that apartheid be replaced by "majority rule in the country as a whole",[23] the Assembly is saying that South Africa and the black homelands form a single political entity which may not be balkanised.

Although the resolutions embodying these objectives are consistently passed with overwhelming majorities, Western powers frequently abstain or register opposition. International consensus on such a highly complex and contentious issue as devising an acceptable new political system for South Africa, is understandably difficult to reach. It can, for example, be asked whether all Western powers perceive the matter as a straight choice between endorsing the *status quo* in South Africa and supporting black majority rule in, most probably, a unitary state. Depending on the party political complexion of the governments in power, some Western states may at times be inclined to favour the kind of liberal democratic objectives formulated by the Myrdal group. Communist states, by contrast, probably have their own ideologically motivated political objectives which they wish to see realised in South Africa. The objectives, as formulated by the General Assembly, could at least be regarded as an accurate expression of the views of black African states.

The UN's position on Namibia has likewise undergone a marked radicalisation since the late 1960s. Thus the General Assembly began calling South West Africa Namibia, revoked South Africa's mandate over the territory and declared the Republic's presence illegal, and conferred on SWAPO the status of sole authentic representative of the people of Namibia. Yet, in the search for an international settlement, South Africa has not been ignored by the UN, while South Africa for its part has conceded a UN role in the process. This mutual recognition found expression in the acceptance by all parties concerned of Security Council resolution 435, which set such objectives as UN-supervised elections and independence for Namibia. But while the UN is engaged in the search for an internationally acceptable diplomatic settlement involving South Africa, the General Assembly keeps up the pressure on the Republic with a continuing string of resolutions condemning its behaviour in the settlement negotiations, calling for sanctions against the country, and pledging support for SWAPO.

South African Perceptions of Foreign Pressure

"In policy making", Holsti rightly pointed out, "the state of the environment does not matter so much as what government officials believe that state to be." The policy formulator therefore acts and reacts "according to his *images* of the environment".[24] When one relates this to foreign pressure on South Africa, it means that the policy formulators respond not on the basis of the "objective" features of the various pressures, but according to their perceptions of the pressures, and particularly of the underlying objectives. Holsti noted that there will always be a discrepancy between *images* of reality, and reality. This is partly the result of physical obstacles to the flow of information (such as lack of time and faulty communications), and partly "a problem of the distortion of reality caused by attitudes, values, beliefs, or faulty expectations".[25]

Faced with a diversity of pressures applied over a very broad front by so many different states and organisations with often conflicting objectives in mind, South African policy formulators might have been expected to distinguish carefully between the various kinds of pressure and those applying it. Official perceptions of pressure are, however, characterised by sweeping generalisations.

At the very least, foreign pressures designed to persuade or force the South African government to change or abolish existing policies are seen as unwelcome external interference. What is more important, foreign demands for drastic political reform in South Africa are easily portrayed as a threat to white survival – in more than a political sense, at that. These views are understandably reinforced when such means of pressure as sanctions and support for the armed "liberation" struggle are employed. Foreign pressure has also become a contentious political issue within South Africa. The result of these features is often a rather distorted picture of the world, caused by obfuscation, over-simplification and exaggeration. But whatever the inadequacies, the fact of the matter is that the policy formulators have certain perceptions of foreign pressure and shape their policies and actions accordingly.

It is an old notion that South Africa is facing an unreasonable, hostile world. Smuts, following his experiences at the infant UN in 1946, spoke of a "solid mass of prejudice against the colour policies of South Africa", which not even the "most efficient publicity" could have overcome.[26] Malan introduced the theme of a world having temporarily lost its senses concerning South Africa, the reason being "a sickly sentimentality with regard to the black man".[27] Verwoerd thought along similar lines, portraying Western countries as being afflicted by a "psychosis" that emphasises only the rights and freedoms of blacks.[28] Many years later, Prime Minister PW Botha diagnosed a "paralysis in the mind of the West", preventing it from acknowledging the importance of South Africa to Western interests and also to the interests of the African continent generally. Like his predecessors, PW Botha hoped Western countries could be cured to regain their "sense of direction" and take up the "fight for Christian civilised standards".[29] The UN is typically portrayed as a major source of evil. Pik Botha, an accomplished exponent of metaphors, has depicted the world body as a "hydra-headed animal" conspiring to "contract us out of existence".[30]

An illuminating official South African "view of the world", c. 1980, is contained in expositions of the "total onslaught" on South Africa. This is a particularly significant source, because the government's total national strategy flows directly from the perception of an all-embracing onslaught.

Defence Minister Malan in 1980 defined the aim of the total onslaught as "the overthrow of the present constitutional order and its replacement by a subject communist-oriented black government." The enemy is applying the whole range of measures it possesses – coercive and persuasive or incentive – in an integrated fashion. Apart from the use of military means, there is action in the political, diplomatic, religious, psychological, cultural/social and sports spheres, Malan explained. Although the onslaught is "communist-inspired", a host of hostile forces is ranged against South Africa. The "political and ideological aspirations" of the UN, the OAU and even "the West" are such that they qualify as elements of the total onslaught. Western powers, Malan maintains, regard the situation in South Africa as a threat to their interests in black Africa. Consequently "the West has accepted, as a point of departure, that the white government of South Africa should be forced into a position where it has no other choice but to abdicate", as had happened in Rhodesia. This perception of Western policy prompted Malan to claim, "justifiably", he said, that "the Western powers make themselves available as handymen of the communists and they are indirectly contributing to the destruction of capitalism and the establishment of world communism."[31]

In his definition of the total onslaught, Malan mentioned the various forms of pressure – coercion, persuasion and the use of incentives – in the same breath, insisting that they are being applied against South Africa in an integrated fashion. By implication, he sees military action, sports boycotts and diplomatic pressure as part of one and the same overall onslaught. Or, as the Defence Minister in fact suggested, Western diplomatic persuasion and communist support for armed conflict against South Africa go hand in hand. There was no attempt on his part to distinguish between the different actors using the different instruments of pressure and pursuing diverging objectives. External pressure, regardless of source, nature or intent, is thus seen as not merely unwelcome but indeed as a threat.

Startling though some of Malan's views might be, they are not new. In August 1977 Vorster, at a particularly low point in relations between South Africa and the United States (under the Carter Administration) said that the end result of American pressure on South Africa "would be exactly the same as if it were subverted by the Marxists. In the one case", he maintained, "it will come about as a result of brute force. In the other case, it will be strangulation with finesse."[32]

Note also the tendency of successive National Party governments since 1948 to group diverse critics together – among them communists, socialists, liberalists, clergymen and Western news media – and to ascribe a mixed bag of unsavoury motives to them. Typical among these are that the critics act out of malice and vindictiveness, indulge in anti-white racism, employ double standards, and suffer from prejudice and ignorance. The most serious charge is that critics are bent on destroying the whites of South Africa.

Attaching labels is however no substitute for a considered policy response and, moreover, tends to convey the false impression that external criticism is simply dismissed. Foreign pressure on the Republic is an abiding feature of the country's external environment, and anything but the transient phenomenon Malan and Verwoerd thought. For South Africans, external hostility has become a way of life. But having learnt to live with it is certainly not to ignore it.

The Impact of Foreign Pressure

In the same way as a state's external environment is not an undifferentiated whole, a national government does not have an undifferentiated internal environment either. A polity can be subdivided into a great many components and linkages traced between them and the sub-environments of the international system.[33] In more practical terms this means that international pressure could have an impact on various different areas of life in a target polity. One of the categories of the domestic environment, identified by Rosenau, is public opinion. In the previous chapter some consideration was given to the connection between South African public opinion and external environmental forces. The present chapter is concerned with official actors' responses to external environmental outputs.

Determining the actual effects of outside pressure on South Africa's foreign and domestic policies is not easy. For one thing, the policy formulators typically deny being influenced by external pressure.[34] While it is politically speaking perfectly understandable that they would not be prepared to offer what might be tantamount to an admission of the effectiveness of foreign pressure, this is not at all helpful to the student of South African foreign policy. South African scholars, for their part, have sadly neglected this particular field of enquiry, which has seemingly become surrounded with taboos.[35] Being an outstanding feature of the Republic's international environment, external pressure cannot but influence its foreign policy in some way. By the same token, the Republic's domestic policies could hardly

have remained wholly unaffected by outside pressure. Insofar as South Africa's behaviour is a response to the behaviour of actors in the external environment, a "reactive" linkage process is in operation. Yet, as Rosenau emphasised, "the life of a polity is conditioned by far more than the purposeful actions that other polities direct at it."[36] This cautions against seeing a straight cause-effect linkage between pressure and policy.

To try to answer the vexed question of the role of external pressure in South African policy formulation – in the realm of domestic as well as foreign policy – a range of government statements and actions will be considered with a view to assessing their possible relationship to outside pressure. The discussion will therefore venture into the area of articulated policies, which is strictly speaking outside the scope of this book; it will furthermore consider domestic policies, which also fall outside the limits of this book. These digressions are however necessary, for the impact of foreign pressure can only be assessed realistically with reference to specific government actions. External pressure being such a complex, relatively neglected subject, this book will merely offer some exploratory, tentative comments and by implication underline the need for further research.

It is interesting to reflect, for a moment, that while South Africa's foreign policy formulators are relatively unfettered by domestic interest group pressure so common in Western states, they are probably subjected to more intense external pressure than their counterparts in any other country in peacetime. Also in the formulation of its domestic policies, the South African government has to contend with considerably less pressure from influential, well organised local interest groups than in Western countries generally, but it is confronted with relentless and tangible external pressure.

The PW Botha government's overall response to the perceived hostile forces ranged against South Africa is expressed in the familiar total national strategy. There is "only one way" of withstanding the total onslaught, the prime minister declared, and that is to formulate a total national strategy.[37] This is the government's counter-strategy, designed to mobilise South Africa's "total national strength" in the face of the total onslaught.[38] Although the total national strategy contains, in the form of the twelve-point plan, some foreign and domestic policy objectives, the strategy is of little use in assessing the influence of foreign pressure on specific government policies and actions. The total national strategy has been institutionalised, as it were, in the SSC and its subsidiary bodies. Viewed in this context, the Council can easily be depicted as an exercise in crisis management, a view strengthened by the Defence Force's prominent role on the SSC. But although the SSC system is clearly related to the government's threat perceptions, it is more than merely a response to external pressure; it is also part of Prime Minister PW Botha's rationalisation of decision making structures and of the public service generally.

The foreign policy realm

To begin with, a number of fairly typical South African responses to external pressure will be considered. These are often on the rhetorical plane, distinct from the substance of foreign policy. The effects of foreign pressure on two major issues in South African foreign policy – Rhodesia and Namibia – will then be examined.

In the diplomatic arena, South Africa's classical response to international pressure over its racial policies has been to seek refuge in the principle of domestic jurisdiction, enshrined in article 2(7) of the UN charter. The "granite-like insistence" that the issues concerned are exclusively South Africa's business, underwent a marked change in the mid-1960s. While still claiming that South Africa's domestic political arrangements are an internal matter, official spokesmen resorted to a new practice of detailed explanations and "spirited defences" of the South African situation in international forums. In 1971 Vorster declared his willingness to discuss South Africa's internal policies with black African leaders.[39] The change in South Africa's general reaction to foreign criticism – i.e. verbal pressures for political reform – was probably due as much to a realisation that the rigid insistence on non-interference in domestic affairs in no way prevented "interference" as to a new confidence in dealing with the outside world. The domestic upheavals of the early 1960s were a thing of the past, the South African economy was buoyant, and moves to impose economic sanctions against the Republic had been a dismal failure.

International pressure on South Africa – expressed in the clamour for economic and social sanctions – has enhanced the importance of its economic and diplomatic links with Western powers. Western states in effect act as South Africa's shield against further mandatory UN punitive measures. To ensure continued Western protection, a central theme of South Africa's foreign policy has long been an emphasis on the country's significance to the Western world. Typical "selling points" are South Africa's importance as a Western trading partner, particularly by supplying raw materials; its strategic location; developed economic infrastructure; domestic political stability and staunch anticommunist and pro-Western orientation.

South Africa's relations with Western states have, however, long been something of a love-hate affair. Often deeply disillusioned about what is typically perceived as Western indifference, if not malice, towards South Africa, government spokesmen have on various occasions suggested a new, non-Western foreign policy orientation. Four options have been mentioned: first, South Africa could become a non-aligned state (sometimes reference is made to a Swiss kind of neutrality); second, it could throw in its lot with other "outcast" states (such as Taiwan and Israel) and form a community of "pariah" states; third, the Republic could begin "looking East", making overtures to its traditional enemies, the communist powers (it has variously been suggested that Moscow and Peking be the object of Pretoria's attentions); finally, South Africa could concentrate on relations with neighbouring countries and promote a regional grouping of states.[40] Such pronouncements often resemble hasty, emotive responses to the actions of Western powers, rather than considered policy statements or serious declarations of intent. The spasmodic utterances reveal a lack of firm foreign policy guidelines and thus support the familiar contention that South Africa's foreign policy is reactive and *ad hoc*.[41]

To be fair, the so-called regional option, the last one mentioned above, has been formulated in some detail by the government and, moreover, implemented to a certain degree in the form of the constellation of states. Of relevance here is the role of external pressure in shaping South Africa's regional policy. The notion of "subcontinental solidarity", as first expounded by Foreign Minister Pik Botha in March 1979,[42] has to be seen against the background of the then prevailing situation in Southern Africa: repeated Western settlement attempts had failed to resolve the Rhodesian and Namibian issues, leaving the wars to escalate. South Africa made no secret of its serious reservations about the Western powers'

211

diplomatic initiatives. Faced on the one side with a "Marxist" enemy and, on the other, with unreliable Western powers, the moderate countries of Southern Africa had to join forces to combat the Marxist threat and, moreover, find their own regional solutions to the problems of the region.[43] Foreign pressure – on the military level from the Marxist enemy and on the diplomatic level from Western powers – was thus supposed to have a cohesive effect on the countries of Southern Africa. In the event, South Africa's coveted regional grouping attracted only independent former homelands. The Rhodesian issue was settled and the new Zimbabwe turned its back on South Africa's constellation.

As far as pressure from black African states – whether direct or indirect – on South Africa is concerned, the government has long been entertaining the idea that "economic realities" would ultimately compel them to abandon or at least soften their hostility towards the Republic and to co-operate with it. Another notion to which Vorster, for one, subscribed, is that the black states are completely misinformed about South Africa's racial policies and that the removal of the misunderstanding would help improve relations.

A response on a completely different level to external pressure was South Africa's resort to a massive secret propaganda offensive. An important objective of the former Department of Information's clandestine activities was to counter South Africa's growing isolation.

Alongside secret ventures went overt, high-profile attempts to counter international pressure. The Department of Information was not the only exponent. There was also Vorster's appeal, over the head of the Carter Administration, to the American public to help stem mounting American pressure on South Africa.

At the peak of the sanctions threat against South Africa in 1977/8, which coincided with the last 18 months of Vorster's premiership, the government seemed resigned to the inevitability of sanctions. It appeared to have run out of innovative capacity. For South Africa it no longer seemed a question of avoiding sanctions but, at best, of surviving them. This defeatist attitude could be seen as another symptom of the kind of political paralysis that characterised the last year or so of Vorster's premiership. An entirely different, perhaps more charitable, reading of the government's position is that it was deliberately designed to call the bluff of the international community, particularly the Western powers. If

that was indeed the purpose, it had largely worked, since the clamour for comprehensive economic sanctions and Western threats of punitive measures over Namibia produced no more than a mandatory arms embargo (not related to the Namibian issue). But whatever South Africa's public stance, there is evidence – as will be seen presently – that Pretoria heeded Western demands over a Namibian settlement in the face of the sanctions threat.

Namibia is an issue that has so long been internationalised that it is impossible to see South Africa's actions in isolation of external factors. The launching of the South African-initiated Turnhalle constitutional conference in Namibia in September 1975 can first be mentioned. The timing of this ethnically-based exercise in constitution making was significant: it coincided with, and was decidedly related to, Vorster's *détente* initiative in Southern Africa. The second track of South Africa's policy on Namibia is participation in UN-sponsored attempts to find an internationally acceptable solution to the conflict over the territory's political future. Various considerations come into play here. South Africa soon realised that the Turnhalle conference, because of its ethnic basis and SWAPO's refusal to participate, would not find international acceptance as the solution to the Namibian issue. Continuing international conflict over Namibia seriously undermines South Africa's foreign relations, particularly with black African states. Without a settlement, the war in Namibia would continue and escalate, causing a drain on South African resources. The Damocles sword of sanctions dangles over South Africa's head as long as it retains control of Namibia. Sanctions (or the threat of sanctions) are indeed the ultimate pressure being brought to bear on South Africa, for the war is still relatively easily containable, albeit costly. The prosecution of the war against SWAPO is in fact the third track of South Africa's Namibia policy. By containing SWAPO militarily, Pretoria hopes, the movement's political influence in Namibia would be checked. More ambitiously, destroying SWAPO as an effective fighting force would hopefully emasculate it politically. SWAPO's guerrilla war, widely supported internationally, is of course a drastic way of exerting pressure on South Africa to at least agree to an early implementation of the UN settlement plan.

While South Africa's willingness to negotiate Namibia's future with the UN cannot be separated from international factors, the latter's influence has by no means worked in one direction only.

Foreign considerations also hamper the search for a settlement. South Africa entertains serious reservations about the UN's impartiality, maintaining that it is favouring SWAPO. A far more substantive stumbling block is South Africa's fear that SWAPO would come to power in an independent Namibia by winning an internationally supervised election – a concern greatly strengthened by Mugabe's spectacular victory in Zimbabwe's pre-independence election. In terms of South African perceptions, a "Marxist" SWAPO regime would provide the Soviet Union with a new foothold on South Africa's doorstep and add the last link in a chain of "Marxist" states around the Republic. Probably more important than these extraneous factors are domestic political considerations. Put in simple terms, the government fears a white backlash at home if a SWAPO regime were to be installed in Windhoek. Of secondary concern is the impact that a SWAPO political victory might have on local black opinion: it might provide a great moral fillip to those dedicated to the overthrow of white rule by violent means. Domestic and foreign considerations are, therefore, mutually reinforcing in obstructing a Namibian settlement. External pressure is neither the only factor shaping South Africa's position on Namibia, nor has it produced only the result intended. Thus, while external pressure may be productive in one respect, it is certainly counter-productive in another.

The **Rhodesian issue** had important features in common with Namibia, being an international dispute in which armed force was used as a principal political instrument. As in Namibia, South Africa featured prominently in repeated attempts at resolving the Rhodesian issue. The Republic had convincing reasons for concerning itself in the 1970s with a settlement of the Rhodesian conflict. First, South Africa realised that the Rhodesian issue could jeopardise its so-called outward movement in Africa. Over a broader front, too, Rhodesia was damaging to South Africa's foreign relations. The Republic was regularly arraigned in international forums for sustaining UDI by keeping embattled Rhodesia's economic lifeline open and its military machine running. Second, South Africa feared, particularly after the independence of Angola and Mozambique, that armed conflict in Rhodesia might escalate to the point of drawing in communist forces, thus obliging the Republic to intervene. Third, there was concern that a protracted war might have a radicalising effect on black Rhodesians similar to that in Angola and Mozambique, eventually producing another Marxist regime on South Africa's borders. What Pretoria therefore desired was an amicably disposed multiracial government in an independent Rhodesia/Zimbabwe, thereby ensuring that the country remained a buffer state on South Africa's northern border.

In the mid-1970s South Africa in partnership with Zambia launched a major diplomatic offensive aimed at settling the Rhodesian conflict. In South Africa it was known as the *détente* initiative, a revival of the outward movement of the late 1960s. Following intense behind-the-scenes diplomatic activity and carefully orchestrated public gestures, Pretoria and Lusaka managed to convene a conference between the Salisbury regime and its black nationalist opponents in August 1975. To show its good faith, South Africa shortly before withdrew the last members of the police force it had despatched to Rhodesia in 1972. The withdrawal probably had another important objective: it was a way of putting pressure on the Rhodesian government to agree to talks with the black nationalists. South Africa is also said to have leaned on Rhodesia to free detained African nationalist leaders to visit Lusaka for talks on the possibility of a conference with the Smith government. Zambia's part of the bargain with South Africa was to secure the black nationalists' participation in such a conference.[44] The upshot was the historic Victoria Falls conference.

Following the collapse of the Pretoria-Lusaka settlement attempt, South Africa became involved in the new Anglo-American diplomatic initiative. Although South Africa's role was secondary to that of the two Western powers, they realised that the Republic had a crucial indirect contribution to make: it could influence the Rhodesian government's response to the Anglo-American settlement plan. This has given rise to the popular notion that the United States, in particular, put strong pressure on South Africa to in turn pressurise Rhodesia to accept the Western proposals. South Africa, it is suggested, was coerced into delivering Rhodesia to Britain and the United States. Prime Minister Smith's acceptance of black majority rule following his meeting with Secretary of State Kissinger in Pretoria in September 1976 was presented as the result of Vorster's pressure on Smith, the former in turn responding – as desired – to American pressure.[45] The United States and also Britain in 1976 certainly exerted diplomatic pressure on South Africa to secure Rhodesia's acceptance of their settlement package. That, however, does not mean that Vorster was reduced to an "agent" of Kissinger's, merely turning the screws on Smith as directed by Kissinger, so as to prevent American punishment against South Africa. For one thing, such subservience is totally alien to South Africa's conduct of foreign policy. Also, South Africa had compelling reasons of its own for wanting a Rhodesian settlement.

Apart from the considerations mentioned earlier, Pretoria in mid-1976 – the time of the first of three series of talks between Vorster and Kissinger – had additional grounds for desiring a speedy resolution of the Rhodesian conflict. Having ended its direct military involvement in the Angolan civil war only months before, South Africa was greatly concerned about the Cuban presence in Southern Africa. Having crossed the threshold to military intervention in an African conflict, the Cubans might be ready for a new adventure in Rhodesia. A further consideration for South Africa was domestic turmoil. With the Soweto riots on its hands – on top of a war in Namibia – Pretoria was hardly in a position to challenge the international community on yet another issue, Rhodesia. Under foreign pressure over Soweto, Vorster was "very definitely prepared to ditch Smith in order to ease the pressure on South Africa", it has been claimed.[46] By then South Africa had accepted the majority rule option for Rhodesia. Politically, Pretoria "had pulled the rug from under Smith".[47] There are strong indications that South Africa supplemented this form of political pressure with more tangible pressure. South Africa is said to have "choked off" oil and military supplies, including the withdrawal of helicopter pilots and mechanics who had served in Rhodesia under the secret "Operation Polo".[48] These actions hit Rhodesia where it hurt most: its capacity to fight the war. South African pressure, so the argument goes, played a decisive role in Smith's dramatic about face in September 1976: majority rule "not in a thousand years" overnight became majority rule in two years. Thus the contention that "John Vorster undermined Rhodesia almost as much as the combined efforts of the insurgents and the OAU did."[49] Kissinger himself confirmed the South African prime minister's crucial role: "The

clincher is Vorster putting the screws on."[50]

Kissinger, however, noted that Smith faced mounting domestic pressures which contributed to his making the ultimate concession: a worsening economic situation (reflected in an escalating budget deficit, among other things), the increasing exodus of whites, the mounting burden of military call-up, difficulties with arms procurement, the worsening security situation and the growing number of war casualties.[51]

Just as South African pressure was not the only factor that brought about Rhodesia's acceptance of majority rule – although such pressure may well have finally tipped the scales – Western pressure on South Africa was not the sole factor behind the latter's pressure on Rhodesia. Domestic considerations weighed heavily with both Pretoria and Salisbury. Important though Western pressure on South Africa may have been, the Republic was far less vulnerable to external pressure than its war torn, economically isolated neighbour. This cautions against looking for any direct cause-effect link between Western pressure on South Africa and South African pressure on Rhodesia.

The limitations of foreign pressure in shaping government behaviour were vividly demonstrated only months after Smith had agreed to the Western settlement terms. The British-sponsored Geneva conference for all the internal and exiled parties involved in the Rhodesian conflict failed to reach agreement on ways of proceeding to majority rule. South Africa subsequently "loosened its armlock" on Rhodesia, restoring the flow of arms.[52] In due course, Pretoria also backed Smith's search for a so-called internal settlement, which culminated in a constitutional agreement between Smith and three black leaders in March 1978. South Africa's previous willingness to co-operate with the Americans and British in resolving the Rhodesian issue had given way to a deep sense of disillusionment, even resentment, particularly about the American role in Southern Africa. South Africa was in a defiant mood, determined to resist Western pressure whether directed at Pretoria's position on Rhodesia, its Namibian policy or its domestic political arrangements. The defiance found its climax in the general election of November 1977, which the government fought in the first place against the Carter Administration. The latter indeed provides the key to Pretoria's hard line: it was largely a reaction to the new Administration's "big stick" approach to South Africa. The Americans appeared to reason that by turning the screws much tighter, the Republic could be coerced into moving in the "right" direction on the three issues simultaneously: Rhodesia, Namibia and apartheid in South Africa. It is alleged that the United States in 1977 threatened South Africa that its oil supplies from Iran would be cut if it did not get Smith to agree to renounce power within two years. The United States would have forced Iran to block the supply of oil to South Africa by threatening an arms embargo.[53] Be that as it may, the most drastic manifestation of Western pressure on South Africa was support for a mandatory UN arms ban against the Republic – a punitive measure however not linked to South Africa's position on Rhodesia.

The important point is the apparent dysfunctionality of foreign pressure. At a time of heightened external pressures on South Africa, its position on Rhodesia was steadily moving in a direction contrary to that desired by the United States and Britain. Far from supporting renewed Anglo-American settlement endeavours, South Africa repeatedly chided the Western powers for their handling of the Rhodesian issue; it openly supported Smith's internal settlement and expressed its solidarity with the Muzorewa government – *inter alia* by reserving a place for it in the constellation of states proposed by Prime Minister Botha – and bolstered rather than undermined Rhodesia's economic and military power.

Such South African support could, however, not prevent the undoing of the Rhodesian rebellion. The Lancaster House conference of 1979, by producing a settlement formula acceptable to all the parties involved, brought an end to UDI. South Africa seemed content to remain in the background, even though it kept in close touch with the (internal) Zimbabwe-Rhodesian delegation. The United Kingdom no doubt appreciated that South Africa could influence the Zimbabwe-Rhodesian side, in much the same way as the Frontline states could influence the Patriotic Front. Yet South Africa was apparently not nearly as instrumental in promoting the Lancaster House settlement as it had been in the case of the 1976 Kissinger-Smith accord. Perhaps this was related to Salisbury's need for a settlement and an end to the war and economic sanctions – a need in all likelihood far greater in 1979 than in 1976.[54] Consequently Salisbury needed less persuasion than previously to settle – even if the terms were unattractive.

These brief overviews show an important simi-larity in South Africa's role in Rhodesia and Namibia: the Republic found itself an intermediary or mediator of sorts. In the case of Rhodesia, South Africa stood between the Western powers and the Smith government; in Namibia, it is between the UN, more particularly the Western contact group, and the internal (non-SWAPO) parties in the territory. For the Western states involved South Africa's role was important, if not indispensable, because the Republic was the only outside power that could exert material influence over the political actors inside the two territories – far more so in the case of Namibia of course. A corollary of this view is the assumption that South Africa, if placed under pressure by the Western powers, would in turn lean on the internal parties in Rhodesia and Namibia to ensure their co-operation with Western settlement attempts.

Although external pressure was a factor shaping South Africa's (shifting) position on a Rhodesian settlement, it was probably less of an influence than on the Namibian issue. Since South Africa did not carry the same direct and formal responsibility in Rhodesia as in Namibia, the international community conceivably had less of a "hold" over the Republic in the former case. Foreign pressure on South Africa over Rhodesia – to in turn persuade or coerce Rhodesia to accept Western settlement terms – was therefore probably less intense than over Namibia, and the threats of punitive measures, such as economic sanctions, correspondingly less credible.

Finally, there is the role of the personal characteristics of some leading political figures in relations between South Africa and Rhodesia – features which reaffirm that deliberately applied foreign pressure was by no means the only determinant of political behaviour. Smith had a legendary reputation for being "a very hard man to pin down"[55] to any firm political or diplomatic commitment. This may well have been one reason for the at times sorely strained relations that reportedly existed between Vorster and Smith. An incident that soured relations between the two was Smith's indirect public attack on Vorster in October 1975, when he suggested that Vorster's *détente* initiative had undermined an internal Rhodesian settlement. Vorster is said to have had even less of a liking for Smith's Foreign Minister, Mr PK van der Byl.[56] These personal animosities might just have encouraged Vorster – or made him feel less constrained – to use the "stick" against the Rhodesians.

Domestic issues

On the domestic front, changes in South Africa's sports policy under Vorster have become the *cause célèbre* of the supposed effectiveness of foreign pressure on South Africa – in this instance taking the form of sports boycotts. South Africa's international sports isolation was caused by the extension of apartheid into South African sport, both at the national and international levels. In due course, the offensive against South African sport became intensely politicised: the objective of depoliticising – that is desegregating – South African sport has become secondary to the much more ambitious objective of promoting fundamental political change in the Republic. Sport is then merely one among several means of external pressure; sports isolation is one of the "social sanctions" imposed on South Africa. Of the array of international measures adopted against South Africa, sports boycotts are probably the most visible and their domestic impact probably the greatest.[57] The results are seen and felt by South Africans of all races.

By the time Vorster became prime minister, efforts to exclude South Africa from international sport had already developed some momentum.[58] The most important development concerned the Olympic movement. In June 1964 the International Olympic Committee presented South Africa with the ultimatum that it would have to alter its sports policy by August, or be excluded from the 1964 Olympic Games in Tokyo. South Africa in the event did not participate. In the same year the International Football Federation decided to suspend all matches with South African teams.[59]

These early moves to isolate South Africa from international sport were in no small measure due to the endeavours of certain "sports protest groups" within the country. The first of these was formed in 1956: the Co-ordinating Committee for International Relations in Sports, led by Mr Dennis Brutus.[60] Although the group was a failure, it paved the way for subsequent "non-white" protest bodies which, with considerable success, championed the cause of non-racial sport, using international sports boycotts as a means of forcing the government to permit non-racial sport. In 1959 the South African Sports Association (SASA) was established, and in its very first year it was instrumental in getting two international sports tours of South Africa cancelled.[61] Three years later the South African

Non-Racial Olympic Committee (SANROC) was founded. An outgrowth of SASA, SANROC soon became the most active and effective of the protest groups. The South African government did not take kindly to SANROC's campaign against foreign sports ties with South Africa. Its leader, Brutus, was served with a banning order. Other leading SANROC figures also fell foul of the authorities, to the extent that the organisation had by 1965 become virtually paralysed. Because of government restrictions on their activities, two SANROC officials went into exile in London. This led to the "rebirth" of SANROC in 1966, when it resumed its activities abroad with a vengeance.[62] Exile gave SANROC a new lease of life and the organisation established itself as the driving force behind the campaign systematically to cut all South Africa's sports links with the outside world. SANROC's methods are varied, ranging from lobbying international sports bodies, appealing to world opinion through the UN and, more recently, helping the Supreme Council of Sport in Africa draw up a blacklist of foreign sportsmen and women who maintain sports contact with South Africa.[63]

SANROC's exile did not spell the end of local "non-white" sports protest groups or non-racial sports bodies. The most prominent of the new generation of organisations is the South African Council on Sport (SACOS). Established in 1973, SACOS was accorded official recognition by the Supreme Council of Sport in Africa. According to a Council statement, SANROC is the "external agent" of SACOS.[64] Abroad, there was a proliferation of protest groups aimed at stopping sports ties with South Africa. These included the "Stop the Seventy Tour" in Britain, the "Halt All Racist Tours" (HART) in New Zealand, and the "Campaign Against Racialism in Sport" (CARIS) in Australia. Among the typical protest methods employed by such groups was the physical disruption of sports fixtures involving visiting South African sportsmen.[65]

To appreciate the significance of the changes in sports policy brought about by Vorster – not least because of the success of the various bodies mentioned – one has to refer briefly to the policy he had inherited from his predecessors. In 1956 the Strijdom government unveiled South Africa's first official sports policy, a blueprint for sports apartheid. Although it contained nothing new, the systematic extension of apartheid into sport was then given the formal stamp of authority. Whites, coloureds, Indians and blacks had to practise and organise their sports separately; South African sportsmen of different races were not allowed to compete with one another either within the country or abroad; South African national teams – Springboks – had to be composed of whites only; and each of the four race groups had to establish its own separate international sports links.[66] In 1965 Prime Minister Verwoerd made his celebrated Loskop Dam speech in which he unambiguously reaffirmed the government's commitment to sports apartheid. Racially mixed sports would not be allowed among South Africans, nor would mixed teams from abroad be permitted to visit the Republic.[67]

Vorster had a mixed record on the sports issue. On the one hand, he began desegregating or normalising sport, at least partly in the hope of countering sports isolation; on the other, he too on occasion adhered to the rigid precepts of apartheid in deciding on sports matters, thus contributing to South Africa's sports isolation. In his first public statement on sports policy after taking office, Vorster in April 1967 declared that the government would not interfere with the composition of foreign sports teams visiting South Africa. This was a clear departure from Verwoerd's Loskop Dam statement. Another change was Vorster's agreeing that South Africa could send a single multiracial team to the Olympic Games; his predecessor had insisted that if South African "non-whites" were to compete, they would do so as a team separate from the all-white Springbok contingent. In what became a feature of government pronouncements on sports matters, Vorster was at pains to present the changes as mere continuations. He wanted to placate his own followers, very many of whom would not have taken kindly to open deviations from the tough Verwoerdian line. What certainly appealed to his constituency was Vorster's forthright declaration – in his April speech – on the question of sports contact between white and "non-white" South Africans. The government adhered to the traditional policy of separate sport: "in respect of this principle we are not prepared to compromise, we are not prepared to negotiate and we are not prepared to make concessions."[68] This was typical of Vorster's sports policy: change (à la continuation) in one area accompanied an unequivocal reaffirmation of the status quo in another. There was another particularly important and frequently overlooked stipulation in Vorster's new sports policy. If it were evident that extraneous (political) motives influenced the selection of foreign sports teams coming to South Africa, the government would have to reconsider its position.[69] It was a highly ironical proviso: South Africa threatened to bar sports organisations from abroad if they dared (as perceived by Pretoria) to resort to a practice so unashamedly followed by South Africa over many years: "playing politics".

The government's bona fides were severely tested with the D'Oliveira case in 1968. A South African coloured cricketer who had moved to Britain, Basil D'Oliveira's skills made him a strong contender for the MCC team due to visit South Africa in 1968. D'Oliveira was, however, not included and this led to a storm of protest in Britain. It was alleged that D'Oliveira had been excluded in deference to South African sensitivities – even though the MCC had earlier assured the British government that its team would be chosen solely on merit, and that the tour would be cancelled if South Africa refused to accept D'Oliveira in the event of his being selected. Within days, one of the cricketers chosen for the tour withdrew, ostensibly because of an injury, and the MCC thereupon included D'Oliveira. This caused a new controversy: Vorster said the government was not prepared to accept a foreign team forced down its throat. By including D'Oliveira the MCC's team had become the "choice of the anti-apartheid movement", he asserted.[70] The tour was cancelled. Vorster's earlier proviso on "playing politics" had been invoked. There had moreover been statements by other Cabinet members in 1967 to the effect that D'Oliveira would not be welcome as a member of an MCC team.[71] The reason was straightforward: sport had to be played according to the rules of apartheid.

Government moves to depoliticise South African sport soon became a highly politicised domestic issue, specifically within National Party ranks. It was a major cause of the split in the National Party in 1969 and the subsequent formation of the Herstigte Nasionale Party.[72] Although the right-wingers' departure from the National Party had to some degree lessened the constraints on the government, the process of sports normalisation has been running far from smoothly. It was often a case of one step forward, one back, and of a patent lack of clear objectives on the part of the political decision makers. Two persuasive explanations for this untidy process are disagreements among ministers and other National Party politicians over the direction and pace of changes in sports policy, and the inhibiting effect of party congresses where the rank-and-file asserted themselves.[73]

There is no need to chronicle the various steps taken on the road to normalisation in the course of the 1970s. Nor is it necessary to catalogue the series of successes achieved by those campaigning for South Africa's exclusion from international sport. What should be mentioned is that "multi-national" sport was gradually permitted, beginning at national level and subsequently extending it to provincial and even club levels. Springbok colours, long the monopoly of white sportsmen, were awarded to blacks and others of colour. Categorical "never" statements were soon forgotten as one concession led to another. Halting and hesitant, the process of desegregation remained a controversial and divisive issue in National Party ranks.[74]

More important for the purposes of this book is to try to identify the reason for the changes in sports policy. GJL Scholtz, Professor of Physical Education at Potchefstroom University, in 1976 offered the following explanation: "In many respects changes and adaptations in our sports relationships were the result of external pressure and the fear of boycotts and isolation."[75] Foreign pressure was indeed the principal motive behind official moves to normalise South African sport – even though the government would never have made such an admission. Given the tangible results of the campaign to isolate South African sport, the widely felt impact on South Africans, and the government's desire to give the country's sportsmen the opportunity of international competition, the normalisation process could not but have been a direct response to these extraneous factors. True, there may have been secondary considerations, such as a realisation by the government that it was unfair to South African sportsmen to subject them to the severe restrictions of apartheid in practising sport. It is, however, doubtful if even such an awareness would have been unconnected to the fact of South Africa's sports isolation. What should not be overlooked, either, is that external moves to exclude South Africa from international sport are reinforced by agitation from within South Africa, from groups such as SACOS. It is a classical case of international sanctions being reinforced by domestic sanctions. Domestic pressure for the desegregation of sport is also brought to bear by local sports organisations endeavouring to break the barriers of inter-national isolation. Particularly active are the national bodies of team sports such as rugby, soccer and cricket.

Progress in the desegregation of South African sport brought no early international break-throughs for the Republic. On the contrary, isolation continues. South Africa failed to return to the Olympic Games, having last participated in 1960. Some of the Republic's traditional sports ties with English-speaking countries were or remained severed, and South African teams that managed to undertake foreign tours were frequently met with hostile demonstrations in the host countries. A further serious setback came with the Commonwealth's adoption of the Gleneagles Agreement in 1977. Commonwealth governments undertook to take "every practical step to discourage contact or competition by their nationals with sporting organisations, teams or sportsmen from South Africa."[76] Four years later came a new punitive measure, this time directed against foreign sportsmen maintaining contact with South Africans: they are now blacklisted.

If the government's "normalisation" moves had as their primary objective the readmission of South Africa to international sport, they have largely failed. The main reason is that South Africa's critics began setting their sights higher as Pretoria began meeting their initial demand, that of desegregating sport. The new cry is that "normal" sport is impossible in an "abnormal" society. Thus society at large first has to be "normalised" before South Africa's sports isolation can be lifted. At issue are what might be termed core values for South Africa's ruling elite: sport, by contrast, represents a peripheral value. A peripheral value could be sacrificed, providing core values remain intact. In official circles there is nonetheless a recognition that certain apartheid measures not directly related to sports activities hamper "normal" sport – thus the Human Sciences Research Council's wide-ranging inquiry into South African sport.[77]

The area of labour relations is another in which changes to established apartheid practices do not affect core values. Other than with sport, there is no clear-cut link between external pressure and domestic change in the labour field. There can nonetheless be little doubt that international pressure has influenced labour reform. South Africa's discriminatory labour practices have long been attracting international censure. A potentially damaging development for South Africa occurred when transnational corporations

218

involved in the Republic became subject to international pressure over their South African connections. They are charged with endorsing and profiting from South Africa's discriminatory labour arrangements and, more seriously, with buttressing apartheid. The corporations are the prime targets of the disinvestment campaign. The South African government probably had these considerations in mind in the late 1970s when it launched a process of labour reform away from apartheid. The Wiehahn Commission enquiring into labour matters was used as the vehicle for reform.[78] However, the factors mentioned are not the only, most probably not even the primary, considerations behind liberalising labour relations. Domestic economic considerations too demand the abolition of ideologically motivated restrictions on economic activity. The government must nonetheless have been hopeful that its labour reforms would produce international dividends, not least by alleviating pressure on transnational corporations to withdraw from South Africa. This consideration might help explain the government's keenness to publicise the Wiehahn reforms abroad.

The effects of foreign pressure on South Africa are most difficult to assess on the level of what might here conveniently be described as high politics. It is in this domain that society's overall political philosophy (or ideology), which embodies its primary values, is formulated and authoritatively interpreted and is given practical expression through the adoption of specific policies. The policies at issue here are those regulating race relations according to the dictates of a separatist ideology.

To the casual observer it might appear that apartheid or separate development is so out of step with the international norms of the day that external pressures have had no noteworthy "positive" or meliorating effects at all. While there is certainly substance to this view, it would nonetheless be wrong to conclude that South African policy makers simply ignore foreign pressure. None other than Verwoerd, the "Architect of Apartheid",[79] in April 1961 told Parliament that the creation of separate black homelands which could develop to "full independence", was a form of fragmentation "which we would not have liked if we were able to avoid it".[80] Ten years earlier Verwoerd, then Minister of Native Affairs, had insisted that the embryonic homelands would not become independent black states in future.[81] Verwoerd explained the radical

new departure in the following terms:

> In the light of the pressure being exerted on South Africa there is however no doubt that eventually this [fragmentation] will have to be done, thereby buying for the White man his freedom and the right to retain domination in what is his country, settled for him by his forefathers.[82]

Verwoerd's implicit hopes of alleviating foreign pressure through the homelands policy have been disappointed. Not even the granting of independence to a number of homelands has led to any reduction in external pressure. What the outside world demands is not the deployment of separate development to its "logical conclusion" of homeland independence, but instead the abolition of the whole policy.

Although in a somewhat different context, it is interesting to point to an example where foreign policy considerations apparently accounted for at least the timing, if not the substance, of a notably *verligte* declaration of intent on the government's domestic policies. Or, put differently, a case where a domestic policy statement was apparently tailored to the exigencies of foreign policy. In October 1974 Pik Botha, then South Africa's UN ambassador, told the UN Security Council that his government was committed to the elimination of racial discrimination.[83] The statement should be read together with Vorster's famous speech only a day earlier, in which he said that "Southern Africa has come to the crossroads" and had to choose between peace and escalating conflict.[84] The pronouncements were both designed to set the scene for the *détente* initiative.

In the event, neither *détente* nor the movement away from racial discrimination got very far. But to be fair, Vorster in subsequent years prepared the groundwork for important political changes. In 1973 the government appointed the Theron Commission of Inquiry into matters affecting the coloured population. A key recommendation of the Commission, accepted by the government, was that South Africa's Westminster-based system had to be changed as part of a process of constitutional adaptation to meet the peculiar needs of the country's plural population.[85] Meanwhile a Cabinet committee, appointed in 1975, was investigating a new constitutional dispensation involving whites and coloureds. Following the Theron Commission's report in

1976, the Cabinet committee's terms of reference were expanded to include the political future of the Indian community. In 1977 the committee produced a set of proposals which, among other things, provided for separate "parliaments" for the three groups and a "cabinet council" representative of the three groups' separate "cabinets". Although the National Party accepted the proposals, both the Coloured Persons' Representative Council and the South African Indian Council rejected them. The next step was the appointment of a parliamentary select committee, subsequently an all-party parliamentary commission of inquiry (the Schlebusch Commission), to give further consideration to a new constitutional arrangement for whites, coloureds and Indians. The Schlebusch Commission reaffirmed the view that South Africa's Westminster system had to be adapted. On the Commission's recommendation, the government abolished the Senate in 1980 and appointed a new body, the President's Council.[86] A nominated body of whites, coloureds and Indians, the Council was to advise the government particularly on the development of new constitutional arrangements.*

There is no evidence to suggest that these various reformist moves were materially inspired by foreign pressure or other external considerations. If anything, they were motivated by the all too glaring inadequacies and iniquities of separate development, highlighted in the very same year by the Theron Commission and the widespread unrest in the black and coloured communities. However reluctant and uncertain these preparatory changes might have been and whatever their shortcomings, they nonetheless represent some movement away from ever greater racial separation. Contrary to the tenets of apartheid, ways of drawing coloureds and Indians into central decision making are being explored. Even if it only means that the racial oligarchy is trying to broaden its base while keeping the (black) majority out, it is nevertheless a departure from the notion that political power is the exclusive

preserve of whites. In a sense, therefore, South Africa is taking a small step in the direction its foreign critics demand. This in itself is highly significant for, as Worrall earlier remarked, "the thrust of change in South Africa has been in the opposite direction from that demanded by the country's critics", all the pressure notwithstanding.[87] Equally significant is that this marginal step towards some convergence of domestic change and external demands is not to any noticeable degree inspired by outside pressure. Pressure for change there certainly is, but the sources are first and foremost domestic.

Hirschmann listed a number of conditions that have to exist for a particular external pressure or category of pressures to produce "even a minor, positive short-term response"; these do not apply to "radical change".[88]

● The foreign influence must be "reinforced by domestic forces working for the same end". Hirschmann cited the improvement of the employment conditions of black labourers as an example: there was a build-up of dissatisfaction among black labourers combined with exposures in the British press about the low wages British firms in South Africa paid their black employees. Sport may be added here because it is an outstanding example of international sanctions being reinforced by domestic sanctions – even though the former are by far the more effective or damaging of the two.
● The particular issue concerned must be one that the government or a "vocal group" in the National Party perceives as a "defect", or that the opposition parties or press have turned into a "potentially sensitive one". Once it was noted outside South Africa that "meaningful contact" between the prime minister and homeland leaders was "almost non-existent", Hirschmann claimed, Vorster moved to rectify this. Whether or not this is true is of lesser relevance; about the need for such a condition there can be little doubt – but with one qualification. Depending on the issue, a "vocal group" in the National Party could be far less important in this process than the voices in and around the SSC.
● The source of pressure must be one to which the government believes it has an "obligation" or an "advantage" to respond. For example, when it is condemned by a conservative Western government, Pretoria finds it both necessary and advantageous to respond, according to Hirschmann. This is a familiar notion, which gained new

*The Constitutional Committee of the President's Council submitted its first report in early 1982. The Committee listed six political options for South Africa, ranging from total territorial partition to full integration. The Committee favoured the continuation of the homelands policy for blacks, combined with a "consociational democracy" for whites, coloureds and Indians.

currency with the advent of the Reagan Administration. South Africa, it is suggested in Pretoria and Washington alike, is more likely to respond favourably to mild pressure from a conservative American government than to harsher pressure from an openly antagonistic liberal government such as Carter's. South African willingness to move forward on a Namibian settlement and to initiate a process of domestic political reform is frequently cited as early fruits of the Reagan Administration's policy of "constructive engagement". Whereas some connection between South African movement on Namibia and constructive engagement might be conceivable, a link between domestic reform and American policy towards the Republic is highly doubtful. (Critics of constructive engagement for their part maintain that America's softer line is counter-productive in that it encourages Pretoria to continue flaunting international demands on both Namibia and apartheid.) If these are nonetheless supposed to be the achievements of moderation, the Vorster government's patent anti-American sentiments – which reached their climax in the November 1977 general election – are typically invoked to "prove" the consequences of trying to lean too hard on South Africa in demand of the impossible (i.e. "full political participation" *à la* Mondale, with simultaneous progress on Namibian and Rhodesian independence). Majority rule would of course involve radical change, and the South African government could be expected to respond negatively – and decisively so – whether the foreign government concerned is conservative or not. In the case of lesser values, the chances are that South Africa would – all things being equal – be more susceptible to the pressures emanating from conservative rather than liberal or socialist Western governments. This also raises the question of a *quid pro quo:* it might be that conservative foreign governments would be more amenable than others to offering South Africa some reward for making desired political changes.

● The development or modification in policy that the government reckons would dilute foreign criticism must also be one that it believes it "can get away with", i.e. that it can "sell" to the electorate and its own right wing. Should the government fear or experience adverse reaction from the right, a concession in one area might be followed up with repression in a related field. Namibia is a popular example where the government is said to have held out against international pressure for a speedy settlement for fear

that a settlement might produce a SWAPO regime – something that the white electorate, not to mention the government's more reactionary critics, would find difficult to digest. While a Namibian settlement may not involve core values similar to those at issue in power-sharing within South Africa, the stakes in Namibia are nonetheless perceived by Pretoria to be far higher than in the case of either labour reform or changes in sports policy, for example. In the case of Namibia, it might be said, intermediary values are at issue. Thus those modifications in policy – in response to foreign pressure – that the government would be able to "sell" domestically, would not concern primary values. Also, such changes might be more readily accepted by the white electorate if these are *not* seen as the direct outcome of external pressure. After all, hardly any government would want to be seen to have openly submitted to outside pressure. In this regard it is worth bearing in mind that the HNP has already charged the government with "selling out" the whites of Namibia because of international pressure. (It is highly ironical that the National Party, which in 1977 fought a resoundingly successful election campaign against foreign pressure on South Africa, should be charged with submitting to such pressure.)

● A particular foreign pressure would impinge on the government only if there is "a background of more extreme pressures linked to more threatening sanctions". The classic example again involves Namibia. The notion of Pretoria moving forward under threat of sanctions is of course the very antithesis of the above-mentioned constraint of domestic white opinion. Although foreign pressure, ultimately in the form of sanctions, is certainly a factor in South Africa's willingness to co-operate with the five Western powers' settlement initiative, this is by no means the only consideration. The reality of a protracted war in Namibia and a desire to improve South Africa's foreign relations, particularly with black African states, may also weigh with Pretoria. It is not inconceivable that Western powers might have tried to elicit South African co-operation on Namibia not only or even primarily through the threat of severe punishment for non-compliance, but also through the promise of substantial rewards for co-operation. This cautions against a single-factor explanation – coercion producing co-operation – of "positive" movement by the Republic on the Namibian issue. South Africa's behaviour can only be explained if allowance is made for several other factors. Similarly, foreign pressure on South Africa was but one consideration – and not the primary one – explaining South Africa's role in promoting a Rhodesian settlement in the 1970s.

The examination of Hirschmann's five conditions has underlined the fact that changes in the South African government's behaviour either internally or externally can very seldom be explained solely in terms of foreign pressures. On its own, an external pressure would rarely be effective or successful; to elicit a positive response, it needs to be reinforced by some form of domestic pressure. These observations apply to intermediary and secondary values, which have indeed been affected by changes in government policies. As far as core values are concerned, they have remained unaffected by years of foreign pressure; this feature reflects the failure of promoting political change by such means.[89] Some primary values may, however, be affected by constitutional reform – a process that apparently bears little direct relation to external pressure.

Hirschmann's model does not allow for the possibility that foreign pressures could produce unintended or undesired results, or could become counter-productive. It is only necessary to recall the role the issue of external pressure played in the National Party's landslide victory in the 1977 general election. Vorster was convinced that the election outcome had strengthened his hand in dealing with outside pressure, and that the Western powers had come to realise that exerting pressure on South Africa – whether over a Rhodesian or a Namibian settlement or domestic reform – would be to no avail.[90] Whether or not the Western powers actually read the election result in this way, the fact is that such was Vorster's perception of the impact of the voters' verdict, and this presumably guided his subsequent dealings with the Western governments.

South African Diplomacy Under Pressure: A Namibian Case Study

The drawn-out international dispute over the political future of Namibia entered a new phase with the formation of the so-called Western contact group in the first half of 1977. It consisted of the then five Western members of the UN Security Council: the United States, France, the United Kingdom, West Germany and Canada. With the Security Council's blessing, the five powers were to join forces in working out proposals for a new constitution for Namibia, which would lead the territory to independence under terms approved by the UN and also accepted by South Africa and SWAPO. A parallel group to the Western contact group was set up in South Africa, consisting of the five powers' ambassadors in the Republic. It was soon dubbed "the Gang of Five".[91]

For South Africa the new Western initiative heralded a period of serious international negotiations, certainly the most intensive talks on a single topic over such a length of time in which the Republic has ever been engaged. South African diplomacy has been put to a severe test. For Pretoria, the stakes in Namibia are very high: an unfavourable outcome could have serious repercussions on both the domestic and foreign policy levels. The fact that the contact group consists of Western powers, of which three are moreover permanent Security Council members, in South African eyes adds weight to the importance of the initiative. And, inevitably, South Africa finds itself under constant international pressure to agree to a speedy resolution of the Namibian issue. Not least does the pressure come from the five Western powers, fearful that a continuation of the armed conflict in Namibia would provide a pretext for Soviet and Cuban involvement in the fighting and thereby give them a political claim to the prize of a future independent Namibia. The contact group, in turn, finds itself under strong pressure, particularly from black African states, to promote a quick settlement. Protecting their political interests in black Africa is a cogent reason for the Western powers' pursuit of a settlement in Namibia.

In using Namibia as a case study, the object is by no means to present a blow-by-blow account of the protracted, tortuous and frustrating negotiations between South Africa and the five Western powers. Instead, a number of salient features of South Africa's diplomatic behaviour under pressure will be considered. Apart from showing some effects of external pressure on South African diplomacy, the investigation will hopefully produce further guides to foreign policy making and reveal a number of interesting aspects of the diplomatic styles of leading South African policy formulators.

Setting the scene: bargaining counters and "counter-counters"

The standard selling points that South Africa uses in its foreign relations feature in the Namibian negotiations too. They are, however, not introduced directly into the discussions by the South African side, nor used deliberately and knowingly as bargaining instruments. Instead they form a prominent part of the backdrop, South Africa making sure that the Western powers are fully aware of these factors.

Typical among the selling points are South Africa's strategic significance; Western countries' economic stake in the Republic; its raw materials, and its anti-communist orientation. In addition South Africa makes great play of the dangers of a "communist" regime in Windhoek – an obvious allusion to SWAPO – to South African as well as Western interests. The Western parties are also made aware of South Africa's economic significance in an African context, as reflected in the economic dependence of black Southern African states on the Republic. The object of the exercise is clearly to impress on the Western powers that South Africa is vitally important to them, that they share some interests with South Africa, and that the Republic's position as a regional power gives it a legitimate role in resolving Southern African conflicts. At best, South Africa wants an open acknowledgement of these considerations; at least, it desires some Western understanding of its position. Either way, South Africa hopes to strengthen its hand in dealings with the five Western powers.

South Africa takes care not to present its perceived attributes as instruments of foreign policy which it is ready to use. The exception, however, is in the case of general economic sanctions against the Republic. Should that happen – over a breakdown of the Namibian initiative – South Africa made it plain that it would cut mineral supplies to the West and also "export" the damaging effects of sanctions to economically vulnerable black states in the region.

Sanctions certainly feature as a weapon of the last resort in the Western arsenal. In 1977 and 1978 the five Western powers on at least three different occasions made it plain to South Africa that they would no longer oppose mandatory UN sanctions if Pretoria refused to change its position on a Namibian settlement. In October 1978 the five powers assembled a group of experts to compile a list of punitive measures that could be imposed against South Africa, in the event of the talks scheduled later that month between Prime Minister PW Botha and the five Western foreign ministers failing to produce positive movement on Pretoria's part. None of the Western participants favoured a total UN economic embargo, but instead considered such limited measures as restrictions on landing rights for South African civil aircraft and on South Africa's access to Western export financing.

In the event, the Western powers never supported the recurring African demands for mandatory sanctions against South Africa over Namibia. One plausible reason is that Pretoria gave way under Western pressure, thus obviating the need for sanctions. On at least one occasion the Western powers believed that South Africa moderated its position under threat of sanctions.[92] There were nonetheless serious constraints on the Western powers regarding the use of sanctions. Doubts existed about the political impact of punitive measures on South Africa; a fear was that sanctions might ruin the whole Western settlement initiative by forcing the Republic to pull out altogether. Britain in particular was concerned about the economic costs that the Western powers would incur through sanctions. Another consideration was public opinion in the Western states, which might be adverse to sanctions against South Africa.

Of course, sanctions need not necessarily be *applied* to achieve a desired political objective; a mere threat to use them under specific circumstances may be sufficient. Considering the constraints on the Western powers, it might be argued that they never seriously contemplated *applying* sanctions, but relied on the *threat* of sanctions, clearly expressed, to induce the desired response from South Africa. To be effective, a sanctions threat has to be credible in the eyes of the target state. Pretoria's (specifically Pik Botha's) apocalyptic statements about the imminence of Western sanctions, it was suggested earlier, might have been designed to call the bluff of the Western powers. The fact that sanctions were never imposed seems to support this view. While there might have been some element of "bluff calling" in South Africa's conduct, it is unlikely that Pretoria always dismissed sanctions talk as Western sabre-rattling. Indications are indeed that South Africa has adapted its behaviour in the face of the sanctions threat.

As regards incentives, the Western powers try to impress upon South Africa that a Namibian settlement would considerably improve the Republic's relations with Western and black African countries alike. A persistent Western theme is that South Africa should make itself acceptable to the international community, and that the Namibian issue provides a major opportunity. It is not inconceivable that South Africa has also been given some reason to believe that the Western powers would reward it for a settlement in Namibia by giving it some respite from pressure over its domestic policies. Another major carrot dangled before South Africa was that President Carter would receive Prime Minister Botha in Washington provided Pretoria gave way on a particular issue regarding a Namibian settlement.[93]

Like South Africa, the Western powers also use the anti-communism argument in the context of Namibia. Delay and a continuation of the war, rather than a settlement that might lead to a SWAPO government in Windhoek, in the Western view create the greatest dangers of communist involvement in Namibia. This would jeopardise both Western and South African interests. On this issue, as will be discussed later, there has been a fundamental difference between South Africa and the Western powers; the two sides find themselves locked in a dialogue of the deaf.

Other South African selling points also meet with a sceptical reception. The contentions about South Africa's strategic significance and the importance of its mineral supplies to the West, particularly as presented by Prime Minister Botha, are typically seen as highly exaggerated.

What causes perhaps more amusement than confusion in the Western camp is the profusion of statements on South Africa's external political orientation. On the one hand, South Africa is anxious to secure Western recognition of its importance to the Western alignment, aspiring to the status of a *de facto* ally; on the other, South Africa speaks about adopting a non-aligned posture largely in response to Western attitudes towards the Republic. Talk of South Africa turning its back on the West is not being taken seriously by the five Western powers.

Hard bargaining: never go soft on concessions

It was Verwoerd, known for his "granite" stance, who once said: "I do not believe in sacrificing principles to obtain support. I do not believe in a policy of conciliation. I believe in a policy of conviction."[94] This led him to the simple premise that others would not try to obtain concessions from one if they knew from the outset that one would not compromise. For South Africa to have adopted such a rigid position in the Namibian negotiations would have doomed them from the outset. Something of the Verwoerdian dictum is nonetheless reflected in the South African negotiators' very tough stance on concessions in talks with the five Western powers.

Concessions are not easily made by the South African side and have to be extracted by the Western powers with considerable effort. Looking for compromises, in the South African view, is primarily the task of the Western negotiators. Once they come up with a proposal, the South African side is very adept at taking it apart. If South Africa itself decides on a concession, it takes care that a back door remains open; its concessions are thus cautious and conditional. Another way South Africa uses to avoid substantive concessions is to keep up a "dialogue on dialogue" with the Western powers, rather than a dialogue on concessions. Given these features, the Western contact group accepts that grand concessions from South Africa are extremely unlikely; South Africa would instead make the minimum concessions to keep the negotiations going. Put differently, South Africa would agree to concessions sufficient to prevent complete breakdown, but insufficient to produce a final breakthrough. Inevitably such tactics resemble brinkmanship. When South Africa, in turn, wins a concession from the Western side, it is usually quick to try to capitalise by asking for another.

South Africa has nonetheless made a number of important concessions, such as accepting the role of the Western contact group, dropping the Turnhalle's constitutional plans and agreeing to the Security Council's resolution 435. And to have kept the Namibian talks alive for five years already means a certain flexibility on South Africa's part. South Africa also shows itself to be adaptable when meeting stiff Western resistence. One factor that strengthens the five Western powers' position *viz à viz* the Republic is that they act in concert – although not without occasional differences – and include people of high standing in their team. The foreign ministers of the United States, Britain, West Germany and Canada have on occasion been personally involved in the talks with South Africa.

In the Western camp there is grudging acknowledgement that South Africa's hard line on concessions could be an effective negotiating posture. But it is decidedly not liked by the Western negotiators, who see a danger of South Africa seriously alienating the other side by persisting with its tactics.

Domestic constraints: the sell-out fear

The South African government's concern about the possibility of adverse domestic (white) reaction to a Namibian settlement has already been mentioned as a very real constraint on Pretoria's involvement in the Western settlement initiative. Here it should be borne in mind that intimate ties exist between whites, particularly Afrikaners, in South Africa and Namibia (although some Germans in the territory might not look to South Africa as their *heimat*). The HNP – which functions in both South Africa and Namibia – tries to capitalise on these ties by linking the political fate of whites in South Africa with that of their brethren in Namibia. Concern over the future of the whites in Namibia is by no means the exclusive preserve of the HNP, but represents a widespread feeling among white South Africans.

These constraints have been formally and informally spelled out to Western negotiators by Vorster and Pik Botha, and also by South African officials. The Western team has felt the effects of the South African government's domestic difficulties, particularly since PW Botha took office – presumably because he was already up against considerable white resistance to his reformist ideas and could not afford a challenge over Namibia too.[95] Although there is much understanding among Western negotiators for the South African government's dilemma, there is also a measure of unease about the government's seeming lack of resolve in dealing with it. It is noted that the government has made little if any attempt – not forgetting the difficulties – to prepare the (white) South African public for the eventuality (or inevitability) of an independent Namibia, one that may not be amicably disposed towards South Africa. This neglect in turn raises doubts about the Republic's true intentions over Namibia.

Their misgivings notwithstanding, the Western powers have tried to help South Africa over its domestic hurdles. A case in point is the Geneva conference held in January 1981. Attended by all the parties involved in the dispute, it was designed by the Western sponsors to discuss the implementation of the Western settlement plan. By having the internal Namibian parties involved in the conference, South Africa could be let off the hook:. these parties would be seen as negotiating in their own right and of their own accord agreeing to settlement terms. The South African government could then hardly have been portrayed as forcing an unpalatable settlement or a "sell-out" onto the whites of Namibia. In the event, the Geneva conference proved a major disappointment for the five Western powers. It soon became apparent that neither South Africa nor its Namibian protégé, the DTA, saw the conference in the first place as an occasion for serious settlement talks with the Western powers and SWAPO. Instead it was used as an opportunity for a major public relations exercise aimed at presenting the DTA to the world as a credible alternative to SWAPO, which had for so long monopolised the international headlines. The home audiences in Namibia and South Africa were of course not forgotten either.

Not only South African party political considerations influence Pretoria in the Namibian talks, but also the views of the internal non-SWAPO Namibian parties. South Africa tries to impress on the Western powers the difficulties it faces in its dealings with the Namibian parties, and has suggested that the contact group's "Gang of Five" should see for themselves by dealing directly with the internal parties (as happened in due course). The views of the internal parties, Pretoria stresses, are decisive and South Africa would be guided by them in the settlement negotiations. On the Western side there are differences of opinion about the influence of the Namibian parties on South Africa's position. One view holds that South Africa has decisive influence over the internal parties, particularly over the ruling DTA,[96] and that the Republic is merely "hiding behind them". The other view is that the DTA and other internal parties are not, or at least no longer, in South Africa's pocket, so to speak, and that they could indeed place serious, even insurmountable obstacles in the way of an international settlement.

If white public reaction makes the South African government wary in the pursuit of an international settlement in Namibia, it faces no similar constraint in its prosecution of the war against SWAPO. The war is not seen as an insufferable burden by white South Africans – at any rate not yet. Such too is the five Western powers' reading of the situation. They and the South African government are nonetheless equally aware that public resistance to the war may develop, should there be a drastic increase in South African loss of life. Analogies with France in Algeria or the United States in Vietnam come to mind.

Playing for time: enter new issues

An outstanding feature of South Africa's conduct of the Namibian negotiations is its tendency to raise new issues, or exaggerate existing ones, just as others have been resolved. The purpose is to stall the negotiations and win time.

Of South Africa's various negotiating tactics, this one is probably most annoying to the Western powers. They have become familiar with, even cynical about, what is depicted as the cycle of South African negotiating tactics, and they are constantly on their guard to try to make sure that all possible issues are covered to prevent South Africa raising new ones. While the Western negotiators protest that South Africa's actions create doubts about its *bona fides* and also undermine the West's credibility in the eyes of the black African countries, they know full well that South Africa is trying to prevent, or at least postpone, a final settlement. South Africa is notably skilful in playing for time, encouraged by the knowledge that the Western powers are reluctant to give up on their settlement initiative and are unwilling to impose sanctions.

Prominent among the delaying issues is that of the UN's partiality towards SWAPO. This is not so much a new issue, but rather one that South Africa has kept in reserve, as it were: it is a fall-back issue in case most or all other issues are resolved.* As regards specific explanations of South African procrastination, the main reason is

---

*In 1981/2, a major new stumbling block emerged: the Cuban presence in Angola. South Africa insisted that the implementation of the Western settlement plan and South Africa's phased military withdrawal from Namibia had to be linked to a Cuban withdrawal from Angola. In fairness, it must be said that the Cuban issue was first introduced into the settlement initiative by the United States; it was raised by Mr William Clark, then Deputy Secretary of State, on his visit to South Africa for talks on Namibia in June 1981. Needless to say, Pretoria immediately seized upon this handy new delaying issue.

the fear that a settlement might lead to SWAPO winning an independence election.[97] By holding out, South Africa hopes to extract more favourable settlement terms – which has indeed happened. Favourable essentially means enhancing the DTA's chances against SWAPO. By gaining time, South Africa hopes to give the DTA an opportunity to strengthen its credibility in Namibia to match SWAPO. Postponing a settlement would furthermore allow South Africa more time to try to further weaken SWAPO militarily, in the hope of thereby damaging the movement politically too. Mugabe's victory in Zimbabwe's pre-independence election gave South Africa added reason to draw out the Namibian negotiations. Mugabe's success added weight to the widespread contention that SWAPO would win an election in Namibia. With a politically highly antagonistic regime in power in Zimbabwe, South Africa experienced renewed concern about being encircled by hostile black states. It is not prepared to see Namibia going the same way as Rhodesia.

When considering South Africa's stalling on an international settlement, it should be remembered that the government has probably not yet irrevocably committed itself to such a negotiated outcome.

A totally different and secondary explanation of South Africa's introduction of new issues is that it results from a lack of communication on the South African side. South African negotiators, particularly Pik Botha, have apparently not always kept others in government sufficiently informed on the talks with the five Western powers. This has led to other decision makers objecting to matters already dealt with around the negotiating table, in turn obliging South African negotiators on occasion to reopen issues.

Western interests: different meanings to different people

By involving themselves in the Namibian issue the five Western powers are certainly not doing the UN, South Africa or SWAPO a "disinterested favour", to paraphrase George Washington. They see the Namibian exercise in terms of its effects on East-West relations and on Western relations with black Africa. While South Africa is aware that the Western states have such wider interests to consider, and even professes to serve some of them, Pretoria interprets them differently. For one thing, South Africa displays a tendency to respond to Western expositions of their interests by emphasising the Republic's importance to the

Western world. Preoccupied with its own supposed significance, South Africa tends to underrate the importance of other considerations to the Western powers. What also complicates the situation is South Africa's peculiar threat perceptions, as expressed in the notion of a total onslaught. It is a view of the world not shared by the five Western powers. In short, South Africa and the five Western powers apply different perceptual frameworks in their assessments of the international implications of the Namibian issue.

South Africa and the Western states both want to keep the communists out of Namibia, but differ fundamentally on how to achieve it. In the Western view a continuing armed conflict provides an open invitation to the Soviet Union and its allies to intervene. The surest way of preventing the communists from gaining influence in Namibia would then be through a speedy, internationally recognised settlement. But keeping the communists out does not mean keeping SWAPO out of power. SWAPO is not regarded as a mere Soviet tool, and the movement's resort to Soviet arms is explained as the force of circumstance, rather than an expression of SWAPO's ideological persuasions. The Western powers are confident that a SWAPO government need not be inimical to Western interests, and that they would be able to keep a SWAPO-ruled Namibia out of the communist fold. In support of such contentions an analogy is drawn between Mr Sam Nujoma's SWAPO and Mugabe's ZANU. Mugabe's record as prime minister is presented as a shining example of the success of an international settlement and a worthwhile precedent for Namibia. All the rationalisations notwithstanding, it would probably suit the Western powers if SWAPO were to lose an internationally supervised election, not least because of their reservations about Nujoma's leadership qualities.

For South Africa, keeping the communists out of Namibia is synonymous with keeping SWAPO out of power. South Africa is convinced that SWAPO is a Marxist organisation, subservient to Moscow. Should it come to power, it would not merely offer the communists a foothold, but would embark on wholesale nationalisation and also ferment unrest and civil war in Namibia, forcing South Africa to invade militarily. South Africa could not allow Namibia to take the "wrong" path and could not countenance the Soviet flag in Windhoek. So committed is South Africa to this position that it appears prepared to pay the price of a continuation of the war and even Western sanctions.[98] And as for the example of Zimbabwe, South Africa is far from encouraged by it; Mugabe is hardly the personification of a friendly, co-operative neighbour or a leader who offers his white subjects a safe and happy haven.

As far as the Western powers' regard for their political interests in black Africa is concerned, South Africa is fond of admonishing them for not facing up to the black states' pressure over Namibia. Yet South Africa knows full well that the Western powers have to weigh up their interests in black Africa against that in South Africa. This is one reason for South Africa so persistently underlining its importance to the West. The Republic does not believe that the whole of black Africa is committed to seeing a SWAPO government installed in Namibia, and Pretoria appears confident that so-called moderate black states support its desire for a different outcome.[99] The implication of such views is that Western interests in black Africa are not irreconcilable with a Namibian "solution" that would keep SWAPO out of power.

For the five Western powers the Namibian negotiations have been a complex affair. They have to consult with South Africa, SWAPO, black southern African (the so-called Frontline) states and the UN, and of course also among themselves. As they have to take account of such a diversity of external interests, together with considering their individual interests, differences of opinion over Namibia have not surprisingly arisen within the Western contact group. South Africa has not been slow in trying to use such Western difficulties to its own advantage. A related tactic employed by South Africa has been to try to play off various American government agencies and officials against each other – something facilitated by the profusion of voices often claiming to speak on behalf of the United States (Carter) government on the Namibian issue.

Government changes in the West: South Africa hopes for better days and better deals

The not uncommon phenomenon of electorates in Western countries changing their governments has often created the hope in South Africa's ruling circles that new governments might be more favourably disposed towards the Republic – also with regard to a Namibian settlement – than their defeated predecessors. It is however a hope mixed with, or tempered by, realism. Major reversals in policy are not expected, but rather shifts or changes in emphasis or style, which might make for a general improvement in relations. For South Africa a key indicator of what to expect of a new Western government is its stance on the use of punitive or coercive measures against South Africa over the Namibian issue. But even if a change in government produces little or no positive change in relations with South Africa, new personalities might create a better climate between the two countries. It is no secret that Dr David Owen, Foreign Secretary in Britain's previous Labour government, and Mr Hans-Dietrich Genscher, West German Foreign Minister, were not popular figures with South Africa's Namibian negotiators.

Two familiar recent cases in which South Africa hoped to benefit from changes of government among members of the Western contact group were the United Kingdom and the United States. The South African government warmly welcomed the coming to power of Mrs Margaret Thatcher's Conservative government in Britain in March 1979. Lord Carrington's appointment as Foreign Secretary met with approval and expectation. However, the Lancaster House agreement on Rhodesia, largely engineered by Lord Carrington, caused considerable disappointment, if not downright dismay, in South Africa; it was not the kind of deal expected of a Conservative government. Nonetheless, the Tories brought some improvement in relations between London and Pretoria, not least because they appeared less "punitively minded" towards South Africa than their Labour predecessors. South Africa, in turn, is apparently more receptive to and appreciative of the diplomatic endeavours of the Conservative government on Namibia, than those of the ousted Labour government.

More important in terms of impact on the Namibian negotiations is a change of government in the United States, the leading member of the Western contact group. It was moreover with the United States, under the Carter Administration, that South Africa's relations were most strained. With the coming to power of the conservative Reagan Administration, there were high hopes in South Africa of a greatly improved relationship between the two countries, also with regard to the Namibian issue. It is widely believed that South Africa's uncooperative role at the Geneva conference was based on the hope that President-elect Reagan would ease the pressure on Pretoria. South Africa's hopes proved well founded, at least

in the short term. The Reagan Administration brought a speedy and marked improvement in United States-South African relations. The new atmosphere has been reflected in the Namibian negotiations, where the United States took the initiative to revise aspects of the settlement plan – not least to make it more acceptable to South Africa. In this case holding out for a change of government has therefore paid off for South Africa, at least for the time being.

It is nonetheless realised in South African decision making circles that it is risky to place too much reliance on government changes in Western countries to produce a favourable, or less unfavourable, Namibian settlement. Whatever the political complexions of Western governments, they have to contend with certain more or less fixed interests which circumscribe their generosity or flexibility in dealing with South Africa over Namibia. Government changes moreover do not let South Africa off the hook as far as an eventual decision on a Western settlement package is concerned – one that is bound to contain elements not appealing to South Africa. It is also recognised that more favourably disposed (conservative) governments in the West would expect some *quid pro quo* from South Africa for their more accommodating position on Namibia. (It is said that South Africa disappointed the Thatcher government on this score.) Even the most sympathetic Western government has a limit to the "diplomatic credit" it can offer South Africa. It seems a fair comment that South Africa had by the end of 1981 already consumed a good deal of its credit with most, if not all, of the Western powers involved in the Namibian settlement initiative.

Pulling out: the threat lacking credibility

The threat of South Africa's withdrawing from the Namibian negotiations with the Western powers is by no means unknown. It was heard more often in the early days of the Western initiative; since then it has occasionally been voiced privately, in exasperation about the state of negotiations, rather than being issued as a direct threat in formal negotiations. In Western diplomatic circles the prospect of South Africa's pulling out is not taken too seriously. The argument is that Pretoria is fully aware of the risks of going it alone on Namibia, not the least of which might be Western-supported economic sanctions. But while this is the general Western view, there is another which regards South Africa's threat of withdrawal as credible, even if it is seen as a highly irresponsible, irrational action. For South Africa it would mean that the perceived risks of withdrawal are outweighed by the dangers of an international settlement.

South Africa's true intentions: keeping them guessing

South Africa's Western negotiating partners, as indeed many other observers, entertain doubts about the Republic's real intentions with regard to a Namibian settlement. Most of the causes of uncertainty and suspicion have already been noted: South Africa's delaying tactics, above all; its three-track policy on Namibia; its secret bilateral talks with Angola on new ways of resolving the Namibian issue, and the seeming impunity with which South Africa continues its military attacks on SWAPO inside Angola.[100]

It is nonetheless beyond doubt in the minds of the five Western powers that South Africa does not want a SWAPO government in an independent Namibia, but desires an amicably disposed one with which South Africa could among other things reach an agreement over the future of Walvis Bay, the South African enclave on the Namibian coast. In the Western powers' eyes this is a legitimate concern. Beyond this basic understanding of South Africa's position the Western powers find themselves in considerable confusion as to what would be acceptable to Pretoria.

One view is that a SWAPO government is a non-negotiable and that South Africa would not agree to any settlement that it fears may lead to SWAPO taking power. Inevitably this raises the spectre of no international settlement being reached, and of South Africa withdrawing to devise a unilateral independence plan. A different view holds that South Africa is in favour of an internationally acceptable settlement – but not yet. The reason is that South Africa thinks SWAPO would win an imminent independence election. This explains South Africa's procrastination, designed to give the DTA an opportunity to become more competitive with SWAPO. Once South Africa is satisfied about the DTA's chances, it would agree to a settlement and accompanying election. A third opinion is that South Africa is not irrevocably committed to seeing a DTA government in an independent Namibia, but is willing to accept a Botswana-type government, one that despite being politically at odds with

South Africa, would adopt a moderate stance towards the Republic by not endangering its security and maintaining strong economic ties. There is however another Western perception, namely that South Africa has decided in favour of an international settlement even if it means a SWAPO government. A crucial consideration would be how SWAPO comes to power. One way in which South Africa wants to soften the blow of a possible SWAPO takeover is through a constitutional conference of all the Namibian parties. The internal parties, including the DTA, would then be seen (by the South African electorate) to have agreed to a settlement package out of their own volition, thus protecting the South African government against subsequently being charged with selling out the whites of Namibia to SWAPO. In support of this fourth view it is said that the South African foreign ministry realises that only an internationally agreed independence plan could finally resolve the Namibian issue.

Finally, there is the belief among Western negotiators that the South African government is not sure of its own position. Not having made a firm decision one way or the other, Pretoria is stalling and keeping all its options open: an international settlement, an internal solution and other alternatives such as a bilateral deal with Angola. It amounts to always having a possible escape route open.

Summing up: the rules of the game

In the five years the Namibian negotiations have been under way a set of tacit "rules" have been developed, understood and respected by the various parties involved.

The first stipulates, *the door remains open.* This is obviously an essential condition for the "game" to be played. However obstructive or uncooperative a party becomes, it still makes it known that the door for further talks has not been shut. In South Africa's case it means that even if it has on occasion not been prepared to use opportunities for negotiations – such as the Geneva conference and Pik Botha's abrupt departure from so-called proximity talks in New York in early 1978 with the UN Secretary-General and representatives from the five Western powers[101] – it is still prepared to continue participating in the settlement initiative.

The second rule is, *the ball is in your court.* It simply means trying to put the blame for setbacks and difficulties on another party, and expecting it to suggest a way out. South Africa stretches this rule far, variously accusing SWAPO, the UN and the Western powers of foul play. More than once South Africa has berated the Western negotiators for alleged duplicity and bad faith, to which they have not surprisingly taken strong exception.[102] It should be said that mistrust on all sides has all along been a major complicating factor in the search for a Namibian settlement.

The third rule reads, paradoxically, *the end of the road is not the end of the road*. More than once have the Western powers had to hear from South Africa that the Namibian negotiations have reached the end of the road. In accordance with rule 2, South Africa would contend that such a grave situation had been brought about by the behaviour of the other parties. Yet rule 1 requires that the negotiations have to be kept going, and ultimatums and threats of withdrawing therefore have to be flexible. Thus, when Vorster announced in February 1978 that South Africa was committed to giving Namibia independence by the end of the year, the deadline had to be readily adaptable. Similarly, when Vorster stated in September 1978 that an internal election would be held in Namibia – in conflict with Western settlement proposals – and that all political options on Namibia's future would be open to the elected constituent assembly,[103] it meant that South Africa would have had to prevent the elected representatives opting out of the Western settlement initiative; some options would thus have been more open than others.

Admittedly these rules are based on the assumption that South Africa – and SWAPO, for that matter – are really committed to an international settlement, however long the route to it may be. The fact that the rules have been observed for some five years, may well inspire confidence in the continuation of the settlement process – although that in itself is no guarantee of a settlement ultimately being reached.

Personal diplomatic styles: they do it differently

South Africa's principal negotiators in the Western settlement initiative have been Prime Ministers Vorster and PW Botha, Foreign Minister Pik Botha, and Fourie, Director-General of Foreign Affairs and Information. How, then, have their Western negotiating partners viewed the South Africans' conduct of diplomacy?

Vorster displayed certain characteristics that commanded wide respect from Western negotiators. He was noted for being straightforward, honest and reliable. With him the opposite parties felt they knew where they stood. Vorster was slow and cautious in negotiations, but the Western side was satisfied that progress could be made. Although willing to listen to the other side's views, he had a tendency to lecture them – something not taken to too kindly. An interesting feature of Vorster's was that he could react emotionally when someone struck a sensitive chord; he made his feelings plain on such occasions.

PW Botha appears to be something of an enigma to Western negotiators. Uncertainties over his domestic power base and leadership style make it difficult to predict how he would influence the Namibian talks. Western representatives on the one hand think that he is seriously encumbered by party political difficulties. On the other hand, they believe that he is more capable of a radical decision on Namibia (by implication agreeing to implement a settlement) than Vorster had been. Another typical dichotomy is that PW Botha's general foreign policy stance is regarded as being much tougher than Vorster's and that Botha is preoccupied with a total onslaught; even so, he is thought to be much more sensitive than his predecessor to the need for a non-military solution to the Namibian problem – an awareness attributed, strangely enough, to the influence the military is believed to carry with him.

Pik Botha's well-known dramatic political style is also reflected in his conduct of diplomacy. A related observation is that he keeps a keen eye on the gallery, so to speak, when negotiating; it is even thought that he is at times more concerned with the party political than the diplomatic effects of negotiations with the West. His propensity for making public statements on the state of negotiations is not welcomed by the opposite side, who believe that it complicates the talks. Pik Botha is also said to be fond of raising domestic political considerations in the course of negotiations. Particularly interesting is that the foreign minister is not regarded by Western negotiators as a decisive figure on the South African side, but more as a "reporter". In the latter capacity his communication with others in government is seen to be unsatisfactory; they are apparently not always fully briefed on the state of the negotiations. A tendency that Pik Botha shares with Vorster is to lecture the Western side. The inescapable conclusion is that the foreign minister is not a popular or highly esteemed negotiator in Western eyes. Western negotiators however appreciate his recognition of wider Western interests in the Namibian negotiations and of the risk for South Africa of relying on government changes in the West to ease matters for it on Namibia.

One of South Africa's longest-serving diplomats, Brand Fourie is someone for whom Western negotiators without fail have the highest regard. He is acknowledged as being enormously skilled, impressive in action and certainly one of South Africa's most accomplished negotiators. Also noted is his great command of the facts of the drawn-out Namibian issue, something born of his long and intimate involvement in the dispute; this is said to give him a distinct advantage over his opposite numbers. Fourie is felt to have a clear understanding of the range of interests that Western powers have to consider in their Namibian settlement initiative. Western negotiators also regard him as someone who could be relied upon as their link with the South African political decision makers when the latter are not personally involved in talks. Fourie is, in short, a man with whom Western negotiators like to deal.

A number of other senior foreign ministry officials have also been heavily involved in the Namibian negotiations, notably Eksteen, Auret and Van Heerden. Although they are sure to have become skilled negotiators, an investigation of their and other officials' conduct of diplomacy is not called for. The salient features of South Africa's handling of the Namibian negotiations should be clear enough from the preceding discussion.

8. Some Perspectives on South African Foreign Policy Making

The facts will eventually test all our theories, and they form, after all, the only impartial jury to which we can appeal.
                                                                Jean Louis Rodolphe Agassiz

The preceding detailed discussion of the structural and functional features of South African foreign policy making is organised in a conventional analytical-descriptive fashion. In this final chapter the explanatory qualities of a number of existing theoretical models or perspectives will be examined against the background of the empirical findings presented. Only a few theoretical insights of direct relevance to the South African case have been selected from the literature; an overview of the wealth of scholarly studies will not be attempted. As will be seen, each model or perspective explains some part of the overall picture, and in this sense they are supplementary. The object of the exercise is to identify what appear to be some key components that ought to feature in any model of foreign policy making in South Africa. No such model has yet been proposed in the handful of studies of South African foreign policy. This book will not do so either. Instead, the modest objective is to suggest some guidelines for such a model.

The Domestic Political Context

"Foreign policy begins at home", therefore the implications of South Africa's domestic form of authority for its foreign policy will first be examined. This particular feature of a political system essentially refers to the measure of popular participation in a state's political processes, and to the manner in which authority is generally exercised.

Wilkinson[1] addressed the question of authority

by analysing the constitutional status and the representative character of a regime. Under the first heading he took into account "the limits, if any, on the domestic social control exercised by the regime." This led Wilkinson to distinguish three types of regime: constitutional, authoritarian and totalitarian. A government is *constitutional* if it is "restricted in ordinary conduct by reference to norms that stipulate individual rights and majoritarianism"; in the case of an *authoritarian* regime there is little if any such effective constitutional limitation on the arbitrary exercise of power, but national convention and the practice of the regime "differentiate between some conventionally bounded 'political' and 'social' spheres", which means that arbitrary government is largely confined to the former, and the latter (family, religion, economy, etc.) is left free from such interference; a *totalitarian* regime is restrained by neither constitutional nor social bounds and generally exercises power in all spheres of life without regard for individual or majority rights.

On the basis of their representative character – using elections as a primary yardstick – regimes are classified into four categories: broadly representative, limited representative, pseudo-representative and non-representative. A regime is *broadly representative* if the state has a broad-based franchise not excluding any large minorities and where the freely elected representatives perform functions not limited or consultative in nature; in the case of a *limited representative* regime the franchise is still broad-based but educationally or regionally or racially discriminatory, allowing representation of the "mass sector" or at least of a very sizeable minority; a *pseudo-representative* regime refers to single-list elections and/or elected representatives vested with limited or consultative functions only; a *non-representative* regime is simply that in both form and substance.

South Africa evidently does not fit neatly into either set of Wilkinson's categories, but displays features of various types of regime. There are of course also numerous other ways of analysing South Africa's form of authority. For example, Munger in his monograph on South Africa's foreign policy formulation typified the Republic as a "democratic oligarchy".[2]

More important than debating the correct classification is to consider the relevance of the generally agreed features of South Africa's form of authority for its foreign policy making. A regime's constitutional status, Wilkinson suggested, will indicate how free it is to formulate foreign policy without regard to norms and limiting measures legislated by previous regimes or inherent in a conventional or written charter. Constitutional status will also tell how free a government is to use the goods and persons of its citizens as instruments of foreign policy. When assessing the significance of a regime's representative character for its foreign policy attention should, according to Wilkinson, be paid to particular limits or changes imposed on policy by elected representatives (especially as the result of new elections and changes in elected office holders), or "changes in policy following a change in the representative character of the regime and emanating from the creation, invigoration, curbing, or expulsion of elected officials." These observations serve as a useful guide to some implications of the Republic's political order for its foreign policy making.

• The South African government's constitutional status, more particularly its representative status, lies at the heart of its international ostracism – its pariah status – thus explaining a major external environmental feature confronting the country's foreign policy formulators. The objective of the unremitting international pressures to which the Republic is subjected is to get its form of authority drastically changed.

• The constitutional and representative status has been characterised by stability. The essential features of the oligarchic form of authority that came into being with the formation of the Union of South Africa in 1910 have remained unchanged. If anything, the regime has since 1948–

when the National Party came to power – become progressively more authoritarian (through vesting the executive with increasing discretionary powers, among other things) and less representative (by abolishing the indirect representation of coloureds and blacks in Parliament). The government has in recent years initiated a process of constitutional restructuring aimed at devising a new dispensation for whites, coloureds and Indians. From a foreign policy point of view a question to ask is whether such a broadening of the regime's representative character would lead to a meaningful improvement in South Africa's international standing. An obvious answer would be that as long as the black majority remains excluded from central decision making, the regime will retain its unrepresentative status and fail to secure material improvements in its international environment. A different question concerns the possible effects on foreign policy of coloured and Indian political elites being "co-opted" into the policy formulating process. While the policy might display some changes in style, it is unlikely to be substantially different from "white foreign policy" as long as the external milieu remains unfavourable.

Despite the features of stability in the regime, there have been innovations – or perhaps aberrations – in South African foreign policy associated with particular individuals, both elected politicians and permanent officials. Best known are the international ventures of the Department of Information under Mulder and Rhoodie and of the Bureau for State Security under Van den Bergh. It should be added that different National Party prime ministers have placed different imprints on foreign policy. Vorster was the architect of the outward movement, whereas the constellation of states is identified with PW Botha. The latter has formalised and regularised key aspects of foreign policy formulation through the SSC, whereas Vorster was content with an untidy, dispersed and uncoordinated process of foreign policy formulation. The National Party-dominated legislature plays a peripheral role in foreign policy making. Neither the appearance of new faces on the National Party benches after general elections nor the PFP's elevation to the official opposition in the place of the United Party, nor the growth in the PFP's parliamentary strength has enhanced Parliament's role in the formulation of foreign policy. Parliament's marginal role is however not primarily, if at all, a function of the "limited representative" status of the regime; it is not an uncommon phenomenon that a legislature plays a much smaller role in foreign than domestic policy making, leaving the executive with a wide margin of discretion.

• The formulation of South African foreign policy is a white monopoly. The implementation had also long been a white preserve, but the foreign ministry has now opened its doors to coloureds and Indians to join the diplomatic service. Earlier the former Department of Information had employed coloureds and Indians in its foreign operations.

• Because of its peculiar representative status, the South African government would find it extremely difficult, if not impossible, to muster the human component of national power, whether for external or domestic purposes. In familiar nomenclature, the government faces severe, if not insurmountable, obstacles in operationalising its total national strategy. Although it might be expected of an authoritarian regime to be more effective in mobilising power than a constitutional one, the problem in South Africa is that the government cannot readily count on the loyalty of the majority of the population because of their exclusion from political power at the central level of government.

• Following from the above, the South African government's legitimacy has been questioned, not least in the UN. The South African government is confronted with a situation where its right to speak on behalf of the people of South Africa is being challenged in international forums. South African foreign policy formulators thus find themselves in the invidious position of not having their backs covered, as it were, by a loyal population at home, while facing an external environment so adverse that their right to formulate the Republic's foreign policy is being disputed. The dilemma can be illustrated as follows: the foreign policy formulators are greatly preoccupied with trying to counter South Africa's growing isolation and to stave off economic sanctions and other punitive measures, and to check the growing influence abroad of the "liberation movements". Whereas whites would certainly applaud the policy formulators' endeavours, the chances are that blacks would generally view these actions negatively, as detrimental to the cause of "liberation", in support of which they see external pressure being applied against South Africa.

• The South African government, notwithstanding its constitutional and representative status and the legislature's feeble influence in foreign affairs, is not unresponsive to white public opinion in its foreign policy. And, as seen in Chapter 6, the government cannot ignore local black opinion either.

Foreign Policy Decision Structures

The structural characteristics and procedures of a state's foreign policy formulation are, according to Charles F Hermann,[3] important influences on both the form and substance of foreign policy. A change in the decision structure frequently changes the decision process, the latter referring to the procedures, norms, decision rules, etc., which the decision makers apply. Then, again, variation in decision processes results in changes in government behaviour or articulated policy. There is, in other words, a linear relationship between structure, process and behaviour.

In his theoretical perspective Hermann distinguished structures according to three properties: physical size (the number of participants), power distribution (represented by the presence or absence of an authoritative leader) and member role (whether participants in a decision unit have the freedom to adopt any position they choose, or whether they represent a government institution whose approval they require). This led him to nine types of decision structure. It now has to be established whether those types relevant to the South African situation are able to explain elements of the process of foreign policy formulation. In other words, can aspects of the decision process be inferred from a knowledge of the decision structures?

The South African Cabinet resembles what Hermann termed a **leader-autonomous group,** including one authoritative decision maker as leader (the prime minister) and members (the ministers), who enjoy some independence from the leader, who have their own political base and also "a perspective for viewing foreign affairs which is different from that of the authoritative decision maker." However, the process and behavioural feature that Hermann hypothesised to be likely in the leader-autonomous group are not typical of the South African Cabinet, at least not in foreign affairs. Hermann compared the process with that of "a judge [the prime minister] hearing and deciding among advocates [the ministers] for various points of view." There is a strong incentive for "careful argumentation" and an advocacy process results in "the introduction of evidence and expert assessment". Another feature of the process is that the decision structure itself does not create pressure for consensus. Hermann depicted the behaviour resulting from the advocacy process as "innovative", which he attributed to "the possibilities for members' open expression of diverse perspectives and the relatively greater ability of members to shift their positions and acknowledge the merits of new ideas."

The SSC approximates Hermann's description of a **leader-delegate group.** He presented it as a small group consisting of an authoritative decision maker and other individuals or delegates (ministers and top officials), most of whom represent some group or agency. "By definition, delegates are spokesmen for their organization or other entity, and the advice they give the leader is not necessarily their personal view." The SSC conforms to this stuctural type in that its permanent members are named – by law – on account of their official positions. But then provision is also made for the co-option of others. (This limited, *ad hoc* co-option cannot be compared with the "co-optation system" of political leadership found in communist states.)[4] Hermann summarised the typical process associated with a leader-delegate group as "persuasion". Since most group members are concerned with advancing the preferred position of their constituencies, each would want to persuade the leader that the position of his particular agency is in the best interests of the government. One way of guarding against an undesired choice by the leader would be the formation of a coalition among all or most delegates before the leader enters the group process. He would thus be faced with agreement that only one course of action is reasonable. If a coalition cannot be formed, a "difference maximisation process" may occur, in which dissatisfied group members are encouraged to maximise the differences between their viewpoints and those of the others, which includes "magnifying the consequences" of failing to adopt their stances.

By its very composition the SSC is representative of different constituencies. Most prominent in the foreign policy field are the foreign ministry and the military, with the (civilian) intelligence service featuring less strongly. It is quite conceivable that the first two, in particular, want to promote their positions and get these adopted as official government positions. Whether there is coalition forming as hypothesised by Hermann is doubtful. For one thing, the prime minister's intimate involvement in the Council's proceedings would make it difficult for members to "caucus" in his absence. By the same token it is even more difficult to imagine members "ganging up" against the prime minister in order to get a particular decision adopted. If there is any kind of manipulation involved, it is more likely to be managed by the prime minister himself, for PW Botha has a reputation as a political tactician. More plausible than coalition forming would be tendencies towards difference maximisation, the two main protagonists being the foreign ministry and the military. Provision is, however, made for ironing out differences between SSC members through the Council's working committee, composed of officials. Here a common position could be worked out and submitted to the Council for final decision. This, of course, is different from the coalition forming process described by Hermann. (The SSC's working committee features in the next type of decision structure.)

Because the process associated with a leader-delegate structure encourages members to protect their respective agencies' position, the resulting behaviour "is unlikely to shift dramatically from reiteration of past actions – that is, the reaffirmation of the status quo", according to Hermann. Should delegates however reach consensus on a new, different course of action, the behaviour "is likely to be stated in broad, vague terms to cover disagreements that might otherwise exist." While it might be true that the SSC has not introduced any major foreign policy changes (since being elevated to its present status by Prime Minister PW Botha), the explanation is not in the first instance to be found in a kind of paralysis caused by members protecting different positions. Similarly, if it is assumed that the government's so-called twelve-point plan was formulated or at least approved by the SSC, and if it is accepted that its 12 policy objectives are indeed couched in "broad, vague terms", the explanation is not to be found in the process of the Council either. The constraints are primarily of an extraneous nature, namely South Africa's peculiar international difficulties and the government's domestic political and ideological commitments.[5] The constraints are operative not because of the SSC, but regardless of it.

The next type of decision structure relevant to South Africa's foreign policy making is what Hermann called a **delegate group.** It consists of a small number of members roughly equal in power, and all or most "act as instructed representatives for some entity with which they are associated that exists outside the decision unit." The decision process of a delegate group is, Hermann suggested, characterised by bargaining. Because it has no authoritative leader to make actual choices, the group's decision process "must include group means of selecting between alternatives." The primary process is therefore one of "incremental bargaining" among members – incremental because of the need of most delegates to consult their agencies before suggesting or consenting to a new position. Because of the incremental nature of the process, quick responses to problems are unlikely. Also unlikely are radical actions or major departures from existing policies. Another feature of the resulting "compromise behaviour" is that compromises contain qualifications or conditions needed to get delegates' agreement and protect their agencies' interests. Where issues cannot be resolved through bargaining, there is a tendency to postpone decisions or pass unresolved problems on to another decision structure.

The official institutions involved with South Africa's foreign policy making which correspond with Hermann's delegate group are the working committee of the State Security Council, the other inter-departmental committees which form part of the security management system, and the Foreign Trade Relations Committee. They are composed of officials representing various different departments, whether on a standing basis or by co-option. Precisely to what extent the processes and behaviour of these bodies conform to Hermann's hypotheses is difficult to tell. A number of general comments can nonetheless be offered. First, incremental bargaining and the need to confer with the constituent organisations are only to be expected in inter-departmental groups composed of officials. Second, although there may be a tendency for delaying responses to some issues, the fact that the SSC meets every fortnight puts pressure on the Council's working committee and the other inter-departmental committees in the security management system to attend to matters and produce some results within a specified time. Third, because the inter-departmental bodies have to refer many matters to the SSC or some other superior institution for final approval, this might however encourage a "pass the buck" attitude, or make it easier to settle for untidy compromises in the knowledge that there is still a higher authority to resolve matters finally. Fourth, it may be true that the delegate groups under discussion are constrained by the decision process from resorting to extreme actions or major reversals of policy. There are, however, also other considerations, such as South Africa's limited freedom of action internationally because of apartheid, and a tradition of continuity in South African foreign policy, which militate against radical changes.

The other South African decision structure, which needs to be mentioned only in passing, is Parliament. It does not neatly fit any of Hermann's four types of "assembly", i.e. structures with a large number of members. (Hermann distinguished between autonomous assembly, delegate assembly, consultative autonomous assembly and consultative delegate assembly.) Neither do the hypothesised processes and behaviour of these four decision structures provide any meaningful explanation of the South African Parliament's marginal role in foreign policy making.

The three properties of decision structures – physical size, power distribution and member role – "increase the probability that certain processes are likely to occur within a given structure", Hermann contended. The preceding discussion shows that some of the processes hypothesised by Hermann actually or possibly occur within certain South African decision structures. As Hermann however admitted – and as the discussion of the South African case clearly reveals – elements other than decision structures also influence decision processes. One of these, which he mentioned, is the "personality characteristics of the participants".

Foreign Policy Making Processes

Closely related to Hermann's theoretical perspectives on decision making are Kohl's models for explaining foreign policy making.[6] In analysing the foreign policy making process of any state, Kohl argued, it is essential first to identify its type of political system, then to understand how political power is distributed within it, particularly with regard to foreign policy formulation, and finally to comprehend the style of key foreign policy formulators. On the basis of these factors, the type of policy making process "most likely to occur" within a specific political system at a given time can be distinguished. Kohl's study dealt with only one political system, the United States; its foreign policy making in a given period, under Nixon and Kissinger; and policy formulation in a more or less defined issue area, US-European relations. Yet, to explain adequately the foreign policy making process involved, Kohl maintains that at least six models (or conceptual frameworks) are required, singly or in some combination. This contention is relevant to the South African case – even allowing for the vast differences between South African and American foreign policy formulation – in that it recognises that the complexities of the policy making process cannot easily be accommodated in a single model.

In the **democratic politics** model foreign policy is closely related to domestic politics. Involved in the process of policy making are not only the White House, Cabinet secretaries and bureaucracies, but also the "public arena", particularly Congress and through it interest groups and attentive publics. Given Parliament's and the public's strictly marginal role in the making of South African foreign policy, this model is of little relevance to South Africa.

The **bureaucratic politics** model focuses solely on the executive branch of government, the contention being that "all or most of foreign policy can be explained as outcomes of organisational decision making and/or intra-governmental bureaucratic bargaining games." In the American context a serious deficiency of the model – which posits that decisions are mostly reached at sub-presidential levels – is that it does not explain foreign policy initiatives taken by Presidents. Applying this argument to South Africa one can similarly say that the model fails to take account of prime ministers' foreign policy initiatives. Nonetheless the model has some applicability to South Africa. The bureaucratic input into foreign policy formulation is important, whether it occurs in an untidy, *ad hoc* fashion as in the Vorster administration or in a regularised and formalised manner through the SSC under PW Botha. The involvement of bureaucrats as not merely expert advisers but also co-decision makers alongside (and sometimes independent of) the political office holders is an outstanding feature of South African foreign policy formulation.

Foreign policy making under the **royal-court** model is highly centralised in a "monarchical mode", dominated by the head of government and/or his key advisors. The personality and operating style of the principal decision maker are vitally important. The elite recruited for the royal court are chosen because they share the leader's views on foreign affairs. There is something of this model in the way foreign policy was formulated during Vorster's premiership, considering the role played by individuals such as Rhoodie and Van

den Bergh. Features of the royal-court model are also to be found in the socio-political status of the principal decision makers, as will be seen presently.

The **multiple-advocacy** model of foreign policy making draws on a "carefully nurtured and structured debate among competing policy advocates [for instance, government departments], managed deliberately at the centre by a neutral custodian." The result is a system of "managed bureaucratic politics". The SSC under PW Botha bears an obvious resemblance to this model, except that the prime minister, as chairman, is more than a neutral custodian; he is the principal decision maker. The multiple-advocacy model also seems to neglect the input of political office holders in decision making.

Kohl's two remaining models focus on the "dangerous and distorted dynamics" that may develop among decision makers. "Groupthink" refers to a situation where group loyalty and cohesion become so strong as to limit the testing of all alternative courses of action and result in bad judgement. Focusing on shared images, perceptions, or mind sets, the other model "is rooted in common socialization processes of certain elites or opinion leaders that result in similar assumptions and outlooks on international affairs." The danger is that "common perceptual lenses" among key policy makers can cloud or foreclose the consideration of alternatives in foreign policy. Examples of this actually happening in American foreign policy, Kohl pointed out, are not difficult to find. In South Africa this is certainly a very real danger, considering the very narrow socio-political spectrum from which the principal foreign policy formulators are drawn. They are, of course, all whites, and most of them are Afrikaner Nationalists and moreover Broederbonders. What may also encourage common outlooks is the peculiar nature of the policy formulators' external environment: in a situation of international hostility South Africa's foreign policy options are in any case very limited. The checks and balances built into the SSC by virtue of its departmental composition may indeed be adversely affected by the cohesive yet distortive effects of mind sets. True, the foreign ministry and the military have their differences on foreign policy issues, but these probably turn more on means than on ends or "world views".

Personal Characteristics of the Decision Makers

The key question to be considered under this heading is whether the decision makers' personal and leadership characteristics help to explain their political behaviour. Personal characteristics, comprehensively defined, refer to "an individual's biographical statistics, training, work experiences, personality traits, beliefs and attitudes, and values";[7] often, however, personal characteristics are limited to the psychological features mentioned.

In using this explanatory device several methodological difficulties arise. An obvious first question is, which personal characteristics should be examined? And then, how? Is quantification essential, or will more traditional methods suffice? Furthermore, which decision makers' characteristics should be considered: only those of political leaders, or of military and intelligence chiefs and other top civil servants as well? And so forth. There are no easy answers. Matters are perhaps even compounded by the wealth of theory; "theoretical overkill"[8] hardly adds to theoretical clarity. This book partially escapes these complexities and controversies, primarily because personal or leadership characteristics are not being presented as the only factors explaining South Africa's foreign policy behaviour. It,therefore does not stand or fall by these particular theoretical perspectives. Under these circumstances certain liberties may be taken: no quantitative analyses will be attempted. Instead the evidence presented in earlier chapters of the book will serve as the "raw material" to test the explanatory powers of the theoretical perspectives. A further self-imposed limitation is that only political leaders will be considered, specifically prime ministers. This greatly simplifies matters but, what is more important, it recognises the major role successive prime ministers have played in South Africa's foreign policy formulation.

Kissinger's leadership typology

It might be appropriate to begin with a typology of leadership formulated by a subsequently prominent foreign policy formulator, Dr Henry Kissinger.[9] He postulated that leadership types are formed by at least three factors: leaders' experiences during their "rise to eminence", the structure in which they operate and the values of their society. He distinguished between three contemporary types. First is the **bureaucratic-pragmatic** leadership type, of which the American elite is the main example. The leaders are shaped by a society without fundamental social schisms and an environment in which most recognised problems have proved soluble. Accordingly their approach is *"ad hoc,* pragmatic and somewhat mechanical"*. Pragmatic thinking is, in short, preoccupied with the manipulation of the environment. These features, Kissinger argued, are "reinforced by the special qualities" of the professions – law and business – which produce the core of American leadership groups. Second is the **ideological** type of leadership, which Kissinger applied to communist states, particularly the Soviet Union. The essence of the Marxist-Leninist view of the world is the belief in the predominance of "objective" factors: social structure, economic process and class struggle are considered far more important than the personal convictions of statesmen. Orthodoxy demands a "posture of ideological hostility" to the non-communist world. Such an outlook, Kissinger maintained, is reinforced by the personal experiences of leadership struggles on the elite's road to eminence. Third is the **charismatic-revolutionary** type of leadership, which is associated with leaders of the new nations. It is their personal experiences in the struggle for independence that have provided the impetus for these leaders.

Using Kissinger's typology, a study has characterised Verwoerd's leadership as "charismatic-ideological".[10] This mixed category was evidently arrived at by using both the ideological and charismatic components in a different context from that suggested by Kissinger. Nonetheless the charismatic-ideological label is useful, for it expresses two outstanding features of Verwoerd's leadership. He undoubtedly had charisma, particularly for the Afrikaners. It was charisma in the sense of being seen to possess exceptional abilities (with regard to intellect, determination, steadfastness, reliability, powers of persuasion, etc.), and certainly not in the form of any theatrical qualities. Verwoerd's ideological fervour was manifested in his passionate belief in the elaborate separate development design. An ideological or dogmatic element also featured strongly in Verwoerd's conduct of foreign affairs. Here one can recall his private encounters with Prime Minister Macmillan during the latter's visit to South Africa in 1960, and the intrigues surrounding Verwoerd's decision to withdraw South Africa from the

Commonwealth in 1961.[11] Another example was Verwoerd's meeting with Chief Jonathan on the eve of Basutoland's independence in 1966. The following year Jonathan also held talks with Verwoerd's successor, Vorster. Comparing the two meetings, Jonathan said he found Vorster "a bit more realistic and practical" than Verwoerd, who had been "a bit difficult, indeed very difficult". Jonathan offered the explanation that Verwoerd was a philosopher, "and philosophers want you to accept their philosophy"; Vorster was more reasonable, "perhaps because he is a lawyer, and they are more amenable".[12] Vorster had indeed been a lawyer, but Verwoerd had not – at least by profession – been a philospher; he had been Professor of Psychology. Nonetheless Jonathan's observation was shrewd, relating – as Kissinger did – behaviour to professional experience.

In contrast to Verwoerd's image of an uncompromising ideologue, Vorster's was that of a pragmatist, both in domestic and foreign affairs. Although some may question Vorster's pragmatism in view of his adherence to the precepts of separate development, it can reasonably be said that he displayed a notable degree of flexibility within these parameters, unlike Verwoerd. Changes to the sports policy are a good example. And in foreign relations Vorster seemed even more of a pragmatist, with his outward movement and his handling of the Rhodesian and Namibian issues. Along with Vorster's pragmatism, or because of it, went such features as an apparent lack of purpose and direction, and "adhocracy" in dealing with foreign policy issues.

It will be recalled that Kissinger suggested that the pragmatism characterising his first leadership typology is reinforced by the "special qualities" of the legal profession. To infer that Vorster displayed pragmatic qualities simply because of his legal background would be extremely rash. For one thing, Kissinger added two other factors that help shape leadership groups, namely the structure in which they operate and the values of their society. The peculiar South African domestic environment provided a particular ideological context, and it can thus be said that Vorster's pragmatism was blended with ideology. The fact that societal values and the broad political structure remained essentially unchanged from Verwoerd to PW Botha might have enhanced the influence of the third of Kissinger's variables – professional background – on the kind of leadership displayed by the three prime ministers.

PW Botha's professional experience is that of a National Party organiser. Kissinger's typology offers no guidance as to the kind of leadership that may be expected of someone with such professional qualities. It is, nonetheless, perhaps not unreasonable to suggest – as has already been done – that the SSC system of decision making is related to the "organisation man" in PW Botha. His early experience as a party organiser was subsequently reinforced by his long association with the Defence Force, a particularly "organisationally-minded" institution, to use a tautology. As for PW Botha's leadership as prime minister, it is considerably more pragmatic than Vorster's. Although there are still obvious ideological parameters, the ideological content of PW Botha's leadership is somewhat smaller than Vorster's had been, just as Vorster's had been smaller than Verwoerd's. Pragmatism seems to increase in proportion to the decline in ideological content. In PW Botha's case the pragmatic element had not yet (by the end of 1981) made the same noticeable impact on articulated foreign policy as it had previously done in Vorster's case. PW Botha's pragmatism has thus far been demonstrated virtually exclusively in the domestic political realm in the shape of reformist rhetoric and a willingness to question some of the tenets of National Party orthodoxy. As with Vorster, PW Botha's pragmatism reveals a certain lack of direction – perhaps the natural consequence of a search for a new (or at least significantly altered) constitutional structure in South Africa. Charisma of the Verwoerd variety is not a description that fits PW Botha's type of leadership. It could be used with some justification in Vorster's case, but less so than in Verwoerd's. If a mixed, seemingly contradictory, typology may be selected, both Vorster's and PW Botha's leadership could be depicted as pragmatic-ideological, with a dose of charisma added in Vorster's case.

Wilkinson's character of leadership

Kissinger's typology can usefully supplemented by the theoretical perspectives offered by the already mentioned Wilkinson.[13] The character of political leadership, Wilkinson argued, is determined by the social status of persons recruited to leadership posts, stability of tenure, and *personalismo* and charisma of those holding such positions. Wilkinson advanced hypotheses about the effects each of the four factors might have on a state's articulated foreign policy. Since the hypotheses do not relate to the way in which policy is formulated, they need not be considered here. Nonetheless, because some of the factors making up Wilkinson's character of political leadership have not been considered in earlier theoretical perspectives, it is worth examining their relevance to the process of policy formulation in South Africa.

Aspects of the influence of social status on South African foreign policy formulation have already been dealt with in the earlier discussion of one of Kohl's models. For the present purposes, that will suffice.

As far as Wilkinson's first quantitative variable, **stability of tenure,** is concerned, a tempting hypothesis would be that the longer a South African prime minister holds office, the greater would be his personal involvement in foreign policy formulation. (Of stability, in the strict sense of the word, there is no doubt: Verwoerd and his successors led a party with a commanding and overwhelmingly loyal majority in Parliament.) In support one might mention Verwoerd's domination of foreign policy formulation after some initial restraint. The reverse of the hypothesis seems to be confirmed by PW Botha: because he is relatively new to the premiership, it might be argued, he relies heavily on the SSC in formulating foreign policy. In due course PW Botha may place a stronger personal imprint on the substance of foreign policy, notwithstanding his team concept of government. If true, it would support the former hypothesis. Vorster's foreign policy role, however, does not conform to either hypothesis. At the beginning of his premiership Vorster – virtually a stranger to foreign affairs – launched his bold outward movement, thus placing a firm personal stamp on foreign policy. In later years, however, despite his considerable experience in foreign affairs, Vorster's personal role – whether by acts of omission or commission on his part – grew weaker and persons like Mulder, Rhoodie and Van den Bergh became increasingly prominent. In Vorster's case a null hypothesis therefore seems more appropriate: that no relationship exists between stability of tenure and involvement in foreign policy formulation.

Wilkinson defines **personalismo** as "the tendency of the politically active sectors of a population to follow or oppose a leader for personal, individual, or family reasons rather than because of the influence of a political idea, program, or party." This is certainly not a feature of political leadership in South Africa and requires no further consideration.

Leadership **charisma**, Wilkinson's final variable, already featured in one of Kissinger's typologies. Here some hypotheses about its effects on foreign policy formulation can be advanced. It might be hypothesised that the more charismatic the prime minister's leadership, the greater his personal role in foreign policy formulation. His charisma might actually encourage him to play a particularly forceful role in foreign policy, giving it a highly personalised character. The records of Smuts and Verwoerd tend to confirm this hypothesis. Vorster possessed a certain degree of charisma, but his role in foreign policy formulation was less pronounced than either Smuts's or Verwoerd's. It would be tempting to hypothesise that Vorster's lesser role was related to his less charismatic leadership (compared with that of his two predecessors). However, the extent of Vorster's personal involvement varied from issue to issue, which could hardly be related to fluctuations in his charisma. In PW Botha's case it might be said that his reliance on the SCC in foreign policy formulation is related to his lack of charisma. Yet, as argued earlier, it could also be connected with his relatively short tenure of office. Charisma, therefore, like social status and stability of tenure, offers at best partial explanations of the role of South African leaders in the formulation of foreign policy.

Hermann's personal political styles

A number of further personal characteristics of political leaders can be found in an analysis of their personal political styles. Margaret G Hermann[14] (not to be confused with Charles F Hermann cited earlier) posited that two personal characteristics form the basis of a leader's "personal political style", namely decision style and interpersonal style. The personal political style of a leader – if he is a head of government – will in turn "affect his government's foreign policy style". Style in the latter sense, according to Hermann, refers to the means or methods a government employs in making its foreign policy, such as the involvement of the bureaucracy, the use of personal diplomacy, the resources and skills used in implementing policy, and the tendency to employ words rather than deeds. The question is whether the foreign policy styles of the Vorster and PW Botha governments can be explained, even only partly, in terms of the two prime ministers' personal political styles.

A definitive answer to this question would require a detailed analysis of the two leaders' political behaviour, also in the domestic political arena. (Hermann employed quantification in her second study of leaders' personal characteristics, but not in the first.) That, however, cannot be attempted here, nor is it necessary. It is only the style of South African foreign policy that is being examined with the help of Hermann's model, and not the entire process of policy making. A fair picture of the personal political styles of Vorster and PW Botha can be painted by considering only the salient aspects of the two personal characteristics mentioned by Hermann.

The two characteristics each comprise a number of aspects. Decision style, according to Hermann, indicates policy formulators' preferred methods of making decisions, and includes such elements as confidence, receptivity to new information, preference for certain levels of risk, capacity for postponing decision without anxiety, preference for compromise, preference for "an optimising as opposed to satisficing mode of decision making", and preference for "planning as opposed to activity". Interpersonal style refers to the typical manner in which a policy formulator deals with other policy formulators and Hermann identified its features as paranoia or suspiciousness; Machiavellianism, which means having a "manipulative way" with other people; means of persuasion; sense of political timing; sensitivity that leaders show to others, and whether or not they are task-oriented or person-oriented.

One of the elements of decision style mentioned by Hermann is openness to new information. With regard to the South African case, it can be remarked that PW Botha, through the formal network of Cabinet committees, planning branches and their supporting bodies, draws on a much wider range of information in decision making than Vorster did. This also applies to foreign policy formulation, where the focus is on the role of the SSC and its subsidiary bodies. Although greater in quantity and probably improved in quality, the information flowing to the policy formulators is still generated by the state machinery, something that is likely – as in all bureaucracies – to affect both the scope and the content of the information.

The postponement of decisions is not an uncommon phenomenon in any political system, and certainly not in South Africa's. Two outstanding instances of postponement concern domestic political reform and an international settlement of the Namibian issue. (This observation of course assumes that decisions on both issues are intended but that the government considers the time inopportune. It is, however, not being suggested that the decisions would involve the abolition of apartheid or a final Namibian settlement.) Whether the postponement is decided without anxiety is an entirely different question. To approach the matter in a roundabout way one can say that postponement is caused by the decision makers' anxiety about possible negative public reaction to "unpopular" decisions on the two issues. (This raises the question of constraints, something not catered for in Hermann's model.)

Compromise is not a feature of the South African government's political style, in the sense of the give-and-take characteristic of Western democratic systems. Verwoerd's disdain for the "politics of conciliation" has already been noted. Vorster and PW Botha have by contrast proven less inflexible and more pragmatic. Yet neither has made any grand concessions on the controversial aspects of the government's domestic racial policies.* In the foreign policy realm this feature is reflected in the government's hard bargaining over Namibia, discussed in Chapter 7. This particular aspect of decision style can also be explained in terms of what Hermann called dogmatism, which emphasises the importance of tradition, rules and principles. A dogmatic leader, who is typically conservative and respects established ideas, will in his foreign policy behaviour "be loath to change any policy that he views as a traditional part of the nation's repertoire of activities." In South Africa's case the latter proposition has to be qualified. While the Republic possesses what may be called a traditional repertoire of foreign policy activities, this is not merely shaped by leaders' political styles, but also by the features of South Africa's external environment – thus the Republic's commitment to the principle of domestic jurisdiction and non-interference, and its pro-Western orientation. But having said that, one has to note that Vorster's dogmatism did not prevent him from agreeing to the Department of Information's secret propaganda offensive – something certainly not part of South Africa's established repertoire of foreign activities. Nor did it prevent South Africa's intervention in a civil war on foreign soil. These observations caution against attaching deterministic properties exclusively to personal characteristics.

---

*The government's new constitutional proposals of 1982 can however be regarded as a major concession in the sense that coloureds and Indians would be drawn into top-level political decision making.

Machiavellianism is an interpersonal style that might be associated with PW Botha, who is an accomplished party "functionary" and doubtless adept at political manipulation. Hermann noted that research found that "the Machiavellian is less successful in using his manipulative tactics when he is not in direct communication with the other party." She then translated this trait into a foreign policy style with the proposition that the more Machiavellian a political leader, "the more face-to-face foreign policy interactions his government will have", such as personal or summit diplomacy conducted by the leader. This, however, has not been a feature of PW Botha's foreign policy style. The primary reason is to be found in South Africa's international political ostracism, which offers him little opportunity for top-level face-to-face diplomatic encounters. Vorster, by contrast, was involved in a good deal of high-level diplomacy, but this is certainly better explained by factors other than any Machiavellian trait he might have had; political considerations were the primary motive.

As far as sense of political timing is concerned, Vorster was renowned for it. An outstanding example was his timing of the 1977 general election, which enabled him to exploit the prevailing intense foreign pressure on South Africa to the full. In PW Botha this quality is less certain. Nonetheless a keen sense of political timing seems to have been shown in the Namibian negotiations – by both PW Botha and Vorster – which has allowed the government to indulge in a form of brinkmanship *vis-à-vis* the five Western powers.

Another aspect of what Hermann termed interpersonal style is whether a leader is task or person-oriented. PW Botha's whole gamut of planning institutions suggests that he is task rather than person-oriented in his leadership. In foreign policy formulation this manifests itself in the SSC system. Vorster, in turn, appeared person-oriented, as witness his use of Van den Bergh in domestic as well as foreign assignments.

PW Botha's elaborate network of policy planning bodies has already prompted the view in South African political circles that planning has become a substitute for action, or at any rate preferred to action. Hermann, it will be recalled, listed a preference for planning as opposed to action as a component of decision style. Considering the energy and resources that have been absorbed by all the planning operations under PW Botha, political action seems to lag well behind, at least until the end of 1981. Vorster was much less planning-oriented. Depending on circumstances he could be either a man of action or a man of inaction, the choice bearing little relation to the presence or absence of planning exercises. When one tries to relate these features to South Africa's foreign policy style, it is difficult to recall a clear instance where planning was preferred to or used as a substitute for action in the foreign policy field. Cases of a discrepancy between rhetoric and action are, however, not hard to find. The constellation of states, *c.* 1981, is but a pale shadow of the grand regional grouping of states which PW Botha and other ministers so confidently and enthusiastically foresaw a few years earlier.[15] Another example, which applies to PW Botha and Vorster, is the frequent talk about changing South Africa's basic foreign policy orientation from its traditional Western alignment to one of neutrality, or non-alignment, or alignment with other "pariah" states. It should however immediately be said that such pronouncements cannot realistically be explained as merely the foreign policy manifestation or extension of a personal political style characterised by an imbalance between rhetoric and action. The main explanation is instead to be found in the state of South Africa's foreign relations, particularly the Republic's disillusionment with the Western powers. This observation touches upon another of the elements of interpersonal style listed by Hermann, namely paranoia or suspiciousness. Whether or not this is a feature of either Vorster's or PW Botha's style in the domestic political arena is hard to judge. But it certainly applies to their dealings with foreign powers. Here one can recall Vorster's celebrated diagnosis of American pressure on South Africa. Its end result, he said in 1977,

> would be exactly the same as if it [South Africa] were subverted by the Marxists. In the one case, it will come about as the result of brute force. In the other case, it will be strangulation with finesse.

Grave concern about the perceived dangers of communism is of course not only associated with Vorster and PW Botha; it has been a major theme in successive Nationalist governments' domestic and foreign policies ever since 1948.

Although the preceding discussion points to some links between personal political style and government foreign policy style, it is clear that several features of the latter cannot be explained in terms of Vorster's and PW Botha's political styles.

Two Broader Perspectives: Barber's Models of British Foreign Policy Making

It is sometimes contended that the making of South African foreign policy is a relatively simple, straightforward, easy-to-understand process. This is based on the notion that relatively few people are involved in policy formulation, that few domestic pressures are brought to bear on them, and that few policy options are open to them. Each of these observations is essentially correct. That is then usually where the "simple" explanation ends, its proponents satisfied that there is little more to be explained once the principal policy formulators have been "identified" (without difficulty) as Vorster, or subsequently PW Botha, Magnus Malan and Pik Botha. The various theoretical perspectives considered in this chapter should have dispelled any such convenient belief. True, South Africa's foreign policy making is a relatively simple process when compared with that of the United States or the United Kingdom. Yet explaining *who* formulates the foreign policy of South Africa, *where, how and why,* is a highly complex matter to which there are few easy answers. Comparisons with other states are not always very useful, considering the special situation in which South Africa's foreign policy formulators find themselves. In a sense they are caught between the (domestic/ideological) devil and the (international/hostile) deep blue sea. Formulating "the foreign policy of apartheid" is certainly not made easy by fewness of options, of people and of domestic pressures.

The problem with the various theoretical perspectives thus far examined is the narrow focus of most of them. However useful they may be as explanatory devices, the areas illuminated are mostly confined. An overall explanation of South African foreign policy making would require a much broader theoretical sweep than provided by any one of the perspectives considered. A good indication of the wide spectrum of features that ought to be included can be found in Barber's study of British foreign policy formation.

In trying to answer the question, "Who makes British foreign policy?", Barber designed four models or "perspectives" as he preferred to call them. [16] The two that are relevant to the South African case are called the "formal office holder perspective" and the "departmental negotiated order perspective". The essence of the first is that foreign policy formulation is dominated by a small group of ministers formally charged with this responsibility. The other is based on the premise that foreign policy embraces a much wider area of government than implied in the first perspective, and that civil servants as well as ministers are directly involved in policy formulation. The two models however have a number of assumptions in common, which can be summarised as follows:

● Foreign policy making is essentially a function of the executive arm of government.
● The process requires specialist knowledge and access to a vast range of information, much of it confidential; those outside the executive could not acquire the necessary knowledge and should not handle sensitive information.
● The general public displays little knowledge of or interest in foreign affairs.
● Parliament, political parties and interest groups play a marginal role in foreign policy making. Their contribution depends on the influence they can exert on the executive.
● The executive not merely reacts to initiatives from domestic and foreign sources, but also plays an initiatory role in foreign policy making.

As regards the differences, the formal office holder perspective assumes that although civil servants play an important part in foreign policy formulation by bringing their expertise and skill to bear in the process, the final responsibility rests with the ministers. The institutional structure of foreign policy formulation resembles a pyramid, with the formal office holders at the top. "The main activity in foreign policy making either is initiated by, or converges upon, the top of the pyramid." A final relevant assumption is that because their number is so small, the personalities, abilities and interests of the formal office holders become significant in policy making.

The departmental negotiated order, by contrast, assumes that foreign policy making cannot be restricted to a particular section of government activity, but is rather an "amalgam of policies" arising from the government's activities in international affairs. The circle of policy formulators, although still in the executive branch of government, is wider than in the first perspective, including also civil servants. The major feature of government structure as it relates to policy formulation is its division into departments. The departments negotiate mutually to achieve their particular objectives "within a government framework which recognizes the need for consensus and cooperation". A bargaining situation is created, with the participating units being approximately equal in power, although there is some recognition of precedence. The activities of ministers are primarily related to those of their departments, and they carry the formal responsibility for policy formulation. In practice, however, "the bulk of policy and decision making is in the hands of civil servants." A final assumption of this perspective is that individual personalities do not play a crucial role, given the large number of policy formulators involved. "The image of foreign policy making is more accurately captured by a co-ordinating committee of departmental officials, than by the personalities of the Prime Minister and Foreign Secretary", according to Barber.

There is no need for a detailed assessment of the applicability of Barber's two perspectives. It is quite obvious that both are relevant to South African foreign policy making. It is also evident that neither perspective can by itself provide an adequate explanation of the South African case. More important, though, is that Barber's perspectives illustrate the wide reach required of a model of South African foreign policy formulation.

So far, a wide theoretical net has been cast. Through the various theoretical perspectives it has been possible to establish a number of important relationships which help explain the making of South African foreign policy. First, the constitutional and representative status of the South African government has direct implications for foreign policy formulation. Second, foreign policy decision processes could in several respects be related to the characteristics of South Africa's policy decision structures. The nature of the processes could, in turn, influence the substance of policy. Third, several features of South Africa's foreign policy behaviour could be related to the personal and leadership characteristics of political leaders. Finally, Barber's theoretical perspectives serve to illustrate how comprehensive a model for explaining even a single state's foreign policy making has to be.

A number of the many factors that influence the making of foreign policy have now been identified. Many more have been dealt with only indirectly or were not considered at all. The theoretical perspectives have not catered for elements of national power or capability, although some of these features have been mentioned in earlier chapters. The concern is not only with the physical components of power, but also with the social elements, principal among them being the values[17] of (white) South African society. "Foreign policy decision making", Holsti pointed out, "is always carried out with some knowledge of a country's immediate or potential capacity to achieve its objectives." The nature of available capability is a guide to what can possibly be achieved in a given situation.[18]

South Africa's Capability

The concept capability, although used in its singular form, is complex, made up of a diversity of components. These elements of national power or determinants of capability, as they are variously called, are typically arranged in two categories alternatively styled tangible and intangible, concrete and abstract, or physical and social environmental factors. The first category usually contains demographic and geographic features, natural resources, economic performance and military power, whereas the second is commonly used to refer to such psychological features as national character, national morale and values, and even socio-political structures.[19] A careful consideration of the determinants of South Africa's capability would obviously require a study of major proportions. Here it will suffice to draw only the contours of South Africa's national power. Some of the factors of capability have been mentioned in earlier chapters, and others, particularly the tangible elements of South Africa's (domestic) power, are fairly well known and have been scrutinised in other studies.[20]

To begin with South Africa's geophysical features: two of them are of particular importance in foreign policy making, namely geographical location and natural resources. It is to a large degree on the basis of South Africa's geographical position that the government has long laid claim to the country's strategic significance to Western powers. South Africa's treasure of raw materials gives the policy formulators a useful foreign policy instrument.

A second component is military power. According to one calculation South Africa in 1979 ranked twenty-third in the world in terms of non-nuclear military capability.[21] Particularly in an African context, though, the foreign policy significance of South Africa's military power becomes evident. It is, in short, a very real instrument of foreign policy, which has in fact been used directly but also has value in its deterrent effect.

Economic power is a third important component of South Africa's national capability. It has obvious foreign policy significance. The Republic's world-wide economic links provide a valuable means of communication with countries that refuse to enter into any overt political relations with Pretoria. The Western countries' economic stake in South Africa and their trade with the country certainly constrain them in expressing their opposition to the Republic's actions and policies at home and abroad. Closer to home, the economic dependence of many surrounding black states on South Africa is an important consideration in their overall relations with Pretoria; the latter, in turn, possesses a formidable foreign policy instrument in this dependence.

The outstanding demographic feature is the plurality of South Africa's population. The mere phenomenon of plurality need not necessarily have an adverse impact on a state's national power. In South Africa's case, however, the ideologisation of population plurality has caused – or at any rate greatly contributed to – racial polarisation. This undermines national power through its negative effect on what has been termed the national will or the national morale. It is perhaps more appropriate to refer to different wills or morales in South Africa, one white and the other, broadly speaking, black. Given such fundamental cleavages, the notion of a total national strategy has a ring of unreality about it. The ideologisation of racial plurality is the basic cause of South Africa's international ostracism and its pariahhood.

The development of an ideology around the (objective) fact of population plurality reflects the value pattern of South Africa's ruling white minority. From a foreign policy perspective, the point is that the "operational value hierarchy"[22] of the white oligarchy is widely rejected by the black majority and is anathema to the rest of the world. This system of values – as expressed in the government's racial policies – conditions the foreign policy formulators' external environment and severely constrains their freedom of action.

Public opinion can be listed as a final component of South Africa's domestic power base. As far as the general, unorganised public is concerned, it is – as with national will – perhaps more correct to speak of a white public and a black public. That the government cannot count on general or popular support among the population as a whole obviously weakens the country's national power. For the foreign policy formulators the "relevant" public is white. Among the unorganised white public it is possible to speak of a mood that constrains the foreign policy formulators, specifically in relations with neighbouring black states. This mood has taken on a more concrete, if extreme, form through the activities of right-wing political groups energetically trying to make a domestic political issue out of South Africa's relations with black states. Interest group activity in the realm of foreign affairs is nonetheless notably limited in South Africa. This frees policy formulators of the manifold pressures that interest groups generate in the Western democracies.

A mere catalogue of a state's capability is not enough. For foreign policy formulators national capability acquires its real significance only when related to the state's international environment. Foreign policy is, after all, not made in a vacuum, but in relation to other actors on the international stage.[23] For the South African foreign policy formulators probably the dominant feature of their external milieu is its hostility. The important intangible component of the international milieu at issue is that of international morality, articulated *inter alia* in the UN charter. South Africa's domestic political arrangements are in the view of its critics fundamentally out of step with international morality, thus eliciting the opprobrium of the international community. The focal point of international adversity is, not surprisingly, the UN. International law, another social component of the international environment, is also commonly invoked against South Africa.[24] Thus it is contended that the Republic has fallen foul of international law by retaining control of Namibia and by dismembering its own territory through the creation of independent homelands.[25]

Whether or not these contentions are valid, South African foreign policy formulators are faced with an extraordinarily unfavourable external environment, which seriously limits their freedom of action. International adversity has taken on numerous tangible forms, such as international boycotts (economic, diplomatic, cultural), a mandatory arms embargo and material foreign support for the "liberation struggle" in both Namibia and South Africa. These external factors combined with those features undermining the Republic's domestic power base explain why South Africa is unable to pursue a foreign policy that corresponds with the tangible components of its national power. Such is the foreign policy of pariahhood.

Features of a Proposed Oligarchic-Bureaucratic Model of South African Foreign Policy Making

The two principal features of South African foreign policy making are the monopolisation of decision making by whites and the growing involvement of professional experts from the public service alongside political office holders in decision making. The first feature is as old as the history of South Africa's foreign policy, whereas the second is a phenomenon of particularly the post-1966 period. Since these are then the key features and many others flow from them, a model of South African policy making might be called the oligarchic-bureaucratic model.

As the construction of a model of South African foreign policy formation is largely *terra incognita,* this book will merely sketch the outlines of a proposed model. Hopefully this will place the search for a model on the agenda as a topic for discussion and research.

• The first feature is South Africa's oligarchic form of authority. In the white oligarchy the foreign policy elite is drawn from the ruling white group. Included are not only the formal decision makers, but also certain businessmen and academics and the Broederbond. But then there is also what might be termed an unofficial foreign policy elite, composed particularly of black political leaders who operate from government-created political platforms. Their input into foreign policy making is, however, very much secondary to that of the white foreign policy elite. (Should coloureds and Indians be brought into top-level decision making alongside whites, the basic oligarchic structure of the political system will remain – albeit with a broader base – as long as the black majority remains excluded from a share in political power at the central level of government.)

• There is a causal relationship between South Africa's oligarchic form of authority and the second feature of its foreign policy making, namely its position as a pariah state.[26] The basic cause of the Republic's pariah status is the fact that it is a racial oligarchy ruled by whites. Seriously at odds with the international norms of the day, South Africa labours under international ostracism. More than that, South Africa as a typical pariah state perceives a constant threat to its security, even its very survival, from a hostile outside world. In short, South Africa is in a chronic state of high tension with its international environment.

• Concern about external security is compounded by an equally strong concern about the maintenance of South Africa's internal security. Like threats to the Republic's external security, internal security threats also derive from the oligarchic form of authority, with the government facing peaceful and violent challenges to its power from elements outside the white community. South Africa's foreign policy formulators have to face a hostile external environment without being backed by a united, supportive populace at home.

• Given the international milieu on the one hand and the South African policy formulators' commitment to upholding internationally rejected values in their domestic policies on the other, it follows that the Republic's foreign policy options are severely circumscribed, and perhaps gradually diminishing. To complicate matters, South Africa as a small power in the world context enjoys only a relatively narrow margin of safety internationally. Its limited resources, compared with the great powers, allow South Africa a strictly limited capacity to absorb serious errors of judgement in its foreign relations.

• There is a direct link between some major tenets of international opinion on South Africa and local black opinion. External opinion essentially champions – or pretends to promote – the cause of black South Africans against the ruling oligarchy. Just as the South African government's right to speak on behalf of all South Africans is widely questioned abroad and by local blacks, so too is Pretoria's foreign policy easily branded by critics as the foreign policy of apartheid. The policy formulators face a crisis of legitimacy both at home and abroad.

• Because of the cleavages in South Africa's body politic, it is appropriate to talk of racially-based opinions in South Africa. There are, in very broad terms, a white and a black public opinion. Insofar as the foreign policy formulators take note of public opinion, they would in the first instance heed white public opinion. Black opinion cannot simply be ignored, though, not least because of the connection between black opinion and international opinion. But although relevant, public opinion in its unorganised, amorphous form plays a marginal role in the making of South African foreign policy. As is the case in many other countries, public opinion in South Africa plays a "negative" role in the formulation of foreign policy by setting limits to the policy formulators' freedom of action. Even the "organised" public –

through political parties and interest groups, among others – carries far less weight in the making of South African foreign policy than in, for example, Britain or the United States. For one thing, overall interest group input into policy formulation in South Africa is relatively small compared to Western countries; another factor is that there are few interest groups active in the foreign policy field in South Africa. Among those that do feature, some are closer to the foreign policy formulators than others; Afrikaner-Nationalist groups typically appear on the list of "insiders". Political parties, including even the ruling National Party, play only a marginal role in the making of foreign policy. The high level of official secrecy and the correspondingly low level of public information characterising the process of foreign policy formulation in South Africa is in no way conducive to public interest in foreign policy.

• The link between domestic black opinion and international opinion, as well as the South African policy formulators' concern about extraneous forces, clearly reveal that the South African political system is being penetrated by external influences. Foreign pressure – whether designed to force the government to meliorate sports apartheid, abolish apartheid altogether or relinquish control of Namibia – is an important factor in the formulation of South Africa's foreign and domestic policies.

• The next feature, paradoxically, complements and contradicts South Africa's pariah status. At issue is the Republic's position within the Southern African region. Its pariah status affects its relations with (black) states in the region, in that the relations are for the most part severely strained; it could be argued that South Africa's pariah status is in large measure made in Southern Africa. The contradiction lies in the fact that South Africa is, in common with other pariahs, a small power in global terms – yet a big power in a regional context. The constraints imposed on South Africa on the wide international stage because of its pariahhood therefore do not apply with nearly the same force in Southern Africa. Notwithstanding its position as regional leviathan, South Africa perceives serious threats to its security from its immediate external environment.

• Concern about such threats have a direct bearing on South Africa's foreign policy decision structures. To begin with, the formulation of foreign policy is the prerogative of the executive branch of government. This universally familiar feature is to a large extent based on the nature of

foreign policy: it deals with matters that are sensitive, often highly confidential, requires specialised knowledge and skills, and can therefore be handled only by a small circle of suitably qualified (and reliable) persons in the executive. As a matter of form ultimate responsibility for South Africa's foreign policy is carried by the Cabinet. In practice, the SSC today plays a vital role in key areas of foreign policy formulation, either by recommending decisions to the Cabinet or by actually taking decisions. Although the Council's involvement in foreign policy formulation is directly related to the policy formulators' threat perceptions – expressed in the notion of a total onslaught – it also owes its position to the personal leadership style of Prime Minister PW Botha. Under Prime Minister Vorster, by contrast, foreign policy formulation was a diffuse process with shifting *loci* of decision making. That this occurred notwithstanding a keen awareness of threats to South Africa's security, can likewise be attributed to leadership style (about which more will be said later).

• Within the executive a crucial role in foreign policy formulation is played by civil servants, not only as expert advisers to the political office holders, but also as *de facto* decision makers. In this sense, there is a technocratic inner group within the bureaucracy. Under Prime Minister PW Botha the SSC is the main forum for expert bureaucratic input. Under Vorster, too, bureaucrats featured in foreign policy decision making, but their role was rather haphazard. In the Botha administration the SSC is but the top of the pyramid, with a whole network of supporting bodies manned by officials. This formalises and regularises the bureaucratic contribution to foreign policy formulation. It is a universal phenomenon that experts are "on tap" in political decision making. These bureaucrats assist the political office holders not only with their specialised knowledge of particular matters, but also with their knowledge of the institutional machinery of government. In these respects the political office holders are greatly dependent on their expert officials in the public service. The extent of the bureaucrats' involvement in decision making is in the final analysis determined by their political masters – which in turn may reflect the latters' leadership styles and the demands of national security, among other considerations.

• The SSC under PW Botha represents a team concept of government, the "players" being politicians and civil servants. They are all representatives of various governments agencies, chaired by the prime minister. His role is not simply that of a neutral referee; he is very much the leader of the team. There is recognition of precedence, with the prime minister indisputably the chief policy formulator, followed by his ministers and backed up by the bureaucratic representatives. In both the latter ranks the foreign ministry representatives regard themselves as first among equals when it comes to foreign policy issues. There are, however, powerful contending voices that are probably not always alive to the foreign ministry's sensitivities. Primary among them is the military. This produces something of a bargaining situation in foreign policy formulation, which involves various government agencies. Moreover a system of checks and balances is (theoretically) created. Under Vorster these various institutions were not involved in policy formulation in such a formalised and regularised fashion. Insofar as Vorster adhered to the team concept of foreign policy formulation, the team was the full Cabinet. Often, however, policy formulation would fall in the hands of small *ad hoc* groups composed of a few political office holders and officials. (The best example of this phenomenon was the handling of the affairs of what was then the Department of Information.)

• Personal characteristics of particularly the head of government have a bearing on South Africa's foreign policy formulation. In this respect South Africa is by no means unique: as Hill pointed out, "we know from the familiar debates about world historial individuals from Napoleon through Stalin to John F Kennedy that bureaucracy has rendered policy making no more impersonal than has democracy."[27] South Africa's foreign policy decision structures can be related to the personal political styles of Prime Ministers Vorster and PW Botha. Among the numerous other personal characteristics that influenced the two leaders' roles in foreign policy formulation, were charisma, ideological commitment, pragmatism, pre-political professional experience, length of tenure as prime minister, interpersonal style (embracing such aspects as suspiciousness and persuasiveness) and decision style (including features such as confidence, receptivity to new information and risk-taking

propensity). In short, the setting of foreign policy decision making in South Africa tends to be highly personalised. Another way in which the personalities of leaders, together with the dynamics of group behaviour, become key factors in the analysis of foreign policy formulation is in the definition of the "psychological environment". The concept "encapsulates the notion that how decision makers perceive the world is at least as important for explaining their actions as is the world's actual condition."[28] In South Africa's case this observation is particularly applicable to the threat perceptions of the decision makers.

• The final feature that ought to be incorporated in the oligarchic-bureaucratic model also concerns the dynamics of group behaviour. A likely result of the common socialisation process of South Africa's foreign policy formulators is the development of mind sets or "similar assumptions and outlooks on international affairs". The danger, as Kohl pointed out, is that common perceptual lenses among key policy formulators can obscure or exclude the consideration of alternatives in foreign policy. In South Africa such distorted dynamics are certainly a very real possibility, considering the narrow socio-political spectrum from which the principal foreign policy formulators are drawn: apart from the obvious prerequisite of race, high premium is placed on political affiliation, language and Broederbond membership.

A number of the above features are by no means unique to South Africa, whereas others derive from the Republic's oligarchic form of authority, its international pariah status and the omnipresent threat perceptions. The country's pariah status is of course the product of its form of authority, and threat perceptions seem to be a feature of pariah states. A model of South African foreign policy making will have to accommodate a diversity of features: elements of foreign policy formulation in Western states, in oligarchic states and in pariah states. It might be rewarding to compare foreign policy making in the Republic with that in other pariah states, so as to establish whether a model of foreign policy formation with a wider applicability than merely South Africa can be devised.

Notes to the Text

CHAPTER 1

1. Rhoodie, DO, *Suid-Afrika: Van Koloniale Onder-horigheid tot Soewereine Onafhanklikheid,* Perskor, Johannesburg, 1974, p.7.
2. In terms of the *South Africa Act,* 1910, the franchise was restricted to white males (in 1930 white women received the franchise), while blacks and coloureds in the Cape Province were placed on a common voters' roll with whites – but only whites could be elected to Parliament. In 1936 Cape blacks were removed from the common roll and were instead to elect three white MPs to represent them. In 1959 the Cape blacks lost also their separate representation in Parliament, leaving them with black homeland legislatures as forums for political representation. In 1956 coloureds too were placed on a separate voters' roll, and in 1968 they lost their parliamentary representation altogether, when the partly elected Coloured Persons Representative Council was established. South African Indians in 1964 for the first time received a modicum of political representation with the creation of a nominated South African Indian Council.
3. Rhoodie, DO, *op. cit.,* p.8 and Bekker, MJ, *Histories-Empiriese Studie van die Suid-Afrikaanse Diplomatieke en Konsulêre Diens as Staatskakelorganisasie,* MA dissertation, University of Potchefstroom, 1973, p.36.
4. Muller, ME, *Suid-Afrika se Buitelandse Verteenwoordiging (1910-1972),* Van Schaik, Pretoria, 1976, p.48.
5. *Loc. cit.,* Bekker, MJ, *op. cit.,* p.37 and Gey van Pittius, EFW, "Die rol van Generaal Hertzog in die ontvoogding van die Unie", in Nienaber, PJ *et al.* (Eds) *Gedenkboek Generaal JBM Hertzog,* Afrikaanse Pers-Boekhandel, Johannesburg, 1965, p.327. For a revealing account of the problems that South Africa's uncertain international status caused its representatives abroad, see Van

der Schyff, PF, *Eric H Louw in die Suid-Afrikaanse Politiek tot 1948,* D. Litt. dissertation, University of Potchefstroom, 1974, pp.221-6.
6. Slee, ATC, *Commonwealth Co-operation 1939-45: South Africa and its London Representation,* D.Phil. dissertation, University of Cape Town, 1959, p.5.
7. Quoted *ibid.,* p.6.
8. Muller, ME, *op. cit.,* pp.50 & 51.
9. Slee, ATC, *op. cit.,* p.6.
10. Muller, ME, *op. cit.,* pp. 48-55. Louw's tenure as trade commissioner in America is discussed in detail in Van der Schyff, PF, *op. cit.,* pp.201ff.
11. In the early days of the League, Prime Minister Smuts appointed Lord Robert Cecil, a prominent British politician, as South Africa's representative in the League Assembly. The move reflected the strength of the imperial connection and the Union's lack of an independent international posture. (Hancock, WK, *Smuts: The Fields of Force, 1919-1950,* Cambridge University Press, London, 1968, pp.36 & 130).
12. Muller, ME, *op. cit.,* pp.49-56.
13. Quoted by Rhoodie, DO, *op. cit.,* p.137.
14. Quoted by Bekker, MJ, *op. cit.,* p.37.
15. Quoted by Rhoodie, DO, *op. cit.,* p.185. See also Scholtz, GD, *Hertzog en Smuts en die Britse Ryk,* Tafelberg, Cape Town, 1975, 158pp.
16. Gey van Pittius, EFW, *op. cit.,* pp.324 & 325.
17. Muller, ME, *op. cit.,* p.57.
18. Union of South Africa, *Debates of the House of Assembly (Hansard)* (hereafter abbreviated HA Deb.), 10/4/1930, col. 3022 & 3023.
19. Muller, ME, *op. cit.,* p.58.
20. Bodenstein was an Afrikaner who hailed from the Western Transvaal and who had, in the Anglo-Boer War, distinguished himself as a Boer scout. Before taking up an academic appointment, he was

a senior journalist with *Die Burger,* the National Party's Cape mouthpiece. (See Du Plessis, WC, *Die Goue Draad: "Op die Trekpad van 'n Nasie",* Afrikaanse Pers-Boekhandel, Johannesburg, 1971, p. 44, and Scholtz, GD "Generaal Hertzog en die internasionale politiek", in Nienaber, PJ, *op. cit.,* p. 338.) Some of Bodenstein's officials remembered him for his modesty; others for his rigorous pedantry. A journalist recalled that Bodenstein was never fond of newspapermen and "had a sarcastic tongue and was often biting about the Press" (Bellwood, WA, *South African Backdrop,* Nasionale Boekhandel, Cape Town, 1969, p.145). Another glimpse of this complex personality was provided by an opposition MP who asked Prime Minister Hertzog when Bodenstein had been elevated to the peerage, for he signed himself only "Bodenstein".

21. In a statement published in a German journal in 1937 Bodenstein said South Africa was a completely sovereign and independent state in the fullest international sense. This prompted the leader of the Dominion Party, Col. CF Stallard, to introduce a motion of censure in Parliament on Bodenstein's action (Rhoodie, DO, *op. cit.,* p.225).

22. Muller, ME, *op. cit.,* pp.61 & 62.

23. Slee, ATC, *op. cit.,* pp.6 & 7.

24. Muller, ME, *op. cit.,* pp.60-65. See also Van der Schyff, PF, *op. cit.,* pp.277-333, on Louw's tenure as first head of mission in Washington.

25. Muller, ME, *op. cit.,* pp.59-65.

26. Pachai, B, *The International Aspects of the South African Indian Question 1860-1971,* Struik, Cape Town, 1971, pp.126, 127 & 154.

27. See Egeland, L, *Bridges of Understanding: A Personal Record in Teaching, Law, Politics and Diplomacy,* Human & Rousseau, Cape Town, 1977, p.148; Rosenthal, E, *South African Diplomats Abroad: The South African Department of External Affairs,* SAIIA, Johannesburg, 1949, p. 22, and Smuts, JC (jr), *Jan Christian Smuts,* Cassell, London, 1952, pp. 451ff.

28. Mulder, PWA, *Die Suid-Afrikaanse Staatsinligtingsdiens, 1936-1977, met Besondere Beklemtoning van sy Buitelandse Doelstellinge en Funksies,* D.Phil. dissertation, University of Potchefstroom, 1977, pp. 55, 56 & 66-9. The post of press officer in London had no connection with that of State Information Officer created in the Union in 1936. The latter post, also in the Department of the Prime Minister, involved liaison between the Union government and the local press.

29. *Ibid.,* p.121.

30. *Ibid.,* p.127.

31. Heaton Nicholls, G, *South Africa in My Time,* George Allen & Unwin, London, 1961, pp.368ff.

32. Egeland, L, *op. cit.,* pp.153ff.

33. Van der Schyff, PF, *op. cit.,* pp.162ff.

34. See Egeland, L, *op. cit.,* p.144.

35. *Ibid,* p.204. Also widely regarded as a diplomatic "dumping" was Smuts's appointment of Mr SF du Toit, Clerk of the Senate, as envoy to Sweden in 1946. For Du Toit's account of his diplomatic career (which in the event lasted until 1960) see his memoirs, *Home and Abroad,* Nasionale Boekhandel, Cape Town, 1969, 222pp.

36. Geldenhuys, DJ, *The Effects of South Africa's Racial Policy on Anglo-South African Relations, 1945-1961,* Ph.D. dissertation, University of Cambridge, 1977, pp.11, 14 & 15.

37. Kavina, SDB, *The South West Africa Dispute: A Political Study,* M.Sc. dissertation, University of Edinburgh, 1967, pp.19, 20 & 57-68.

38. Quoted by Geldenhuys, DJ, *Anglo-South African Relations, op. cit.,* p.36.

39. See Ezejiofor, G, *Protection of Human Rights under the Law,* Butterworth, London, 1964, pp.52ff., and Luard, E (Ed), *The International Protection of Human Rights,* Thames & Hudson, London, 1967, pp.14ff.

40. See Hancock, WK, *op. cit.,* pp.467-72.

41. Smuts in a letter to F Lamont, 31/3/1947, in Van der Poel, J (Ed), *Selections from the Smuts Papers,* Vol. VII (August 1945-October 1950), Cambridge University Press, London, 1973, p.129.

42. Smuts in a letter to MC Gillett, 14/1/1947, *ibid.,* p.116. See also Smuts, JC (jr), *op. cit.,* p.499.

43. Geldenhuys, DJ, *Anglo-South African Relations, op. cit.,* pp.91 & 92.

44. Quoted in HA Deb., 12/5/1959, col. 5604.

45. Hancock, WK, *op. cit.,* p.473.

46. See Mansergh, N, *South Africa 1906-1961: The Price of Magnanimity,* George Allen & Unwin, London, 1962, pp.64-98.

47. Meintjes, J, *General Louis Botha: A Biography,* Cassell, London, 1970, p.279.

48. Miller, JDB, *The Commonwealth in the World,* Gerald Duckworth, London, 1965, p.32.

49. Krüger, DW, *The Age of the Generals: A Short Political History of the Union of South Africa,* Dagbreekpers, Johannesburg, 1961, pp.106 & 107.

50. Published by Hodder & Stoughton, London, 1918, 71pp.

51. See Smuts, JC (jr), *op. cit.,* pp.219-38 and Hancock, WK, *op. cit.,* pp.3-20.

52. Smuts, JC (jr), *op. cit.,* p.422.

53. *Ibid.,* pp.421, 429, 449 & 461.

54. See Slee, ATC, *op. cit.,* pp.43 & 44, Heaton Nicholls, G, *op. cit.,* p.387 and Smuts, JC (jr), *op. cit.,* p.432.

55. For the text of Smuts's original draft preamble, see Smuts, JC (jr), *op. cit.,* p.478.

56. *Ibid.,* p.475.

57. Cockram, B, "General Smuts and South African Diplomacy", address to a meeting of the Witwatersrand branch of the South African Institute of International Affairs, 16 September 1970, Roneoed, p. 6.

58. Hancock, WK, *op. cit.*, p. 433.
59. See Friedman, B, *Smuts: A Reappraisal,* Hugh Keartland Publishers, Johannesburg, 1975, p.178.
60. See Lawrence, J, *Harry Lawrence,* David Philip Publishers, Cape Town, 1978, pp.87 & 198-212.
61. Smuts, JC (jr), *op. cit.*, pp.449, 461 & 491.
62. Hancock, WK, *op. cit.*, pp.36 & 131-49.
63. Smuts, JC (jr), *op. cit.*, pp.491-7 and Egeland, L, *op. cit.*, p.193.
64. Among the reasons for Hertzog's attendance were his deep concern about the worldwide economic recession and political tensions in Europe, and his keenness to enhance South Africa's status internationally (Scholtz, GD, "Generaal Hertzog", *op. cit.*, pp.339 & 340; Van Vuuren, DJ, *Eric H Louw en sy Bydrae tot die Internasionale Betrekkinge van Suid-Afrika,* D.Phil. dissertation, University of the Orange Free State, 1972, p.41, and HA Deb., 10/4/1930, col. 3019).
65. Van Vuuren, DJ., *op. cit.*, p.vii.
66. Van den Heever, CM, *General JBM Hertzog,* APB Bookstore, Johannesburg, 1946, pp.208, 231, 232, 266 & 271.
67. See Pirow, O, *James Barry Munnik Hertzog,* Howard Timmins, Cape Town, undated, pp.227-41 and Watt, DC, "South African attempts to mediate between Britain and Germany, 1935-1938", in Bourne, K & DC Watt (Eds), *Studies in International History,* Longman, London, 1967, pp.402-22.
68. Watt, DC, *op. cit.*, p.421.
69. Munger, ES, *Notes on the Formation of South African Foreign Policy,* Castle Press, Pasadena, 1965, p.16.
70. See Rhoodie, DO, *op. cit.*, pp.122ff.
71. See Hyam, R, *The Failure of South African Expansion, 1908-1948,* Macmillan, London, 1972, pp.42-4 and Van der Schyff, PF, *op. cit.*, p.258.
72. Munger, ES, *Foreign Policy, op. cit.*, p.16.
73. Geldenhuys, DJ, *Anglo-South African Relations, op. cit.*, pp.63 & 64.
74. *Ibid.*, pp.76-9.
75. Van den Heever was not only an accomplished jurist (specialising on the SWA mandate and issues arising from South Africa's dominion status) and a member of several official South African delegations abroad, but also a noted Afrikaans poet and as closely identified as Hertzog with the Afrikaans language movement. (See Jooste, GP, *Diensherinneringe,* Perskor, Johannesburg, 1977, pp.30 & 31 and Du Plessis, WC, *op. cit.*, pp.46 & 47.) Van den Heever was also known for his sharp wit. At a social function in London a British lady raised the question of the Hertzog government's insistence on South Africa's right to neutrality and secession from the Commonwealth and asked Van den Heever, "What is the use of a right which you don't exercise?" Van den Heever is said to have replied: "But madam, is that not the essence of virginity?"
76. Jooste, a former private secretary of Havenga's, wrote that the tie between Hertzog and Havenga "was one of intimate friendship and intense loyalty – the general always the leader and Mr Havenga always the adviser and follower" (Jooste, GP, *op. cit.*, p.26).
77. Van der Schyff, PF, *op. cit.*, pp.201ff. and Van Vuuren, DJ, *op. cit.*, pp.20-50.
78. See Egeland, L, *op. cit.*, pp.145, 169 & 170.
79. De Beer, KJ, *Dr DF Malan as Minister van Buitelandse Sake,* M.A. dissertation, University of the Orange Free State, 1977, p.99.
80. See Paton, A, *Hofmeyr* (Abridged edition), Oxford University Press, London, 1971, p.298.
81. *Ibid.*, p.310.
82. Egeland, L, *op. cit.*, p.196. Egeland records the following telling anecdote: when Smuts visited London in 1947 Egeland, then high commissioner, suggested Smuts should delay his return to South Africa for a few days to have a rest. "No, my boy," was his reply, "I must get back. When I'm away none of my Ministers take decisions."
83. Friedman, B, *op. cit.*, p.158. See also Hancock, WK, *op. cit.*, pp.333 & 387, and Jooste, GP, *op. cit.*, p.104.
84. Quoted by De Beer, KJ, *op. cit.*, p.99.
85. Quoted by Mulder, PWA, *op. cit.*, p.167.
86. Personal interview with Mr DD Forsyth.
87. Dugard, CJR (Ed), *The South West Africa/Namibia Dispute; Documents and Scholarly Writings on the Controversy between South Africa and the United Nations,* University of California Press, Berkeley, 1973, pp.106-9.
88. Personal interview with Mr L Egeland.
89. Slee, ATC, *op. cit.*, pp.44 & 45 and Van der Schyff, PF, *op. cit.*, p.326.
90. Quoted by Mulder, PWA, *op. cit.*, pp.117 & 118.
91. HA Deb., 10/4/1930, col. 3018.
92. Olivier, GC, *Suid-Afrika se Buitelandse Beleid,* Akademica, Pretoria, 1977. p.181.
93. Quoted by Mulder, PWA, *op. cit.*, p.117.
94. Quoted by Geldenhuys, DJ, *Anglo-South African Relations, op. cit.*, p.189.
95. HA Deb., 12/5/1949, col. 5663 & 5717. The fascinating story of Te Water's unique mission has yet to be recorded in detail. Here it can be related only very briefly. Although combating foreign criticism – which in effect meant trying to explain the Malan government's policies abroad – was the only publicly announced purpose of Te Water's mission, it was by no means the sole reason for his appointment. Te Water, it seems, was also asked to assist in negotiating a loan for South Africa in the United States, to attend the third session of the United Nations General Assembly in Paris and to redress the damage caused to South Africa's relations with the Low Countries by The Netherlands' refusal to grant *agrément* for Dr Otto du Plessis, Malan's nominee as South African

ambassador to The Hague. This was an ill-advised nomination, for Du Plessis was a controversial political figure who had openly displayed Nazi sentiments during the war. The Dutch made it plain to Te Water that a career diplomat would be more agreeable than such a controversial political nominee. Te Water also held talks with the government and political leaders in the United Kingdom, France, Belgium, Portugal, Spain, Greece, Italy, Egypt, the United States and Canada, and had an audience with Pope Pius XII in the Vatican. He paid flying visits to Northern and Southern Rhodesia, Nyasaland, Tanganyika, Kenya, Uganda and the Sudan, and consulted with the governors and senior officials of these territories.

Te Water's own diplomatic style was not exactly suited to the new times. He was a representative of the old school of pre-war diplomacy with all its pomp and ceremony, and Te Water placed a heavy reliance on his own powers of persuasion. Though a seasoned diplomat – and someone who had closely identified with Hertzog's attempts to resolve the issue of South Africa's international status – Te Water was something of an anachronism in the post-war world and the "shirt-sleeve" diplomacy that characterised it. His task was made no easier by the uncertainty still surrounding the real meaning of the incoming government's apartheid policy; it was hardly possible to "sell" such a vaguely formulated policy abroad. It is also doubtful whether Te Water had much enthusiasm for this part of his assignment, for he was said not to be a (Malan) Nationalist. To complicate matters for him even further, he found himself heavily at odds with Louw, the Malan government's "expert" on international affairs and leader of the Union's mission to the United Nations General Assembly in 1948. Personality clashes between the two probably played a role in Malan's decision not to extend Te Water's appointment beyond July 1949. (Most of this information was obtained in a personal interview with Mr Louis Gerber, who was Te Water's aide on his missions overseas. References to Te Water's missions are also contained in De Beer, KJ, *op. cit.*, pp.194 & 265; Egeland, L, *op. cit.*, p.145 and Muller, ME, *op. cit.*, p.85.)

96. See note 2, above.
97. Quoted by Geldenhuys, DJ, *South Africa's Black Homelands: Past Objectives, Present Realities and Future Developments*, SAIIA, Johannesburg, 1981, pp.5 & 6.
98. HA Deb., 10/4/1961, col. 4191 and Scholtz, GD, *Dr Hendrik Frensch Verwoerd, 1901-1966*, Vol. 2, Perskor, Johannesburg, 1974, p.134. See also Chapter 7 in this book, in which the role of foreign pressure in South African policy making is discussed.
99. Du Plessis, E, *Die Buitelandse Beleid van Dr HF Verwoerd (1958-1966)*, M.A. dissertation, University of Pretoria, 1978, p.142.
100. Feit, E, *Urban Revolt in South Africa 1960-1964: A Case Study*, Northwestern University Press, 1971, pp.3-7.
101. The complete text of the speech is appended to Macmillan, H, *Pointing the Way, 1959-1961*, Macmillan, London, 1967, pp.473-82.
102. See Geldenhuys, DJ, *Anglo-South African Relations, op. cit.*, pp.416ff.
103. Muller, ME, *op. cit.*, p.101.
104. Louw, in HA Deb., 15/7/1958, col. 351.
105. Muller, ME, *op. cit.*, pp.102, 141 & 142.
106. De Beer, KJ, *op. cit.*, pp.499 & 526.
107. Schoeman, BJ, *My Lewe in die Politiek*, Perskor, Johannesburg, 1978, p.284. (The author served as minister in successive Nationalist governments from 1948 to 1974.)
108. Dugard, CJR, *South West Africa, op. cit.*, pp.239-325 & 379-81.
109. See Labuschagne, GS, *Suid-Afrika en Afrika: Die Staatkundige Verhouding in die Tydperk 1945-1966*, Centre for International Politics, Potchefstroom, 1969, pp.33ff.
110. Muller, ME, *op. cit.*, pp.105-7.
111. Van Vuuren, DJ, *op. cit.*, p.153.
112. Bekker, MJ, *op. cit.*, p.54. The establishment of such a division had already been proposed by Te Water in 1949 (De Beer, KJ, *op. cit.*, p.371).
113. Quoted by Barber, J, *South Africa's Foreign Policy 1945-1970*, Oxford University Press, London, 1973, p.106.
114. Quoted by Du Plessis, E, *op. cit.*, p.90.
115. Olivier, GC, *op. cit.*, p.131.
116. Quoted by Van Vuuren, DJ, *op. cit.*, p.161.
117. Quoted by Geldenhuys, DJ, *Anglo-South African Relations, op. cit.*, p.417.
118. Quoted *loc. cit.*
119. See Olivier, GC, *op. cit.*, p.135.
120. *Loc. cit.*
121. *Ibid.*, p.136.
122. Muller, ME, *op. cit.*, p.96.
123. Du Plessis, E, *op. cit.*, p.82.
124. Olivier, GC, *op. cit.*, p.137, and Du Plessis, E, *op. cit.*, p.83.
125. See *ibid.*, pp.137 & 138.
126. Bekker, MJ, *op. cit.*, p.45.
127. Van den Berghe, PL, *South Africa: A Study in Conflict*, Wesleyan University Press, Middletown, 1965, p.311.
128. Cervenka, Z., *The Unfinished Quest for Unity: Africa and the OAU*, Julian Friedman, London, 1977, p.111.
129. See Labuschagne, GS, *op. cit.*, pp.55, 56, 69 & 70, and Du Plessis, E, *op. cit.*, pp.85-7.
130. Muller, ME, *op. cit.*, pp.143-4.
131. Figures obtained from Union of South Africa, *Department of External Affairs List*, July 1948 and July 1955, and *Department of Foreign Affairs List*, February 1966 (all published by Government

Printer, Pretoria); Muller, ME, *op. cit.*, p.87, and *Yearbook of the United Nations,* 1948, 1955, 1961 and 1966 (UN, New York).

132. De Beer, KJ, *op. cit.*, p.297.

133. Muller, ME, *op. cit.*, pp.85 & 123-7, and Bekker, MJ, *op. cit.*, p.44.

134. Muller, ME, *op. cit.*, pp.94 & 132.

135. *Ibid.*, pp.88-93 & 128-32.

136. De Beer, KJ, *op. cit.*, p.488, and Schoeman, BJ, *op. cit.*, p.218.

137. See HA Deb., 4/5/1972, col. 6514 & 6533.

138. Muller, ME, *op. cit.*, pp.89 & 137.

139. *Ibid.*, pp.89, 137 & 138.

140. In 1950 South Africa first appointed a high commissioner in Southern Rhodesia. With the creation of the Central African Federation three years later, he became South Africa's representative in the Federation. With the dissolution of the Federation in 1963 and the subsequent independence of Northern Rhodesia (Zambia) and Nyasaland (Malawi), South Africa was left with representation only in Southern Rhodesia and established diplomatic ties with Malawi in 1967. When Rhodesia, as it subsequently became known, declared UDI in 1965, South Africa's representation in Salisbury remained unaffected (Muller, ME, *op. cit.*, pp.88 & 138).

141. Pachai, B, *op. cit.*, p.192, and Geldenhuys, DJ, *Anglo-South African Relations, op. cit.*, p.170.

142. See Egeland, L, *op. cit.*, p.200, and Geyer, AL, *Vier Jaar in Highveld,* Tafelberg, Cape Town, 1969, pp.17 & 18.

143. Confidential communication.

144. See note 95, above. The Du Plessis incident revealed Malan's ignorance of diplomatic formality in more ways than one. None other than Malan informed *Die Burger* – which published it as a scoop – that Du Plessis had been nominated for the ambassadorship, at a stage when the matter was supposed to be strictly confidential, i.e. before the Dutch Queen had granted her *agrément* (De Beer, KJ, *op. cit.*, p.416).

145. Egeland, L, *op. cit.*, p.212, and personal interview. Geyer, Egeland's successor, thought that in view of the British people's caricaturish image of the Afrikaner and their consequent negative attitude towards the Malan government, the latter had made a mistake "to wait for a full two years before it recalled a fervent admirer of General Smuts [i.e. Egeland] as High Commissioner" (Geyer, AL, *op. cit.*, p.24).

146. Geyer, a close friend of Malan's, had in 1923 succeeded the latter as editor of *Die Burger*. As for Geyer's diplomatic appointment, Malan probably felt the time had arrived to have an Afrikaner-Nationalist – one who would make a favourable impression – representing South Africa in London. Geyer proved eminently suited to the task. (See De Beer, KJ, *op. cit.*, pp.11ff., and Schoeman, BJ, *op. cit.*, p.184.)

147. Jooste, GP, *op. cit.*, pp.170 & 171, wrote that Malan told him he had been selected for the high commissionership to assist Erasmus, Minister of Defence, in negotiations with the United Kingdom over the Simonstown naval base, and to try to resolve the dispute between South Africa and Britain over the future of the high commission territories. (In a country where relatively few public figures write their memoirs, it is a truly amazing coincidence that four successive holders of the Union's high commissionership in London published theirs: Heaton Nicholls, Egeland, Geyer and Jooste.)

148. Wilkins, I & H Strydom, *The Super-Afrikaners: Inside the Afrikaner Broederbond,* Jonathan Ball Publishers, Johannesburg, 1978, p.119.

149. See Schoeman, BJ, *op. cit.*, pp.252, 253, 278 & 313.

150. *Ibid.*, pp.243 & 244.

151. *Ibid.*, p.309.

152. Confidential communication.

153. See Mulder, PWA, *op. cit.*, pp.171-206.

154. Quoted *ibid.*, p.209. The endeavours of the State Information Office were from early on acclaimed in official circles. In his annual report of 1950 Du Plessis confidently asserted that the efforts of South Africa's information attachés abroad to eliminate "ignorance, prejudice and hostility against South Africa, have in the short space of one year already produced a noticeable change in the tide" (of foreign opinion). (Quoted *ibid.*, p.218.) Malan spoke in similar vein in 1953, arguing that foreign attitudes towards South Africa were undoubtedly becoming more positive, and he attributed this in the first place to the work of the State Information Office (*ibid.*, p.254). As it subsequently turned out, such improvements or advances were little more than temporary respites, caused probably more by events abroad (distracting attention from South Africa), than by South Africa's information activities. Another factor was some lessening in the incidence of controversial government measures in South Africa, so that there was less cause for unfavourable publicity abroad. There was no fundamental, consistent improvement in South Africa's international standing in these years; the general trend was instead towards gradually increasing international unpopularity.

155. *Ibid.*, pp.171 & 207-32.

156. *Ibid.*, p.175.

157. *Ibid.*, pp.270, 278, 279 & 294. See also Meiring, P, *Inside Information,* Howard Timmins, Cape Town, 1973, pp.133ff. (The author served as Director of the State Information Office.)

158. De Villiers, D, "The cowcatcher of diplomacy: South Africa's overseas information services", *New Nation,* Vol. 4, No. 7, February 1971, p.16.

159. Meiring, P, *Information, op. cit.*, p.137.

160. Mulder, PWA, *op. cit.*, pp.341-3 & 352. For Du

Plessis's account of his appointment, see Du Plessis, WC, *op. cit.*, pp.218-21.

161. Mulder, PWA, *op. cit.*, pp.353-71.

162. On Malan's performance at the two Commonwealth summits, see Egeland, L, *op. cit.*, p.210, and Geyer, AL, *op. cit.*, pp.94-122.

163. De Beer, KJ, *op. cit.*, pp.266, 383, 421, 437-41 & 461, and Mulder, PWA, *op. cit.*, p.234.

164. Meiring, P, *Ons Eerste Ses Premiers: 'n Persoonlike Terugblik,* Tafelberg, Cape Town, 1972, p.112.

165. Jooste, GP, *op. cit.*, p.190.

166. Mulder, PWA, *op. cit.*, pp.326-9; Meiring, P, *Information, op. cit.*, p.162, and Meiring, P, *Ses Premiers, op. cit.*, p.113. According to an official document of the South African Information Service dealing with its activities at the 1961 Commonwealth Conference, Verwoerd's personal image had in past years "suffered gross distortion through deliberate caricaturisation and the figure which the average Briton could be expected to visualise would be dour, inaccessible, bigoted, humourless, tyrannical and authoritarian, the living embodiment of every characteristic which made the dictators of recent memory such unloved figures in Britain." (Quoted by Mulder, PWA, *op. cit.*, p.326.)

167. Van Vuuren, DJ, *op. cit.*, p.vii.

168. Munger, ES, *Foreign Policy, op. cit.*, p.88.

169. Van Vuuren, DJ, *op. cit.*, p.153.

170. Geyer, AL, *op. cit.*, pp.89-91.

171. Geldenhuys, DJ, *Anglo-South African Relations, op. cit.*, pp.200 & 201.

172. De Beer, KJ, *op. cit.*, pp.421 & 422.

173. *Ibid.*, p.403.

174. See Dugard, CJR, *South West Africa, op. cit.*, pp.229-31.

175. Schoeman, BJ, *op. cit.*, p.281.

176. The government was so concerned about the possibility of Jonathan's visit causing "incidents" or domestic political embarrassment for itself that Verwoerd decided to receive his guest in Pretoria rather than in Cape Town where Parliament was in session. Verwoerd tried to keep publicity to a minimum. He even decided not to join Jonathan for a lunch, but instead sent a retired top official to accompany Jonathan (confidential communication).

178. Geyer, AL, *op. cit.*, p.14.

179. Consider, for example, Egeland, L, *op. cit.*, p.145: Malan "had little experience of foreign affairs other than on issues affecting the dominions *inter se*"; Geyer, AL, *op. cit.*, pp.14 & 15: "essentially he did not have much interest in foreign affairs and his knowledge of international politics and the world situation was not particularly great . . . a great Minister of External Affairs he was not"; Munger, ES, *Foreign Policy, op. cit.*, p.92, recalled an interview with Malan after the latter's retirement: "Although shrewd in his comments on many aspects of world affairs, particularly in inter-

Commonwealth matters which he knew so well, the former Prime Minister did surprise me with his limited and hazy comprehension of the geography, and contemporary events, throughout much of black Africa"; Olivier, GC, *op. cit.*, p.184: "Malan did not share Smuts's interest and competence with regard to international politics"; Thom, HB, *op. cit.*, pp.212 & 213: by 1948 Malan "had not yet made a particular study of international affairs", and Meiring, P, *Ses Premiers, op. cit.*, p.92: "Dr Malan was . . . not particularly interested in foreign affairs and was not always familiar with overseas thinking".

180. De Beer, KJ, *op. cit.*, pp.89 & 90; Walker, EA, *A History of Southern Africa,* Longman, London, 1968, p.569, and *The Round Table,* No. 35, June 1919, pp.620-29 & No. 37, December 1919, pp.186-91. The purpose of the deputation was to seek "independence" for the Union or, if not granted, for the two former Boer republics or, in the final resort, for the Orange Free State only. Among the other members of the delegation were none other than Hertzog and Havenga and Dr EG Jansen, a later (post-1948) Cabinet member and governor-general.

181. See Meiring, P, *Smuts the Patriot,* Tafelberg, Cape Town, 1975, pp.174ff.

182. Egeland, L, *op. cit.*, p.145.

183. See *loc. cit.* and Munger, ES, *Foreign Policy, op. cit.*, p.92.

184. Malan's endeavours to get the high commission territories transferred is in fact the only foreign policy matter that his biographer examined in any detail – Thom, HB, *op. cit.*, pp.226-48. See also De Beer, KJ, *op. cit.*, pp.342-60; Geldenhuys, DJ, *Anglo-South African Relations, op. cit.*, pp.276-90; Geyer, AL, *op. cit.*, pp.123-8 and Hyam, R, *op. cit.*, pp.72ff.

185. Geyer, AL, *op. cit.*, pp.60, 120 & 125, and HA Deb., 13/4/1954, col. 3966.

186. See De Villiers, D & J, *Paul Sauer,* Tafelberg, Cape Town, 1977, p.108.

187. See *ibid.*, p.91 and Schoeman, BJ, *op. cit.*, p.181.

188. See Schoeman, BJ, *op. cit.*, pp.181 & 216; Thom, HB, *op. cit.*, p.218 and De Villiers, D & J, *op. cit.*, p.91.

189. Personal interview with Mr DD Forsyth.

190. A number of former South African diplomats have commented favourably on Forsyth's abilities. See Du Plessis, WC, *op. cit.*, p.100; Egeland, L, *op. cit.*, p.145 and Jooste, GP, *op. cit.*, p.186.

191. See Schoeman, BJ, *op. cit.*, p.158 and Mulder, PWA, *op. cit.*, pp.240-44.

192. For analyses of the Simonstown Agreement, see Dugard, CJR, "The Simonstown Agreement: South Africa, Britain and the United Nations", and Lawrie, GG, "The Simonstown Agreement: South Africa, Britain and the Commonwealth", both in *South African Law Journal,* Vol. 85, May 1968, pp.142-77; and Tunstall, WCB, *The*

Commonwealth and Regional Defence, Athlone Press, London, 1959, p.51.

193. HA Deb., 18/4/1955, col. 4020.
194. See HA Deb., 5/5/1955, col. 5072 & 5073.
195. Strydom gave Louw two of the most important portfolios, Finance (previously held by Havenga) and subsequently also External Affairs. Finding the combination too onerous a burden, Louw in 1956 relinquished Finance.
196. See De Beer, KJ, *op. cit.,* p.165.
197. See Geyser, O, *Dr HF Verwoerd die Republikein: Hoofartikels uit Die Transvaler, 1937-1948,* Tafelberg, Cape Town, 1972, 100pp.
198. See Du Plessis, E, *op. cit.,* pp.4 & 168 and Schoeman, BJ, *op. cit.,* p.294.
199. See Schoeman, BJ, *op. cit.,* pp.246, 253 and 254 and Du Plessis, E, *op. cit.,* p.4. Verwoerd tended to interfere in the workings of two Departments in particular: Bantu Administration and Development (having been Minister of Native Affairs) and Defence (presumably because of his concern with the arms embargo).
200. See Schoeman, BJ, *op. cit.,* p.245 and Jooste, GP, *op. cit.,* p.187.
201. Schoeman, BJ, *op. cit.,* pp.218, 219 & 294.
202. See Scholtz, GD, *Verwoerd, op. cit.,* pp.67-71; Schoeman, BJ, *op. cit.,* pp.256-9 and Jooste, GP, *op. cit.,* pp.188-90.
203. Quoted by Geldenhuys, DJ, *Anglo-South African Relations, op. cit.,* p.334.
204. HA Deb., 20/5/1960, col. 8337 & 8338.
205. Barber, J, *South African Foreign Policy, op. cit.,* pp.133 & 134.
206. Quoted by Kenney, H, *Architect of Apartheid: HF Verwoerd – An Appraisal,* Jonathan Ball Publishers, Johannesburg, 1980, p.260.
207. Du Plessis, E, *op. cit.,* pp.155ff.
208. Quoted by Kenney, H, *op. cit.,* p.255.
209. Personal interview with Mr BJ Schoeman.
210. Cordier, AW and W Foote, *Public Papers of the Secretaries-General of the United Nations,* Vol. 5, *Dag Hammarskjöld 1960-1961,* Columbia University Press, New York, 1975, pp.317-19; Zacher, MW, *Dag Hammarskjöld's United Nations,* Columbia University Press, New York, 1970, pp.106, 107, 130; Munger, ES "South Africa: are there silver linings?", *Foreign Affairs,* Vol. 47, No. 2, January 1969, p.379, and Verwoerd, HA Deb., 23/1/1961, col. 15 & 16.
211. The day after informing the Commonwealth Conference of South Africa's withdrawal, Verwoerd instructed Meiring (Director of the State Information Service) to leave immediately for South Africa to tell Mr Jack Steyl, the National Party's Transvaal secretary, "that he must lay on a big show at the airport when we arrive. There must be no doubt about the outcome of the conference." On arrival Meiring was told by Steyl that it was unnecessary to organise a demonstration: "This is going to be the biggest show Jan Smuts [Airport] has ever seen and it will be entirely spontaneous." (Quoted by Meiring, P, *Information, op. cit.,* p.168.)
212. Quoted by Pelzer, AN, *Verwoerd Speaks: Speeches 1948-1966,* Afrikaanse Pers, Johannesburg, 1966, p.516. See also Schoeman, BJ, *op. cit.,* pp.271-5.
213. HA Deb., 28/3/1961, col. 3845.
214. Olivier, GC, *op. cit.,* p.184.
215. See Hill, CR, "UDI and South African Foreign Policy", *Journal of Commonwealth Political Studies,* Vol. 8, No. 2, July 1969, pp.96-103; Scholtz, GD, *Verwoerd, op. cit.,* pp.254-60; Du Plessis, E, *op. cit.,* pp.110-44 and Rossouw, CJ, *Wapenverkope aan Suid-Afrika: 'n Beslissingsprobleem in Britse Buitelandse Beleid (1963-1973),* MA dissertation, University of Pretoria, 1975, pp.37-56.
216. Quoted by Scholtz, GD, *Verwoerd, op. cit.,* p.258.
217. Quoted *ibid.,* p.294.
218. Republic of South Africa, *Dr HF Verwoerd on: I. Crisis in World Conscience; II. The Road to Freedom for Basutoland, Bechuanaland, Swaziland,* Fact Paper 107, Department of Information, Pretoria, undated, pp.14 & 15.
219. Schoeman, BJ, *op. cit.* p.292.
220. *Ibid.,* p.308.
221. Du Plessis, E, *op. cit.,* p.174.
222. Schoeman, BJ, *op. cit.,* p.308.
223. *Ibid.,* p.272.
224. Mr Robert Menzies, commenting on Verwoerd's behaviour at the 1961 Commonwealth Conference, in Menzies, R, *Afternoon Light: Some Memories of Men and Events,* Penquin, Harmondsworth, 1970, p.212. Macmillan paid Verwoerd a similar compliment in Parliament – United Kingdom, *Parliamentary Debates (Hansard), House of Commons,* 16/3/1961, col. 1752.
225. Quoted by Geldenhuys, DJ, *Anglo-South African Relations, op. cit.,* pp.380 & 382.
226. Quoted by Du Plessis, E, *op. cit.,* p.153.
227. Biermann, HH, *The Case for South Africa as Put Forth in the Public Statements of Eric H Louw, Foreign Minister of South Africa,* Macfadden Books, New York, 1963, pp.82-95.
228. *Ibid.,* p.79.
229. Van Vuuren, DJ, *op. cit.,* p.137.
230. Quoted by Jooste, GP, *op. cit.,* p.157.
231. See *loc. cit.* and Schoeman, BJ, *op. cit.,* p.220.
232. Munger, ES, *Foreign Policy, op. cit.,* pp.30 & 31. PO Sauer, one of Louw's Cabinet colleagues (and a man renowned for his wit) was once asked about Louw's attributes by a Dutch journalist. Said Sauer: "Look, Eric Louw is an exceptional person. It is he who laid the foundations for our foreign diplomatic service. He is a tireless worker and redoubtable fighter. He has already given great service to the National Party and the Government, as a member of the Opposition, as diplomat and as minister. He is often reviled, and under the

sharpest attacks he is at his most brilliant. A real pillar in the most difficult circumstances. And he is a little shit." (Quoted by De Villiers, D & J, *op. cit.*, p.114.)

233. Schoeman, BJ, *op. cit.*, p.294.
234. See Egeland, L, *op. cit.*, p.144 & 145, and Jooste, GP, *op. cit.*, p.186.
235. See Jooste, GP, *op. cit.*, p.187.
236. Meiring, P, *Information, op. cit.*, p.137.
237. Quoted by Spence, JE, *Republic under Pressure: A Study of South African Foreign Policy,* Oxford University Press, London, 1965, pp.40 & 41.
238. Munger, ES, *Foreign Policy, op. cit.*, p.48.
239. *Ibid.*, pp.34-69.
240. *Ibid.*, p.38.
241. See, for example, the deliberately provocative article by "a prominent Afrikaner" (presumably the paper's own editor, Cillié) in *Die Burger (Byvoegsel)*, 20/7/1957, on the question of diplomatic ties between South Africa and black states. The caption read: "Black states – bring it to a head: Don't let us whisper, but talk it through".
242. See Jooste, GP, *op. cit.*, p.134.
243. By the time the Press Commission submitted its extremely detailed report it was already badly dated, for it dealt with the years 1950-55. The Commission found that only four countries received substantial quantities of general and political news from South Africa, namely the United Kingdom, United States, India and Australia, in that order. As for the British press's reporting on "politics and race" in South Africa, the Commission judged 46,70% as "very bad", 29,25% as "bad", 14,63% as "faulty" and only 9,42% as "good". South Africa, *Report of the Commission of Inquiry into the Press,* Government Printer, 1964, Annexure XX, pp.479 & 1175.
244. Munger, ES, *Foreign Policy, op. cit.*, p.54.
245. See Gerber, L, *Friends and Influence: The Diplomacy of Private Enterprise,* Purnell, Cape Town, 1973, pp.6ff.
246. Munger, ES, *Foreign Policy, op. cit.*, p.86.
247. Wilkins, I & H Strydom, *op. cit.*, pp.58-72, 83 & 119. See also Du Plessis, WC, *op. cit.*, pp.104-11: in a celebrated incident, Du Plessis resigned from his senior post in the foreign ministry rather than end his *Broederbond* membership – a choice he had to make under Smuts's ultimatum.
248. Pelzer, AN, *Die Afrikaner-Broederbond: Eerste 50 Jaar,* Tafelberg, Cape Town, 1979, pp.169 & 170.
249. Quoted by Serfontein, JHP, *Brotherhood of Power: An Exposé of the secret Afrikaner Broederbond,* Rex Collings, London, 1979, p.85.
250. Quoted by Wilkins, I & H Strydom, *op. cit.*, p.136.
251. Pelzer, AN, *Broederbond, op. cit.*, pp.91-3.
252. Wilkins, I & H Strydom, *op. cit.*, pp.401-7.
253. Pelzer, AN, *Broederbond, op. cit.*, p.171.
254. Serfontein, JHP, *op. cit.*, p.150.
255. *Ibid.*, p.151. See also Wilkins, I & H Strydom, *op. cit.*, p.370.

256. Pelzer, AN, *Broederbond, op. cit.*, pp.167 & 168.
257. Quoted by Wilkins, I & H Strydom, *op. cit.*, p.4.
258. Pelzer, AN, *Broederbond, op. cit.*, p.33. A breakdown by profession of the *Broederbond's* membership in 1968 revealed that of the 8 191 members, 1 806 (22,1%) were farmers, making it the single largest group. Thereafter followed the teaching profession (20,6%), commerce (10,2%) and the church (8,2%). No fewer than 210 members (2,6%) fell in the category "Politics", while 419 were employed in the civil service and 154 in the police. An interesting feature is that the average age of Broederbond members varied between 48,4 and 50,3 years between 1955 and 1966 *(ibid.,* pp.33-5).

CHAPTER 2

1. Quoted by D'Oliveira, J, *Vorster – Die Mens,* Perskor, Johannesburg, 1977, p.113.
2. *Ibid.,* pp.69-162 and Botha, MC, *Premiersverkiesings Sedert 1910,* Perskor, Johannesburg, 1979, pp.139-45.
3. Quoted by Barber, J, *South Africa's Foreign Policy, op. cit.,* p.213.
4. Scholtz, JJJ, "Die Republiek van Suid-Afrika, 1961-1967", in Van der Walt, AJH, *et al., Geskiedenis van Suid-Afrika,* Nasou, Cape Town, 1978, pp.609 & 610.
5. See Heard, KA, *General Elections in South Africa: 1943-1970,* Oxford University Press, London, 1974, pp.180-88 and Serfontein, JHP, *Die Verkrampte Aanslag,* Human & Rousseau, Cape Town, 1970, pp.118-218.
6. Heard, KA, *op. cit.*, pp.207 & 208.
7. Scholtz, JJJ, *op. cit.*, pp.616 & 617.
8. Heard, KA, *op. cit.*, p.189.
9. *Loc. cit.*
10. Scholtz, JJJ, *op. cit.*, p.615.
11. Theron, E, & JB du Toit, *Kortbegrip van die Theron-verslag,* Tafelberg, Cape Town, 1977, pp.85ff.
12. Scholtz, JJJ, *op. cit.*, p.627.
13. Republic of South Africa, *South Africa 1980-1981,* Official Yearbook of the Republic of South Africa, Chris van Rensburg Publications, Johannesburg, 1980, pp.183 & 184.
14. South Africa Foundation, *1978 Information Digest,* SA Foundation, Johannesburg, 1978, p.51.
15. Gordon, L (Ed), *A Survey of Race Relations in South Africa 1977,* South African Institute of Race Relations (hereafter abbreviated SAIRR), Johannesburg, 1978, pp.3, 4, 10, 21 & 22.
16. Ries, A & E Dommisse, *Broedertwis: Die Verhaal van die 1982-Skeuring in die Nasionale Party,* Tafelberg, Cape Town, 1982, pp.8-24.
17. *Survey of Race Relations 1977, op. cit.*, p.3.
18. The conferences were named after their venues: the Carlton Hotel in Johannesburg and Good Hope Centre in Cape Town. The Prime Minister, Cabinet members, top officials and leading

258

businessmen attended the gatherings, at which PW Botha delivered the key-note address. See *Address by the Honourable PW Botha, Prime Minister, Carlton Centre, Johannesburg: 22 November 1979*, Roneoed, Department of Foreign Affairs.

19. Duff, T, "Recent political developments", *South Africa International*, South Africa Foundation, Vol. 11, No. 3, January 1981, p.144.

20. See South Africa Foundation, *1980 Information Digest*, SA Foundation, Johannesburg, p.4.

21. Herbst, DAS, "Election 1981: In Facts and Figures", *Position Paper*, Southern Africa Forum, Vol. 4, No. 12, June 1981.

22. Ries, A & E Dommisse, *op. cit.*, pp.75ff.

23. See Geldenhuys, DJ, *Some Foreign Policy Implications of South Africa's Total National Strategy, with Particular Reference to the 12-Point Plan*, SAIIA, Johannesburg, 1981, 63pp.

24. See Vorster, BJ, "South Africa's Outward Policy", one of a series of lectures delivered at the Annual General Meeting of the *Suid-Afrikaanse Akademie vir Wetenskap en Kuns* in July 1969 in Pretoria, published as *South Africa in the World*, Tafelberg, Cape Town, 1970, pp.94-104.

25. See Cockram, G-M, *Vorster's Foreign Policy*, Academica, Pretoria, 1970, pp.116ff.

26. Tötemeyer, GKH, *Namibia Old and New: Traditional and Modern Leaders in Ovamboland*, Hurst, London, 1978, p.194.

27. See Strack, HR, *Sanctions: The Case of Rhodesia*, Syracuse University Press, 1978, pp.85-189.

28. Nolutshungu, SC, *South Africa in Africa: A Study in Ideology and Foreign Policy*, Manchester University Press, Manchester, 1975, pp.181 & 182.

29. *Ibid.*, pp.173 & 263.

30. HA Deb., 15/9/1970, col. 4208.

31. Vorster, *ibid.*, col. 4207.

32. Barratt, CJA, *Dialogue in Africa*, SAIIA, Johannesburg, 1971, 23pp.

33. HA Deb., 4/2/1974, col. 59 & 60.

34. Quoted by Geldenhuys, DJ, & TD Venter, "Regional co-operation in Southern Africa: A Constellation of States?", *International Affairs Bulletin*, Vol. 3, No. 3, December 1979, p.49.

35. Legum, C, *Vorster's Gamble for Africa – How the Search for Peace Failed*, Rex Collings, London, 1976, pp.13 & 14.

36. *Ibid.*, pp.23-5.

37. Scholtz, JJJ, *op. cit.*, p.622.

38. See Vorster, HA Deb., 30/1/1976, col. 375.

39. See *Survey of Race Relations 1977, op. cit.*, pp.572-5.

40. See the parliamentary debate on the Vorster-Mondale meeting, HA Deb., 13/6/1977, col. 9968ff.

41. Gordon, L (Ed), *Survey of Race Relations in South Africa 1980*, SAIRR, Johannesburg, 1981, pp.635-8.

42. Gordon, L (Ed), *Survey of Race Relations in South Africa 1979*, SAIRR, Johannesburg, 1980, pp.604-7.

43. See Geldenhuys, DJ, *Total National Strategy, op. cit.*, pp.18-22.

44. Quoted by Geldenhuys, DJ, & TD Venter, *op. cit.*, pp.54 & 55.

45. *Ibid.*, p.56 and *Rand Daily Mail*, 23/11/1979.

46. *Die Vaderland*, 20/4/1979 and *Die Transvaler*, 13/6/1979.

47. *Survey of Race Relations 1980, op. cit.*, pp.656-64.

48. Geldenhuys, DJ, *The Constellation of Southern African States and the Southern African Development Coordination Council: Towards a New Regional Stalemate?* SAIIA, Johannesburg, 1981, pp.10-31.

49. Spence, JE, *The Strategic Significance of Southern Africa*, Royal United Service Institution, London, 1970, pp.27 & 28.

50. On the two prime ministers' conduct of personal diplomacy, see Chapter 3.

CHAPTER 3

1. *Die Transvaler*, 31/1/1975 and *Beeld*, 23/8/1978.

2. *Senate Debates*, 6/6/1967, col. 3746-60 and 7/6/1976, col. 3830-37.

3. *Ibid.*, 17 & 18/5/1976, col. 2314-431.

4. *Ibid.*, 20/3/1969, col. 1053-66. Muller made a statement in regard to UN criticism of South Africa's administration of Namibia, choosing the upper house as forum. No debate followed the statement.

5. *Ibid.*, 14/3/1967, col. 1990-96. The occasion was the second reading of the Foreign Affairs Special Account Bill.

6. *Ibid.*, 21/2/1979, col. 133-44.

7. *Ibid.*, 20/4/1978, col. 1504-6, 1510 & 1511 (second reading of the Diplomatic Privileges Amendment Bill); 12/6/1979, col. 2411-16 & 2422-8 (second reading of the State Trust Board Bill) and 21/5/1980, col. 1800-1805 (second reading of the State Trust Board Amendment Bill).

8. In 1978 special sessions of both the House of Assembly and the Senate were convened to discuss the *Report of the Commission of Inquiry into Alleged Irregularities in the Former Department of Information*, RP 113/1978, Government Printer, Pretoria. (This was the first of three reports submitted by the commission chaired by Mr Justice RPB Erasmus. This report is hereafter referred to as Erasmus Report 1, *op. cit.*) See *Senate Debates*, 7/12/1978, col. 1-7 and 8/12/1978, col. 7-104.

9. HA Deb., 17/5/1976, col. 2316 & 2318.

10. *Ibid.*, 21/2/1979, col. 144.

11. *Ibid.*, 20/4/1978, col. 1509.

12. Olivier, GC, *Die Grondslae van Suid-Afrika se Buitelandse Beleid*, D. Phil. dissertation, University of Pretoria, 1973, p.73. This study was subsequently published in revised form as *Suid-Afrika se Buitelandse Beleid, op. cit.* In this book all other references to Olivier relate to his book, not the dissertation.

13. Frankel, J, *The Making of Foreign Policy: An*

Analysis of Decision-Making, Oxford University Press, London, 1967, p.25.

14. Richards, PG, *Parliament and Foreign Affairs,* George Allen & Unwin, London, 1967, pp.13 & 48-63.

15. *Ibid.,* pp.13 & 14.

16. *Ibid.,* p.164.

17. HA Deb., 1/9/1970, col. 3113.

18. *Ibid.,* 6/2/1974, col. 225.

19. See *ibid.,* 29/5/1968, col. 6265.

20. JD du P Basson, *ibid.,* 6/2/1974, col. 229.

21. *Ibid.,* 6/2/1974, col. 227.

22. *Ibid.,* 6/2/1974, col. 220; 30/5/1968, col. 6319 and 1/9/1970, col. 3122.

23. See *ibid.,* 6/2/1974, col. 213 & 222.

24. H Muller, *ibid.,* 1/9/1970, col. 3121 & 3122.

25. *Ibid.,* 6/2/1974, col. 224.

26. *Ibid.,* 1/9/1970, col. 3123.

27. H Muller, *ibid.,* 30/5/1968, col. 6319 and 1/9/1970, col. 3116 & 3121.

28. *Ibid.,* 11/9/1974, col. 2642.

29. *Ibid.,* 1/9/1970, col. 3113.

30. *Ibid.,* 1/9/1970, col. 3124.

31. *Ibid.,* 11/9/1974, col. 2632 & 2633. See also 1/9/1970, col. 3116; 6/2/1974, col. 212-20; 11/9/1974, col. 2629 & 2632 and 26/4/1976, col. 5426.

32. JD du P Basson, *ibid.,* 1/9/1970, col. 3131 & 3132.

33. HH Schwarz, *ibid,.* 11/9/1974, col. 2624 and *ibid.,* 6/2/1974, col. 212.

34. *Ibid.,* 1/9/1970, col. 3120 & 3121; 6/2/1974, col. 216-18; 11/9/1974, col. 2630, 2631 & 2635-9 and 26/4/1976, col. 5426 & 5427.

35. *Ibid.,* 6/2/1974, col. 212 & 213.

36. *Ibid.,* 11/9/1974, col. 2639 & 2640.

37. *Ibid.,* 1/9/1970, col. 3114 & 3115. See also 26/4/1976, col. 5416.

38. *Ibid.,* 1/9/1970, col. 3132.

39. *Ibid.,* 30/5/1968, col. 6321.

40. *Ibid.,* 1/9/1970, col. 3107.

41. *Ibid.,* 29/5/1968, col. 6269 & 6270.

42. *Ibid.,* 30/5/1968, col. 6321.

43. *Ibid.,* 29/5/1968, col. 6272 & 6273.

44. *Ibid.,* 30/5/1968, col. 6323.

45. Schoeman, BJ, *op. cit.,* p.292.

46. See HA Deb., 29/5/1968, col. 6271; 30/5/1968, col. 6318 and 1/9/1970, col. 3113, 3116 & 3130.

47. JD du P Basson, *ibid.,* 1/9/1970, col. 3113.

48. *Ibid.,* 17/4/1975, col. 4306; 25/4/1975, col. 4840 and 16/6/1975, col. 8424. For the United Party's attitude towards Rhodesia in the aftermath of UDI, see Cockram, G-M, *op. cit.,* pp.178-86 and Vandenbosch, A, *South Africa and the World: The Foreign Policy of Apartheid,* University Press of Kentucky, 1970, pp.149-51.

49. HA Deb, 1/9/1970, col. 3116.

50. *Ibid.,* 11/9/1974, col. 2652 & 2662.

51. *Ibid.,* 11/9/1974, col. 2637.

52. *Loc. cit.*

53. *Ibid.,* 30/1/1976, col. 366 & 367.

54. *Ibid.,* 27/1/1976, col. 104. See also CW Eglin, *ibid.,* 26/4/1976, col. 5392 & 5393. For Graaff's contribution to the January 1976 Angola debate, which was part of the no-confidence vote, see *ibid.,* 26/1/1976, col. 24ff.

55. See *ibid.,* 29/5/1968, col. 6272.

56. See *ibid.,* 13/6/1977, col. 9963 & 9964.

57. *Ibid.,* 13/6/1977, col. 9965 & 9966.

58. *Ibid.,* 13/6/1977, col. 9968 & 9969.

59. *Ibid.,* 13/6/1977, col. 10000, 10005 & 10006.

60. *Rand Daily Mail,* 11/11/1976.

61. HA Deb., 3/4/1979, col. 3911-14 & 3965.

62. *Ibid.,* 3/4/1979, col. 3912-19.

63. *Ibid.,* 19/4/1979, col. 4472-80.

64. *Ibid.,* 3/4/1979, col. 3912 & 3913 and 19/4/1979, col. 4483 & 4484.

65. *Ibid.,* 3/4/1979, col. 3918.

66. Hugh Leggatt in *The Star,* 17/4/1979. See also *The Citizen,* 11/4/1979; *Die Transvaler,* 12/4/1979; *Die Vaderland* 21/4/1979 and *Weekend Argus,* 21/4/79.

67. HA Deb., 29/1/1981, col. 312-17.

68. *Beeld,* 2/9/1981.

69. HA Deb., 7/8/1981, col. 449-52.

70. *Beeld,* 13/8/1981.

71. HA Deb., 4/4/1979, col. 3962 & 3963.

72. *Ibid.,* 5/6/1979, col. 7806; 4/4/1979, col. 3962 and 5/6/1979, col. 7806. See also *ibid.,* 19/5/1980, col. 6578. In the no-confidence motion in the House of Assembly in January 1981 IFA de Villiers (PFP) questioned some of the conventional establishment views about the role of the UN in a Namibian settlement and about SWAPO's nature and objectives. It was, however, done with great circumspection and his views were anything but radical (*ibid.,* 27/1/1981, col. 199-208). The Foreign Minister, nonetheless, took strong exception to De Villiers's speech and *inter alia* charged him with playing politics on the Namibian issue and, moreover, displaying a "spirit of abdication" with regard to the territory (*ibid.,* 29/1/1981, col. 304 & 305).

73. IFA de Villiers, *ibid.,* 19/5/1980, col. 6666 and *ibid.,* 20/5/1980, col. 6725.

74. *Ibid.,* 5/6/1979, col. 7859.

75. For example, Mr DJ Dalling, PFP MP, declared that he "did not believe that there was a total onslaught against South Africa" (*ibid.,* 28/1/1981, col. 226).

76. *Ibid.,* 19/4/1979, col. 4470 & 4471.

77. *Ibid.,* 19/5/1980, col. 6588. See also *ibid.,* 19/5/1980, col. 6586; 5/6/1979, col. 7825, 7826 & 7850, and 6/6/1979, col. 7898.

78. *Ibid.,* 19/5/1980, col. 6589 and 20/5/1980, col. 6718.

79. *Ibid.,* 5/6/1979, col. 7823 & 7851.

80. See *ibid.,* 5/6/1979, col. 7821-4.

81. See New Republic Party, *1st Anniversary 1978,* Commemoration publication, 13pp.

82. See *Address by the Honourable PW Botha, Prime Minister, Minister of Defence and of the National Intelligence Service at the opening ceremony of the*

summit meeting in Pretoria on 23 July 1980, Roneoed, Department of Foreign Affairs and Information, p.7.

83. See HA Deb., 27/1/1981, col. 198.

84. For a seminal quantitative analysis of the political beliefs of South African MPs, including questions of inter-party trust and hostility, see Kotzé, HJ, *Konsensus en Klowings in die Politieke Oortuigings van Suid-Afrikaanse Volksraadslede*, D. Phil. dissertation, Rand Afrikaans University, 1981, pp.99ff.

85. HA Deb., 9/2/1979, col. 460 and 28/2/1979, col. 1499.

86. *The Citizen*, 2/3/1979.

87. Conducted by the author in 1980 and 1981.

88. In personal interviews conducted by the author in 1980 and 1981.

89. HA Deb., 26/1/1976, col. 25.

90. HA Deb., 27/1/1976, col. 100ff.

91. JD du P Basson, *ibid.*, 27/1/1976, col. 120 & 121.

92. HEJ van Rensburg, *ibid.*, 29/1/1976, col. 296.

93. *Ibid.*, 30/1/1976, col. 366-74.

94. *Ibid.*, 26/1/1976, col. 53.

95. *Ibid.*, 6/6/1979, col. 7876 & 7894.

96. See Nolutshungu, SC, *op. cit.*, pp.181 & 182, and Schoeman BJ, *op. cit.*, pp.337 & 338. In August 1975, as part of South Africa's *détente* initiative, its policemen were withdrawn from Rhodesia.

97. De Villiers, LES, *Secret Information*, Tafelberg, Cape Town, 1980, pp.58 & 151. See also HA Deb., 7/12/1978, col. 52 and 8/12/1978, col. 290.

98. HA Deb., 4/5/1976, col. 5955 & 5956.

99. De Villiers, LES, *op. cit.*, p.58.

100. CW Eglin, HA Deb., 7/12/1978, col. 66. See also col. 54 and 83.

101. *Ibid.*, 7/12/1978, col. 8.

102. *Ibid.*, 7/12/1978, col. 12, 39, 40 & 81.

103. See *ibid.*, 7/12/1978, col. 8 & 75-9; 8/12/1978, col. 237, 238 & 519.

104. Olivier, GC, *op. cit.*, pp.181, 182 & 202.

105. The Foreign Minister replied in writing, in September 1981, to a questionnaire submitted by the author. The extracts appearing in the text have been translated from Afrikaans.

106. The analysis of the roles of the National Party caucus and foreign affairs study group is based on wide-ranging personal interviews with present and former Cabinet members and MPs conducted in 1980 and 1981.

107. Consider Pik Botha's address in the UN Security Council in October 1974, in which he expressed the South African government's commitment to move away from racial discrimination, and his maiden speech in Parliament in 1970, in which he argued in favour of South Africa's identifying itself "to a greater extent" with the Universal Declaration of Human Rights of 1948 (HA Deb., 20/8/1970, col. 2164-6). South Africa has never signed the Declaration.

108. See Rees, M and C Day, *Muldergate: The Story of the Info Scandal*, Macmillan, Johannesburg, 1980, pp.75 & 76.

109. Information by courtesy of Christopher Hill.

110. Richards, PG, *op. cit.*, pp. 48-63.

111. *Die Transvaler*, 22/5/1980.

112. See HA Deb., 6/6/1979, col. 7911-14 (Worrall); 19/5/1980, col. 6606-9 (Marais); 19/5/1980, col. 6603-6 (Durr); and 19/5/1980 col. 6619-23 (Malan).

113. See F. Herman, *ibid.*, 5/6/1979, col. 7813-7; WD Kotzé, *ibid.*, 5/6/1979, col. 7817-20 and GPD Terblanche, *ibid.*, 5/6/1979, col. 7829-32. Consider Herman's statement, *ibid.*, 19/5/1980, col. 6582: "I think the cry of human rights has become a force in the world – what country gives more recognition to human rights and complies to a greater extent with the requirements of human rights than South Africa does?"

114. See HA Deb., 27/1/1977, col. 327-32; 1/2/1978, col. 203 & 204; 5/6/1978, col. 8479-82 and 19/5/1980, col. 6624-7.

CHAPTER 4

1. D'Oliveira, J, *op. cit.*, pp.102-14.

2. See, for example, *Uittreksel uit die 1977-Nuwejaarsboodskap van die Suid-Afrikaanse Minister van Verdediging, Sy Edele PW Botha*, in *Southern Africa Record* (SAIIA), No 9, July 1977, pp.4 & 5; and PW Botha in HA Deb., 6/2/1975, col. 297 and 18/2/1972, col. 1389ff.

3. See Olivier, GC, *op. cit.*, p.184.

4. See D'Oliveira, J *op. cit.*, pp.200ff; Serfontein, JHP, *Die Verkrampte Aanslag, op. cit.*, 197pp; Schoeman, BM, *Vorster se 100 Dae*, Human & Rousseau, Cape Town, 1974, pp.18-32 and 268-80; and Ries, A & E Dommisse, *op. cit.*, pp.75ff. In a personal interview with the present author Vorster singled out the inclusion of Maoris in an All Black rugby team due to visit South Africa and the establishment of diplomatic ties with Malawi as the two main issues featuring in the breakaway of four rightwing Nationalist MPs in 1969. He also referred to the "absurdity" of these disaffected elements saying that the South African government should talk to black African leaders "but you should do it under a tree".

5. On 20 September 1978 Vorster held a major press conference to outline the government's position on the Namibian issue. This was, however, not the only matter to feature: Vorster on this occasion also announced his retirement as prime minister. As for PW Botha, it might be that apart from convention he has another reason for not holding frequent open press conferences: his well-known quick temper and brusque manner are not the ideal qualities for handling the rough-and-tumble of a high visibility news conference.

6. Vorster confirmed that Verwoerd did not dine with Jonathan after seeing the black leader in 1966, and sent other people instead. When Vorster joined Jonathan for a meal the following year, some

261

people "raised eyebrows", he recalled (personal interview with Mr BJ Vorster).

7. D'Oliveira, J, *op. cit.*, pp.197ff., and Cockram, G-M, *op. cit.*, pp.116ff.

8. See Geldenhuys, DJ and TD Venter, *op. cit.*, pp.45-50.

9. Vorster focused on Malawi, he said, because close ties had long existed between churches in the two countries, many Malawians were employed on South African mines, and President Hastings Banda was a "realist" – a reference to Banda's staunch pro-Western attitude and his willingness to co-operate with South Africa (personal interview with Mr BJ Vorster).

10. See *Die Burger,* 15/8/1975, and *The Star,* 21/8/1975.

11. An expression used by Munger, ES, *Foreign Policy, op. cit.,* p.86.

12. See Vital, D, *The Making of British Foreign Policy,* George Allen & Unwin, London, 1968, p.54.

13. Barber, J, *Who Makes British Foreign Policy?,* Open University Press, Milton Keynes, 1976, p.13.

14. See PW Botha, HA Deb., 8/12/1978, col. 518; *Die Aanvullende Verslag van die Kommissie van Ondersoek na Beweerde Onreëlmatighede in die Voormalige Departement van Inligting,* May 1979, par. 3.66. (Published as a special supplement to *Die Transvaler/Oggendblad,* 5/6/1979.) This was the final of the three reports of the Erasmus Commission and will hereafter be referred to as Erasmus Report 3, *op. cit.*

15. Botha, MC, *op. cit.,* pp.153-5.

16. In August 1975 Vorster received the Toastmasters International communication and leadership award "for the qualities of communication and leadership which he has demonstrated in his dedicated pursuit of the ideal of *détente*" (*The Star,* 14/8/1975).

17. Hallett, R, "The South African intervention in Angola 1975-76", *African Affairs,* Vol. 77, No. 303, July 1978, pp.356 & 357.

18. See HA Deb., 26/1/1976, col. 46-8.

19. South Africa, Defence Headquarters, *Nature and Extent of the SADF's Involvement in the Angolan Conflict,* Press Release, Roneoed, Pretoria, 3 February 1977, p.1.

20. Hallett, R, *op. cit.,* p.357.

21. Defence Headquarters Press Release, *op. cit.,* p.2.

22. Hallett, R, *op. cit.,* p.363.

23. Defence Headquarters Press Release, *op. cit.,* pp.2 & 3.

24. *Ibid.,* pp.3-7.

25. *Ibid.,* p.8.

26. Hallett, R, *op. cit.,* p.361.

27. See *ibid.,* p.370 and Defence Headquarters Press Release, *op. cit.,* p.8.

28. Hallett, R, *op. cit.,* pp.370 & 371, and De Villiers, LES, *op. cit.,* p.146.

29. Defence Headquarters Press Release, *op. cit.,* p.8.

30. See *ibid.,* pp.8-10.

31. Hallett, R, *op. cit.,* p.371.

32. *Ibid.,* p.380.

33. See *loc. cit.*

34. See *ibid.,* p.371.

35. *Ibid.,* p.372.

36. Defence Headquarters Press Release, *op. cit.,* p.10.

37. Hallett, R, *op. cit.,* p.382.

38. *Ibid.,* p.384.

39. HA Deb., 30/1/1976, col. 366.

40. Through the Alvor Agreement, signed in the Algarve on 15 January 1975, Portugal hoped that a government of national unity would be formed in Angola. Such hopes had however been in vain. Another attempt was made through the Nakuru Agreement of 15 June, but this too proved abortive in the face of the power struggle between the MPLA, FNLA and UNITA (Legum, C & T Hodges, *After Angola: The War over Southern Africa,* Rex Collings, London, 1976, p.13).

41. Quoted by Van Rensburg, APJ, *The Tangled Web: Leadership and Change in Southern Africa,* HAUM, Cape Town, 1977, p.29.

42. For details of the poll, see the section on public opinion in Chapter 6.

43. HA Deb., 30/1/1976, col. 368 & 369.

44. Quoted by Hallett, R, *op. cit.,* p.382.

45. See Hallett, R, *op. cit.,* pp.380-83.

46. See HA Deb., 27/1/1976, col. 110-32. Vorster, *ibid.,* 30/1/1976, col. 365-9, listed some key objectives: "to chase the MPLA and the Cubans away from the borders for which we are responsible"; to prevent the MPLA, with Russian and Cuban help, subjugating the entire Angolan population; to prevent Angola becoming "a base for attacks on South West Africa", and "to bring to the notice of the free world and of Africa the fact that an unwilling people was being driven into the communist fold at the point of a bayonet." (The last consideration already seems to cast doubt on the second one.)

47. HA Deb., 30/1/1976, col. 375.

48. *Ibid.,* col. 359 & 366.

49. Dr RA Schrire, quoted by Hallett, R, *op. cit.,* p.366.

50. Steenkamp, W, *Borderstrike! South Africa into Angola,* Butterworth, Durban, 1983, pp.5-11.

51. *Ibid.,* from the Foreword.

52. Winter, G, *Inside BOSS: South Africa's Secret Police,* Penguin, Middlesex, 1981, pp.545-53.

53. See Nolutshungu, SC, *op. cit.,* pp.264-6.

54. Personal interview with Dr EM Rhoodie (hereafter referred to as Rhoodie interview) and confidential communication.

55. De Villiers, LES, *op. cit..,* 182pp., and Rees, M and C Day, *op. cit.,* 222pp. A forthcoming book is Rhoodie's *The Real Information Scandal,* Orbis Publishers, Pretoria and Atlanta, 1983.

56. De Villiers, LES, *op. cit.,* pp.13-17 & 38, and Rees, M and C Day, *op. cit.,* p.22.

57. Personal interview with Dr CP Mulder (hereafter

referred to as Mulder interview).

58. *Ibid.*
59. De Villiers, LES, *op. cit.,* pp.44-6 and Mulder interview. See also Erasmus Report 3, *op. cit.,* par. 14.13.
60. Rees, M and C Day, *op. cit.,* p.167.
61. De Villiers, LES, *op. cit.,* pp.46 & 47. On the two Rhoodie brothers finding themselves in the top jobs, see Erasmus Report 3, *op. cit.,* par. 14.13 and 14.14.
62. Rhoodie interview.
63. Mulder and Rhoodie interviews.
64. Mulder interview.
65. Rhoodie interview.
66. See HA Deb., 10/5/1978, col. 6555, on the prime minister's admission that it was decided in 1972 to canalise funds to the Department of Information through other departments.
67. Quoted by De Villiers, LES, *op. cit.,* p.62, and Rhoodie interview. See also Erasmus Report 3, *op. cit.,* par. 3.21.
68. Consider the following statement attributed to Rhoodie by Les de Villiers, who was also present: "Mr Prime Minister, when I say that this should be a campaign where no rules apply, I mean every word of it. If it is necessary, for instance, for me to give an important person's wife a fur coat, I should be able to do so. And if it is necessary to send a man on holiday to Hawaii with his mistress, I should be allowed to." (Quoted by De Villiers, LES, *op. cit.,* p.74.)
69. See Republic of South Africa, *Tussentydse Verslag van die Kommissie van Ondersoek na Beweerde Onreëlmatighede in die Voormalige Departement van Inligting,* Government Printer, Pretoria, 1979, par. 10-23. This was the second of the three Erasmus Commission reports and will hereafter be referred to as Erasmus Report 2, *op. cit.*
70. Mulder interview.
71. Erasmus Report 2, *op. cit.,* par. 15-23.
72. Republic of South Africa, *Evidence and Exhibits of the Commission of Inquiry into Alleged Irregularities in the Former Department of Information,* Vol. 14, Issued by the Office of the Prime Minister, undated, pp.4814 & 4815.
73. Mulder interview. See also Rees, M and C Day, *op. cit.,* pp.22,23 & 175.
74. De Villiers, LES, *op. cit.,* pp.153-6.
75. Mulder interview.
76. See Rees, M and C Day, *op. cit.,* p.27.
77. De Villiers, LES, *op. cit.,* p.148, and Erasmus Report 1, *op. cit.,* par. 2.13. Although a minimum of R15 million a year was initially promised, it was on two occasions below that; on another it was under the R20 million Information had asked, and on a fourth occasion the requested amount of R23,9 million was reduced to R15 million. This, Finance Minister Horwood explained, he had deliberately done. Not only did he refuse to commit himself (which Diederichs, on the contrary, had done) to providing R15 million per annum, he also insisted that the Treasury be given details of the expenditure by Information. These were not forthcoming, he said (HA Deb., 7/12/1978, col. 109).

78. Rhoodie interview.
79. Rhoodie interview. See also De Villiers, LES, *op. cit.,* p.148, and Rees, M and C Day, *op. cit.,* 222pp.
80. Erasmus Report 3, *op. cit.,* par. 3.26-33 & 3.69.
81. *Ibid.,* par. 3.29 and HA Deb., 7/12/1978, col. 15 & 16. See also De Villiers, LES, *op. cit.,* p.149.
82. Erasmus Report 3, *op. cit.,* par. 3.29.
83. HA Deb., 16/3/1978, col. 3138ff. and 7/12/1978, col. 16, 94, 95, 103 & 104.
84. Erasmus Report 3, *op. cit.,* par. 3.31.
85. *Ibid.,* par. 4.15.
86. See HA Deb., 7/12/1978, col. 94-112.
87. See note 73 above.
88. Erasmus Report 3, *op. cit.,* par. 3.33. For Horwood's explanation of his involvement, see HA Deb., 7/12/1978, col. 100-112.
89. See Rees, M and C Day, *op. cit.,* pp.169-78.
90. Mulder interview.
91. Rhoodie interview.
92. Quoted by Rees, M and C Day, *op. cit.,* p.133.
93. HA Deb., 7/12/1978, col. 87.
94. *Ibid.,* 7/12/1978, col. 24.
95. *Ibid.,* 7/12/1978, col. 122.
96. Erasmus Report 3, *op. cit.,* par 3.60, 3.65 and 3.69.
97. *Ibid.,* par. 4.15. See also PW Botha, HA Deb., 8/12/1978, col. 518.
98. Personal interview with Mr BJ Vorster.
99. See Rees, M and C Day, *op. cit.,* pp.121 & 214.
100. Erasmus Report 3, *op. cit.,* par. 4.8.
101. See Geldenhuys, DJ and TD Venter, *op. cit.,* pp.49ff.
102. See Frankel, P, "Race and counter-revolution: South Africa's 'total strategy' ", *Journal of Commonwealth and Comparative Politics,* Vol. 28, No. 3, October 1980, pp.272-92, and Geldenhuys, DJ, *Total National Strategy, op. cit.,* 63pp.
103. See Republic of South Africa, *White Paper on Defence and Armament Production, 1973,* laid before Parliament by the Minister of Defence, p.1.
104. A public opinion poll conducted among whites on the eve of the election of Vorster's successor in September 1978 found that 83,9% favoured Pik Botha (*Rand Daily Mail,* 29/9/1978). Just over six months later, whites were asked in a similar poll who they would trust to lead South Africa. Of the five politicians listed, Pik Botha received a 65% endorsement, followed by PW Botha with only 19,4% (*Sunday Times,* 8/4/1979).
105. This refers specifically to his reluctance to follow up the Department of Information's contacts in Francophone Africa with personal visits. The same later happened with regard to Israel. In the end Vorster was persuaded to go. (See Chapter 5.)
106. See Giliomee, H, *The Parting of the Ways: South African Politics 1976-82,* David Philip Publishers, Cape Town, 1983, pp.14ff.

107. Schoeman, BJ, *op. cit.*, pp.312 & 313, recalls a revealing incident in early 1966, when Verwoerd discussed a forthcoming Cabinet reshuffle with Schoeman. Verwoerd wanted to give Schoeman the Defence portfolio in addition to Transport, which he had already held for some years. Schoeman, however, suggested that PW Botha, then one of the deputy ministers, be made Minister of Defence. Verwoerd's immediate reaction was: "But does he not also have the party organiser's mentality like [FC] Erasmus? Erasmus always remained the party organiser and you know in what problems we landed from time to time, particularly because of his ill-considered handling of personnel." Schoeman assured Verwoerd that PW Botha was of a different calibre and would prove a success. Verwoerd subsequently appointed PW Botha as Minister of Defence.

108. See *Beeld*, 4/10/1978, and *The Star*, 31/10/1978.

109. Quoted by Geldenhuys, DJ, *Total National Strategy, op. cit.*, p.37.

110. *Ibid.*, p.10.

111. Du Plessis, JE, "Die Veranderende Rol van die Kantoor van die Eerste Minister", Paper presented at a meeting at the University of Port Elizabeth, 8/5/1980, Roneoed, by courtesy of Dr du Plessis, pp.3 & 4. A condensed version was subsequently published under the title, "Kantoor van die Premier: so verander sy rol", *UPE FOKUS*, June 1980, pp.6 & 29. (Du Plessis was Director-General of the Office of the Prime Minister.) See also PW Botha, HA Deb., 6/2/1980, col. 233 & 234, and Botes, PS, "Die sentrale administrasie", in Nieuwoudt, CF, GC Olivier and M Hough (Eds), *Die Politieke Stelsel van Suid-Afrika*, Academica, Pretoria, 1981, pp.170 & 171.

112. Du Plessis, JE, *op. cit.*, pp.5 & 6, and HA Deb., 6/2/1980, col. 234.

113. Du Plessis, JE, *op. cit.*, pp.8 & 9.

114. *Ibid.*, pp.13 & 14.

115. *Ibid.*, pp.6 & 7 (source for the fifth and final points listed).

116. *Toespraak deur Generaal Magnus Malan voor die Instituut vir Strategiese Studies, Universiteit van Pretoria, 3 September 1980*, Roneoed, by courtesy of the Institute for Strategic Studies, University of Pretoria, p.16.

117. *Ibid.*, pp.16 & 17.

118. See Du Plessis, JE, *op. cit.*, pp.4ff. and HA Deb., 6/2/1980, col. 234.

119. Frankel, J, *op. cit.*, p.40 and Vital, D, *op. cit.*, pp.59-61.

120. PW Botha, HA Deb., 7/12/1978, col. 17-19.

121. Du Plessis, JE, *op. cit.*, pp.7 & 11.

122. See *ibid.*, p.9.

123. See Schoeman, BJ, *op. cit.*, pp.343 & 421, for a first-hand account from a former Cabinet colleague of PW Botha's.

124. PW Botha was dubbed "Pangaman", according to Rhoodie, because "you'd never know when he was going to lash out at you" (quoted by Rees, M and C Day, *op. cit.*, p.174). In similar vein, Les de Villiers explained that PW Botha earned this nickname, for he was "not a man to be trifled with" (De Villiers, LES, *op. cit.*, pp.96 & 168). As Defence Minister PW Botha was popularly known as "Piet Skiet" or "Piet Wapen". (Pieter is his first name; "skiet" means shoot and "wapen" weapon.)

125. See Chapter 3. In September 1948 Prime Minister Malan said that while the Declaration contained much that was acceptable, a great deal was not; for example, freedom of marriage and freedom of movement (HA Deb., 1/9/1948, col. 1365).

126. "Statement by Ambassador RF Botha, Permanent Representative of South Africa, to the United Nations Security Council on 24 October 1974", in *Southern Africa Record* (SAIIA), No. 1, March 1975, p.21.

127. *Senate Debates*, 23/10/1974, col. 3340 & 3346.

128. Quoted in HA Deb., 13/6/1977, col. 9971.

129. HA Deb., 13/6/1977, col. 9998, 10009 & 10010.

130. HA Deb., 13/6/1977, col. 9994. Compare this statement with Pik Botha's speech, *ibid.*, 19/2/1974, col. 1244-6, where he took the popular government line that South Africa's international problems began under Smuts in the wake of the war.

131. *Ibid.*, 13/6/1977, col. 9995 & 9998.

132. See *ibid.*, 14/6/1977, col. 10094-7.

133. See note 104 above.

134. Written answers supplied by the Minister of Foreign Affairs and Information to the author's questionnaire, September 1981.

135. See *Namibia and the Sanctions Controversy*, SAIIA Brief Report, No. 30, 20 November 1980, 4pp.

136. Personal interview with Dr Hilgard Muller. When Vorster was asked whether he appointed Pik Botha to succeed Muller because he wanted someone with a different style, he nonchalantly replied: "No, every man kisses his wife in his own way" (personal interview with Mr BJ Vorster).

137. Written answers supplied by the Minister of Foreign Affairs and Information to the author's questionnaire, September 1981. The Foreign Minister wrote: "It is probably not known that for the full duration of Dr H Muller's term of office, I worked very closely with him; that we displayed the same approach to domestic and foreign affairs; that Dr Muller more than any of his other colleagues was familiar with my style; that it was his desire that I should succeed him; that we attended the same school, Volkskool Potchefstroom, studied at the same university, University of Pretoria, where he was for a time my lecturer in Latin, and that we moreover from mother's side descend from the same Dreyers."

138. Written answers supplied by the Minister of Foreign Affairs and Information to the author's questionnaire, September 1981.

139. Following the Maputo raid, the South African

government released a strongly worded note the Foreign Minister had sent to the Mozambique government nearly a year earlier, warning it against providing bases to insurgents. This warning followed in the wake of a terrorist attack on a trading store in northern Zululand in February 1980. The note stated that South Africa had "conclusive evidence that terrorists were being harboured in Mozambique" and that South Africa held the Mozambique government "responsible for the presence of these terrorists on its territory and for their actions". The South African government reserved the right "to take whatever steps may, in its view, be necessary, whenever and wherever", to safeguard South African life and property (*Rand Daily Mail*, 31/1/1981).

140. See Du Plessis, SPJ, *Handelsverdrae as Instrument van die Suid-Afrikaanse Regering se Ekonomiese Beleid*, MA dissertation, University of Pretoria, 1967, 222pp.

141. South African Foreign Trade Organisation (SAFTO), *Sixteenth Annual Report 1978-79*, Johannesburg, p.6.

142. See *Rand Daily Mail*, 26/3/1981, and *The Star*, 26 & 28/3/1981, on the controversy over South Africa's withdrawal of locomotives loaned to Zimbabwe. The latter saw it as a political move, which Pretoria denied.

143. Neethling, DC, *The Geopolitics of Mineral Supply: Access to and Availability of the Mineral Resources of Southern Africa*, Paper read at the Conference on Southern African Metals in a World Context, Johannesburg, 11 and 12 May 1981, Roneoed, by courtesy of the author, pp.7 & 8 (Dr Neethling is Chief Director: Energy, in the Department of Mineral and Energy Affairs), and Etheredge, DA, *Presidential Address*, 90th Annual General Meeting, Chamber of Mines of South Africa, Johannesburg, 24 June 1980, published by the Chamber of Mines, pp.3 & 10.

144. Neethling, DC, *op. cit.*, p.8.

145. *Ibid.*, p.9. See also *Toespraak deur Sy Edele FW de Klerk, Minister van Mineraal- en Energiesake, by die Amptelike Opening van die Matla-steenkoolmyn, op Vrydag, 15 Mei 1981 om 12h30*, Roneoed, by courtesy of the Department of Mineral and Energy Affairs, 21pp.

146. See Vale, PCJ, *The Atlantic Nations and South Africa: Economic Constraints and Community Fracture*, Ph.D. dissertation, University of Leicester, 1981, 446pp.

147. See *Notas vir Toespraak deur Sy Edele FW de Klerk, Minister van Mineraal- en Energiesake, by Geleentheid van die Twintigste Algemene Jaarvergadering van die Suid-Afrikaanse Instituut vir Organisasie en Metode, op Donderdag, 26 Junie 1980 om 09h00*, Roneoed, by courtesy of the Department of Mineral and Energy Affairs, p.13; Neethling, DC, *op. cit.*, pp.9 & 10, and personal interview with Mr FW de Klerk.

148. See *Speech by the South African Minister of Mines and of Environmental Planning and Energy, Mr FW de Klerk, at a Mini Seminar on Wednesday, 28 November 1979, the Gold Room, Pierre Hotel, New York*, Roneoed, by courtesy of the Department of Mineral and Energy Affairs, pp.11-19, and Neethling, DC, *op. cit.*, pp.4 & 5.

149. See "The South African dilemma", *Metal Bulletin*, London, 22/8/1980.

150. See *Notas vir Toespraak deur Sy Edele FW de Klerk, op. cit.*, pp.6-10, and *Openingsrede deur Sy Edele FW de Klerk, Minister van Mineraal- en Energiesake, by Geleentheid van die 36ste Jaarkongres van die Afrikaanse Handelsinstituut, op 23 Mei 1981 te Bloemfontein*, Roneoed, by courtesy of the Department of Mineral and Energy Affairs, 17pp.

151. See Geldenhuys, DJ, "Some strategic implications of regional economic relationships for the Republic of South Africa", *ISSUP Strategic Review*, University of Pretoria, January 1981, pp.17ff.

152. See Geldenhuys, DJ, "South Africa and the West", in Schrire, R (Ed), *South Africa: Public Policy Perspectives*, Juta, Cape Town, 1982, pp.309-12.

153. Mulder interview.

154. De Villiers, LES, *op. cit.*, pp.103 & 104.

155. Mulder interview.

156. *Toespraak deur Generaal Magnus Malan, op. cit.*, p.5, and written answers supplied by the Minister of Foreign Affairs to the author's questionnaire, September 1981. The Foreign Minister wrote as follows: "Foreign issues confronting South Africa do not hold implications for the white electorate only. The onslaught on South Africa is decidedly in the first instance directed at the white government, but not exclusively. The ultimate objective of the onslaught is to dismantle and destroy all forms of democratic power structures."

157. See Pik Botha, HA Deb., 19/5/1980, col. 6627 & 6628.

158. Written answers supplied by the Minister of Foreign Affairs and Information to the author's questionnaire, September 1981.

159. Quoted by Geldenhuys, DJ, *Total National Strategy, op. cit.*, pp.18-20.

160. Quoted by Shaw, JA, "The evolving framework for functional co-operation in Southern Africa", paper delivered at a seminar on economic co-operation held at Thohoyandou, Venda, on 2 July 1981, Roneoed, by courtesy of the author, p.13.

161. *Beeld*, 12/4/1979.

162. Written answers supplied by the Minister of Foreign Affairs and Information to the author's questionnaire, September 1981.

163. *Rand Daily Mail*, 2/2/1981, and *The Sowetan*, 2/2/1981.

164. *Beeld*, 3/2/1981. See also *Rapport*, 1/2/1981, *Die Volksblad*, 2/2/1981, and *Die Transvaler*, 3/2/1981.

For the rather different reaction of the anti-government English press, see *The Star,* 2/2/1981, *The Cape Times,* 2/2/1981, and *Rand Daily Mail,* 3/2/1981.

165. *Rand Daily Mail,* 3/1/1981, and *The Cape Times,* 31/1/1981.
166. *Rand Daily Mail,* 3/2/1981.
167. HA Deb., 27/1/1976, col. 121.

CHAPTER 5

1. Mulder, PWA, *op. cit.,* pp.394-8.
2. *Ibid.,* pp.396-407.
3. De Villiers, LES, *op. cit.,* pp.13-16 & 38; Rees, M & C Day, *op. cit.,* pp.42, 43, 165 & 167, and Erasmus Report 3, *op. cit.,* par. 11.19-24.
4. The four divisions were Foreign, Domestic, Audio-Visual Services and Publications, and Press Liaison. After the reorganisation the Department consisted of the following eight divisions: Planning, Foreign Information, Domestic Information, Foreign Publications, Audio-Visual Services and Production, Administration, Press Liaison, and Training (Mulder, PWA, *op. cit.,* pp.433 & 434).
5. See De Villiers, LES, *op. cit.,* pp.46ff, and Republic of South Africa, Department of Information, *Report for the Period 1 January 1974 to 31 December 1974,* Government Printer, Pretoria, p.10. De Villiers has also written another book, *South Africa: A Skunk Among Nations,* Universal Tandem, London, 1975, 186pp. Only his book on Information is cited in the present work.
6. Mulder, PWA, *op. cit.,* p.436.
7. Personal interview with Dr EM Rhoodie (hereafter referred to as Rhoodie interview). When Mulder, himself a *Broederbonder,* was asked whether Rhoodie's non-membership was not brought into consideration, he replied: "It was of no concern to me whether he was a member or not. I was looking for a professional expert who could do the work." (Personal interview with Dr CP Mulder – hereafter referred to as Mulder interview.)
8. Books by EM Rhoodie: *Penal Systems of the Commonwealth: A Criminological Survey against the Background of the Cornerstones for a Progressive Correctional Policy,* Academica, Pretoria, 1967, 257pp.; *South West Africa: The Last Frontier in Africa,* Voortrekkerpers, Johannesburg, 1967, 254pp.; *The Third Africa,* Nasionale Boekhandel, Cape Town, 1968, 313pp., and *The Paper Curtain,* Voortrekkerpers, Johannesburg, 1969, 212pp.
9. Quoted by Rees, M & C Day, *op. cit.,* p.29.
10. Mulder, PWA, *op. cit.,* p.436.
11. Quoted *ibid.,* pp.485 & 486.
12. Quoted *ibid.,* p.447.
13. See Chapter 4, p.86.
14. The following points of criticism are based on personal interviews with persons involved, and published sources. Where necessary, a specific source will be listed.
15. Rhoodie interview.

16. At the South African mission in Stockholm Mulder and Rhoodie, on an official visit, discovered that the staff were too afraid to hoist the South African flag lest they attract demonstrations. On his return Mulder protested and it took an instruction from Vorster to get the flag displayed (Rhoodie interview; Mulder interview, and De Villiers, LES, *op. cit.,* p.28).
17. Consider the following list of former diplomats who became active in opposition politics: Mr IFA de Villiers (first United Party, then PFP MP); Mr John Maree (NRP candidate in 1981 general election); Dr John Widdowson (NRP candidate in 1981 election); Dr Charles Fincham (active in the PFP); Mr Louis Gerber (PFP candidate); and Mr Elias Olivier (Democratic Party candidate). A rather extreme case is that of Mr Patrick van Rensburg, who was active in the Liberal Party and subsequently went into voluntary exile for his opposition to government policies.
18. Rhoodie interview.
19. In his very early days as a South African Information officer, then serving in Australia, Rhoodie complained to a number of visiting National Party MPs about the anti-government utterances the high commissioner, Mr Anthony Hamilton, had made in the presence of Australian Prime Minister Robert Menzies and Rhoodie. Two of the MPs subsequently raised the matter with Eric Louw. Three weeks later Rhoodie received a message from Louw, conveyed by Mr Piet Meiring, Director of the Information Service, in which he was bluntly told not to concern himself with the political attitude of the high commissioner; Louw could not care whether Hamilton was a liberal (meaning a Progressive Party supporter) or a Nationalist (Rhoodie interview).
20. Rhoodie interview.
21. Rees, M & C Day, *op. cit.,* p.171.
22. Rhoodie interview.
23. Mulder interview. Mulder was, and is, something of a political enigma. Although as minister he had a distinctly conservative public image, he is known to have cut a strongly *verligte* figure in private conversations with visiting foreigners. What adds to the confusion is that Mulder, after his expulsion from the National Party, established the right-wing National Conservative Party. He made a big issue of attacking the Botha government's moves to devise a new constitution, which would to some degree involve coloureds and Indians in the central processes of government – something that he had endorsed when still in office.
24. Republic of South Africa, Department of Information, *Report for the Period 1 January 1976 to 31 December 1976,* Government Printer, Pretoria, p.10.
25. Consider, in particular, Republic of South Africa, Department of Information, *Report for the Period 1 January 1977 to 31 December 1977,* Government

Printer, Pretoria, pp.3-8. See the comments of Basson, HA Deb., 4/5/1976, col. 5919, on this matter.

26. Rhoodie interview.

27. De Villiers, LES, *op. cit.,* p.107.

28. *Ibid.,* pp.110 & 142.

29. Mulder, PWA, *op. cit.,* p.439.

30. Mulder, PWA, *op. cit.,* pp.463-5, and HA Deb., 4/5/1976, col. 5956. In employing coloured and Indian Information officers, the Department acted according to the precepts of separate development. Mulder, in a personal interview, explained that if an Indian or coloured Information officer returned to South Africa after a tour of duty abroad, he could be placed in a regional office where he would work among his own population group, and not among whites in head office. Blacks were not considered on the same basis, the assumption presumably being that they should serve homeland governments and not that of "white South Africa".

31. Mulder, PWA, *op. cit.,* pp.415 & 416.

32. *To the Point,* 11/7/1975.

33. *Die Transvaler,* 14/7/1975.

34. *The Star,* 23/1/1976. See also De Villiers, LES, *op. cit.,* pp.92 & 93.

35. See HA Deb., 4/5/1976, col. 5919, and 13/6/1977, col. 10013.

36. *Ibid.,* 4/5/1976, col. 5957 & 5958.

37. A case in point was Mulder's meeting with Vice President Gerald Ford in Washington in January 1974. On Mulder's arrival in the American capital South Africa's ambassador, Mr Frikkie Botha, expressed his annoyance about being completely in the dark about Mulder's plans. Les de Villiers, who accompanied Mulder and who had been involved in arrangements for the meeting with Ford, explained: "When the visit was first conceived and Ford's office approached, the signal came back loud and clear: There should be no involvement on the part of the South African embassy in Washington as this in turn would require participation by the State Department, the very institution we were trying to bypass. It was obvious to Ford's office and to us that the State Department would have killed the project at the outset. So it was decided in South Africa and in Washington to steer clear of normal diplomatic channels at all costs. It was left to Foreign Minister Hilgard Muller or his Secretary, Brand Fourie, to inform their Ambassador about developments in their own way." (De Villiers, LES, *op. cit.,* p.68.)

38. HA Deb., 20/5/1980, col. 6738.

39. Rhoodie interview. See also De Villiers, LES, *op. cit.,* p.66.

40. De Villiers, LES, *op. cit.,* pp.70 & 71.

41. See Department of Information, *Report . . . 1974, op. cit.,* p.41, which shows a picture of Governor Carter receiving a publication from a South African Information officer.

42. De Villiers, LES, *op. cit.,* p.103.

43. See *The Star,* 6/8/1977.

44. Rhoodie interview.

45. Mulder interview.

46. Probably sensing the value of a public relations-type approach to diplomacy in America, Pik Botha twice requested Rhoodie and De Villiers that he, like the Department of Information, be allowed to engage a lobbyist paid from Information's secret funds. Rhoodie insisted that Pik Botha channel the request through the Secretary of Foreign Affairs, which the ambassador was unwilling to do (Rhoodie interview).

47. Department of Information, *Report . . . 1977, op. cit.,* pp.5-40. The Department had offices in the following countries: Argentina, Australia, Belgium, France, Israel, Italy, Canada, The Netherlands, New Zealand, Austria, Portugal, Rhodesia, Spain, Switzerland, Transkei, United Kingdom, United States and West Germany.

48. Rhoodie told the authors of the book *Muldergate* that the number of secret projects eventually totalled nearly 180 (Rees, M & C Day, *op. cit.,* p.186). An interdepartmental committee, the Pretorius committee, which was appointed by the government to investigate the secret projects of the dismantled Department of Information, after a month reported that it had already identified 138 projects (HA Deb., 7/12/1978, col. 17 & 18).

49. Rhoodie placed the secret projects in two categories. If the secrets of those in category A leaked out, it would seriously embarrass all and even lead to the resignation of some officials and their minister. Should the secret projects in category AA be revealed, there could be a grave political crisis and the government could fall, accompanied with international punitive action against South Africa; what is more, it could even lead to the assassination of Information officials who were intimately involved with certain projects – the fear was not that the South African authorities would try to liquidate them, but other parties desperately wanting to protect their own vital interests (Rhoodie interview).

50. De Villiers, LES, *op. cit.,* pp.54 & 55, and Rees, M, & C Day, *op. cit.,* pp.32-40.

51. Rees, M & C Day, *op. cit.,* pp.188 & 189, and Rhoodie interview.

52. Rhoodie interview. See also Rees, M & C Day, *op. cit.,* pp.200 & 201.

53. Erasmus Report 3, *op. cit.,* par. 9.4-33.

54. Rhoodie interview, and Rees, M & C Day, *op. cit.,* pp.198 & 206.

55. Rhoodie interview, and Rees, M & C Day, *op. cit.,* p.206.

56. Rhoodie interview.

57. *Loc. cit.,* and Rees, M & C Day, *op. cit.,* p.199.

58. De Villiers, LES, *op. cit.,* pp.85 & 86, and Rees, M & C Day, *op. cit.,* p.200.

59. Rhoodie interview.

60. *Loc. cit.* See also Rees, M & C Day, *op. cit.,* p.200.

61. Rees, M & C Day, *op. cit.,* p.201.

62. Erasmus Report 3, *op. cit.*, par. 10.1-31.
63. Rhoodie interview. One such book was AW Steward's *The World, The West and Pretoria*, David McKay, New York, 1977, 308pp. Steward was a former South African Information officer and subsequently became a well-known – and controversial – radio commentator in South Africa.
64. Rees, M & C Day, *op. cit.*, pp.200, 201 & 205.
65. See *Rapport*, 2/3/1980.
66. Rhoodie interview.
67. Mulder interview. In 1977, at one of the periodic low points in South Africa's relations with the Western powers, Mulder suggested that South Africa might decide to "sail under a different flag" because of negative Western attitudes (*Die Burger*, 15/4/1977). His subsequent allusion to the proverb, "my enemy's enemy is my friend" (*The Star*, 17/6/1977), was seen as a clear reference to Peking. The common enemy Mulder had in mind was not the West but the Soviet Union. Nonetheless, it was intended to warn Western countries that they were driving South Africa towards China.
68. Rhoodie interview.
69. Mulder interview.
70. Rhoodie interview. So concerned was the Department of Foreign Affairs about possible adverse Arab reaction to South Africa's relations with Israel that it instructed Dr CBH Fincham not to give a farewell function in Pretoria before leaving to take up his position as Consul-General in Israel in 1972.
71. *Loc. cit.*
72. De Villiers, LES, *op. cit.*, p.102. Mr Shimon Peres, Israeli Minister of Defence, on 22 November 1974 wrote to Rhoodie acknowledging the latter's "significant personal role" in promoting ties between Israel and South Africa, and said that it was largely due to Rhoodie's "perspicacity, foresight and political imagination that a vitally important co-operation between our two countries has been initiated." (Shown in Rhoodie interview.)
73. Rhoodie interview.
74. De Villiers, LES, *op. cit.*, pp.102, 105 & 106, and Rhoodie interview.
75. De Villiers, LES, *op. cit.*, p.106.
76. *Loc. cit.*
77. Rhoodie interview.
78. *Loc. cit.*, and Rees, M & C Day, *op. cit.*, p.179-81.
79. Rhoodie interview, and Rees, M & C Day, *op. cit.*, p.181.
80. Rhoodie interview, and De Villiers, LES, *op. cit.*, pp.49 & 75.
81. It was Vorster's hesitation and prevarication in following up Information's diplomatic breakthroughs in Francophone Africa that prompted Rhoodie's unflattering assertion that he had to "drag Vorster screaming and kicking into Africa". (See Rees, M & C Day, *op. cit.*, p.181 & 182.)
82. It was only in November 1974 that Houphouet-Boigny agreed to confirm publicly his meeting with Vorster by releasing pictures taken on the occasion and issuing an official statement. Senghor, however, insisted that his participation remain secret. He therefore had to be cut out from the pictures released to the press. The excision almost worked, but for one widely publicised picture in which Senghor's amputated arm appeared. In African diplomatic circles the riddle of the day was whose arm it was (De Villiers, LES, *op. cit.*, p.79, and Mulder interview).
83. Rhoodie interview.
84. *Loc. cit.*, and De Villiers, LES, *op. cit.*, pp.142-5.
85. Rhoodie interview.
86. *Loc. cit.*
87. *Loc. cit.*
88. *Loc. cit.*
89. *Loc. cit.* For the controversy caused by Rhoodie's revelations about the Church's involvement with Information, see *Beeld*, 17/8/1979, *Die Transvaler*, 17/8/1979, and *Rand Daily Mail*, 23/8/1979. See also Geldenhuys, FE O'Brien, *In die Stroomversnellings: Vyftig Jaar van die NG Kerk*, Tafelberg, Cape Town, 1982, pp.72-7; the author had been associated with the Ecumenical Bureau at the time of Information's financial support.
90. Department of Information, *Report . . . 1974, op. cit.*, p.3.
91. Quoted by Mulder, PWA, *op. cit.*, p.490.
92. *Loc. cit.*
93. HA Deb., 4/5/1976, col. 5952-4.
94. Department of Information, *Report . . . 1977, op. cit.*, p.3
95. *Rapport*, 2/3/1980.
96. HA Deb., 7/12/1978, col. 24. In December 1978 PW Botha revealed that the interdepartmental committee of investigation had reported on 125 secret Information projects. On the basis of these findings, the State Security Council decided to terminate 57 projects for various reasons, "such as having become redundant or totally unacceptable"; 68 would be continued, 56 of which as secret projects (*ibid.*, 7/12/1978, col. 19). Among the projects that would be openly financed were South African institutions engaged in foreign affairs research, namely the Institute for Strategic Studies at the University of Pretoria, the Centre for International Politics at the University of Potchefstroom, and the Southern African Freedom Foundation (subsequently renamed the Southern Africa Forum) in Johannesburg (Rees, M & C Day, *op. cit.*, p.209).
97. Personal interview with Mr BJ Vorster.
98. See Pik Botha's interview with *Rapport*, 2/3/1980, under the self-explanatory heading, *"Pik Loop Connie"* ("Pik Flays Connie"), and Rhoodie's reaction in a lengthy letter to *Rapport*, 16/3/1980. A vivid illustration of the acrimony of the conflict between the National Party and Mulder can be found in *Pro-Nat*, an official National Party publication. In its March 1980 issue considerable atten-

tion was devoted to Mulder and Information, under the caption, *"Dr Connie Mulder se politieke spel blootgelê"* ("Dr Connie Mulder's political game exposed").

99. Lerche, CO & AA Said, *Concepts of International Politics,* Prentice-Hall, Englewood Cliffs, 1970, p.43.

100. Padelford, NJ & GA Lincoln, *The Dynamics of International Politics,* Second Edition, Macmillan, New York, 1967, p.313.

101. Lerche, CO & AA Said, *op. cit.,* p.43.

102. Mulder, PWA, *op. cit.,* p.416.

103. Rhoodie interview.

104. De Villiers, LES, *op. cit.,* p.99.

105. The Department of Information was dissolved on 1 July 1978, following a government decision based on a recommendation from the Public Service Commission. On that day the Bureau of National and International Communication came into being. In a strange arrangement the Bureau fell under the Ministry of Foreign Affairs – Pik Botha thus being the minister responsible – but not under the Secretary of Foreign Affairs; instead it was placed under the Secretary of Plural Relations and Development, whose department dealt exclusively with black affairs. From 1 September 1978 the Bureau was assigned to the Department of Foreign Affairs. On 1 February 1979 it was renamed the Information Service of South Africa, and it merged with Foreign Affairs in April 1980. Mr AJ Engelbrecht served as Director-General of National and International Communication and subsequently of the Information Service. For the activities of the Bureau/Information Service, see Republic of South Africa, Information Service of South Africa, *Report for the Period 1 April 1978 to 31 March 1979,* Government Printer, Pretoria, and Republiek van Suid-Afrika, Inligtingsdiens van Suid-Afrika, *Verslag vir die tydperk 1 April 1979 tot 31 Desember 1979,* Government Printer, Pretoria.

106. Barratt, CJA, "The Department of Foreign Affairs", in Worrall, DJ (Ed), *South Africa: Government and Politics,* second edition, Van Schaik, Pretoria, 1975, pp.336-8. See also Bekker, MJ, *op. cit.,* pp.52ff. and Olivier, GC, *op. cit.,* pp.186-90.

107. *South African Panorama,* a prestige magazine first published 25 years ago, appears in Afrikaans, English and six European languages, with a circulation of some 300 000 per edition. *South African Digest* appears in Afrikaans, English, French and German, the bulk of its circulation being abroad. Nearly 200 000 editions in English are published weekly.

108. The more recent occasional publications include *Dynamic Change in South Africa,* Government Printer, Pretoria, 1980, 136pp; *Economic Co-operation in Southern Africa,* Government Printer, Pretoria, 1981, 80pp., and *Republic of South Africa: 20 Years of Progress,* Government Printer,

Pretoria, 1981, 89pp.

109. Among the regular publications issued by South African embassies are *South African News and Views* (Canberra); *Beelden* (Brussels); *Zuid-Afrika in Focus* (The Hague) and *Heute aus Süd-afrika* (Vienna).

110. The seven publications in the series are: *Inqubela* (Xhosa), *Intuthoko* (Zulu), *Mvelapanda* (Venda), *Nhluvuko* (Tsonga), *Tswelopele* (North Sotho), *Tswelopele* (South Sotho) and *Tswelelopele* (Tswana).

111. These publications are *Alpha* (for coloureds), *Fiat Lux* (for Indians) and *Educamus* (for the Department of Education and Training).

112. These include *Ngwane,* aimed at Swazi readers, and the "official" journals of urban black councils, such as the *Diepmeadow News, Dobsonville Mirror* and *Soweto News.*

113. See Inligtingsdiens van Suid-Afrika, *Verslag . . . 1979, op. cit.,* p.28.

114. The missions are based in the following cities: Buenos Aires (also accredited to Chile, Bolivia, Paraguay and Uruguay), Canberra, Sydney, Brussels (Belgium and EC), Paris, Tel Aviv, Rome, Ottawa, The Hague, Wellington, Vienna, Lisbon, Madrid, Berne, London, Washington, Los Angeles, Chicago, Houston, New York (US and UN) and Bonn.

115. Pik Botha decided to terminate the services of Donald de Kieffer (appointed by Mulder) as American lobbyist, and instead appointed Mr Kimberley Hallamore. A new public relations consultant, Mr John Sears, was also appointed in the place of Sydney Baron. In what was a highly ironical instance of musical chairs, De Kieffer was subsequently appointed as trade adviser in the Reagan Administration, whereas Sears was sacked as Reagan's campaign manager in the course of the presidential election.

116. PW Botha, HA Deb., 7/12/1978, col. 34ff. On the basis of information given to Parliament by the prime minister in December 1978 the Department of Foreign Affairs and Information was continuing over 50 of the former Department of Information's secret projects.

117. Shaw, JA, "The evolving framework", *op. cit.,* pp.6ff. See also Shaw, JA, "The prospects for economic integration in Southern Africa", Inaugural lecture delivered by Dr JA Shaw, Chargé d'Affaires of South Africa in Malawi, at the Kamuzu Academy, Kasungu, on Saturday, 28 November 1981, Roneoed, by courtesy of the author, 21pp. Before taking up his appointment in Malawi, Dr Shaw was co-ordinator at the interim regional secretariat of the constellation, attached to the economic and development co-operation branch, Department of Foreign Affairs and Information.

118. Information on KEOSSA from Shaw, JA, "The evolving framework", *op. cit.,* pp. 21 & 22, and

personal interview with Mr GJ Richter.

119. Barratt, CJA, *op. cit.,* p.340.

120. See *ibid.,* pp.340 & 343.

121. Information on South Africa's foreign representation obtained from Republic of South Africa, *Department of Foreign Affairs List,* February 1966 and December 1975, Government Printer, Pretoria, and Republic of South Africa, *South Africa 1980/1,* Official Yearbook of the Republic of South Africa, Chris van Rensburg Publications, Johannesburg, pp. 232-6, and also by courtesy of the Protocol Division, Department of Foreign Affairs and Information.

122. Republic of South Africa, *Diplomatic List,* July 1976 and January 1981, Government Printer, Pretoria, and information by courtesy of the Department of Foreign Affairs and Information.

123. Information by courtesy of the Department of Foreign Affairs and Information.

124. *South Africa 1980/1, op. cit.,* pp.232-6. Consular missions with the status of consulate-generals and consulates have been included in the numbers given.

125. Information by courtesy of the Department of Foreign Affairs and Information.

126. Coetzee, formerly Minister of Community Development and of Public Works in Vorster's Cabinet, gave a colourful account of his duties as ambassador to Rome: "After six months I can say that I slowly had to discover what exactly the work of an ambassador is, and I still don't know what the work of an ambassador is. All I know is that he has very, very little to do. He has great difficulty in keeping himself occupied. You have correspondence and you make at the most one or two visits a day. For the rest of the day you read newspapers and try to keep yourself informed." (Quoted by Olivier, GC, *op. cit.,* p. 198.)

127. From the written replies of the Minister of Foreign Affairs and Information to the author's questionnaire.

128. The observations described are based on interviews with former South African diplomats.

129. The following are some of the English-speakers who served as ambassadors in recent years: Messrs DB Sole, N Best, AJ Oxlee, RH Coaton, HLT Taswell, AAM Hamilton, P Philip, J Stewart, FD Tothill and Drs CBH Fincham and HJ Widdowson.

130. Munger, ES, *Foreign Policy, op. cit.,* p.26.

131. *Loc. cit.*

132. *Ibid.,* p.24.

133. *The Star,* 25/9/1979.

134. The questionnaire submitted to the Minister of Foreign Affairs and Information read: "Reference is sometimes made to a 'Washington Mafia' in your Department, as if it were an inner circle consisting of officials who had served under you in Washington. What are your comments?" The curt reply was: "It is not correct." Someone who believed differently was Hogarth, the *Sunday Times* columnist. Under the caption, "Dwindling band" (11/7/1982), he asked: "Whatever happened to Mr Pik Botha's 'Washington Mafia', that happy little group who dominated foreign affairs after Mr Botha's elevation from ambassador to Minister?" Hogarth noted that several members of the group had been posted to South African missions abroad, including Van Heerden and Auret. "If the gang goes," Hogarth wondered, "can the godfather be far behind?"

135. See *Rapport,* 7/12/1980, and *Sunday Times,* 6/9/1981.

136. *Rapport,* 7/12/1980.

137. Lerche, CO & AA Said, *op. cit.,* p.43.

138. Republic of South Africa, *Estimate of Revenue and Estimate of Expenditure from State Revenue and South West Africa Accounts,* various years, Government Printer, Pretoria, and further information by courtesy of the Department of Foreign Affairs and Information.

139. Quoted by Mulder, PWA, *op. cit.,* pp.480 & 481.

140. Information by courtesy of the Department of Foreign Affairs and Information.

141. Jensen, L, *Explaining Foreign Policy,* Prentice-Hall, Englewood Cliffs, 1982, p.130.

142. Republic of South Africa, *White Paper on Defence ... 1973, op. cit.,* p. 1.

143. Republic of South Africa, *White Paper on Defence and Armament Production, 1975,* Tabled in the Senate and the House of Assembly by the Minister of Defence, Government Printer, Pretoria, pp.3 & 4.

144. Republic of South Africa, *White Paper on Defence, 1977,* Tabled in the Senate and the House of Assembly by the Minister of Defence, Government Printer, Pretoria, p.5.

145. *Toespraak deur Generaal Magnus Malan . . . 3 September 1980, op. cit.,* pp.7ff.

146. *Address by the Honourable PW Botha, Prime Minister, Minister of Defence and of National Security, on the Occasion of a National Party Congress in Durban on 15 August 1979,* Roneoed, Information Service of South Africa, pp.24-7.

147. Information by courtesy of the South African Defence Force.

148. Information on the three institutions by courtesy of the South African Defence Force.

149. Jaster, R, *South Africa's Narrowing Security Options,* Adelphi Papers, International Institute for Strategic Studies, Nr. 159, Spring 1980, p.16.

150. Republic of South Africa, *Estimate of the Expenditure to be Defrayed from the State Revenue Account,* various years, Government Printer, Pretoria.

151. *Sunday Times,* 11/7/1982. For an overview of the development of South Africa's own arms industry, see Jaster, R, *op. cit.,* pp. 12-17, and Crocker, CA, "Current and projected military balances in Southern Africa", in Bissell, RE & CA Crocker (Eds), *South Africa into the 1980s,* Westview Press,

Boulder, 1979, pp.81-8.

152. Republic of South Africa, *White Paper on Defence and Armaments Supply 1979,* Tabled in the Senate and the House of Assembly by the Minister of Defence, Government Printer, Pretoria, pp.22-5, and *Sunday Times,* 11/7/1982. See also Republic of South Africa, White Paper on Defence, 1965-67, Government Printer, Pretoria, p.8, on the origins of local armaments production.

153. *Die Afrikaner* (24/4/1981), mouthpiece of the HNP, tried to cast suspicions on the members of the Defence Advisory Council by insinuating that some were anti-Afrikaner, even disloyal to South Africa. (See the reaction of Magnus Malan to the HNP's "smear tactics", *Beeld,* 11/4/1981.)

154. Vosloo, T, *Schalk Pienaar: 10 Jaar Politieke Kommentaar,* Tafelberg, Cape Town, 1975, pp.68 & 76.

155. See Admiral HH Biermann (chief of the Defence Force, 1972-6), reported in *Die Burger,* 25/9/1974, and Magnus Malan, reported in *The Cape Times,* 24/1/1978.

156. *The Cape Times,* 26/4/1980, and *White Paper on Defence . . . 1979, op. cit.,* p.16.

157. *Sunday Times,* 23/3/1980; *Beeld,* 26/3/1980; *Die Burger,* 26/3/1980; *The Star,* 26/3/1980; *Sunday Express,* 30/3/1980; *The Cape Times,* 25 & 26/4/1980.

158. See *South Africa 1980/1, op. cit.,* p.285.

159. See Geldenhuys, DJ, *The Constellation, op. cit.,* p.6.

160. For details, see Geldenhuys, DJ, *South Africa's Black Homelands, op. cit.,* pp.39 & 40.

161. See Shaw, JA, "The evolving framework", *op. cit.,* pp.13 & 14.

162. *Rand Daily Mail,* 20/4/1979, and *International Herald Tribune,* 21/4/1979. For a historical overview of the role of military attachés, including South Africa's, see Van der Waals, WS, *Die Weermag-Attaché – 'n Studie in Internasionale Verhoudinge,* M.A. dissertation, University of the Orange Free State, 1970, 303pp.

163. *The Daily News,* 10/4/1981.

164. *The Star,* 30/3/1981 and 2/4/1981.

165. *Sunday Tribune,* 19/4/1981.

166. Frankel, J, *op. cit.,* pp.51 & 52.

167. See *The Star,* 14/1/1980; "The BOSS/DONS story", *Rand Daily Mail,* 1 & 2/2/1980; and *Sunday Times,* 24/5/1981.

168. "The BOSS/DONS story", *Rand Daily Mail,* 1/2/1980.

169. "The BOSS/DONS story", *Rand Daily Mail,* 2/2/1980.

170. Erasmus Report 3, *op. cit.,* Annexure A, par. 1-16, and Rees, M & C Day, *op. cit.,* pp.134 & 135.

171. HA Deb., 8/12/1978, col. 361.

172. *Ibid.,* 7/12/1978, col. 12.

173. De Villiers, LES, *op. cit.,* pp.75-8.

174. Erasmus Report 1, *op. cit.,* par. 12.448. See also Winter, G., *op. cit.,* pp.335-41.

175. De Villiers, LES, *op. cit.,* pp.76 & 78.

176. Rees, M & C Day, *op. cit.,* p.181.

177. See Martin, D & P Johnson, *The Struggle for Zimbabwe: The Chimurenga War,* Faber and Faber, London, 1981, pp.129ff.

178. General van den Bergh bluntly refused the author an interview – the only ex-official approached to have done so.

179. De Villiers, LES, *op. cit.,* p.77.

180. See Winter, G, *op. cit.,* pp.394-410 & 454-9; *The Star,* 14/1/1980 & 29/6/1981, and "The BOSS/DONS Story", *Rand Daily Mail,* 2/2/1980.

181. See Erasmus Report 3, *op. cit.,* Annexure A, par. 6, and HA Deb., 7/12/1978, col. 57.

182. See Barnard, LD, *Die Magsfaktor in Internasionale Verhoudinge,* D.Phil. dissertation, University of the Orange Free State, 1975, 1072 pp.; Barnard, LD (Ed), *Konflik en Orde in Internasionale Verhoudinge,* Perskor, Johannesburg, 1978, 298pp. *The Star,* 14/11/1979, contains a review of some of Barnard's published articles.

183. See Olivier, GC, *op. cit.,* p.195.

184. *South Africa 1980/1, op. cit.,* p.481.

185. South Africa is the dominant trading partner of Botswana, Lesotho and Swaziland. It supplies some 80% of Botswana's essential imports and provides outlets for its principal export commodities. Lesotho conducts 90% of its external trade with the Republic, while South Africa supplies over 90% of Swaziland's import requirements. When Zimbabwe became independent in April 1980 South Africa was its major trading partner, providing the bulk of its imports and serving as the main market for its industrial exports *(Quarterly Economic Review of Southern Africa: Annual Supplement 1979,* The Economist Intelligence Unit, pp.44, 55 & 60, and *Quarterly Economic Review of Zimbabwe-Rhodesia, Malawi,* 1st Quarter 1980, The Economist Intelligence Unit, p.12).

186. *South Africa 1980/1, op. cit.,* p.409.

187. *Ibid.,* p.529.

188. *Ibid.,* p.416. The territories are Namibia, Transkei, Bophuthatswana, Venda, Lesotho, Swaziland, Zimbabwe and Mozambique.

189. *Ibid.,* pp.323, 330 & 412.

190. *Ibid.,* p.662, and *The Star,* 30/6/1981.

191. *South Africa 1980/1, op. cit.,* pp.410-12.

192. See Walker, EA, *op. cit.,* pp.406ff.

193. See Cockram, G-M, *op. cit.,* p.141.

194. Since the story of the discussions between Vorster, Kaunda and Smith on the reopening of the Zambia-Rhodesian border is so intriguing, it is related here in some detail, as told by Vorster in a personal interview with the author. It is largely a verbatim (albeit translated) transcript.

(After Vorster and Kaunda had met in Livingstone, Zambia, early on the morning of 25 August 1975, they made an unscheduled visit to the Rhodesian side of the border – the first time Kaunda had set foot in Rhodesia since 1962. They drove to the Victoria Falls and then on to the railway station where the coach of the General Manager of the South African Railways (Loubser) stood.)

And I told him [Kaunda] we should go and see if we can get tea at Kobus Loubser's. I then introduced him to Kobus Loubser and told him [Kaunda]: "This is the man with whom you will have talks about the opening of the railway line between South Africa and Zambia." He then told me he did not intend opening it. I said, "Yes, you will some time or other; we will talk about it." We in any case had tea there and went back to Zambia where we had lunch. In the afternoon we returned to the coach and there we had serious talks. I tried to persuade him to open the railway line and impressed it very strongly upon him that it was in his economic interests to open the line. His reply to me was that he had irrevocably turned his back on the south, and that his future lay north. I told him it was not his future that lay north. I said: "It's your bankruptcy that lies to the north, not your future." We argued about it all afternoon, discussed it from all angles. It was fairly late, probably about half past four in the afternoon, when he told me that I had convinced him that it was probably in his interests to open the railway line, but that he had two difficulties in this regard. One was political in nature and the other practical. I then asked him: "Now what is your political problem?" He said it was not a matter he could discuss with me, because it was only for the people of Africa, for the black people. Then I said: "And who is now the racist, if you don't want to discuss it with me?" He felt very embarrassed. I said to him, "Will you take it amiss if I take a shrewd guess as to what your political problem is?" He said to me, "No, not at all." Then I said: "Julius Nyerere won't allow you to do it." One need not see an antelope fall to know you've hit it.

In any case, I said, "Let us now forget about that. What is your practical problem?" He said his practical problem was this: suppose he opened the railway line to the south, he was of course going to give offence to the north, and it may be that he burns all his bridges to the north. And suppose that at a point in time for him [Kaunda] the most inconvenient, Mr Smith were to close his route to the south, then he would have nothing. I said: "No, that I can understand very well. And you know that Rhodesia relies very heavily on South Africa. I am prepared to say this to you: if you and Mr Smith agree, short of war, to open the railway line, I am prepared to endorse ("onderskrywe") it." Then I added, "If he drops you, I'll ditch him."

I went out and asked someone to go and call Mr Smith to leave the conference room of the train – the dining coach – and come to the compartment. He came to the compartment and there were the three of us. I repeated the whole story in Mr Smith's presence and I told him, "This is what I said to the President, and this is what he said." Then Mr Smith in my presence told Kaunda: "I am quite prepared to give you the assurance that, short of war, I will keep the railway line open under all circumstances." He said, "To tell you the truth, I am prepared to give it to you in writing." I then told Kaunda that I was prepared to co-sign that written document. He said, "Very well," he would let me know within 14 days. He did let me know within 14 days, and the message simply read: he's very sorry, but he cannot overcome his political problem.

It was three years later, Vorster added, when Kaunda eventually had to negotiate with Loubser over the opening of the railway line. "But that is the tempo of Africa; the tempo of Africa is slow. It took him three years to realise that his bankruptcy was such that he had to get the railway line opened."

195. Loubser, JGH, "Vervoerdiplomasie met spesiale verwysing na Suider-Afrika", *Politikon*, Vol. 6, No. 2, December 1979, p.146.
196. *Ibid.*, pp.148 & 149.
197. Written response from the Minister of Foreign Affairs and Information to the author's questionnaire.
198. Loubser, JGH, "Vervoerdiplomasie", *op. cit.*, pp.145ff., and Loubser, JGH, "The function of transport as a line of communication between states in Southern Africa", Draft speech for Dr Loubser to be delivered in October 1980 in Germany, Roneoed, by courtesy of the Director of Public Relations, SAR & H, pp. 10ff.
199. Loubser, JGH, "Vervoerdiplomasie", *op. cit.*, p.143, and "Function of transport" *op. cit.*, p.10.
200. Loubser, JGH, "Vervoerdiplomasie", *op. cit.*, pp.137ff.
201. *Sunday Express*, 27/9/1981.
202. Shaw, JA, "The evolving framework", *op. cit.*, pp.8 & 9.
203. *South Africa 1980/1, op. cit.*, p.896.
204. Quoted by Du Plessis, DT, "The creation of job opportunities for the Black labour force of South Africa within the policy of multinational development", *Development Studies Southern Africa*, BENSO, Pretoria, Vol. 2, No. 4, July 1980, p.449.
205. *South Africa 1980/1, op. cit.*, p.895.
206. *Beeld*, 6/8/1981.
207. *South Africa 1980/1, op. cit.*, p.895.
208. Shaw, JA, "The evolving framework", *op. cit.*, pp.12 & 15.

209. *South Africa 1980/1, op. cit.,* p.549.

210. Official statistics for 1976/7 show that black states purchased 187 000 tons of maize products, 29 200 tons of wheat, 2 300 tons of oats and 161 200 cartons of eggs (each containing 30 dozen) from South Africa (*ibid.,* p.894).

211. See *ibid.,* pp.892 & 894.

212. Shaw, JA, "The evolving framework", *op. cit.,* pp.6 & 7.

213. *South Africa 1980/1, op. cit.,* p.569.

CHAPTER 6

1. See Frankel, J, *op. cit.,* pp.70 & 71.

2. *Ibid.,* p.70.

3. Holsti, KJ, *International Politics: A Framework for Analysis,* Third Edition, Prentice-Hall, New Jersey, 1977, pp.393 & 394.

4. The concept was introduced by Gabriel A. Almond in *The American People and Foreign Policy,* Harcourt Brace Jovanovich, New York, 1950, 269pp.

5. See Wallace, W, *The Foreign Policy Process in Britain,* Royal Institute of International Affairs, London, 1975, p.88.

6. Barber, J, *British Foreign Policy, op. cit.,* p.92.

7. See Vital, D, *op. cit.,* p.82.

8. Barber, J, *British Foreign Policy, op. cit.,* p.70.

9. Holsti, KJ (1977), *op. cit.,* pp.393 & 394.

10. Abravanel, MD and B Hughes, "Public attitudes and foreign policy behaviour in Western democracies", in Chittick, WO (Ed), *The Analysis of Foreign Policy Outputs,* Charles E Merrill Publishing Company, Columbus, 1975, p.54.

11. Barber, J, *British Foreign Policy, op. cit.,* p.92.

12. Frankel, J, *op. cit.,* p.70.

13. Almond, GA, *op. cit.,* pp.5 & 6.

14. Barber, J, *British Foreign Policy, op. cit.,* p.95.

15. *Opening Address by the Prime Minister, the Honourable PW Botha at the Annual Congress of the Associated Chambers of Commerce (ASSOCOM) in Johannesburg on 21 October, 1980,* Roneoed, Department of Foreign Affairs and Information, p.2.

16. *Toespraak deur Sy Edele PW Botha DVD LV, Eerste Minister, Minister van Verdediging en van Nasionale Intelligensiediens tydens die Opening van die 35e Jaarkongres van die Afrikaanse Handelsinstituut te Port Elizabeth op 7 Mei 1980,* Roneoed, Department of Foreign Affairs and Information, pp.4 & 5.

17. *Toespraak deur Generaal Magnus Malan, op. cit.,* pp.12 & 13.

18. See *Toespraak deur Sy Edele PW Botha . . . Port Elizabeth op 7 Mei 1980, op. cit.,* p.17.

19. *Address by the Honourable PW Botha . . . Carlton Centre, Johannesburg: 22 November 1979, op. cit.,* pp.31 & 32.

20. See *ibid.,* p.23 and *Toespraak deur Sy Edele PW Botha . . . Port Elizabeth op 7 Mei 1980, op. cit.,* p.6.

21. The lengthy declaration is reproduced in Shaw, JA, "The evolving framework", *op. cit.,* pp.15-17. The four parties *inter alia* resolved to restrict the public sector's direct role in the economy "mainly to the provision of collective and strategic goods and services and to the co-ordination of regional development"; to provide "as much scope as possible to private business enterprises to decide what, how, where and for whom to produce", and to give private business enterprises the assurance "that they will not be nationalised and that their ability to make profits and to repatriate dividends will not be arbitrarily restricted".

22. *Toespraak deur Sy Edele PW Botha . . . Port Elizabeth op 7 Mei 1980, op. cit.,* pp.15 & 16.

23. *Opening Address by the Prime Minister . . . Johannesburg on 21 October 1980, op. cit.,* pp.14-21.

24. See Geldenhuys, DJ and TD Venter, *op. cit.,* pp.55 & 56.

25. See *Opening Address by the Prime Minister . . . Johannesburg on 21 October 1980, op. cit.,* pp.22 & 37.

26. Etheredge, DA, *op. cit.,* pp.12 & 13; *The ASSOCOM Executive Council Response to the Concept of a Southern African Constellation of States – As Outlined by the Prime Minister, the Hon. PW Botha,* Issued by the Association of Chambers of Commerce of South Africa, Johannesburg, 21 May 1980, 3pp.; and *The Constellation of States, Sanctions, and Southern Africa,* Address to the Witbank Chamber of Commerce and Industries by Mr Raymond Parsons, Chief Executive of the Association of Chambers of Commerce (ASSOCOM), on Wednesday, March 18, 1981, Roneoed, ASSOCOM, 9pp.

27. *Address by the Honourable PW Botha . . . Carlton Centre, Johannesburg: 22 November 1979, op. cit.,* 60pp.; subsequently reproduced in Republic of South Africa, *Towards a Constellation of States in Southern Africa,* Information Service of South Africa, 1980, pp.6-23.

28. *Towards a Constellation, op. cit.,* p.25.

29. *Ibid.,* pp.24-41.

30. Confidential communication.

31. See *Die Transvaler,* 13 & 14/11/1981; *The Star,* 13/11/1981; *Beeld,* 13/11/1981; *Sunday Tribune,* 15/11/1981; and *Rapport,* 15/11/1981.

32. "Business Diplomacy", editorial in *ASSOCOM Review,* First Quarter 1981, ASSOCOM, Johannesburg, pp.1 & 2.

33. Republic of South Africa, *South Africa 1982,* Official Yearbook of the Republic of South Africa, Chris van Rensburg Publications, Johannesburg, 1982, p.514.

34. *Ibid.,* p.495, and an official brochure, *The FCI.*

35. Information obtained in a personal interview with Mr FF de W Stockenstrom, Executive Director of

the AHI, and from various AHI publications.

36. Personal interview with Mr E Verburg, Johannesburg Chamber of Commerce.

37. Information obtained in a personal interview with Dr PJ Kieser, General Manager of SAFTO; from SAFTO publications, and from *South Africa 1982, op. cit.*, pp.527 & 528.

38. See *Towards a Constellation, op. cit.*, pp.28 & 29, and Etheredge, DA, *op. cit.*, pp.12 & 13.

39. Established in 1965, SABRITA has about 400 companies – both British and South African – as members. In common with other inter-country chambers, SABRITA's object is the promotion of mutual trade and the encouragement of British investment in South Africa (information by courtesy of Ms Y Roux, Executive Manager of SABRITA).

40. Some 250 companies, including a good many South African enterprises, belong to the American Chamber of Commerce. (Personal interview with Mr CM Else, Executive Director of AMCHAM.)

41. The South Africa-German Chamber has some 700 institutional and individual members. It is part of a network of similar German chambers in 43 states, maintained by the *Deutscher Industrie und Handelstag* based in Bonn. These chambers, partly financed by the Federal German government, normally handle all trade matters between the host country and West Germany. (Personal interview with Mr A Stracke, Senior Executive of the South Africa-German Chamber of Trade and Industry.)

42. The American Chamber of Commerce, for example, initiated and substantially financed a project to build a private commercial high school for 600 pupils in Soweto, known as Pace Commercial College.

43. See Giliomee, H, *op. cit.*, pp.131-5.

44. Stultz, NM, *Who Goes to Parliament?* Institute for Social and Economic Research, Rhodes University, Grahamstown, 1975, p.13.

45. For details of unions and of work stoppages, see the *Official Trade Union Directory, 1980-1981*, published by the Trade Union Council of South Africa (TUCSA), Johannesburg.

46. *Beeld*, 29/1/1980 & 26/6/1981, and *Die Afrikaner*, 27/6/1980.

47. Stultz, NM, *op. cit.*, p.13.

48. *South Africa 1982, op. cit.*, p.583.

49. Figures obtained in a personal interview with Mr C Cilliers, Director of the South African Agricultural Union.

50. *South Africa 1980/1, op. cit.*, pp.555 & 556.

51. *Die Volksblad*, 9/10/1980, and personal interview with Mr C Cilliers.

52. See *Southern Africa Record* (SAIIA), No. 1, March 1975, p.20.

53. See "Mieliediplomasie en nasionale strategie", *Die Afrikaner*, 11/7/1980. *Die Afrikaner* is the mouthpiece of the *Herstigte Nasionale Party*.

54. Personal interview with Mr BJ Vorster.

55. *South Africa 1982, op. cit.*, p.739.

56. *Loc. cit.*

57. Munger, ES, *Foreign Policy, op. cit.*, pp.34-6 & 51-3.

58. For example, Van Aswegen, HJ, *Geskiedenis van Afrika: Van die Vroegste Oorspronge tot Onafhanklikheid*, Academica, Pretoria, 1980, 557pp. A very recent publication by a Pretoria University historian who has written several books on aspects of contemporary African history is Van Rensburg, APJ, *Moderne Afrika*, De Jager-HAUM, Pretoria, 1983, 317pp.

59. For example, Prinsloo, DS, *United States Foreign Policy and the Republic of South Africa*, Foreign Affairs Association, Pretoria, 1978, 141pp.; Spring, GM, *Confrontation: The Approaching Crisis between the United States and South Africa*, Valiant Publishers, Sandton, 1977, 181pp., and Steward, AW, *op. cit.*, 308pp.

60. The Africa Institute and the SAIIA are two of the most prolific producers of studies on South Africa's relations with black states.

61. Olivier, GC, *op. cit.*, 236pp. The author is Professor in the Department of Political Science and International Politics, Pretoria University. In August 1983 his university seconded him for two years to the foreign ministry.

62. Spence, JE, *Republic under Pressure, op. cit.*, 132pp.

63. See Willers, D & S Begg (Eds), *South Africa and Sanctions: Genesis and Prospects*, South African Institute of Race Relations/South African Institute of International Affairs, Johannesburg, 1979, 95pp.

64. Munger, ES, *Foreign Policy, op. cit.*, p.52.

65. *Loc. cit.*

66. In discussing Soviet designs in Africa, PW Botha in at least two public addresses approvingly cited the views of "an authority on these matters, namely Prof. Connaught [*sic* – he meant Kunert], of the Witwatersrand University, Department of International Relations". *Toespraak deur Sy Edele PW Botha DVD LV, Eerste Minister, tydens 'n Openbare Vergadering te Durban, op 21 April 1981*, p.5., and *Toespraak deur Sy Edele PW Botha DVD LV, Eerste Minister, tydens 'n Openbare Vergadering te Randburg op 25 April 1981*, p.10, both Roneoed, Department of Foreign Affairs and Information.

67. Quoted by Wilkins, I & H Strydom, *op. cit.*, p.345.

68. Quoted *ibid.*, p.410. Pelzer's official history of the *Broederbond* has been cited in Chapter 1.

69. Serfontein, JHP, *op. cit.*, p.98.

70. See *ibid.*, pp.99-125, and Wilkins I & H Strydom, *op. cit.*, pp.5-7 & 190.

71. Serfontein, JHP, *op. cit.*, 278pp., and Wilkins I & H Strydom, *op. cit.*, 597pp. According to a former spy of the Bureau for State Security, the *Broederbond* was so anxious to stop the latter book being

published that the authors were offered a bribe of over R30 000 (Winter, G, *op. cit.*, p.87). The *Broederbond's* published official history (Pelzer, AN, *op. cit.*, 193pp.), though useful, is not surprisingly far less revealing than the other two books on the organisation's influence in the corridors of power.

72. Munger, ES, *Foreign Policy, op. cit.*, pp.56 & 82.
73. See Chapter 1.
74. Serfontein, JHP, *op. cit.*, p.145.
75. Wilkins, I & H Strydom, *op. cit.*, p.30.
76. A breakdown of the *Broederbond's* membership figures for 1977 showed that the teaching profession represented the largest group (including university and school teachers) – 20,36%; followed by farmers – 18,81%; clergymen – 7,12%, and the public service – 4,35%. In 1968 16 managers of newspaper groups and 22 editors were *Broederbonders*; by 1977 these figures may well have increased. (Quoted *ibid.*, p.366.) Membership in 1968 stood at 8 154. (Quoted by Serfontein, JHP, *op. cit.*, p.105.)
77. Quoted by Serfontein, JHP, *op. cit.*, p.110.
78. Quoted by Wilkins, I & H Strydom, *op. cit.*, p.356.
79. Viljoen, quoted *loc. cit.*
80. Serfontein, JHP, *op. cit.*, pp.101, 102, 105, 123 & 153, and Wilkins, I & H Strydom, *op. cit.*, pp.239-52.
81. Quoted by Wilkins, I & H Strydom, *op. cit.*, p.28. See also Serfontein, JHP, *op. cit.*, pp.123, 146 & 156.
82. Quoted by Wilkins, I & H Strydom, *op. cit.*, p.29.
83. *Ibid.*, p.356.
84. *Ibid.*, p.27.
85. *Ibid.*, p.31.
86. Quoted *ibid.*, p.441.
87. Quoted by Serfontein, JHP, *op. cit.*, p.156.
88. Quoted *ibid.*, p.155.
89. *Ibid.*, p.156.
90. See Wilkins, I & H Strydom, *op. cit.*, pp.157ff.
91. *Ibid.*, p.1.
92. HA Deb., 8/12/1978, col. 532.
93. See Wilkins, I & H Strydom, *op. cit.*, p.440.
94. Quoted by Serfontein, JHP, *op. cit.*, p.101.
95. *Toespraak deur Sy Edele PW Botha . . . te Randburg op 25 April 1981, op. cit.*, p.6.
96. Wilkins, I & H Strydom, *op. cit.* (title of the book).
97. For details about the origins of the South Africa Foundation, see Gerber, LB, *op. cit.*, pp.1-22. Gerber in May 1960 joined the Foundation as Assistant Director and subsequently became Director.
98. In 1981 the Committees were the following: American, Australian, Austrian, Belgian, Canadian, Danish, Finnish, French, German, Hellenic, Israeli, Italian, Lebanese, Netherlands, New Zealand, Norwegian, Portuguese, Swedish and Swiss.
99. Beck, WF de la Harpe, Presidential Address to the South Africa Foundation, 11 March 1981, reprinted in *South Africa International*, Vol. II, No. 4, April 1981, pp.177ff. One of the Founda-

tion's main activities was sponsoring visits to South Africa by eminent foreigners. The extent to which the programme has reached into the corridors of power is seen in the fact that every Foundation-sponsored guest from Westminster between 1968 and 1970 became a member of the Heath Cabinet, except for one, who became Speaker of the House of Commons (Gerber, LB, *op. cit.*, p.150).
100. It is only necessary to read the regular *SA Foundation News*, the quarterly *South Africa International*, and such occasional publications as Breytenbach, WJ (Ed), *The Constellation of States: A Consideration*, SA Foundation, Johannesburg, 1980, 81pp.
101. Munger, ES, *Foreign Policy, op. cit.*, p.78.
102. Gerber, LB, *op. cit.*, pp.13, 152 & 164.
103. See Beck, WF de la Harpe, *op. cit.*, pp.180-83.
104. Munger, ES, *Foreign Policy, op. cit.*, p.57.
105. See Mulder, PWA, *op. cit.*, p.417.
106. *The Star*, 12/3/1981.
107. *Natal Witness*, 21/3/1981.
108. Munger, ES, *Foreign Policy, op. cit.*, pp.76-8.
109. *The USSALEP Story 1958-1980*, USSALEP brochure, Washington DC.
110. See *Beeld*, 12/2/1981.
111. See Chapter 5.
112. United Nations, *Resolutions of the General Assembly, Twenty-Third Session, 24 September to 21 December 1968*, p.20.
113. United Nations, *Resolutions of the General Assembly, Twenty-Eighth Session, 18 September to 18 December 1973*, p.33; *Resolutions . . . Thirty-First session, 21 September to 22 December 1976*, p.15, and *Resolutions . . . Thirty-Second Regular Session, 20 September to 21 December 1977*, pp.63 & 69.
114. Gordon, L (Ed), *Survey of Race Relations in South Africa 1981*, SAIRR, Johannesburg, 1982, p.25.
115. *Survey of Race Relations 1980, op. cit.*, pp.60 & 61.
116. *Toespraak deur Sy Edele PW Botha . . . te Randburg op 25 April 1981, op. cit.*, p.8. See also *Toespraak deur Generaal Magnus Malan, op. cit.*, pp.6 & 7.
117. *Survey of Race Relations 1981, op. cit.*, p.26.
118. *Survey of Race Relations 1979, op. cit.*, pp.41-3; *Survey of Race Relations 1980, op. cit.*, p.53, and *Survey of Race Relations 1981, op. cit.*, p.27.
119. *Survey of Race Relations 1979, op. cit.*, p.20.
120. *Ibid.*, pp.50 & 51.
121. *Survey of Race Relations 1980, op. cit.*, p.56 and *Survey of Race Relations 1981, op. cit.*, p.30.
122. See *Survey of Race Relations 1981, op. cit.*, pp.28 & 29.
123. Republic of South Africa, *Report of the Commission of Inquiry into the Mass Media* (Steyn Commission), Vol. 3, 1982, Roneoed, p.981, and Herbst, DAS, *Die Dilemma van die Moderne Koerant: 'n Historiese Ondersoek met Toespitsing op Maatskaplike, Ekonomiese en Politieke Aspekte,*

D. Phil. dissertation, University of Potchefstroom, 1973, pp.215 & 216.

124. Williams, F, *The Right to Know: The Rise of the World Press,* Longman, London, 1969, p.148, quoted by Steyn Commission, Vol. 3. *op. cit.,* p.970.

125. Sussens, A, "The English language press", in *South Africa Today, Financial Mail* publication, 1966, p.77, quoted by Herbst, DAS, *op. cit.,* p.222.

126. Steyn Commission, Vol. 3. *op. cit.,* p.974.

127. Potter, E, *The Press as Opposition: The Political Role of South African Newspapers,* Chatto & Windus, London, 1975, p.31.

128. On the history of *Die Burger,* see Scannell, JP (Ed), *Keeromstraat 30,* Nasionale Boekhandel, Cape Town, 1965, 267pp.

129. Steyn Commission, Vol. 3. *op. cit.,* p.974 & 975.

130. *Ibid.,* pp.977-80.

131. *South Africa 1982, op. cit.,* p.782.

132. Broughton, M, *Press and Politics of South Africa,* Purnell & Sons, Cape Town, 1961, p.7.

133. Potter, E, *op. cit.,* p.170.

134. *Loc. cit.,* and Broughton, M, *op. cit.,* p.7.

135. Steyn Commission, Vol. 3, *op. cit.,* pp.1073 & 1075.

136. *Average sales per issue:*

Newspaper	January-June 1981	July-December 1981
Argus	101 700	99 843
Beeld	66 197	67 963
Die Burger*	69 788	68 641
Cape Times*	64 095	63 486
The Citizen*	60 833	65 051
Daily News*	87 425	88 928
Hoofstad*	14 409	13 628
Pretoria News*	25 849	24 876
Rand Daily Mail	109 819	106 759
Rapport	412 294	407 215
Sowetan	65 315	72 846
The Star*	173 206	168 511
Sunday Times	470 116	464 989
Die Transvaler*	45 942	44 109
Die Vaderland*	40 199	40 998
*only weekday editions		

Source: Audit Bureau of Circulations of South Africa Limited, Johannesburg. (Schedule based on certificates received until closing date as at 12 February 1982.)

137. See Republic of South Africa, *Verslag van die Kommissie van Ondersoek na Beriggewing oor Sekerheidsaangeleenthede Rakende die Suid-Afrikaanse Weermag en die Suid-Afrikaanse Polisiemag,* RP 52/1980, Government Printer, Pretoria, 1980, pp.102, 154-6. This Commission, like the Commission of Inquiry into the Mass Media, was chaired by Mr Justice MT Steyn.

138. The Steyn Commission, Vol. 3, *op. cit.,* p.943, took the rather questionable view that "the overall effect of the restrictive legislation has been widely exaggerated and even sloganised", claiming that "certain members of the media and certain of their minions", had overzealously created "a false image of 'press oppression and censorship' ". For a different view, see Duff, T, "A legislated erosion of freedom", *Ecquid Novi,* Vol. 1, No. 2, 1980, pp.128-35.

139. On the Council and Press Code, see Steyn Commisson, Vol. 3. *op. cit.,* pp.992 & 993.

140. For details, see *ibid.,* pp.1045-50 and *South Africa 1982, op. cit.,* pp.778-80.

141. Steyn Commission, Vol. 3, *op. cit.,* pp.984 & 985.

142. Mulder, CE, "Interessant of belangrik?", *Ecquid Novi,* Vol. 2, No. 2, 1981, pp.69-90.

143. The series was subsequently published as a booklet: Parker, A, *Secret U.S. War Against South Africa,* SA Today, Johannesburg, 1977, 76pp.

144. Quoted in HA Deb., 19/4/1960, col. 5558.

145. Quoted in HA Deb., 12/5/1959, col. 5604.

146. See *Report of the Commission of Inquiry into the Press, op. cit.,* Annexure XX. Useful background information on the Commission's origins, terms of reference, proceedings and eventual findings is contained in Potter, E, *op. cit.,* pp.102-8.

147. *Department of Information Report 1974, op. cit.,* pp.3 & 5.

148. *Department of Information Report 1976, op. cit.,* p.3.

149. *Loc. cit.*

150. *Report of the Commission of Inquiry into the Press, op. cit.,* pp.479 & 1175.

151. Mulder, CE, "World focus on South Africa", *South Africa International,* Vol. 12, No. 2, October 1981, pp.384-93. For an earlier content analysis of Austrian press reporting by the same author, see "Some stereotyped images of South Africa", *Politikon,* Vol. 1, No. 1, June 1974, pp.15-27.

152. Steyn Commission, Vol. 3, *op. cit.,* p.1032.

153. Potter, E. *op. cit.,* p.130.

154. Steyn Commission, Vol. 3, *op. cit.,* pp.950 & 951. The Defence Force responded to Angolan reports of a massive South African invasion by issuing dismissals, denials and non-committal replies. Only after the military thrust had been well under way did the military authorities openly admit South African involvement and provide the press with official and reliable information.

155. See Vosloo, T, *Schalk Pienaar: 10 Jaar Politieke Kommentaar,* Tafelberg, Cape Town, 1975, pp.22, 41 & 42. (Pienaar was at the time – 1968-9 – editor of *Die Beeld,* Nasionale Pers's Sunday paper.)

156. Cillié, PJ, *Tydgenote,* Tafelberg, Cape Town, 1980, pp.16-23.

157. Steyn Commission, Vol. 3, *op. cit.,* pp.1073 & 1227. The Commission (Vol. 2, *op. cit.,* p.816), in its peculiar phraseology, directed the following admonition at the English papers: "The South African English-language press will . . . do well . . . to exert themselves in preventing South Africa from being strangled by a cross-weave of erroneous and destructive perceptions."

158. "Dawie" (columnist), *Die Burger,* 22/9/1973, quoted in Steyn Commission, Vol. 3, *op. cit.,* pp.1037 & 1038. See also Herbst, DAS, *op. cit.,* pp.351 &

360.

159. See *Beeld*, 4/9/1981, quoted in Steyn Commission, Vol. 3, *op. cit.*, pp.796-9.
160. See Potter, E, *op. cit.*, p.170.
161. *The Times*, 17/9/1958, quoted by Geldenhuys, DJ, *Anglo-South African Relations, op. cit.*, p.232.
162. *Rand Daily Mail*, 27/4/1974.
163. *Die Transvaler*, 26/4/1974.
164. *The Star*, 26/4/1974.
165. *Rand Daily Mail*, 26/8/1975.
166. *The Star*, 27/8/1975.
167. *Die Transvaler*, 26/8/1975.
168. *Rand Daily Mail*, 23/3/1976.
169. *Die Transvaler*, 26/3/1976.
170. *Die Burger*, 22/3/1976.
171. *Rand Daily Mail*, 26/6/1976.
172. *Die Burger*, 28/6/1976.
173. *Die Transvaler*, 28/6/1976.
174. *Rand Daily Mail*, 21/5/1977.
175. *Die Burger*, 23/5/1977.
176. *Die Transvaler*, 23/5/1977.
177. *Die Burger*, 7/11/1977.
178. *Die Transvaler*, 5/11/1977.
179. *Rand Daily Mail*, 8/11/1977.
180. *The Star*, 7/11/1977.
181. *The Star*, 2/10/1978.
182. *Rand Daily Mail*, 4 & 13/12/1978.
183. *Die Burger*, 11/12/1978.
184. *Die Burger*, 6/3/1980.
185. *Die Transvaler*, 5/3/1980.
186. *Beeld*, 5/3/1980.
187. *Rand Daily Mail*, 6/3/1980.
188. *The Star*, 5/3/1980.
189. *Sunday Post*, 16/3/1980.
190. *Post*, 5/3/1980.
191. *Sunday Post*, 9/3/1980.
192. *Post*, 6/3/1980.
193. See Seiler, J, "The world perspectives of South African media", *Communications in Africa*, Vol. 1, No. 5, March 1974, pp.26-8, for a content analysis of *To the Point's* news coverage.
194. Steyn Commission, Vol. 3, *op. cit.*, pp.1094-1101.
195. *Ibid.*, pp.1101-9.
196. *Ibid.*, p.1073. In April 1980 the prime minister told Parliament that the television service, falling under state control, "will in future be instructed not to feature reports of the onslaughts on South Africa by revolutionary elements as main news items" (Quoted *ibid.*, p.1050). On the content of SABC radio news broadcasts, see Seiler, J, *op. cit.*, pp.28-32.
197. The opinion survey was conducted by Market and Opinion Surveys (Pty) Ltd (M & M) of Bellville, Cape, at the request of the South African Institute of International Affairs. Self-completion questionnaires were sent to the approximately 2 400 members of M & M's nationally representative white consumer panel in February 1982; 1 999 responded. The findings of the survey have in the meantime been published, under the name of the present author, titled *What Do We Think? A Survey of White Opinion on Foreign Policy Issues*, SAIIA, Johannesburg, 1982. This publication provides a far more detailed analysis of the results than the present book can; the latter is no more than a brief summary of the former. Further information on the methodology used, the composition of the sample and the questionnaire can be found in the SAIIA publication.
198. Adam, H, *South Africa: Sociological Perspectives*, Oxford University Press, London, 1971, pp.90ff.
199. Hudson, W, GF Jacobs & S Biesheuvel, *Anatomy of South Africa: A Scientific Study of Present Day Attitudes*, Purnell, Cape Town, 1966, p.27.
200. Lever, H, "Public opinion and voting", in De Crespigny, ARC & R Schrire, (Eds), *The Government and Politics of South Africa*, Juta, Cape Town, 1978, p.144.
201. Quoted by Lever, H, *op. cit.*, pp.144 & 145.
202. Quoted by Schlemmer, L, "External pressures and local attitudes and interests", in Clifford-Vaughan, F McA (Ed), *International Pressures and Political Change in South Africa*, Oxford University Press, Cape Town, 1978, p.79.
203. Adam, H, *op. cit.*, pp.90ff.
204. Schlemmer, L, *op. cit.*, p.79.
205. In an opinion poll conducted for *Rapport* in 1974 respondents were asked, "What three issues should the government give its attention to after the coming general election?" "Terrorism" was mentioned by 25%, a further 14,9% mentioned "security" or "defence". (Quoted by Lever, H, *op. cit.*, p.144.)
206. Hanf, T, H Weiland & G Vierdag, *South Africa: The Prospects of Peaceful Change – An Empirical Enquiry into the Possibility of Democratic Conflict Regulation*, David Philip Publishers, Cape Town, 1981, pp.206ff.
207. Having noted whites' fears of the future, one should reflect on the findings of a survey that probed the reactions of whites in Pretoria to a terrorist siege of a bank in the city in January 1980. In the incident three terrorists were killed by police, and a white bank employee also died. The survey, conducted by the Human Sciences Research Council shortly after the unprecedented act of terrorism, found that 92% of the respondents said that before as well as after the incident they felt whites will survive in South Africa. Nearly 89% had, before the incident, thought there was a future for them and their children in South Africa; afterwards, 87,7% still felt that way. No less than 96,3% of the respondents believed that terrorists would not be able to defeat South African security forces, and 88,6% were of the opinion that terrorists could not destroy whites' morale. An interesting finding was that 76,7% of white Pretorians did not think that blacks generally condoned such acts of terrorism as

the bank siege (*Die Afrikaner*, 13/1/1982).

208. Hanf, T, *et al., op. cit.*, p.210.
209. Hudson, W, *et al., op. cit.*, p.37.
210. Conducted by Market Research Africa and published in *The Argus*, 12/5/1976, cited in Hallett, R, *op. cit.*, p.384.
211. Quoted by Schlemmer, L, *op. cit.*, p.79.
212. Quoted by Frankel, J, *op. cit.*, p.73.
213. Schlemmer, L, *op. cit.*, p.79.
214. Hanf, T, *et al., op. cit.*, pp.321ff.
215. *The Quail Report, Feb 8 80,* Report of the Ciskei Commission, Conference Associates, Pretoria, 1980, p.225.
216. *The Buthelezi Commission, The Requirements for Stability and Development in KwaZulu and Natal,* Vol. 1, H & H Publications, Durban, 1982, p.203.
217. Hanf, T, *et al., op. cit.*, pp.321ff.
218. *The Quail Report, op. cit.*, pp.109, 195 & 242.
219. Cited in *The Buthelezi Commission, op. cit.*, p.244.
220. *Ibid.*, p.245.
221. *Pretoria News*, 23/9/1981, and *The Star*, 23/9/1981 & 25/9/1981.
222. See *Beeld*, 24/9/1981.
223. *The Buthelezi Commission, op. cit.*, pp.244 & 245.
224. Hanf, T, *et al., op. cit.*, pp.325 & 326.
225. *The Buthelezi Commission, op. cit.*, pp.210-13.
226. *The Markinor South African Social Value Study,* in association with Gallup International, Markinor, Johannesburg, March 1982, pp.90-93.
227. *The Star*, 22/2/1980. See note 207 above, for white reaction.
228. *The Buthelezi Commission, op. cit.*, pp.204-7.
229. *The Star*, 21/5/1980, and *Beeld* 22/5/1980.
230. *The Buthelezi Commission, op. cit.*, p.207.
231. *Daily Dispatch*, 12/4/1982.
232. Edelstein, ML, *What Do Coloureds Think?,* Labour and Community Consultants, Johannesburg, 1974, p.60.
233. *The Star*, 23/9/1981.
234. *The Star*, 25/9/1981.
235. *The Markinor South African Social Value Study, op. cit.*, pp.90-93.

CHAPTER 7

1. See Johnston, AM, "Domestic concerns and international pressures: the evolution of the new international relations", in Clifford-Vaughan, F McA, *op. cit.*, pp.9-26.
2. Rosenau, JN, "Toward the study of national-international linkages", in Rosenau, JN (Ed), *Linkage Politics: Essays on the Convergence of National and International Systems,* The Free Press, New York, 1969, p.45.
3. *International Convention on the Suppression and Punishment of the Crime of Apartheid,* adopted by the UN General Assembly at its 2185th plenary meeting, 30 November 1973.
4. Rosenau, JN, *Linkages, op. cit.*, p.45.
5. *Ibid.*, p.53. Rosenau distinguished six "subenvi-ronments": the contiguous, regional, cold war, racial, resource and organisational.
6. United Nations, *Resolutions Adopted by the General Assembly during its Fifteenth Session, Vol. 2, 7 March to 21 April 1961,* pp.5 & 6.
7. United Nations, *Resolutions Adopted by the General Assembly during its Seventeenth Session, 18 September to 20 December 1962,* p.9.
8. United Nations, *Resolutions and Decisions of the Security Council 1963 (Eighteenth Year),* p.7. See also *Resolutions and Decisions of the Security Council 1960 (Fifteenth Year),* p.1, for the resolution (No. 134, 1 April 1960) adopted after the Sharpeville shooting.
9. Resolution 418, adopted by the Security Council at its 2046th meeting on 4 November 1977.
10. See United Nations, *Resolutions and Decisions of the Security Council 1976 (Thirty-First Year),* pp.10 & 11; *Resolutions and Decisions Adopted by the General Assembly during its Thirty-First Session,* Vol. 1, 21 September to 22 December 1976, pp.10-19, and *Report of the World Conference for Action against Apartheid, Lagos, 22-26 August 1977,* Vol. 1, pp.31-6.
11. Bissell, RE, *Apartheid and International Organizations,* Westview Press, Boulder, 1977, pp.32, 33, 161, 162 & 167.
12. *Report of the World Conference for Action against Apartheid, op. cit.*, pp.31-6.
13. *Department of Information Report . . . 1977, op. cit.*, pp.17 & 18. A case for American punitive measures against South Africa, including an inventory of instruments, was made by Ferguson, C & WR Cotter, "South Africa: what is to be done?", *Foreign Affairs*, Vol. 56, No. 2, January 1978, pp.253-74. For a searching assessment of this kind of approach to influencing South Africa from outside, see Stultz, NM, "Foreign pressures on South Africa: the thumb-screw as conceptual frame", *International Affairs Bulletin,* Vol. 4, No. 1, 1980, pp.27-42.
14. See Shepherd, GW, *Anti-Apartheid: Transnational Conflict and Western Policy in the Liberation of South Africa,* Greenwood Press, Westpoint, 1977, pp.24ff., and Soref, H and I Greig, *The Puppeteers,* Tandem Books, London, 1965, 127pp.
15. Bissell, RE, *op. cit.*, pp.32ff. See also note 3, above.
16. See Vosloo, WB, "Die implikasies van buitelandse druk op Suid-Afrika", *Politikon*, Vol. 5, No. 2, December 1978, pp.125-41.
17. Dale, R, "South Africa and the international community", *World Politics*, Vol. 18, No. 2, January 1966, p.305.
18. Austin, D, *Britain and South Africa,* Oxford University Press, London, 1966, p.12, and Macdonald, R St J, "The resort to economic coercion by international political organisations", *University of Toronto Law Journal,* Vol. 17, 1967, pp. 113 &

114.

19. Dale, R, *op. cit.,* p.306. See also Schrire, RA, "South Africa and the world: which way now?", *International Affairs Bulletin,* Vol. 2, No. 1, 1978, pp.32 & 33.

20. United Nations, *Security Council Official Records, Nineteenth Year, Supplement for April, May and June 1964,* pp.23-43.

21. United Nations, *Resolutions of the General Assembly, Twenty-Fifth Session, 16 September to 17 December 1969,* p.24.

22. See United Nations, *Resolutions of the General Assembly, Twenty-Eighth Session, 18 September to 18 December 1973,* p.33, and *Resolutions of the General Assembly, Thirty-Second Regular Session, 20 September to 21 December 1977,* pp.63 & 69.

23. United Nations, *Resolutions of the General Assembly, Twenty-Fifth Session, 15 September to 17 December 1970,* p.34, and *Resolutions of the General Assembly, Thirtieth Session, 16 September to 17 December 1975,* p.37.

24. Holsti, KJ (1977), *op. cit.,* p.367.

25. *Ibid.,* p.368. See also Jervis, R, *The Logic of Images in International Relations,* Princeton University Press, Princeton, 1970, p.12.

26. Quoted by Smuts, JC (jr), *op. cit.,* p.498.

27. HA Deb., 4/5/1954, col. 4495 and 4496.

28. HA Deb., 9/3/1960, col. 3013-18.

29. HA Deb., 21/3/1980, col. 3319, and 20/4/1979, col. 4606.

30. HA Deb., 6/6/1979, col. 7956-60.

31. *Toespraak deur Generaal Magnus Malan, op. cit.,* p.1ff.

32. *The Star,* 30/8/1977.

33. Rosenau, JN, *Linkages, op. cit.,* pp.49-54. See also note 5, above.

34. The author's questionnaire to the Minister of Foreign Affairs and Information read: "The claim is commonly made that changes to South Africa's sports policy have largely been the result of foreign pressure. What role does foreign pressure play in the shaping of both domestic and foreign policies?" The Minister replied: "No government worth its salt allows itself to be prescribed to on how to handle its affairs. Foreign policy is formulated with the goal of protecting and promoting South Africa's interests abroad in the best way. Because the international community continuously undergoes changes and the environment in which foreign policy has to be applied consequently also changes continuously, it is imperative that foreign policy should be adaptable without surrendering overall goals." His predecessor, Muller, insisted that, "We never allowed ourselves to be dictated to by the outside world in my time", but he significantly added that he had often stated in public that South Africa's first duty was "to get our own house in order". He had always been convinced, Muller said, that South Africa would only normalise its position in the world once its domestic situation had been normalised and its peoples enjoyed peaceful co-existence (personal interview). One Cabinet minister, in a personal interview, was frank enough to declare that South African foreign policy was not initiated by the policy formulators in the first instance, but rather consisted of reactions to foreign impulses – by implication also external pressures.

35. Best known of the few studies by local authors are Hirschmann, D, "Pressures on apartheid", *Foreign Affairs,* Vol. 52, No. 1, October 1973, pp.168-79; Worrall, D, "South Africa's reactions to external criticism", in Rhoodie, NJ (Ed), *South African Dialogue,* McGraw-Hill, Johannesburg, 1973, pp.562-89, and the collection of essays published under the already cited title, *International Pressures and Political Change in South Africa,* edited by F McA Clifford-Vaughan. Reference can also be made to a study by a well-known South African-born scholar: Nolutshungu, SC, "The impact of external opposition on South African politics" in Thompson, LM & J Butler (Eds), *Change in Contemporary South Africa,* University of California Press, Berkeley, 1975, pp.369-99.

36. Rosenau, JN, *Linkages, op. cit.,* pp.46 & 55.

37. HA Deb., 21/3/1980, col. 3321.

38. PW Botha, HA Deb., 1/5/1980, col. 5298.

39. Worrall, D, in Rhoodie, N, *op. cit.,* pp.572-7.

40. These options are considered in some detail in Geldenhuys, DJ, *Total National Strategy, op. cit.,* pp.25-37.

41. Olivier, GC, *op. cit.,* p.213.

42. *Address by the Hon. RF Botha, South African Minister for Foreign Affairs, to Members and Guests of the Swiss-South African Association in Zurich, on 7th March 1979,* Press Section, South African Embassy, Berne, pp.24 & 25.

43. See Geldenhuys, DJ & TD Venter, *op. cit.,* pp.51ff.

44. Martin, D & P Johnson, *op. cit.,* pp.145 & 194, and Moorcraft, PL & P McLaughlin, *Chimurenga! The War in Rhodesia 1965-1980: A Military History,* Sygma/Collins, Johannesburg, 1982, p.31.

45. See Johnson, RW, *How Long Will South Africa Survive?,* Macmillan, Johannesburg, 1977, pp.243-86.

46. Martin, D & P Johnson, *op. cit.,* p.239.

47. Moorcraft, PL & P McLaughlin, *op. cit.,* p.36.

48. *Ibid.,* pp.27 & 167.

49. *Ibid.,* p.27.

50. Quoted by Martin, D & P Johnson, *op. cit.,* p.253.

51. *Ibid.,* pp.248 & 253.

52. Moorcraft, PL & P McLaughlin, *op. cit.,* p.39.

53. Johnson, HC, *Rhodesia to Zimbabwe: Roadblocks on the Path to Majority Rule,* M.A. dissertation, California State University, Fullerton, 1979, p.250.

54. See Martin, D & P Johnson, *op. cit.*, pp.308 & 309.
55. *Ibid.*, p.153.
56. *Ibid.*, pp.236-8.
57. Bissell, RE, *op. cit.*, p.126.
58. See Lapchick, RE, *The Politics of Race and International Sport: The Case of South Africa,* Ph.D. dissertation, University of Denver, 1973, pp.60ff.
59. Bissell, RE, *op. cit.*, p.127.
60. Lapchick, RE, *op. cit.*, pp.69-73.
61. *Ibid.*, pp.74 & 75.
62. *Ibid.*, pp.110ff.
63. *Ibid.*, pp.162ff., and Saaiman, GB, *Suid-Afrika se Sportisolasie en die Invloed op die Binnelandse Politiek,* M.A. dissertation, University of the Orange Free State, 1981, p.42.
64. Saaiman, GB, *op. cit.*, pp.42 & 43.
65. See *ibid.*, pp.53-74.
66. Kotzé, G, *Sport en Politiek,* Makro, Pretoria, 1978, pp.39 & 40.
67. *Ibid.*, pp.59 & 60.
68. Quoted by Lapchick, RE, *op. cit.*, pp.180-82. See also Kotzé. G, *op. cit.*, pp.65 & 66.
69. Kotzé, G, *op. cit.*, p.66.
70. Quoted *ibid.*, pp.68 & 69.
71. Lapchick, RE, *op. cit.*, pp.171 & 172.
72. Saaiman, GB, *op. cit.*, pp.182-4.
73. Kotzé, G, *op. cit.*, p.90.
74. See *ibid.*, pp.89ff., and Saaiman, GB, *op. cit.*, pp.187-281.
75. Quoted by Saaiman, GB, *op. cit.*, p.187.
76. Quoted *ibid.*, p.77.
77. In February 1980 the government gave a mandate to the Human Sciences Research Council to investigate the structure of South African sport. The first report was submitted in September 1980 by the committee, which specifically investigated legislation that hampered sport in South Africa. The committee recommended the repeal or amendment of several pieces of legislation *(Survey of Race Relations 1980, op. cit.*, pp.585-8). The main report on the investigation was published in 1982.
78. The Commission of Inquiry into Labour Legislation was appointed in June 1977. Chaired by Prof. NE Wiehahn, the Commission was to inquire into existing labour legislation, *inter alia* with a view to adjusting the present system of labour relations to "provide more effectively for the needs of our changing times". The first of a series of reports was presented in May 1979, and outlined principles of change in existing discriminatory labour practices *(South Africa 1982, op. cit.*, pp.463ff.).
79. Kenney, H, *op. cit.*, 278pp.
80. HA Deb., 10/4/1961, col. 4191 and Pelzer, AN, *Verwoerd Speaks, op. cit.*, p.278.
81. Quoted by Austin, D, *op. cit.*, p.10.
82. HA Deb., 10/4/1961, col. 4191.
83. Statement by Ambassador RF Botha, Permanent Representative of South Africa to the United Nations, in the Security Council on 24 October 1974, in *Southern Africa Record,* No. 1, March 1975, p.21.
84. *Senate Debates,* 23/10/1974, col. 3340 & 3346.
85. Theron, E & JB du Toit, *op. cit.*, pp.104 & 105.
86. *South Africa 1982, op. cit.*, pp.137 & 138.
87. Worrall, D, in Rhoodie, NJ, *op. cit.*, p.585.
88. Hirschmann, D, *op. cit.*, pp.175 and 176.
89. See Bissell, RE, *op. cit.*, pp.167-9.
90. Personal interview with Mr BJ Vorster.
91. Scott, D, *Ambassador in Black and White: Thirty Years of Changing Africa,* Weidenfeld & Nicolson, London, 1981, p.197.
92. See Vance, C, *Hard Choices: Critical Years in American Foreign Policy,* Simon & Schuster, New York, 1983, pp.277ff.
93. *Ibid.*, p.308.
94. Quoted by Geldenhuys, DJ, *Anglo-South African Relations, op. cit.*, p.416.
95. An interesting speculation in Western diplomatic circles was that Vorster had agreed to the internal Namibian election of December 1978 before he resigned the premiership in September in order to promote Pik Botha's chances in the succession contest. By insisting that the election go ahead despite strong Western objections, Pik Botha would then presumably have cut a strong figure with the National Party caucus (and thus hopefully countered suspicions about his being submissive to foreign pressures).
96. It was widely rumoured that only strong South African pressure eventually got the DTA leader, Mr Dirk Mudge, to the Geneva conference.
97. Dr Gerrit Viljoen, who served as (South African-appointed) Administrator-General of Namibia (1979-80), is said to have reported to Pretoria that SWAPO was certain to win an election, largely because of its massive support among the majority Ovambo ethnic group.
98. This summary of South African views is based on the minutes of a discussion between Pik Botha and Dr Chester Crocker, US Assistant Secretary of State for African Affairs, on Namibia in April 1981. The secret American minutes were published by the left-wing American journal *Covert Action,* and reported in *Beeld,* 8/7/1981. It was rumoured (not in the *Beeld* report) that when Crocker in April visited South Africa for talks on Namibia, PW Botha refused to receive him because Crocker's views on SWAPO differed so profoundly from the prime minister's.
99. See *ibid.*
100. To date South Africa's biggest cross-border attack on SWAPO occurred in May 1978, when it raided SWAPO's Cassinga base with heavy enemy loss of life. For the five Western powers "this raid could scarcely have been more disastrously timed", according to Sir David Scott, then British ambassador to South Africa. It was certain to make progress on a settlement package in the UN Security Council extremely difficult. He however acknowledged that South Africa had made it absolutely

clear "where the military balance of power lay, and this message was not entirely lost on SWAPO" (Scott, D, *op. cit.*, p.213).

101. See *ibid.*, p.210.
102. See *ibid.*, pp.216, 232 & 233.
103. *Ibid.*, pp.210, 216 & 217.

CHAPTER 8

1. Wilkinson, DO, *Comparative Foreign Relations: Framework and Methods*, Dickinson, California, 1969, pp.110-13.
2. Munger, ES, *Foreign Policy, op. cit.*, p.51.
3. Hermann, CF, "Decision structure and process influences on foreign policy", in East, MA, *et al.* (Eds), *Why Nations Act: Theoretical Perspectives for Comparative Foreign Policy Studies*, Sage Publications, Beverley Hills, 1978, pp.69-90.
4. See Fleron, FJ, "System attributes and career attributes: the Soviet political leadership system, 1952 to 1965", in Beck, C *et al.*, *Comparative Communist Political Leadership*, David McKay, New York, 1973, pp.43-53. In a co-optation system, according to Fleron's definition, the necessary technical skills required for running society "are acquired by coopting into the political elite members of various specialized elites in society, thus giving them direct access to the policy-making process". The co-opted specialists enter into the political or party elite midway or late in their careers, i.e. after having spent at least seven years in a non-political sector of society.
5. For an analysis of the 12-point plan, see Geldenhuys, DJ, *Total National Strategy, op. cit.*, pp.10ff.
6. Kohl, WL, "The Nixon-Kissinger foreign policy system and US-European relations: patterns of policy making", *World Politics*, Vol. 28, No. 1, October 1975, pp.1-43. Kohl served as a member of the National Security Council staff during 1970-71.
7. Hermann, MG, "Effects of personal characteristics of political leaders on foreign policy", in East, MA, *et al., op. cit.*, p.64.
8. Expression used by Russett, BM & EC Hanson, *Interest and Ideology*, WH Freeman, San Francisco, 1975, p.7. For overviews of the relevant literature, see Hermann, CF, *op. cit.*, pp.74-6, and Hermann, MG, in East, MA *et al., op. cit.*, pp.50-56.
9. Kissinger, HA, "Domestic structure and foreign policy", in Rosenau, JN (Ed), *International Politics and Foreign Policy: A Reader in Research and Theory*, The Free Press, New York, 1969, pp.261-75. (Kissinger's study was first published in 1966 before his appointment as Special Assistant for National Security Affairs and later as Secretary of State.)
10. Du Plessis, E, *op. cit.*, pp.6 & 7.
11. See Geldenhuys, DJ, *Anglo-South African Relations, op. cit.*, pp.354ff.

12. Quoted by Cockram, G-M, *op. cit.*, p.124.
13. Wilkinson, DO, *op. cit.*, pp.113 & 114.
14. Hermann, MG, in East, MA, *et al., op. cit.*, pp.49-68, and Hermann, MG, "Explaining foreign policy behaviour using the personal characteristics of political leaders", *International Studies Quarterly*, Vol. 24, No. 1, March 1980, pp.7-46. The exposition of the conceptual framework is taken from the earlier study.
15. See Geldenhuys, DJ, *Constellation, op. cit.*, pp.2ff.
16. Barber, J, *British Foreign Policy, op. cit.*, pp.7-9 & 34-7. The two models not considered are the "pluralist perspective", which assumes that "power is dispersed, that a variety of individuals, parties and groups inside and outside government are involved", and the "public control perspective", of which the principal premise is that "political activity and policy making take place within a setting of broad public awareness and response to government decisions".
17. See Frankel, J, *op. cit.*, pp.111-47, on values in foreign policy making.
18. Holsti, KJ, *International Politics: A Framework for Analysis*, Second Edition, Prentice-Hall, Englewood Cliffs, 1967, p.175.
19. Olivier, GC, *op. cit.*, pp.10 & 11, provides a useful summary of various conceptualisations of capability.
20. In particular, see *ibid.*, pp.33-55. The summary offered in the present book is partly based on the categories used by Olivier.
21. Cline, RS, *World Power Trends and US Foreign Policy for the 1980s*, Westview Press, Boulder, 1980, p.136.
22. Olivier, GC, *op. cit.*, p.49.
23. See Reynolds, PA, *An Introduction to International Relations*, Longman, London, 1971, p.97.
24. Frankel, J, *op. cit.*, p.63.
25. See Norman, GE, "The Transkei: South Africa's illegitimate child", *New England Law Review*, Vol. 12, No. 3, Winter 1977, pp.614ff., and Witkin, MF, "Transkei: an analysis of the practice of recognition – political or legal?", *Harvard International Law Journal*, Vol. 18, No. 3, Summer 1977, pp.621-6.
26. See Adelman, K, "South Africa/Israel: the club of pariahs", *Africa Report*, Vol. 25, No. 6, November-December 1980, pp.8-11; Harkavy, RE, "The pariah state syndrome", *Orbis*, Vol. 21, No. 3, 1977, pp.623-49, and Vale, PCJ, "South Africa as a pariah international state", *International Affairs Bulletin*, Vol. 1, No. 3, 1977, pp.121-41.
27. Hill, C, "Theories of foreign policy making for the developing countries", in Clapham, C (Ed), *Foreign Policy Making in Developing States: A Comparative Approach*, Saxon House, Westmead, 1977, p.6.
28. *Ibid.*, p.8.

Index of Proper Names

Subject Index

Non-aggression pacts, 39, 146
Non-alignment (for South Africa), 211, 224, 243
Norway, 115, 133
Nuclear arms, 206

Oil, 109, 116, 117, 152, 215. Also see *Mineral and Energy Affairs.*
Oligarchy, South Africa as, 234, 247-9
Organisation of African Unity (OAU), 39, 78, 81, 117, 118, 148, 209
Outward movement: see *Black African states*

Palestine, 4
Pan-Africanist Congress (PAC), 11, 72, 147, 179, 180, 208
Paraguay, 42, 73
Pariah state, 102, 116, 211, 243, 246, 247, 249
Paris Match, 114
Parliament, 44-69
  Angolan war, 81, 82
  businessmen as MPs, 165
  foreign affairs/policy, 2, 9, 10, 25, 28, 29, 59, 234
  Hermann's typology, 237
  House of Assembly, 46-69
  Information, Department of, 58, 108, 110
  Senate, 44-6
  Kohl's typology, 238
Personal characteristics (of political leaders), 215, 239-43, 249
Personal diplomacy (of prime ministers), 6, 7, 9, 17-19, 72, 73, 90, 95, 243
Petroleum Products Amendment Act, 1979, 144
Planning Branches (in Prime Minister's Office), 91, 150, 151, 171
Political Science Association of South Africa, 169. Also see *Universities.*
Portugal, 4, 25, 26, 73
Post, 184, 191
President's Council, 36, 220
Press, 182-92
  access to information, 186, 187
  Afrikaans press, 182 *passim*
  Angolan war, 186, 188, 189
  Argus Printing and Publishing Company, 182
  arms embargo, 190
  black press, 182, 191
  English press, 182 *passim*
  foreign affairs, 30, 184-8
  foreign press reporting on South Africa, 186
  freedom, 184, 187
  Information, Department of, 112, 116
  international opinion, 188
  Nasionale Pers, 182
  outward movement, 187
  Perskor, 182
  political support, 182-4
  Portuguese *coup d'état,* 188

Rhodesia, 190
South African Associated Newspapers (SAAN), 182
SWA/Namibia, 190
structure, 182
United States, 189, 190
Pretoria News, 185
Prime Minister's Economic Advisory Council, 150, 162, 163, 167
Private Sector Export Advisory Committee, 151, 162, 163, 167
Progressive Federal Party (PFP)/Progressive Reform Party (PRP)/Progressive Party, 36, 37, 45, 49, 51-5, 58, 67, 68, 82, 144
Public opinion, 29, 238, 246, 247
  black opinion, 10, 29, 199-201, 213
  coloured opinion, 10, 201, 202
  Indian opinion, 10, 201, 202
  white opinion, 10, 79, 80, 193-9, 213, 221, 225, 226, 235

Quail Commission, 199, 200

Racial policies, 5, 8, 11, 25, 26, 28, 35, 36. Also see *Black homelands, Coloureds* and *Indians.*
Rand Daily Mail, 184 *passim*
Rand Mines, 164
Rapport, 111, 112, 183
Rapportryers, 169
Reform Party, 181
Regional policy: see *Black African states*
Rembrandt Group, 163, 165
Republicanism, 11, 22, 31
Reuters, 185
Rhodesia, 40. Also see *Victoria Falls conference* and *Zimbabwe.*
  Anglo-American initiative, 73
  black homeland leaders briefed, 104
  détente, 39, 118
  Geneva conference, 40, 214
  Information, Department of, 118, 119
  invasion by South Africa, 57
  international pressure on South Africa, 213-15, 222
  parliamentary debates, 28, 50, 51, 54, 62
  press comment, 185, 190, 191
  relations with South Africa, 15, 25, 72, 118, 132, 133, 153, 206, 240
Ruacana hydro-electric scheme, 75, 76, 78

Sacramento Union, 115
Sanctions, 36, 63, 169, 207, 212, 235. Also see *International opinion and pressure.*
  ANC, 179
  arms embargo, 11, 25, 27, 40, 190, 205, 206, 212
  economic sanctions, 27, 100, 156
  Foreign Affairs, Department of, 83
  Inkatha, 181